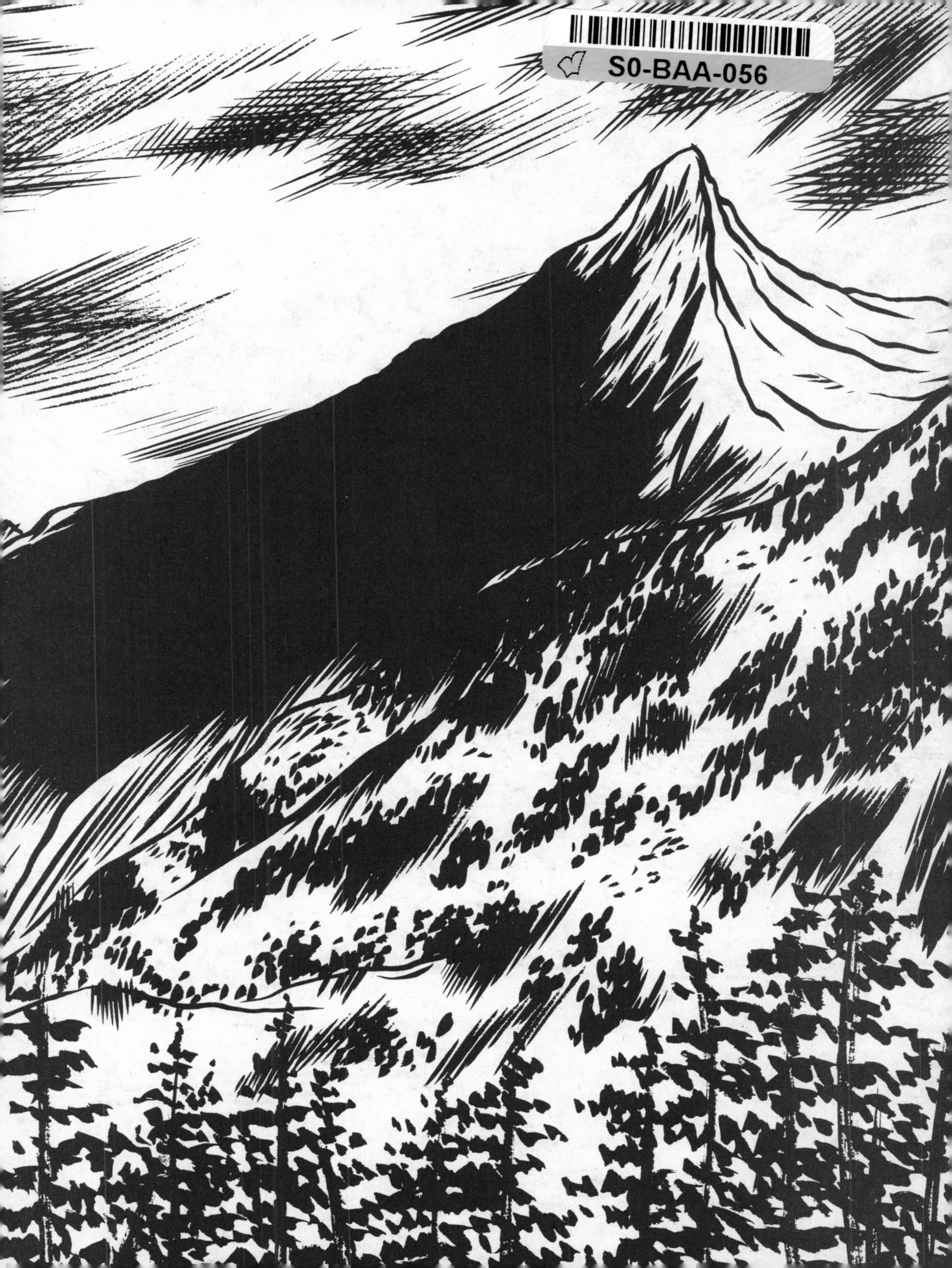

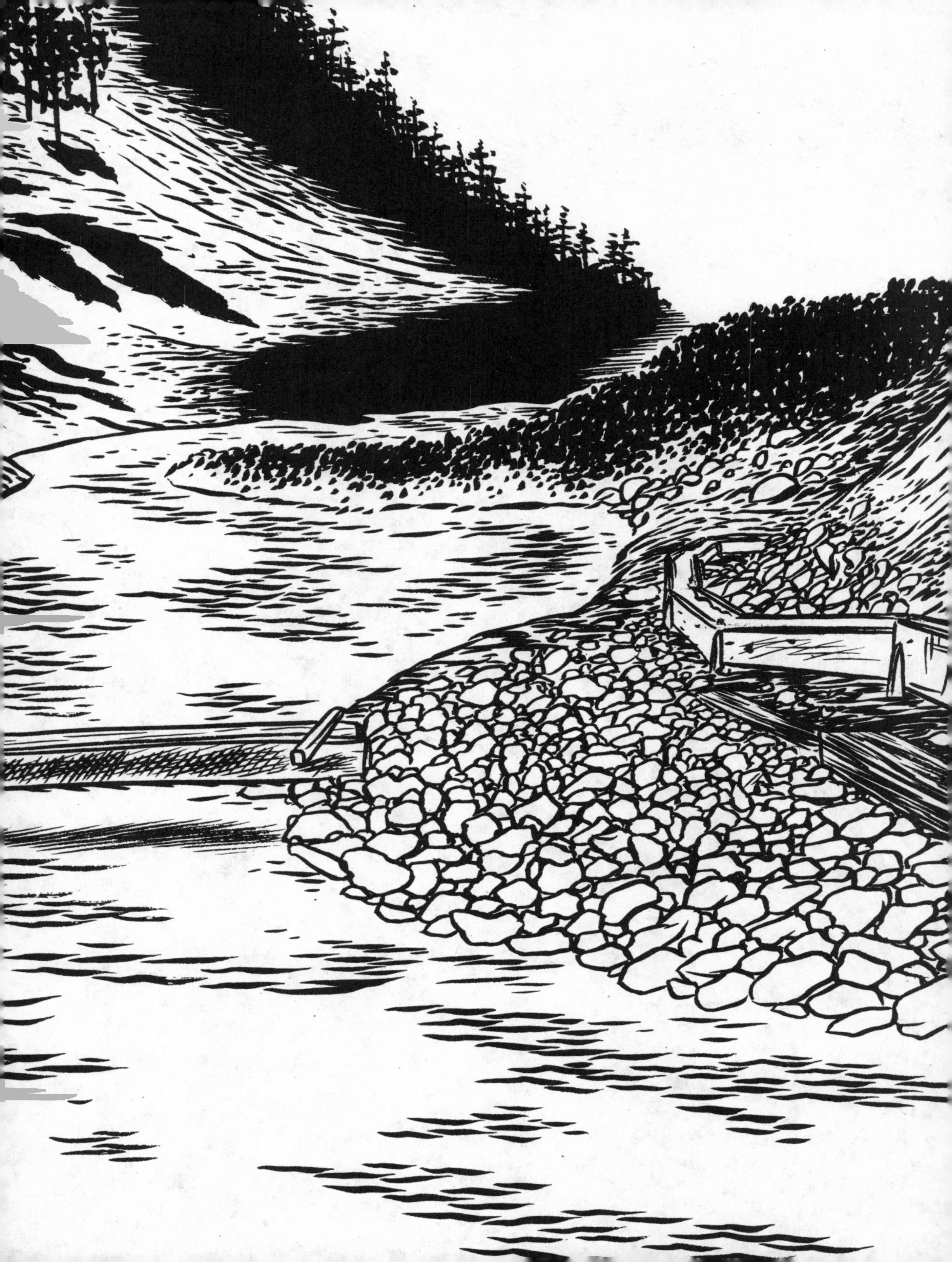

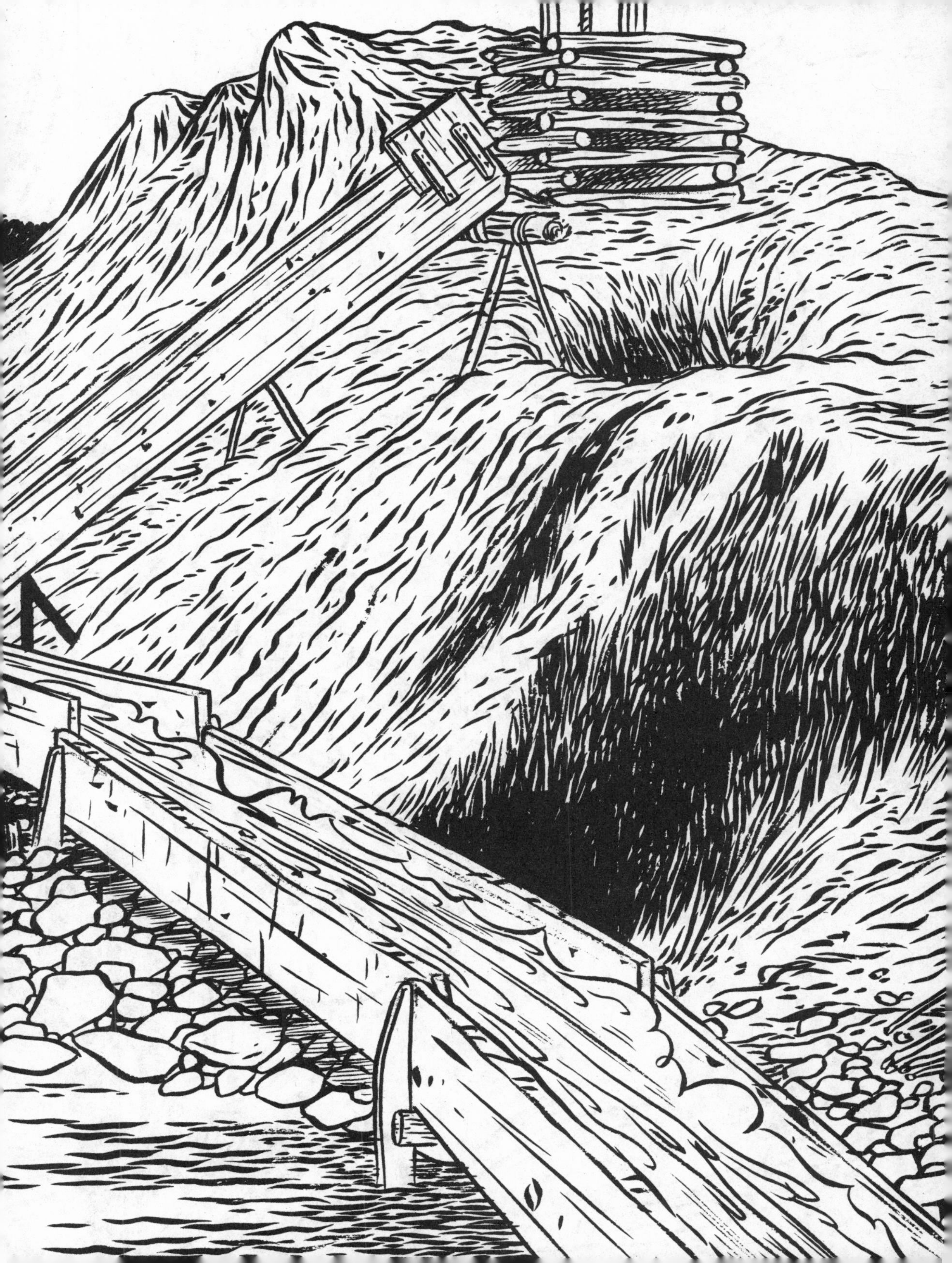

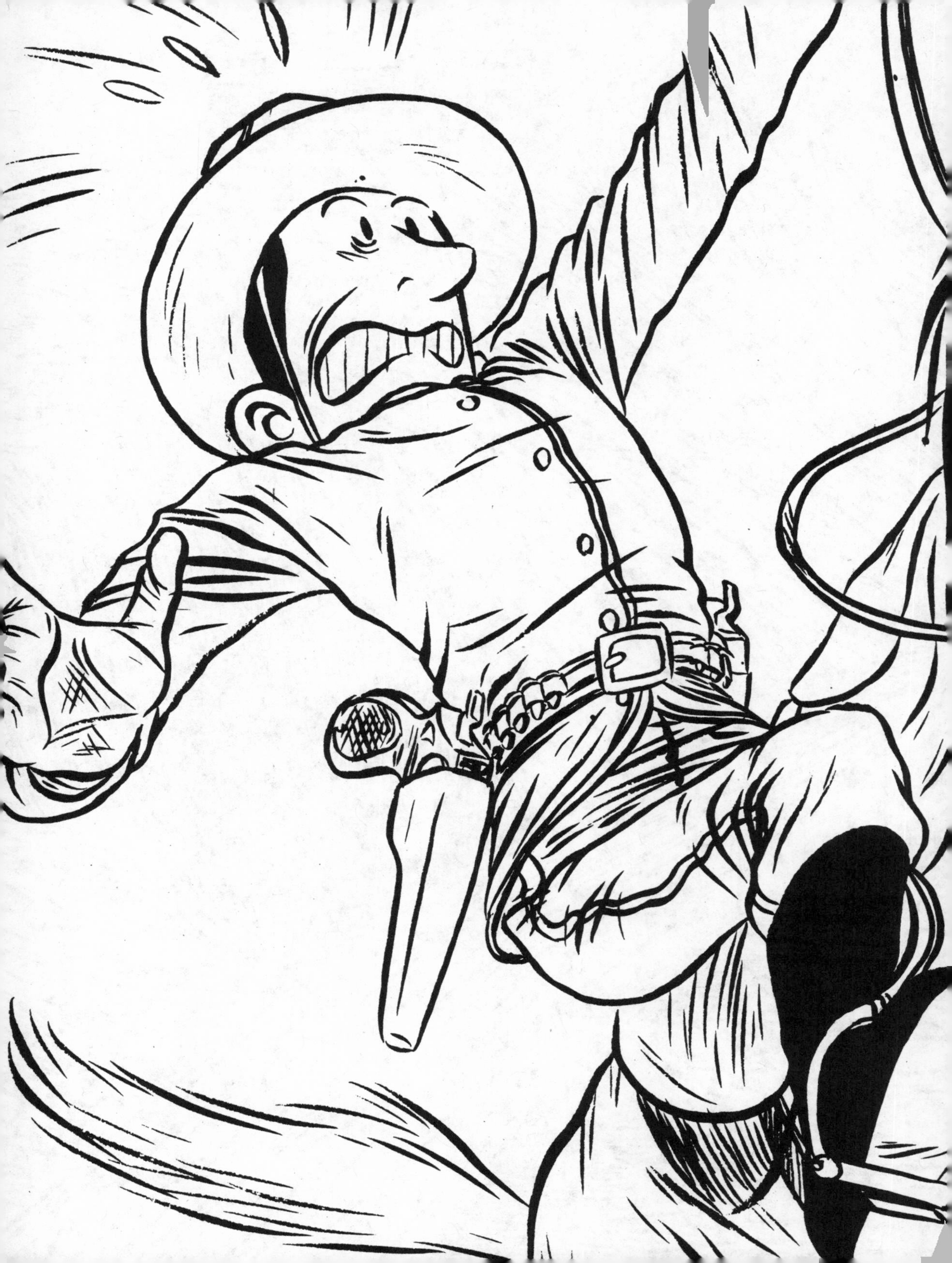

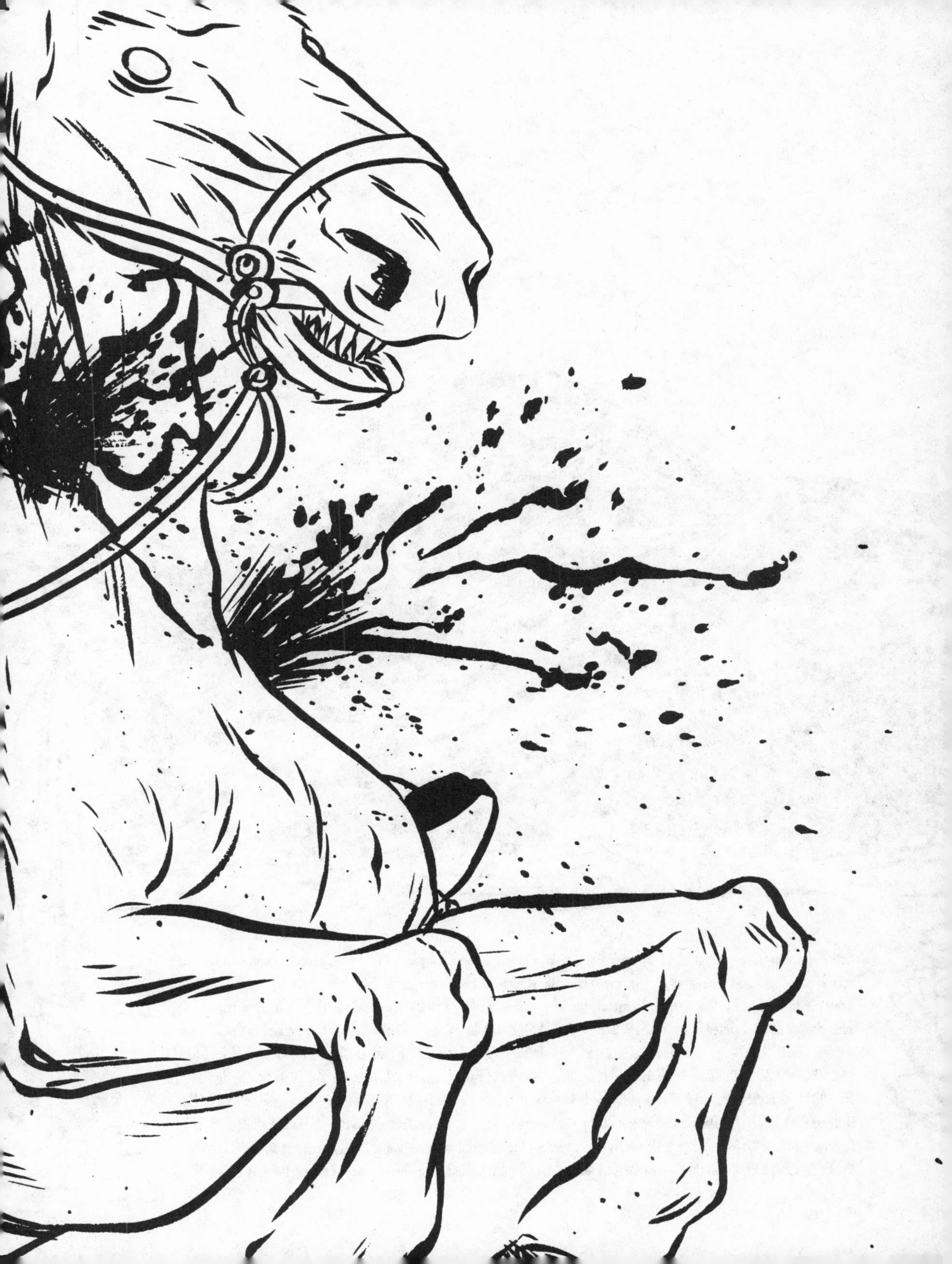

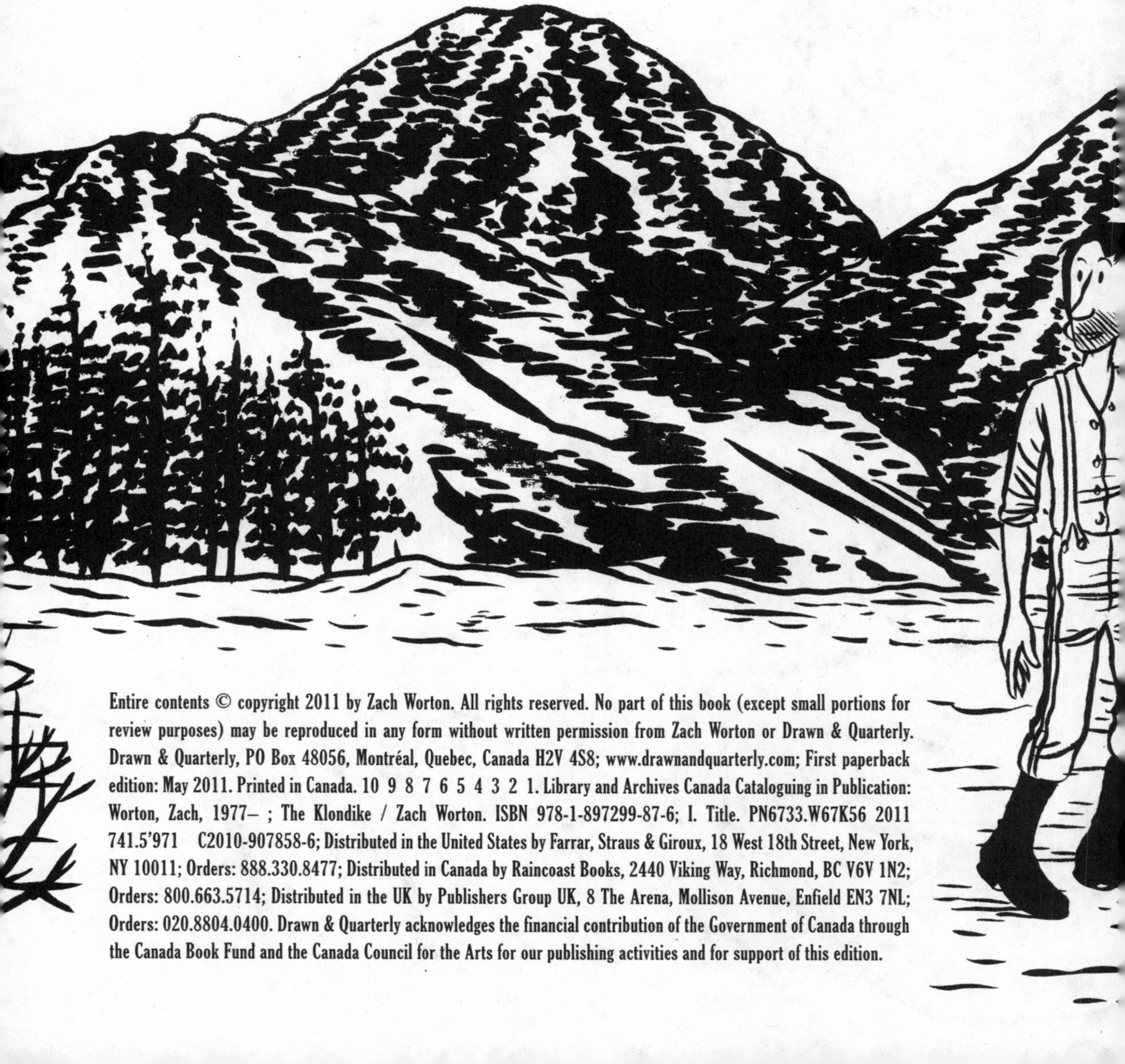

Drawn & Quarterly, PO Box 48056, Montréal, Quebec, Canada H2V 4S8; www.drawnandquarterly.com; First paperback edition: May 2011. Printed in Canada. 10 9 8 7 6 5 4 3 2 1. Library and Archives Canada Cataloguing in Publication: Worton, Zach, 1977– ; The Klondike / Zach Worton. ISBN 978-1-897299-87-6; I. Title. PN6733.W67K56 2011 741.5'971 C2010-907858-6; Distributed in the United States by Farrar, Straus & Giroux, 18 West 18th Street, New York, NY 10011; Orders: 888.330.8477; Distributed in Canada by Raincoast Books, 2440 Viking Way, Richmond, BC V6V 1N2; Orders: 800.663.5714; Distributed in the UK by Publishers Group UK, 8 The Arena, Mollison Avenue, Enfield EN3 7NL; Orders: 020.8804.0400. Drawn & Quarterly acknowledges the financial contribution of the Government of Canada through the Canada Book Fund and the Canada Council for the Arts for our publishing activities and for support of this edition.

THE KLONDIKE

ZACH WORTON

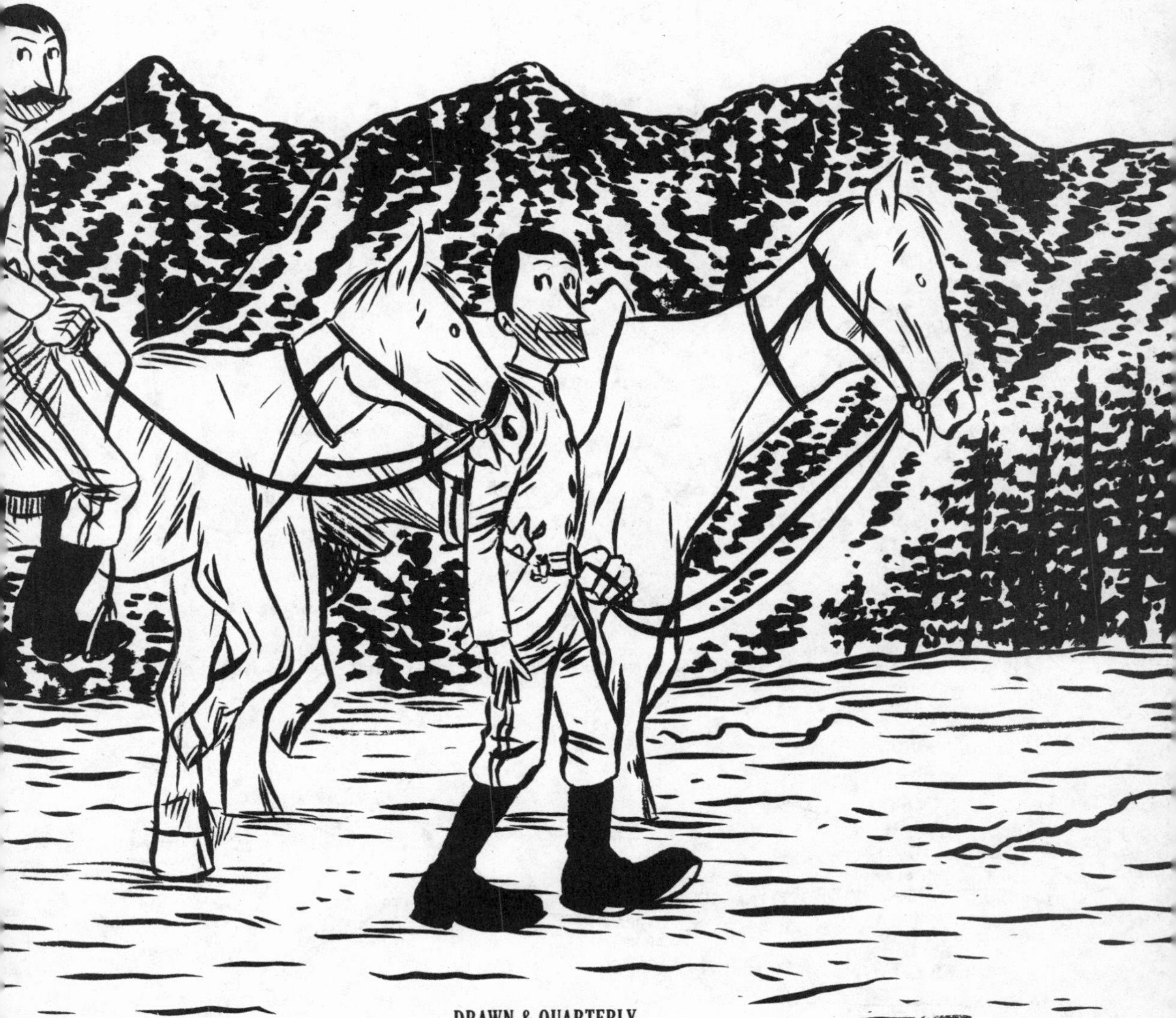

DRAWN & QUARTERLY
MONTRÉAL

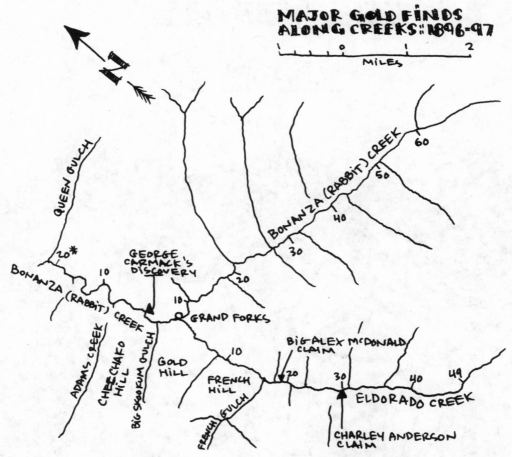

MAJOR GOLD FINDS ALONG CREEKS 1896-97

0   1   2
MILES

N

QUEEN GULCH

BONANZA (RABBIT) CREEK

60
50
40
30
20

20 *

10

GEORGE CARMACK'S DISCOVERY

BONANZA (RABBIT) CREEK

10

GRAND FORKS

ADAMS CREEK

CHEECHAKO HILL

BIG SKOOKUM GULCH

GOLD HILL

FRENCH HILL

FRENCH GULCH

10

BIG ALEX McDONALD CLAIM

20

30

40

49

ELDORADO CREEK

CHARLEY ANDERSON CLAIM

＊ NUMBERS ALONG CREEKS INDICATE DISCOVERY CLAIM

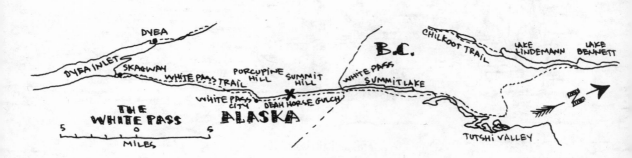

DYEA

DYEA INLET

SKAGWAY

WHITE PASS TRAIL

PORCUPINE HILL

SUMMIT HILL

B.C.

CHILKOOT TRAIL

LAKE LINDEMANN

LAKE BENNETT

WHITE PASS CITY

DEAD HORSE GULCH

WHITE PASS

SUMMIT LAKE

THE WHITE PASS

ALASKA

TUTSHI VALLEY

N

5   0   5
MILES

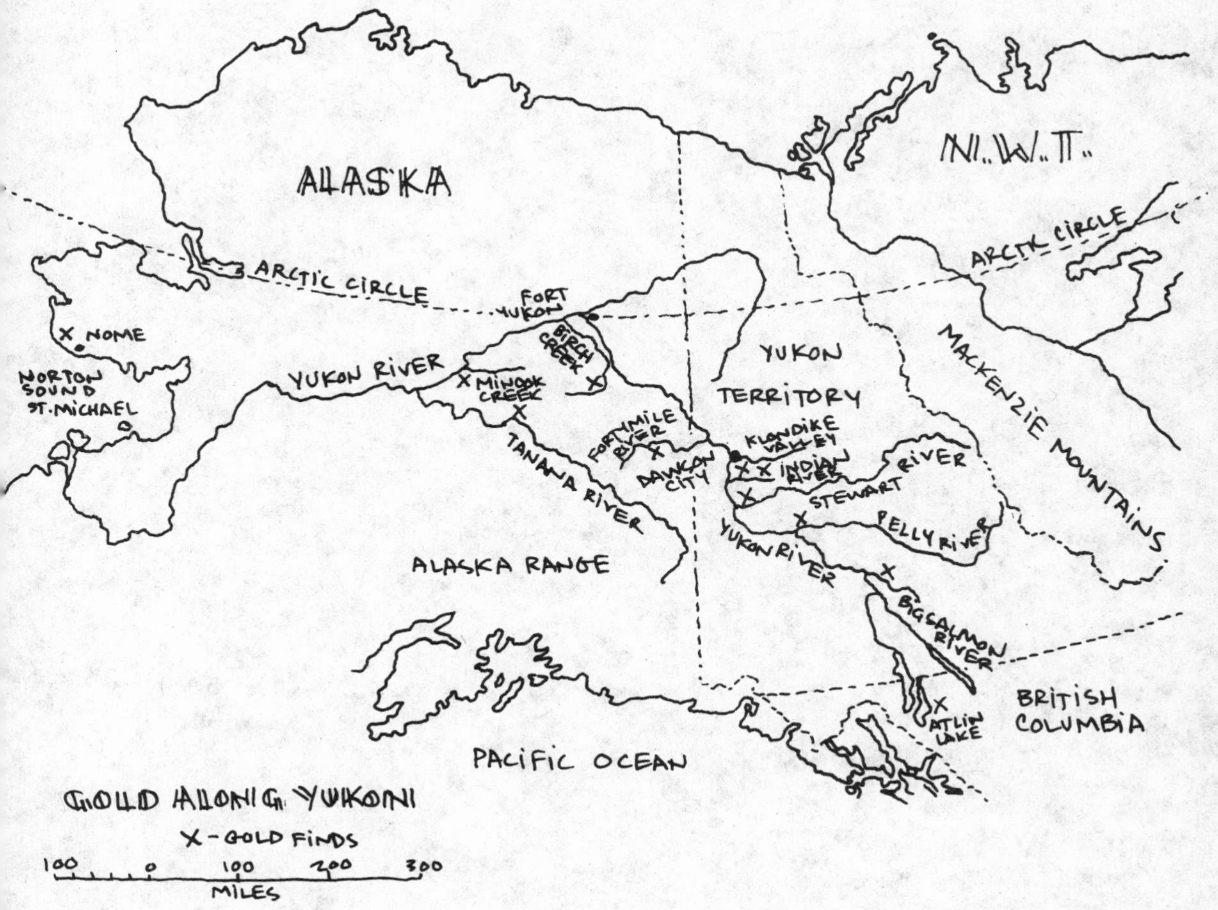
ALASKA
N.W.T.
ARCTIC CIRCLE
ARCTIC CIRCLE
FORT YUKON
X NOME
NORTON SOUND
ST. MICHAEL
YUKON RIVER
BIRCH CREEK
X MINOOK CREEK
YUKON
TERRITORY
MACKENZIE MOUNTAINS
FORTYMILE RIVER
KLONDIKE VALLEY
INDIAN RIVER
DAWSON CITY
STEWART RIVER
TANANA RIVER
PELLY RIVER
YUKON RIVER
ALASKA RANGE
BIG SALMON RIVER
BRITISH COLUMBIA
ATLIN LAKE
PACIFIC OCEAN
GOLD ALONG YUKON
X - GOLD FINDS
100 0 100 200 300
MILES

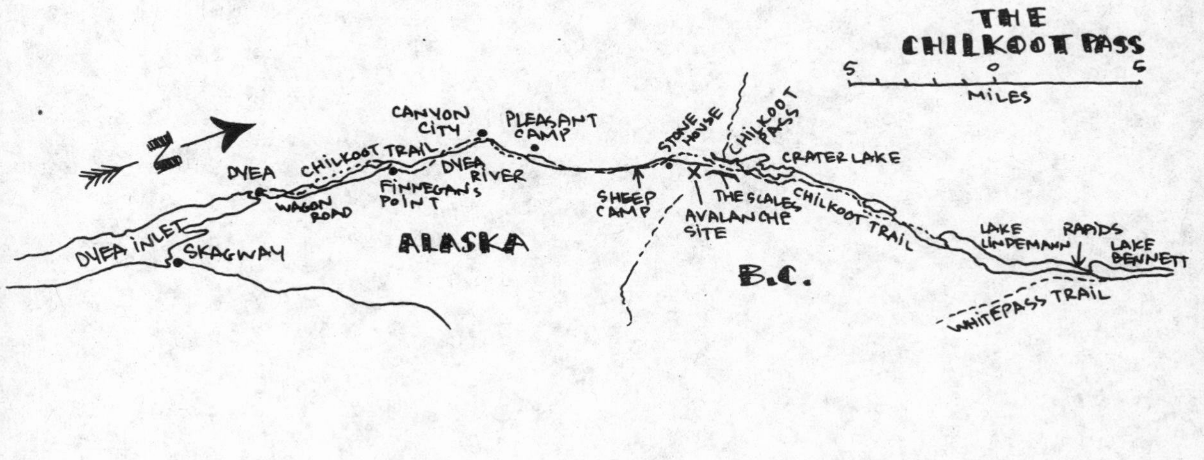
THE CHILKOOT PASS
5 0 5
MILES
N
CANYON CITY
PLEASANT CAMP
STONE HOUSE
CHILKOOT PASS
CRATER LAKE
DYEA
CHILKOOT TRAIL
DYEA RIVER
FINNEGAN'S POINT
WAGON ROAD
SHEEP CAMP
THE SCALES
AVALANCHE SITE
CHILKOOT TRAIL
DYEA INLET
SKAGWAY
ALASKA
B.C.
LAKE LINDEMANN
RAPIDS
LAKE BENNETT
WHITEPASS TRAIL

GEORGE HOLT DID SOMETHING NO WHITE MAN
HAD DONE AT THE TIME: CROSSED THE CHILKOOT AND
LIVED TO TELL THE TALE. THE CHILKOOT TRAIL
WAS FIERCELY GUARDED BY THE CHILKAT INDIANS
WHO WERE KNOWN FOR KILLING INTRUDERS
ON SIGHT. SURVIVING THE CONDITIONS OF A
YUKON WINTER WAS A FEAT IN AND OF ITSELF,
AS THE FIERCE WINDS WERE KNOWN TO ACT-
UALLY CARVE HOLES INTO ROCKS. SUCH
CONDITIONS DID NOT STOP A DETERMINED MAN
LIKE HOLT.

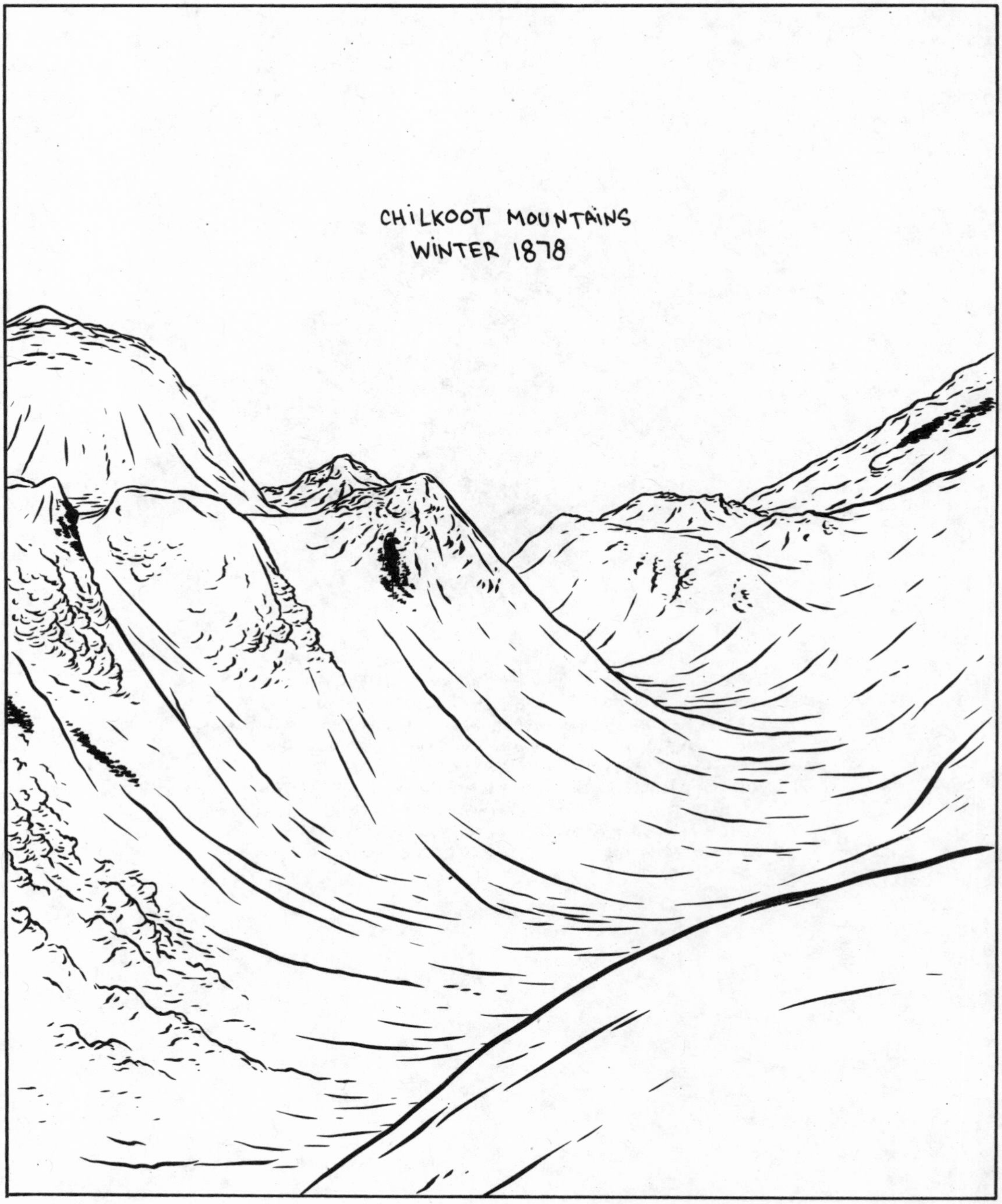
CHILKOOT MOUNTAINS
WINTER 1878

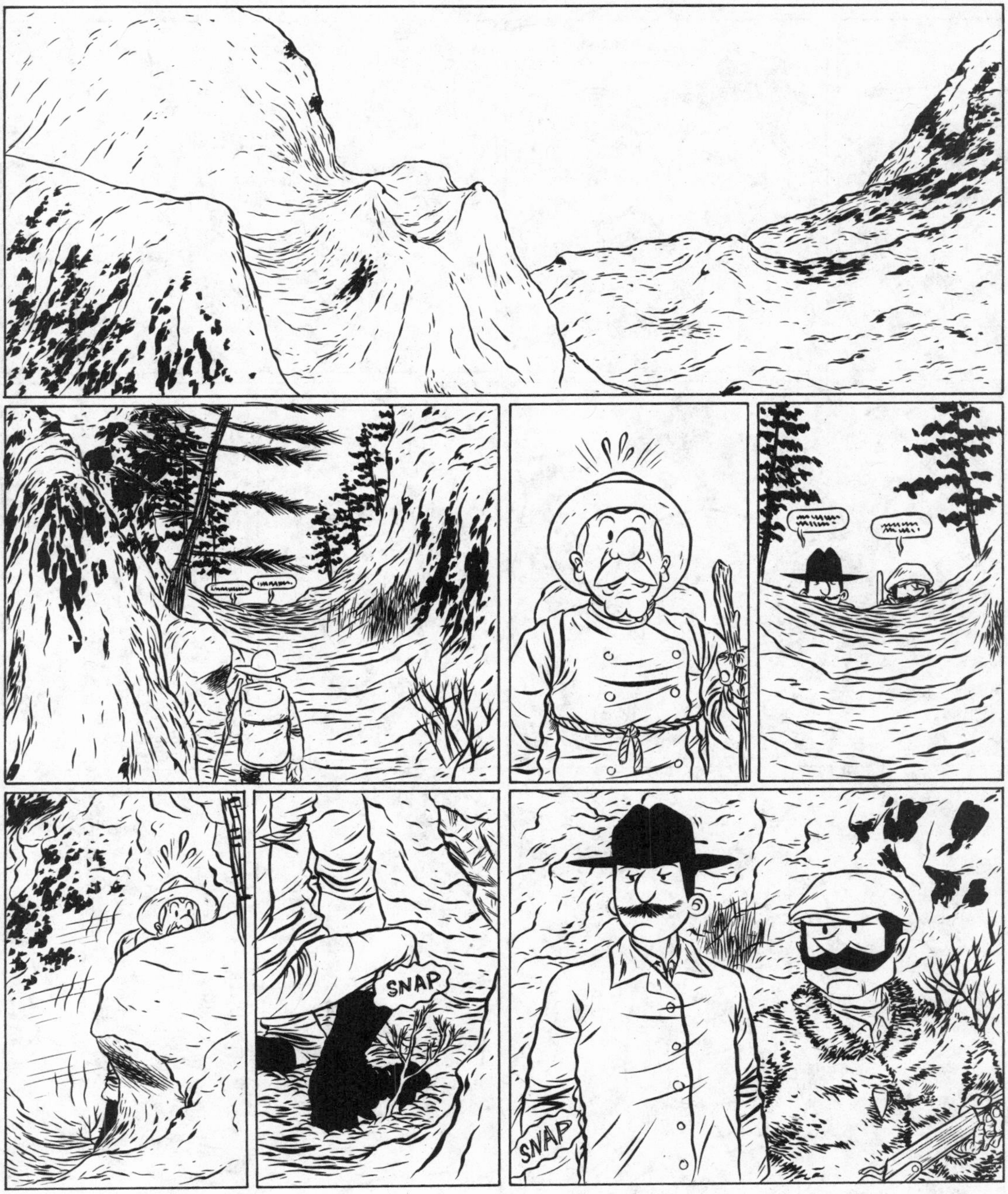
SNAP
SNAP

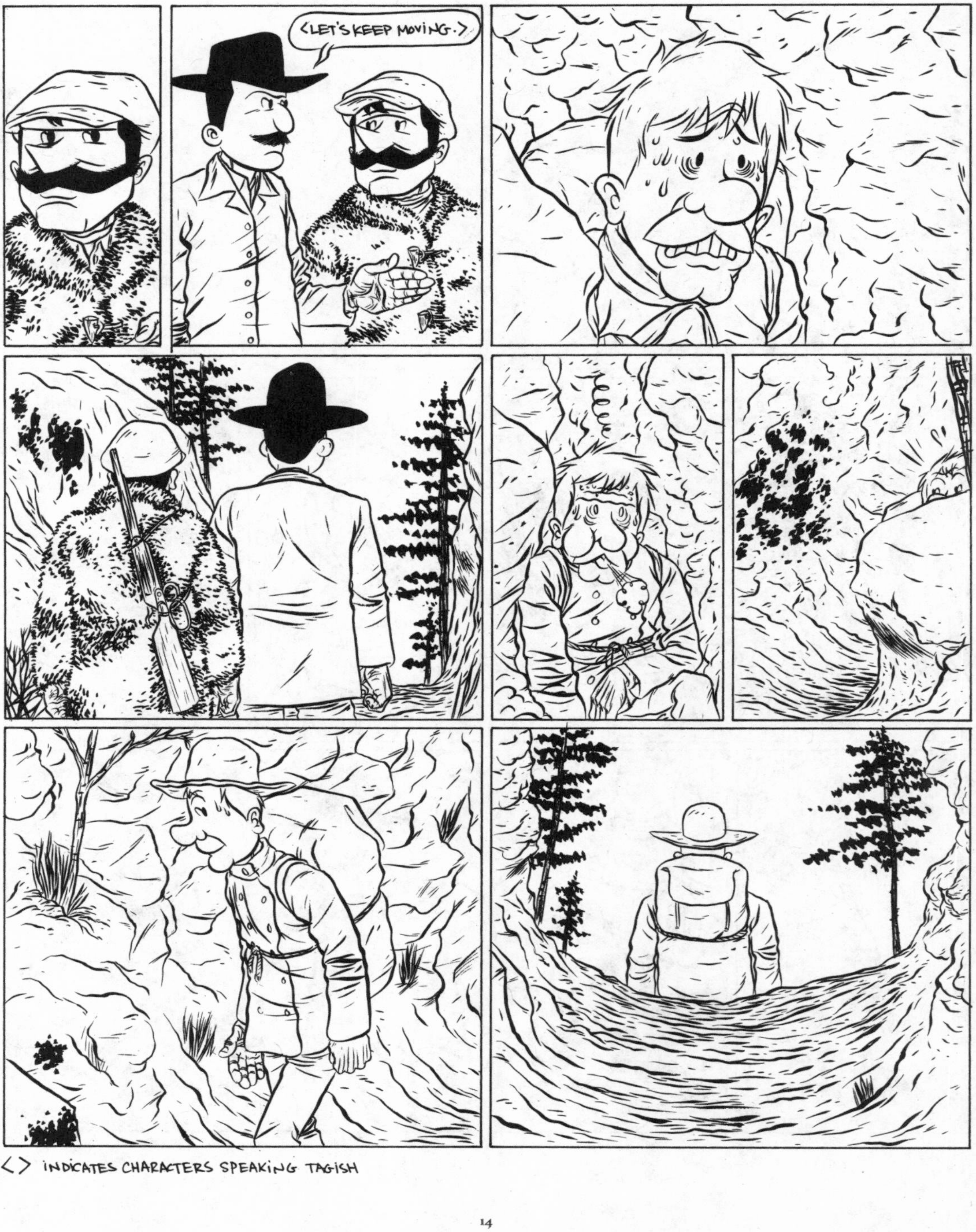
<LET'S KEEP MOVING.>

<> INDICATES CHARACTERS SPEAKING TAGISH

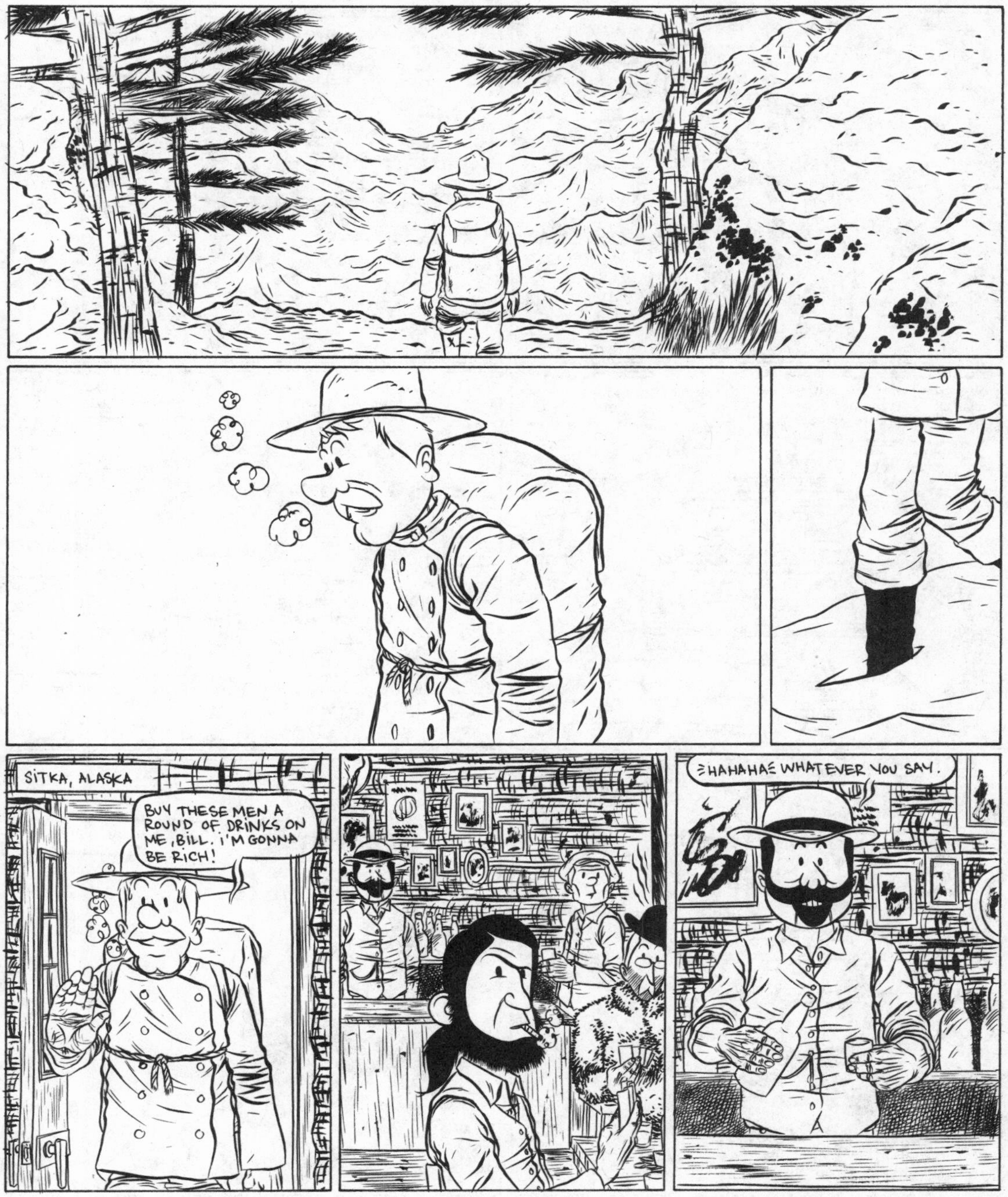
SITKA, ALASKA
BUY THESE MEN A ROUND OF DRINKS ON ME, BILL. I'M GONNA BE RICH!
HAHAHA! WHATEVER YOU SAY.

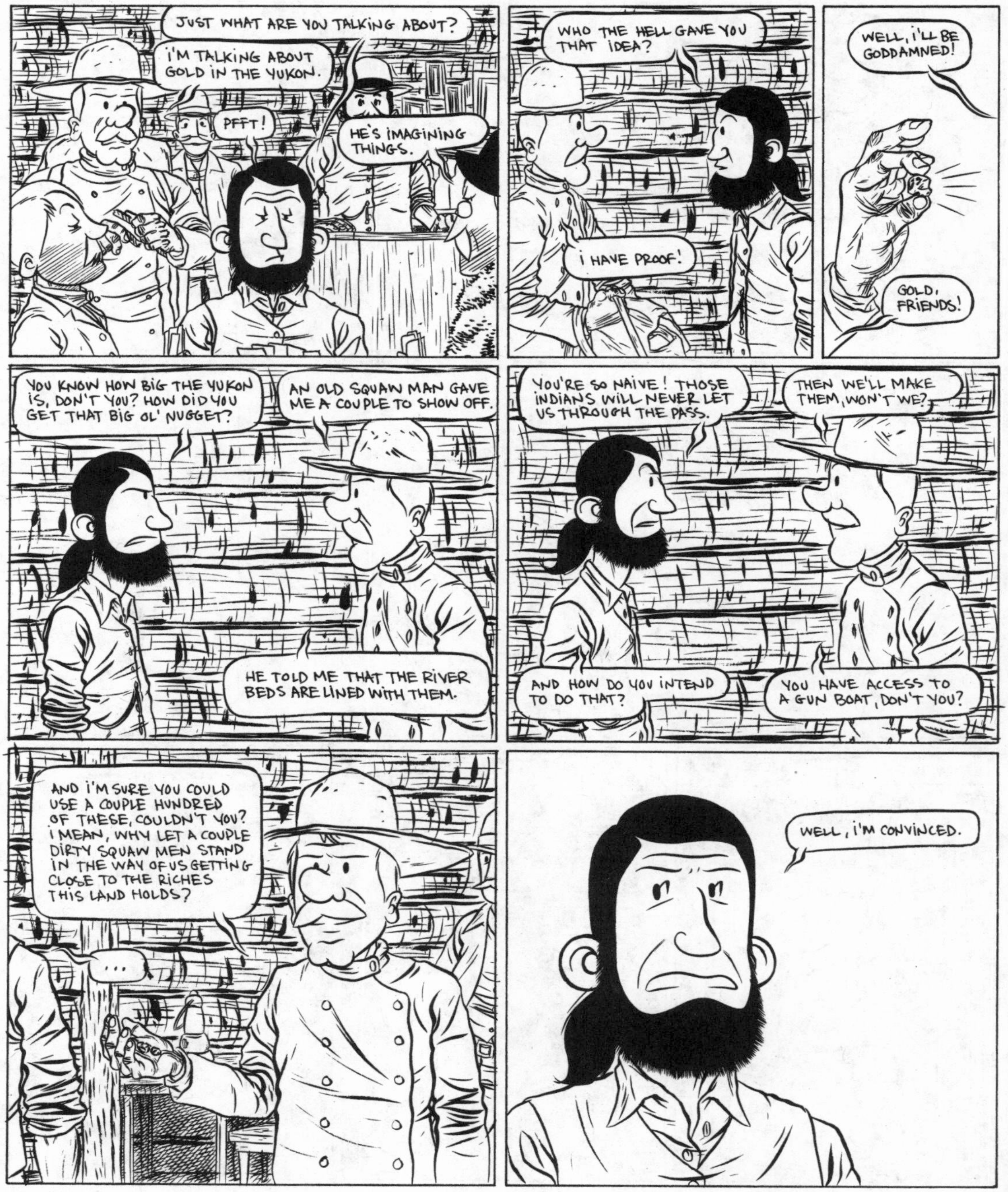
JUST WHAT ARE YOU TALKING ABOUT?
I'M TALKING ABOUT GOLD IN THE YUKON.
PFFT!
HE'S IMAGINING THINGS.
WHO THE HELL GAVE YOU THAT IDEA?
I HAVE PROOF!
WELL, I'LL BE GODDAMNED!
GOLD, FRIENDS!
YOU KNOW HOW BIG THE YUKON IS, DON'T YOU? HOW DID YOU GET THAT BIG OL' NUGGET?
AN OLD SQUAW MAN GAVE ME A COUPLE TO SHOW OFF.
HE TOLD ME THAT THE RIVER BEDS ARE LINED WITH THEM.
YOU'RE SO NAIVE! THOSE INDIANS WILL NEVER LET US THROUGH THE PASS.
THEN WE'LL MAKE THEM, WON'T WE?
AND HOW DO YOU INTEND TO DO THAT?
YOU HAVE ACCESS TO A GUN BOAT, DON'T YOU?
AND I'M SURE YOU COULD USE A COUPLE HUNDRED OF THESE, COULDN'T YOU? I MEAN, WHY LET A COUPLE DIRTY SQUAW MEN STAND IN THE WAY OF US GETTING CLOSE TO THE RICHES THIS LAND HOLDS?
...
WELL, I'M CONVINCED.

ANY OF YOU FEEL LIKE GETTING RICH? WE'RE LEAVING IN AN HOUR!
AND SO...
<WHY ARE THOSE MEN COMING WITH GUNS?>
<THE ONLY THING THIS LAND HOLDS, MEN WILL KILL FOR.>
DROP THE ANCHOR, READY THE LIFE BOATS AND BE FAST ABOUT IT, FELLAS.
MAKE SURE YOU TWO ARE READY TO SHOOT AT ANY POINT, GOT IT?
BWAHAHA
HEHEHEHE GONNA BAG US A COUPLE INDIANS!
AH, WHAT THE HELL? GIVE 'EM A TASTE, GUNNER!
WITH PLEASURE!
<DON'T BE AFRAID. I WON'T LET MY PEOPLE COME TO HARM.>
<YOU MAY WANT TO TELL THEM THAT. I DOUBT THEY CARE FOR OUR HEALTH!>

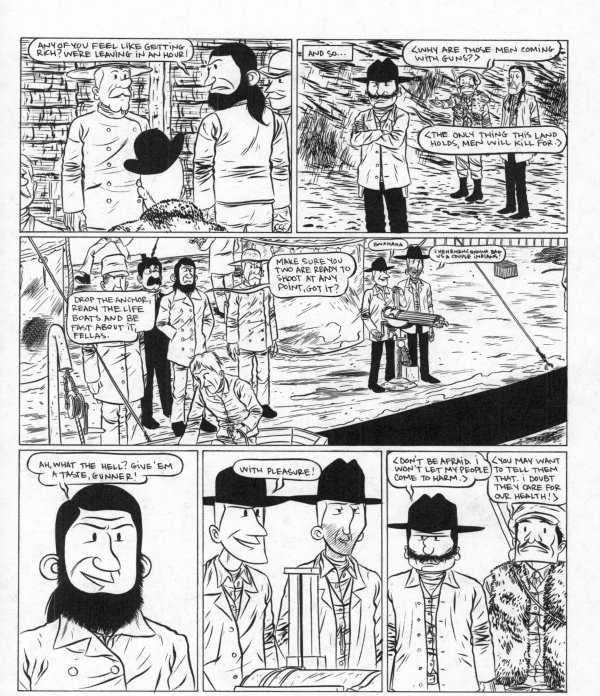

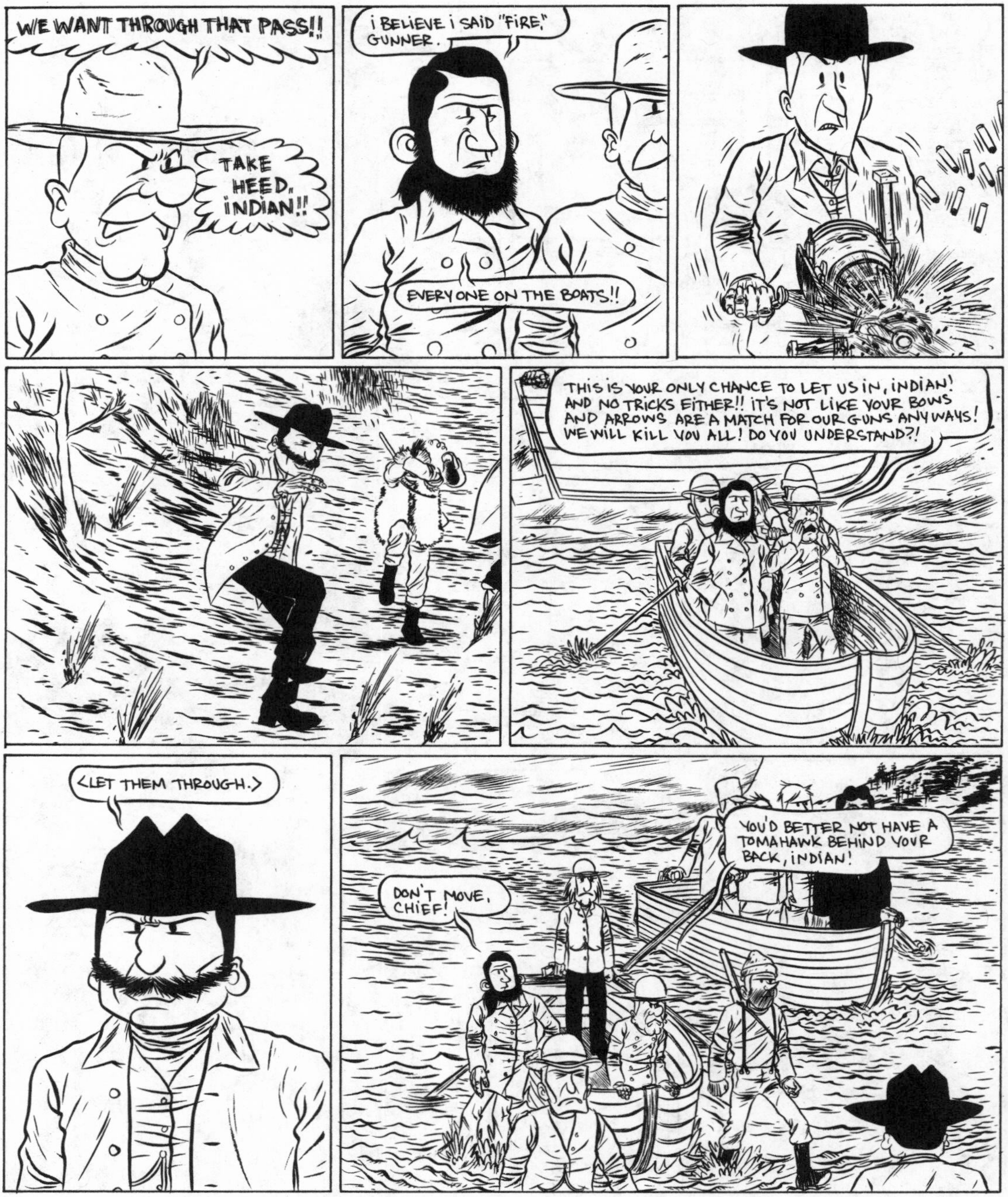
WE WANT THROUGH THAT PASS!!
TAKE HEED, INDIAN!!
I BELIEVE I SAID "FIRE," GUNNER.
EVERYONE ON THE BOATS!!
THIS IS YOUR ONLY CHANCE TO LET US IN, INDIAN! AND NO TRICKS EITHER!! IT'S NOT LIKE YOUR BOWS AND ARROWS ARE A MATCH FOR OUR GUNS ANYWAYS! WE WILL KILL YOU ALL! DO YOU UNDERSTAND?!
<LET THEM THROUGH.>
YOU'D BETTER NOT HAVE A TOMAHAWK BEHIND YOUR BACK, INDIAN!
DON'T MOVE, CHIEF!

I KNEW YOU'D SEE IT OUR WAY.
COME ALONG NOW, CHIEF.
YOU'D BETTER BE RIGHT ABOUT THIS. YOU'VE PUT THE ENTIRE CAMP AT RISK WITH THIS PLAN OF YOURS. I'M ALL FOR GETTING RICH, BUT WE WILL ALL HANG--
LOOK, IT'S GOING TO BE FINE AND THERE'S NO NEED FOR THREATS! IF I'M RIGHT ABOUT THIS, THE ONLY THING YOU'LL NEED TO BE CONCERNED WITH IS WHERE TO PUT ALL THEM SACKS OF GOLD!
DON'T TELL ME WHAT I SHOULD BE CONCERNED ABOUT.
ALL YOU NEED TO BE CONCERNED ABOUT IS FINDING THE GODDAMNED GOLD! MAKE SURE YOU REMEMBER THAT.
I SAID YOU DON'T HAVE TO THREATEN ME. THAT OLD INDIAN MAN TOLD ME THE RIVERS SHINE WITH IT!
RIGHT. AND DID THAT OLD INDIAN TELL YOU WHERE THOSE SHINING RIVERS ARE? SEEMS LIKE HE DIDN'T.

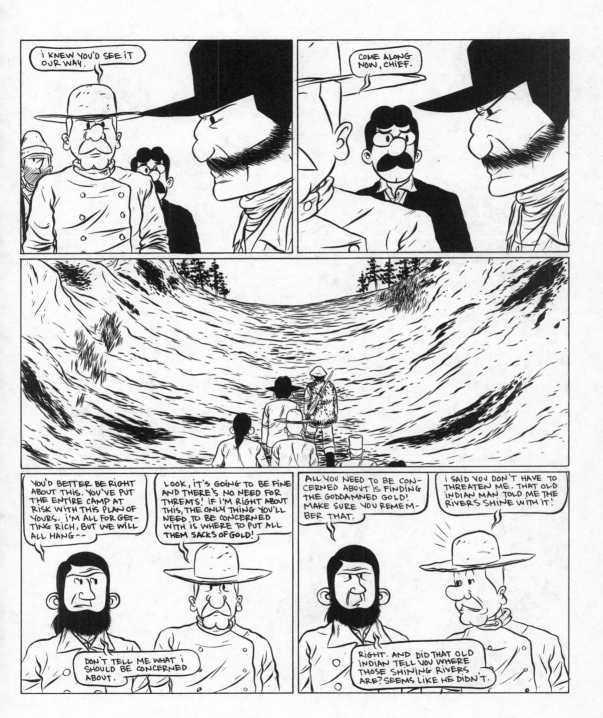

EVENTUALLY...
nothing...
JUST ROCKS AND DIRT. YOU ARE A STUPID SON OF A BITCH! THERE'S NOTHING HERE.
SO IT SEEMS.
"SO IT SEEMS"...
THERE'S NOTHING HERE AND YOU'LL BE LUCKY IF SITKA ISN'T BURNED TO THE GROUND BY THE TIME WE GET BACK!!
AND ANYBODY WHO WANTS TO STAY AND WASTE TIME PLAYING IN THE DIRT MAY DO SO... YOU WILL ALL BE FOOLS THOUGH!!

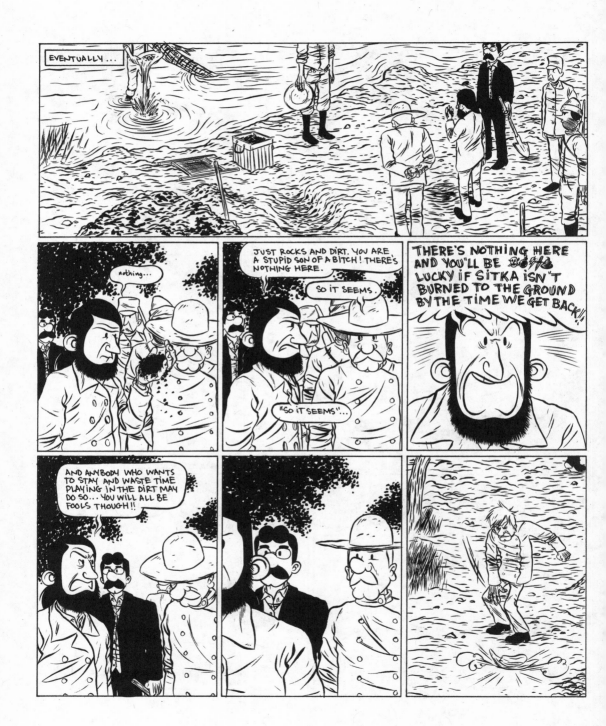

AS A TWELVE-YEAR-OLD BOY, ED SCHIEFFELIN,
FOUNDER OF TOMBSTONE, ARIZONA, JOINED HIS
FIRST GOLD RUSH, THUS BEGINNING HIS LIFE AS
A PROSPECTOR. BY THE TIME SCHIEFFELIN
WENT TO THE YUKON, HE HAD ALREADY MADE
WELL OVER A MILLION DOLLARS MINING SILVER
IN ARIZONA. HE BELIEVED THAT THE YUKON
WAS PART OF A WORLD ENCOMPASSING MINERAL
BELT, BUT COULD NEVER PROVE IT. DESPITE HIS
AMBITION, AS AUTUMN APPROACHED, SCHIEFFELIN
REALIZED THE CHILLY CONDITIONS WERE TOO
MUCH FOR HIM. YEARS LATER, AS THE GOLD RUSH
WAS BEGINNING, SCHIEFFELIN'S LIFE WAS
ENDING. STILL PROSPECTING, HE DIED OF A HEART
ATTACK OUTSIDE OF HIS CABIN IN THE TEMPERATE
FORESTS OF OREGON.

ST. MICHAEL, ALASKA
1883

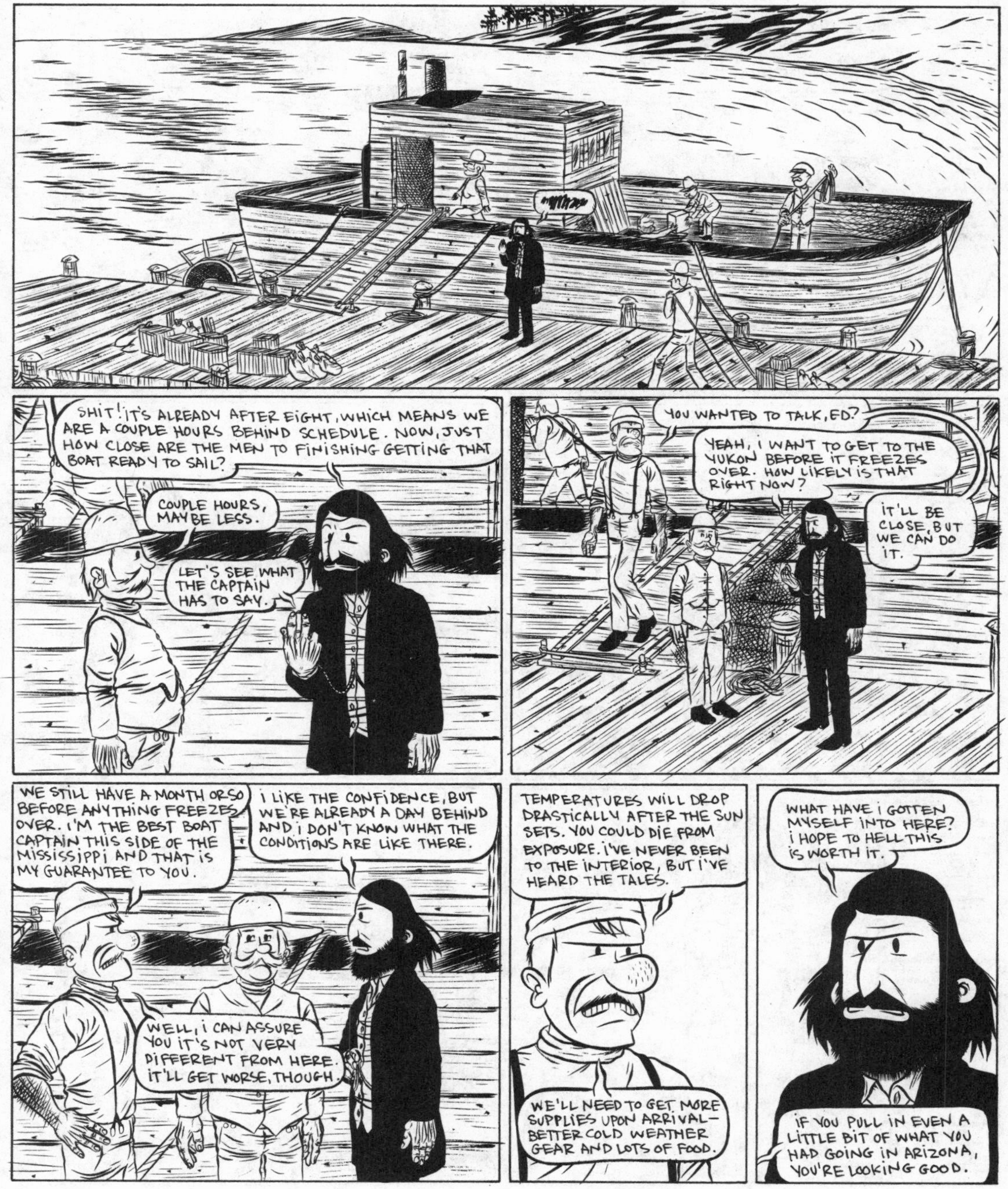
SHIT! IT'S ALREADY AFTER EIGHT, WHICH MEANS WE ARE A COUPLE HOURS BEHIND SCHEDULE. NOW, JUST HOW CLOSE ARE THE MEN TO FINISHING GETTING THAT BOAT READY TO SAIL?
COUPLE HOURS, MAYBE LESS.
LET'S SEE WHAT THE CAPTAIN HAS TO SAY.
YOU WANTED TO TALK, ED?
YEAH, I WANT TO GET TO THE YUKON BEFORE IT FREEZES OVER. HOW LIKELY IS THAT RIGHT NOW?
IT'LL BE CLOSE, BUT WE CAN DO IT.
WE STILL HAVE A MONTH OR SO BEFORE ANYTHING FREEZES OVER. I'M THE BEST BOAT CAPTAIN THIS SIDE OF THE MISSISSIPPI AND THAT IS MY GUARANTEE TO YOU.
I LIKE THE CONFIDENCE, BUT WE'RE ALREADY A DAY BEHIND AND I DON'T KNOW WHAT THE CONDITIONS ARE LIKE THERE.
WELL, I CAN ASSURE YOU IT'S NOT VERY DIFFERENT FROM HERE. IT'LL GET WORSE, THOUGH.
TEMPERATURES WILL DROP DRASTICALLY AFTER THE SUN SETS. YOU COULD DIE FROM EXPOSURE. I'VE NEVER BEEN TO THE INTERIOR, BUT I'VE HEARD THE TALES.
WE'LL NEED TO GET MORE SUPPLIES UPON ARRIVAL— BETTER COLD WEATHER GEAR AND LOTS OF FOOD.
WHAT HAVE I GOTTEN MYSELF INTO HERE? I HOPE TO HELL THIS IS WORTH IT.
IF YOU PULL IN EVEN A LITTLE BIT OF WHAT YOU HAD GOING IN ARIZONA, YOU'RE LOOKING GOOD.

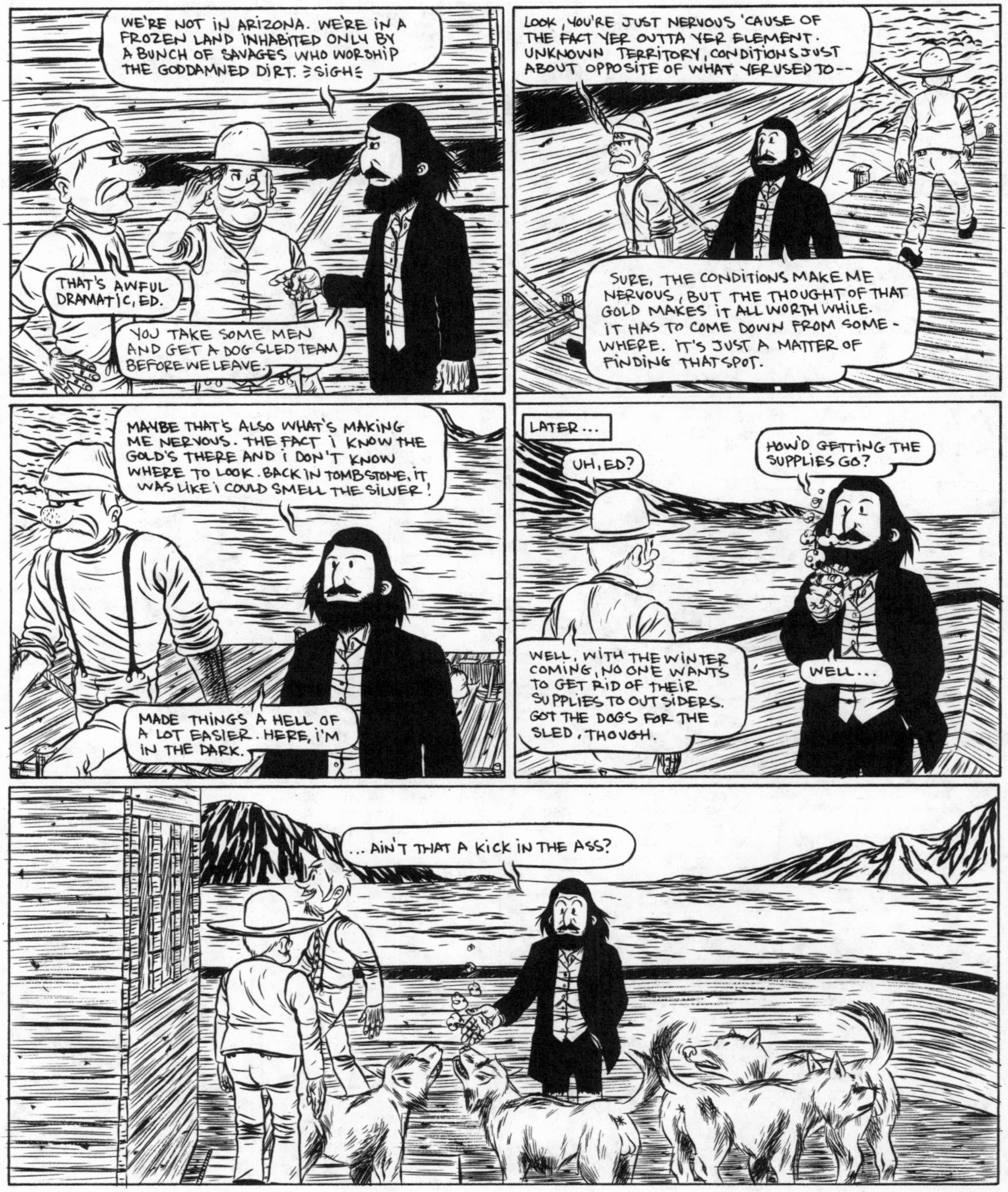
WE'RE NOT IN ARIZONA. WE'RE IN A FROZEN LAND INHABITED ONLY BY A BUNCH OF SAVAGES WHO WORSHIP THE GODDAMNED DIRT. ⋮SIGH⋮
THAT'S AWFUL DRAMATIC, ED.
YOU TAKE SOME MEN AND GET A DOG SLED TEAM BEFORE WE LEAVE.
LOOK, YOU'RE JUST NERVOUS 'CAUSE OF THE FACT YER OUTTA YER ELEMENT. UNKNOWN TERRITORY, CONDITIONS JUST ABOUT OPPOSITE OF WHAT YER USED TO--
SURE, THE CONDITIONS MAKE ME NERVOUS, BUT THE THOUGHT OF THAT GOLD MAKES IT ALL WORTH WHILE. IT HAS TO COME DOWN FROM SOME-WHERE. IT'S JUST A MATTER OF FINDING THAT SPOT.
MAYBE THAT'S ALSO WHAT'S MAKING ME NERVOUS. THE FACT I KNOW THE GOLD'S THERE AND I DON'T KNOW WHERE TO LOOK. BACK IN TOMBSTONE, IT WAS LIKE I COULD SMELL THE SILVER!
MADE THINGS A HELL OF A LOT EASIER. HERE, I'M IN THE DARK.
LATER...
UH, ED?
HOW'D GETTING THE SUPPLIES GO?
WELL, WITH THE WINTER COMING, NO ONE WANTS TO GET RID OF THEIR SUPPLIES TO OUTSIDERS. GOT THE DOGS FOR THE SLED, THOUGH.
WELL...
...AIN'T THAT A KICK IN THE ASS?

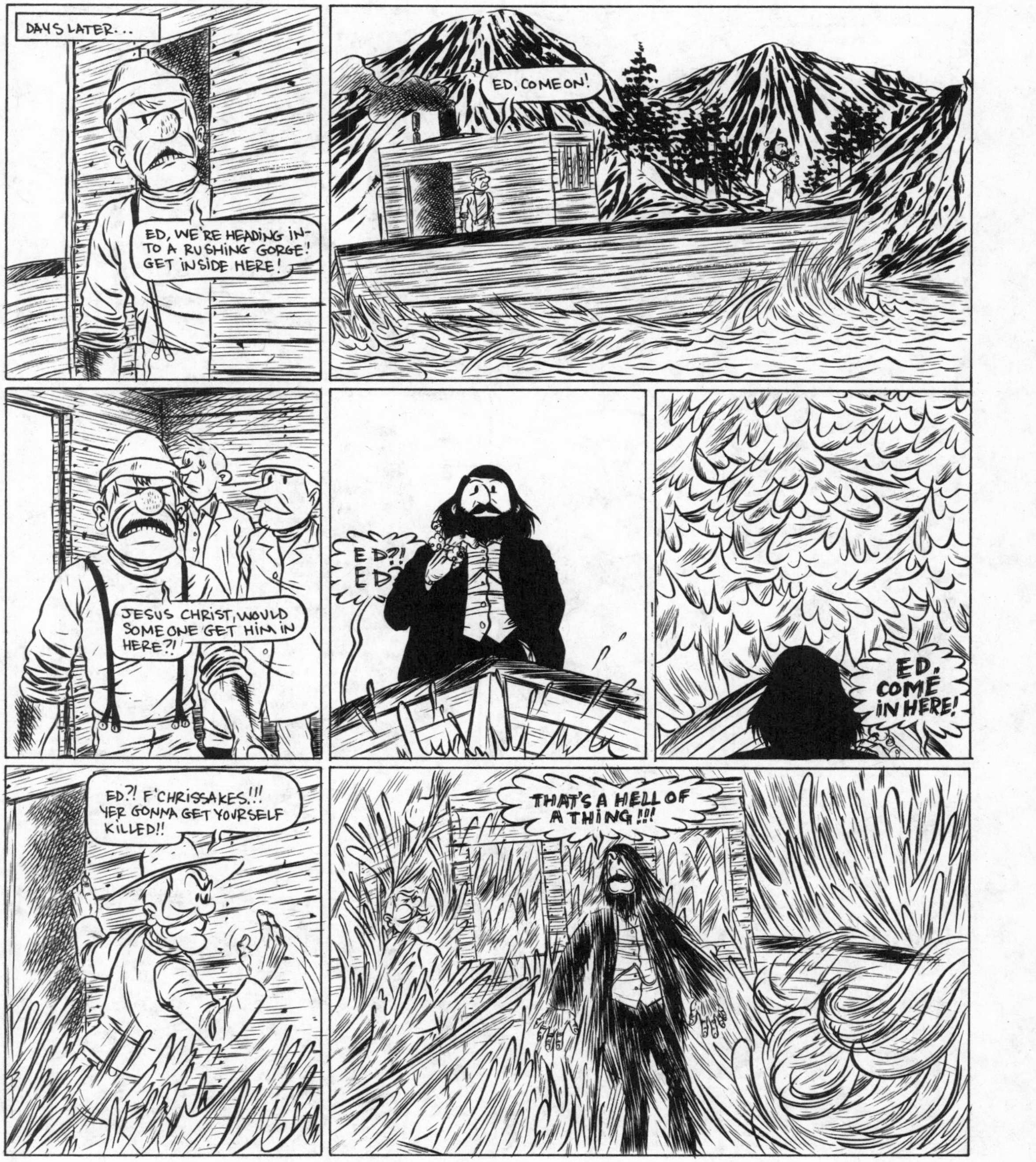
DAYS LATER...
ED, WE'RE HEADING IN-TO A RUSHING GORGE! GET INSIDE HERE!
ED, COME ON!
JESUS CHRIST, WOULD SOMEONE GET HIM IN HERE?!
ED?! ED!
ED, COME IN HERE!
ED?! F'CHRISSAKES!!! YER GONNA GET YOURSELF KILLED!!
THAT'S A HELL OF A THING!!!

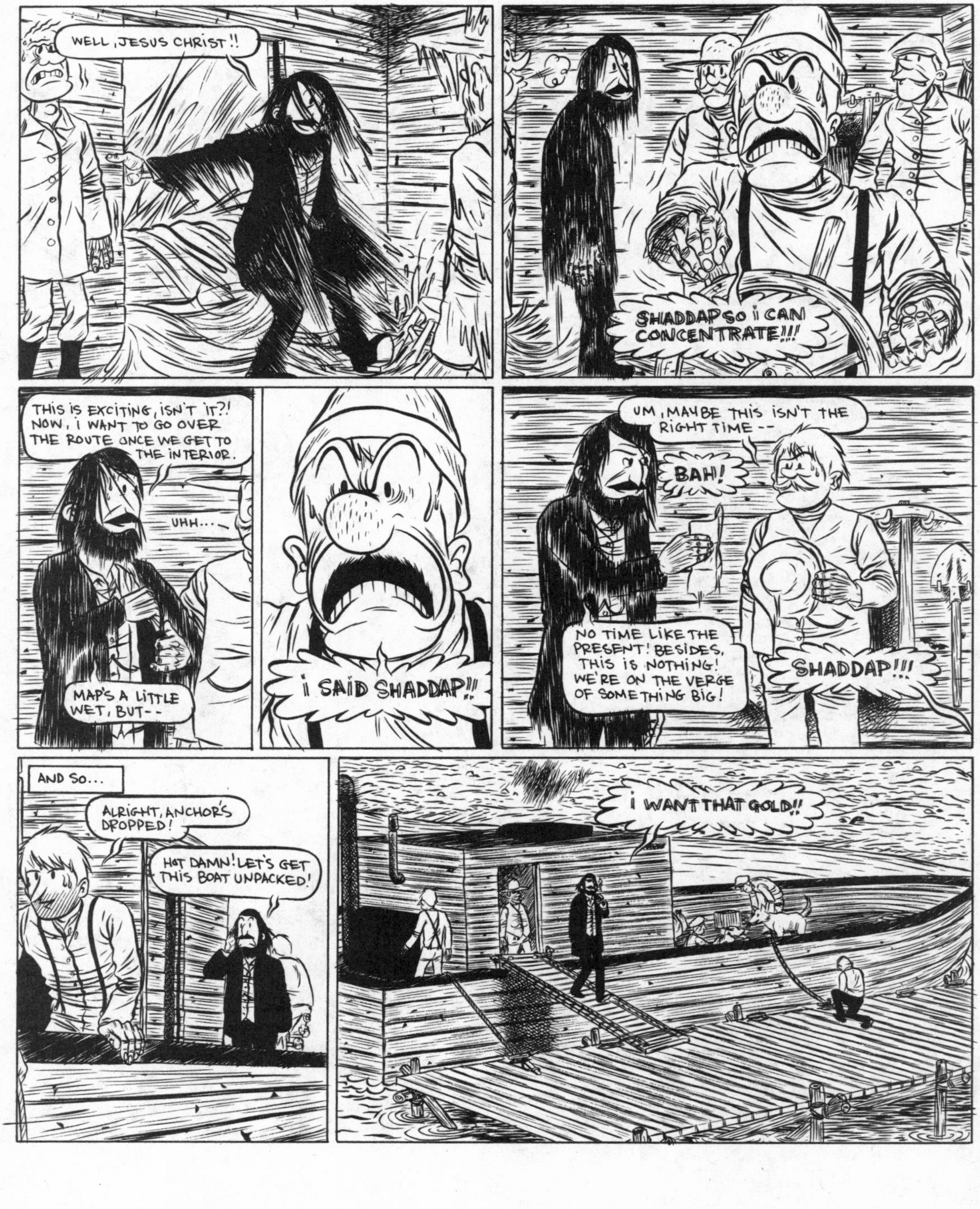

WELL, JESUS CHRIST!!
SHADDAP SO I CAN CONCENTRATE!!!
THIS IS EXCITING, ISN'T IT?! NOW, I WANT TO GO OVER THE ROUTE ONCE WE GET TO THE INTERIOR.
UHH...
MAP'S A LITTLE WET, BUT--
I SAID SHADDAP!!
UM, MAYBE THIS ISN'T THE RIGHT TIME--
BAH!
NO TIME LIKE THE PRESENT! BESIDES, THIS IS NOTHING! WE'RE ON THE VERGE OF SOMETHING BIG!
SHADDAP!!!
AND SO...
ALRIGHT, ANCHOR'S DROPPED!
HOT DAMN! LET'S GET THIS BOAT UNPACKED!
I WANT THAT GOLD!!

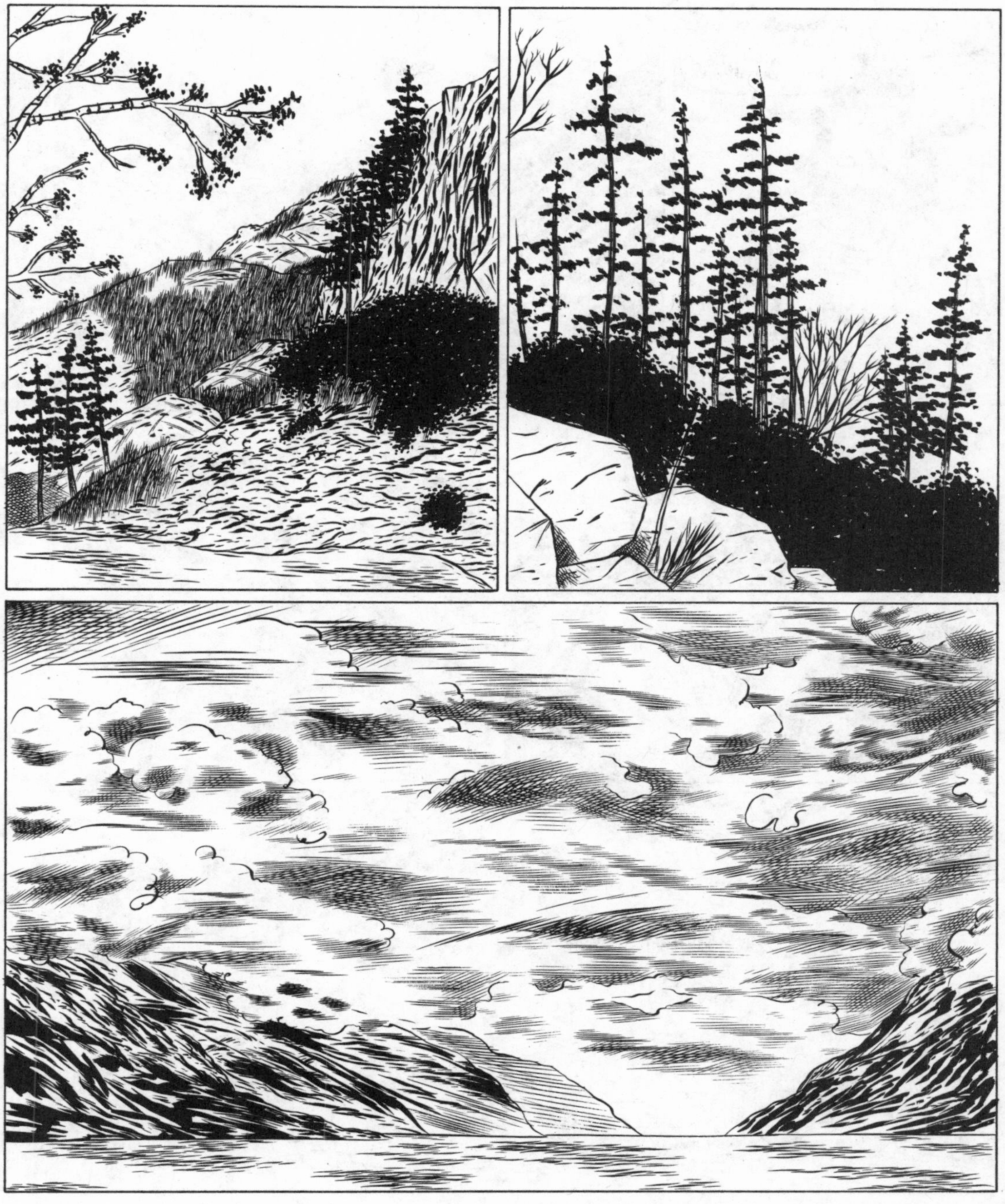

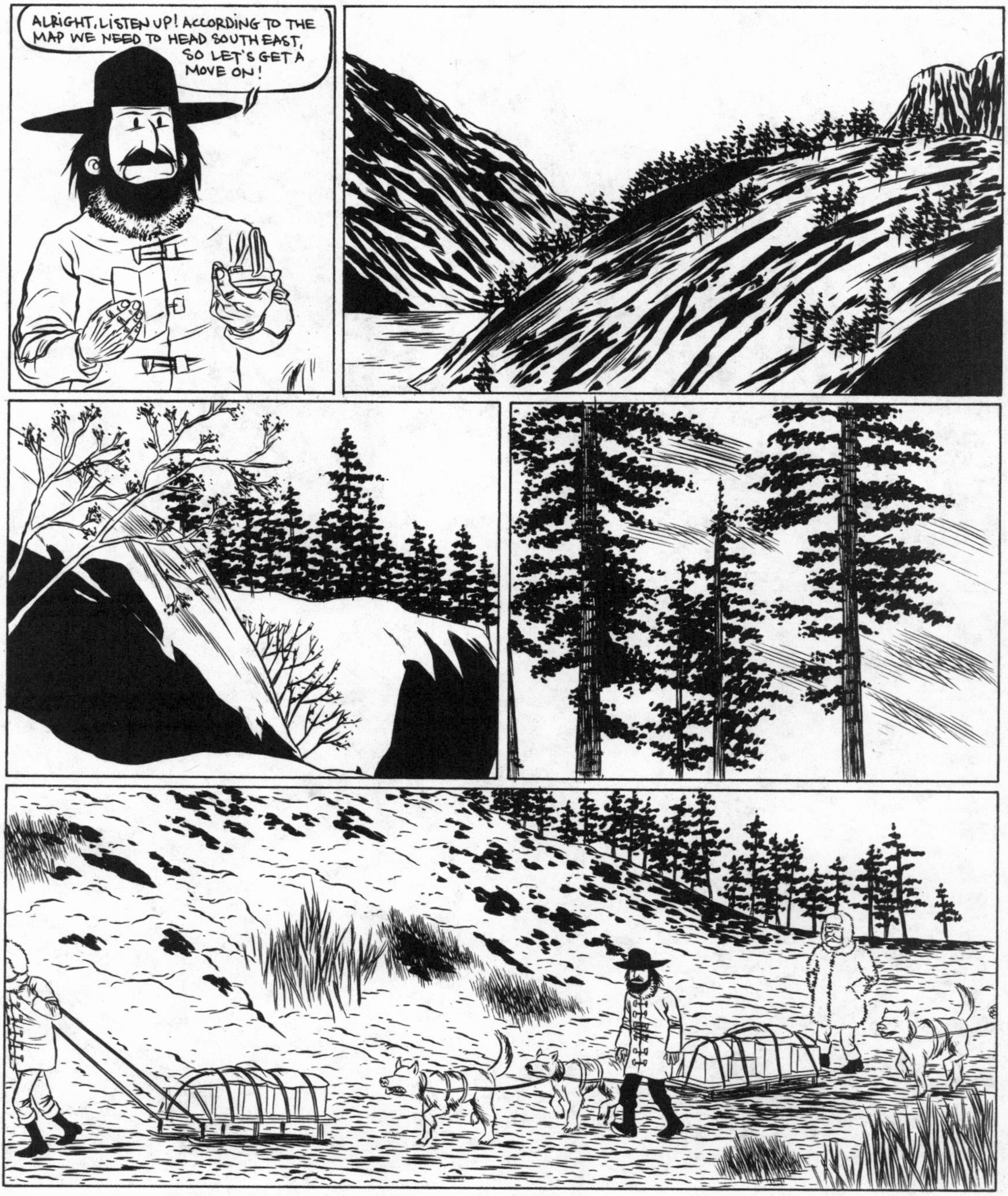
ALRIGHT, LISTEN UP! ACCORDING TO THE MAP WE NEED TO HEAD SOUTH EAST, SO LET'S GET A MOVE ON!

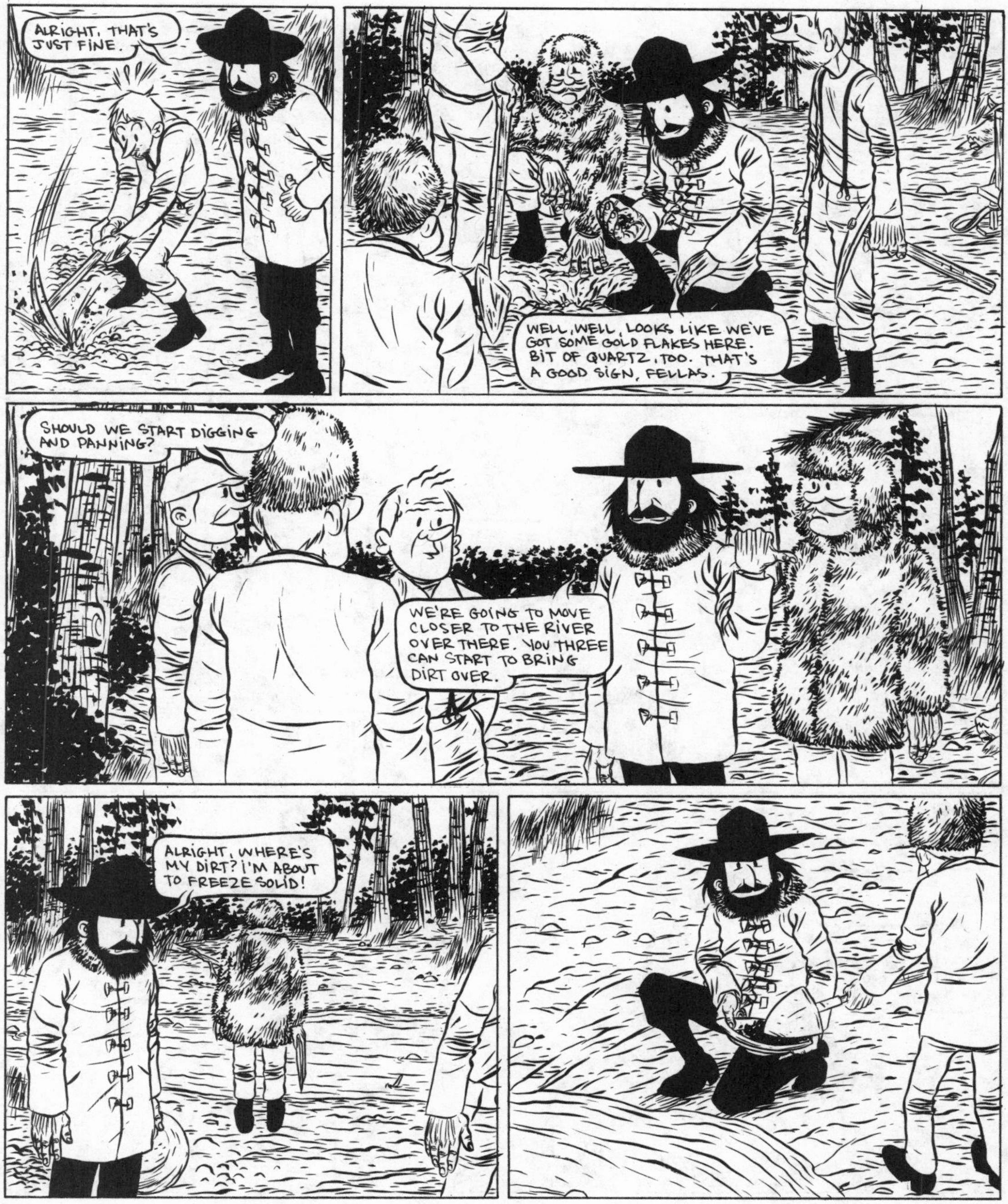
ALRIGHT. THAT'S JUST FINE.
WELL, WELL, LOOKS LIKE WE'VE GOT SOME GOLD FLAKES HERE. BIT OF QUARTZ, TOO. THAT'S A GOOD SIGN, FELLAS.
SHOULD WE START DIGGING AND PANNING?
WE'RE GOING TO MOVE CLOSER TO THE RIVER OVER THERE. YOU THREE CAN START TO BRING DIRT OVER.
ALRIGHT, WHERE'S MY DIRT? I'M ABOUT TO FREEZE SOLID!

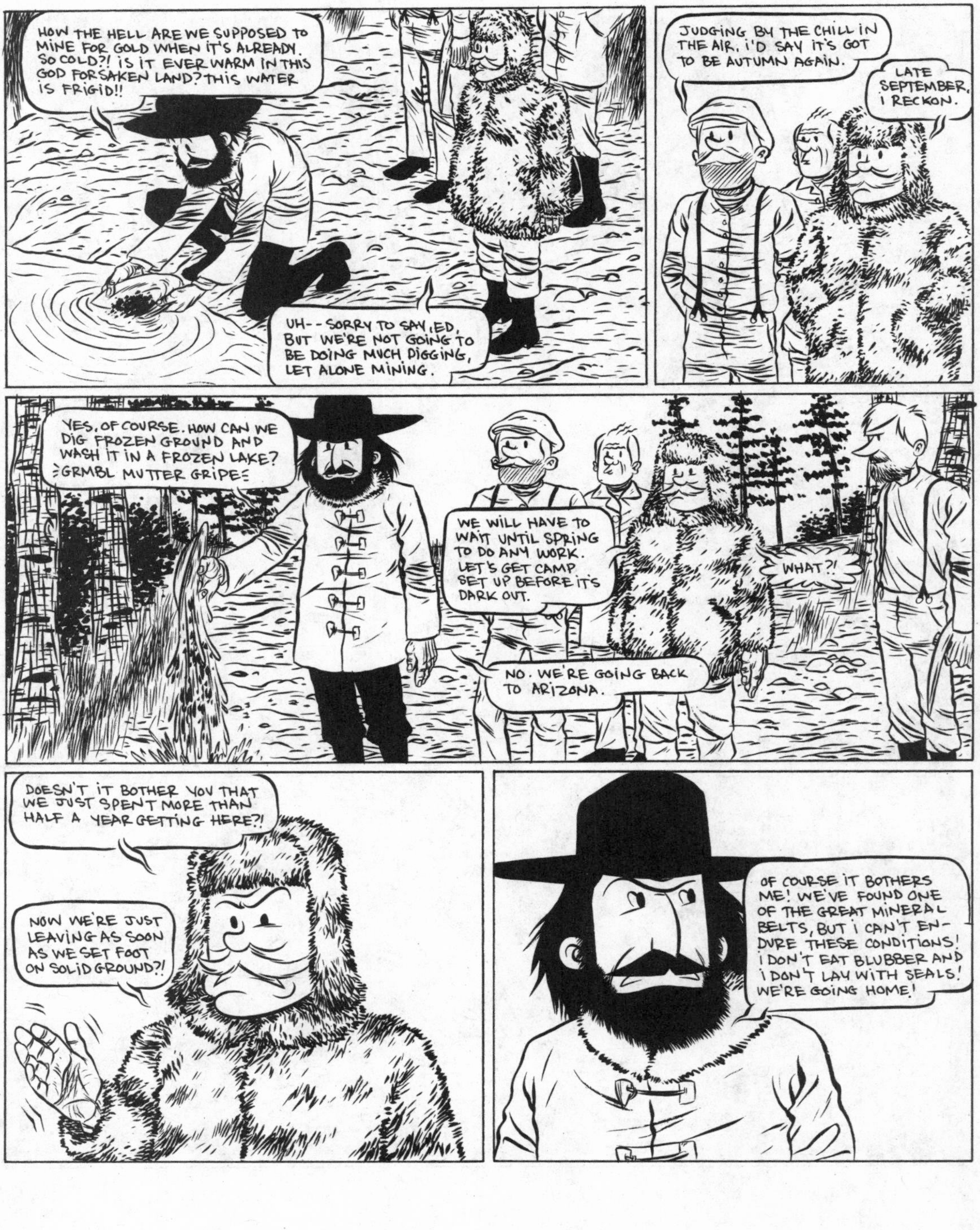
HOW THE HELL ARE WE SUPPOSED TO MINE FOR GOLD WHEN IT'S ALREADY SO COLD?! IS IT EVER WARM IN THIS GOD FORSAKEN LAND? THIS WATER IS FRIGID!!
UH-- SORRY TO SAY, ED, BUT WE'RE NOT GOING TO BE DOING MUCH DIGGING, LET ALONE MINING.
JUDGING BY THE CHILL IN THE AIR, I'D SAY IT'S GOT TO BE AUTUMN AGAIN.
LATE SEPTEMBER, I RECKON.
YES, OF COURSE. HOW CAN WE DIG FROZEN GROUND AND WASH IT IN A FROZEN LAKE? ≷GRMBL MUTTER GRIPE≶
WE WILL HAVE TO WAIT UNTIL SPRING TO DO ANY WORK. LET'S GET CAMP SET UP BEFORE IT'S DARK OUT.
NO. WE'RE GOING BACK TO ARIZONA.
WHAT?!
DOESN'T IT BOTHER YOU THAT WE JUST SPENT MORE THAN HALF A YEAR GETTING HERE?!
NOW WE'RE JUST LEAVING AS SOON AS WE SET FOOT ON SOLID GROUND?!
OF COURSE IT BOTHERS ME! WE'VE FOUND ONE OF THE GREAT MINERAL BELTS, BUT I CAN'T ENDURE THESE CONDITIONS! I DON'T EAT BLUBBER AND I DON'T LAY WITH SEALS! WE'RE GOING HOME!

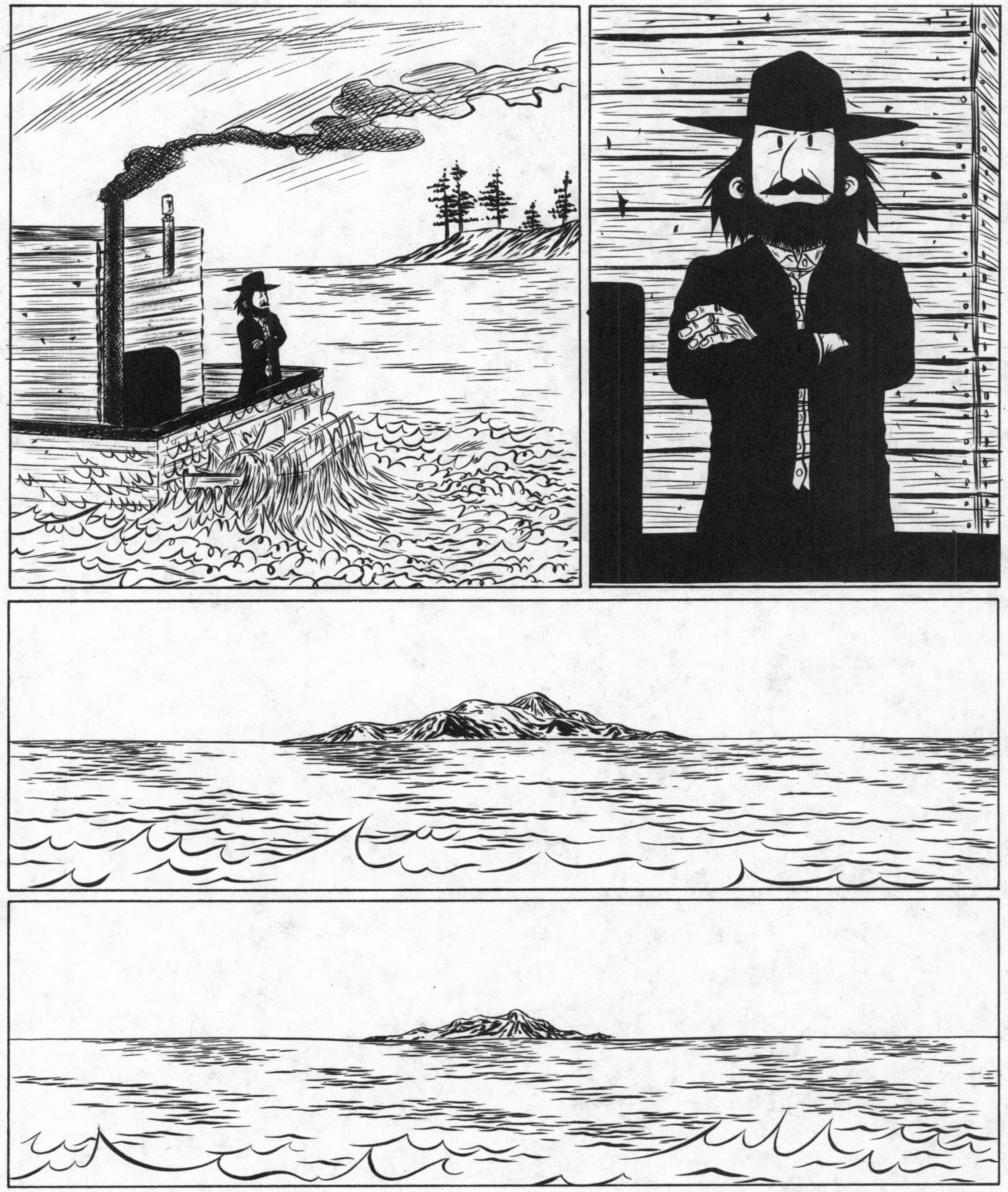

BY THE TIME MANY PEOPLE REACHED THE
YUKON, THEY COULD BARELY AFFORD TO FEED
THEMSELVES, LET ALONE PROSPECT; ROBERT
HENDERSON WAS NO DIFFERENT. HE HAD BEEN
PROSPECTING SINCE HE WAS A CHILD ON "BIG
ISLAND," JUST OFF THE COAST OF NOVA SCOTIA. AS
A TEENAGER, HENDERSON TRAVELLED TO NEW
ZEALAND, AUSTRALIA AND BACK UP THROUGH
COLORADO IN SEARCH OF GOLD. AFTER ABOUT
FOURTEEN YEARS OF PROSPECTING THE WORLD
OVER, HENDERSON WOUND UP IN ALASKA WHERE
HE MET DAWSON CITY FOUNDER, JOE LADUE,
WHOM HE WORKED FOR, BRIEFLY. LADUE WAS,
BY ALL RIGHTS, A VERY CLEVER BUSINESSMAN
AND THROUGH VARIOUS ENTERPRISES EMPLOYED
SEVERAL KEY PLAYERS IN THE GOLD RUSH.
THE JOBS WERE GENERALLY MANUAL LABOUR,
SUCH AS MILL WORK, PACKING FOR OTHER
PROSPECTORS AND HAULING LUMBER. IN EXCHANGE
FOR THEIR LABOUR, LADUE WOULD SUPPLY OUTFITS
FOR THE PROSPECTORS. THE OUTFITS INCLUDED
EQUIPMENT SUCH AS PANS, PICKS, SHOVELS,
FOOD, TOOLS (TO BUILD DEVICES LIKE SLUICE BOXES)
AND THE EQUALLY IMPORTANT SLED FOR TRANS-
PORTING THE OUTFIT.

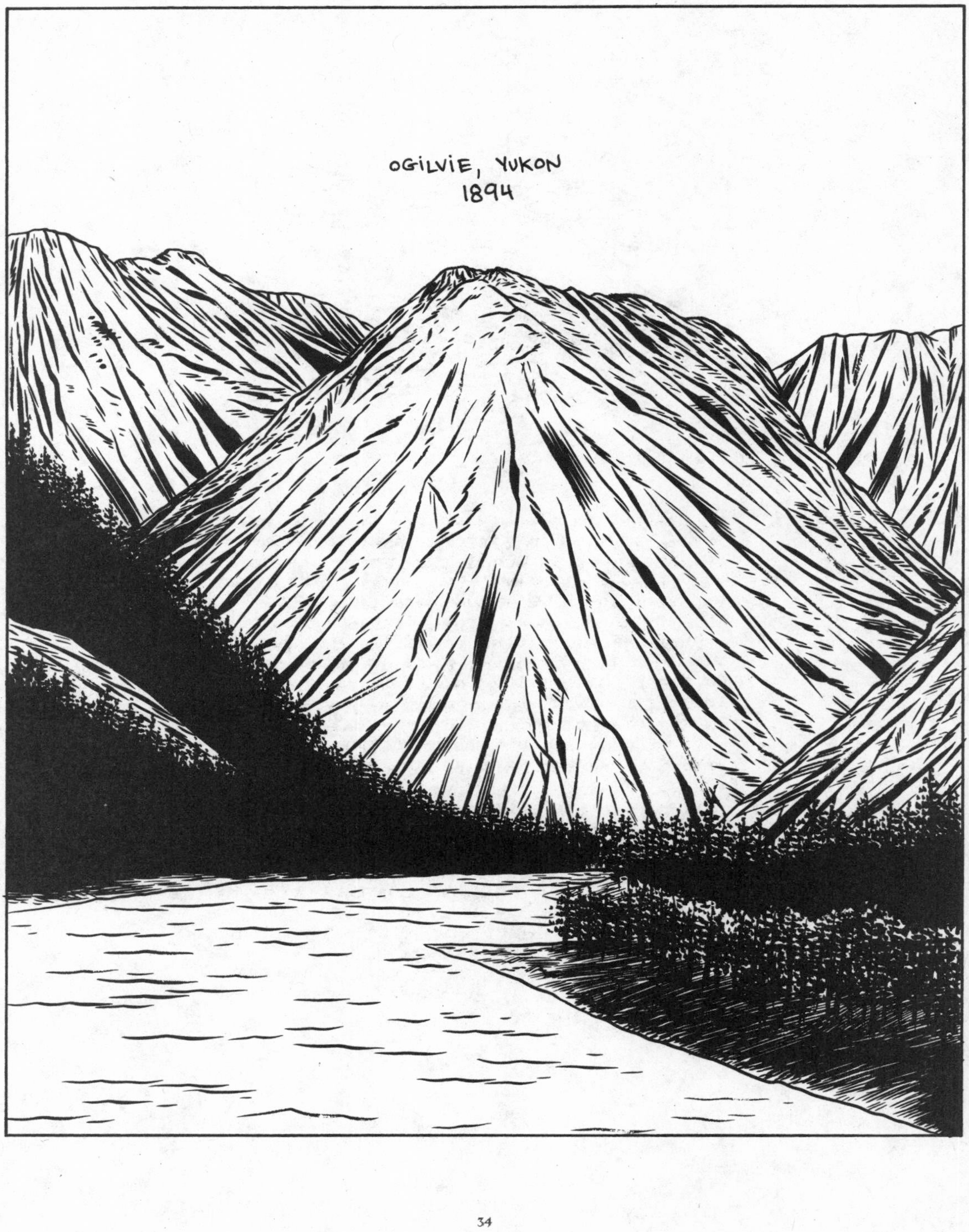
OGILVIE, YUKON
1894

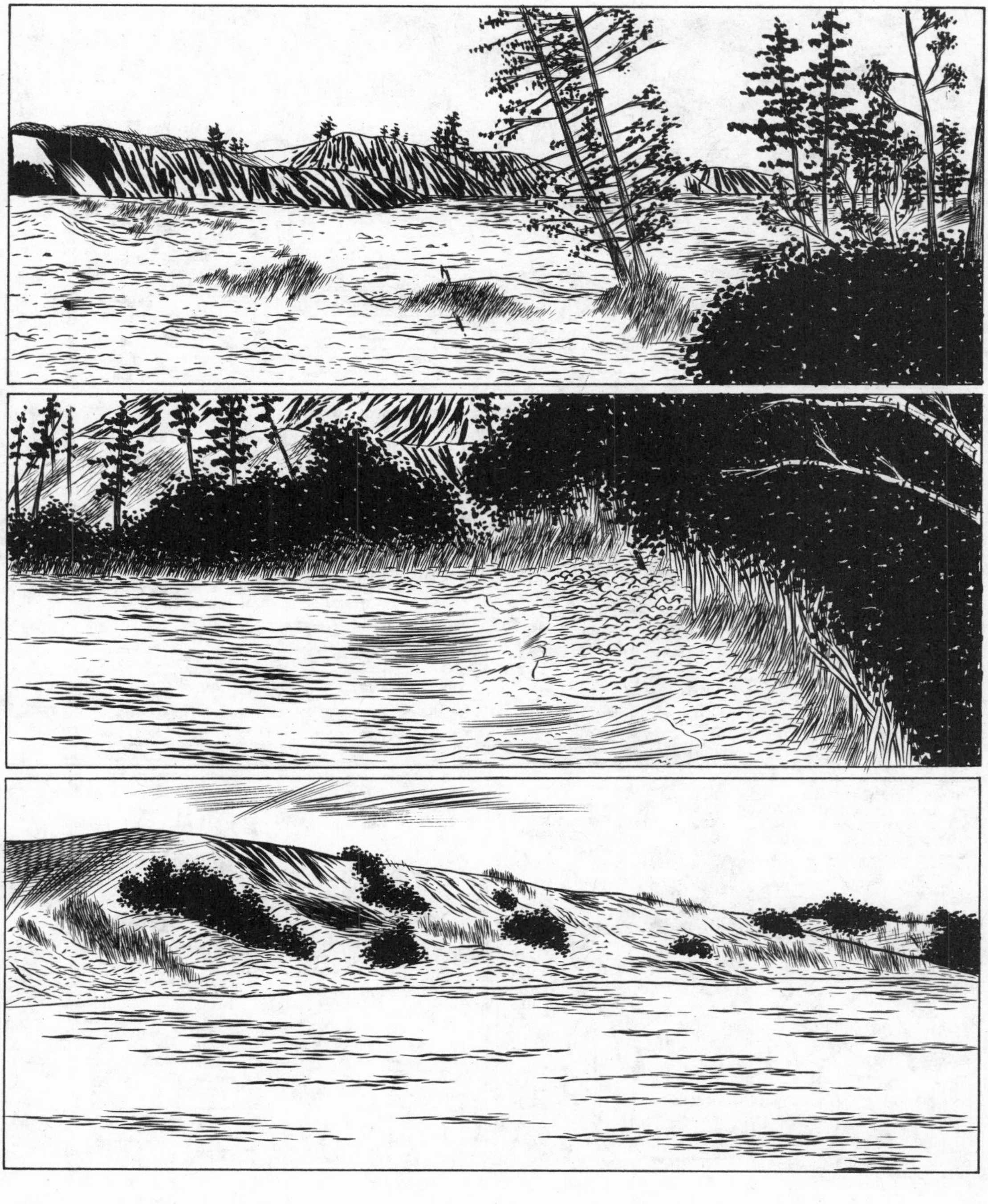

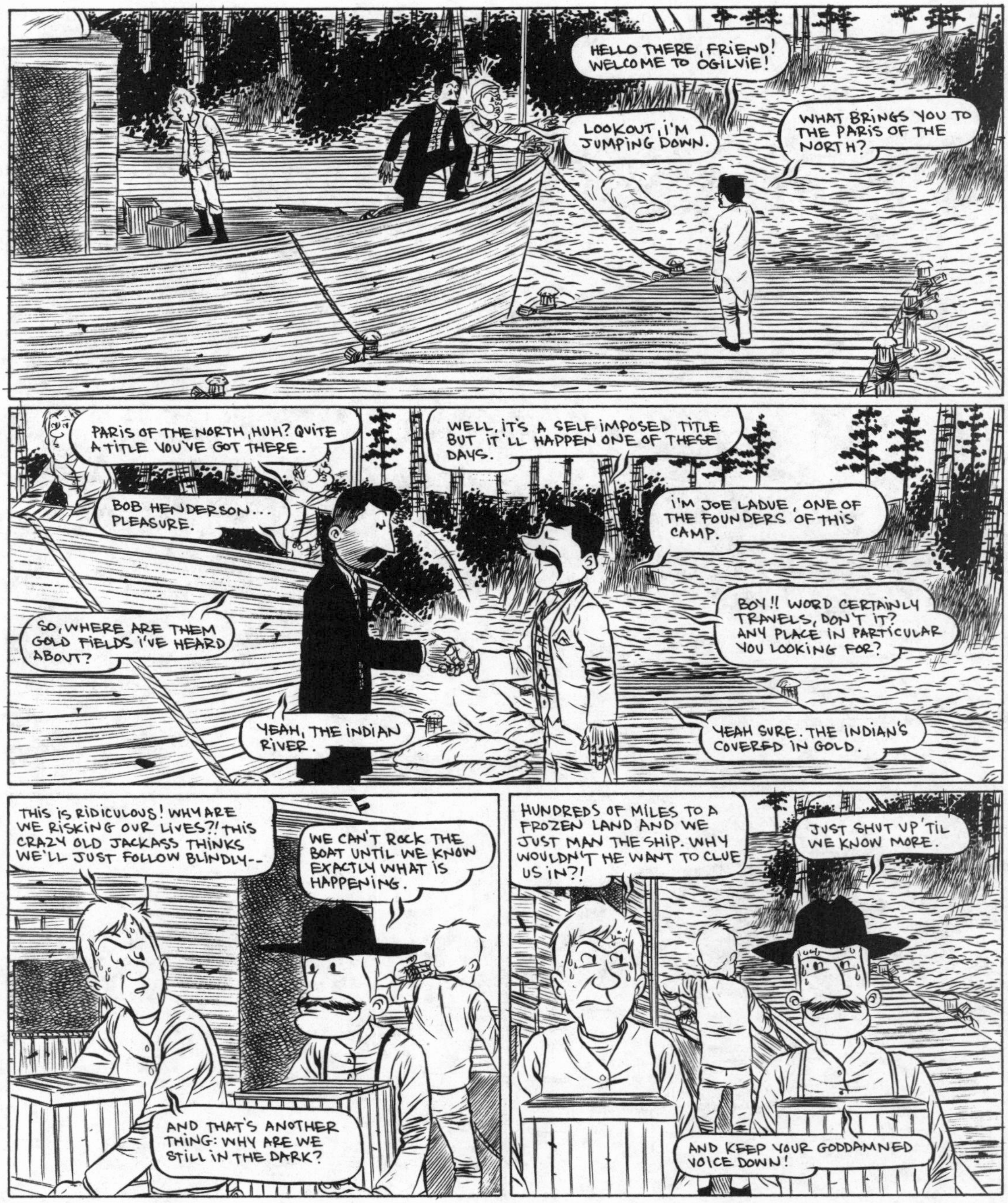
HELLO THERE, FRIEND! WELCOME TO OGILVIE!
LOOKOUT, I'M JUMPING DOWN.
WHAT BRINGS YOU TO THE PARIS OF THE NORTH?
PARIS OF THE NORTH, HUH? QUITE A TITLE YOU'VE GOT THERE.
WELL, IT'S A SELF IMPOSED TITLE BUT IT'LL HAPPEN ONE OF THESE DAYS.
BOB HENDERSON... PLEASURE.
I'M JOE LADUE, ONE OF THE FOUNDERS OF THIS CAMP.
SO, WHERE ARE THEM GOLD FIELDS I'VE HEARD ABOUT?
BOY!! WORD CERTAINLY TRAVELS, DON'T IT? ANY PLACE IN PARTICULAR YOU LOOKING FOR?
YEAH, THE INDIAN RIVER.
YEAH SURE. THE INDIAN'S COVERED IN GOLD.
THIS IS RIDICULOUS! WHY ARE WE RISKING OUR LIVES?! THIS CRAZY OLD JACKASS THINKS WE'LL JUST FOLLOW BLINDLY--
WE CAN'T ROCK THE BOAT UNTIL WE KNOW EXACTLY WHAT IS HAPPENING.
AND THAT'S ANOTHER THING: WHY ARE WE STILL IN THE DARK?
HUNDREDS OF MILES TO A FROZEN LAND AND WE JUST MAN THE SHIP. WHY WOULDN'T HE WANT TO CLUE US IN?!
JUST SHUT UP 'TIL WE KNOW MORE.
AND KEEP YOUR GODDAMNED VOICE DOWN!

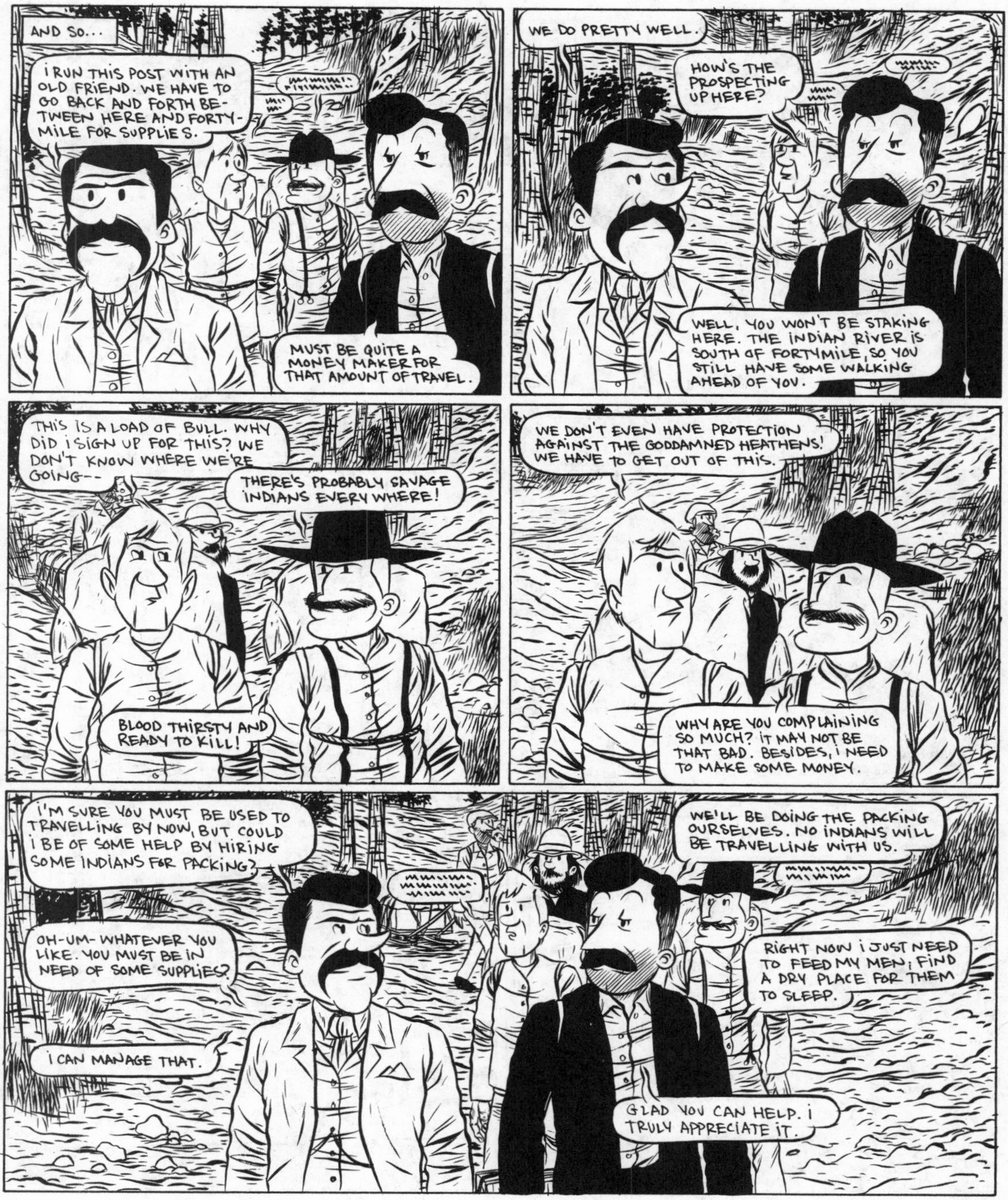
AND SO...
I RUN THIS POST WITH AN OLD FRIEND. WE HAVE TO GO BACK AND FORTH BETWEEN HERE AND FORTYMILE FOR SUPPLIES.
MUST BE QUITE A MONEY MAKER FOR THAT AMOUNT OF TRAVEL.
WE DO PRETTY WELL.
HOW'S THE PROSPECTING UP HERE?
WELL, YOU WON'T BE STAKING HERE. THE INDIAN RIVER IS SOUTH OF FORTYMILE, SO YOU STILL HAVE SOME WALKING AHEAD OF YOU.
THIS IS A LOAD OF BULL. WHY DID I SIGN UP FOR THIS? WE DON'T KNOW WHERE WE'RE GOING--
THERE'S PROBABLY SAVAGE INDIANS EVERY WHERE!
BLOOD THIRSTY AND READY TO KILL!
WE DON'T EVEN HAVE PROTECTION AGAINST THE GODDAMNED HEATHENS! WE HAVE TO GET OUT OF THIS.
WHY ARE YOU COMPLAINING SO MUCH? IT MAY NOT BE THAT BAD. BESIDES, I NEED TO MAKE SOME MONEY.
I'M SURE YOU MUST BE USED TO TRAVELLING BY NOW, BUT COULD I BE OF SOME HELP BY HIRING SOME INDIANS FOR PACKING?
WE'LL BE DOING THE PACKING OURSELVES. NO INDIANS WILL BE TRAVELLING WITH US.
OH-UM- WHATEVER YOU LIKE. YOU MUST BE IN NEED OF SOME SUPPLIES?
RIGHT NOW I JUST NEED TO FEED MY MEN; FIND A DRY PLACE FOR THEM TO SLEEP.
I CAN MANAGE THAT.
GLAD YOU CAN HELP. I TRULY APPRECIATE IT.

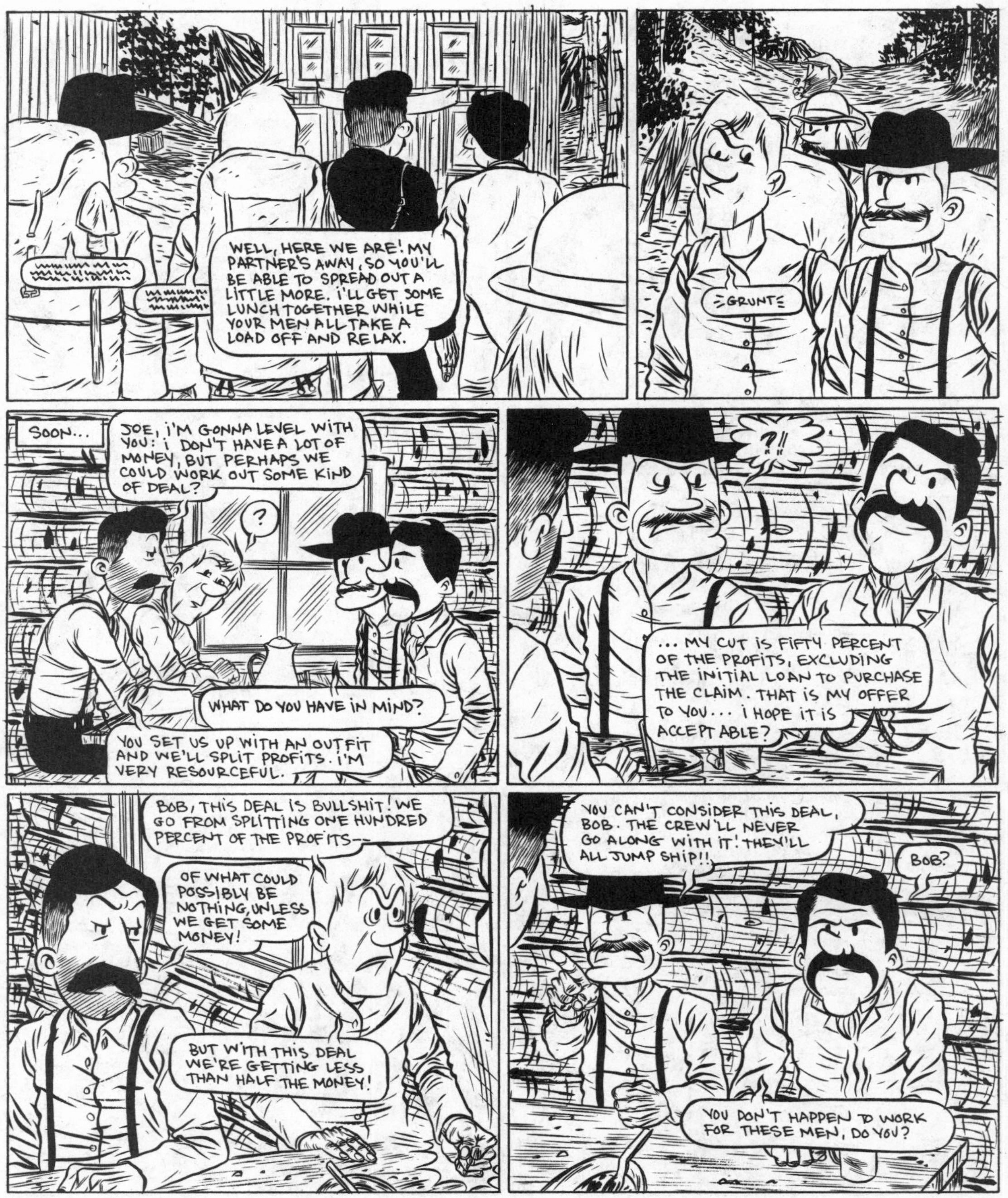
WELL, HERE WE ARE! MY PARTNER'S AWAY, SO YOU'LL BE ABLE TO SPREAD OUT A LITTLE MORE. I'LL GET SOME LUNCH TOGETHER WHILE YOUR MEN ALL TAKE A LOAD OFF AND RELAX.
GRUNT
SOON...
JOE, I'M GONNA LEVEL WITH YOU: I DON'T HAVE A LOT OF MONEY, BUT PERHAPS WE COULD WORK OUT SOME KIND OF DEAL?
?
WHAT DO YOU HAVE IN MIND?
YOU SET US UP WITH AN OUTFIT AND WE'LL SPLIT PROFITS. I'M VERY RESOURCEFUL.
?!!
... MY CUT IS FIFTY PERCENT OF THE PROFITS, EXCLUDING THE INITIAL LOAN TO PURCHASE THE CLAIM. THAT IS MY OFFER TO YOU... I HOPE IT IS ACCEPTABLE?
BOB, THIS DEAL IS BULLSHIT! WE GO FROM SPLITTING ONE HUNDRED PERCENT OF THE PROFITS--
OF WHAT COULD POSSIBLY BE NOTHING, UNLESS WE GET SOME MONEY!
BUT WITH THIS DEAL WE'RE GETTING LESS THAN HALF THE MONEY!
YOU CAN'T CONSIDER THIS DEAL, BOB. THE CREW'LL NEVER GO ALONG WITH IT! THEY'LL ALL JUMP SHIP!!
BOB?
YOU DON'T HAPPEN TO WORK FOR THESE MEN, DO YOU?

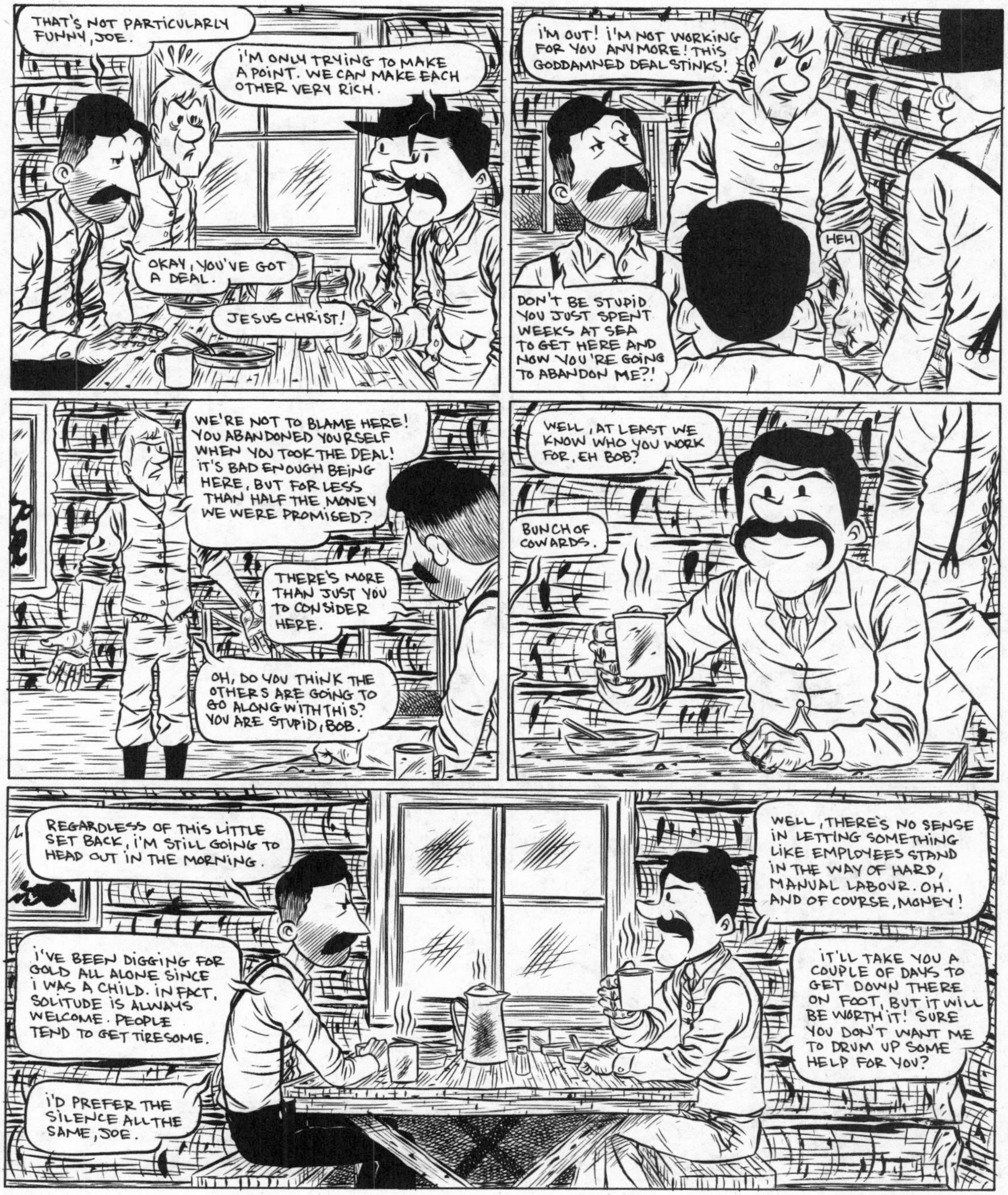

THAT'S NOT PARTICULARLY FUNNY, JOE.
I'M ONLY TRYING TO MAKE A POINT. WE CAN MAKE EACH OTHER VERY RICH.
OKAY, YOU'VE GOT A DEAL.
JESUS CHRIST!
I'M OUT! I'M NOT WORKING FOR YOU ANYMORE! THIS GODDAMNED DEAL STINKS!
HEH
DON'T BE STUPID YOU JUST SPENT WEEKS AT SEA TO GET HERE AND NOW YOU'RE GOING TO ABANDON ME?!
WE'RE NOT TO BLAME HERE! YOU ABANDONED YOURSELF WHEN YOU TOOK THE DEAL! IT'S BAD ENOUGH BEING HERE, BUT FOR LESS THAN HALF THE MONEY WE WERE PROMISED?
THERE'S MORE THAN JUST YOU TO CONSIDER HERE.
OH, DO YOU THINK THE OTHERS ARE GOING TO GO ALONG WITH THIS? YOU ARE STUPID, BOB.
WELL, AT LEAST WE KNOW WHO YOU WORK FOR, EH BOB?
BUNCH OF COWARDS.
REGARDLESS OF THIS LITTLE SET BACK, I'M STILL GOING TO HEAD OUT IN THE MORNING.
WELL, THERE'S NO SENSE IN LETTING SOMETHING LIKE EMPLOYEES STAND IN THE WAY OF HARD, MANUAL LABOUR. OH. AND OF COURSE, MONEY!
I'VE BEEN DIGGING FOR GOLD ALL ALONE SINCE I WAS A CHILD. IN FACT, SOLITUDE IS ALWAYS WELCOME. PEOPLE TEND TO GET TIRESOME.
IT'LL TAKE YOU A COUPLE OF DAYS TO GET DOWN THERE ON FOOT, BUT IT WILL BE WORTH IT! SURE YOU DON'T WANT ME TO DRUM UP SOME HELP FOR YOU?
I'D PREFER THE SILENCE ALL THE SAME, JOE.

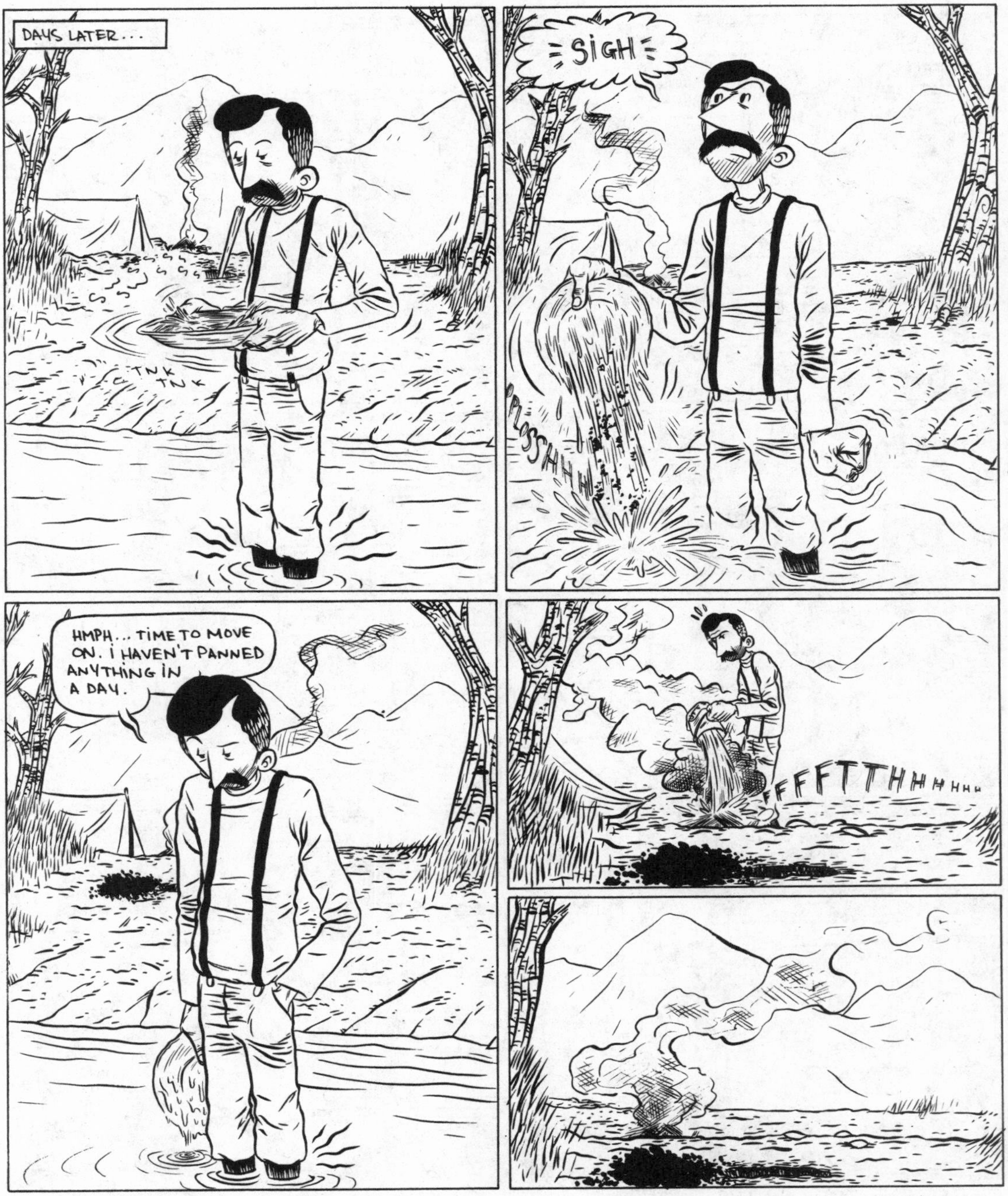
DAYS LATER...
TNK TNK
SIGH
PLOOSHHH
HMPH... TIME TO MOVE ON. I HAVEN'T PANNED ANYTHING IN A DAY.
FFFFTTHHHHHH

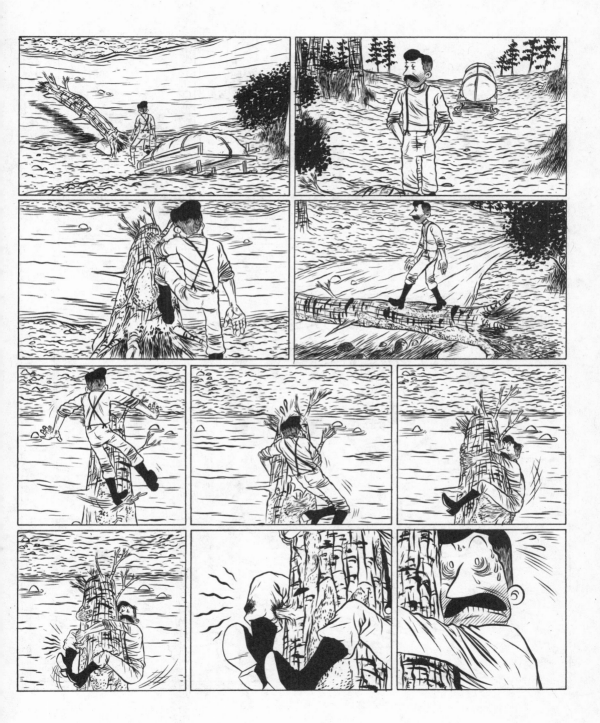

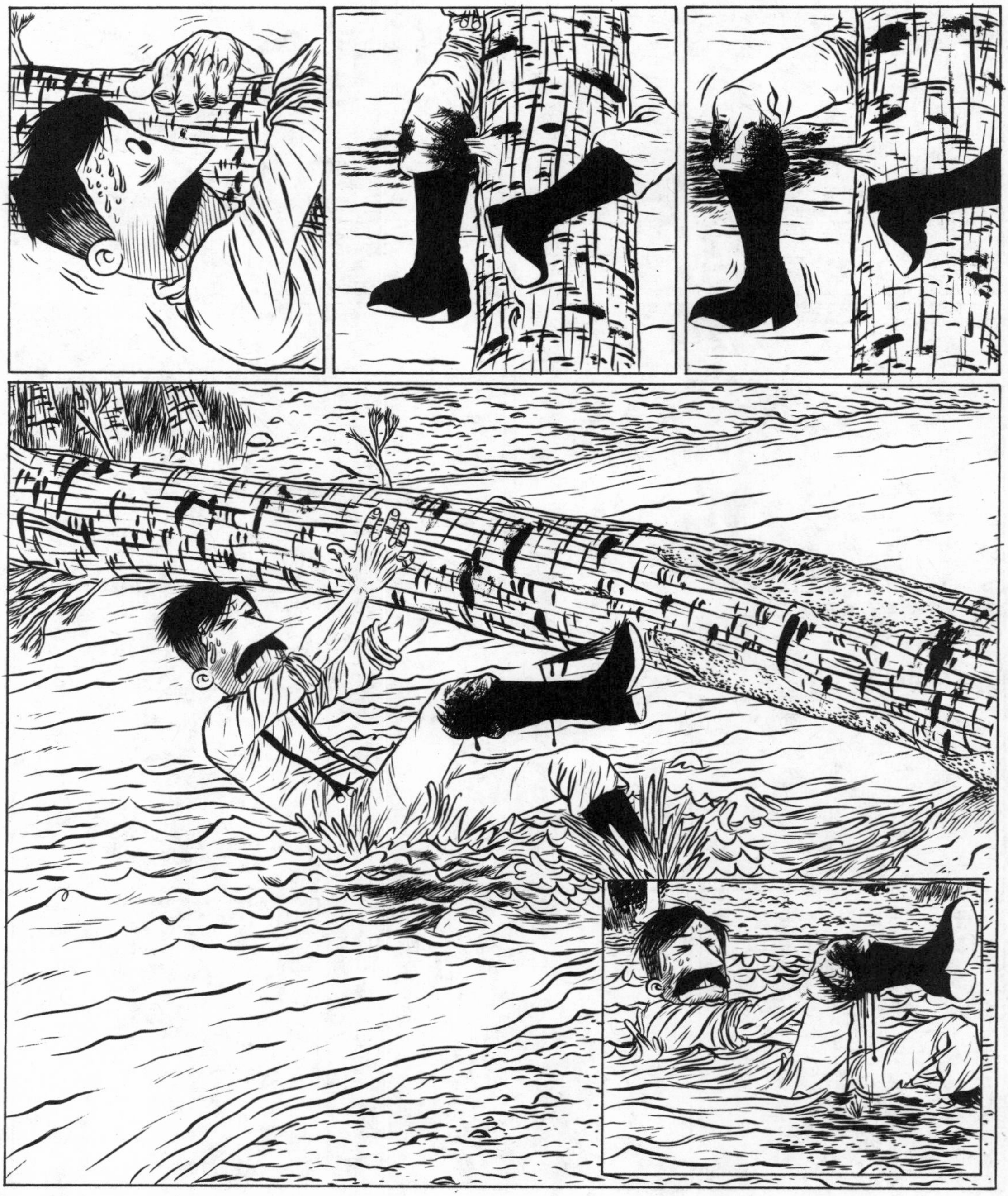

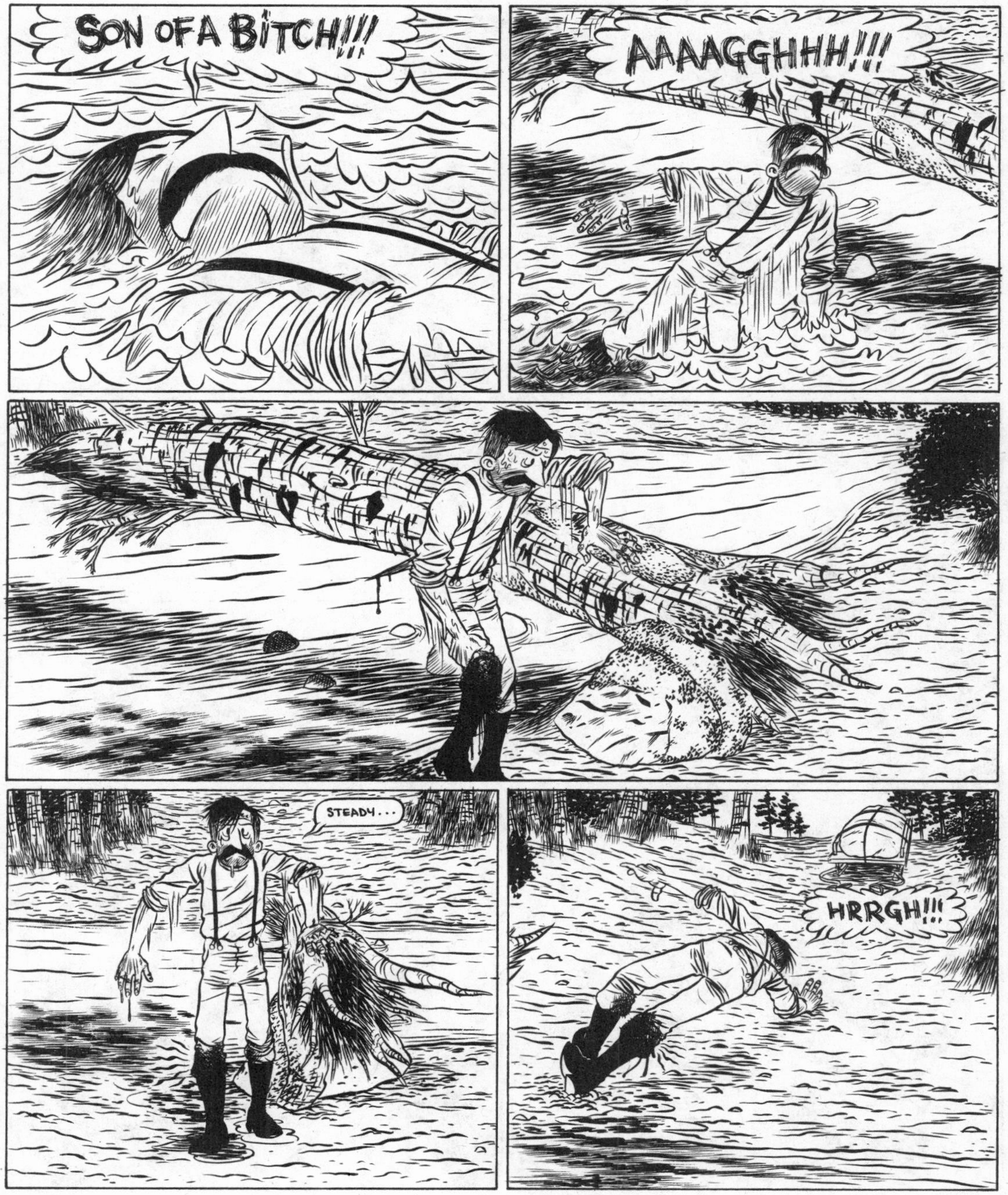
SON OF A BITCH!!!
AAAAGGHHH!!!
STEADY...
HRRGH!!!

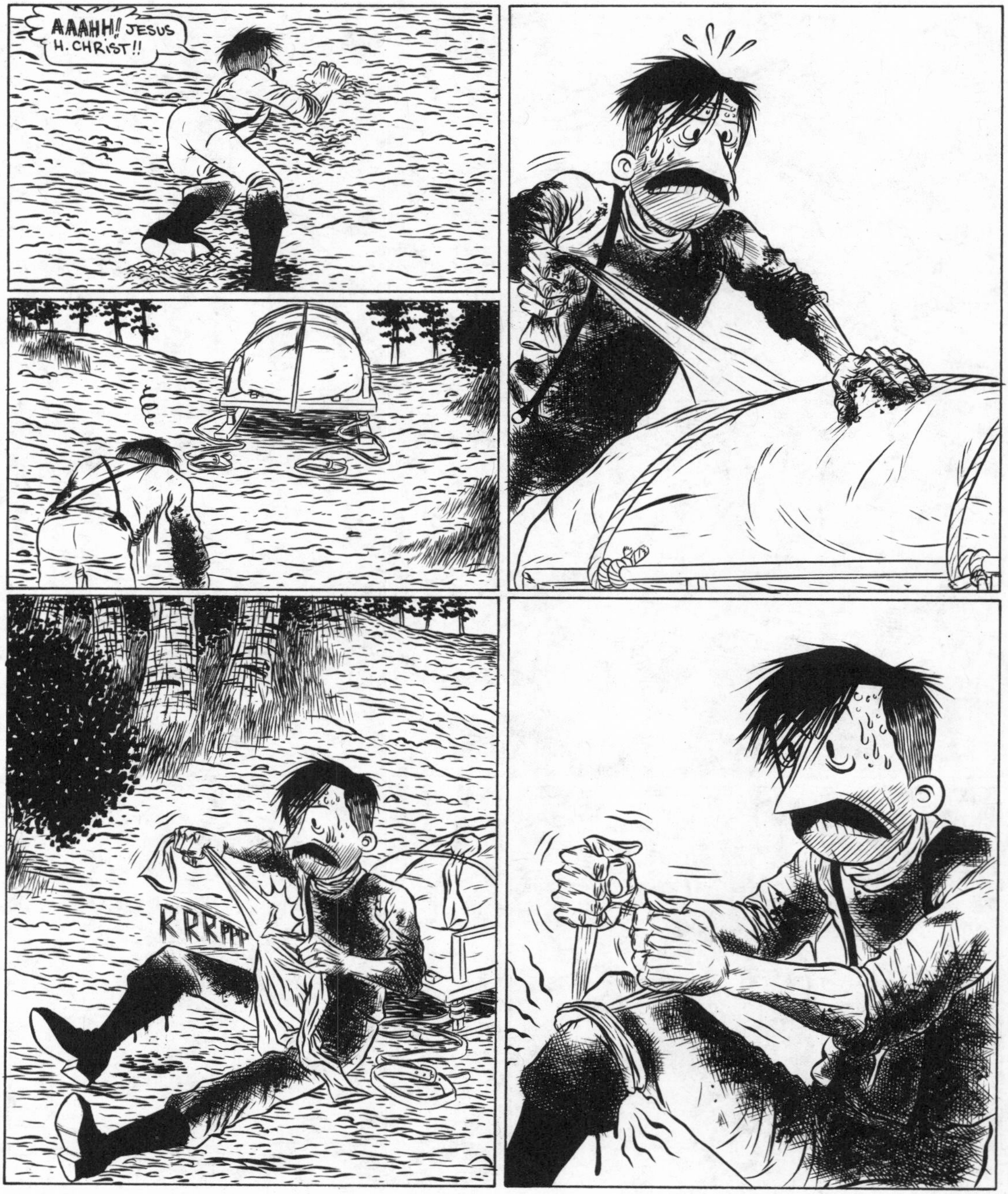

AAAHH!! JESUS H. CHRIST!!
RRRPPP

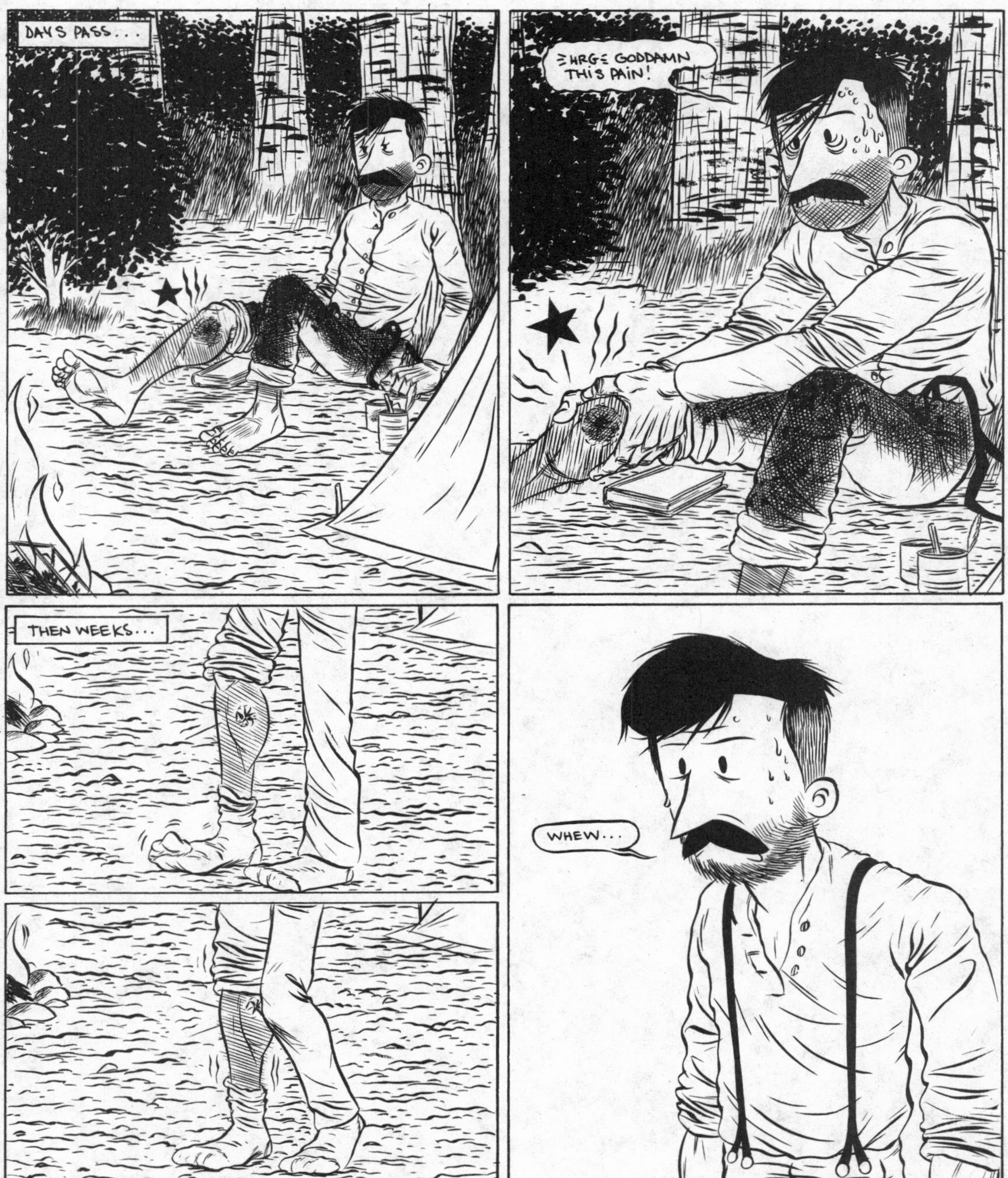
DAYS PASS...
≡HRG≡ GODDAMN THIS PAIN!
THEN WEEKS...
WHEW...

GEORGE CARMACK WAS WELL KNOWN IN THE NORTH AS "LYING GEORGE," A NICKNAME EARNED THROUGH HIS REPUTATION OF STRETCHING THE TRUTH. HE WAS ALSO KNOWN FOR LIVING AS A TAGISH INDIAN, TAKING A TAGISH WOMAN AS HIS BRIDE. CARMACK DID MOST OF HIS WORK AND TRAVELLING WITH HIS BROTHER IN LAW, A LARGE TAGISH MAN CALLED "SKOOKUM" JIM. HE GOT HIS NICKNAME-- WHICH MEANS STURDY-- BECAUSE OF HIS WORK AS A PACKER. JIM COULD CARRY 200 POUNDS ON HIS BACK WITH LITTLE OR NO BREAK.

ANOTHER MAJOR PLAYER IN THE KLONDIKE WAS "BIG" ALEX McDONALD. HE OWNED LAND IN DAWSON AND HAD CLAIMS ON ALL OF THE RICHEST CREEKS. HE WAS CONSIDERED SLOW WITTED BY MANY, YET WAS ONE OF THE RICHEST MEN DURING THE GOLD RUSH. ONE MIGHT ATTRIBUTE McDONALD'S SUCCESS TO THE FACT THAT HE ABSTAINED FROM DRINKING ALL TOGETHER; AN INSATIABLE APPETITE FOR MONEY AND PROPERTY WAS HIS ONLY VICE. McDONALD WAS NEVER TERRIBLY POPULAR AS HE SAW MOST PEOPLE ONLY AS A WAY TO MAKE MONEY. CARMACK HAD THE SAME PROBLEMS WITH POPULARITY. HIS LIFESTYLE AT THE TIME WAS SEEN AS VERY UNDESIRABLE AND EVEN THOUGH THE YUKON WAS MAINLY POPULATED BY VARIOUS INDIAN TRIBES, THEY WERE TREATED POORLY BY THE INFLUX OF WHITES FROM NORTH AMERICA AND EUROPE.

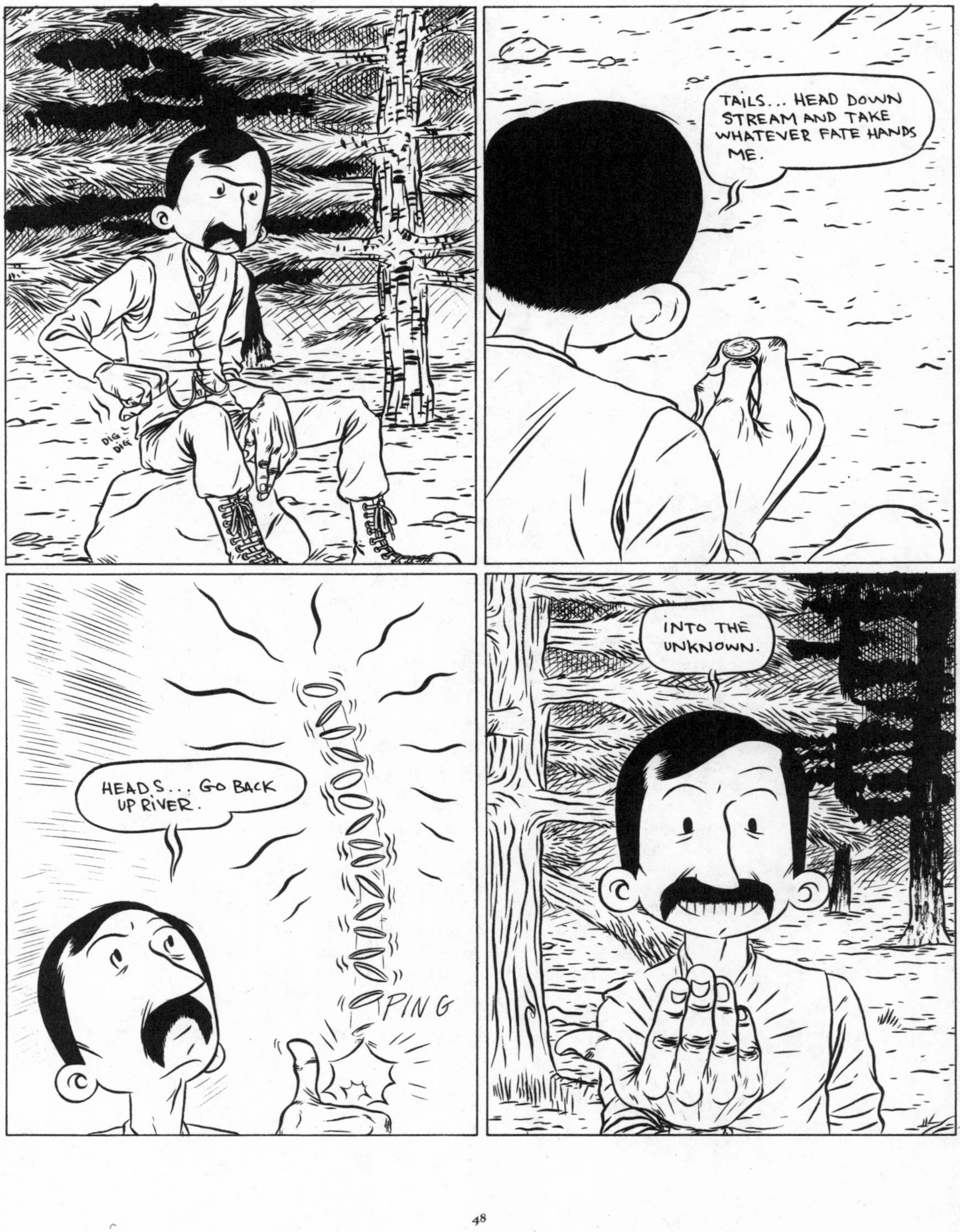
DIG DIG
TAILS... HEAD DOWN STREAM AND TAKE WHATEVER FATE HANDS ME.
HEADS... GO BACK UP RIVER.
PING
INTO THE UNKNOWN.

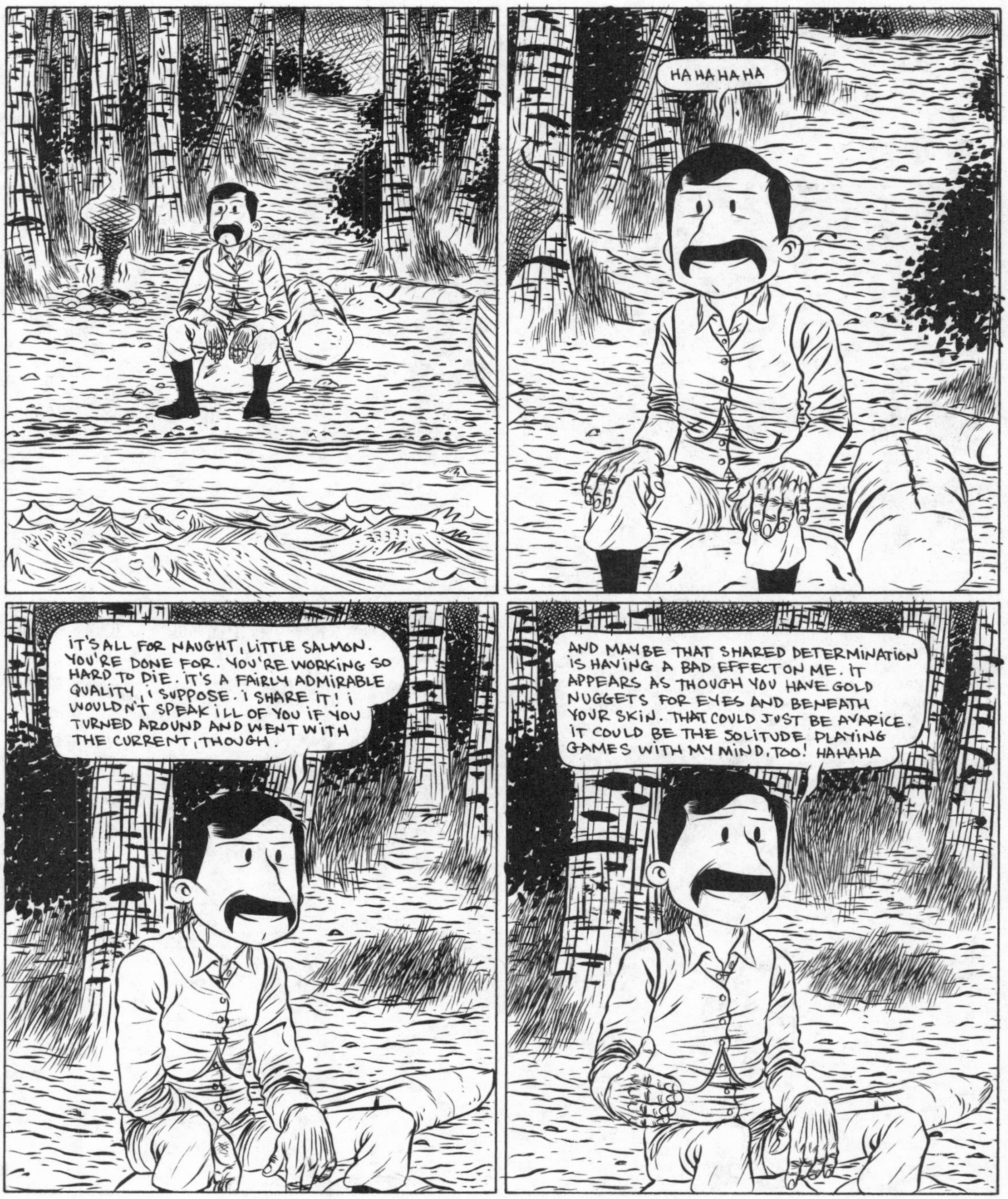
HA HA HA HA
IT'S ALL FOR NAUGHT, LITTLE SALMON. YOU'RE DONE FOR. YOU'RE WORKING SO HARD TO DIE. IT'S A FAIRLY ADMIRABLE QUALITY, I SUPPOSE. I SHARE IT! I WOULDN'T SPEAK ILL OF YOU IF YOU TURNED AROUND AND WENT WITH THE CURRENT, THOUGH.
AND MAYBE THAT SHARED DETERMINATION IS HAVING A BAD EFFECT ON ME. IT APPEARS AS THOUGH YOU HAVE GOLD NUGGETS FOR EYES AND BENEATH YOUR SKIN. THAT COULD JUST BE AVARICE. IT COULD BE THE SOLITUDE PLAYING GAMES WITH MY MIND, TOO! HAHAHA

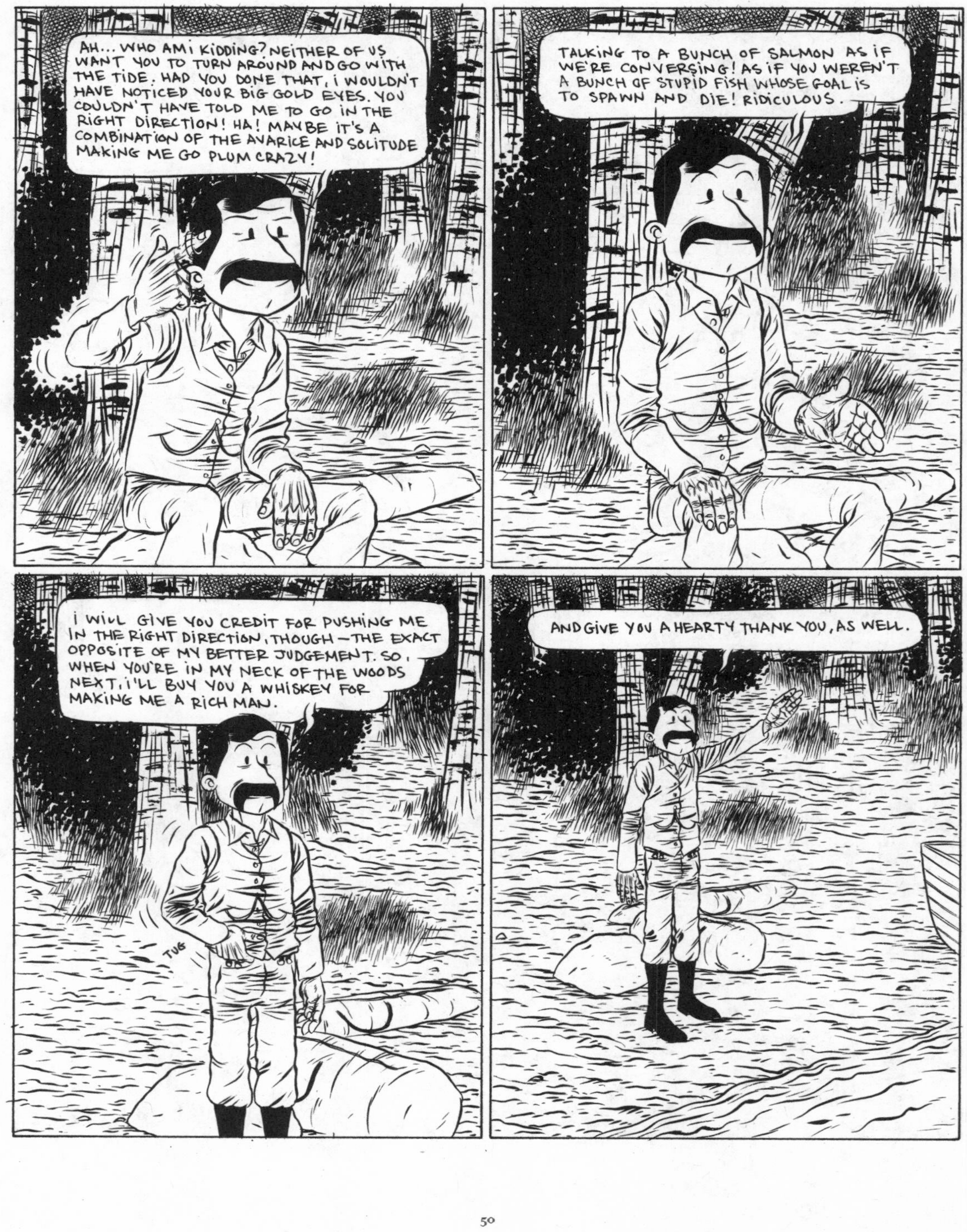
AH... WHO AM I KIDDING? NEITHER OF US WANT YOU TO TURN AROUND AND GO WITH THE TIDE. HAD YOU DONE THAT, I WOULDN'T HAVE NOTICED YOUR BIG GOLD EYES. YOU COULDN'T HAVE TOLD ME TO GO IN THE RIGHT DIRECTION! HA! MAYBE IT'S A COMBINATION OF THE AVARICE AND SOLITUDE MAKING ME GO PLUM CRAZY!
TALKING TO A BUNCH OF SALMON AS IF WE'RE CONVERSING! AS IF YOU WEREN'T A BUNCH OF STUPID FISH WHOSE GOAL IS TO SPAWN AND DIE! RIDICULOUS.
I WILL GIVE YOU CREDIT FOR PUSHING ME IN THE RIGHT DIRECTION, THOUGH—THE EXACT OPPOSITE OF MY BETTER JUDGEMENT. SO, WHEN YOU'RE IN MY NECK OF THE WOODS NEXT, I'LL BUY YOU A WHISKEY FOR MAKING ME A RICH MAN.
TUG
AND GIVE YOU A HEARTY THANK YOU, AS WELL.

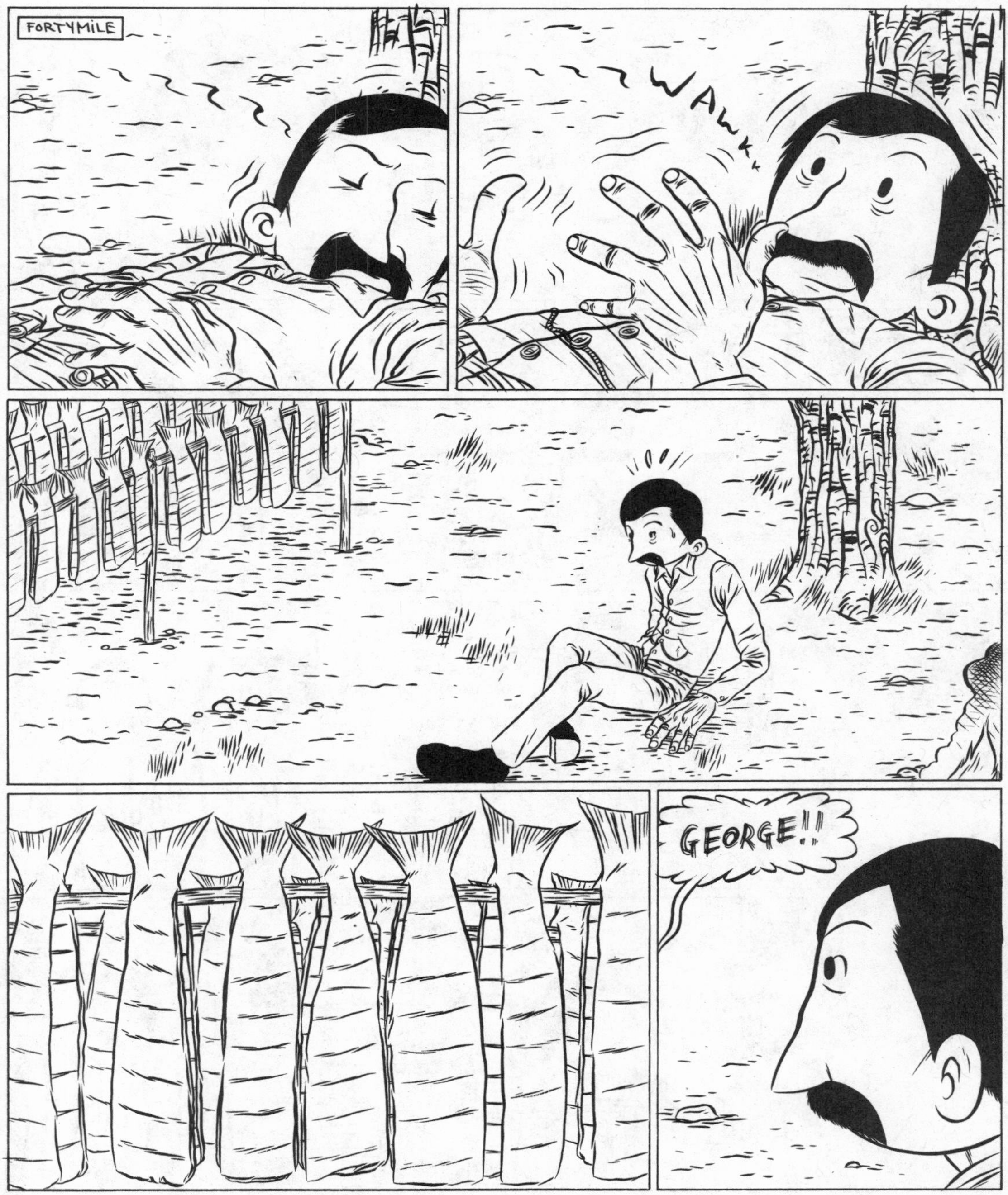
FORTYMILE
WAWK
GEORGE!!

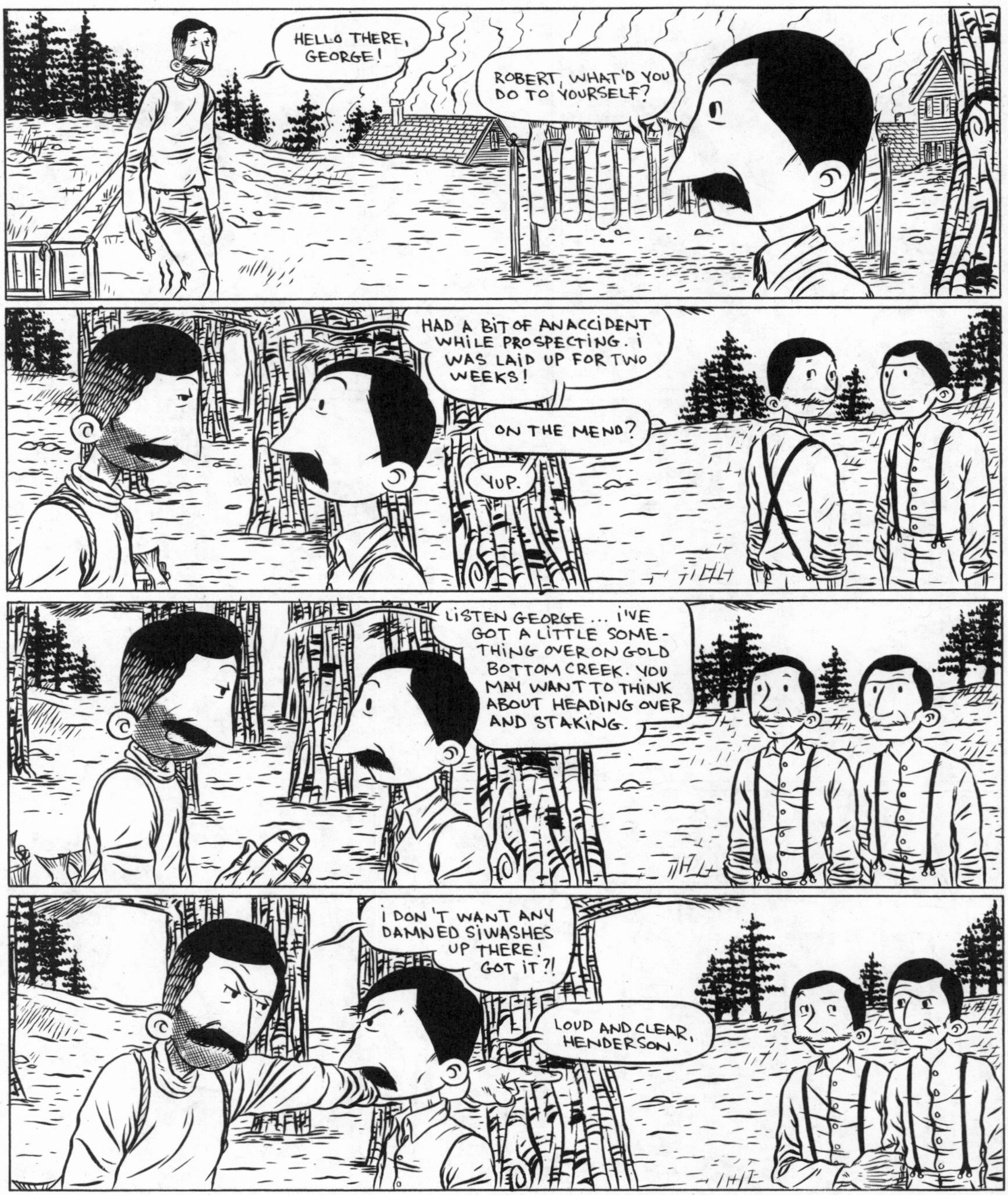
HELLO THERE, GEORGE!
ROBERT, WHAT'D YOU DO TO YOURSELF?
HAD A BIT OF AN ACCIDENT WHILE PROSPECTING. I WAS LAID UP FOR TWO WEEKS!
ON THE MEND?
YUP.
LISTEN GEORGE... I'VE GOT A LITTLE SOME-THING OVER ON GOLD BOTTOM CREEK. YOU MAY WANT TO THINK ABOUT HEADING OVER AND STAKING.
I DON'T WANT ANY DAMNED SIWASHES UP THERE! GOT IT?!
LOUD AND CLEAR, HENDERSON.

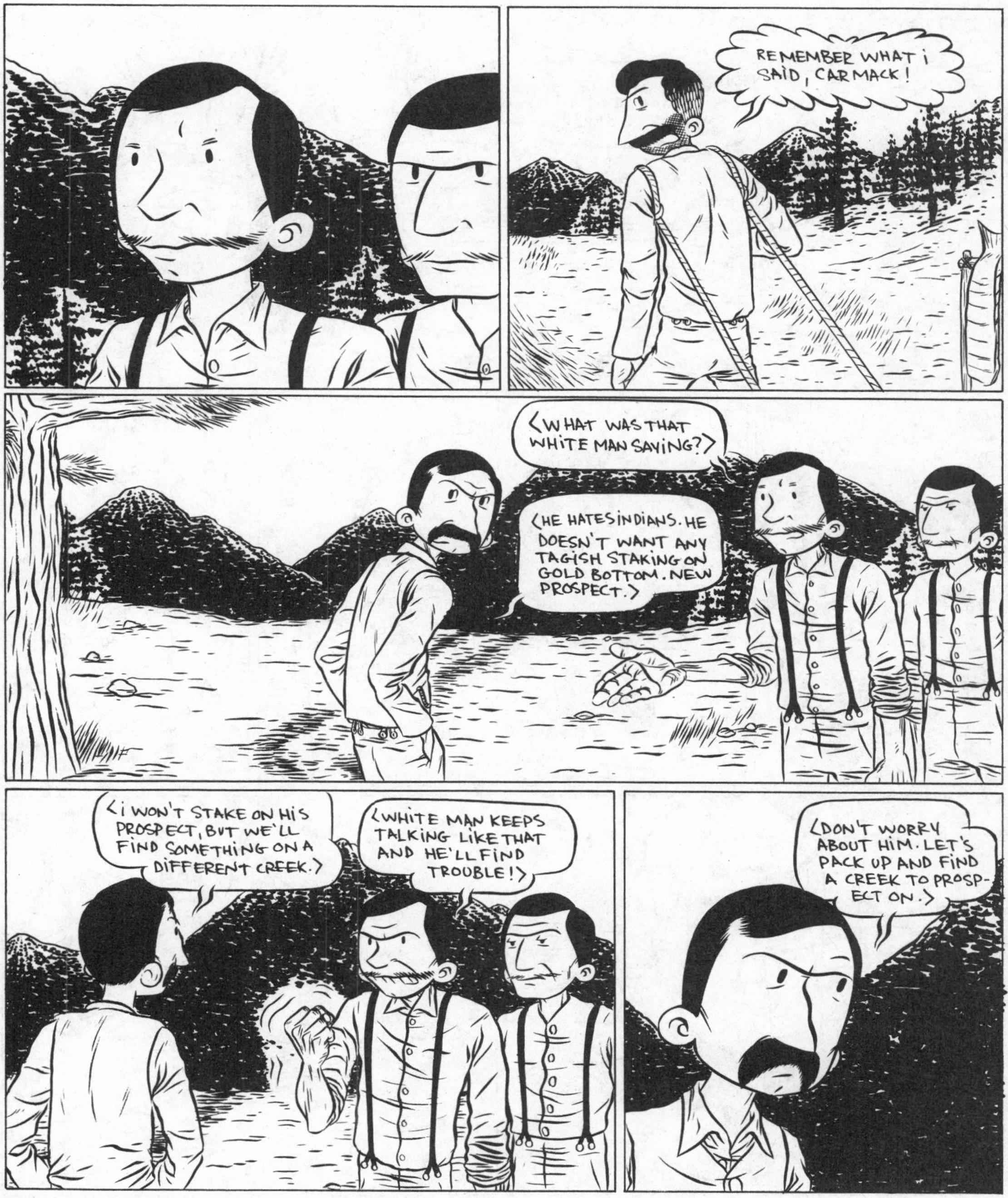
REMEMBER WHAT i SAID, CARMACK!
<WHAT WAS THAT WHITE MAN SAYING?>
<HE HATES INDIANS. HE DOESN'T WANT ANY TAGISH STAKING ON GOLD BOTTOM. NEW PROSPECT.>
<i WON'T STAKE ON HIS PROSPECT, BUT WE'LL FIND SOMETHING ON A DIFFERENT CREEK.>
<WHITE MAN KEEPS TALKING LIKE THAT AND HE'LL FIND TROUBLE!>
<DON'T WORRY ABOUT HIM. LET'S PACK UP AND FIND A CREEK TO PROSPECT ON.>

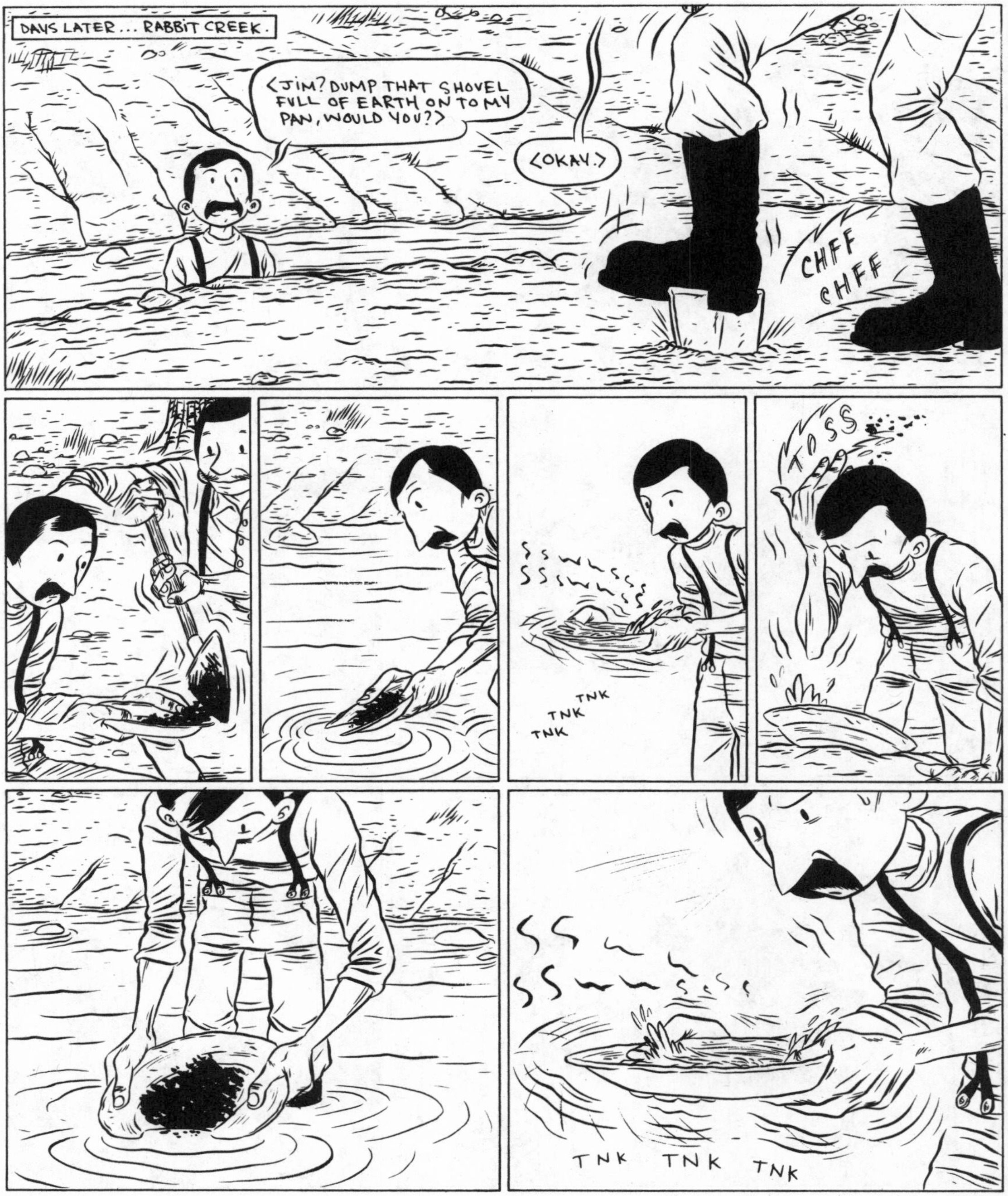

DAYS LATER... RABBIT CREEK.
<JIM? DUMP THAT SHOVEL FULL OF EARTH ON TO MY PAN, WOULD YOU?>
<OKAY.>
CHFF CHFF
SSWLSSS
TNK TNK TNK
TOSS
TNK TNK TNK

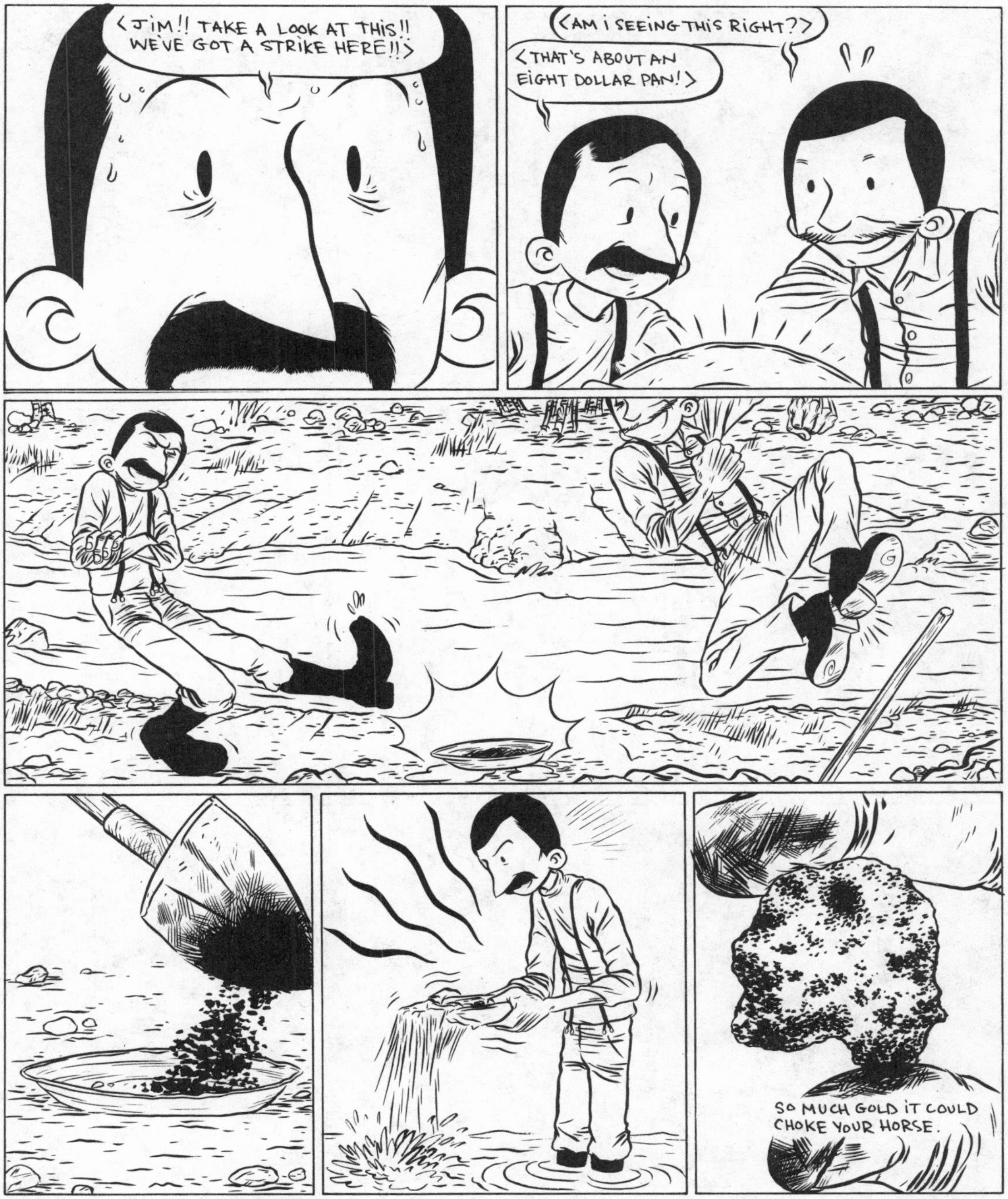
<JIM!! TAKE A LOOK AT THIS!! WE'VE GOT A STRIKE HERE!!>
<AM I SEEING THIS RIGHT?>
<THAT'S ABOUT AN EIGHT DOLLAR PAN!>
SO MUCH GOLD IT COULD CHOKE YOUR HORSE.

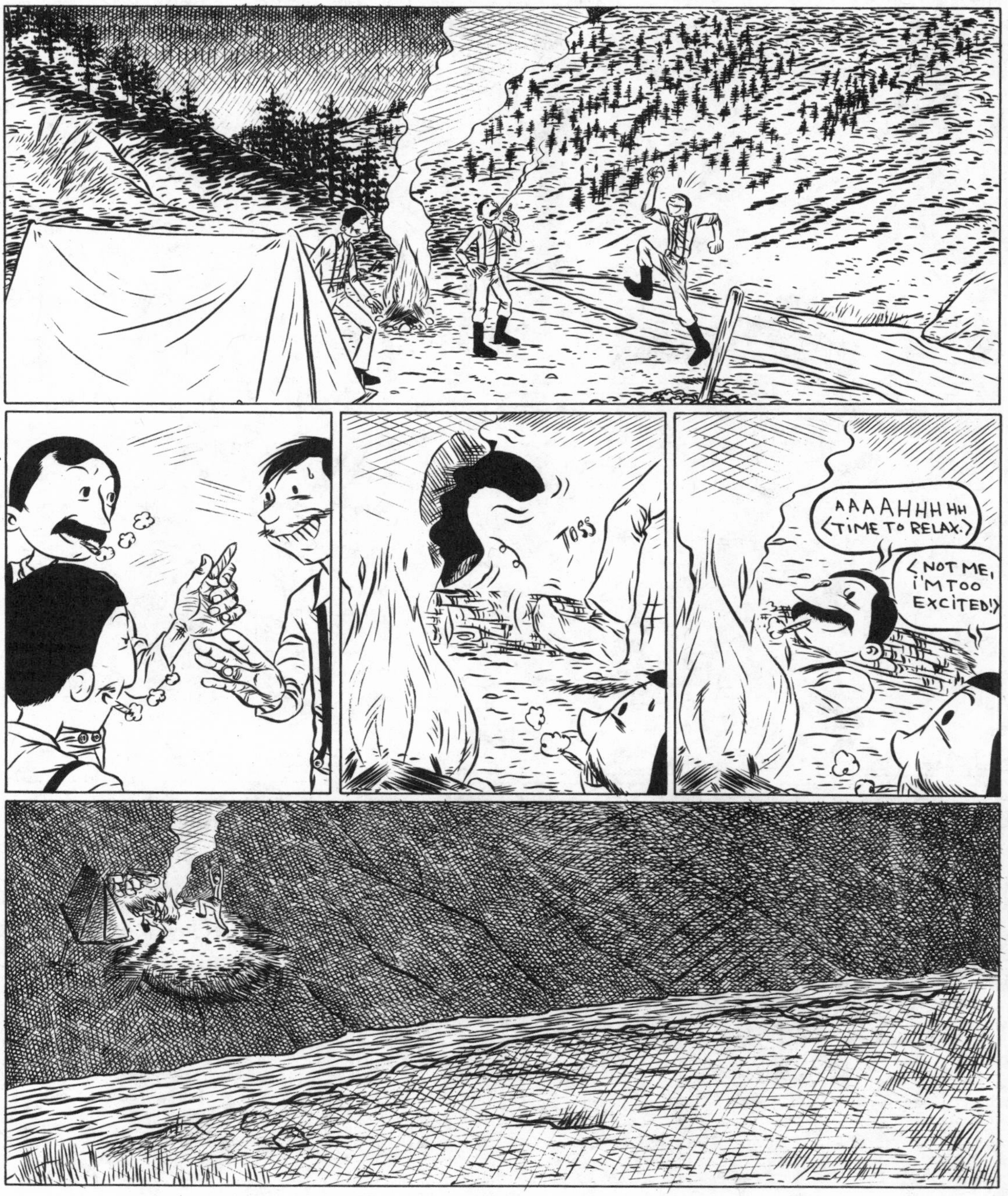
TOSS
AAAAHHHHH
<TIME TO RELAX.>
<NOT ME, I'M TOO EXCITED!>

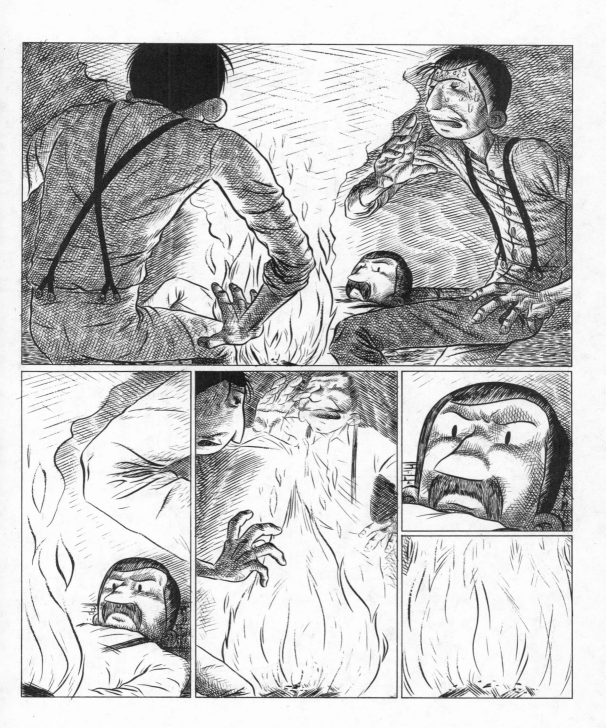

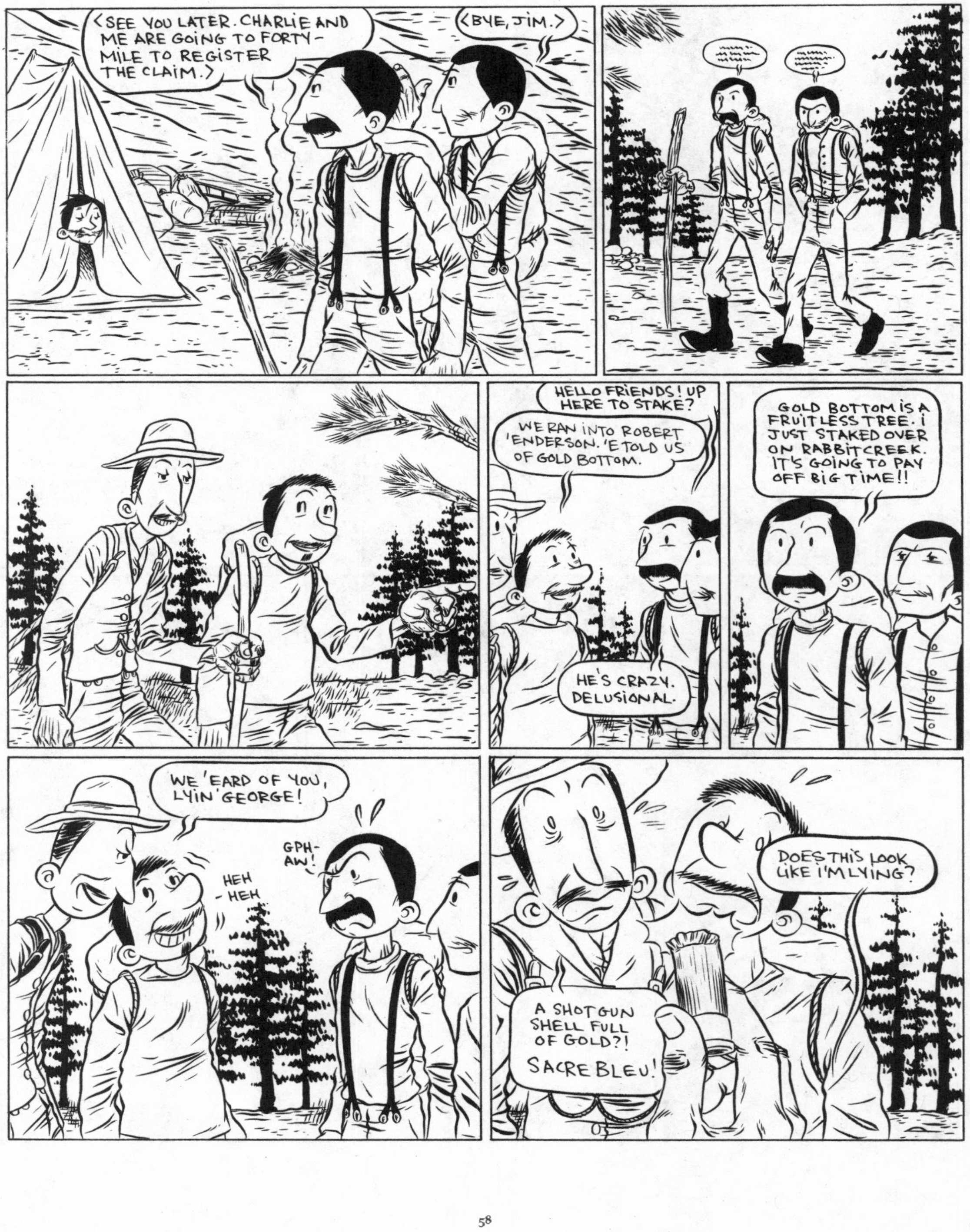
<SEE YOU LATER. CHARLIE AND ME ARE GOING TO FORTY-MILE TO REGISTER THE CLAIM.>
<BYE, JIM.>
HELLO FRIENDS! UP HERE TO STAKE?
WE RAN INTO ROBERT 'ENDERSON. 'E TOLD US OF GOLD BOTTOM.
HE'S CRAZY. DELUSIONAL.
GOLD BOTTOM IS A FRUITLESS TREE. I JUST STAKED OVER ON RABBIT CREEK. IT'S GOING TO PAY OFF BIG TIME!!
WE 'EARD OF YOU, LYIN' GEORGE!
HEH - HEH
GPH-AW!
DOES THIS LOOK LIKE I'M LYING?
A SHOTGUN SHELL FULL OF GOLD?!
SACRE BLEU!

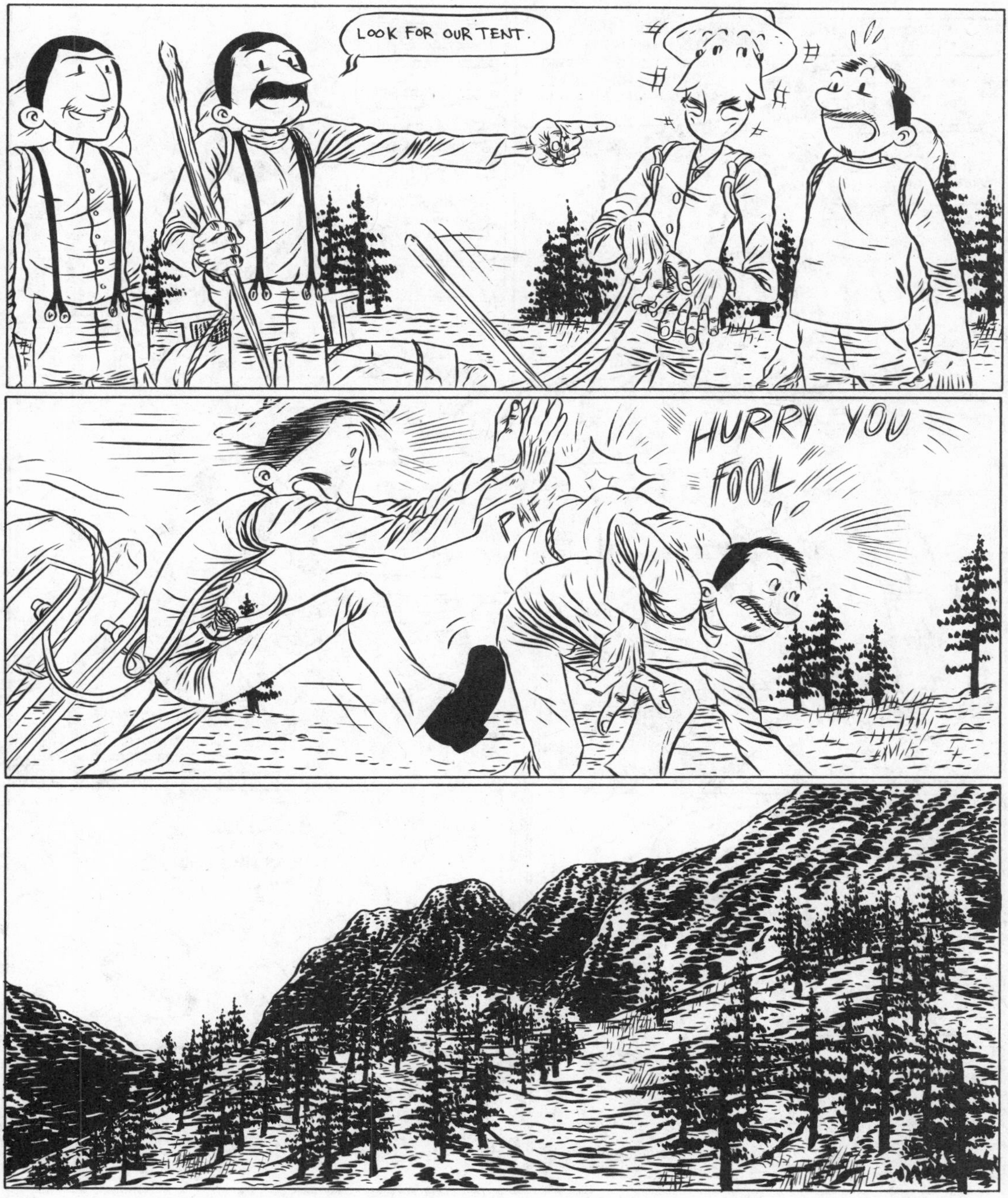
LOOK FOR OUR TENT.
HURRY YOU FOOL
PAF

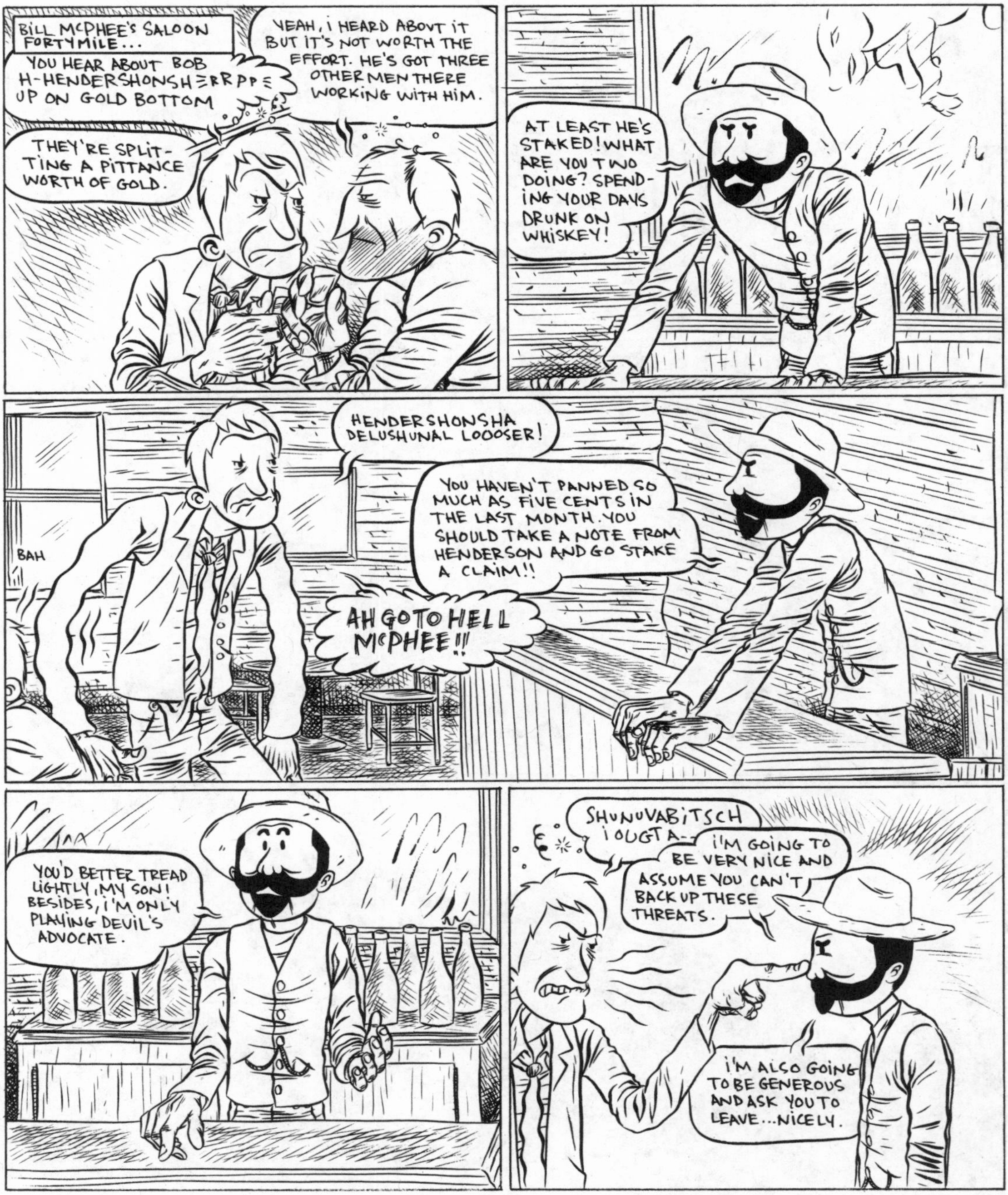
BILL McPHEE'S SALOON FORTYMILE...
YOU HEAR ABOUT BOB H-HENDERSHONSHERRPP UP ON GOLD BOTTOM
YEAH, I HEARD ABOUT IT BUT IT'S NOT WORTH THE EFFORT. HE'S GOT THREE OTHER MEN THERE WORKING WITH HIM.
THEY'RE SPLIT-TING A PITTANCE WORTH OF GOLD.
AT LEAST HE'S STAKED! WHAT ARE YOU TWO DOING? SPEND-ING YOUR DAYS DRUNK ON WHISKEY!
HENDERSHONSHA DELUSHUNAL LOOOSER!
YOU HAVEN'T PANNED SO MUCH AS FIVE CENTS IN THE LAST MONTH. YOU SHOULD TAKE A NOTE FROM HENDERSON AND GO STAKE A CLAIM!!
BAH
AH GO TO HELL McPHEE!!
YOU'D BETTER TREAD LIGHTLY, MY SON! BESIDES, I'M ONLY PLAYING DEVIL'S ADVOCATE.
SHUNUVABITSCH I OUGTA...
I'M GOING TO BE VERY NICE AND ASSUME YOU CAN'T BACK UP THESE THREATS.
I'M ALSO GOING TO BE GENEROUS AND ASK YOU TO LEAVE...NICELY.

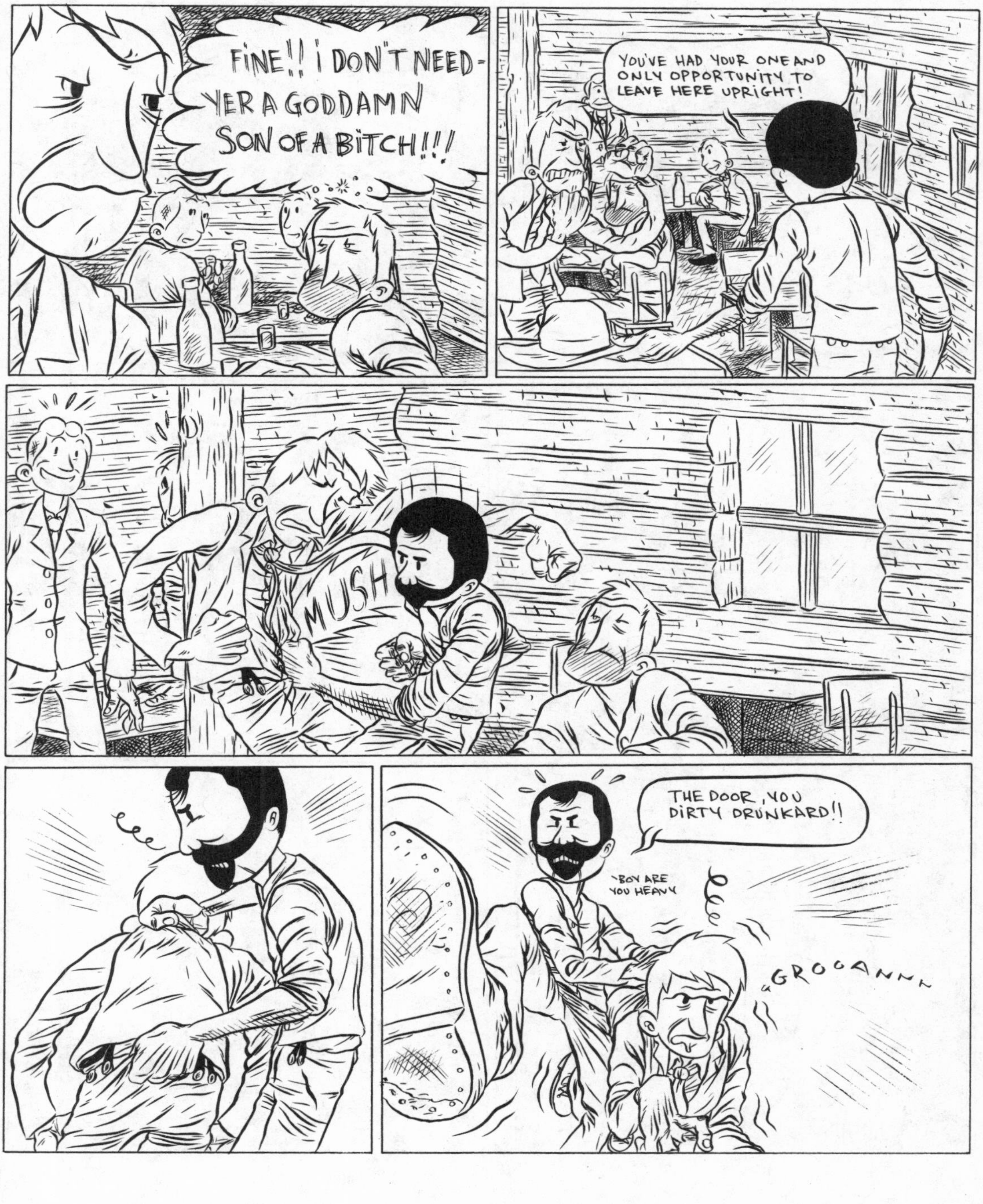

FINE!! I DON'T NEED-
YER A GODDAMN
SON OF A BITCH!!!
YOU'VE HAD YOUR ONE AND ONLY OPPORTUNITY TO LEAVE HERE UPRIGHT!
MUSH
THE DOOR, YOU DIRTY DRUNKARD!!
BOY ARE YOU HEAVY
GROOANNK

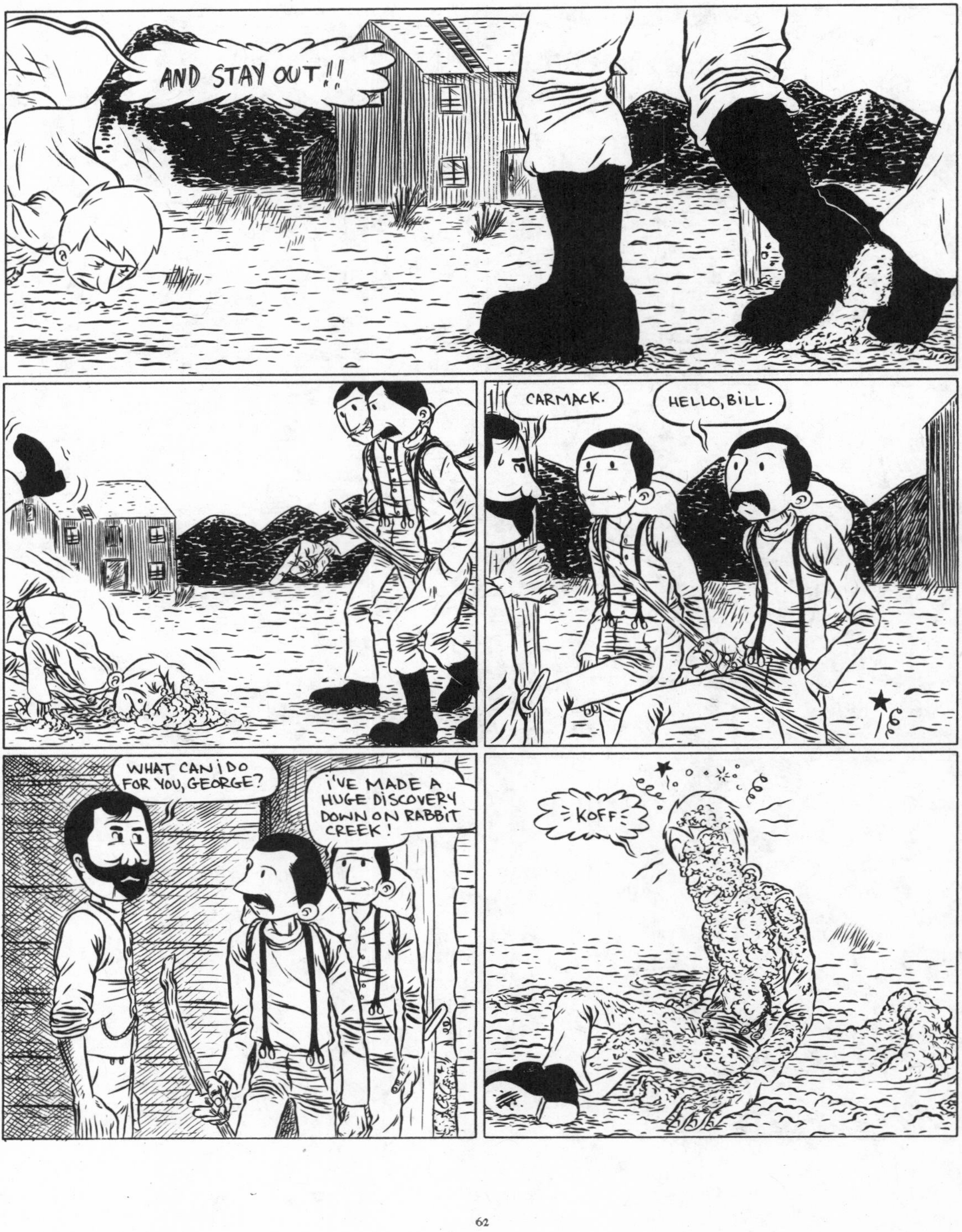
AND STAY OUT!!
CARMACK.
HELLO, BILL.
WHAT CAN I DO FOR YOU, GEORGE?
I'VE MADE A HUGE DISCOVERY DOWN ON RABBIT CREEK!
KOFF

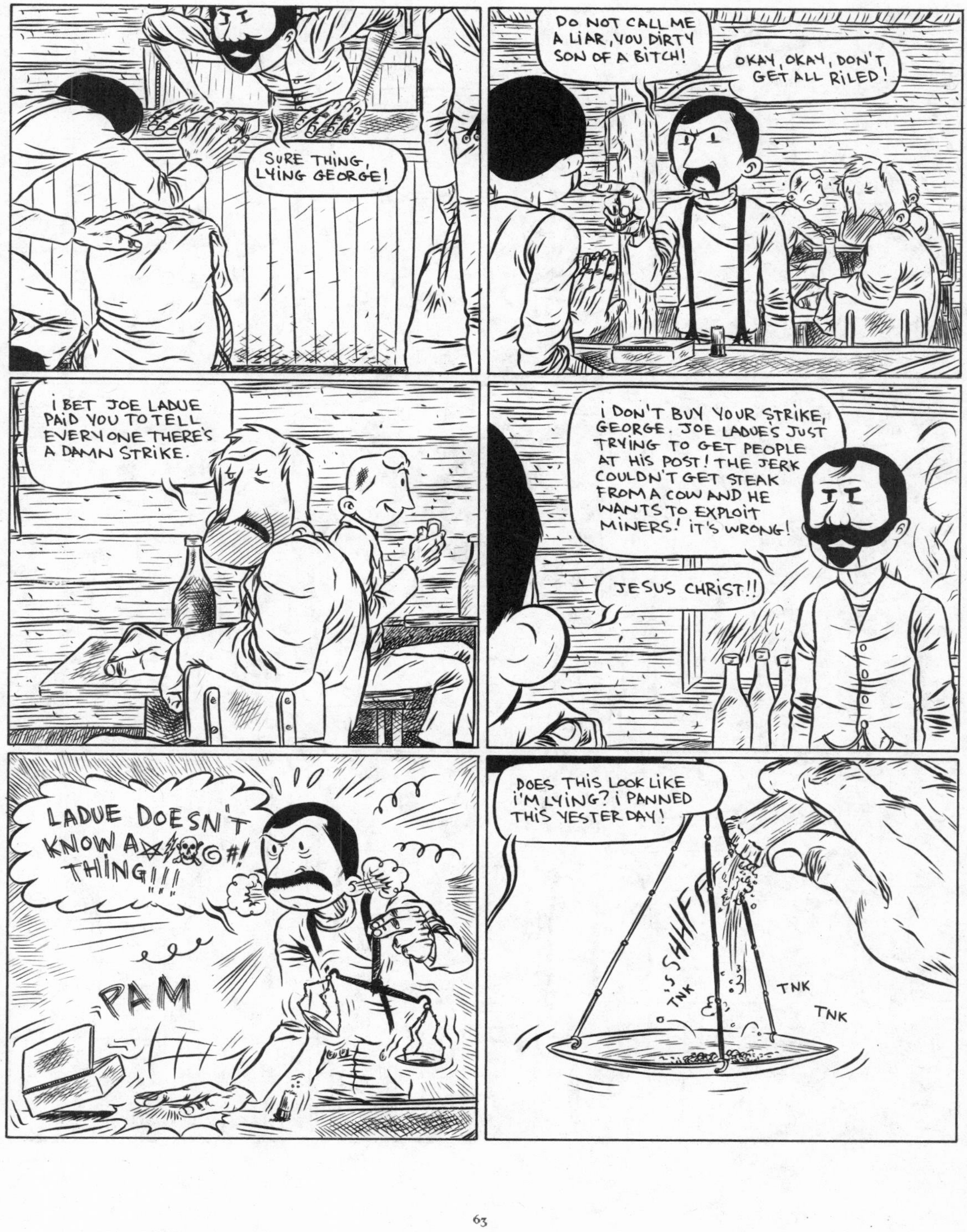
SURE THING, LYING GEORGE!
DO NOT CALL ME A LIAR, YOU DIRTY SON OF A BITCH!
OKAY, OKAY, DON'T GET ALL RILED!
I BET JOE LADUE PAID YOU TO TELL EVERYONE THERE'S A DAMN STRIKE.
I DON'T BUY YOUR STRIKE, GEORGE. JOE LADUE'S JUST TRYING TO GET PEOPLE AT HIS POST! THE JERK COULDN'T GET STEAK FROM A COW AND HE WANTS TO EXPLOIT MINERS! IT'S WRONG!
JESUS CHRIST!!
LADUE DOESN'T KNOW A ✡⚡☠©#! THING!!!
PAM
DOES THIS LOOK LIKE I'M LYING? I PANNED THIS YESTERDAY!
SHHFFF
TNK
TNK
TNK

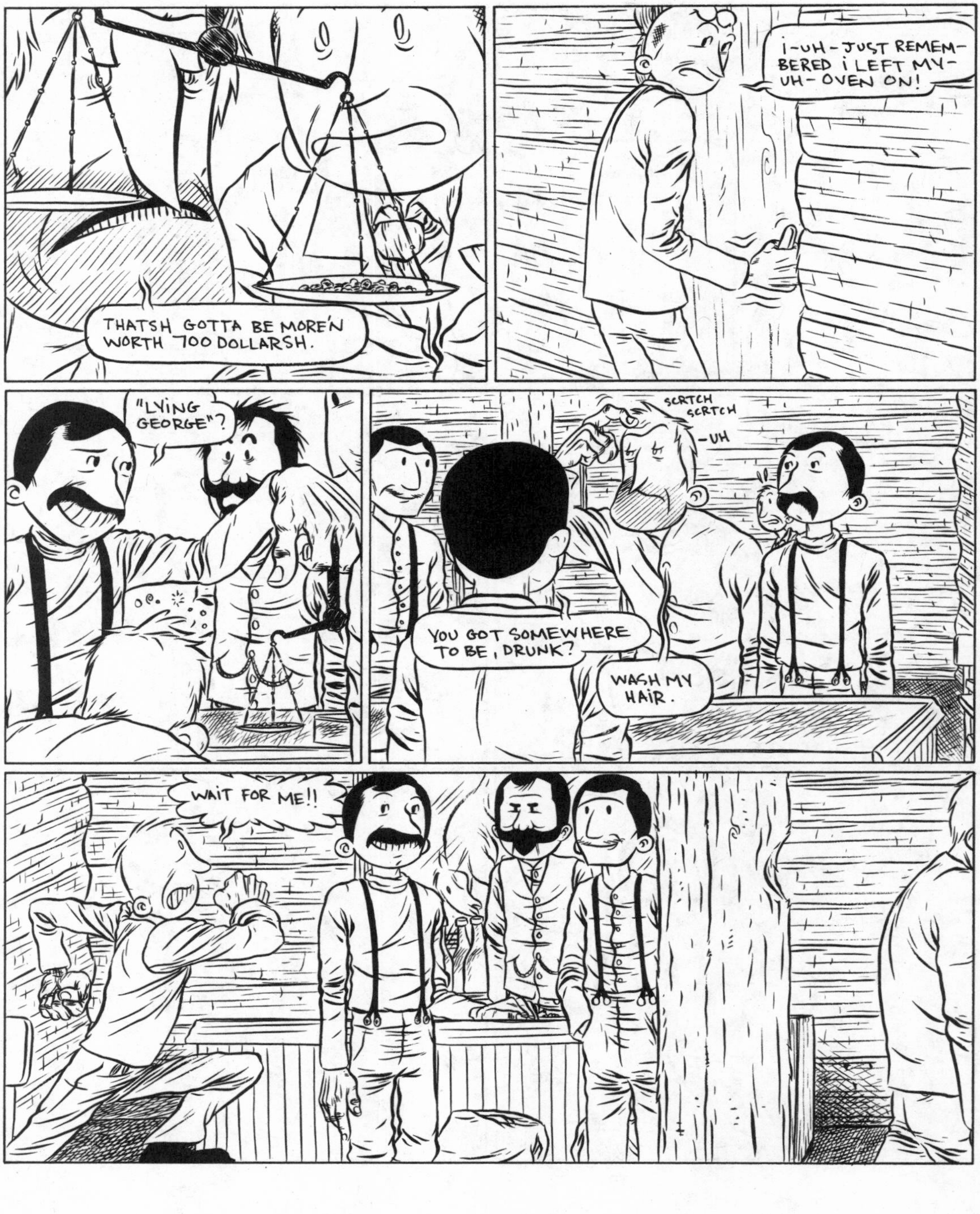
THATSH GOTTA BE MORE'N WORTH 700 DOLLARSH.
I-UH-JUST REMEMBERED I LEFT MY-UH-OVEN ON!
"LYING GEORGE"?
SCRTCH SCRTCH
-UH
YOU GOT SOMEWHERE TO BE, DRUNK?
WASH MY HAIR.
WAIT FOR ME!!

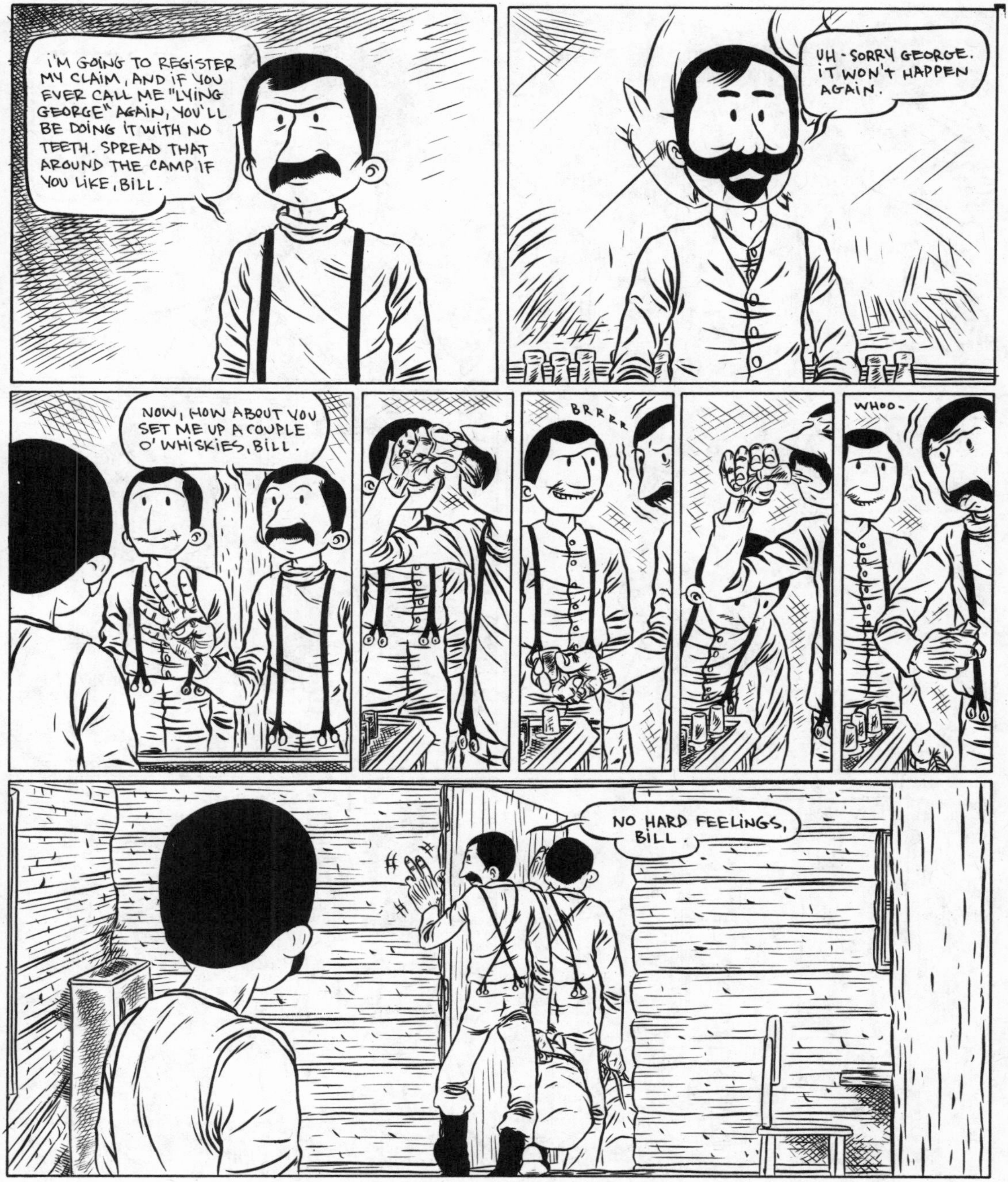
I'M GOING TO REGISTER MY CLAIM, AND IF YOU EVER CALL ME "LYING GEORGE" AGAIN, YOU'LL BE DOING IT WITH NO TEETH. SPREAD THAT AROUND THE CAMP IF YOU LIKE, BILL.
UH - SORRY GEORGE. IT WON'T HAPPEN AGAIN.
NOW, HOW ABOUT YOU SET ME UP A COUPLE O' WHISKIES, BILL.
BRRRR
WHOO-
NO HARD FEELINGS, BILL.

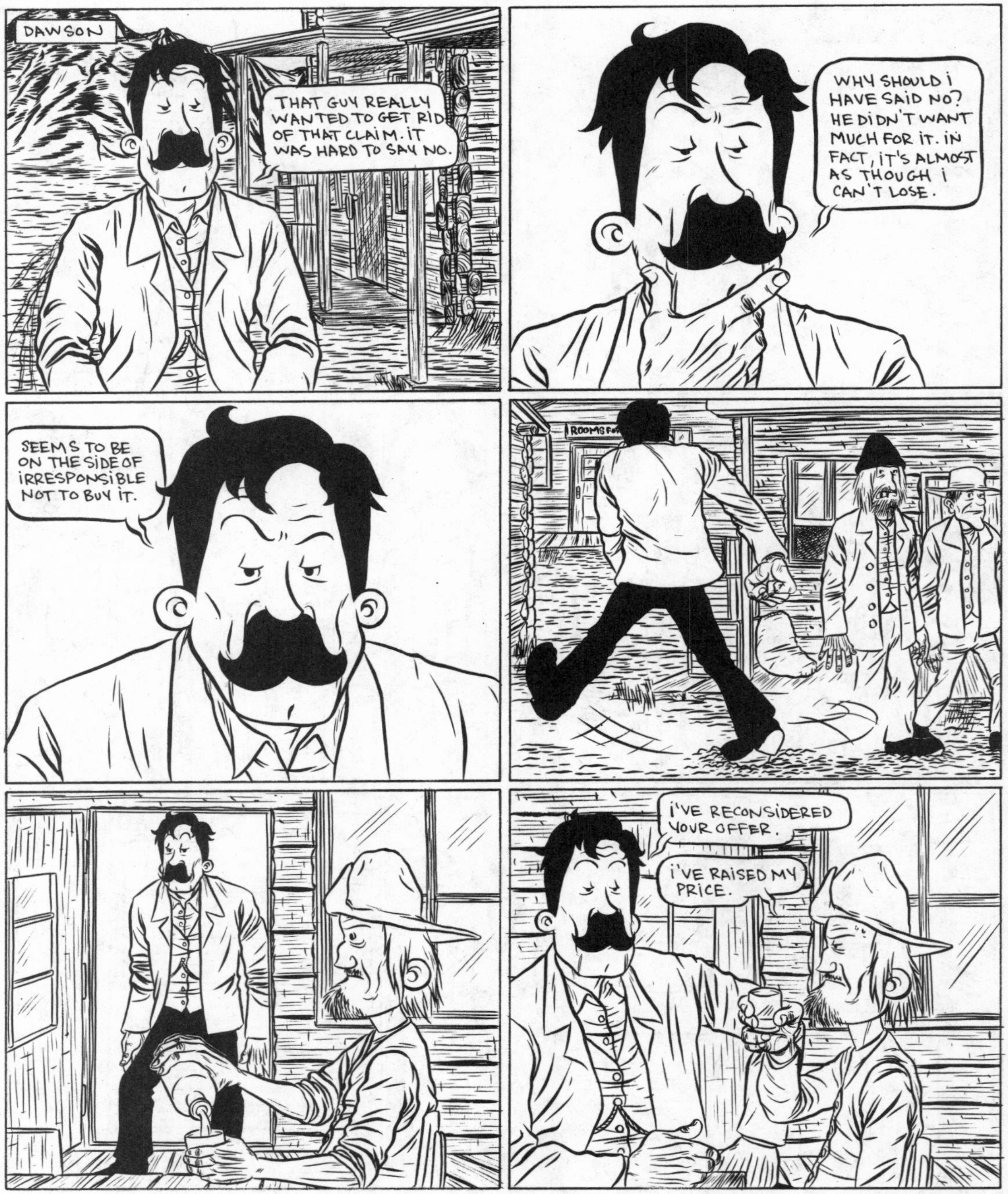
DAWSON
THAT GUY REALLY WANTED TO GET RID OF THAT CLAIM. IT WAS HARD TO SAY NO.
WHY SHOULD I HAVE SAID NO? HE DIDN'T WANT MUCH FOR IT. IN FACT, IT'S ALMOST AS THOUGH I CAN'T LOSE.
SEEMS TO BE ON THE SIDE OF IRRESPONSIBLE NOT TO BUY IT.
I'VE RECONSIDERED YOUR OFFER.
I'VE RAISED MY PRICE.

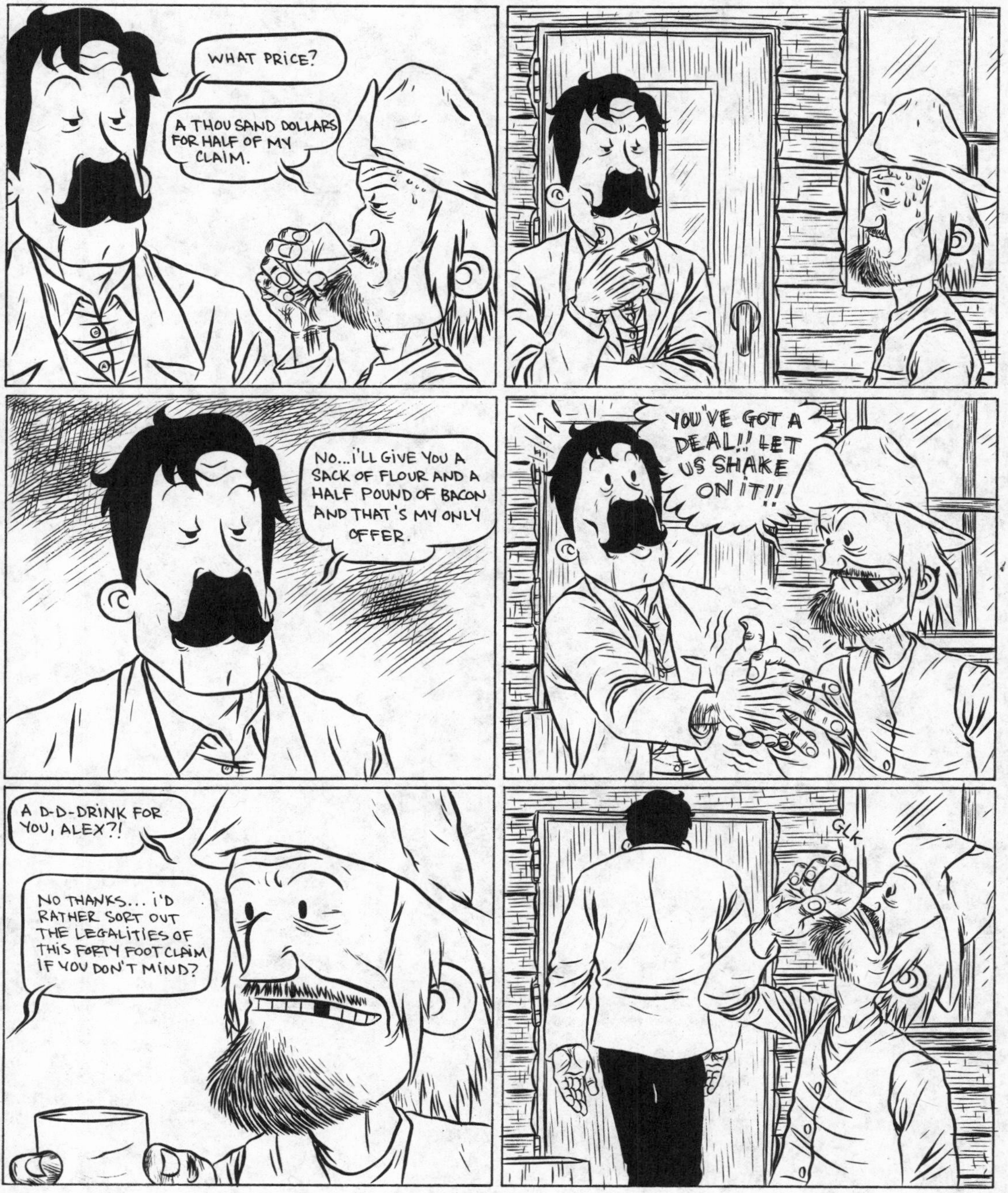
WHAT PRICE?
A THOUSAND DOLLARS FOR HALF OF MY CLAIM.
NO... I'LL GIVE YOU A SACK OF FLOUR AND A HALF POUND OF BACON AND THAT'S MY ONLY OFFER.
YOU'VE GOT A DEAL!! LET US SHAKE ON IT!!
A D-D-DRINK FOR YOU, ALEX?!
NO THANKS... I'D RATHER SORT OUT THE LEGALITIES OF THIS FORTY FOOT CLAIM IF YOU DON'T MIND?
GLK

BY THE TIME THE RUSH STARTED, INSPECTOR CHARLES CONSTANTINE OF THE NORTHWEST MOUNTED POLICE HAD DONE HIS BEST TO BAN MINERS' MEETINGS. AT THE MEETINGS, WHERE THERE WERE TRIALS TO PUNISH CRIMINALS, LAW AND ORDER WAS DOLED OUT BY PROSPECTORS AND MINERS AS THEY SAW FIT, DEPENDING ON THE SEVERITY OF THE CRIMES. WHIPPINGS IN FRONT OF A CROWD WERE STANDARD PRACTISE. OF COURSE, THERE WERE THOSE WHO FELT THAT THE MINERS' MEETINGS--WHICH FLEW IN THE FACE OF TRADITIONAL GOVERNMENTAL LAW--DEALT WITH CRIME MORE EFFECTIVELY THAN THE N.W.M.P., MAKING THE MOUNTIES' JOB THAT MUCH MORE DIFFICULT.

BELINDA MULROONEY, WHO WAS MAKING HER FIRST FAILED ATTEMPT TO CROSS THE CHILKOOT PASS, FACED THE SAME DIFFICULTIES AS THE MOUNTIES. HER FAILURE WAS DUE TO THE FACT THAT SHE UNDERESTIMATED THE HARSHNESS OF THE CONDITIONS, HER CLOTHING BEING TOO HEAVY AND BULKY, AND THE LACK OF SUPPLIES. SHE QUICKLY TURNED BACK AND LEARNED FROM HER MISTAKES. MULROONEY EMPLOYED MEN THAT SHE KEPT IN LINE WITH AN IRON FIST. SHE ONCE CAUGHT A MAN STEALING FROM HER, SO SHE HAD A FEW OF HER MEN HOLD HIM DOWN WHILE SHE WHIPPED HIM, MAKING IT ABUNDANTLY CLEAR THAT SHE WAS NOT TO BE CROSSED.

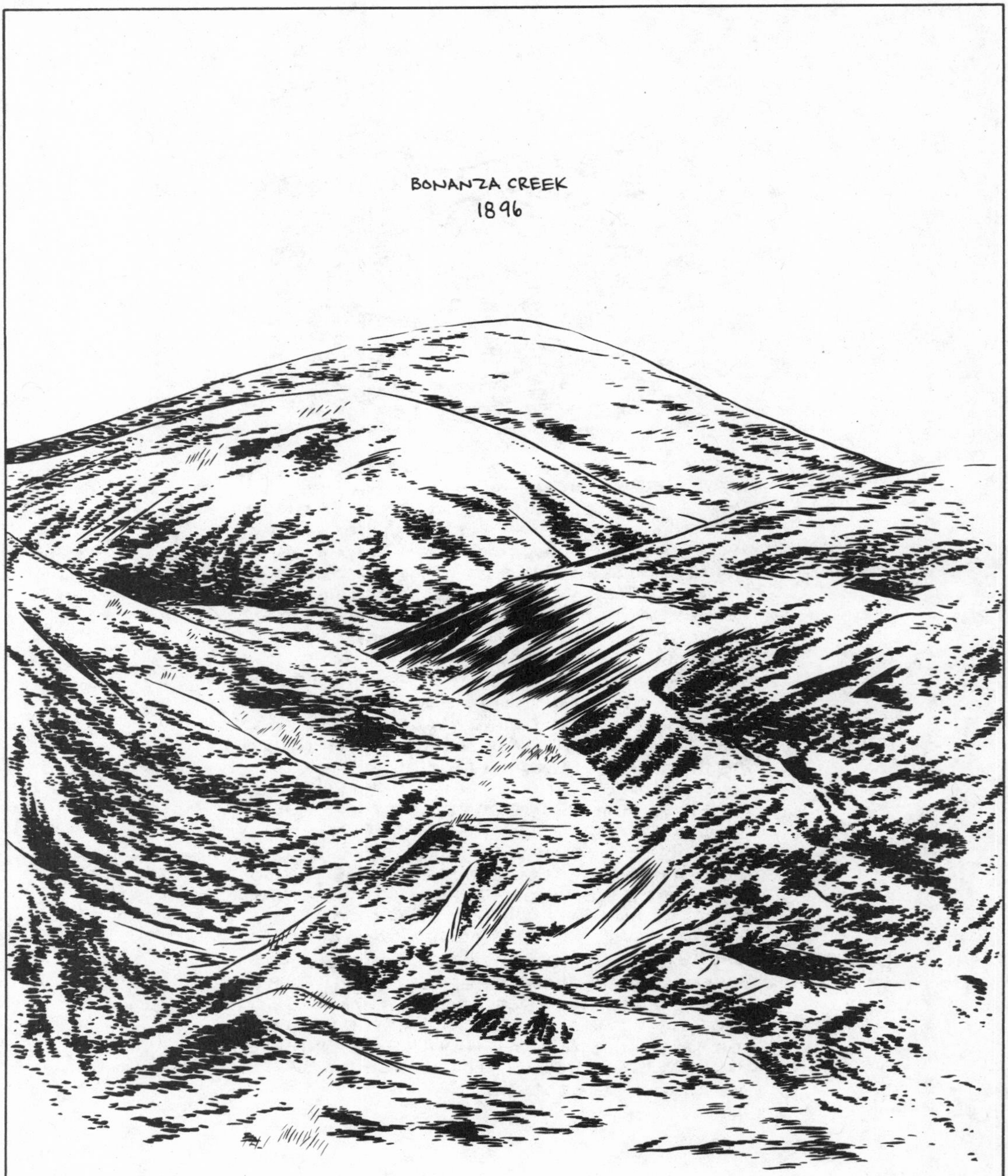
BONANZA CREEK
1896

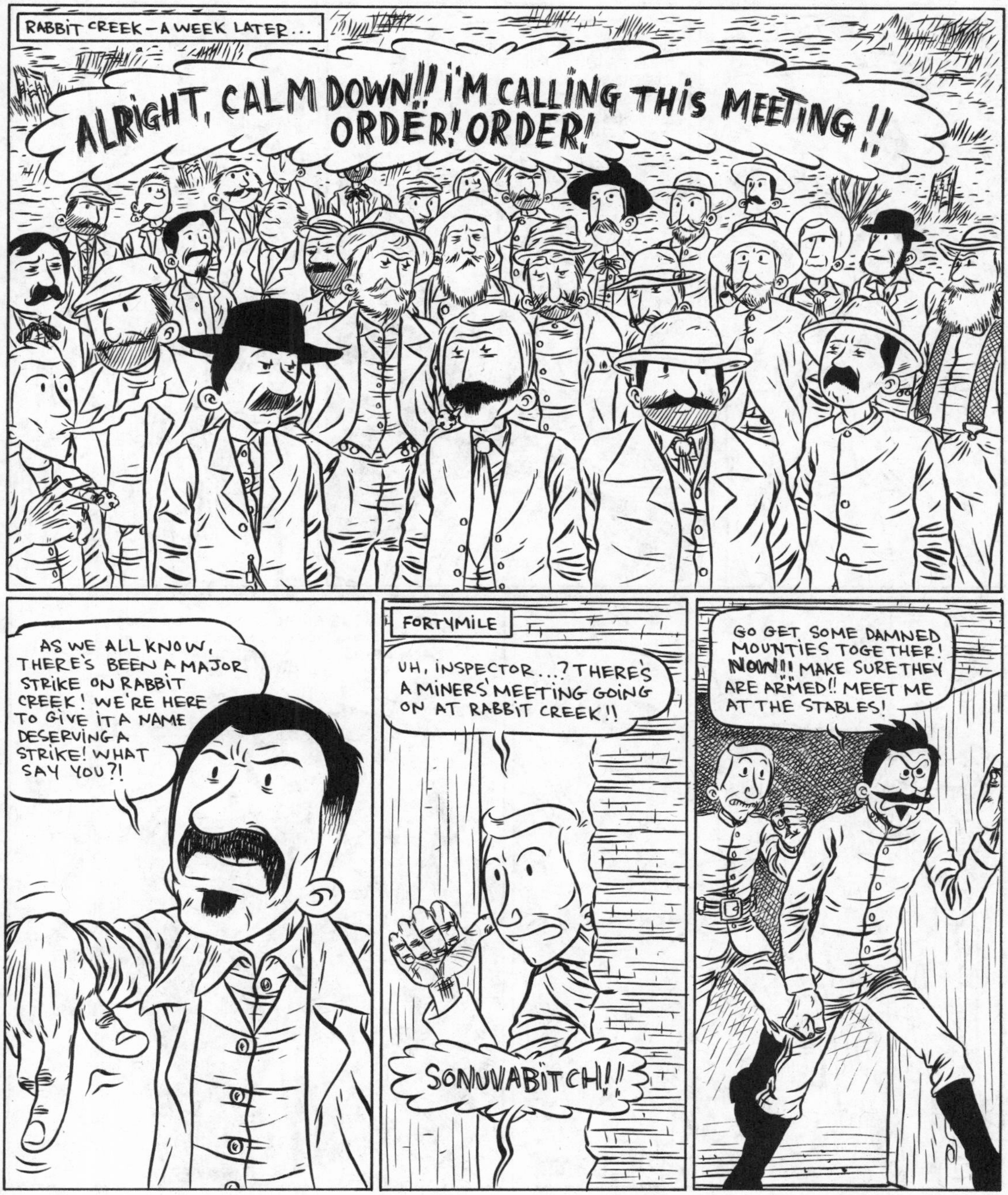
RABBIT CREEK—A WEEK LATER...
ALRIGHT, CALM DOWN!! I'M CALLING THIS MEETING!! ORDER! ORDER!
AS WE ALL KNOW, THERE'S BEEN A MAJOR STRIKE ON RABBIT CREEK! WE'RE HERE TO GIVE IT A NAME DESERVING A STRIKE! WHAT SAY YOU?!
FORTYMILE
UH, INSPECTOR...? THERE'S A MINERS' MEETING GOING ON AT RABBIT CREEK!!
SONUVABITCH!!
GO GET SOME DAMNED MOUNTIES TOGETHER! NOW!! MAKE SURE THEY ARE ARMED!! MEET ME AT THE STABLES!

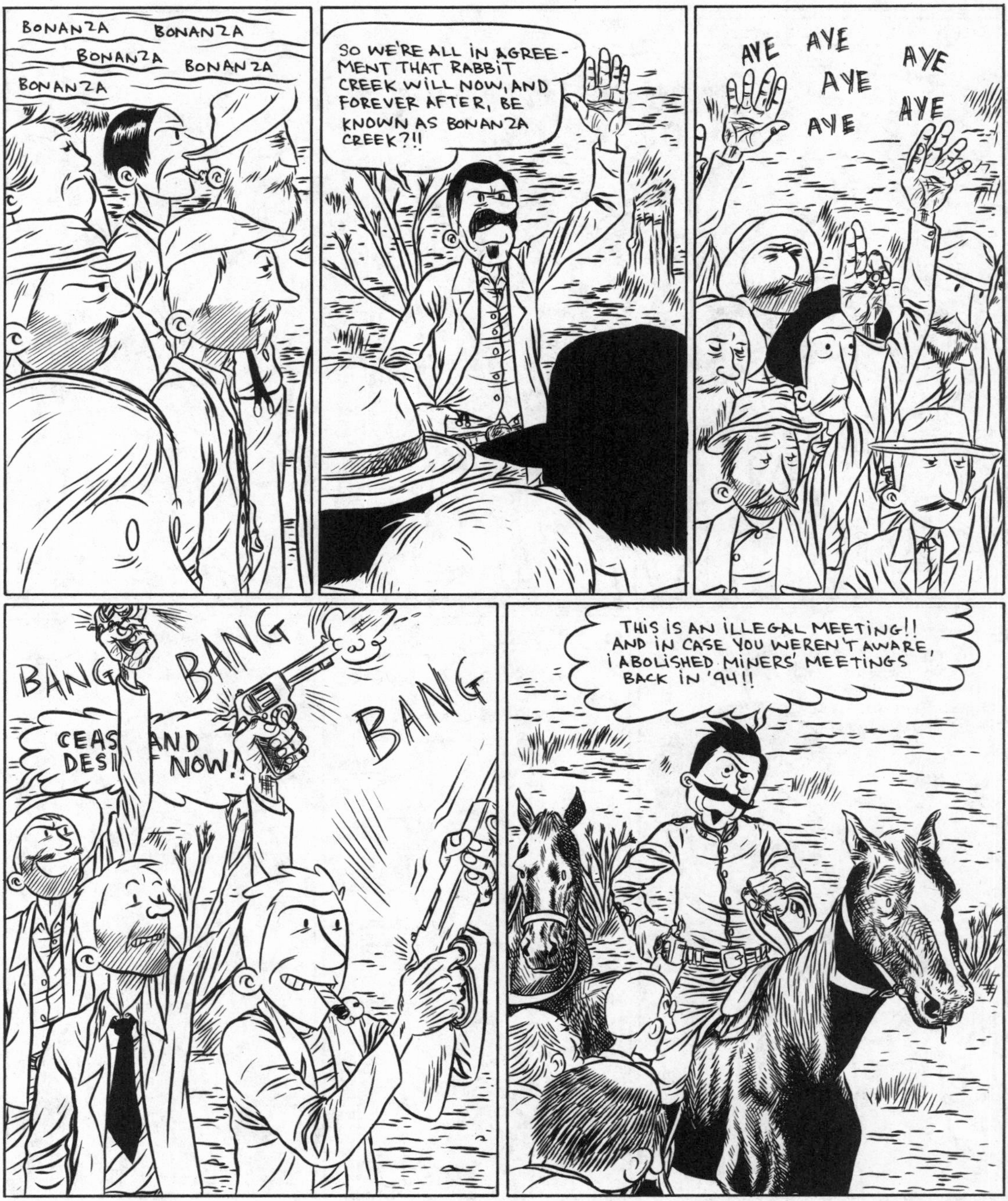
BONANZA BONANZA
BONANZA BONANZA
BONANZA
SO WE'RE ALL IN AGREEMENT THAT RABBIT CREEK WILL NOW, AND FOREVER AFTER, BE KNOWN AS BONANZA CREEK?!!
AYE AYE AYE
AYE
AYE AYE
BANG BANG
BANG
CEASE AND DESIST NOW!!
THIS IS AN ILLEGAL MEETING!! AND IN CASE YOU WEREN'T AWARE, I ABOLISHED MINERS' MEETINGS BACK IN '94!!

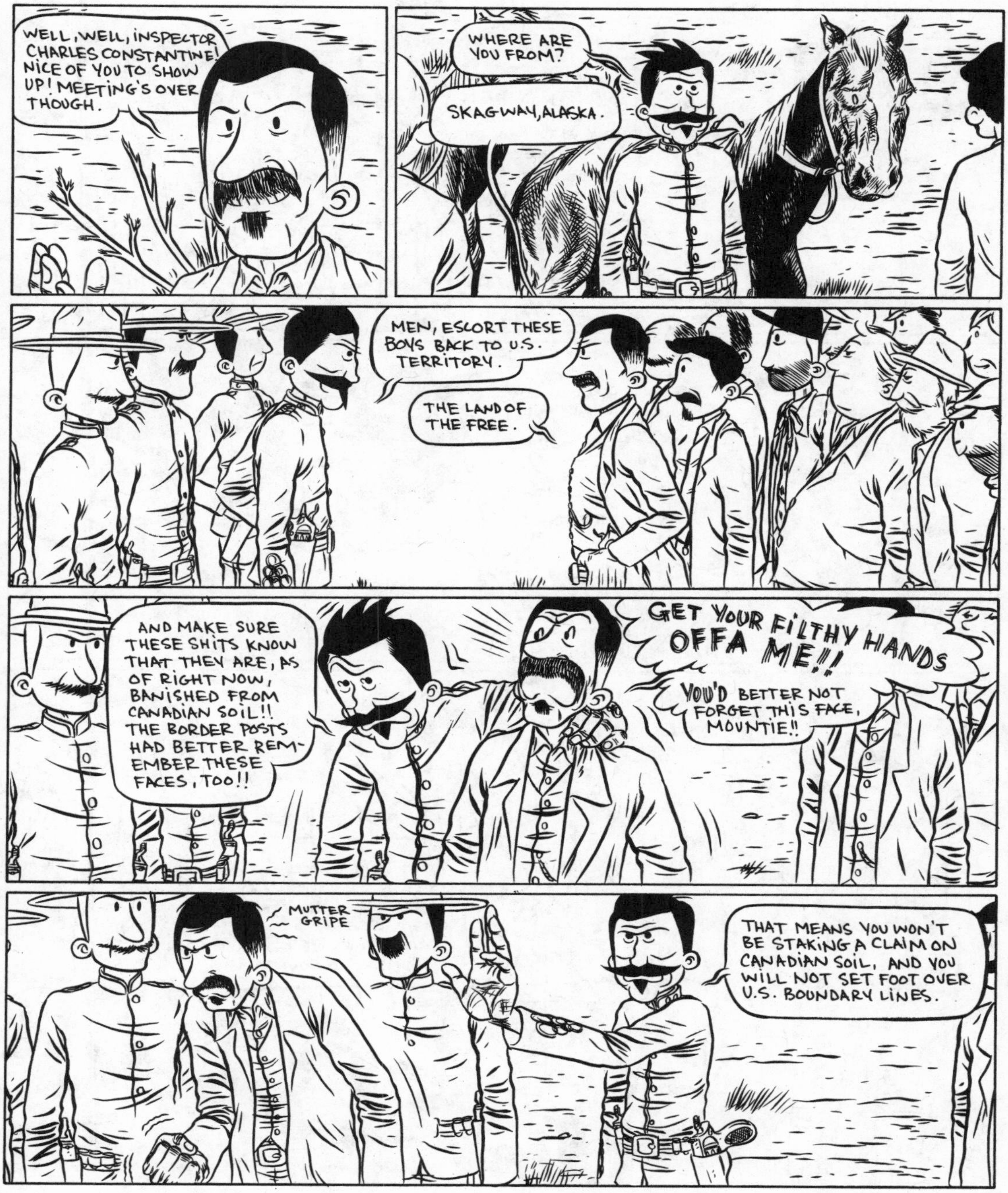
WELL, WELL, INSPECTOR CHARLES CONSTANTINE! NICE OF YOU TO SHOW UP! MEETING'S OVER THOUGH.
WHERE ARE YOU FROM?
SKAGWAY, ALASKA.
MEN, ESCORT THESE BOYS BACK TO U.S. TERRITORY.
THE LAND OF THE FREE.
AND MAKE SURE THESE SHITS KNOW THAT THEY ARE, AS OF RIGHT NOW, BANISHED FROM CANADIAN SOIL!! THE BORDER POSTS HAD BETTER REMEMBER THESE FACES, TOO!!
GET YOUR FILTHY HANDS OFFA ME!!
YOU'D BETTER NOT FORGET THIS FACE, MOUNTIE!!
MUTTER GRIPE
THAT MEANS YOU WON'T BE STAKING A CLAIM ON CANADIAN SOIL, AND YOU WILL NOT SET FOOT OVER U.S. BOUNDARY LINES.

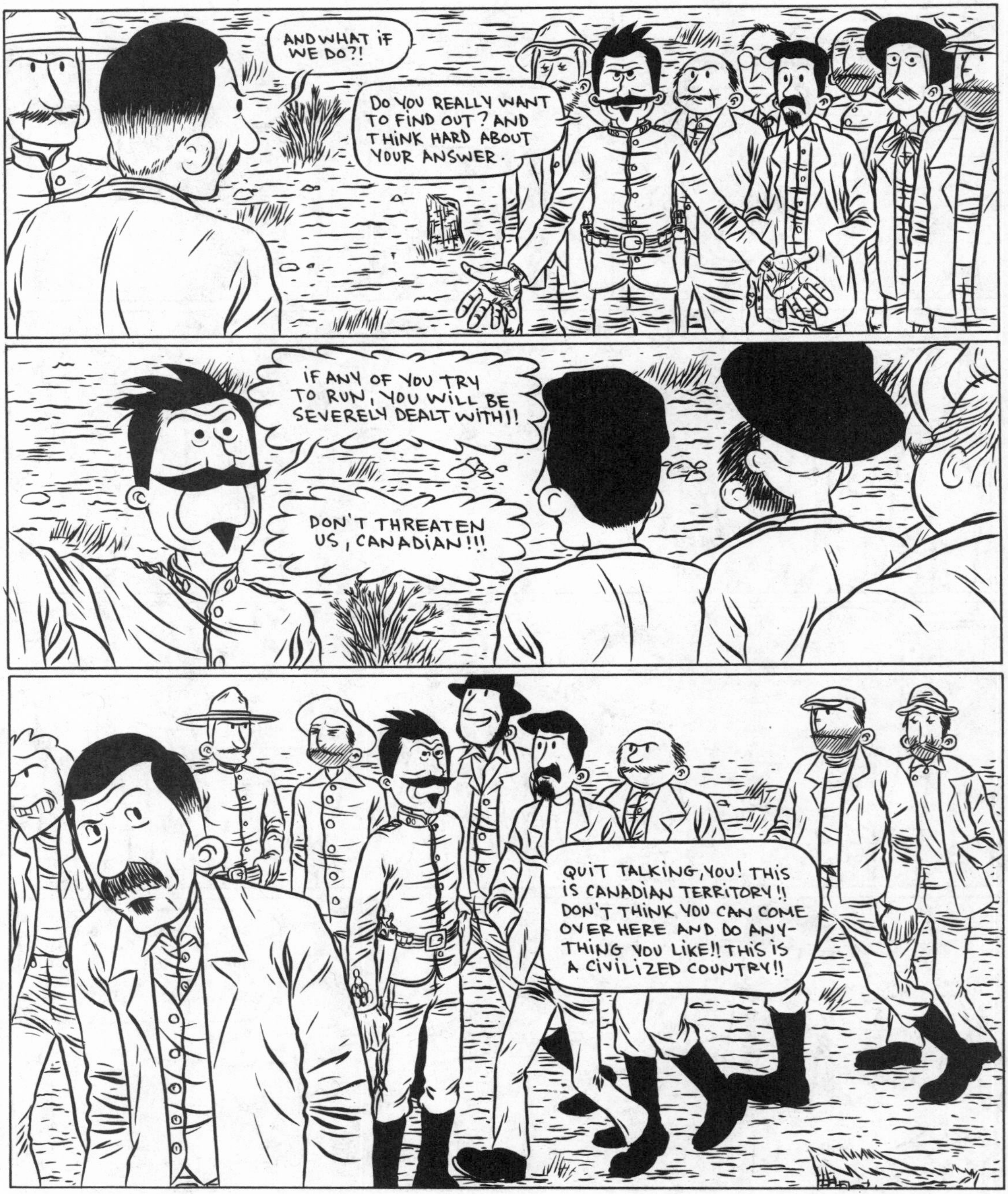
AND WHAT IF WE DO?!
DO YOU REALLY WANT TO FIND OUT? AND THINK HARD ABOUT YOUR ANSWER.
IF ANY OF YOU TRY TO RUN, YOU WILL BE SEVERELY DEALT WITH!!
DON'T THREATEN US, CANADIAN!!!
QUIT TALKING, YOU! THIS IS CANADIAN TERRITORY!! DON'T THINK YOU CAN COME OVER HERE AND DO ANYTHING YOU LIKE!! THIS IS A CIVILIZED COUNTRY!!

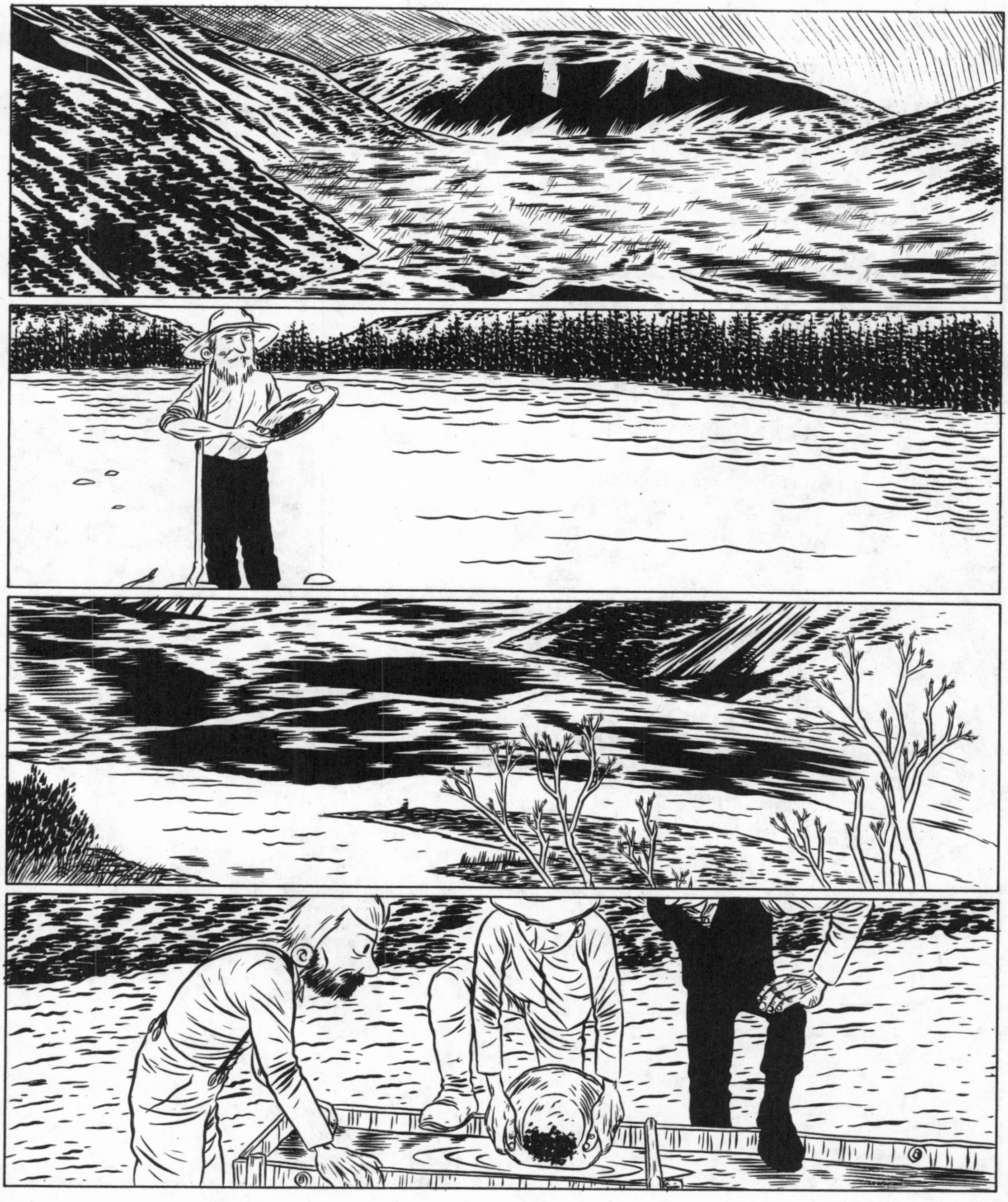

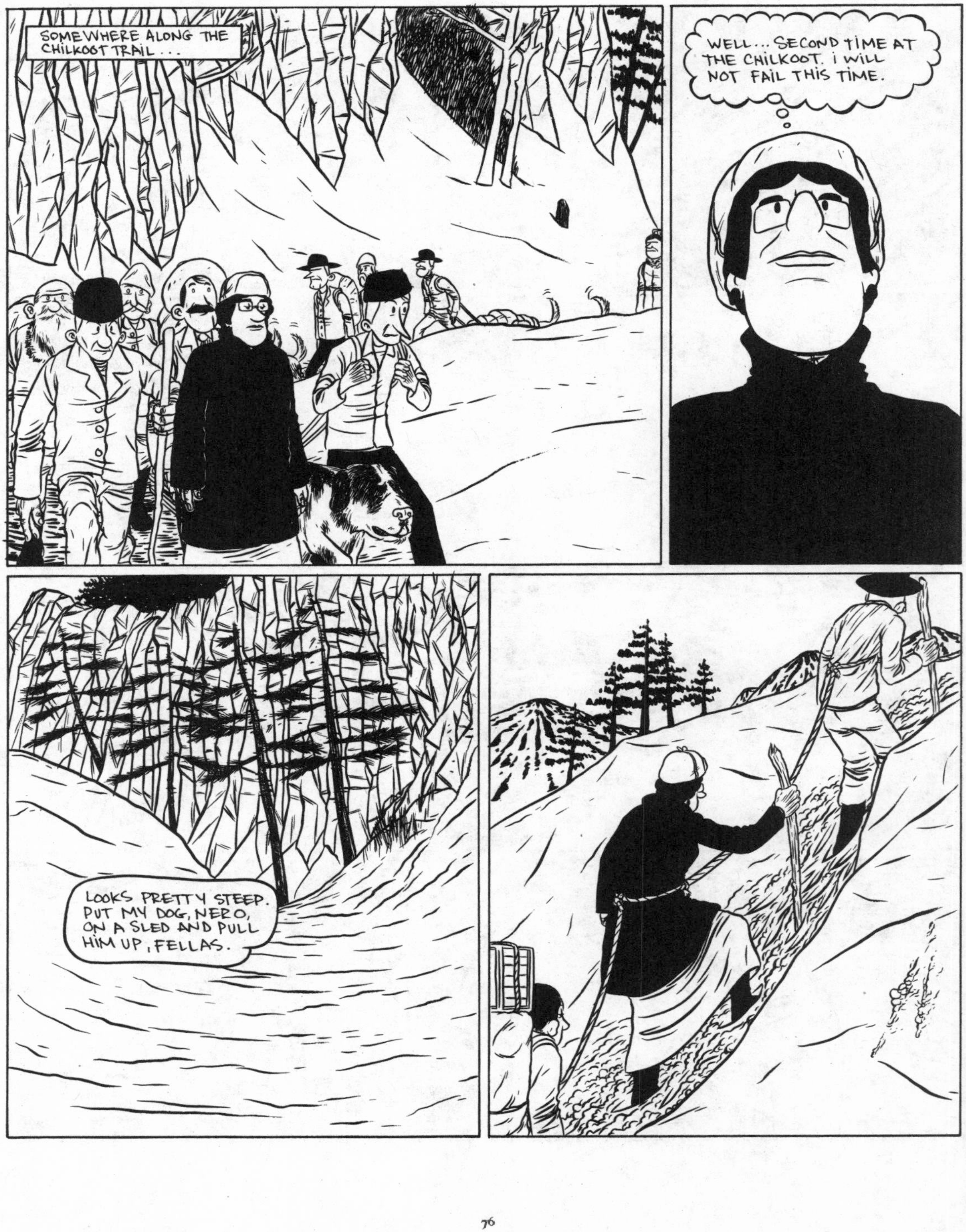
SOMEWHERE ALONG THE CHILKOOT TRAIL . . .
WELL... SECOND TIME AT THE CHILKOOT. I WILL NOT FAIL THIS TIME.
LOOKS PRETTY STEEP. PUT MY DOG, NERO, ON A SLED AND PULL HIM UP, FELLAS.

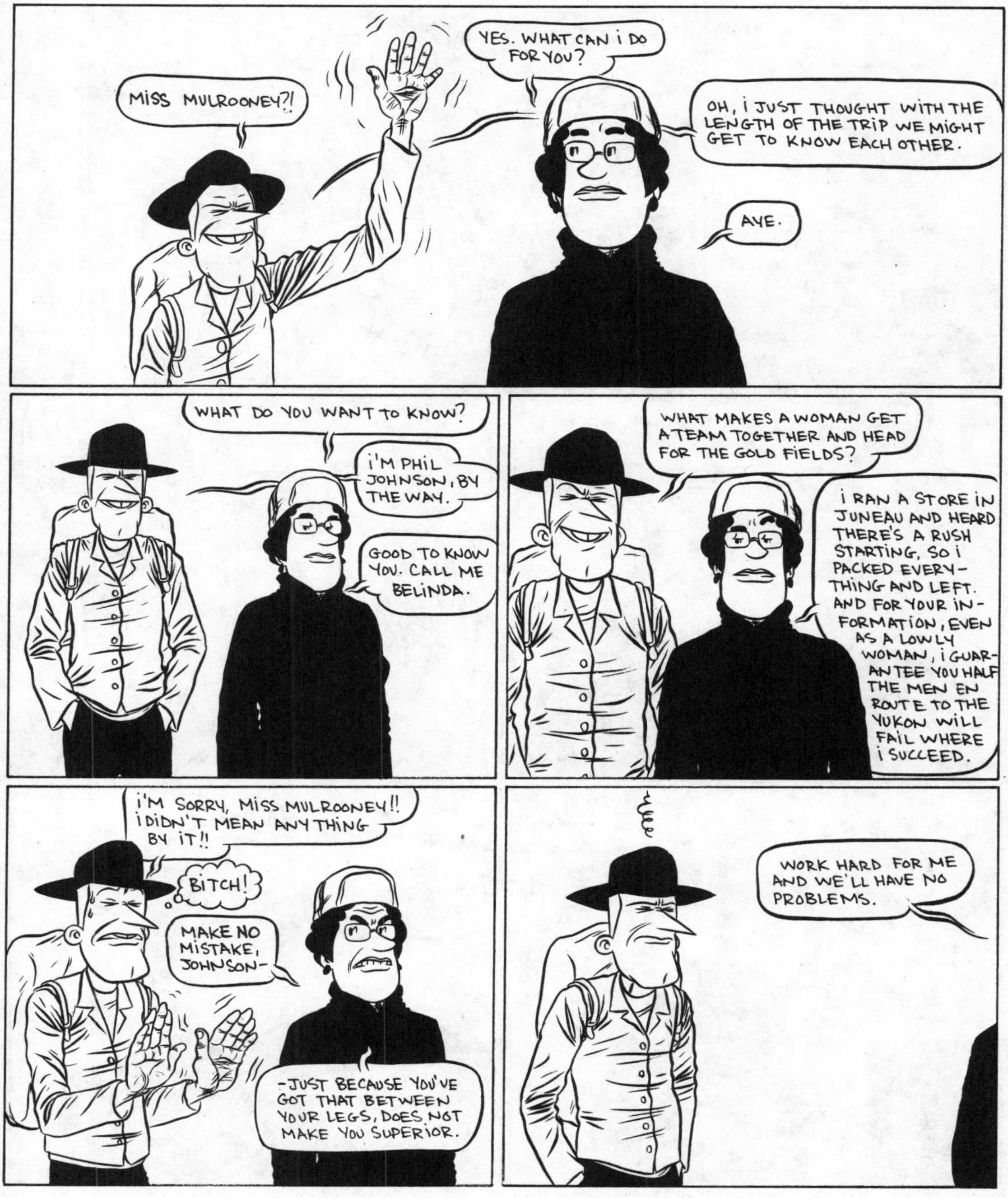
MISS MULROONEY?!
YES. WHAT CAN I DO FOR YOU?
OH, I JUST THOUGHT WITH THE LENGTH OF THE TRIP WE MIGHT GET TO KNOW EACH OTHER.
AYE.
WHAT DO YOU WANT TO KNOW?
I'M PHIL JOHNSON, BY THE WAY.
GOOD TO KNOW YOU. CALL ME BELINDA.
WHAT MAKES A WOMAN GET A TEAM TOGETHER AND HEAD FOR THE GOLD FIELDS?
I RAN A STORE IN JUNEAU AND HEARD THERE'S A RUSH STARTING, SO I PACKED EVERYTHING AND LEFT. AND FOR YOUR INFORMATION, EVEN AS A LOWLY WOMAN, I GUARANTEE YOU HALF THE MEN EN ROUTE TO THE YUKON WILL FAIL WHERE I SUCCEED.
BITCH!
I'M SORRY, MISS MULROONEY!! I DIDN'T MEAN ANYTHING BY IT!!
MAKE NO MISTAKE, JOHNSON-
-JUST BECAUSE YOU'VE GOT THAT BETWEEN YOUR LEGS, DOES NOT MAKE YOU SUPERIOR.
WORK HARD FOR ME AND WE'LL HAVE NO PROBLEMS.

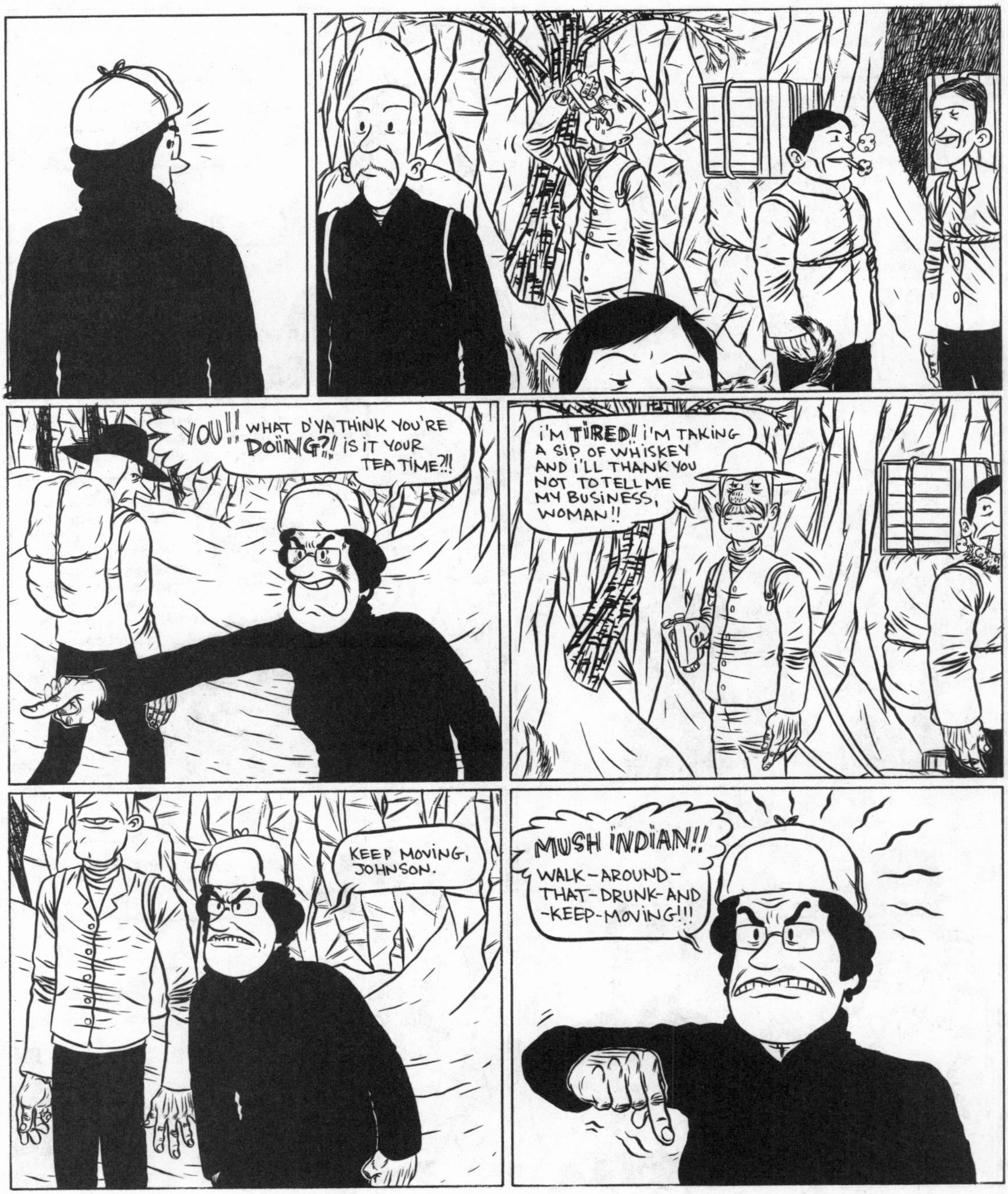
YOU!! WHAT D'YA THINK YOU'RE DOiiNG?!! IS IT YOUR TEA TIME?!!
i'M TiRED!! i'M TAKiNG A SiP OF WHiSKEY AND i'LL THANK YOU NOT TO TELL ME MY BUSINESS, WOMAN!!
KEEP MOViNG, JOHNSON.
MUSH iNDiAN!!
WALK-AROUND-THAT-DRUNK-AND-KEEP-MOViNG!!!

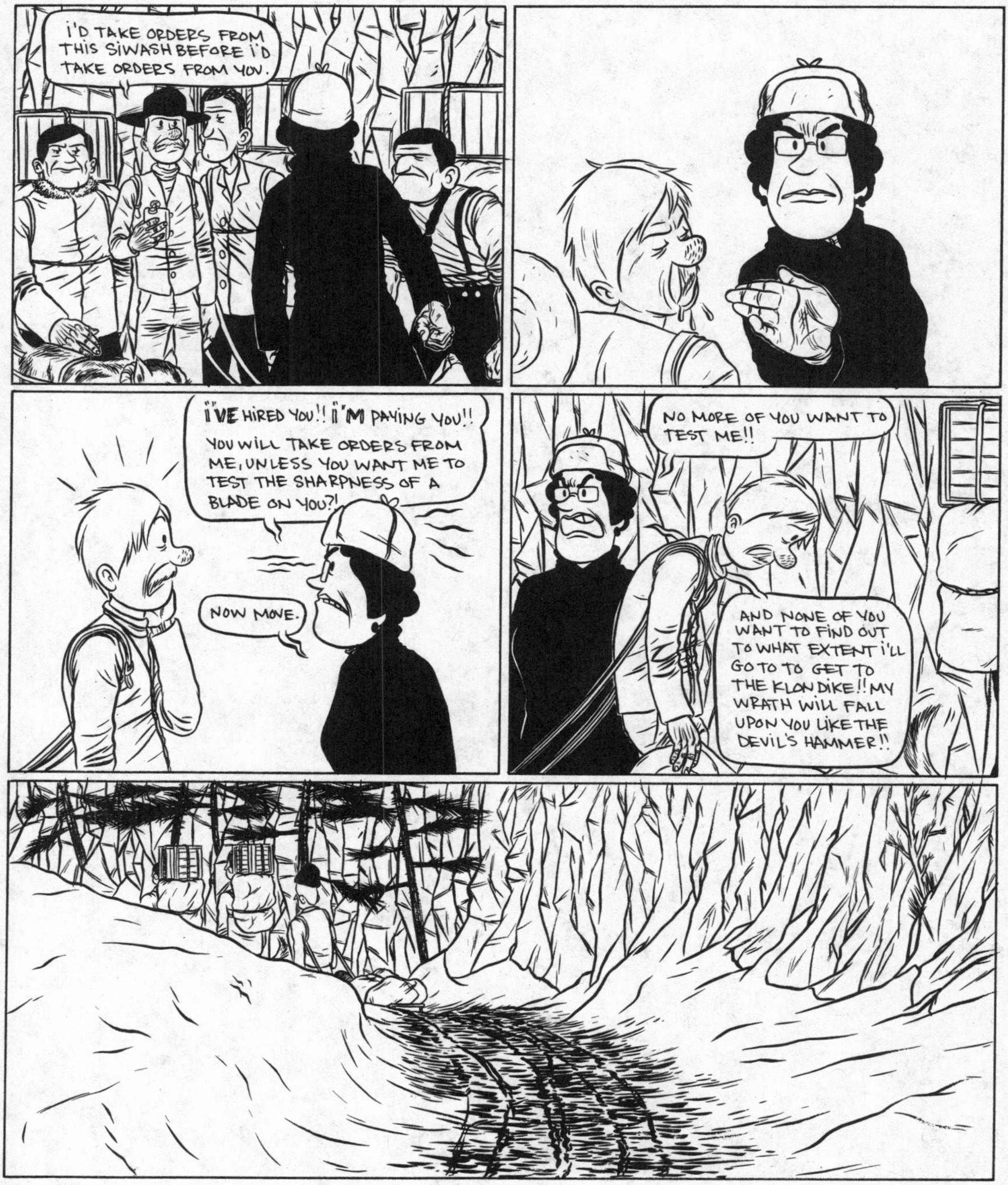

I'D TAKE ORDERS FROM THIS SIWASH BEFORE I'D TAKE ORDERS FROM YOU.
I'VE HIRED YOU!! I'M PAYING YOU!! YOU WILL TAKE ORDERS FROM ME, UNLESS YOU WANT ME TO TEST THE SHARPNESS OF A BLADE ON YOU?!
NOW MOVE.
NO MORE OF YOU WANT TO TEST ME!!
AND NONE OF YOU WANT TO FIND OUT TO WHAT EXTENT I'LL GO TO TO GET TO THE KLONDIKE!! MY WRATH WILL FALL UPON YOU LIKE THE DEVIL'S HAMMER!!

THE RECENT DISCOVERY ON BONANZA CREEK
KEPT THE SURVEYORS OF THE GOLD FIELDS BUSY
ADJUSTING AND RE-ADJUSTING CLAIMS. THE LAND
WAS BOUGHT UP HASTILY AND NOT PROPERLY
PLOTTED, WHICH LED TO TURMOIL IN THE FIELDS.
PROSPECTORS ON NEIGHBOURING CLAIMS COM-
PLAINED THAT THEIR CLAIMS WEREN'T FAIRLY
DIVIDED. THE N.W.M.P. HAD TO STEP IN AND
MANAGE THE SITUATION THE BEST THEY COULD.
DESPITE THEIR DESIRE TO HELP, THE MOUNTIES
PRESENCE ONLY RESULTED IN MORE PROBLEMS
AS MANY PROSPECTORS FELT IT WAS NOT THE
MOUNTIES' PLACE TO INTERFERE IN THESE MATTERS.
FIGHTS BROKE OUT AMONGST PROSPECTORS; THE
MOUNTIES AND SURVEYORS MOVED QUICKLY TO
AVOID ANY FURTHER OUTBURSTS. THEY HAD
THINGS SETTLED WITHIN A FEW WEEKS.

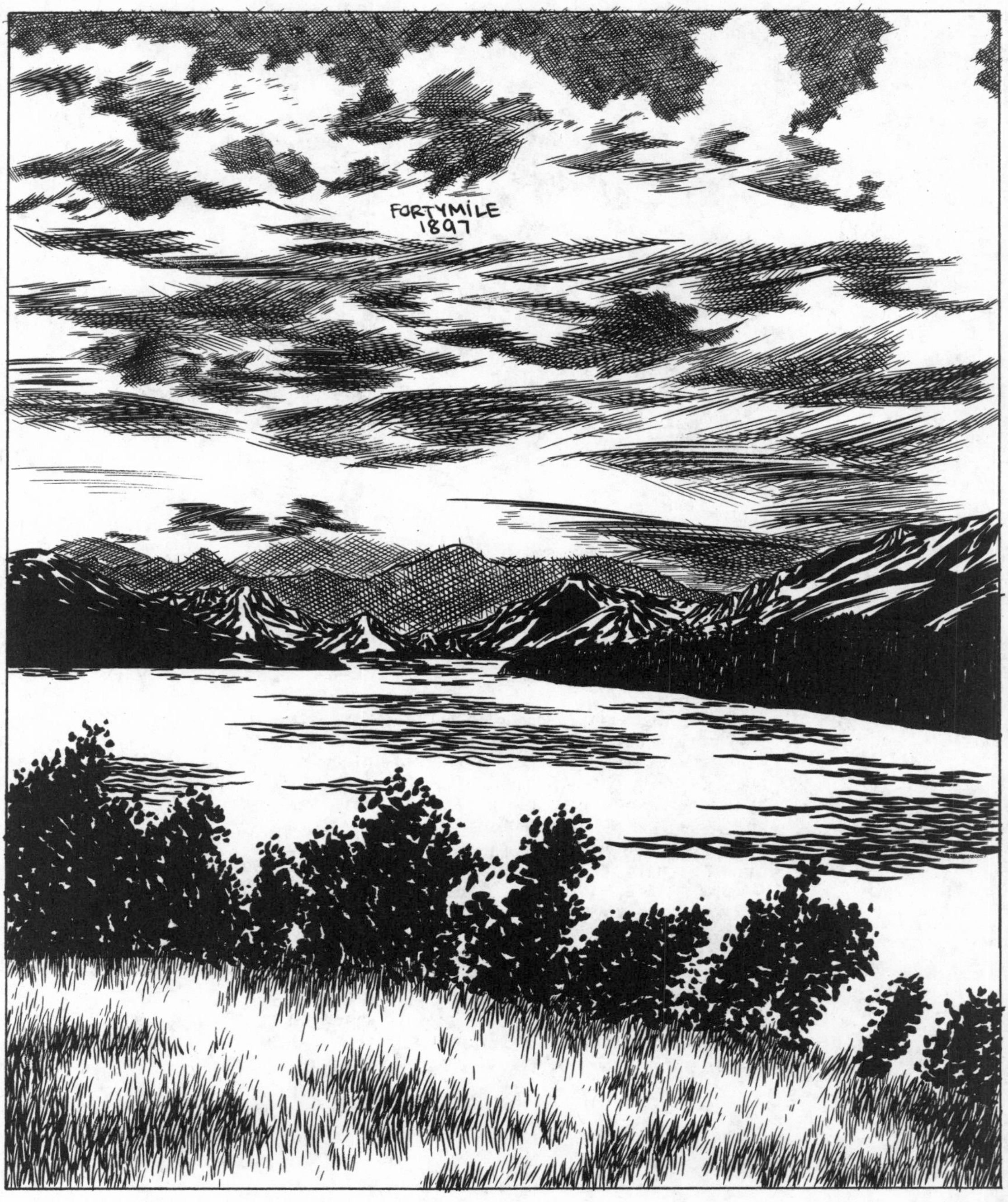
FORTYMILE
1897

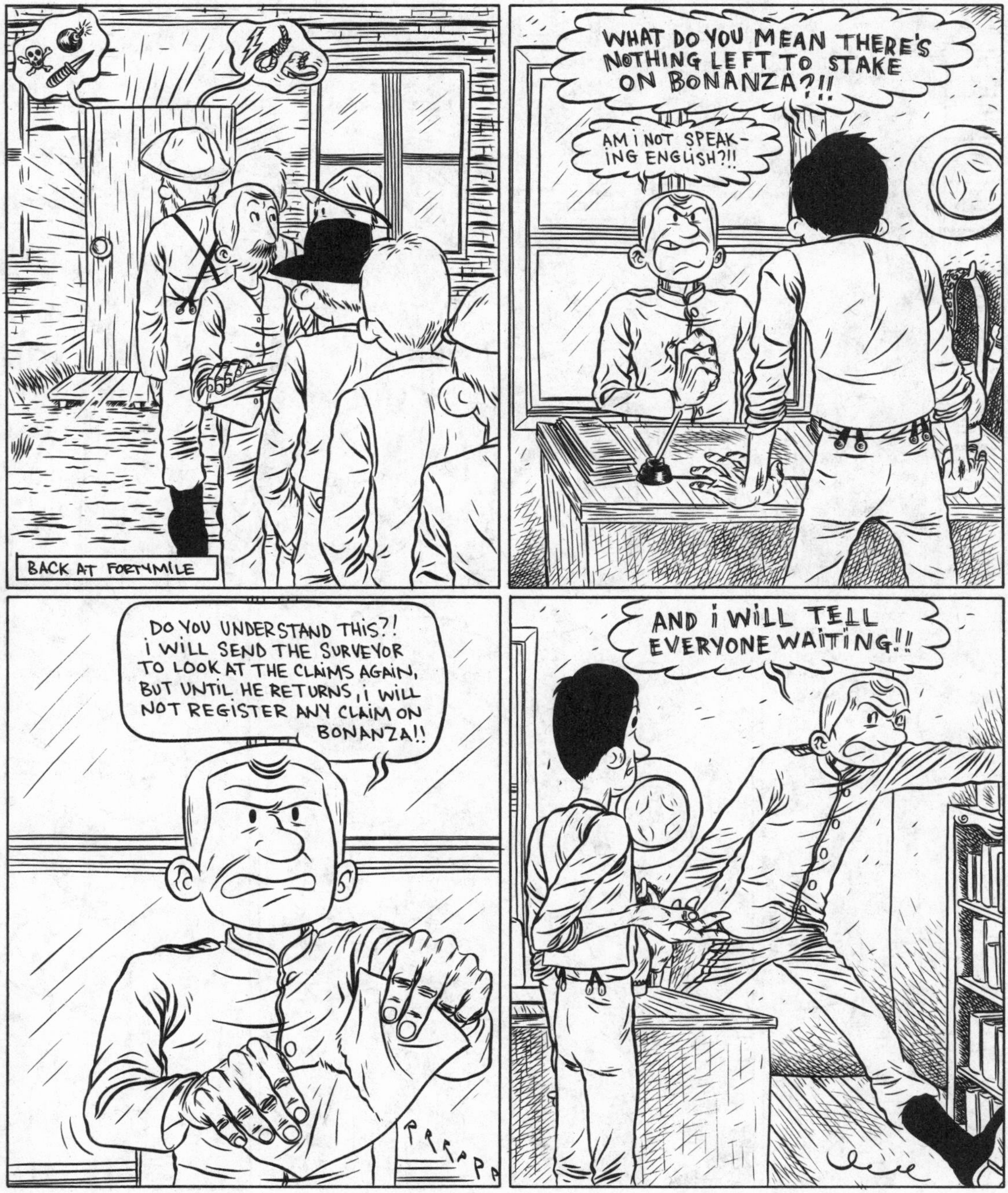
BACK AT FORTYMILE
WHAT DO YOU MEAN THERE'S NOTHING LEFT TO STAKE ON BONANZA?!!
AM I NOT SPEAKING ENGLISH?!!
DO YOU UNDERSTAND THIS?! I WILL SEND THE SURVEYOR TO LOOK AT THE CLAIMS AGAIN, BUT UNTIL HE RETURNS, I WILL NOT REGISTER ANY CLAIM ON BONANZA!!
RRRAPPA
AND I WILL TELL EVERYONE WAITING!!

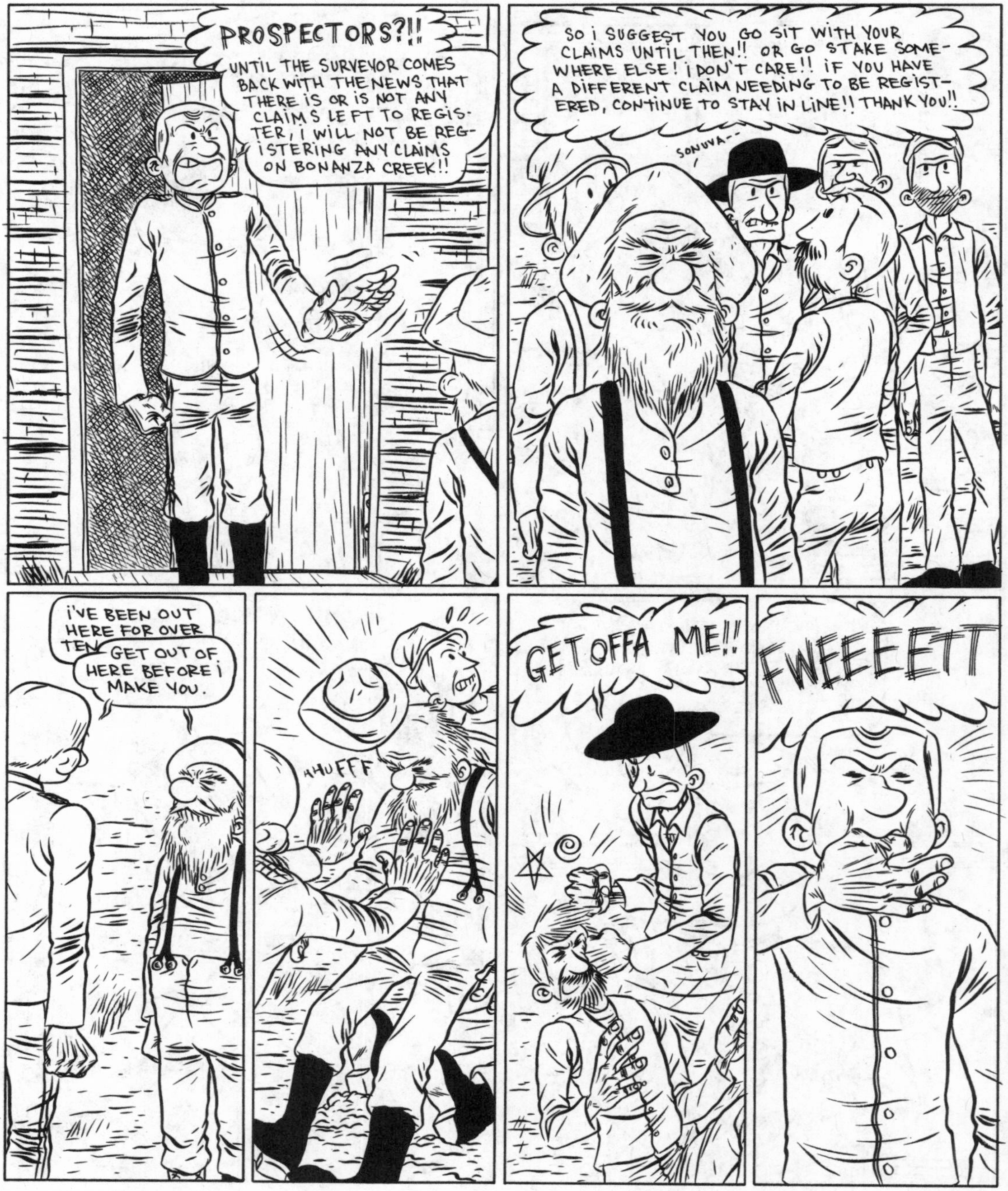
PROSPECTORS?!!
UNTIL THE SURVEYOR COMES BACK WITH THE NEWS THAT THERE IS OR IS NOT ANY CLAIMS LEFT TO REGISTER, I WILL NOT BE REGISTERING ANY CLAIMS ON BONANZA CREEK!!
SO I SUGGEST YOU GO SIT WITH YOUR CLAIMS UNTIL THEN!! OR GO STAKE SOMEWHERE ELSE! I DON'T CARE!! IF YOU HAVE A DIFFERENT CLAIM NEEDING TO BE REGISTERED, CONTINUE TO STAY IN LINE!! THANK YOU!!
SONUVA--
I'VE BEEN OUT HERE FOR OVER TEN
GET OUT OF HERE BEFORE I MAKE YOU.
AHUFFF
GET OFFA ME!!
FWEEEEETT

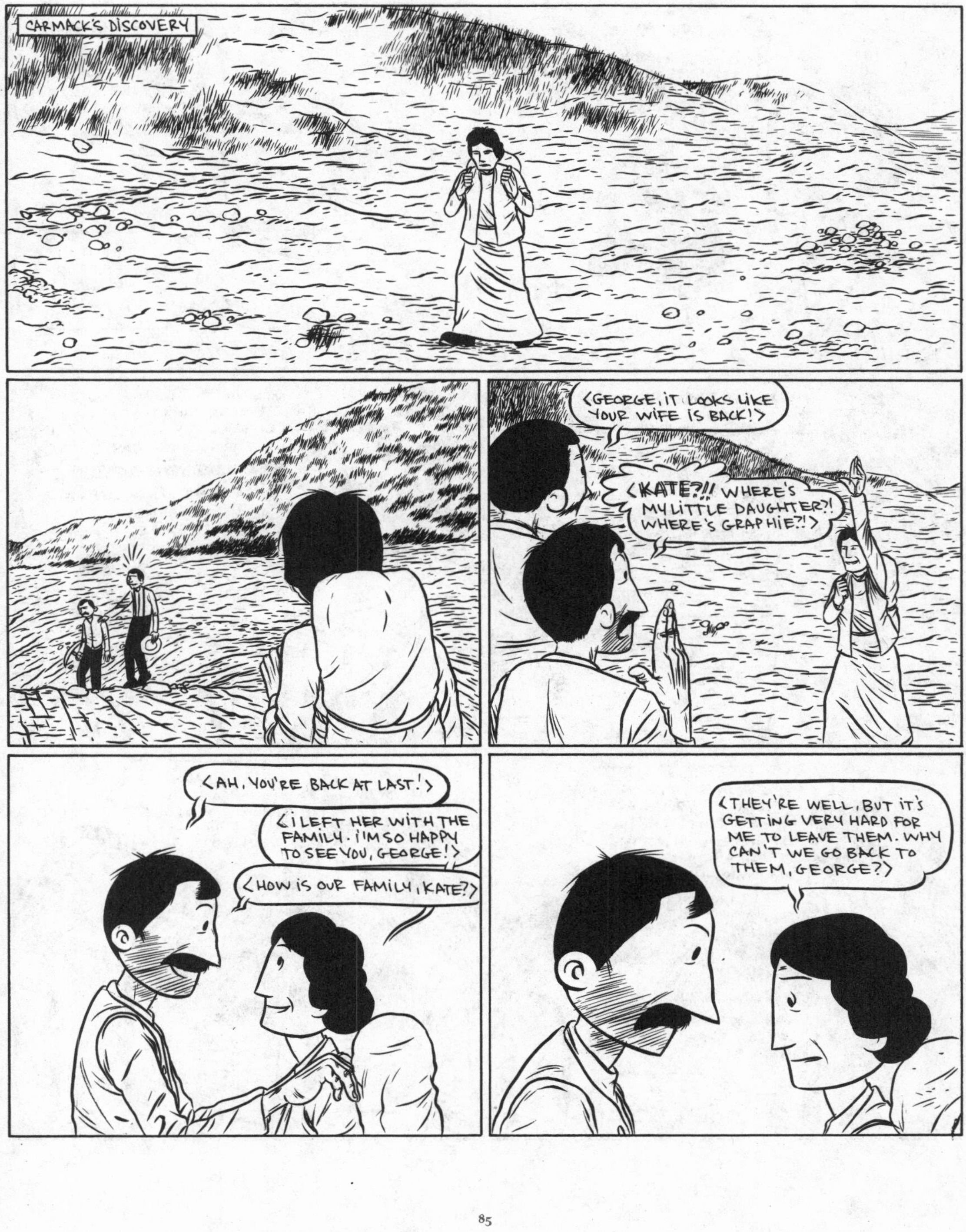
CARMACK'S DISCOVERY
<GEORGE, IT LOOKS LIKE YOUR WIFE IS BACK!>
<KATE?!! WHERE'S MY LITTLE DAUGHTER?! WHERE'S GRAPHIE?!>
<AH, YOU'RE BACK AT LAST!>
<I LEFT HER WITH THE FAMILY. I'M SO HAPPY TO SEE YOU, GEORGE!>
<HOW IS OUR FAMILY, KATE?>
<THEY'RE WELL, BUT IT'S GETTING VERY HARD FOR ME TO LEAVE THEM. WHY CAN'T WE GO BACK TO THEM, GEORGE?>

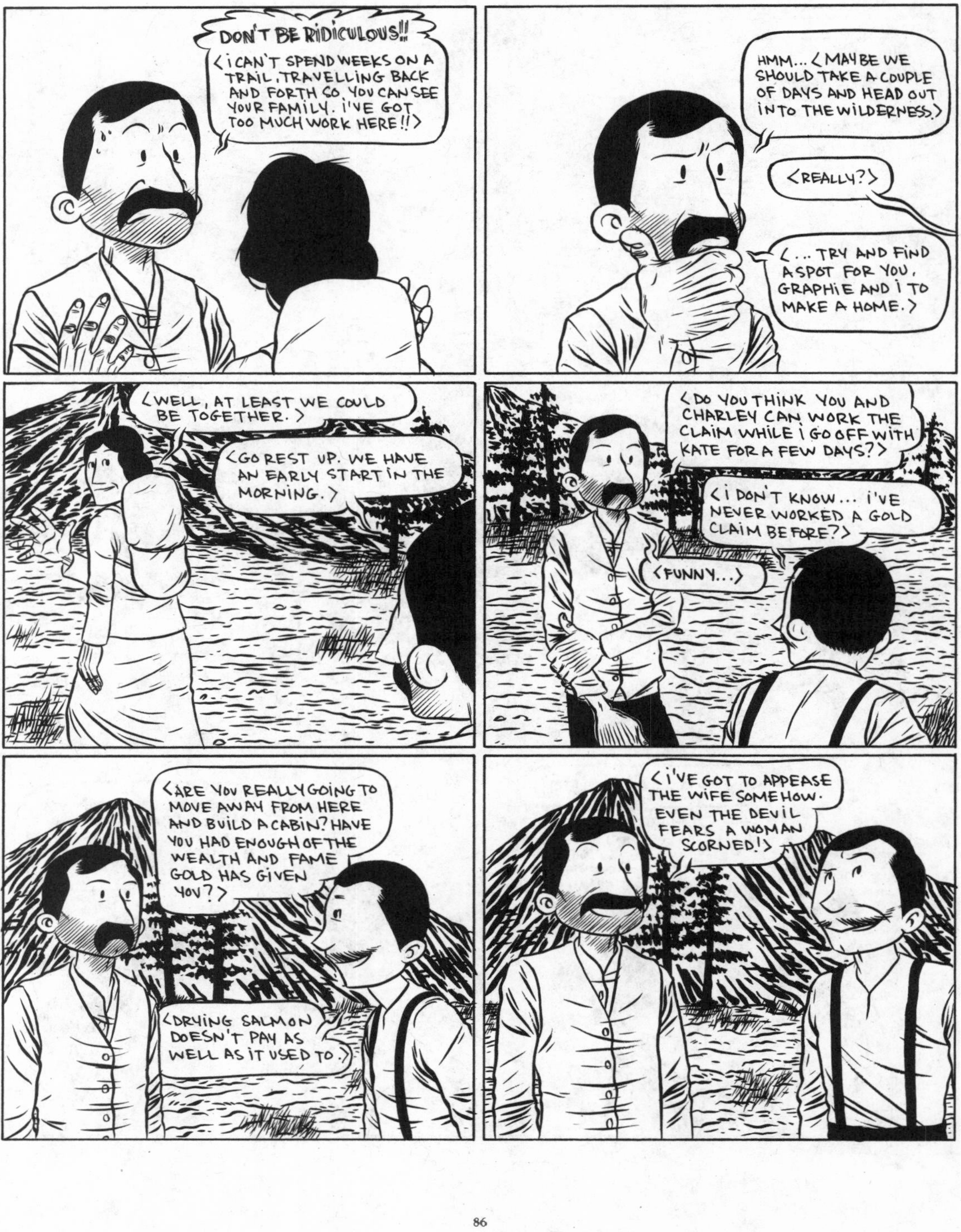
DON'T BE RIDICULOUS!!
<i CAN'T SPEND WEEKS ON A TRAIL, TRAVELLING BACK AND FORTH SO YOU CAN SEE YOUR FAMILY. i'VE GOT TOO MUCH WORK HERE!!>
HMM... <MAYBE WE SHOULD TAKE A COUPLE OF DAYS AND HEAD OUT INTO THE WILDERNESS>
<REALLY?>
<... TRY AND FIND A SPOT FOR YOU, GRAPHIE AND I TO MAKE A HOME.>
<WELL, AT LEAST WE COULD BE TOGETHER.>
<GO REST UP. WE HAVE AN EARLY START IN THE MORNING.>
<DO YOU THINK YOU AND CHARLEY CAN WORK THE CLAIM WHILE i GO OFF WITH KATE FOR A FEW DAYS?>
<i DON'T KNOW... i'VE NEVER WORKED A GOLD CLAIM BEFORE?>
<FUNNY...>
<ARE YOU REALLY GOING TO MOVE AWAY FROM HERE AND BUILD A CABIN? HAVE YOU HAD ENOUGH OF THE WEALTH AND FAME GOLD HAS GIVEN YOU?>
<DRYING SALMON DOESN'T PAY AS WELL AS IT USED TO.>
<i'VE GOT TO APPEASE THE WIFE SOMEHOW. EVEN THE DEVIL FEARS A WOMAN SCORNED!>

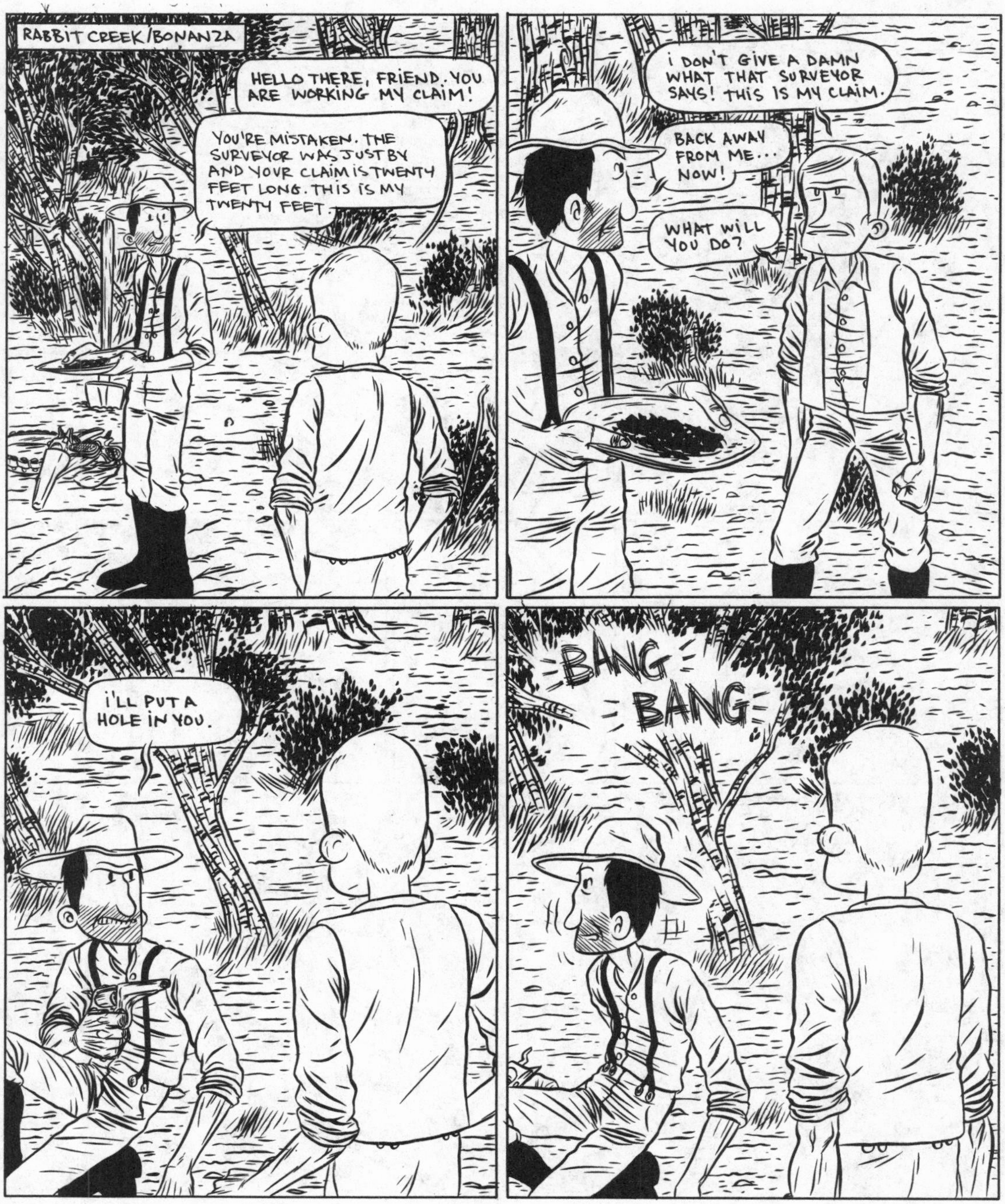
RABBIT CREEK/BONANZA
HELLO THERE, FRIEND. YOU ARE WORKING MY CLAIM!
YOU'RE MISTAKEN. THE SURVEYOR WAS JUST BY AND YOUR CLAIM IS TWENTY FEET LONG. THIS IS MY TWENTY FEET.
I DON'T GIVE A DAMN WHAT THAT SURVEYOR SAYS! THIS IS MY CLAIM.
BACK AWAY FROM ME... NOW!
WHAT WILL YOU DO?
I'LL PUT A HOLE IN YOU.
BANG
BANG

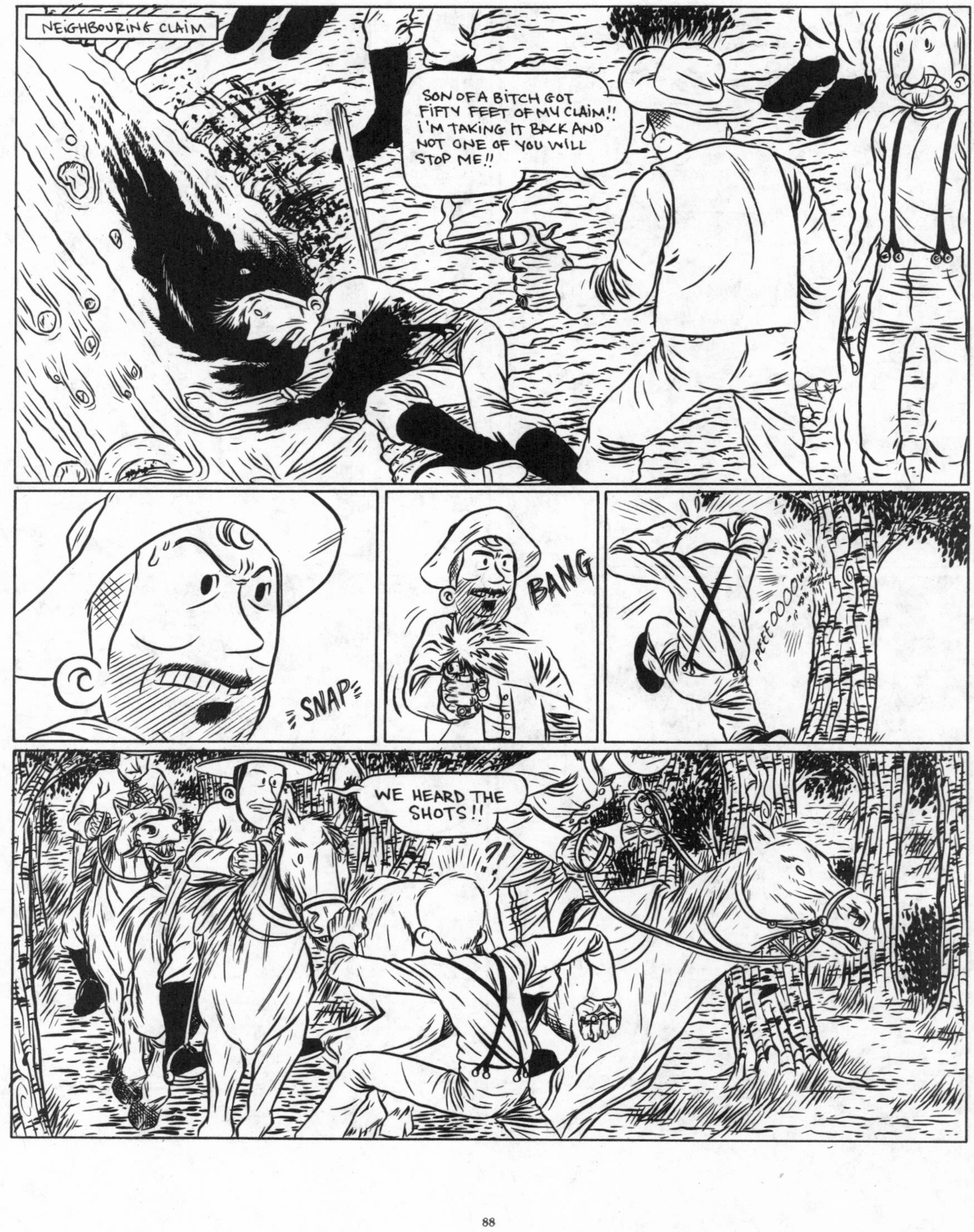
NEIGHBOURING CLAIM
SON OF A BITCH GOT FIFTY FEET OF MY CLAIM!! I'M TAKING IT BACK AND NOT ONE OF YOU WILL STOP ME!!
SNAP
BANG
PPFEEOOOOW
WE HEARD THE SHOTS!!
?!

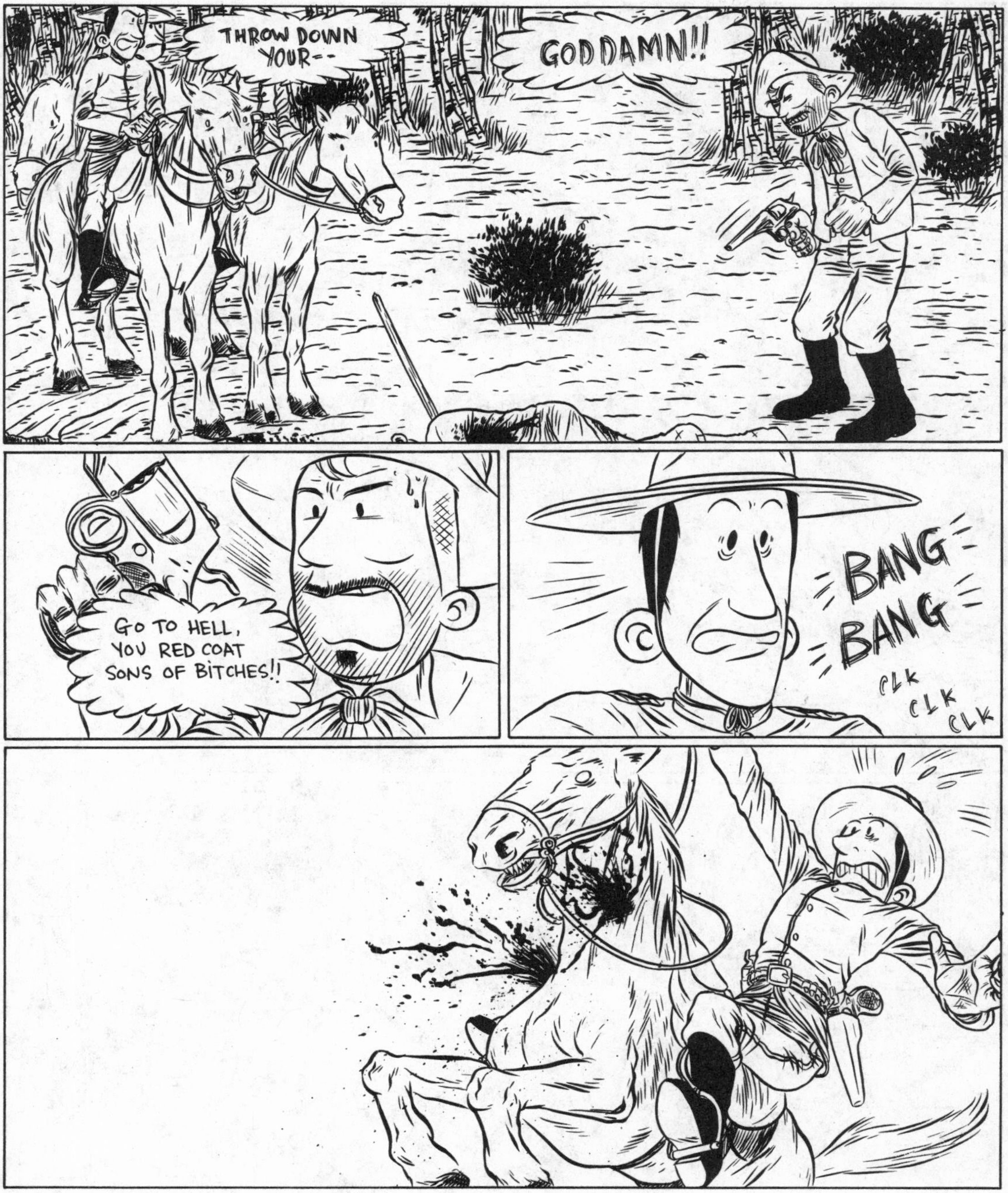

THROW DOWN YOUR--
GODDAMN!!
GO TO HELL, YOU RED COAT SONS OF BITCHES!!
BANG BANG
CLK CLK CLK

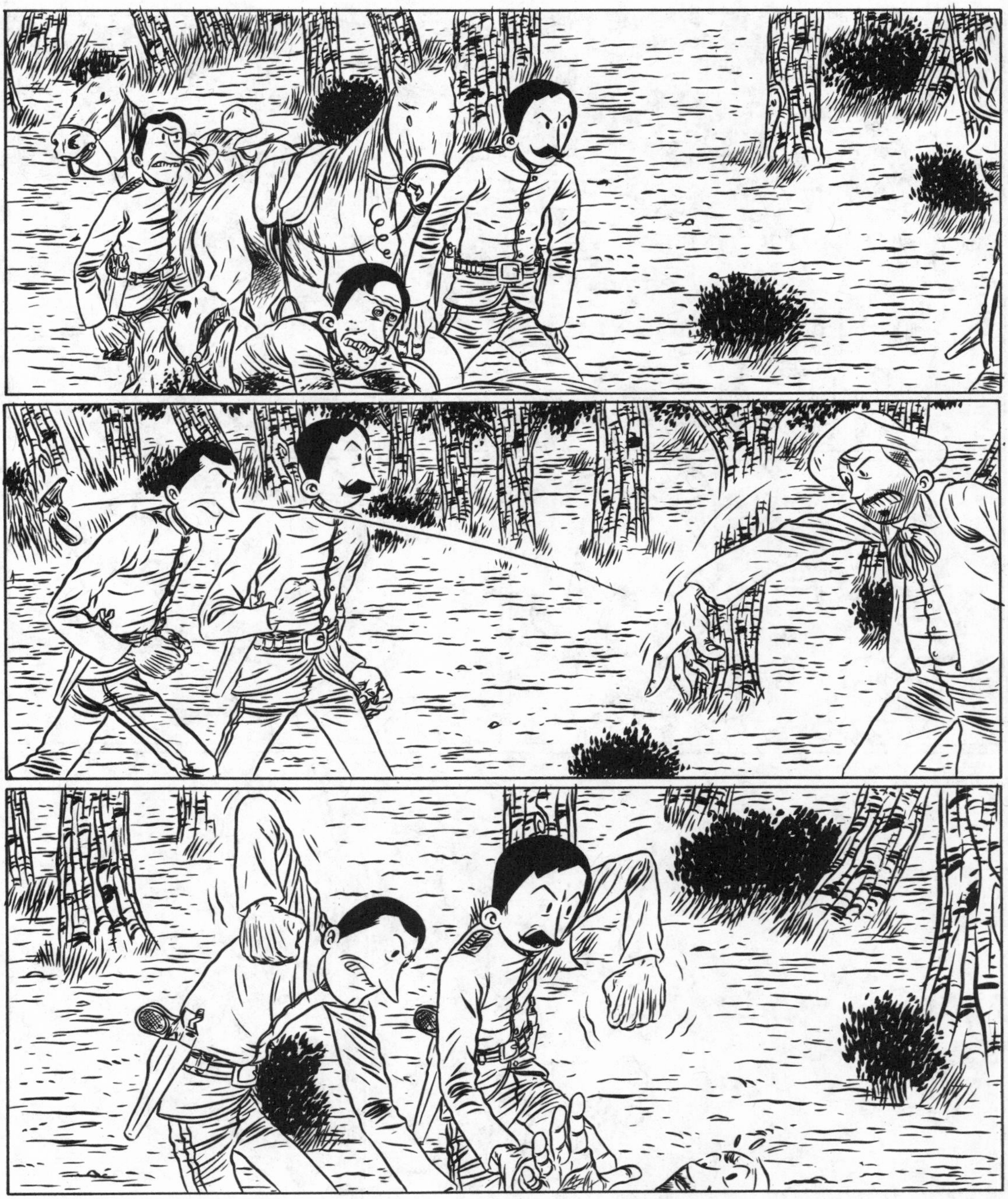

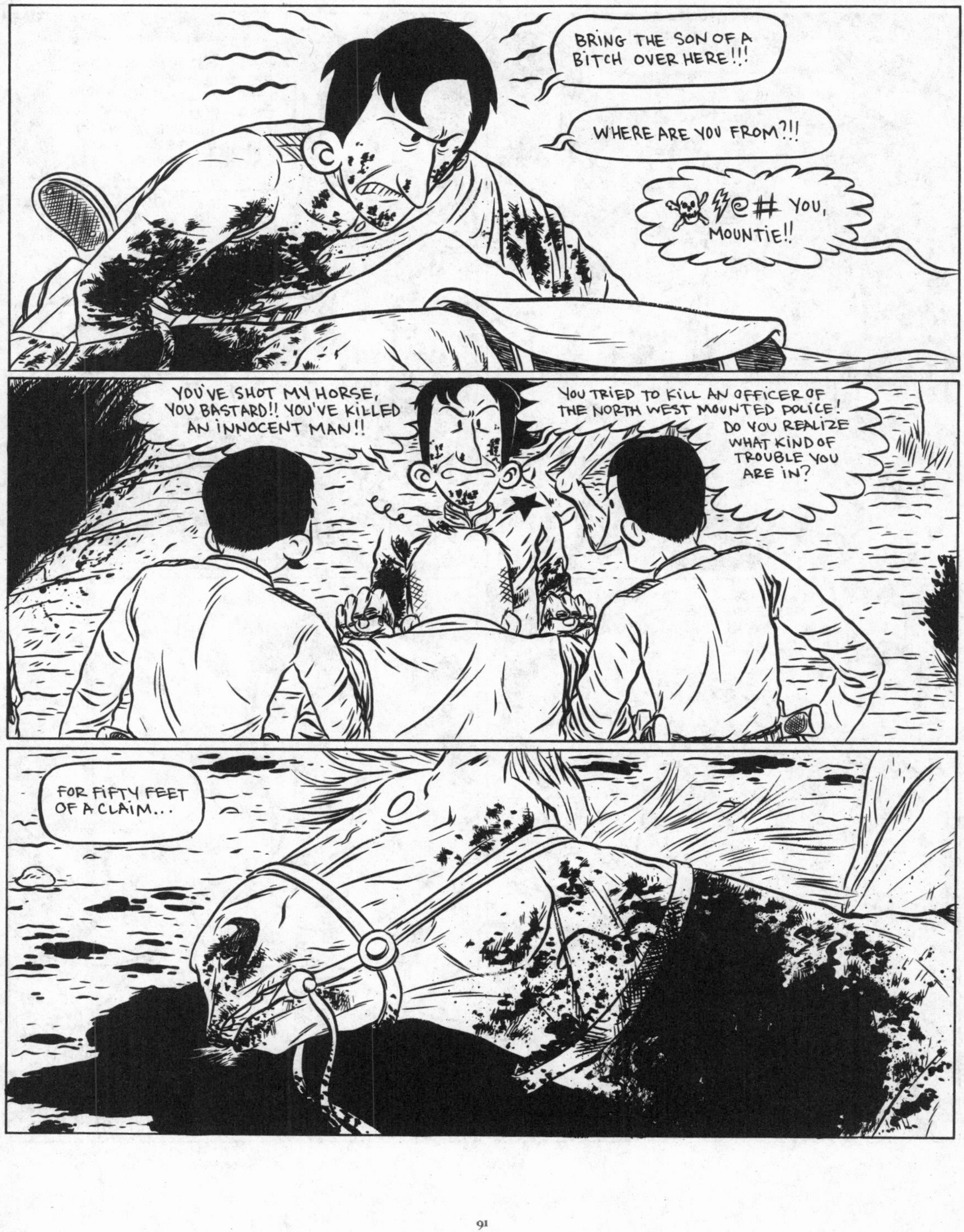
BRING THE SON OF A BITCH OVER HERE!!!
WHERE ARE YOU FROM?!!
@# YOU, MOUNTIE!!
YOU'VE SHOT MY HORSE, YOU BASTARD!! YOU'VE KILLED AN INNOCENT MAN!!
YOU TRIED TO KILL AN OFFICER OF THE NORTH WEST MOUNTED POLICE! DO YOU REALIZE WHAT KIND OF TROUBLE YOU ARE IN?
FOR FIFTY FEET OF A CLAIM...

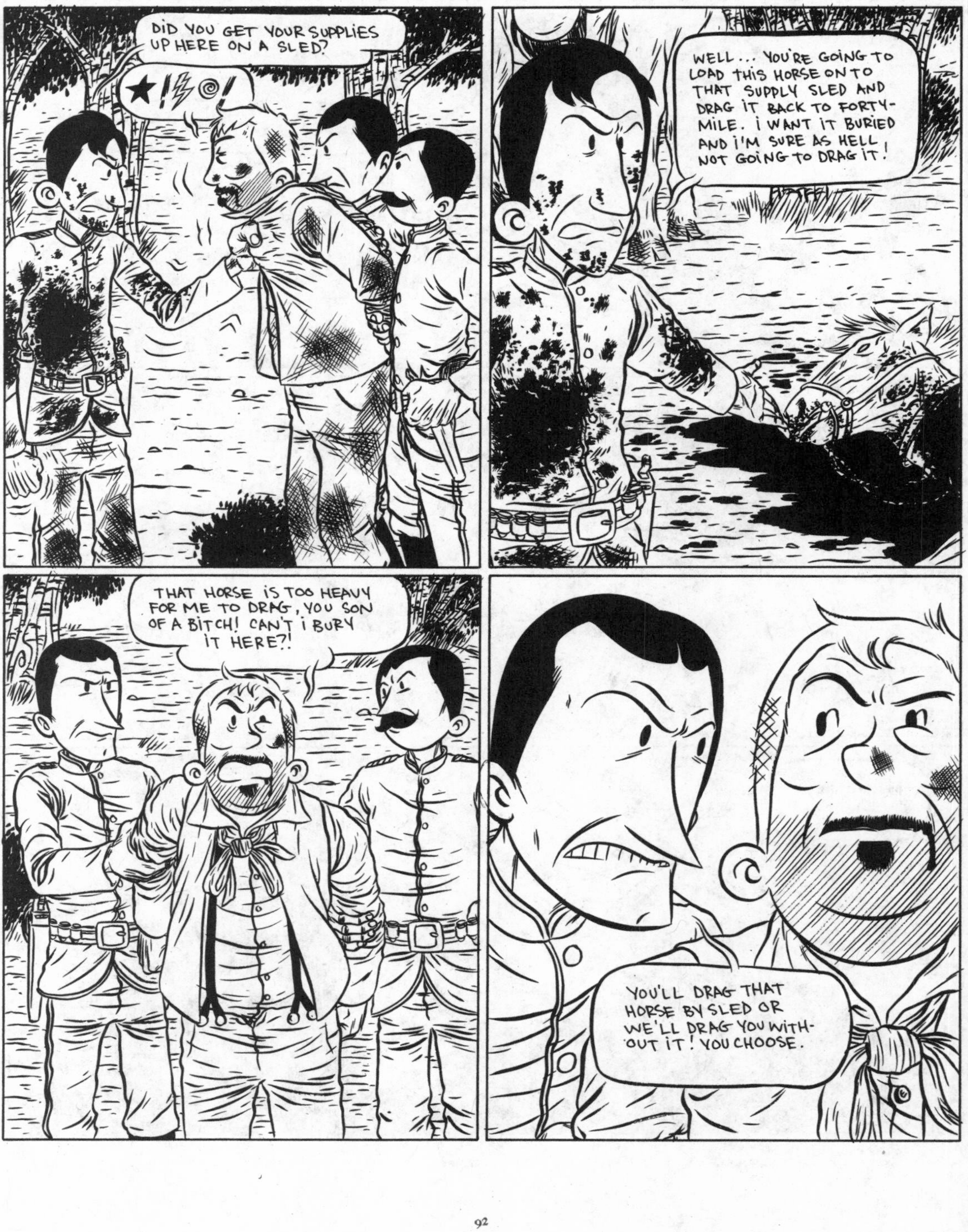
DID YOU GET YOUR SUPPLIES UP HERE ON A SLED?
★!⚡◎!
WELL... YOU'RE GOING TO LOAD THIS HORSE ON TO THAT SUPPLY SLED AND DRAG IT BACK TO FORTY-MILE. I WANT IT BURIED AND I'M SURE AS HELL NOT GOING TO DRAG IT!
THAT HORSE IS TOO HEAVY FOR ME TO DRAG, YOU SON OF A BITCH! CAN'T I BURY IT HERE?!
YOU'LL DRAG THAT HORSE BY SLED OR WE'LL DRAG YOU WITH-OUT IT! YOU CHOOSE.

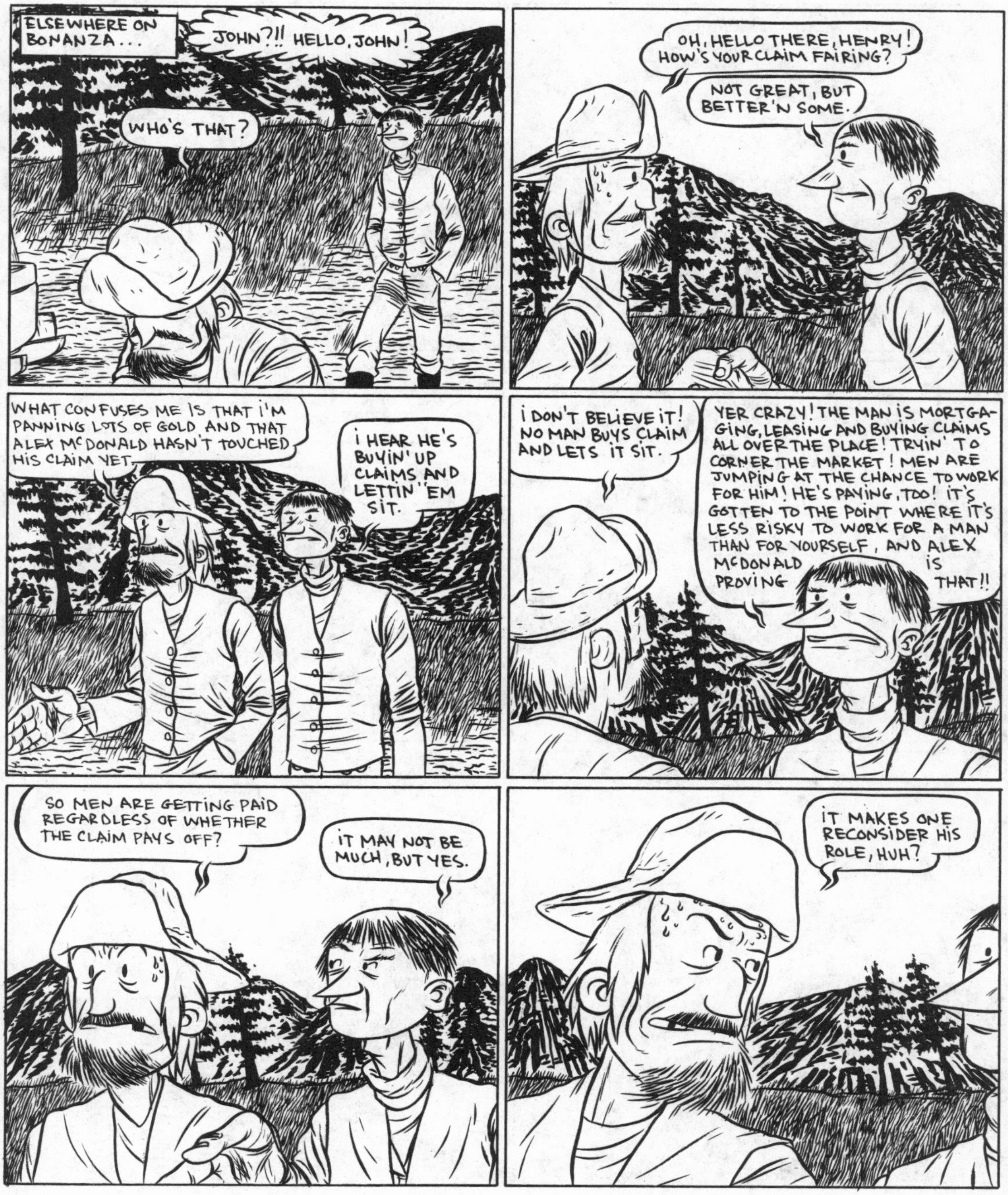
ELSEWHERE ON BONANZA...
JOHN?!! HELLO, JOHN!
WHO'S THAT?
OH, HELLO THERE, HENRY! HOW'S YOUR CLAIM FAIRING?
NOT GREAT, BUT BETTER'N SOME.
WHAT CONFUSES ME IS THAT I'M PANNING LOTS OF GOLD, AND THAT ALEX McDONALD HASN'T TOUCHED HIS CLAIM YET.
I HEAR HE'S BUYIN' UP CLAIMS AND LETTIN' 'EM SIT.
I DON'T BELIEVE IT! NO MAN BUYS CLAIM AND LETS IT SIT.
YER CRAZY! THE MAN IS MORTGAGING, LEASING AND BUYING CLAIMS ALL OVER THE PLACE! TRYIN' TO CORNER THE MARKET! MEN ARE JUMPING AT THE CHANCE TO WORK FOR HIM! HE'S PAYING, TOO! IT'S GOTTEN TO THE POINT WHERE IT'S LESS RISKY TO WORK FOR A MAN THAN FOR YOURSELF, AND ALEX McDONALD IS PROVING THAT!!
SO MEN ARE GETTING PAID REGARDLESS OF WHETHER THE CLAIM PAYS OFF?
IT MAY NOT BE MUCH, BUT YES.
IT MAKES ONE RECONSIDER HIS ROLE, HUH?

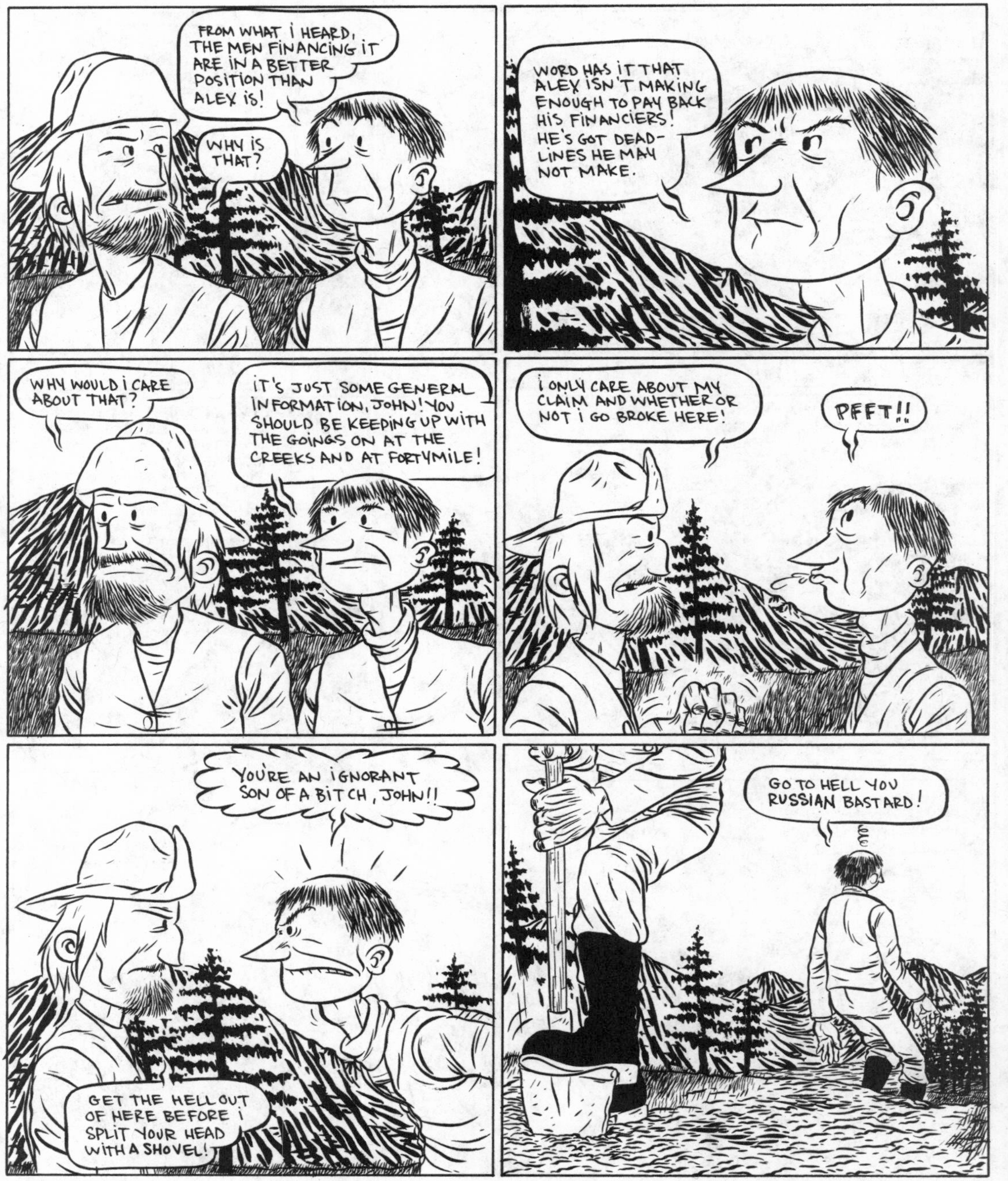
FROM WHAT I HEARD, THE MEN FINANCING IT ARE IN A BETTER POSITION THAN ALEX IS!
WHY IS THAT?
WORD HAS IT THAT ALEX ISN'T MAKING ENOUGH TO PAY BACK HIS FINANCIERS! HE'S GOT DEAD-LINES HE MAY NOT MAKE.
WHY WOULD I CARE ABOUT THAT?
IT'S JUST SOME GENERAL INFORMATION, JOHN! YOU SHOULD BE KEEPING UP WITH THE GOINGS ON AT THE CREEKS AND AT FORTYMILE!
I ONLY CARE ABOUT MY CLAIM AND WHETHER OR NOT I GO BROKE HERE!
PFFT!!
YOU'RE AN IGNORANT SON OF A BITCH, JOHN!!
GET THE HELL OUT OF HERE BEFORE I SPLIT YOUR HEAD WITH A SHOVEL!
GO TO HELL YOU RUSSIAN BASTARD!

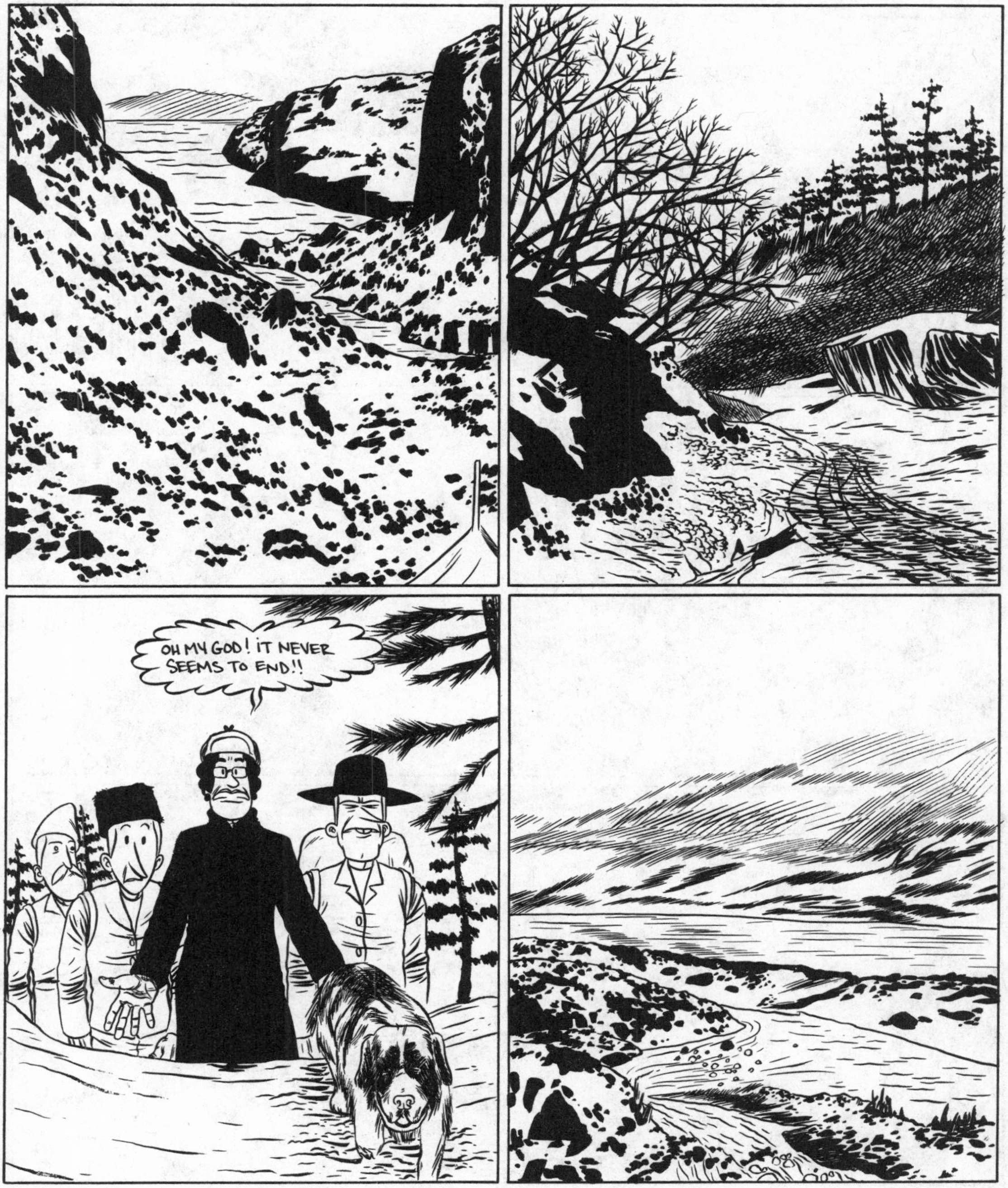
OH MY GOD! IT NEVER SEEMS TO END!!

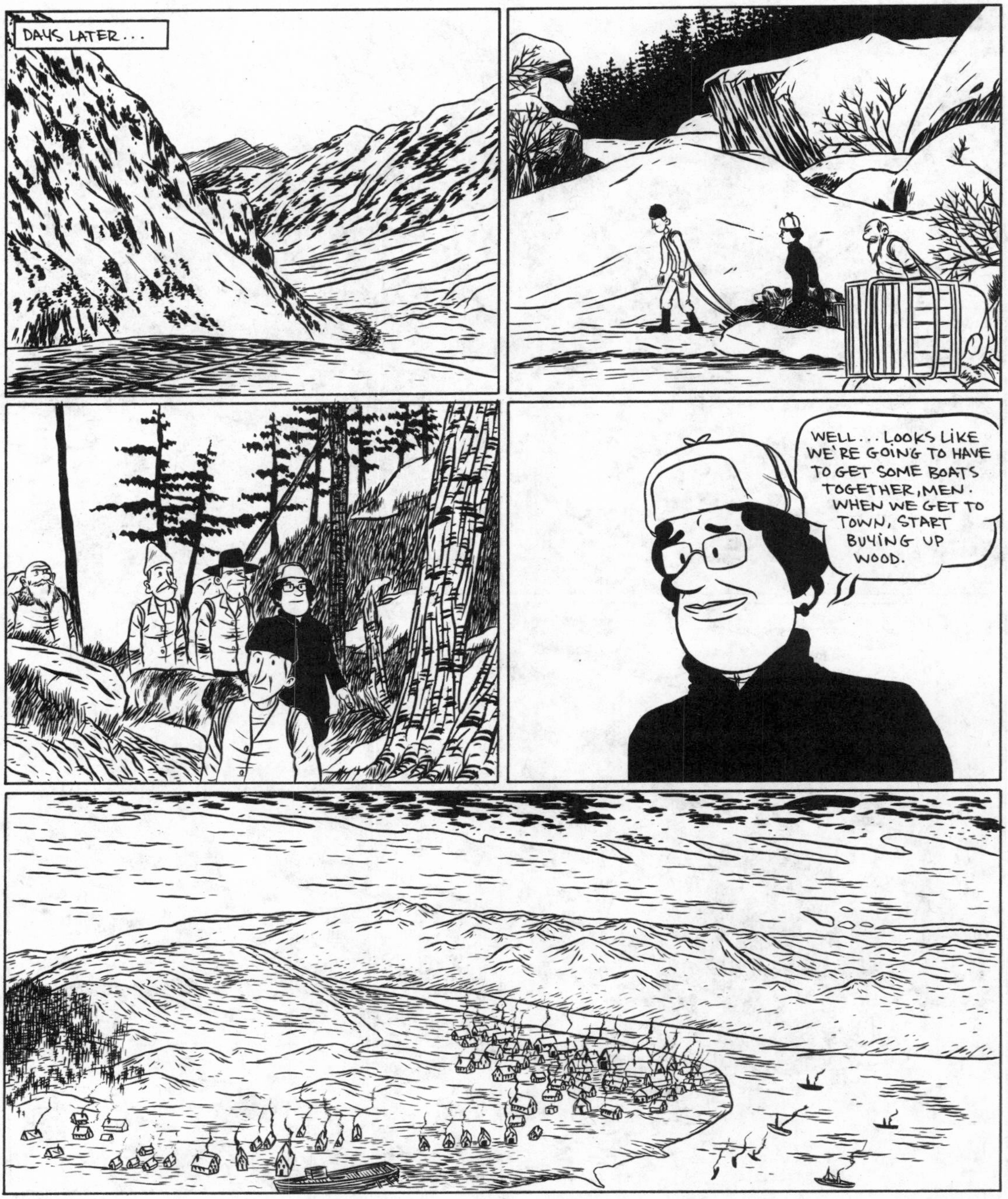
DAYS LATER...
WELL... LOOKS LIKE WE'RE GOING TO HAVE TO GET SOME BOATS TOGETHER, MEN. WHEN WE GET TO TOWN, START BUYING UP WOOD.

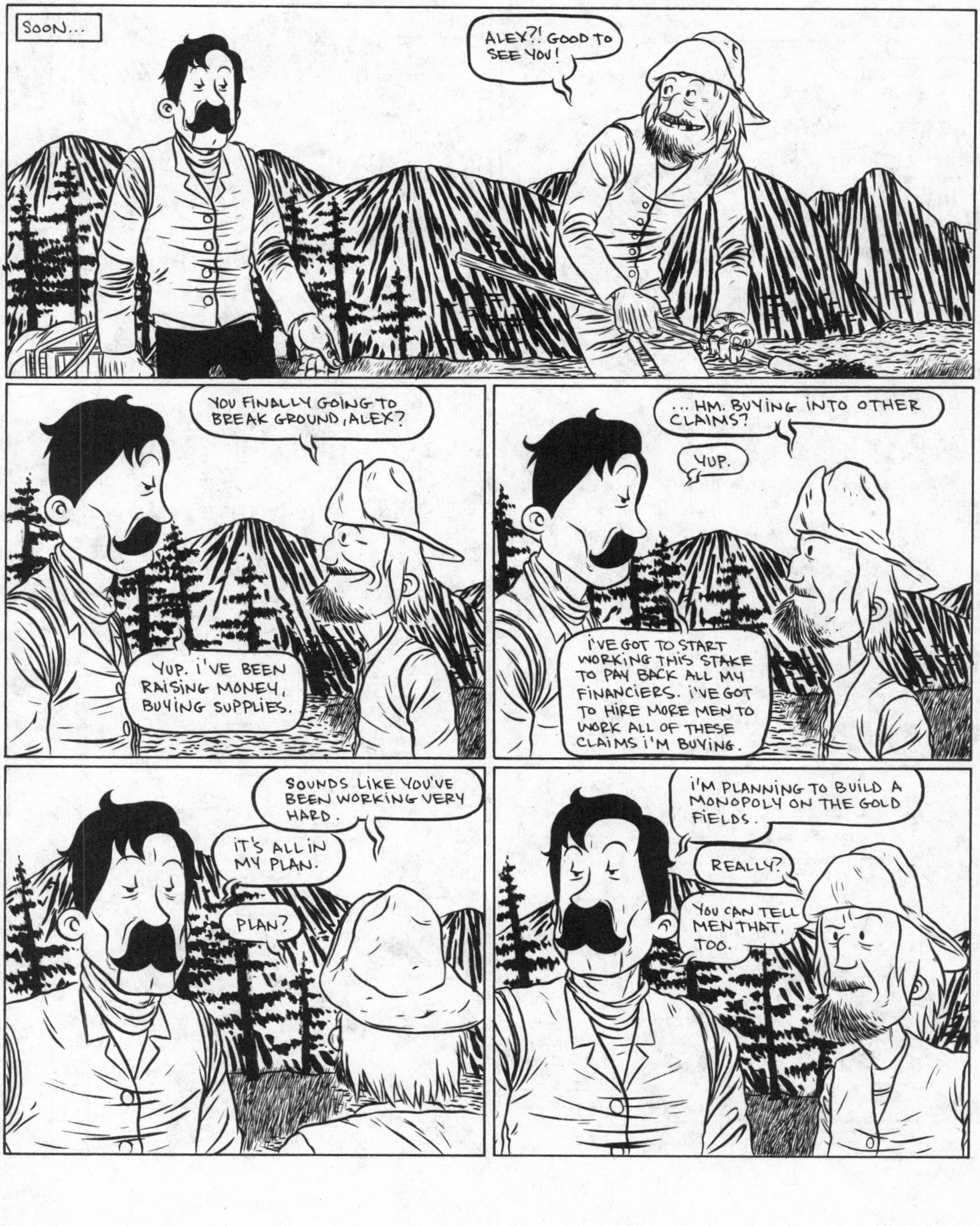
SOON...
ALEX?! GOOD TO SEE YOU!
YOU FINALLY GOING TO BREAK GROUND, ALEX?
YUP. I'VE BEEN RAISING MONEY, BUYING SUPPLIES.
... HM. BUYING INTO OTHER CLAIMS?
YUP.
I'VE GOT TO START WORKING THIS STAKE TO PAY BACK ALL MY FINANCIERS. I'VE GOT TO HIRE MORE MEN TO WORK ALL OF THESE CLAIMS I'M BUYING.
SOUNDS LIKE YOU'VE BEEN WORKING VERY HARD.
IT'S ALL IN MY PLAN.
PLAN?
I'M PLANNING TO BUILD A MONOPOLY ON THE GOLD FIELDS.
REALLY?
YOU CAN TELL MEN THAT, TOO.

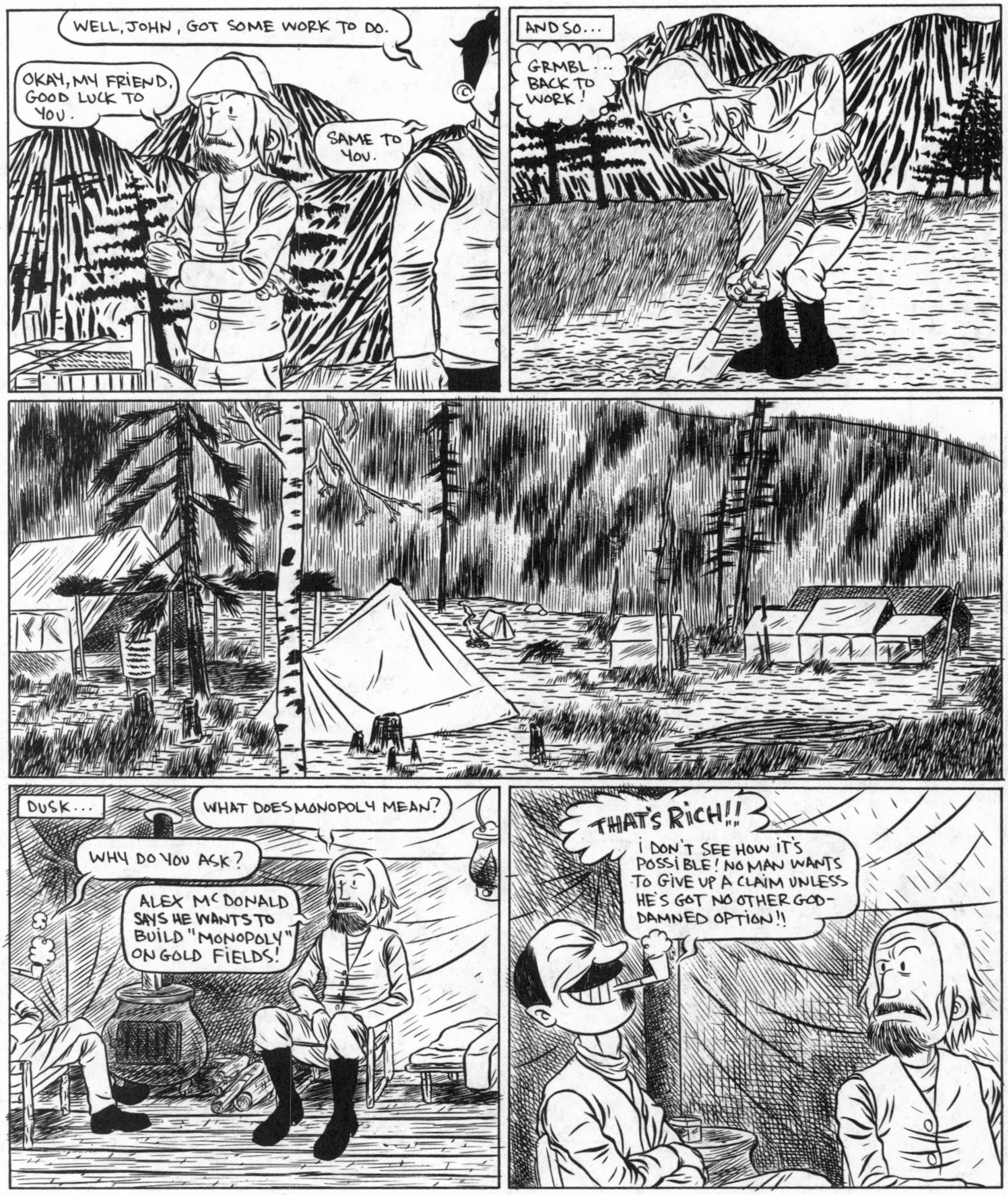
WELL, JOHN, GOT SOME WORK TO DO.
OKAY, MY FRIEND, GOOD LUCK TO YOU.
SAME TO YOU.
AND SO...
GRMBL... BACK TO WORK!
DUSK...
WHAT DOES MONOPOLY MEAN?
WHY DO YOU ASK?
ALEX McDONALD SAYS HE WANTS TO BUILD "MONOPOLY" ON GOLD FIELDS!
THAT'S RICH!!
I DON'T SEE HOW IT'S POSSIBLE! NO MAN WANTS TO GIVE UP A CLAIM UNLESS HE'S GOT NO OTHER GOD-DAMNED OPTION!!

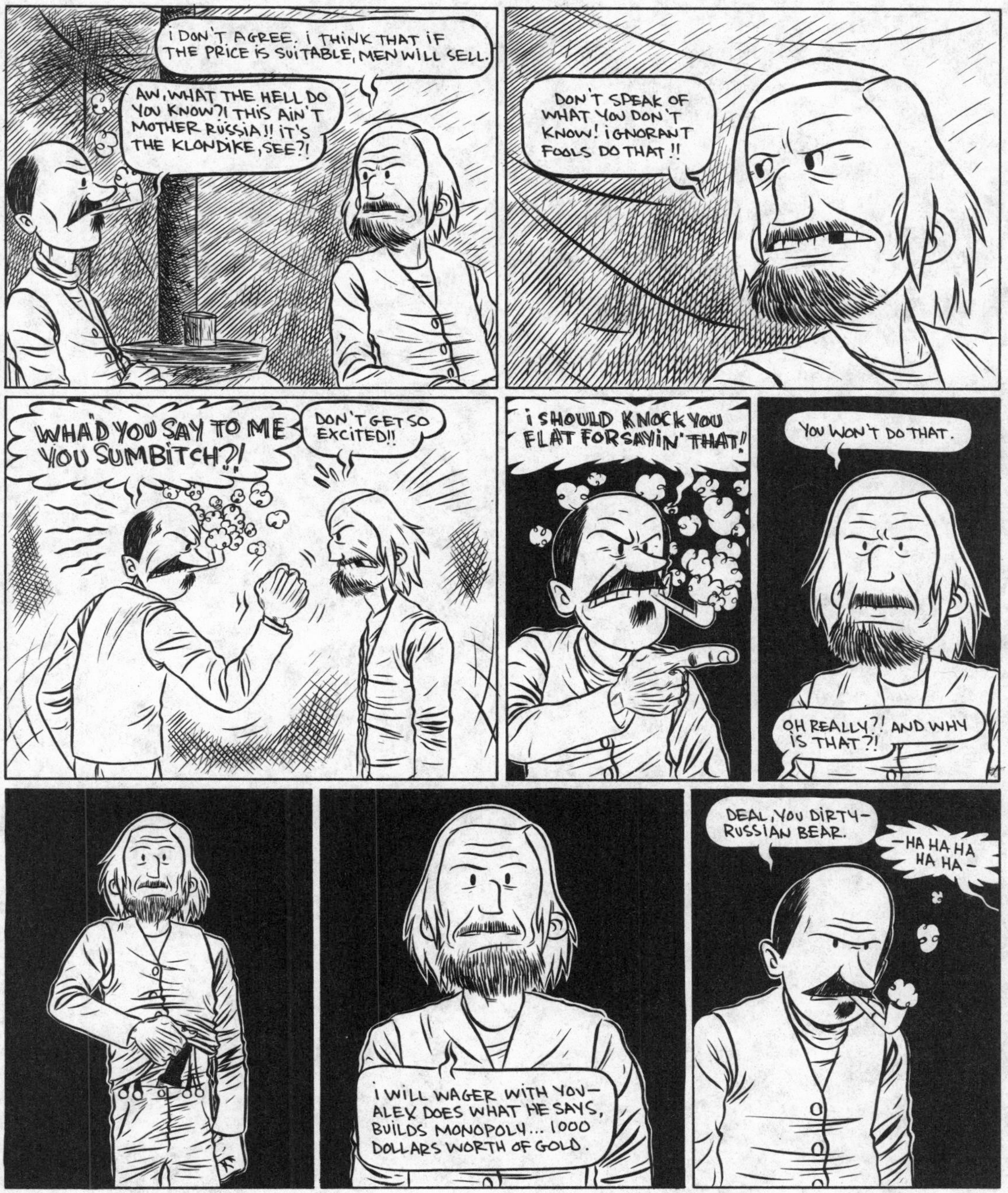
I DON'T AGREE. I THINK THAT IF THE PRICE IS SUITABLE, MEN WILL SELL.
AW, WHAT THE HELL DO YOU KNOW?! THIS AIN'T MOTHER RUSSIA!! IT'S THE KLONDIKE, SEE?!
DON'T SPEAK OF WHAT YOU DON'T KNOW! IGNORANT FOOLS DO THAT!!
WHA'D YOU SAY TO ME YOU SUMBITCH?!
DON'T GET SO EXCITED!!
I SHOULD KNOCK YOU FLAT FOR SAYIN' THAT!
YOU WON'T DO THAT.
OH REALLY?! AND WHY IS THAT?!
I WILL WAGER WITH YOU- ALEX DOES WHAT HE SAYS, BUILDS MONOPOLY... 1000 DOLLARS WORTH OF GOLD.
DEAL, YOU DIRTY- RUSSIAN BEAR.
-HA HA HA HA HA-

UPON LEARNING OF THE MAJOR DISCOVERY ON THE BONANZA, ROBERT HENDERSON HANDED HIS YUKON ORDER OF PIONEERS BADGE (A FRATERNAL ORGANIZATION THAT HELD THE MOTTO "DO UNTO OTHERS AS YOU WOULD BE DONE BY") OVER TO "HARPER'S ILLUSTRATED WEEKLY" CORRESPONDENT TAPPAN ADNEY. ADNEY WAS RESPONSIBLE FOR WRITING HUNDREDS OF PAGES OF MATERIAL ON THE GOLD RUSH. HE BASICALLY WENT EVERYWHERE THE WOULD-BE PROSPECTORS WENT, INCLUDING THE TRAILS, CAMPS, MINERS' MEETINGS AND SPECIAL EVENTS.

WHILE HENDERSON'S LUCK WAS GETTING WORSE, AL THAYER AND WINFIELD OLER'S WAS ABOUT TO TAKE A TURN EVEN THEY COULDN'T HAVE EXPECTED. THEY WERE TWO SHIFTY MORONS WHO GOT COLD FEET WHEN THEY THOUGHT THEY WERE IN POSSESSION OF A WORTHLESS CLAIM. SELLING IT TO AN INEBRIATED CHARLEY ANDERSON SEEMED LIKE A GOOD IDEA AT THE TIME, BUT THE FUTURE TOLD A DIFFERENT STORY. AT ONE POINT ANDERSON HAD SO MUCH MONEY THAT HE BOUGHT A SINGLE NEWSPAPER FROM A LOCAL BOY FOR FIFTY-NINE DOLLARS, A FORTUNE IN THE 1890S.

HELLO BOB, HOW'S LIFE?
IT'S GOOD. I'VE MADE A NICE LITTLE DISCOVERY ON GOLD BOTTOM.
GOLD BOTTOM?
WHY? DO YOU HAVE SOMETHING ELSE?
SURE! OVER ON BONANZA! IT WAS A HUGE STRIKE AND EVERYONE'S GETTING RICH OFF OF IT!
BONANZA?!!
WHERE'S THAT?! I KNOW ALL THE CREEKS!!
THEY'VE RENAMED RABBIT CREEK.

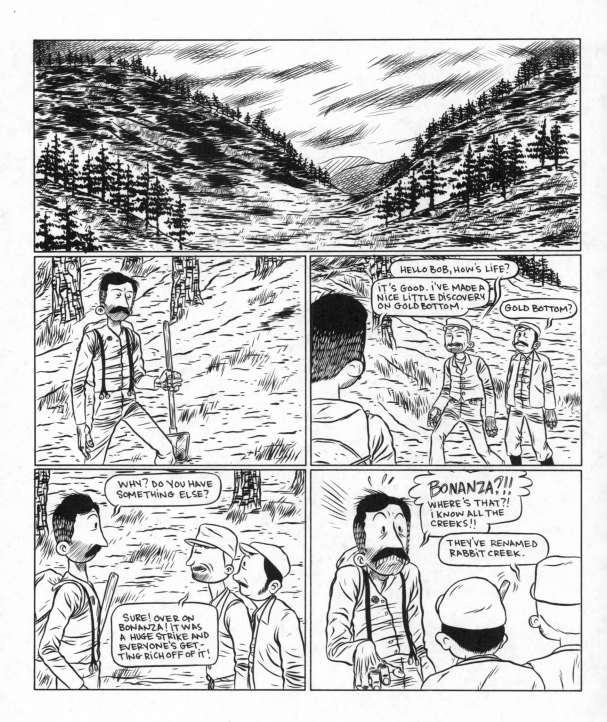

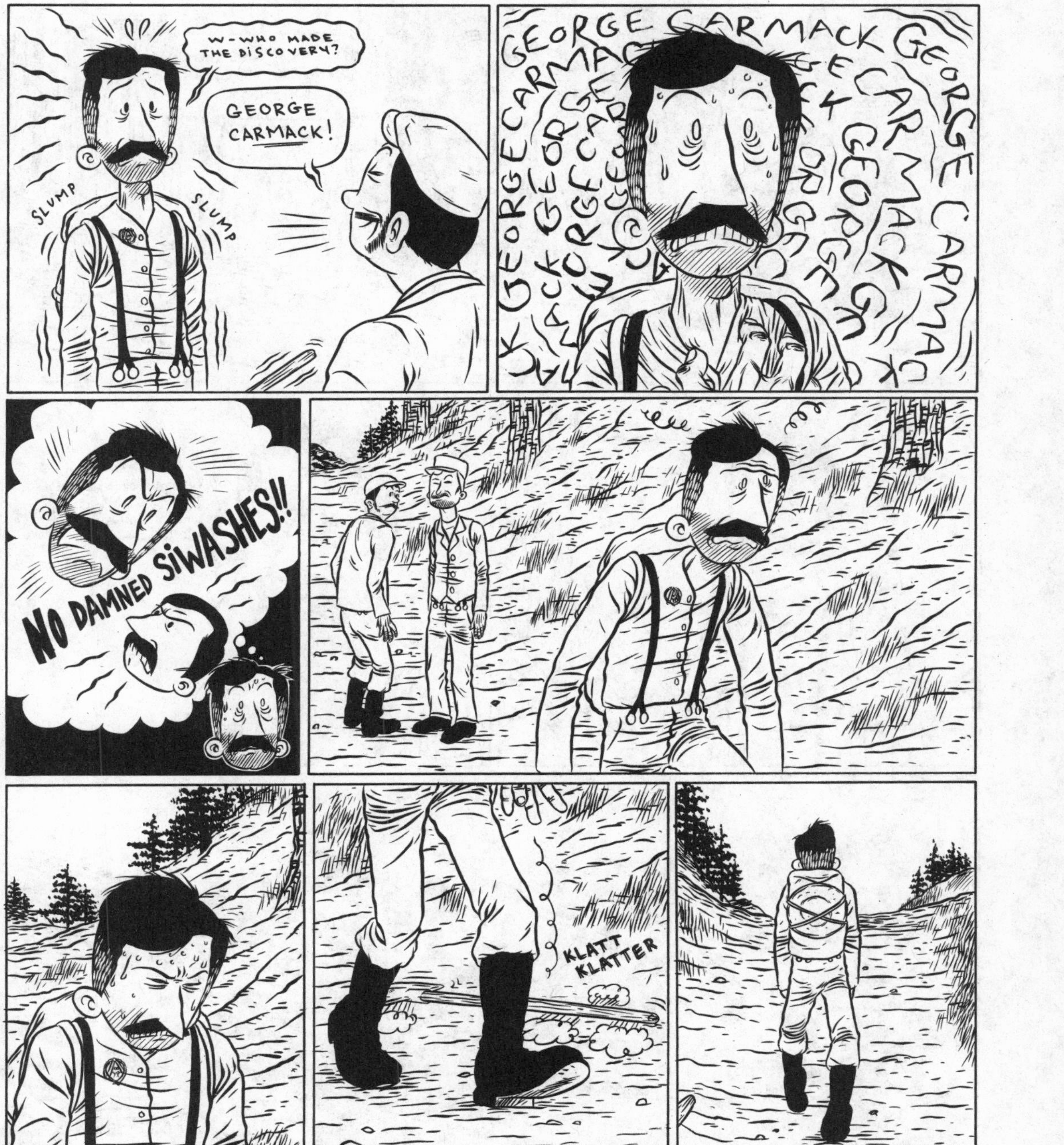
W-WHO MADE THE DISCOVERY?
GEORGE CARMACK!
SLUMP
SLUMP
GEORGE CARMACK GEORGE CARMACK
NO DAMNED SIWASHES!!
KLATT KLATTER

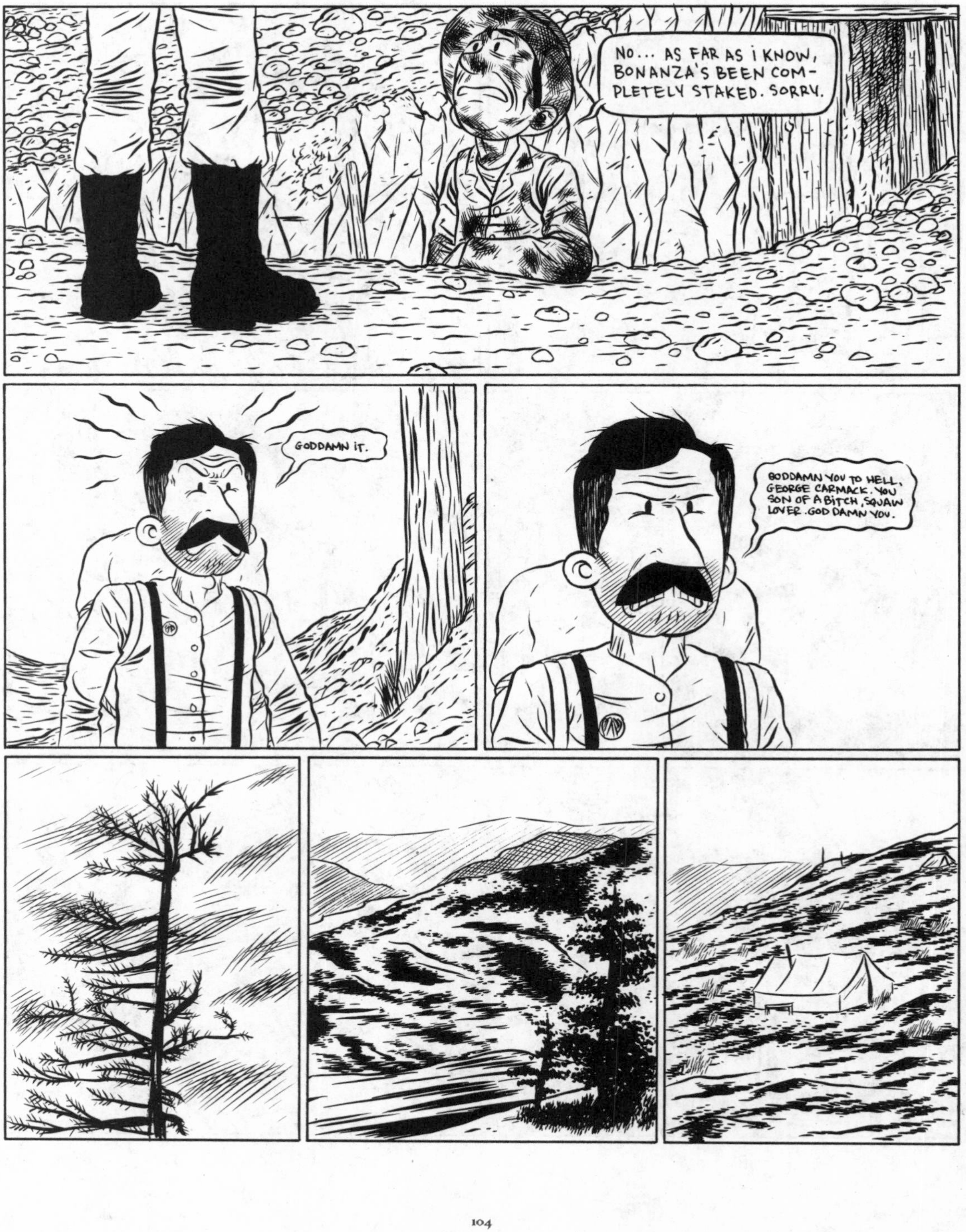
NO... AS FAR AS i KNOW, BONANZA'S BEEN COMPLETELY STAKED. SORRY.
GODDAMN iT.
GODDAMN YOU TO HELL, GEORGE CARMACK. YOU SON OF A BITCH, SQUAW LOVER. GOD DAMN YOU.

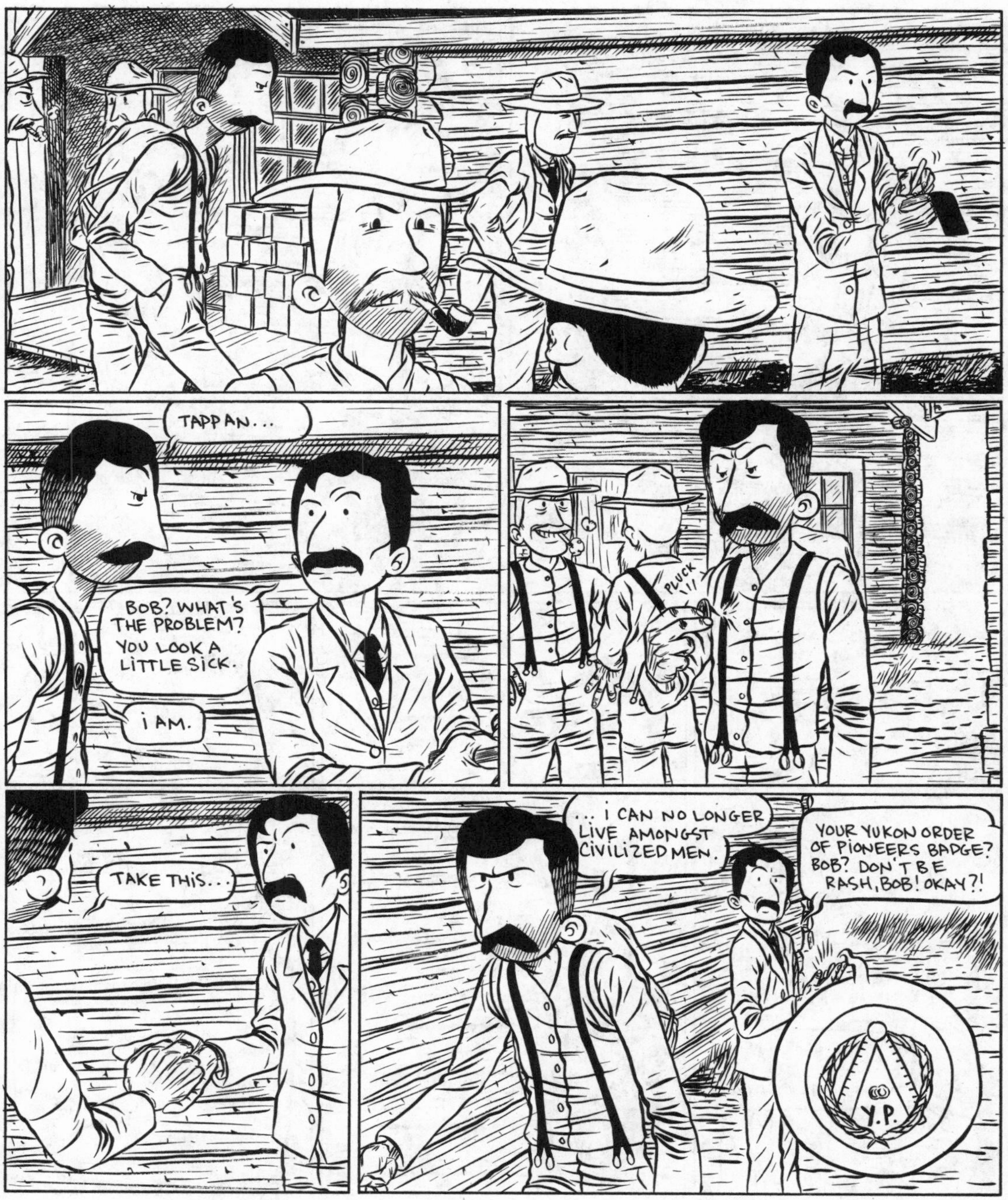

TAPPAN...
BOB? WHAT'S THE PROBLEM? YOU LOOK A LITTLE SICK.
I AM.
PLUCK
TAKE THIS...
...I CAN NO LONGER LIVE AMONGST CIVILIZED MEN.
YOUR YUKON ORDER OF PIONEERS BADGE? BOB? DON'T BE RASH, BOB! OKAY?!
Y.P.

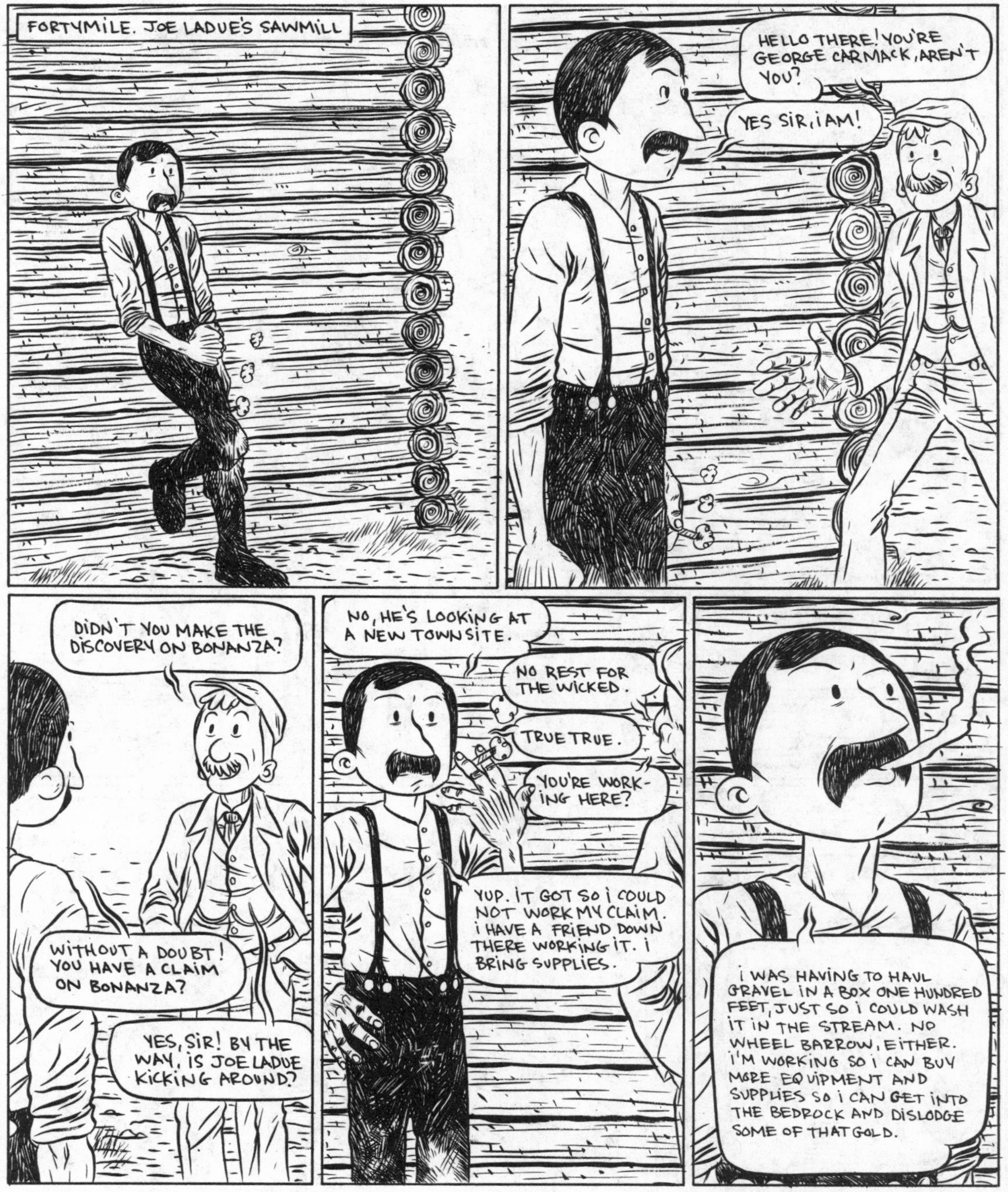
FORTYMILE. JOE LADUE'S SAWMILL
HELLO THERE! YOU'RE GEORGE CARMACK, AREN'T YOU?
YES SIR, I AM!
DIDN'T YOU MAKE THE DISCOVERY ON BONANZA?
WITHOUT A DOUBT! YOU HAVE A CLAIM ON BONANZA?
YES, SIR! BY THE WAY, IS JOE LADUE KICKING AROUND?
NO, HE'S LOOKING AT A NEW TOWNSITE.
NO REST FOR THE WICKED.
TRUE TRUE.
YOU'RE WORKING HERE?
YUP. IT GOT SO I COULD NOT WORK MY CLAIM. I HAVE A FRIEND DOWN THERE WORKING IT. I BRING SUPPLIES.
I WAS HAVING TO HAUL GRAVEL IN A BOX ONE HUNDRED FEET, JUST SO I COULD WASH IT IN THE STREAM. NO WHEEL BARROW, EITHER. I'M WORKING SO I CAN BUY MORE EQUIPMENT AND SUPPLIES SO I CAN GET INTO THE BEDROCK AND DISLODGE SOME OF THAT GOLD.

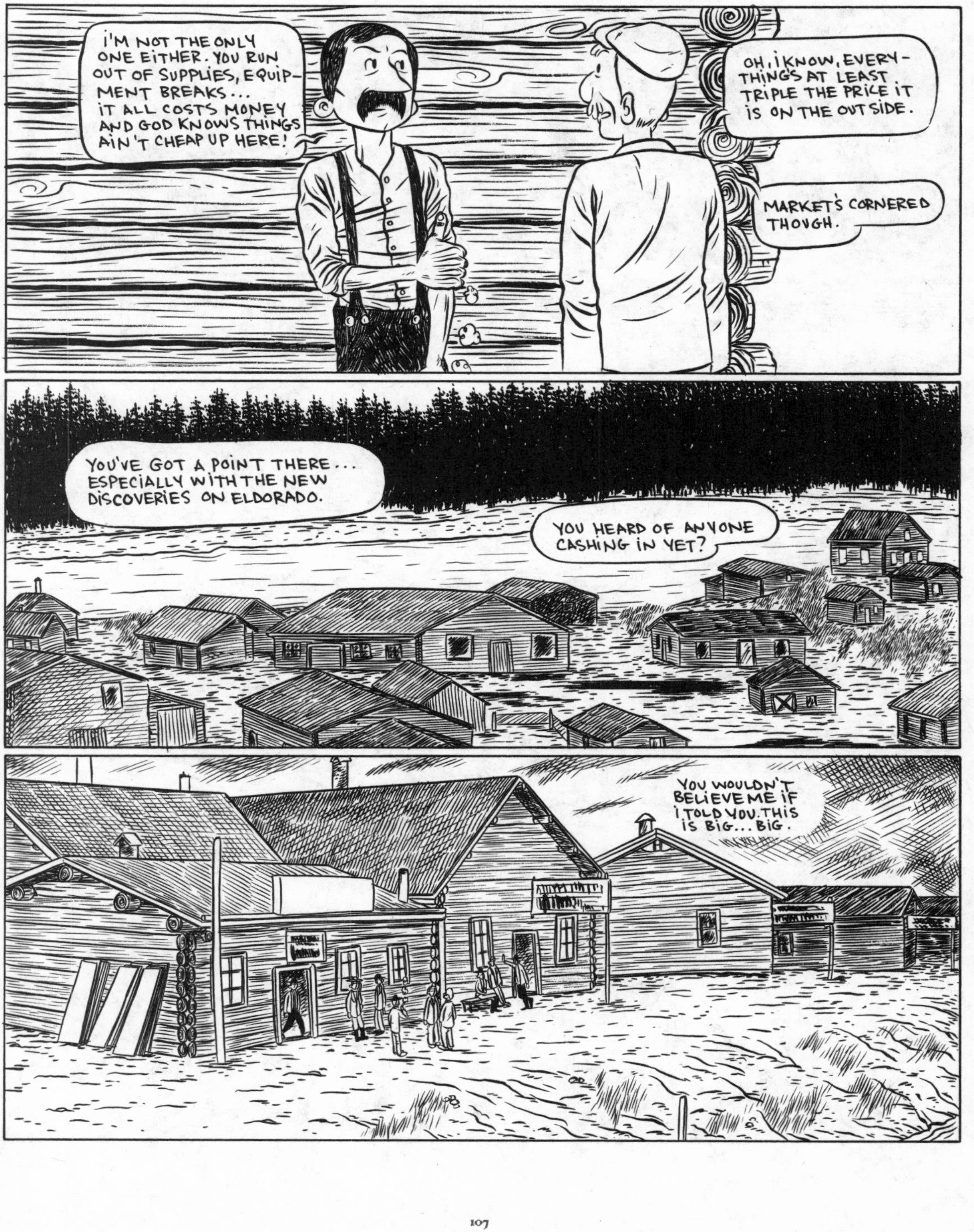
I'M NOT THE ONLY ONE EITHER. YOU RUN OUT OF SUPPLIES, EQUIPMENT BREAKS... IT ALL COSTS MONEY AND GOD KNOWS THINGS AIN'T CHEAP UP HERE!
OH, I KNOW, EVERYTHING'S AT LEAST TRIPLE THE PRICE IT IS ON THE OUTSIDE.
MARKET'S CORNERED THOUGH.
YOU'VE GOT A POINT THERE... ESPECIALLY WITH THE NEW DISCOVERIES ON ELDORADO.
YOU HEARD OF ANYONE CASHING IN YET?
YOU WOULDN'T BELIEVE ME IF I TOLD YOU. THIS IS BIG... BIG.

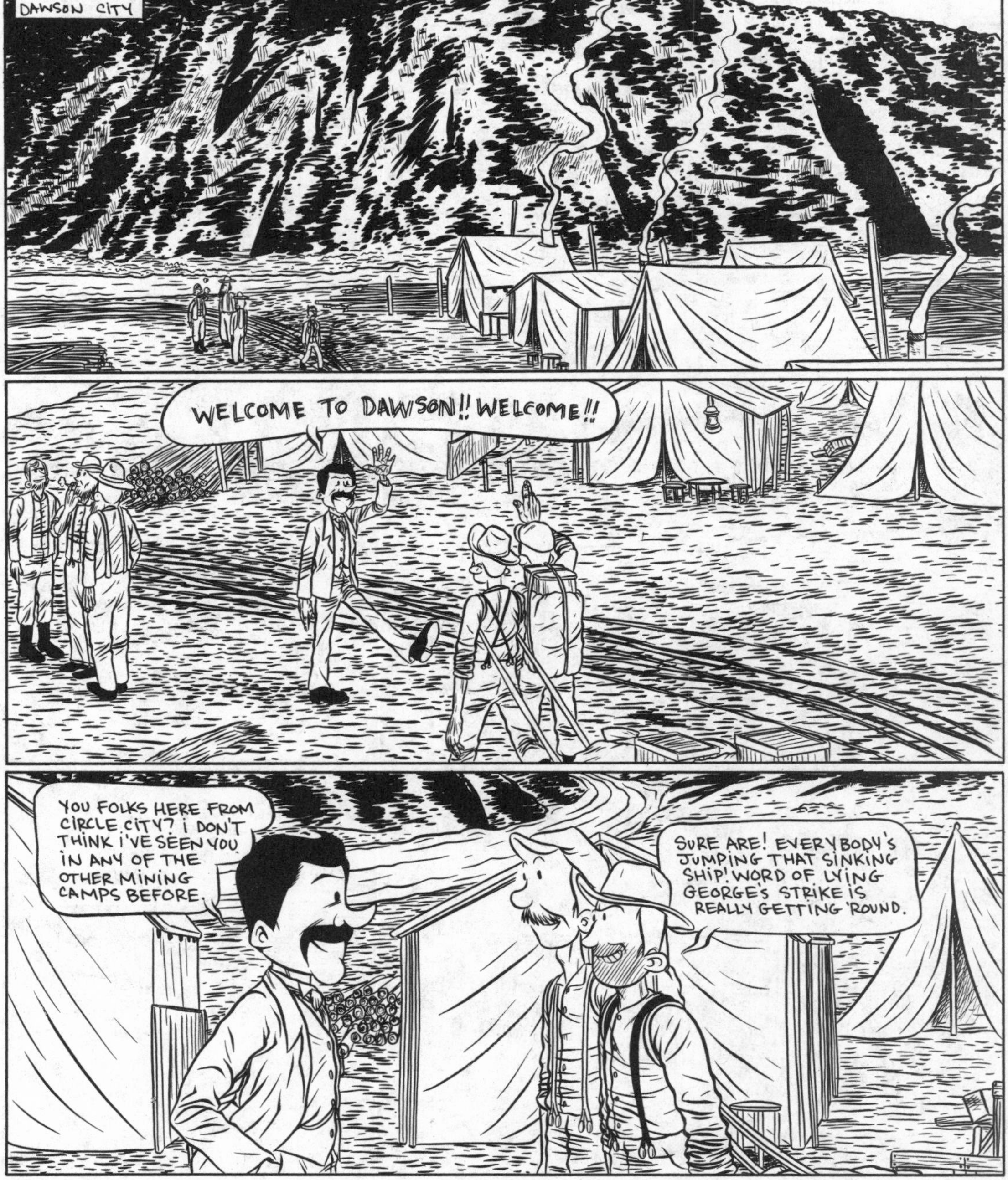
DAWSON CITY
WELCOME TO DAWSON!! WELCOME!!
YOU FOLKS HERE FROM CIRCLE CITY? I DON'T THINK I'VE SEEN YOU IN ANY OF THE OTHER MINING CAMPS BEFORE.
SURE ARE! EVERYBODY'S JUMPING THAT SINKING SHIP! WORD OF LYING GEORGE'S STRIKE IS REALLY GETTING 'ROUND.

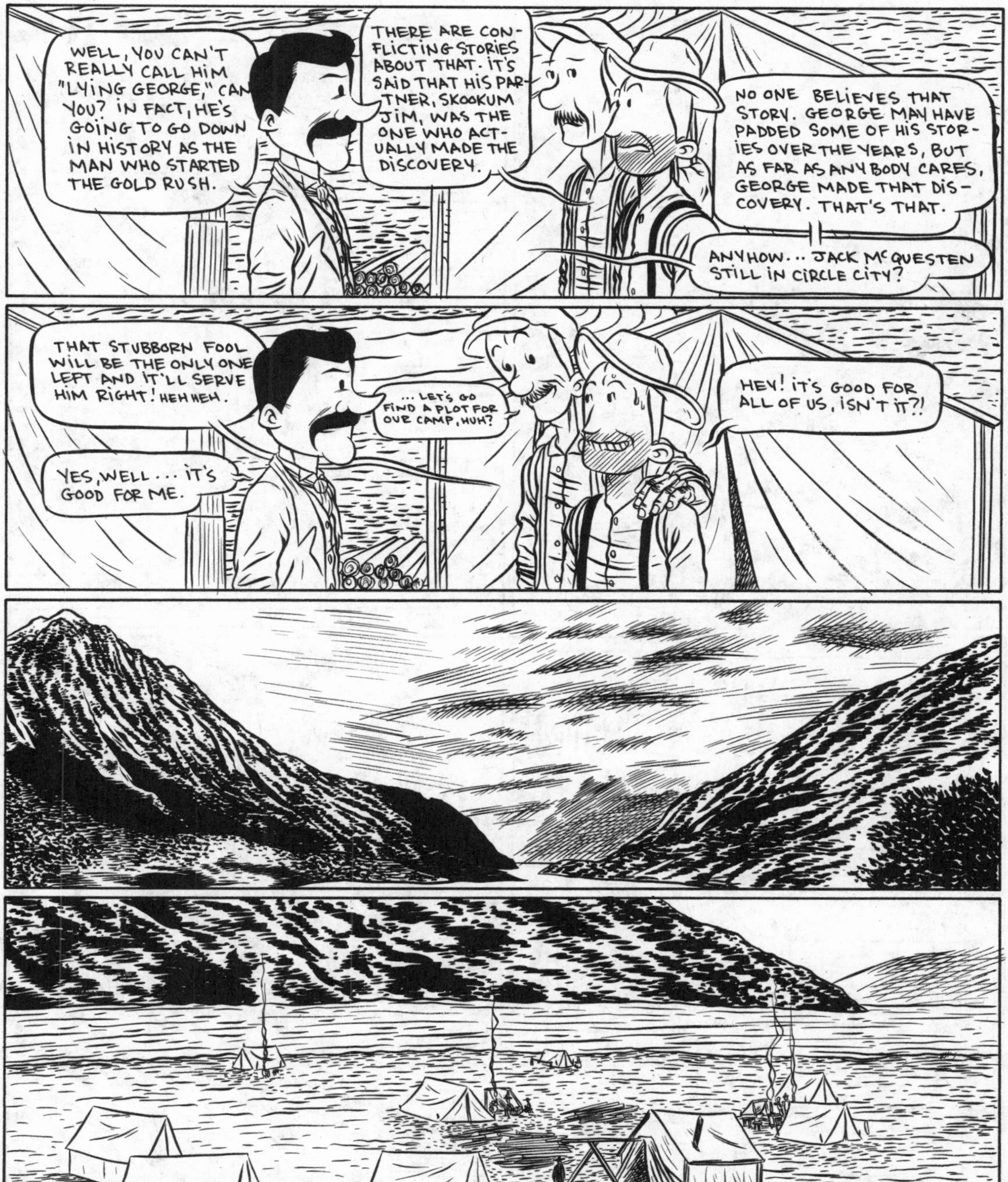
WELL, YOU CAN'T REALLY CALL HIM "LYING GEORGE," CAN YOU? IN FACT, HE'S GOING TO GO DOWN IN HISTORY AS THE MAN WHO STARTED THE GOLD RUSH.
THERE ARE CONFLICTING STORIES ABOUT THAT. IT'S SAID THAT HIS PARTNER, SKOOKUM JIM, WAS THE ONE WHO ACTUALLY MADE THE DISCOVERY.
NO ONE BELIEVES THAT STORY. GEORGE MAY HAVE PADDED SOME OF HIS STORIES OVER THE YEARS, BUT AS FAR AS ANYBODY CARES, GEORGE MADE THAT DISCOVERY. THAT'S THAT.
ANYHOW... JACK McQUESTEN STILL IN CIRCLE CITY?
THAT STUBBORN FOOL WILL BE THE ONLY ONE LEFT AND IT'LL SERVE HIM RIGHT! HEH HEH.
YES, WELL... IT'S GOOD FOR ME.
...LET'S GO FIND A PLOT FOR OUR CAMP, HUH?
HEY! IT'S GOOD FOR ALL OF US, ISN'T IT?!

WORD'S REACHED THE OUTSIDE WITH NEWS OF CARMACK'S DISCOVERY, AS WELL AS THE STRIKES ON ELDORADO.
DAW
Harp
WORDS CAN'T EVEN BEGIN TO DESCRIBE THE JOY THAT SWELLS IN MY GUT!!
FROM WHAT I KNOW, PEOPLE ARE GOING ALMOST INSANE UPON HEARING NEWS OF THE GOLD! SEATTLE, SAN FRANCISCO, NEW YORK, LONDON, PARIS, AFRICA... IT'S WORLD WIDE, FELLAS!
I WILL BE FAMOUS, FRIENDS!! DAWSON WILL BE THE GREATEST CITY IN THE YUKON. THIS GOLD RUSH WILL GO INTO THE HISTORY BOOKS! MARK MY WORDS YOU MAGNIFICENT BASTARDS!!
OFFICE
ON TOWN
Harper & La

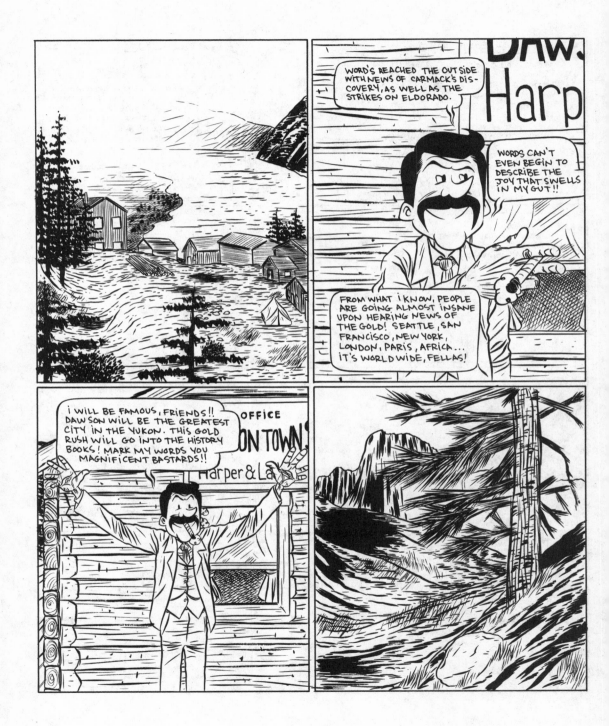

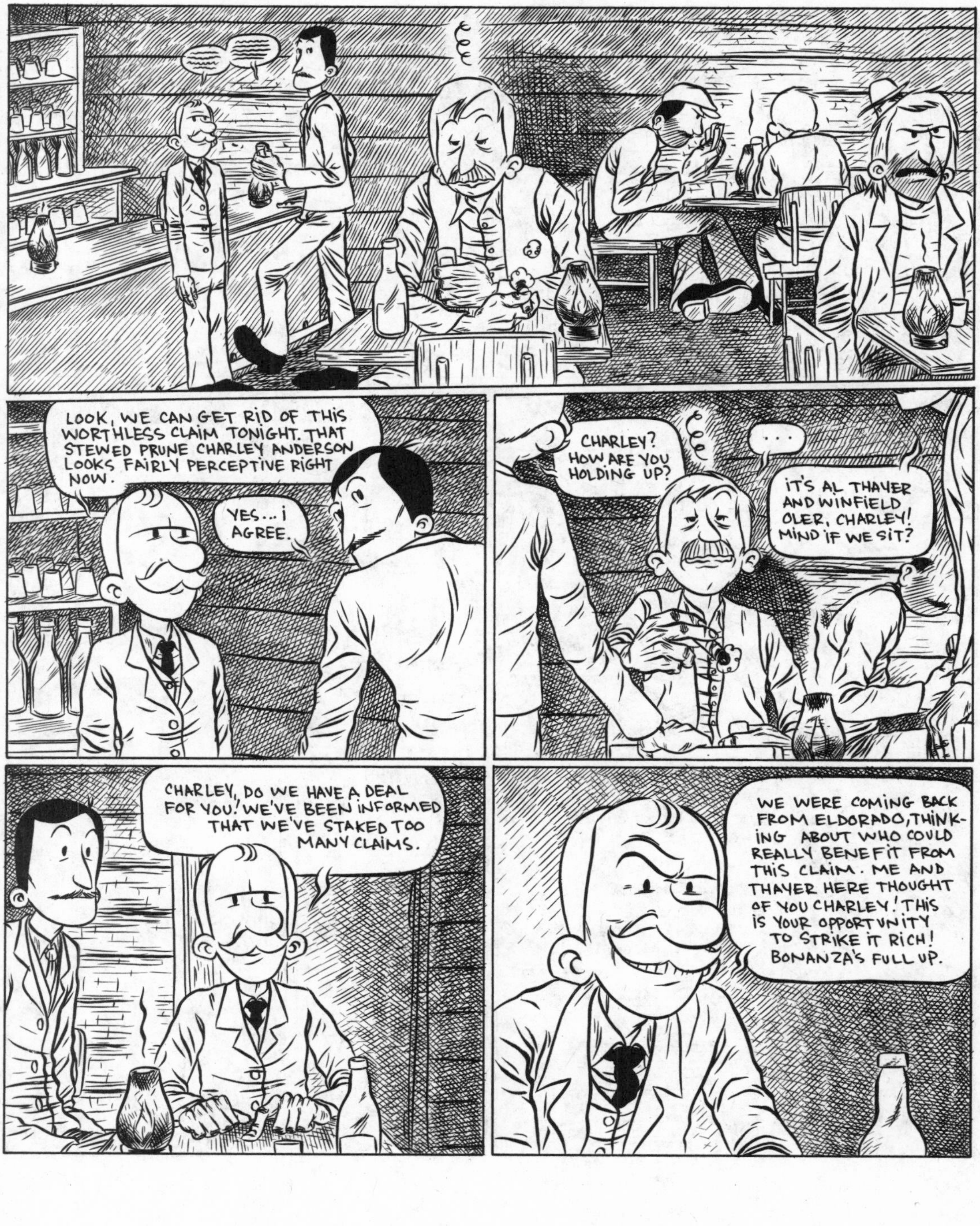
LOOK, WE CAN GET RID OF THIS WORTHLESS CLAIM TONIGHT. THAT STEWED PRUNE CHARLEY ANDERSON LOOKS FAIRLY PERCEPTIVE RIGHT NOW.
YES... I AGREE.
CHARLEY? HOW ARE YOU HOLDING UP?
...
IT'S AL THAYER AND WINFIELD OLER, CHARLEY! MIND IF WE SIT?
CHARLEY, DO WE HAVE A DEAL FOR YOU! WE'VE BEEN INFORMED THAT WE'VE STAKED TOO MANY CLAIMS.
WE WERE COMING BACK FROM ELDORADO, THINK-ING ABOUT WHO COULD REALLY BENEFIT FROM THIS CLAIM. ME AND THAYER HERE THOUGHT OF YOU CHARLEY! THIS IS YOUR OPPORTUNITY TO STRIKE IT RICH! BONANZA'S FULL UP.

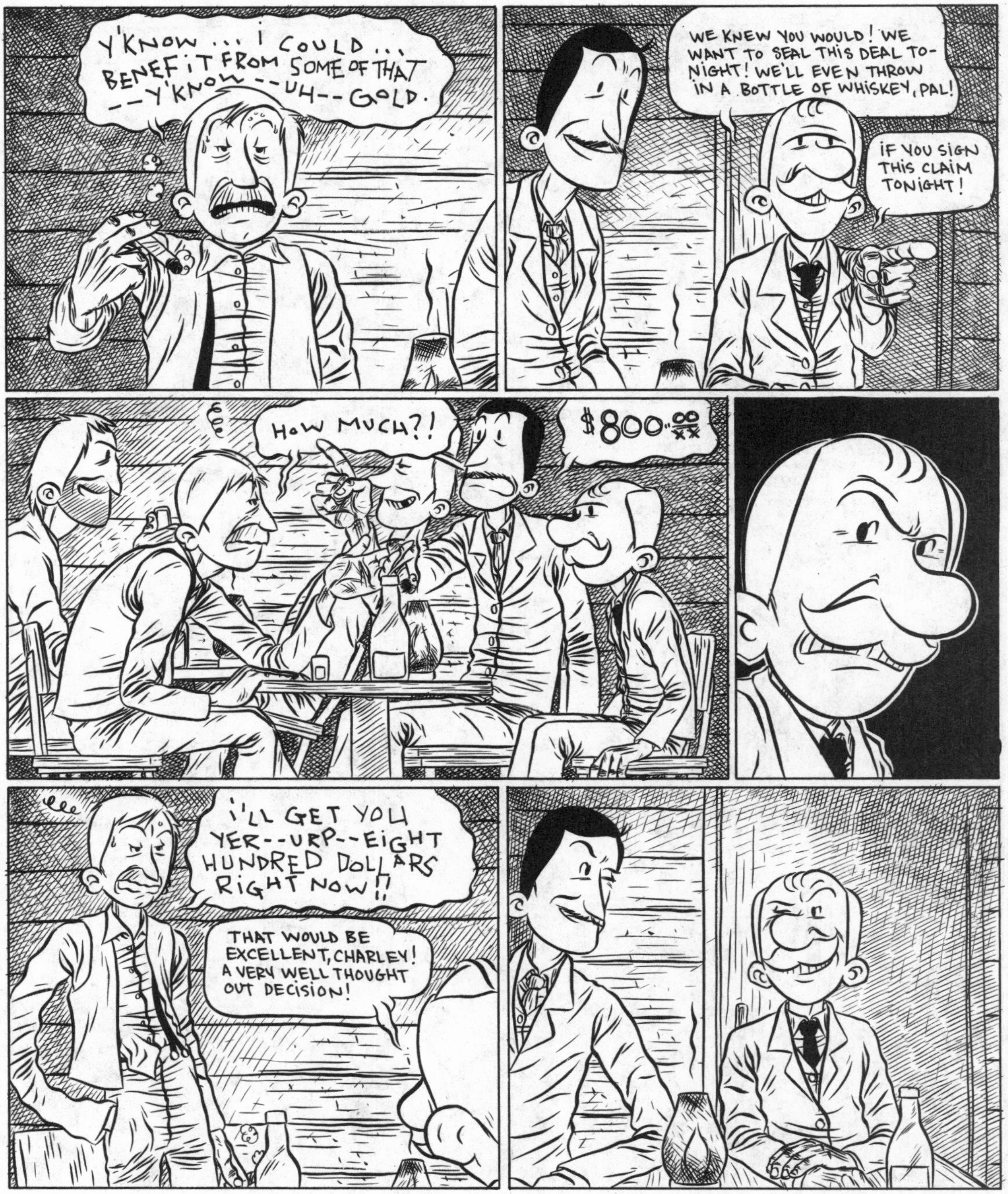
Y'KNOW... I COULD... BENEFIT FROM SOME OF THAT --Y'KNOW--UH--GOLD.
WE KNEW YOU WOULD! WE WANT TO SEAL THIS DEAL TONIGHT! WE'LL EVEN THROW IN A BOTTLE OF WHISKEY, PAL!
IF YOU SIGN THIS CLAIM TONIGHT!
HOW MUCH?!
$800.00
I'LL GET YOU YER--URP--EIGHT HUNDRED DOLLARS RIGHT NOW!!
THAT WOULD BE EXCELLENT, CHARLEY! A VERY WELL THOUGHT OUT DECISION!

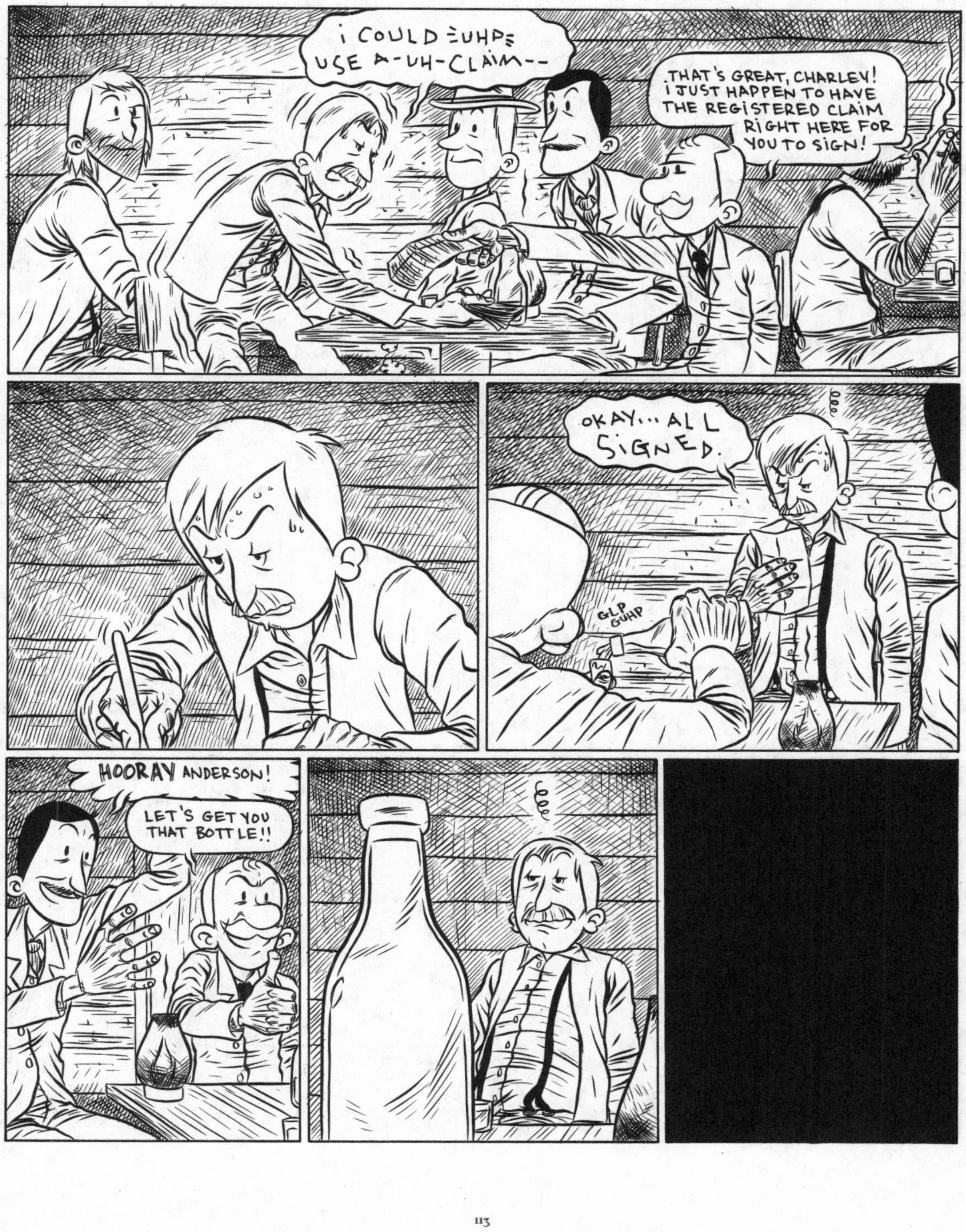
I COULD =UHP= USE A-UH-CLAIM--
THAT'S GREAT, CHARLEY! I JUST HAPPEN TO HAVE THE REGISTERED CLAIM RIGHT HERE FOR YOU TO SIGN!
OKAY... ALL SIGNED.
GLP GUHP
HOORAY ANDERSON!
LET'S GET YOU THAT BOTTLE!!

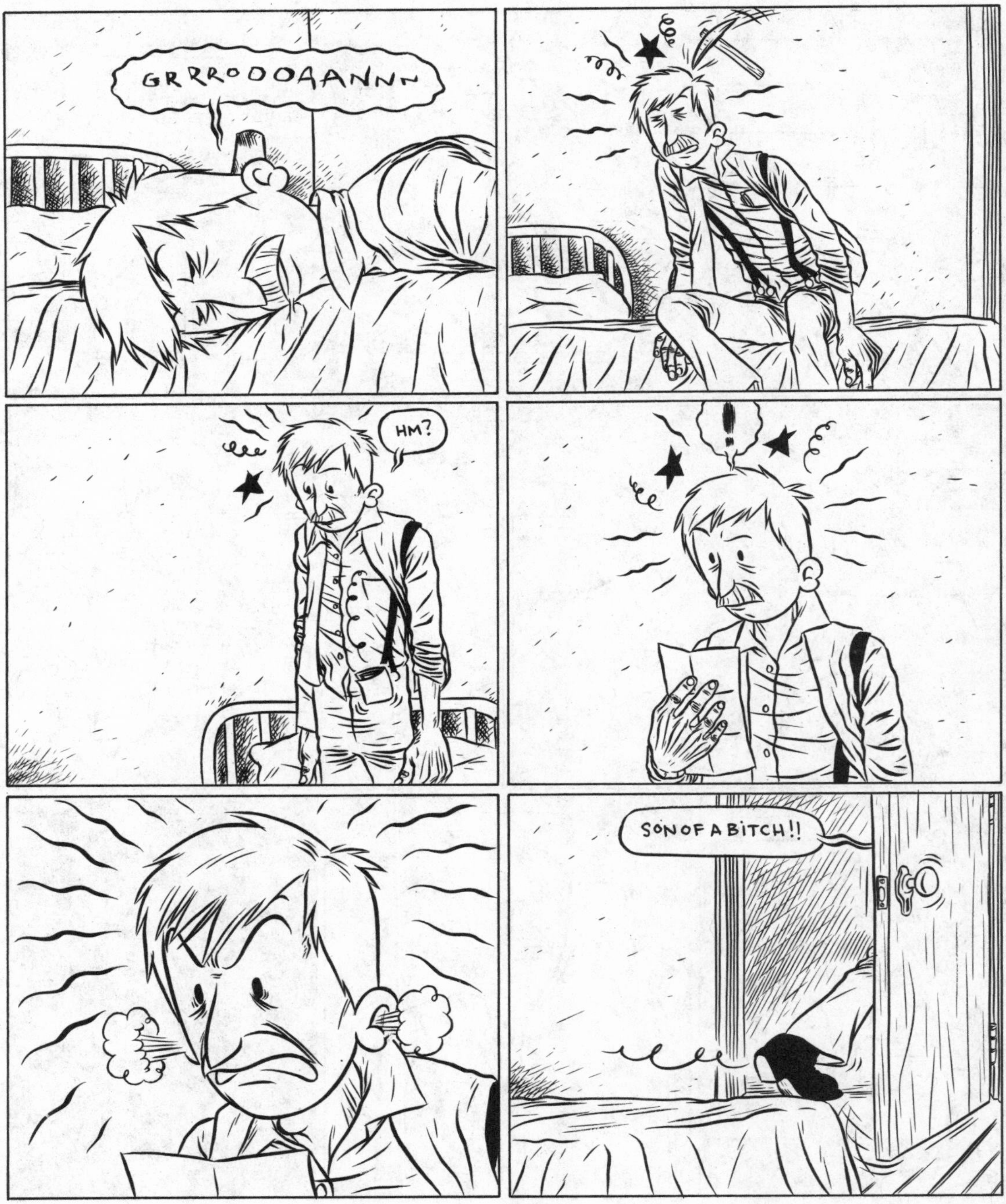
GRRROOOAANNN
HM?
!
SONOFABITCH!!

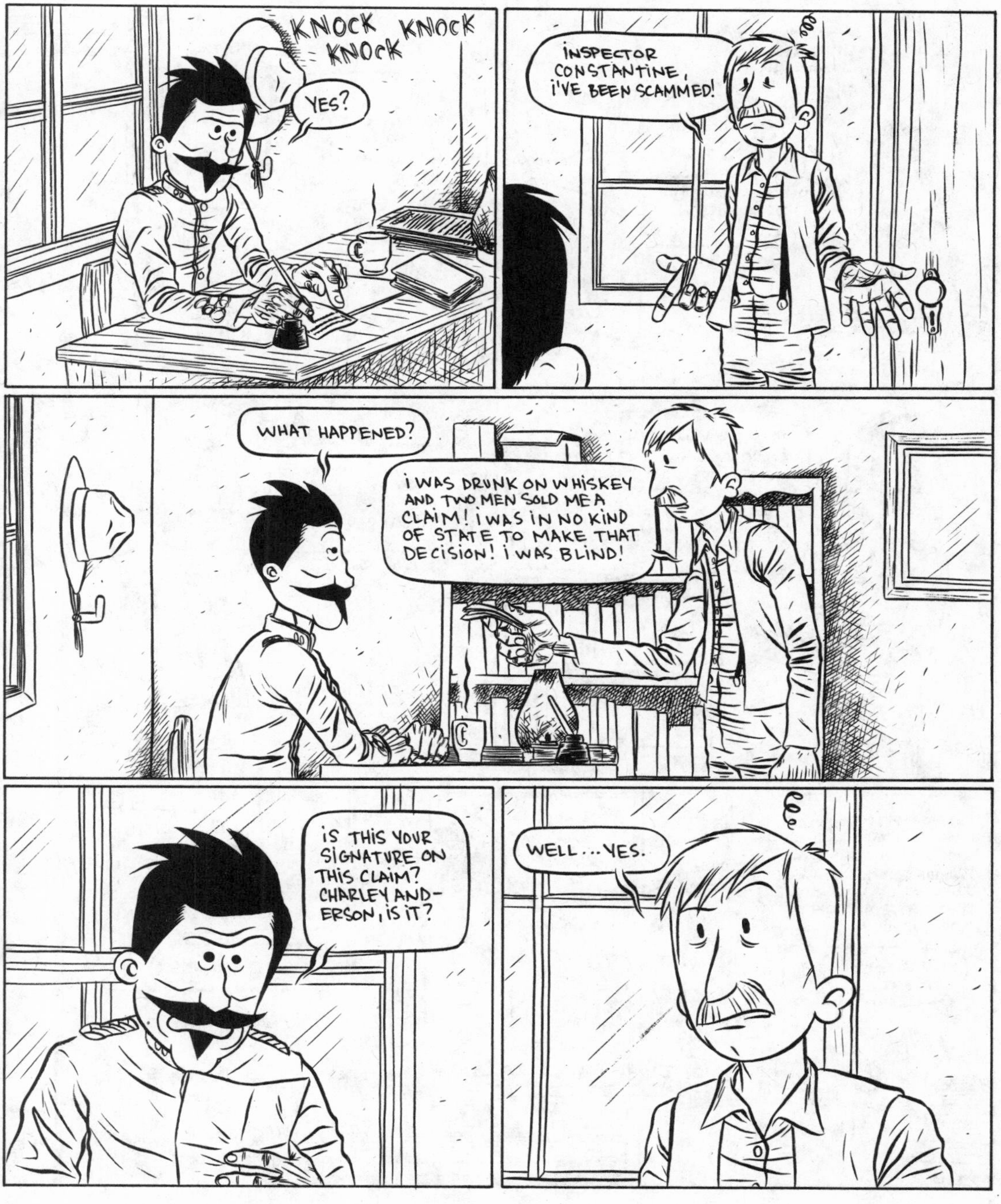
KNOCK KNOCK KNOCK
YES?
INSPECTOR CONSTANTINE, I'VE BEEN SCAMMED!
WHAT HAPPENED?
I WAS DRUNK ON WHISKEY AND TWO MEN SOLD ME A CLAIM! I WAS IN NO KIND OF STATE TO MAKE THAT DECISION! I WAS BLIND!
IS THIS YOUR SIGNATURE ON THIS CLAIM? CHARLEY ANDERSON, IS IT?
WELL... YES.

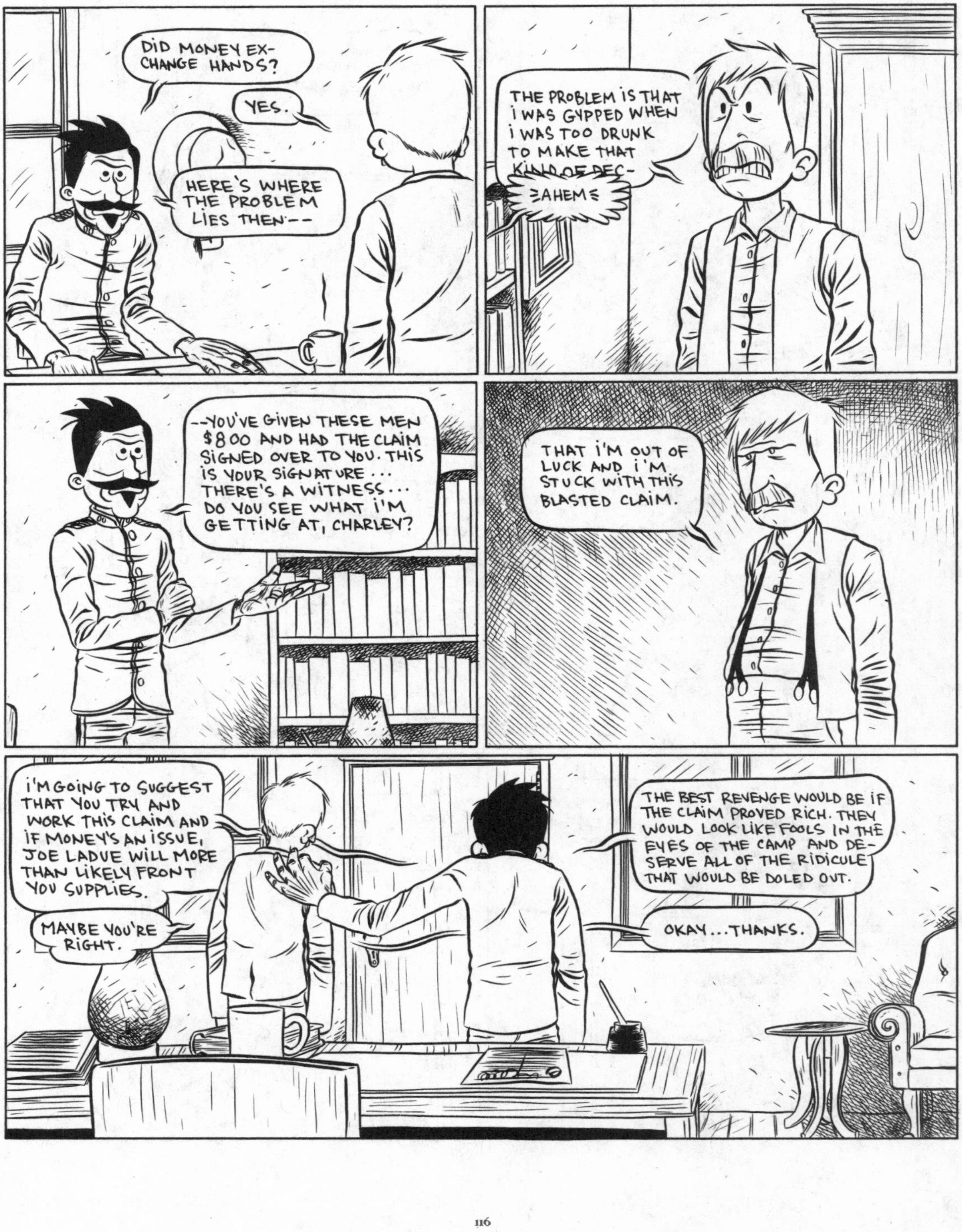
DID MONEY EX-CHANGE HANDS?
YES.
HERE'S WHERE THE PROBLEM LIES THEN--
THE PROBLEM IS THAT I WAS GYPPED WHEN I WAS TOO DRUNK TO MAKE THAT KIND OF DEC-
AHEM
--YOU'VE GIVEN THESE MEN $800 AND HAD THE CLAIM SIGNED OVER TO YOU. THIS IS YOUR SIGNATURE... THERE'S A WITNESS... DO YOU SEE WHAT I'M GETTING AT, CHARLEY?
THAT I'M OUT OF LUCK AND I'M STUCK WITH THIS BLASTED CLAIM.
I'M GOING TO SUGGEST THAT YOU TRY AND WORK THIS CLAIM AND IF MONEY'S AN ISSUE, JOE LADUE WILL MORE THAN LIKELY FRONT YOU SUPPLIES.
THE BEST REVENGE WOULD BE IF THE CLAIM PROVED RICH. THEY WOULD LOOK LIKE FOOLS IN THE EYES OF THE CAMP AND DE-SERVE ALL OF THE RIDICULE THAT WOULD BE DOLED OUT.
MAYBE YOU'RE RIGHT.
OKAY...THANKS.

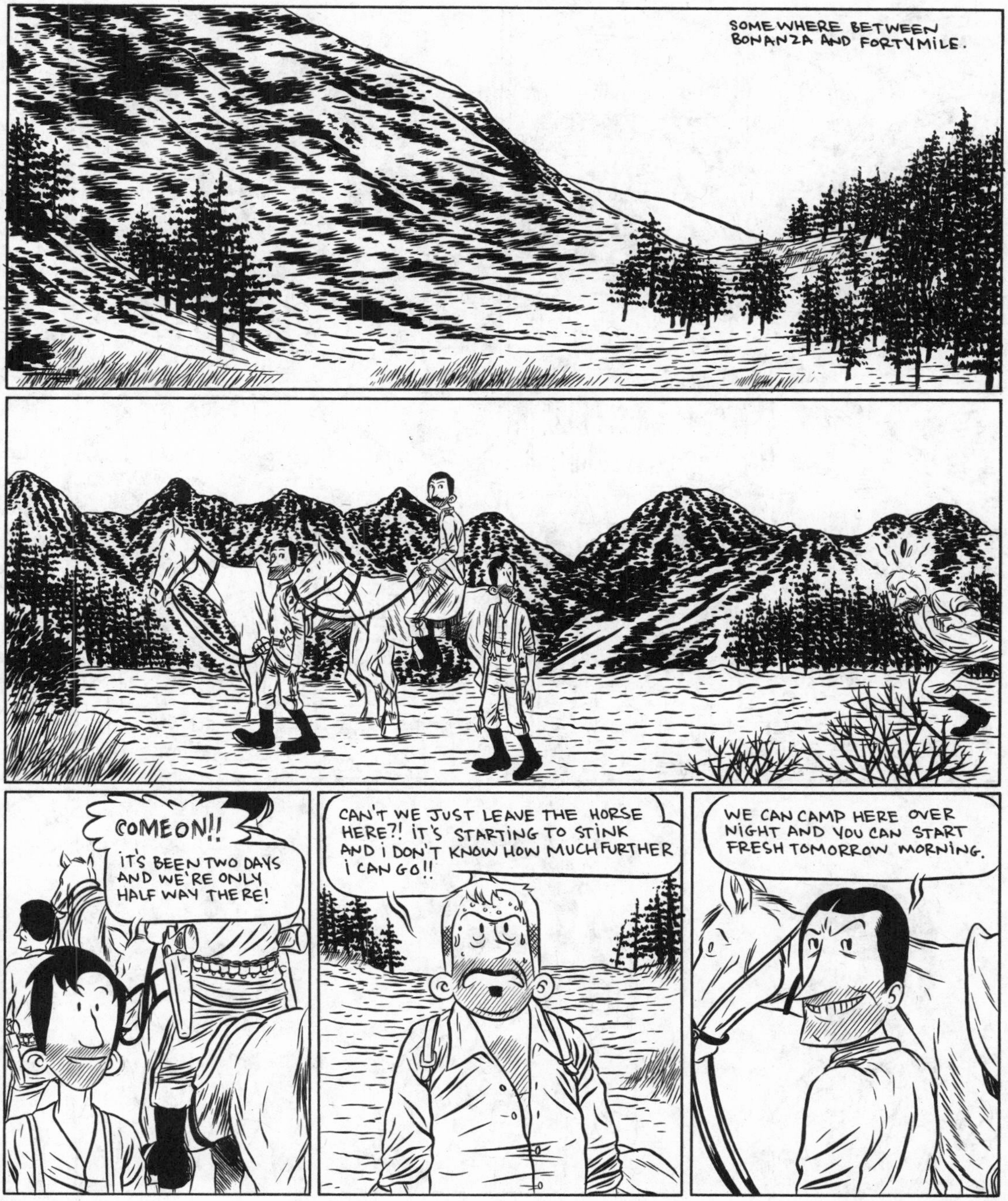
SOMEWHERE BETWEEN BONANZA AND FORTYMILE.
COMEON!!
IT'S BEEN TWO DAYS AND WE'RE ONLY HALF WAY THERE!
CAN'T WE JUST LEAVE THE HORSE HERE?! IT'S STARTING TO STINK AND I DON'T KNOW HOW MUCH FURTHER I CAN GO!!
WE CAN CAMP HERE OVER NIGHT AND YOU CAN START FRESH TOMORROW MORNING.

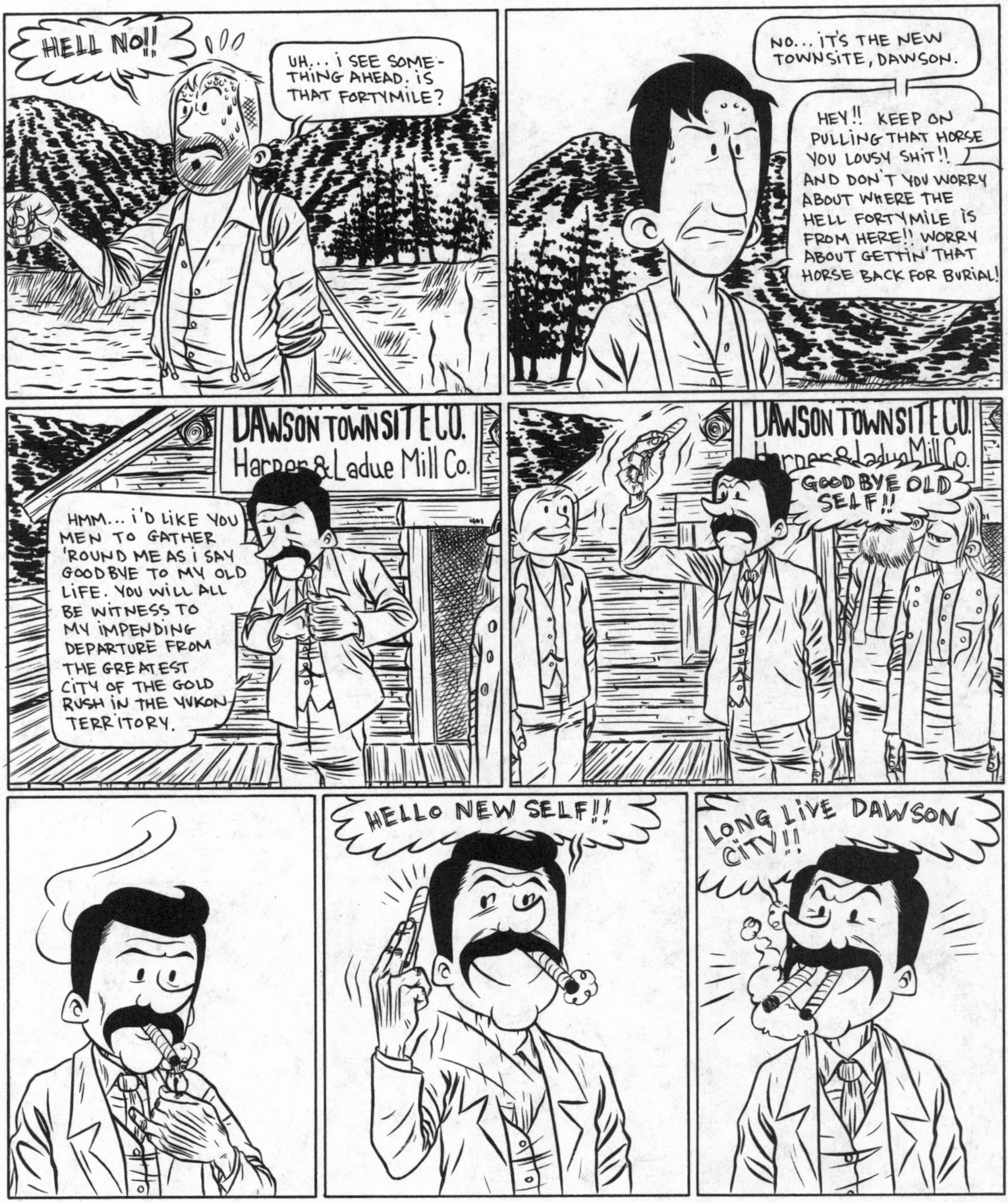

HELL NO!!
UH... I SEE SOME-THING AHEAD. IS THAT FORTYMILE?
NO... IT'S THE NEW TOWNSITE, DAWSON.
HEY!! KEEP ON PULLING THAT HORSE YOU LOUSY SHIT!! AND DON'T YOU WORRY ABOUT WHERE THE HELL FORTYMILE IS FROM HERE!! WORRY ABOUT GETTIN' THAT HORSE BACK FOR BURIAL!
DAWSON TOWNSITE CO.
Harper & Ladue Mill Co.
HMM... I'D LIKE YOU MEN TO GATHER 'ROUND ME AS I SAY GOODBYE TO MY OLD LIFE. YOU WILL ALL BE WITNESS TO MY IMPENDING DEPARTURE FROM THE GREATEST CITY OF THE GOLD RUSH IN THE YUKON TERRITORY.
DAWSON TOWNSITE CO.
GOOD BYE OLD SELF!!
HELLO NEW SELF!!
LONG LIVE DAWSON CITY!!

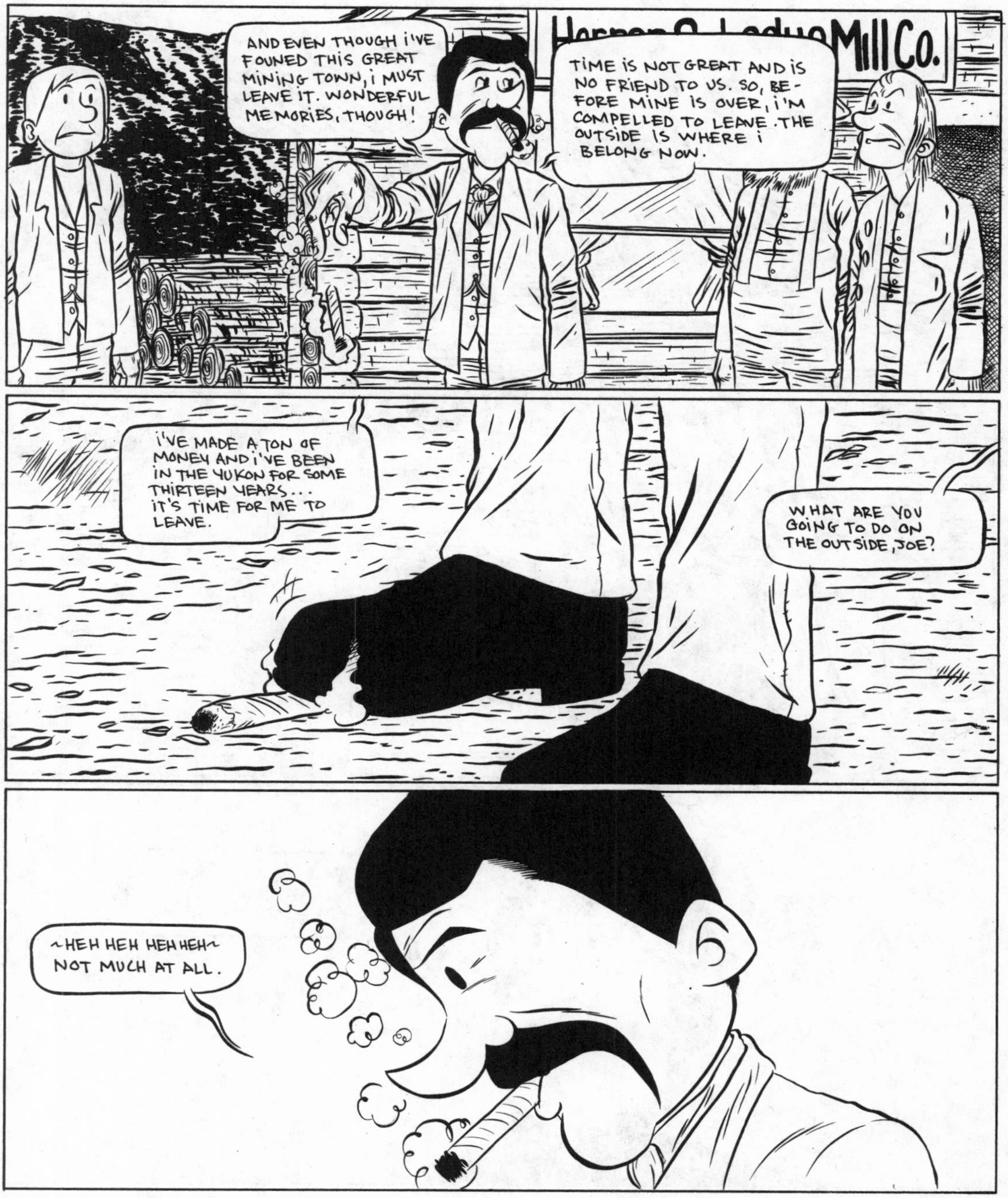
Herman & Ledue Mill Co.
AND EVEN THOUGH I'VE FOUNED THIS GREAT MINING TOWN, I MUST LEAVE IT. WONDERFUL MEMORIES, THOUGH!
TIME IS NOT GREAT AND IS NO FRIEND TO US. SO, BEFORE MINE IS OVER, I'M COMPELLED TO LEAVE. THE OUTSIDE IS WHERE I BELONG NOW.
I'VE MADE A TON OF MONEY AND I'VE BEEN IN THE YUKON FOR SOME THIRTEEN YEARS... IT'S TIME FOR ME TO LEAVE.
WHAT ARE YOU GOING TO DO ON THE OUTSIDE, JOE?
~HEH HEH HEH HEH~ NOT MUCH AT ALL.

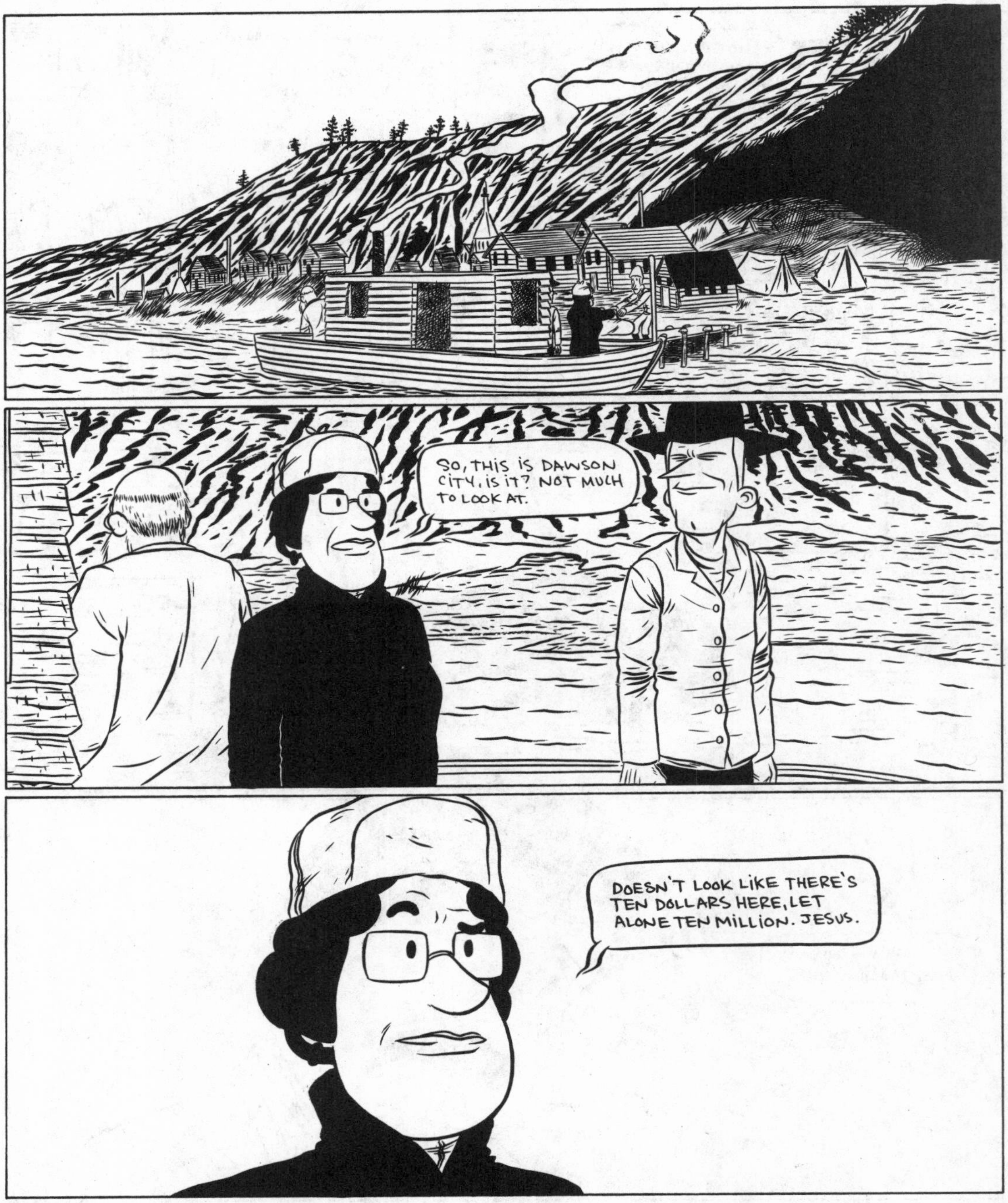
SO, THIS IS DAWSON CITY, IS IT? NOT MUCH TO LOOK AT.
DOESN'T LOOK LIKE THERE'S TEN DOLLARS HERE, LET ALONE TEN MILLION. JESUS.

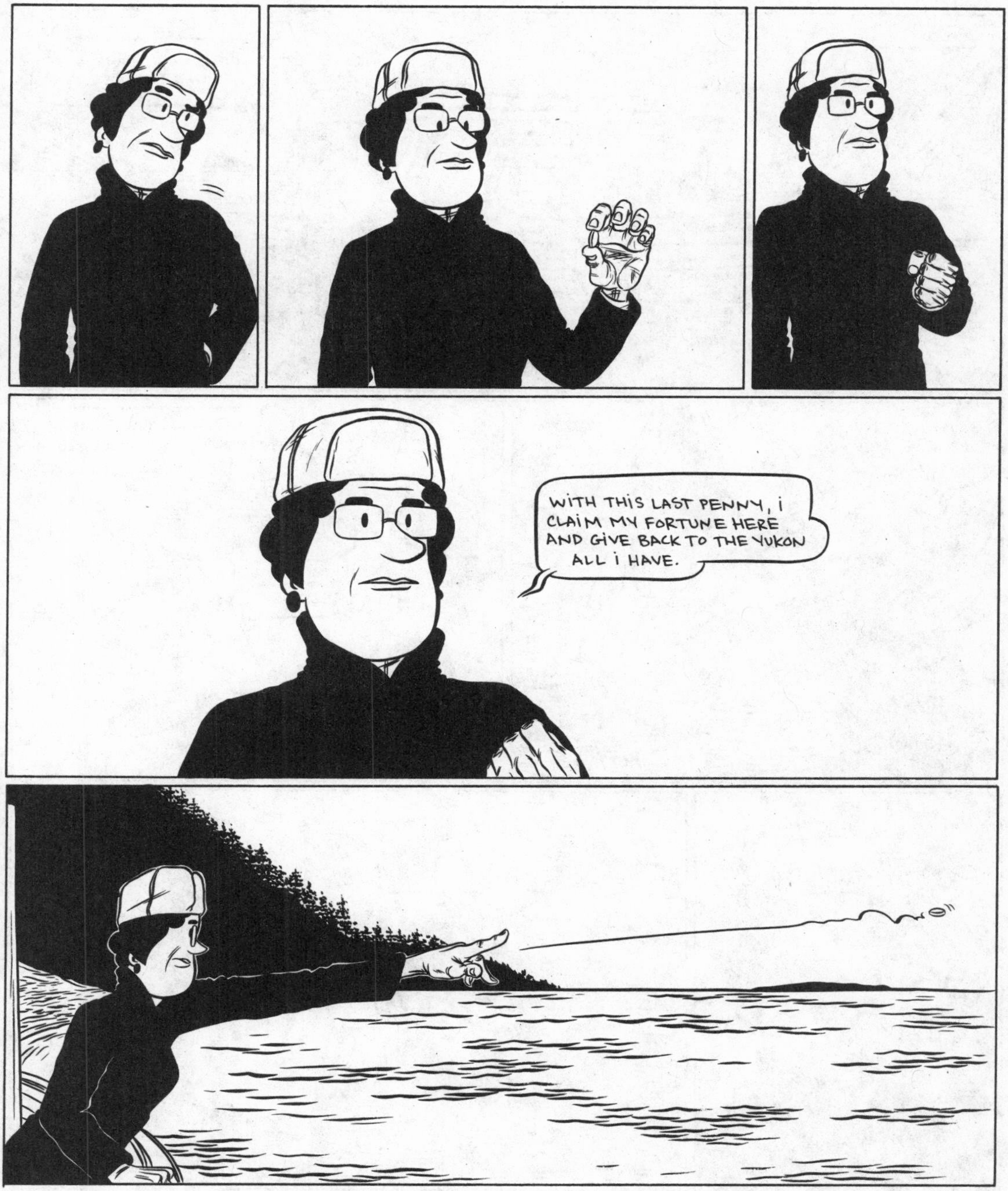
WITH THIS LAST PENNY, I CLAIM MY FORTUNE HERE AND GIVE BACK TO THE YUKON ALL I HAVE.

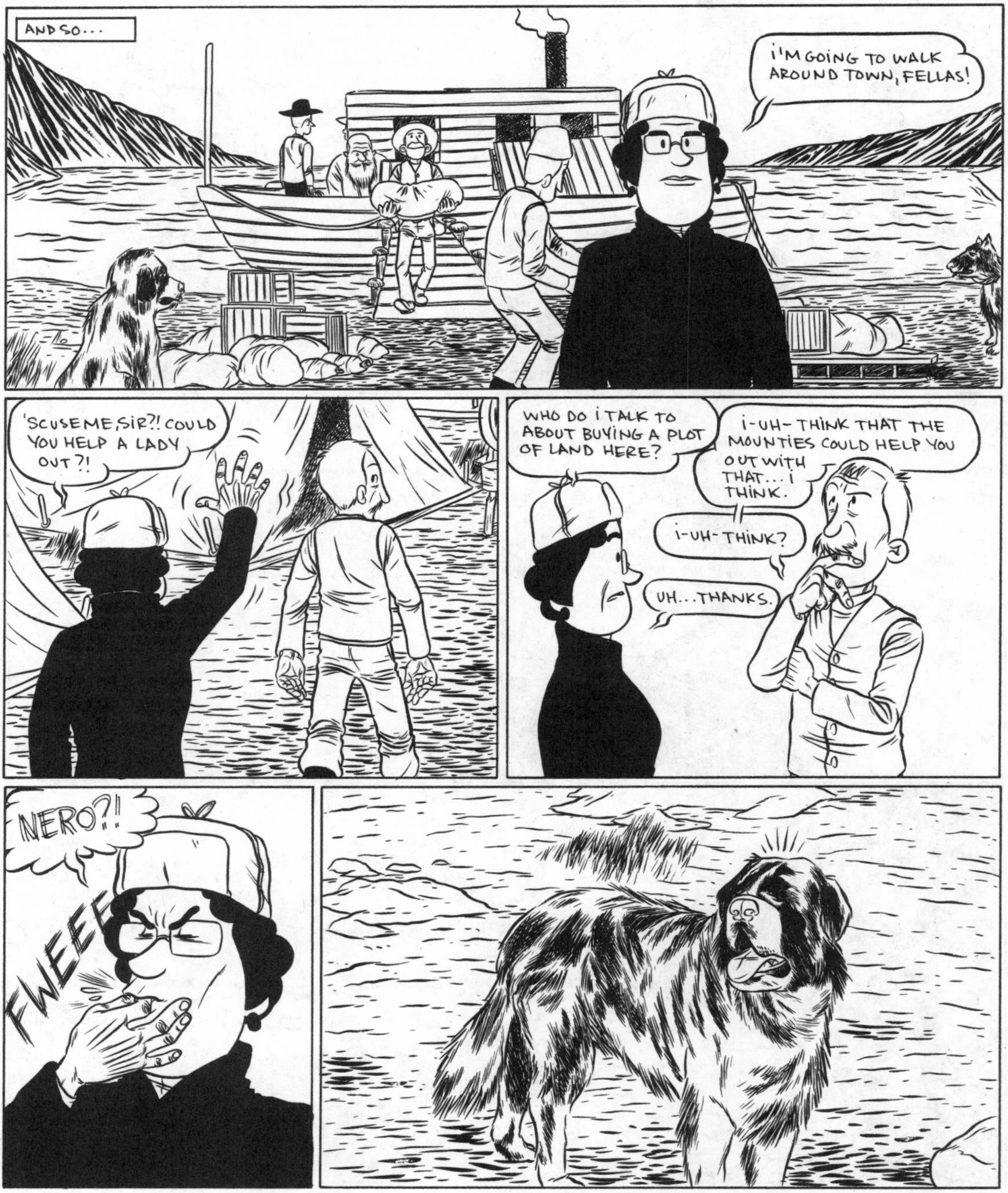
AND SO...
I'M GOING TO WALK AROUND TOWN, FELLAS!
'SCUSE ME, SIR?! COULD YOU HELP A LADY OUT?!
WHO DO I TALK TO ABOUT BUYING A PLOT OF LAND HERE?
I-UH- THINK THAT THE MOUNTIES COULD HELP YOU OUT WITH THAT... I THINK.
I-UH-THINK?
UH... THANKS.
NERO?!
FWEEE

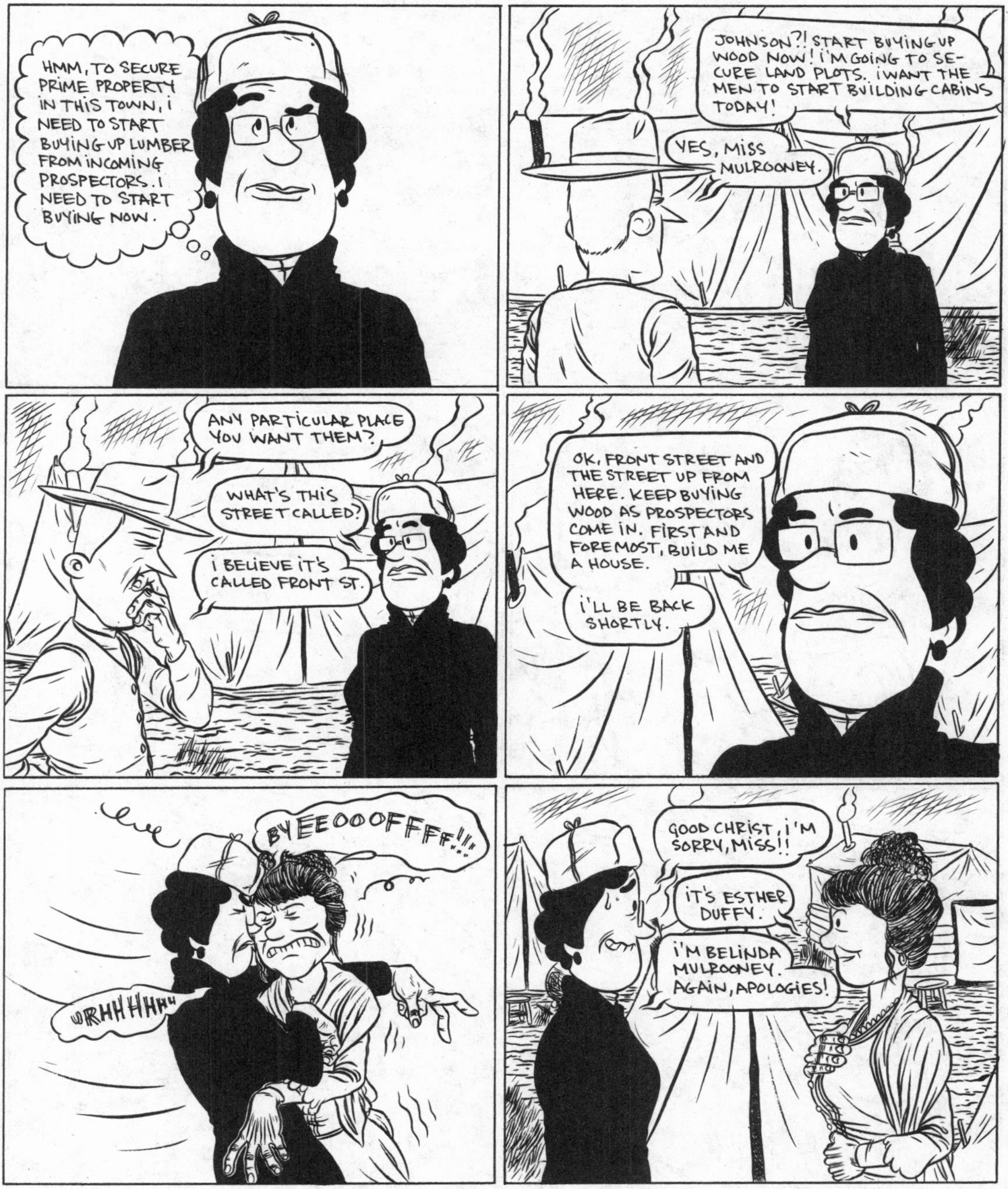
HMM, TO SECURE PRIME PROPERTY IN THIS TOWN, I NEED TO START BUYING UP LUMBER FROM INCOMING PROSPECTORS. I NEED TO START BUYING NOW.
JOHNSON?! START BUYING UP WOOD NOW! I'M GOING TO SECURE LAND PLOTS. I WANT THE MEN TO START BUILDING CABINS TODAY!
YES, MISS MULROONEY.
ANY PARTICULAR PLACE YOU WANT THEM?
WHAT'S THIS STREET CALLED?
I BELIEVE IT'S CALLED FRONT ST.
OK, FRONT STREET AND THE STREET UP FROM HERE. KEEP BUYING WOOD AS PROSPECTORS COME IN. FIRST AND FOREMOST, BUILD ME A HOUSE.
I'LL BE BACK SHORTLY.
BYEEOOOFFFF!!!
URHHHHH
GOOD CHRIST, I'M SORRY, MISS!!
IT'S ESTHER DUFFY.
I'M BELINDA MULROONEY. AGAIN, APOLOGIES!

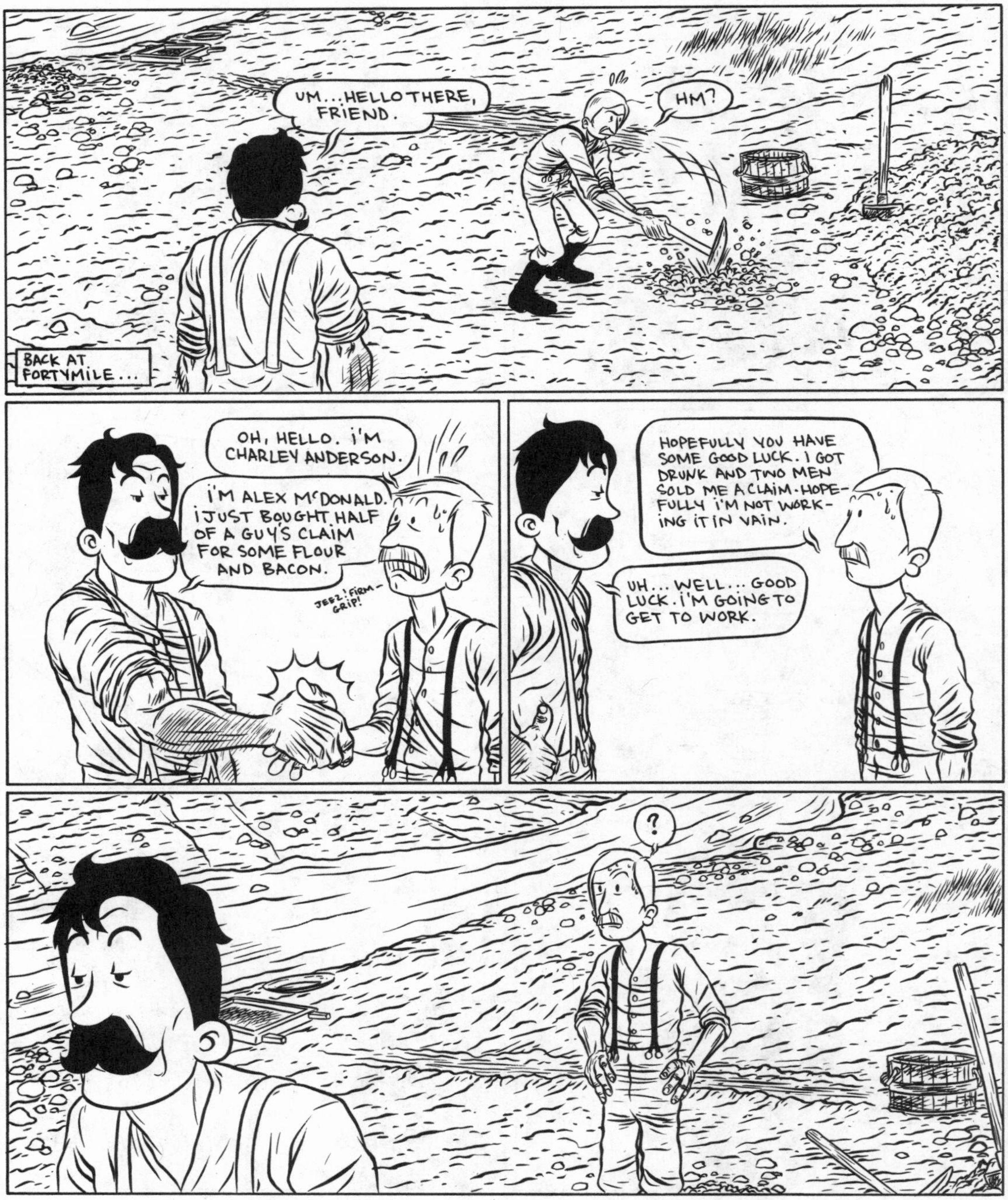

BACK AT FORTYMILE...
UM...HELLO THERE, FRIEND.
HM?
OH, HELLO. I'M CHARLEY ANDERSON.
I'M ALEX McDONALD. I JUST BOUGHT HALF OF A GUY'S CLAIM FOR SOME FLOUR AND BACON.
JEEZ! FIRM GRIP!
HOPEFULLY YOU HAVE SOME GOOD LUCK. I GOT DRUNK AND TWO MEN SOLD ME A CLAIM. HOPEFULLY I'M NOT WORKING IT IN VAIN.
UH... WELL... GOOD LUCK. I'M GOING TO GET TO WORK.
?

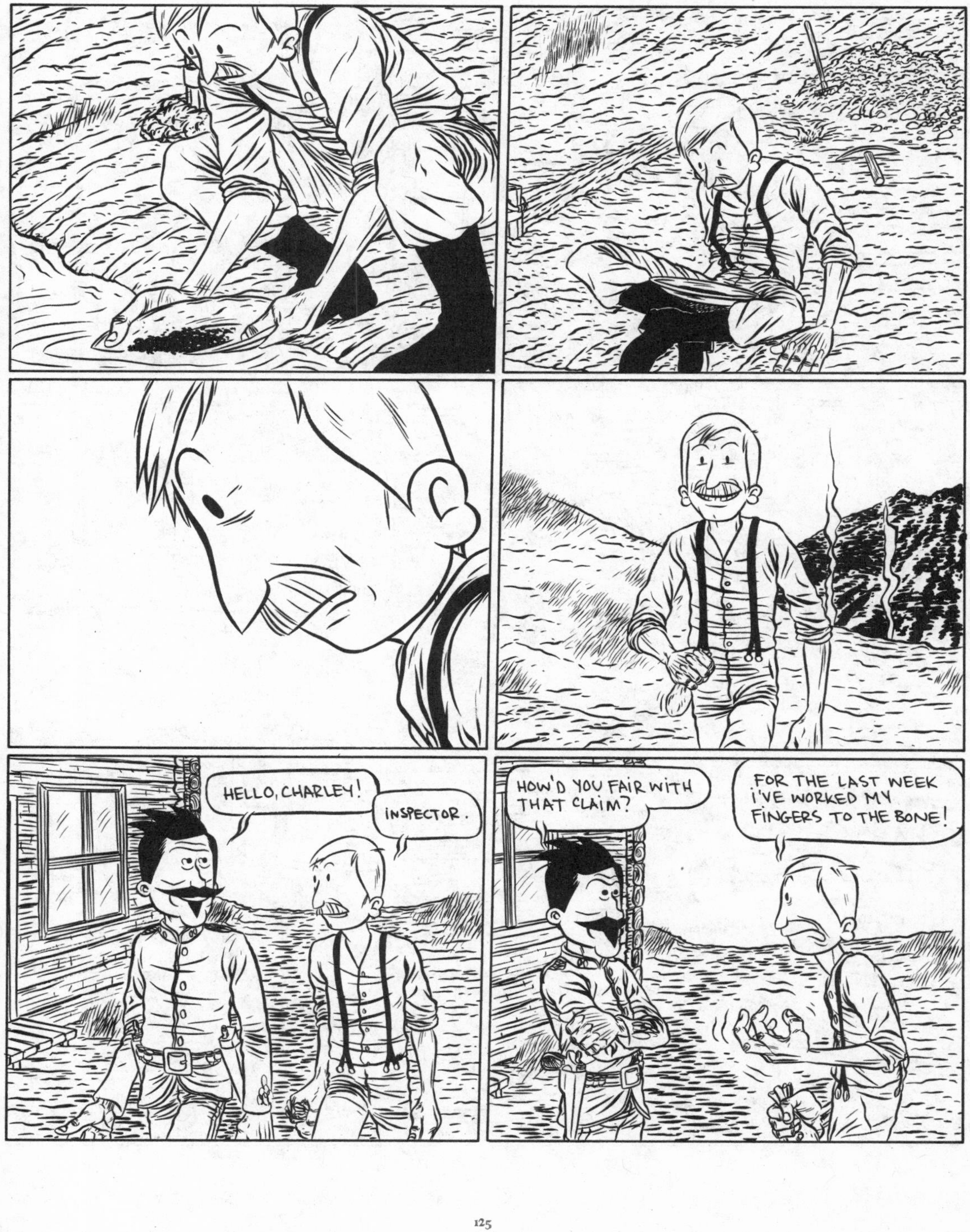
HELLO, CHARLEY!
INSPECTOR.
HOW'D YOU FAIR WITH THAT CLAIM?
FOR THE LAST WEEK I'VE WORKED MY FINGERS TO THE BONE!

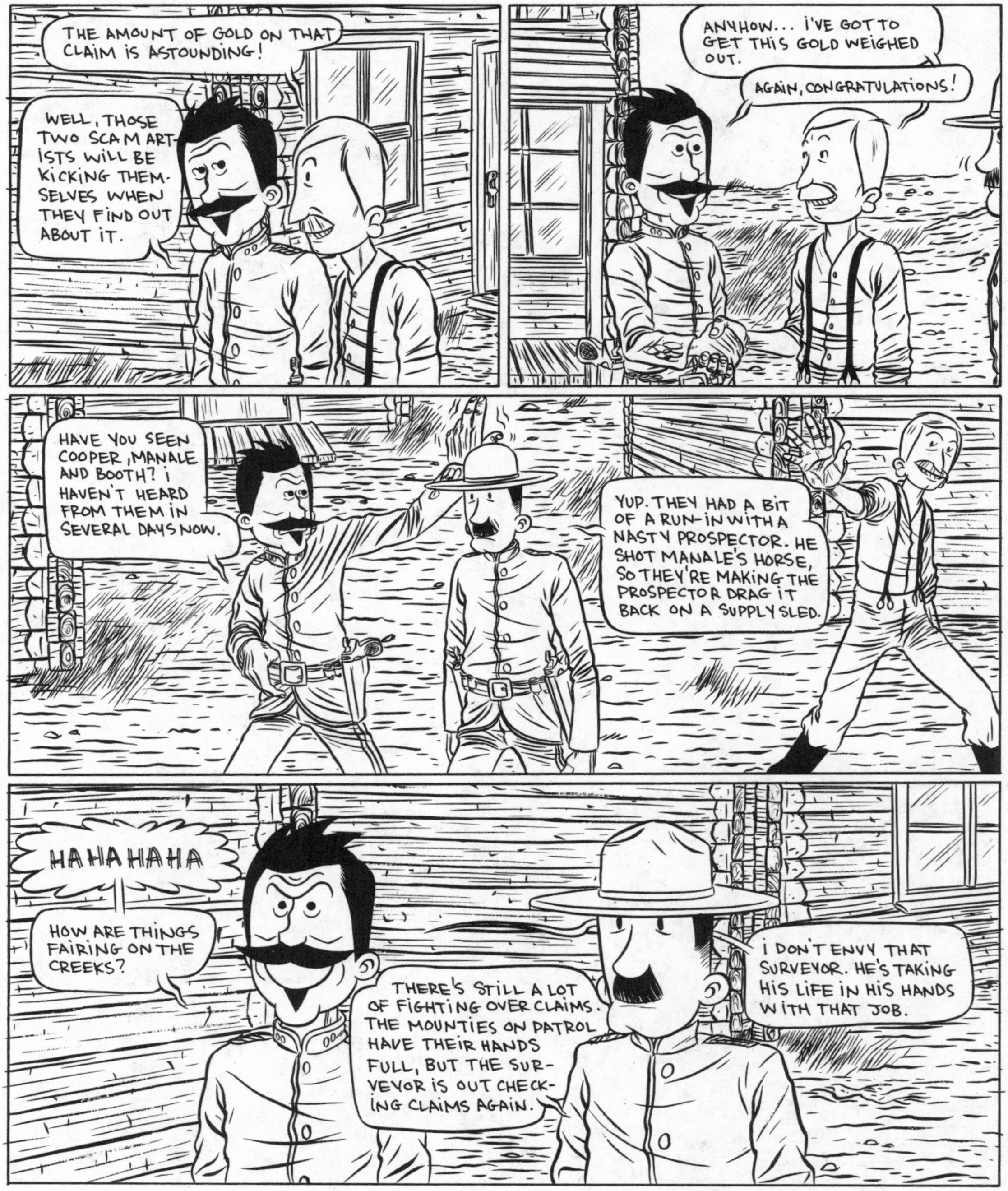
THE AMOUNT OF GOLD ON THAT CLAIM IS ASTOUNDING!
WELL, THOSE TWO SCAM ARTISTS WILL BE KICKING THEMSELVES WHEN THEY FIND OUT ABOUT IT.
ANYHOW... I'VE GOT TO GET THIS GOLD WEIGHED OUT.
AGAIN, CONGRATULATIONS!
HAVE YOU SEEN COOPER, MANALE AND BOOTH? I HAVEN'T HEARD FROM THEM IN SEVERAL DAYS NOW.
YUP. THEY HAD A BIT OF A RUN-IN WITH A NASTY PROSPECTOR. HE SHOT MANALE'S HORSE, SO THEY'RE MAKING THE PROSPECTOR DRAG IT BACK ON A SUPPLY SLED.
HAHAHAHA
HOW ARE THINGS FAIRING ON THE CREEKS?
THERE'S STILL A LOT OF FIGHTING OVER CLAIMS. THE MOUNTIES ON PATROL HAVE THEIR HANDS FULL, BUT THE SURVEVOR IS OUT CHECKING CLAIMS AGAIN.
I DON'T ENVY THAT SURVEYOR. HE'S TAKING HIS LIFE IN HIS HANDS WITH THAT JOB.

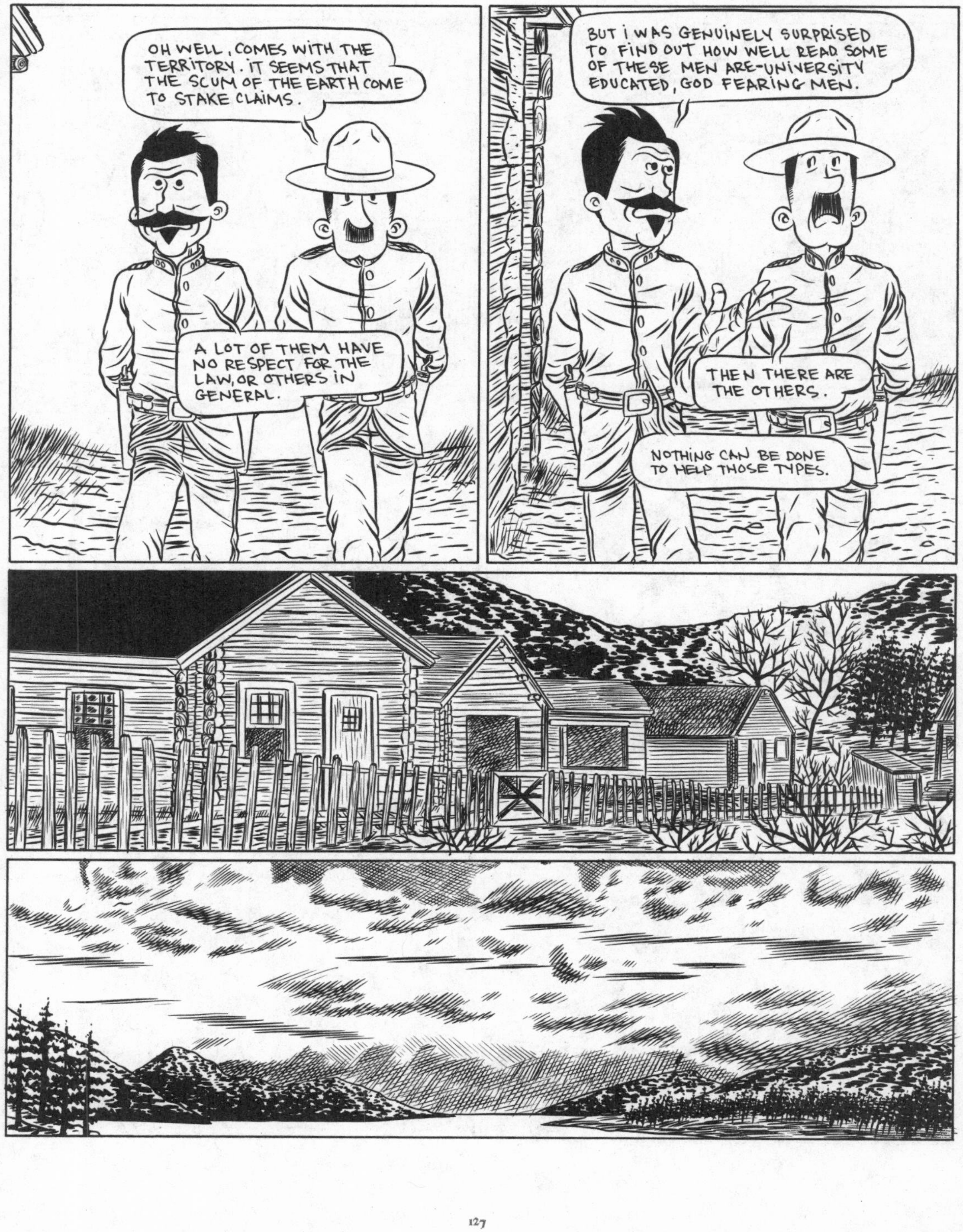
OH WELL, COMES WITH THE TERRITORY. IT SEEMS THAT THE SCUM OF THE EARTH COME TO STAKE CLAIMS.
A LOT OF THEM HAVE NO RESPECT FOR THE LAW, OR OTHERS IN GENERAL.
BUT I WAS GENUINELY SURPRISED TO FIND OUT HOW WELL READ SOME OF THESE MEN ARE-UNIVERSITY EDUCATED, GOD FEARING MEN.
THEN THERE ARE THE OTHERS.
NOTHING CAN BE DONE TO HELP THOSE TYPES.

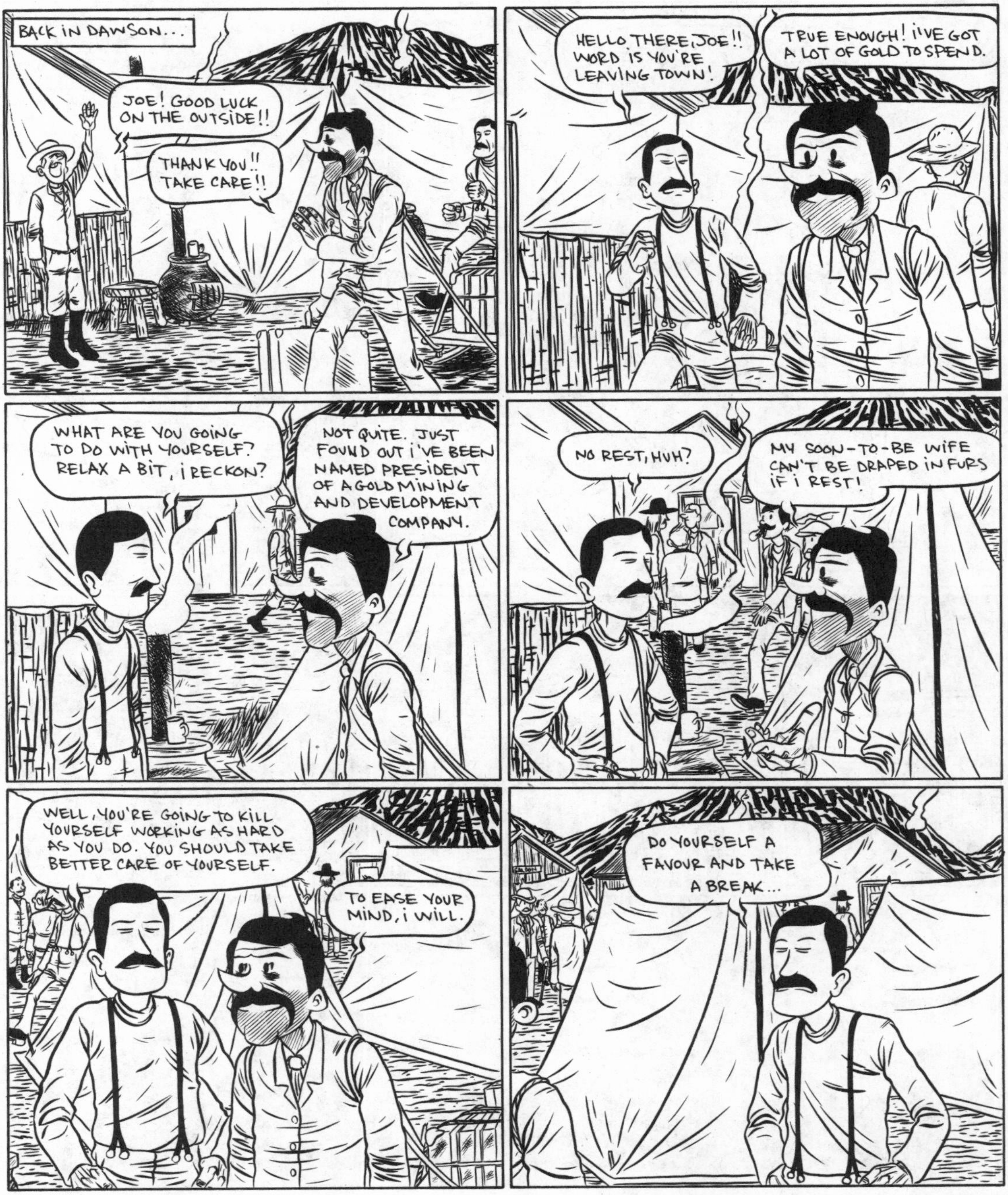
BACK IN DAWSON...
JOE! GOOD LUCK ON THE OUTSIDE!!
THANK YOU!! TAKE CARE!!
HELLO, THERE, JOE!! WORD IS YOU'RE LEAVING TOWN!
TRUE ENOUGH! I'VE GOT A LOT OF GOLD TO SPEND.
WHAT ARE YOU GOING TO DO WITH YOURSELF? RELAX A BIT, I RECKON?
NOT QUITE. JUST FOUND OUT I'VE BEEN NAMED PRESIDENT OF A GOLD MINING AND DEVELOPMENT COMPANY.
NO REST, HUH?
MY SOON-TO-BE WIFE CAN'T BE DRAPED IN FURS IF I REST!
WELL, YOU'RE GOING TO KILL YOURSELF WORKING AS HARD AS YOU DO. YOU SHOULD TAKE BETTER CARE OF YOURSELF.
TO EASE YOUR MIND, I WILL.
DO YOURSELF A FAVOUR AND TAKE A BREAK...

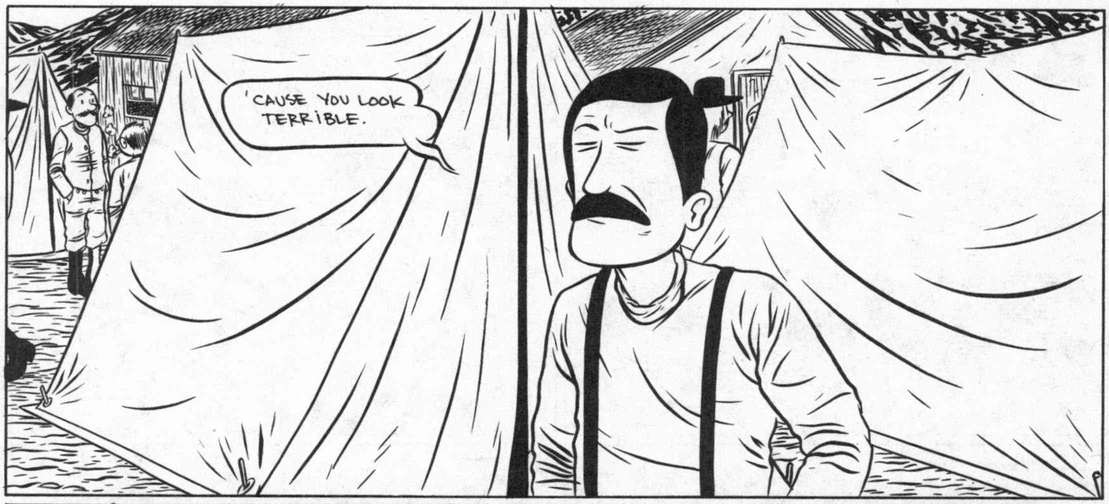
'CAUSE YOU LOOK TERRIBLE.

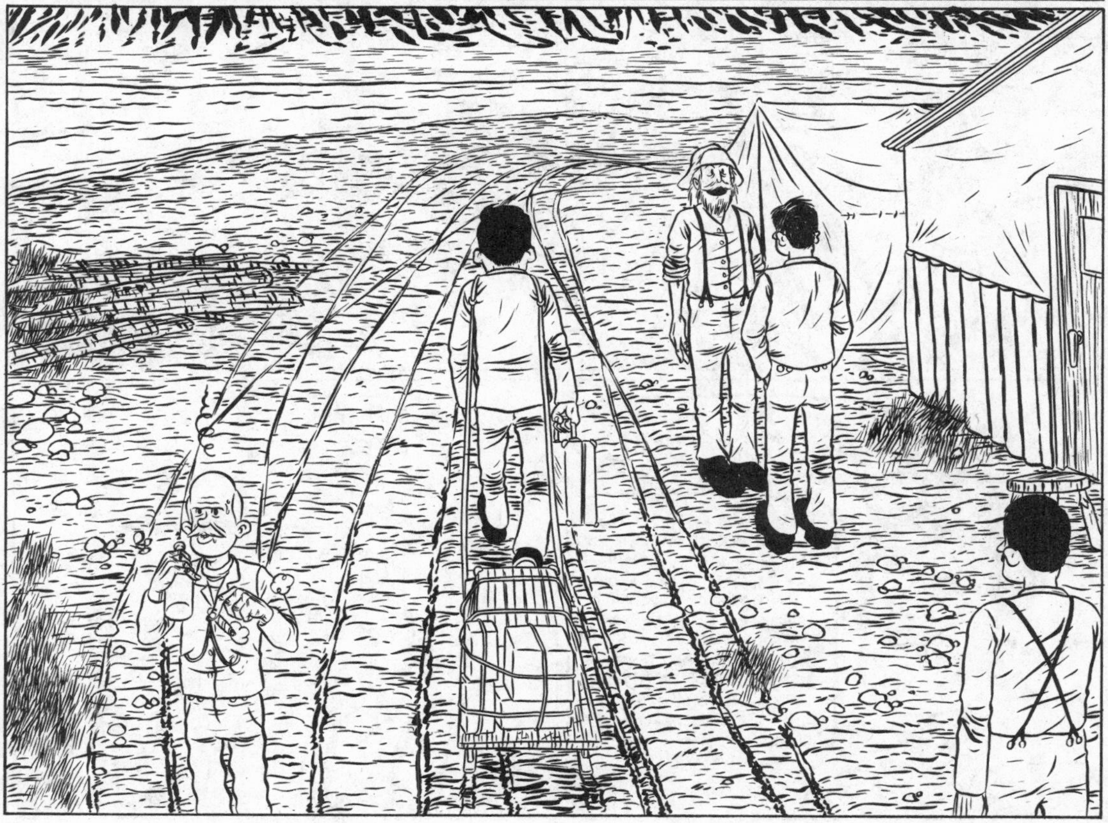

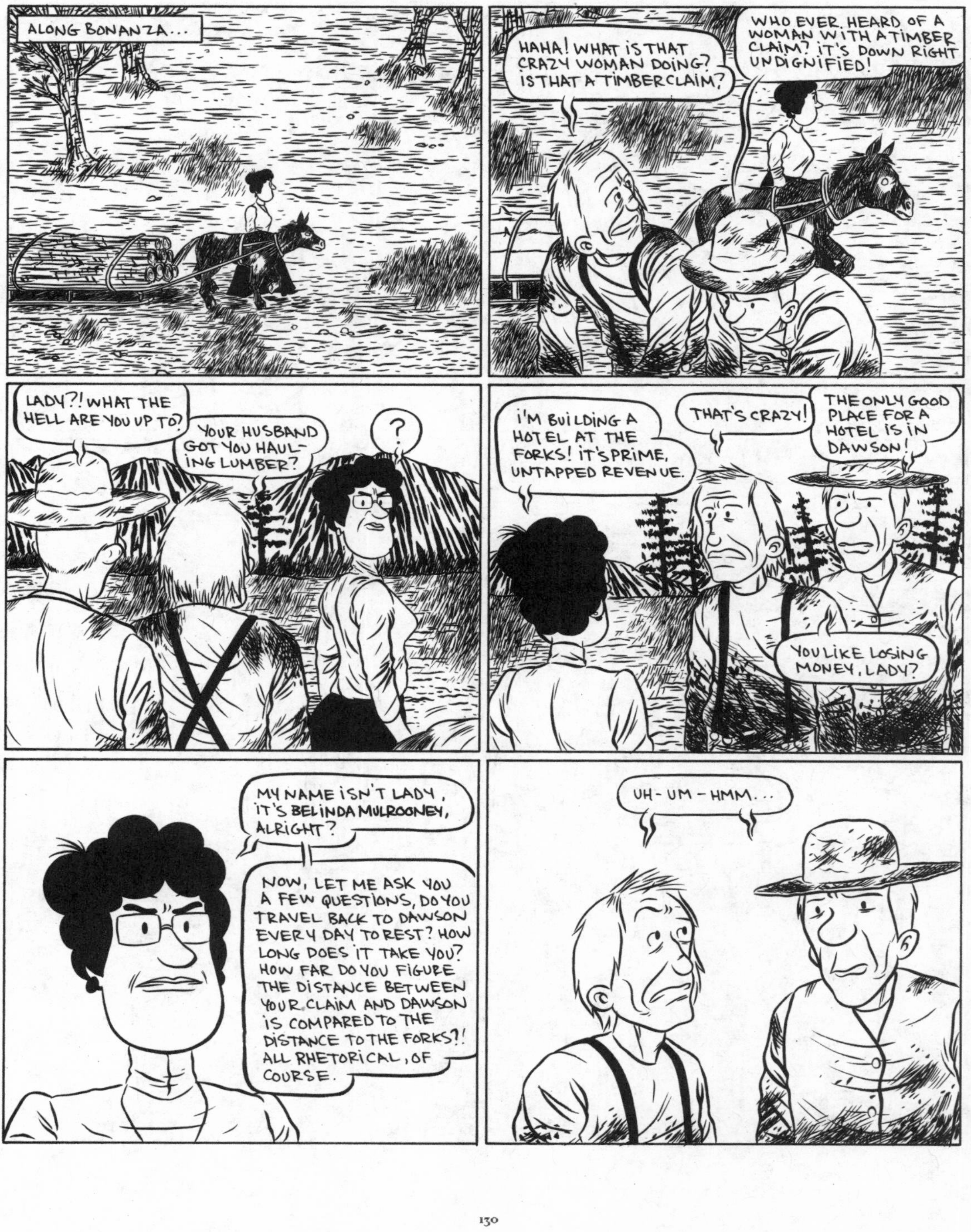
ALONG BONANZA...
HAHA! WHAT IS THAT CRAZY WOMAN DOING? IS THAT A TIMBER CLAIM?
WHO EVER HEARD OF A WOMAN WITH A TIMBER CLAIM? IT'S DOWN RIGHT UNDIGNIFIED!
LADY?! WHAT THE HELL ARE YOU UP TO?
YOUR HUSBAND GOT YOU HAULING LUMBER?
?
I'M BUILDING A HOTEL AT THE FORKS! IT'S PRIME, UNTAPPED REVENUE.
THAT'S CRAZY!
THE ONLY GOOD PLACE FOR A HOTEL IS IN DAWSON!
YOU LIKE LOSING MONEY, LADY?
MY NAME ISN'T LADY, IT'S BELINDA MULROONEY, ALRIGHT?
NOW, LET ME ASK YOU A FEW QUESTIONS, DO YOU TRAVEL BACK TO DAWSON EVERY DAY TO REST? HOW LONG DOES IT TAKE YOU? HOW FAR DO YOU FIGURE THE DISTANCE BETWEEN YOUR CLAIM AND DAWSON IS COMPARED TO THE DISTANCE TO THE FORKS?! ALL RHETORICAL, OF COURSE.
UH-UM-HMM...

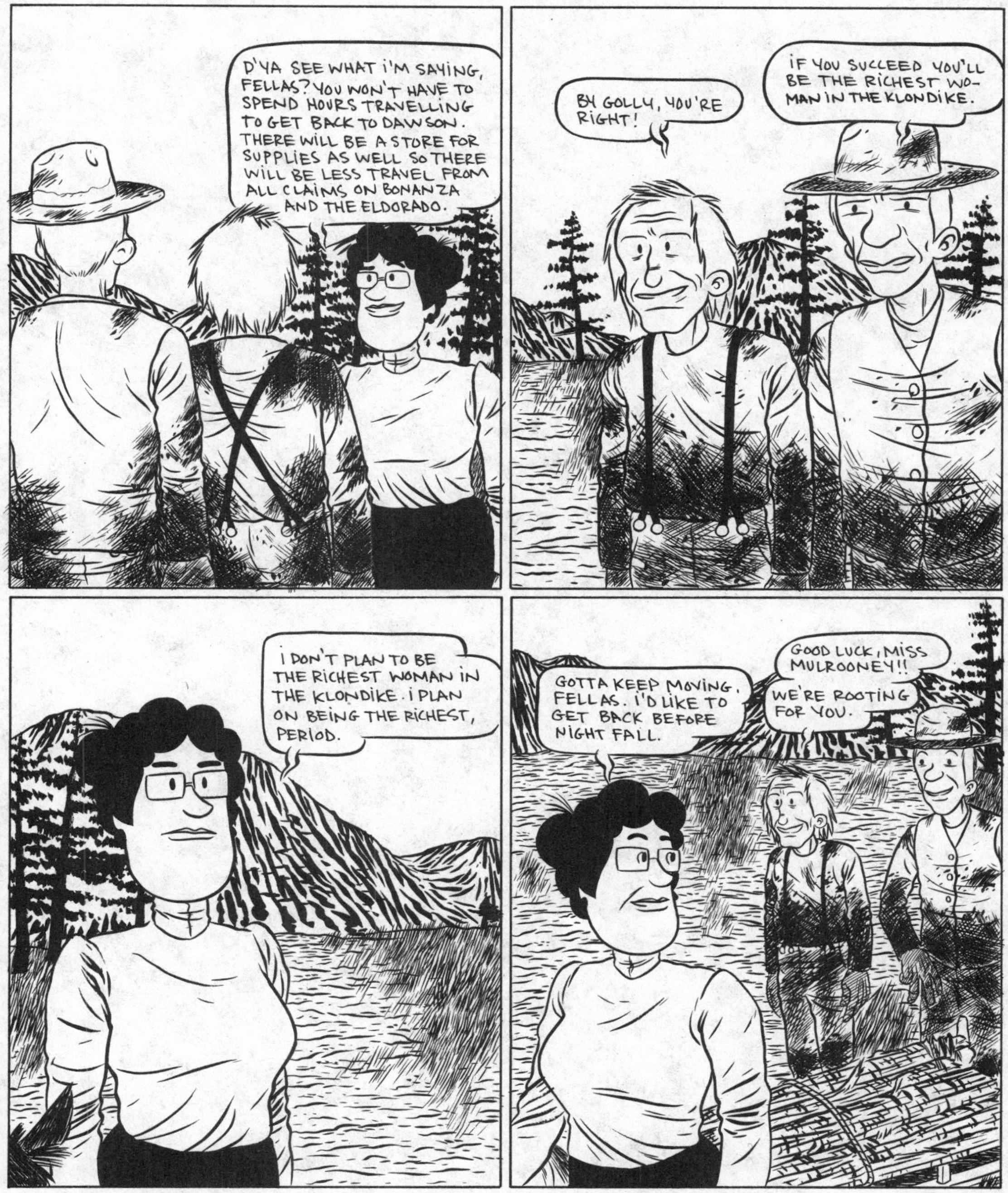
D'YA SEE WHAT I'M SAYING, FELLAS? YOU WON'T HAVE TO SPEND HOURS TRAVELLING TO GET BACK TO DAWSON. THERE WILL BE A STORE FOR SUPPLIES AS WELL SO THERE WILL BE LESS TRAVEL FROM ALL CLAIMS ON BONANZA AND THE ELDORADO.
BY GOLLY, YOU'RE RIGHT!
IF YOU SUCCEED YOU'LL BE THE RICHEST WOMAN IN THE KLONDIKE.
I DON'T PLAN TO BE THE RICHEST WOMAN IN THE KLONDIKE. I PLAN ON BEING THE RICHEST, PERIOD.
GOTTA KEEP MOVING, FELLAS. I'D LIKE TO GET BACK BEFORE NIGHT FALL.
GOOD LUCK, MISS MULROONEY!!
WE'RE ROOTING FOR YOU.

AS JEFFERSON RANDOLPH "SOAPY" SMITH, A NOTORIOUS BUNKO MAN FROM DENVER, TRIED TO CONVINCE EX-POLICEMAN WILLIS LOOMIS TO BE CHIEF OF POLICE IN SKAGWAY, A DIRECT TRAIL FROM EDMONTON, ALBERTA TO THE YUKON WAS BEING PROMOTED. THE PITCH WAS THAT ONE COULD GET TO THE YUKON BY HORSE IN NINETY DAYS-- AN INSANE NOTION CONSIDERING NO ONE HAD ACTUALLY TRAVELLED THE EDMONTON TRAIL. IT WAS PLOTTED BY AMATEUR CARTOGRAPHERS, WITH NO REFERENCE TO SPEAK OF, IN AN ATTEMPT TO BRING REVENUE INTO THE ECONOMY. THE CANADIANS THAT USED THE TRAIL DID SO MOSTLY OUT OF PATRIOTISM. THE TALES TOLD TO ENTICE THE TRAVELLERS CLAIMED IT WAS AS GOOD AS AN EXTENDED CAMPING TRIP. AS A RESULT OF NO ONE ACTUALLY WALKING THE TRAIL TO CHART IT, DOZENS OF MEN LOST THEIR LIVES. ASIDE FROM THE HUMAN TRAVELLERS THAT DIED, EVERY SINGLE HORSE USED DIED EN ROUTE. WHAT HAD PROMISED TO BE AN EASY THREE MONTH CAMPING TRIP TURNED OUT TO BE CLOSER TO ONE AND A HALF YEARS THROUGH UNCHARTED TERRAIN. IN SOME CASES, MEN HAD TO CHOP THEIR WAY THROUGH THREE HUNDRED MILES OF FALLEN TIMBER, AVOID FOREST FIRES AND, OF COURSE, DEAL WITH THE BRUTAL NORTHERN CANADIAN WINTERS.

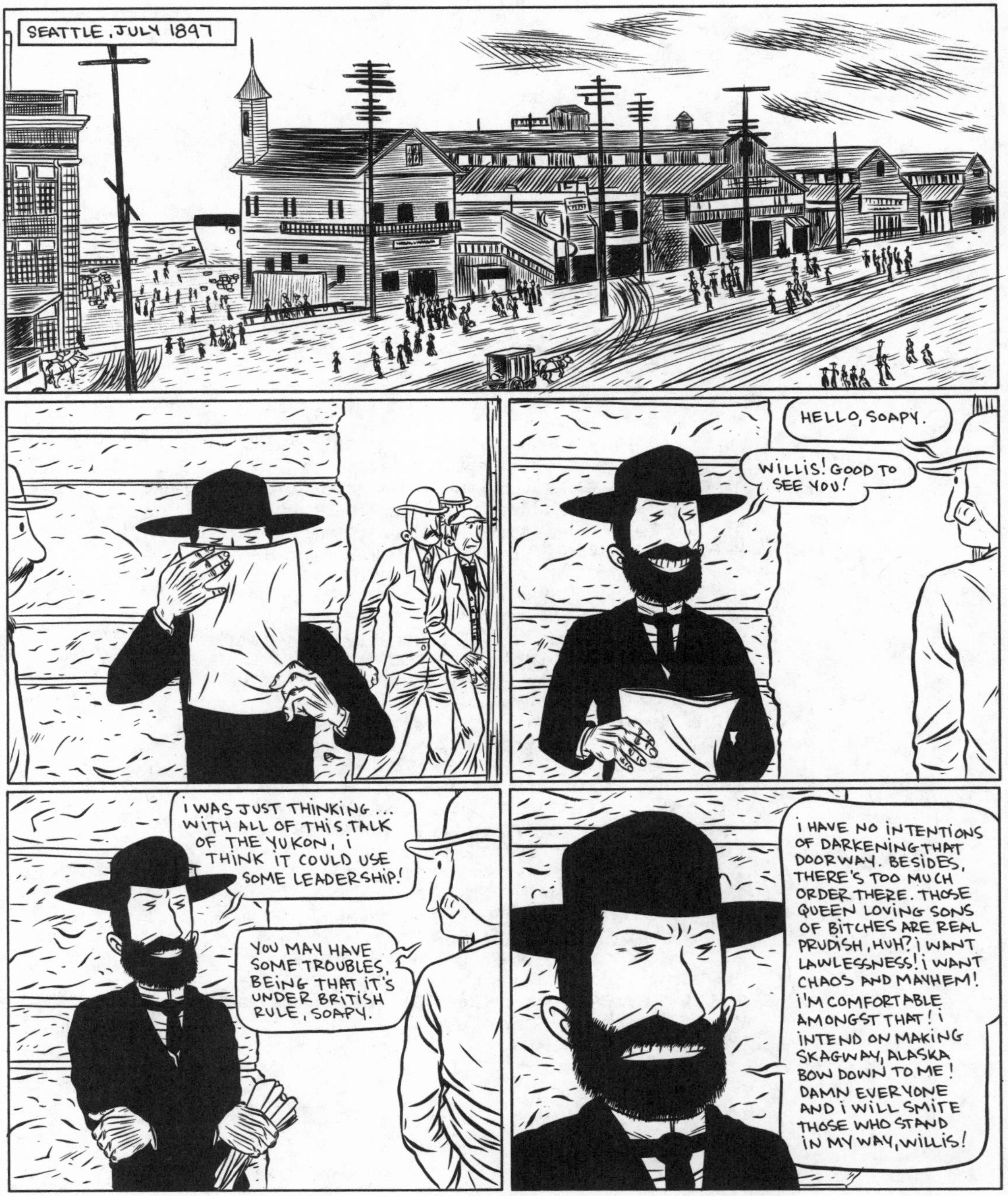
SEATTLE, JULY 1897
HELLO, SOAPY.
WILLIS! GOOD TO SEE YOU!
I WAS JUST THINKING ... WITH ALL OF THIS TALK OF THE YUKON, I THINK IT COULD USE SOME LEADERSHIP!
YOU MAY HAVE SOME TROUBLES, BEING THAT IT'S UNDER BRITISH RULE, SOAPY.
I HAVE NO INTENTIONS OF DARKENING THAT DOORWAY. BESIDES, THERE'S TOO MUCH ORDER THERE. THOSE QUEEN LOVING SONS OF BITCHES ARE REAL PRUDISH, HUH? I WANT LAWLESSNESS! I WANT CHAOS AND MAYHEM! I'M COMFORTABLE AMONGST THAT! I INTEND ON MAKING SKAGWAY, ALASKA BOW DOWN TO ME! DAMN EVERYONE AND I WILL SMITE THOSE WHO STAND IN MY WAY, WILLIS!

LET'S TAKE A WALK.

WHY NOT.

YOU SEE ALL THESE PEOPLE? THESE ARE THE PEOPLE I'M GOING TO THE KLONDIKE FOR. THOUSANDS OF DOCTORS, LAWYERS, CITY WORKERS... DO YOU SEE WHAT I MEAN?

NO, I DON'T.

MOST OF THESE PEOPLE HAVE NEVER BEEN IN A MINING CAMP OR BORDER TOWN. THE NAÏVETY IS ASTOUNDING! THESE PEOPLE HAVE GOLD IN THEIR EYES AND NOTHING IN THEIR GODDAMNED HEADS!

SO, YOUR INTENTIONS ARE TO PREY ON PEOPLE WHO DON'T KNOW ANY BETTER?

I'D SAY "PREYING" IS A BIT HARSH, THOUGH. I'M LIBERATING IGNORANT BUFFOONS OF WHAT THEY SHOULDN'T HAVE. I'M TEACHING...

I'M TEACHING THEM THAT WHAT THEY DREAM, WHAT THEY WANT, WHAT THEY NEED—WHICH IN THIS CASE IS MONEY—IS OUTWEIGHED BY WHAT I WANT.

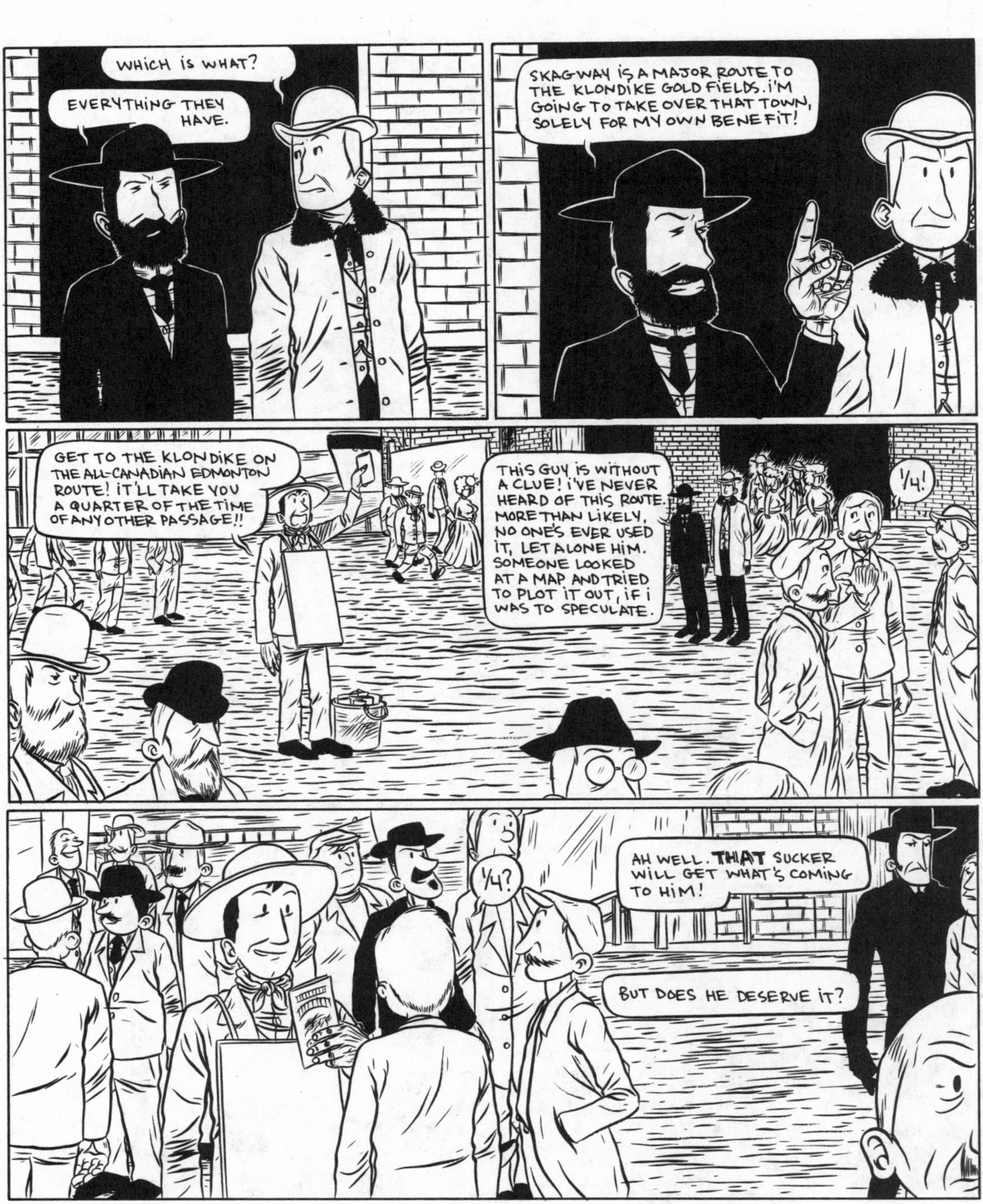
WHICH IS WHAT?
EVERYTHING THEY HAVE.
SKAGWAY IS A MAJOR ROUTE TO THE KLONDIKE GOLD FIELDS. I'M GOING TO TAKE OVER THAT TOWN, SOLELY FOR MY OWN BENEFIT!
GET TO THE KLONDIKE ON THE ALL-CANADIAN EDMONTON ROUTE! IT'LL TAKE YOU A QUARTER OF THE TIME OF ANY OTHER PASSAGE!!
THIS GUY IS WITHOUT A CLUE! I'VE NEVER HEARD OF THIS ROUTE. MORE THAN LIKELY, NO ONE'S EVER USED IT, LET ALONE HIM. SOMEONE LOOKED AT A MAP AND TRIED TO PLOT IT OUT, IF I WAS TO SPECULATE.
1/4!
1/4?
AH WELL. THAT SUCKER WILL GET WHAT'S COMING TO HIM!
BUT DOES HE DESERVE IT?

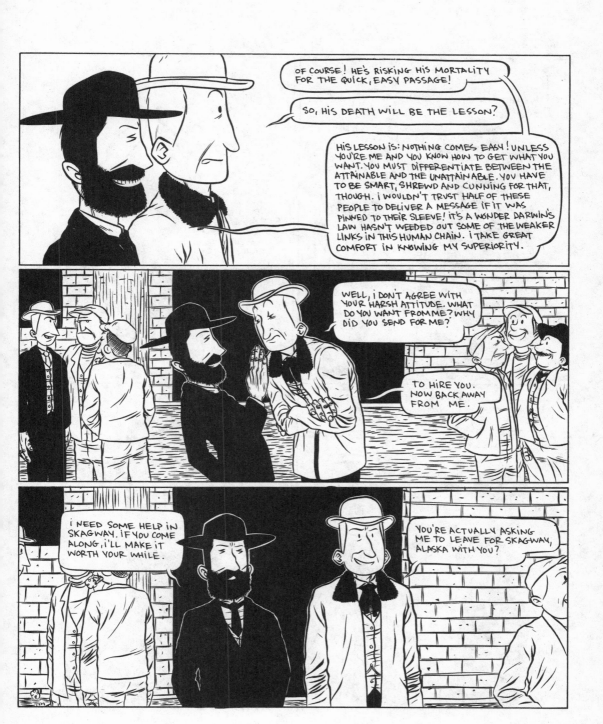

OF COURSE! HE'S RISKING HIS MORTALITY FOR THE QUICK, EASY PASSAGE!

SO, HIS DEATH WILL BE THE LESSON?

HIS LESSON IS: NOTHING COMES EASY! UNLESS YOU'RE ME AND YOU KNOW HOW TO GET WHAT YOU WANT. YOU MUST DIFFERENTIATE BETWEEN THE ATTAINABLE AND THE UNATTAINABLE. YOU HAVE TO BE SMART, SHREWD AND CUNNING FOR THAT, THOUGH. I WOULDN'T TRUST HALF OF THESE PEOPLE TO DELIVER A MESSAGE IF IT WAS PINNED TO THEIR SLEEVE! IT'S A WONDER DARWIN'S LAW HASN'T WEEDED OUT SOME OF THE WEAKER LINKS IN THIS HUMAN CHAIN. I TAKE GREAT COMFORT IN KNOWING MY SUPERIORITY.

WELL, I DON'T AGREE WITH YOUR HARSH ATTITUDE. WHAT DO YOU WANT FROM ME? WHY DID YOU SEND FOR ME?

TO HIRE YOU. NOW BACK AWAY FROM ME.

I NEED SOME HELP IN SKAGWAY. IF YOU COME ALONG, I'LL MAKE IT WORTH YOUR WHILE.

YOU'RE ACTUALLY ASKING ME TO LEAVE FOR SKAGWAY, ALASKA WITH YOU?

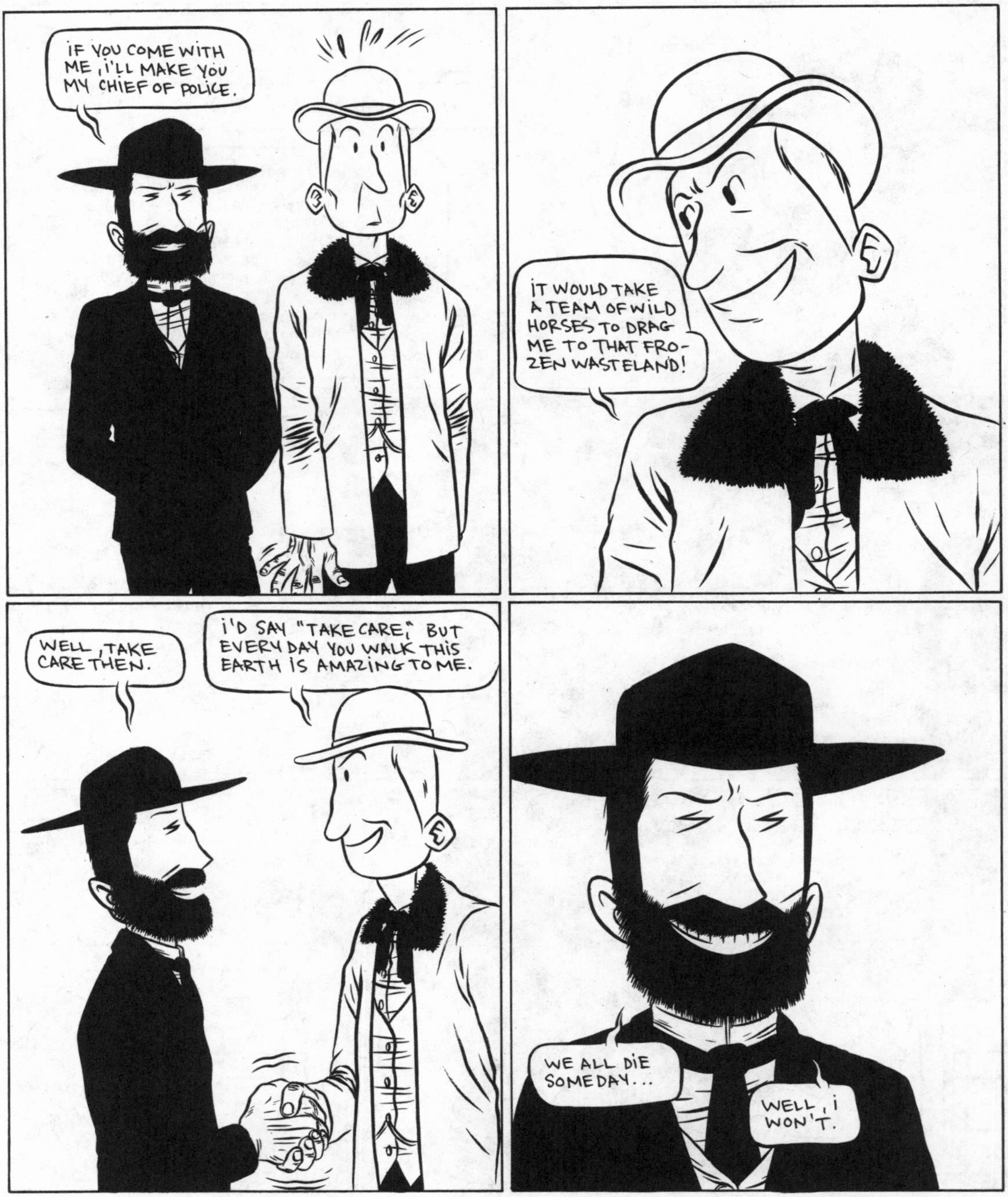
IF YOU COME WITH ME, I'LL MAKE YOU MY CHIEF OF POLICE.
IT WOULD TAKE A TEAM OF WILD HORSES TO DRAG ME TO THAT FROZEN WASTELAND!
WELL, TAKE CARE THEN.
I'D SAY "TAKE CARE," BUT EVERY DAY YOU WALK THIS EARTH IS AMAZING TO ME.
WE ALL DIE SOMEDAY...
WELL, I WON'T.

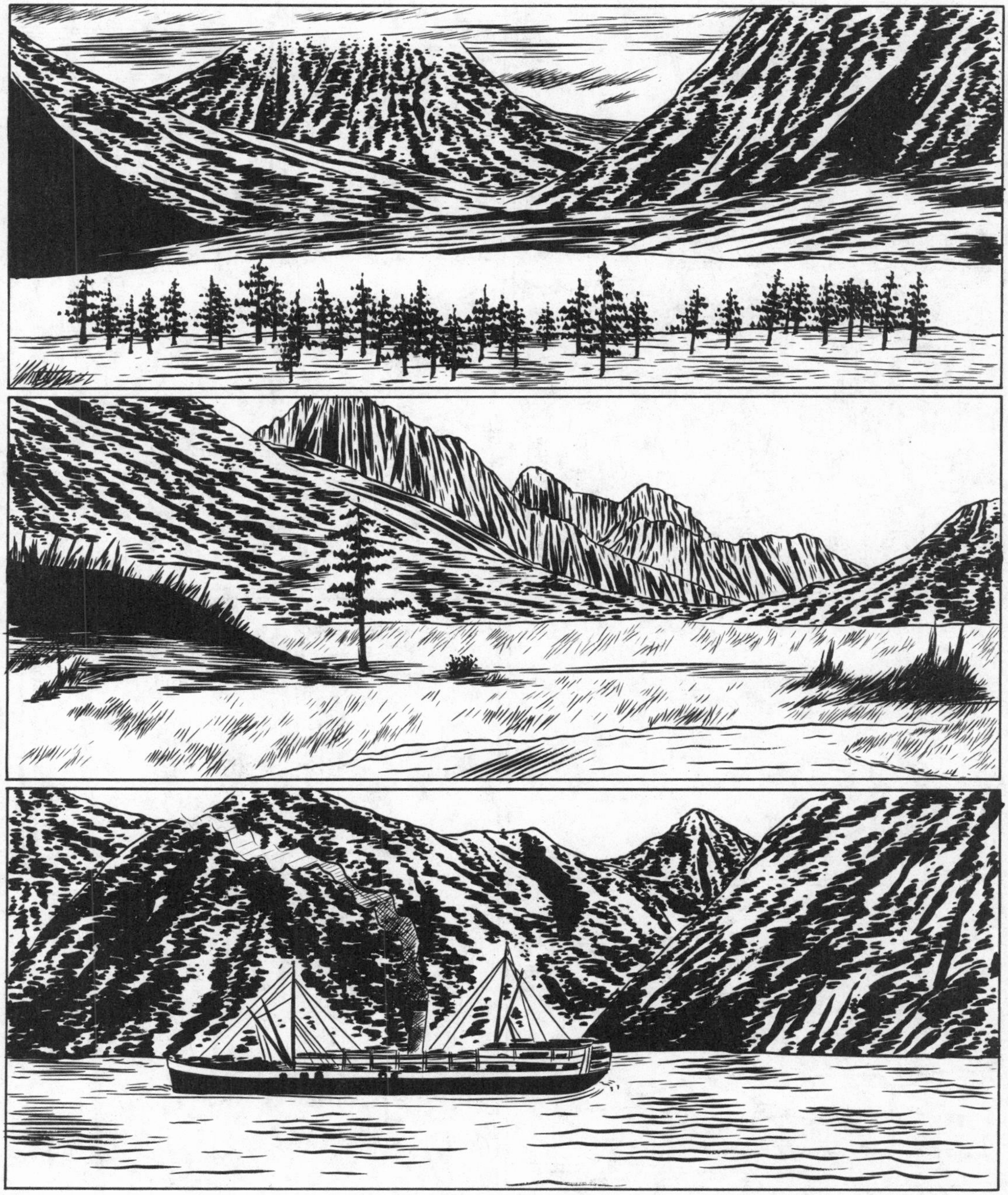

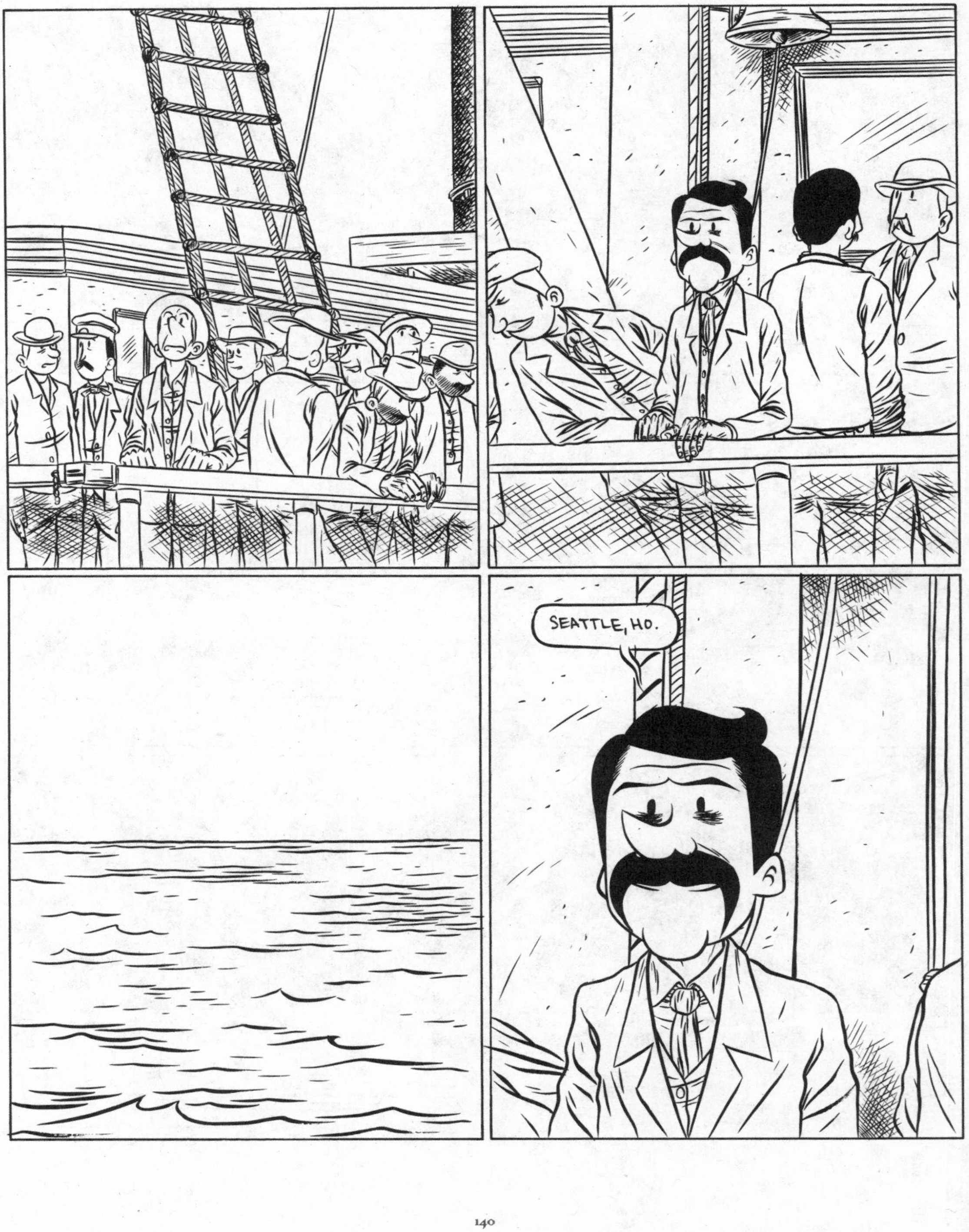
SEATTLE, HO.

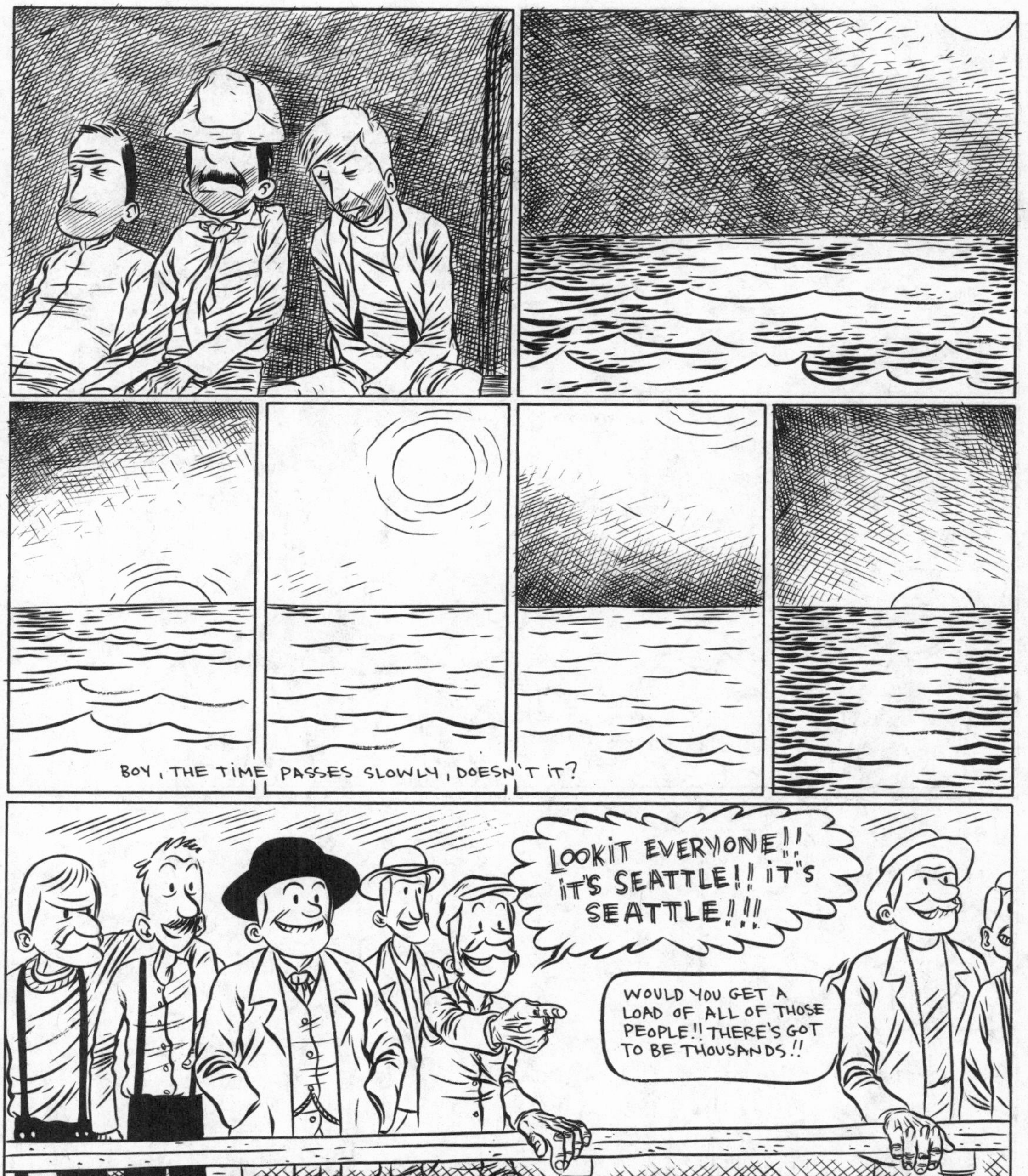
BOY, THE TIME PASSES SLOWLY, DOESN'T IT?
LOOKIT EVERYONE!! IT'S SEATTLE!! IT'S SEATTLE!!!
WOULD YOU GET A LOAD OF ALL OF THOSE PEOPLE!! THERE'S GOT TO BE THOUSANDS!!

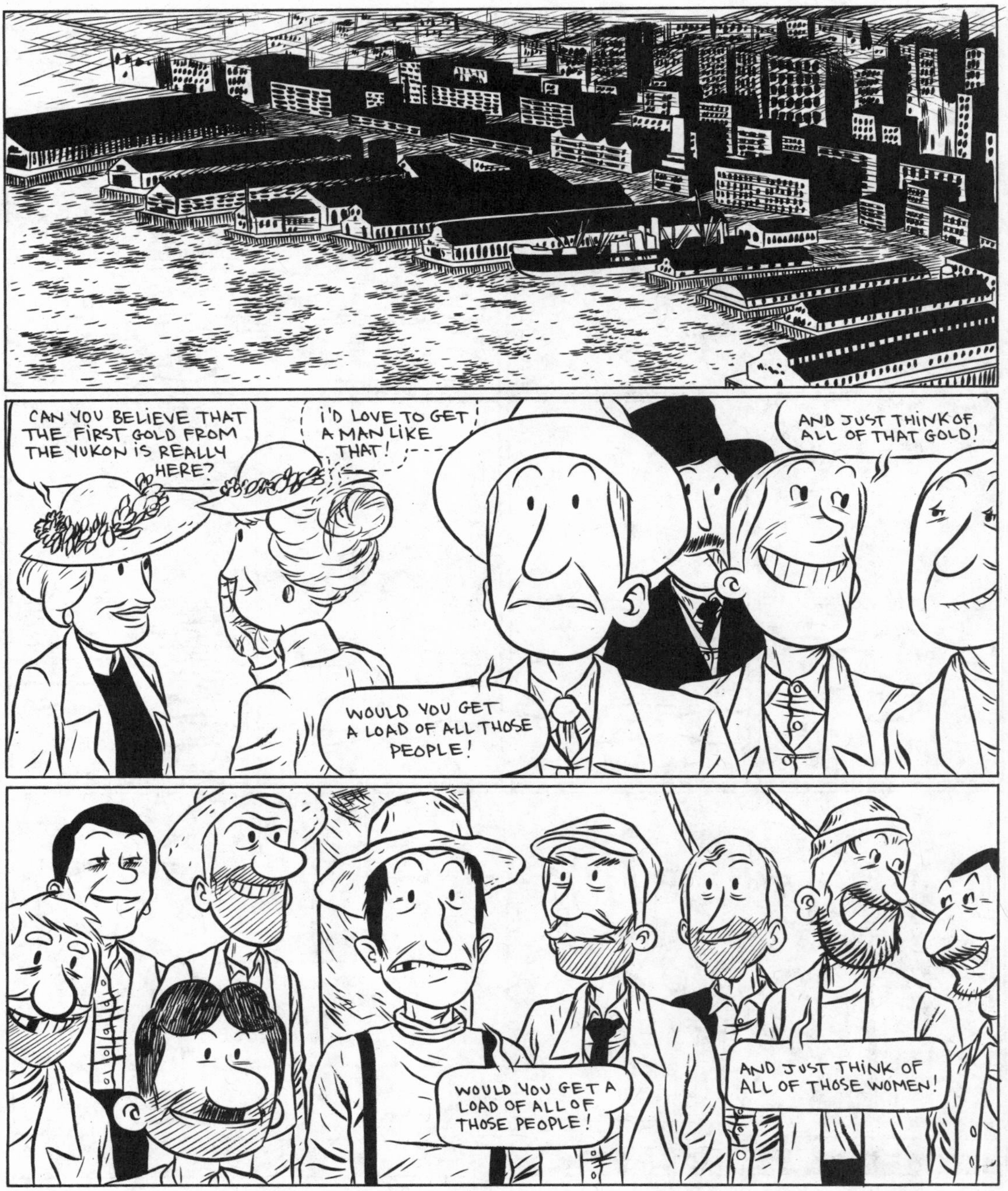
CAN YOU BELIEVE THAT THE FIRST GOLD FROM THE YUKON IS REALLY HERE?
I'D LOVE TO GET A MAN LIKE THAT!
AND JUST THINK OF ALL OF THAT GOLD!
WOULD YOU GET A LOAD OF ALL THOSE PEOPLE!
WOULD YOU GET A LOAD OF ALL OF THOSE PEOPLE!
AND JUST THINK OF ALL OF THOSE WOMEN!

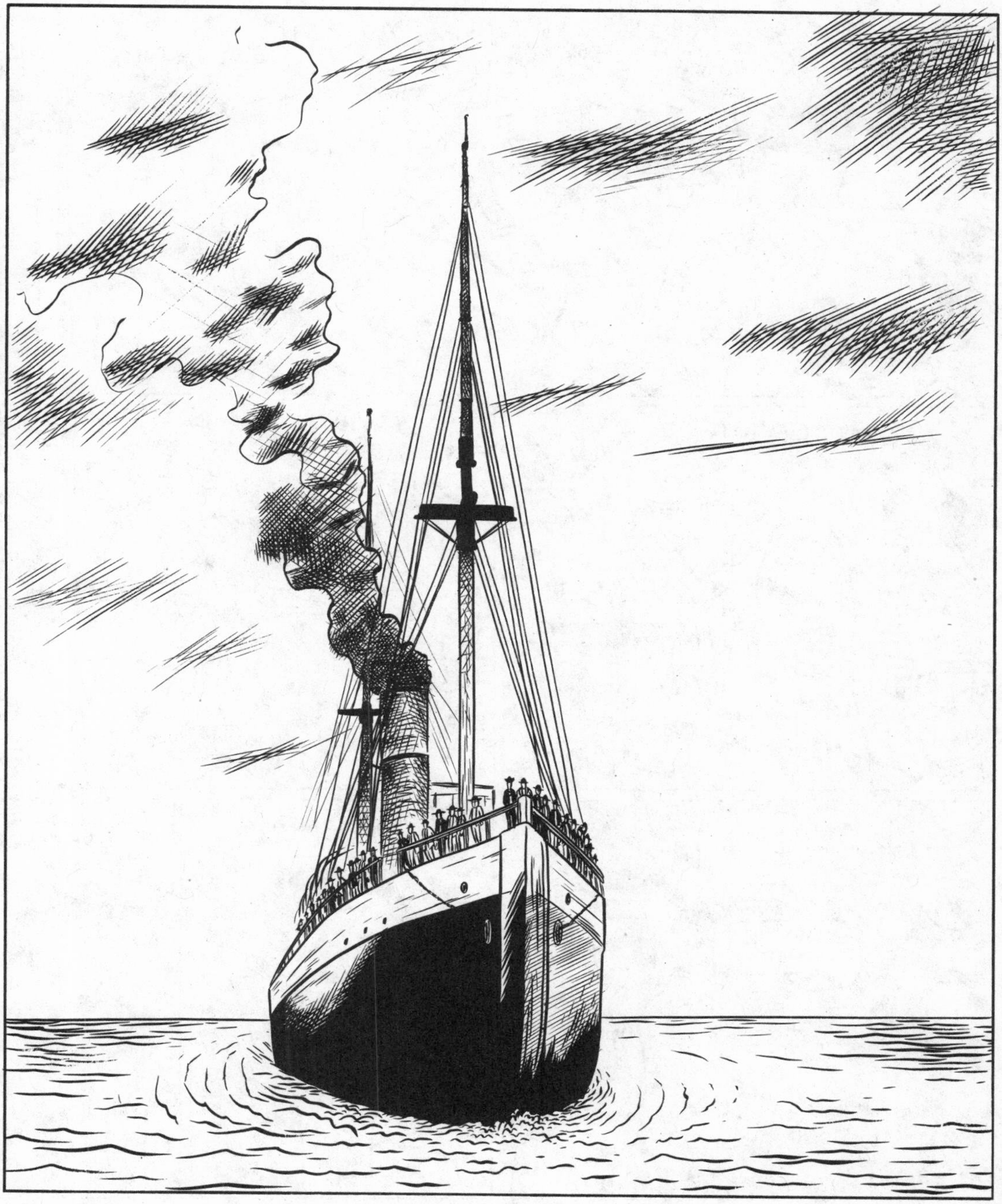

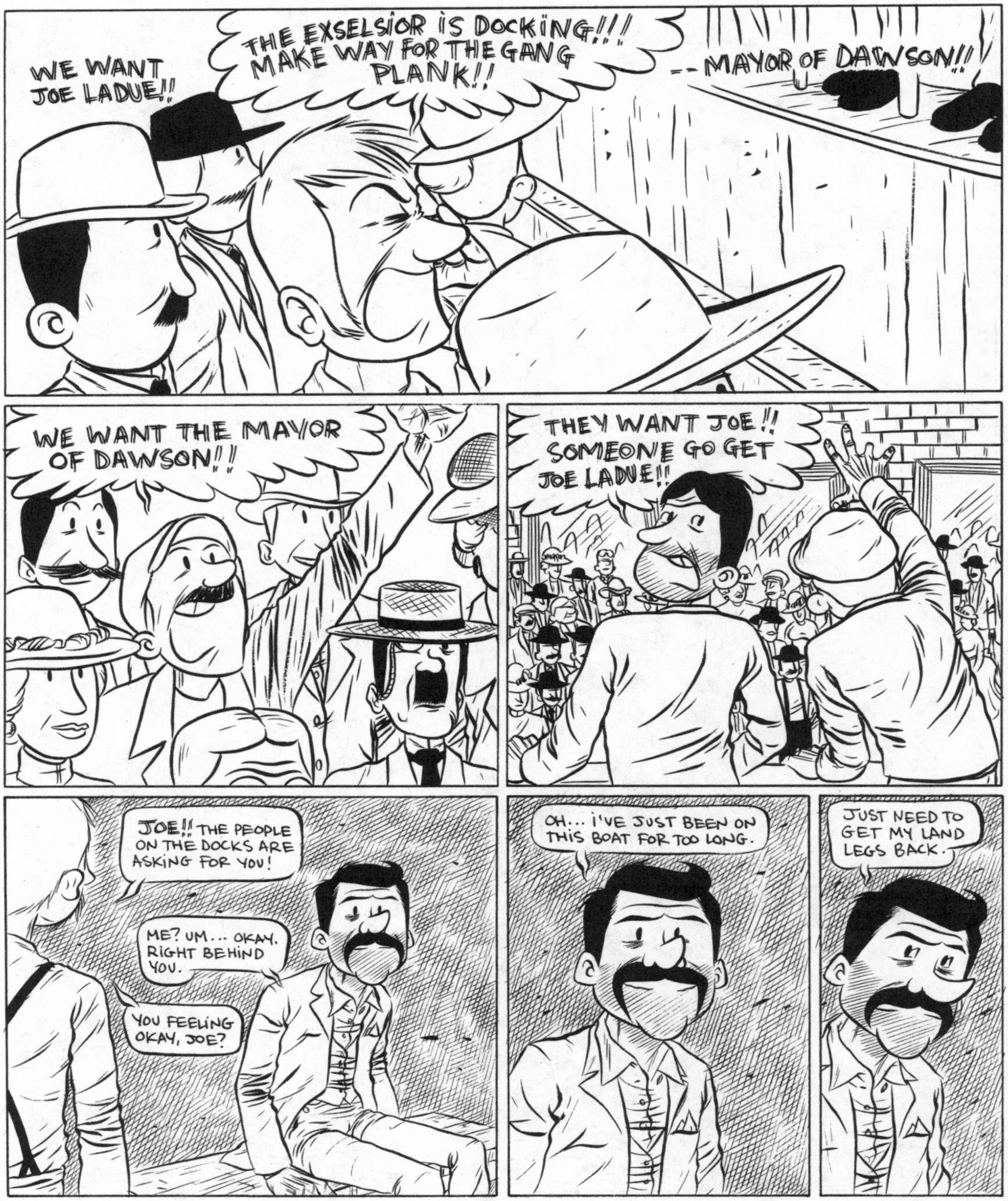
WE WANT JOE LADUE!!
THE EXSELSIOR IS DOCKING!!! MAKE WAY FOR THE GANG PLANK!!
-- MAYOR OF DAWSON!!
WE WANT THE MAYOR OF DAWSON!!
THEY WANT JOE!! SOMEONE GO GET JOE LADUE!!
JOE!! THE PEOPLE ON THE DOCKS ARE ASKING FOR YOU!
ME? UM... OKAY. RIGHT BEHIND YOU.
YOU FEELING OKAY, JOE?
OH... I'VE JUST BEEN ON THIS BOAT FOR TOO LONG.
JUST NEED TO GET MY LAND LEGS BACK.

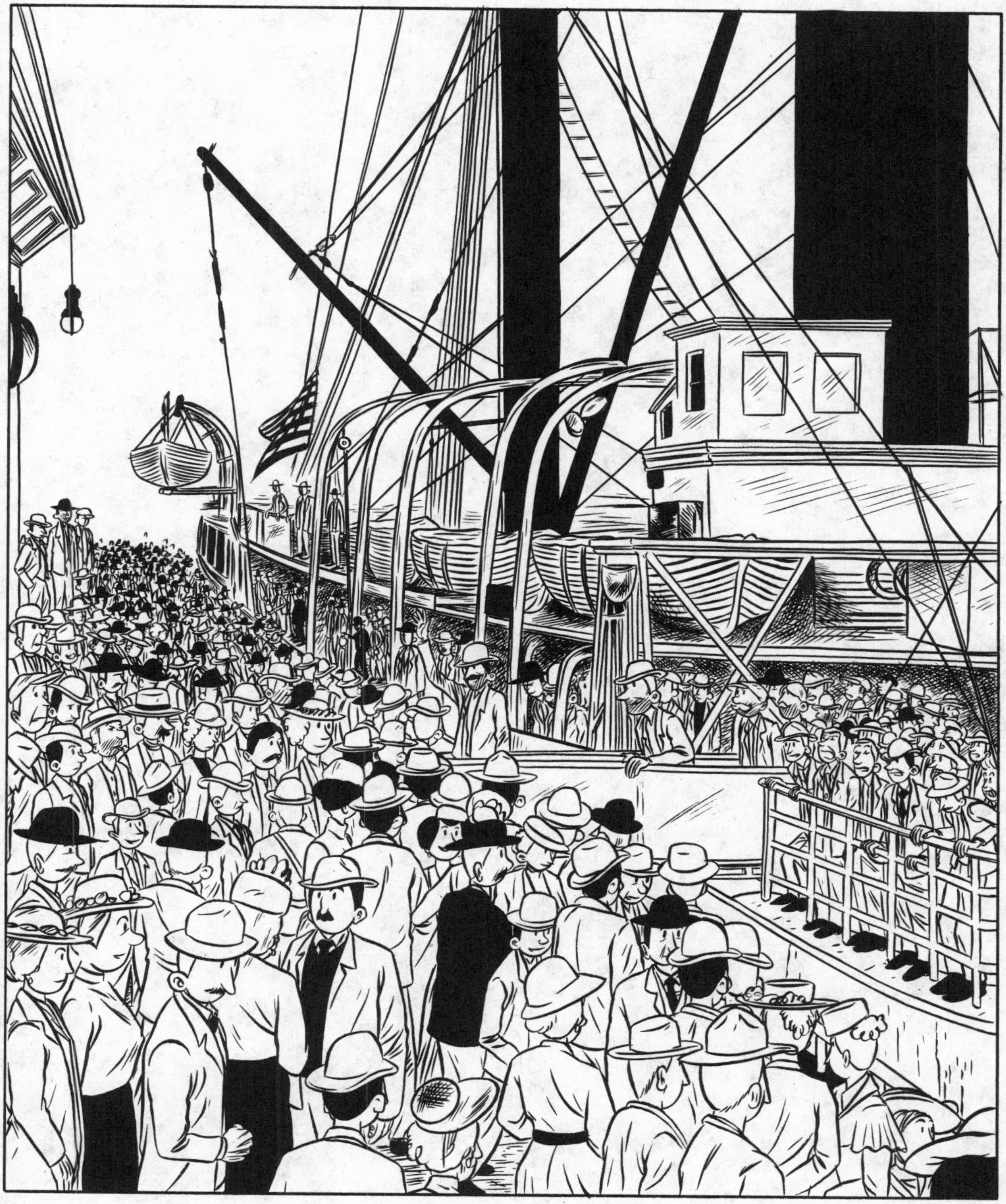

SEATTLE WAS ONE OF THE MAJOR PORTS FOR THOSE TRYING TO GET TO THE YUKON AND THUS ATTRACTED PEOPLE FROM ALL WALKS OF LIFE: SOURDOUGHS (LONG TIME PROSPECTORS), GREENHORNES (BUSINESSMEN, WOULD-BE PROSPECTORS, GET-RICH-QUICK TYPES AND SO-CALLED ADVENTURERS), THIEVES, THUGS, KILLERS, GAMBLERS, ACTORS, PRIESTS, PIMPS AND PROSTITUTES. THEY ALL HAD THEIR REASONS FOR SAYING, "YUKON, HO!"

AMONGST THE THIEVES AND THUGS WAS THE MAN RESPONSIBLE FOR THE SOAP GAME: SOAPY SMITH. HE WOULD SELL BARS OF SOAP WITH A PRIZE INSIDE -- THE SCAM WAS THAT HE HAD PLANTS, MEMBERS OF HIS GANG IN THE CROWD WHO WOULD WIN THE PRIZES, USUALLY MONETARY. THE REGULAR FOLKS WOULD NEVER WIN THE PRIZES AND THE MONEY FROM THE PLANTS, ALONG WITH ALL THE EARNINGS, WENT STRAIGHT BACK INTO SOAPY'S POCKET. LIKE MOST NOTORIOUS FIGURES, SMITH WAS WELL KNOWN ACROSS THE COUNTRY. HE POSSESSED VERY UNIQUE TALENTS IN THE ART OF MANIPULATION. HE HAD A DEEP, ALMOST MELLOW, VOICE AND A VERY COOL WAY OF SPEAKING THAT COULD CHARM JUST ABOUT ANYONE. THIS INCLUDED POLITICIANS, JUDGES AND SENATORS, WHICH HE HAD MANY OF AS CLOSE FRIENDS, EVEN CONFIDANTS.

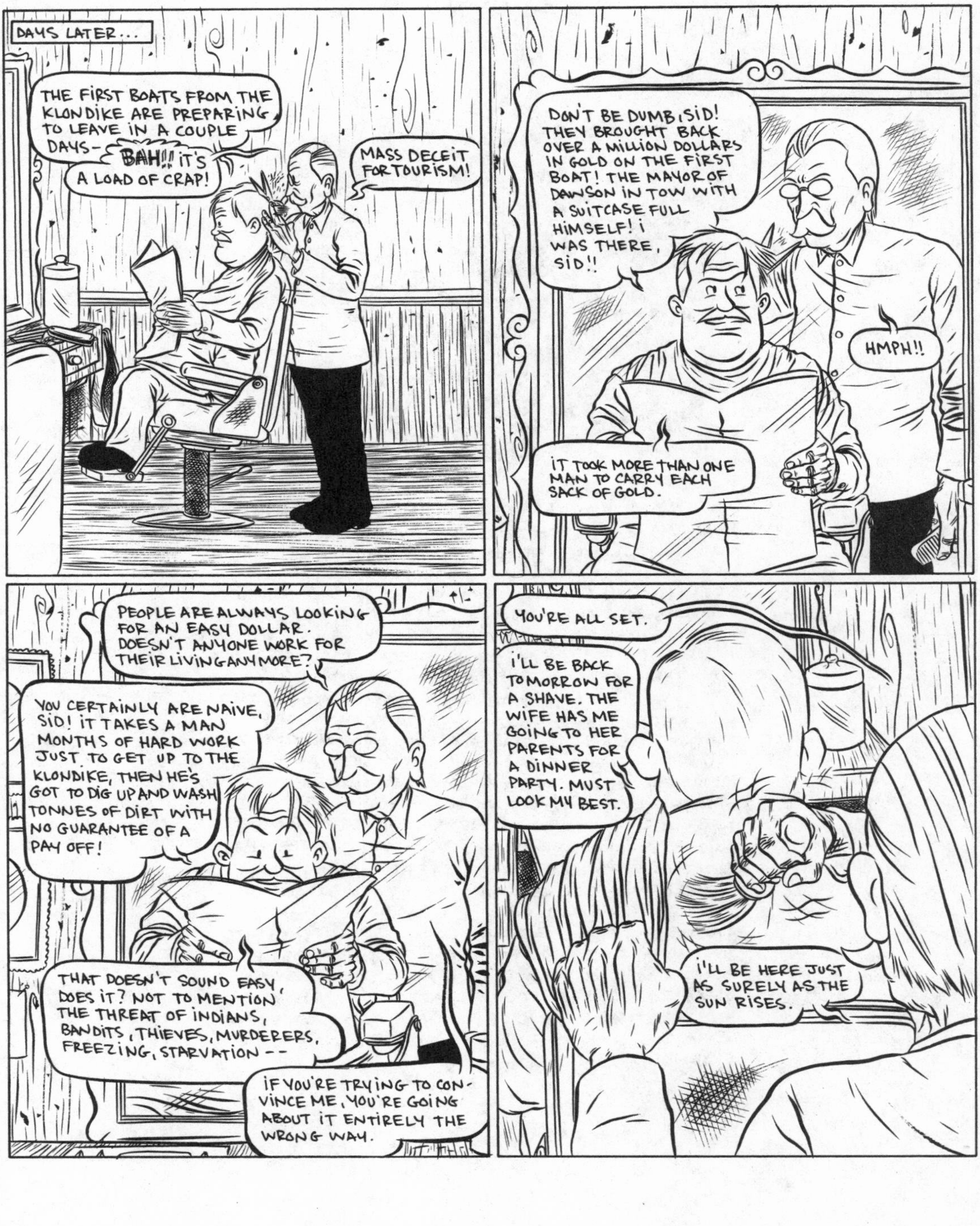
DAYS LATER...
THE FIRST BOATS FROM THE KLONDIKE ARE PREPARING TO LEAVE IN A COUPLE DAYS—
BAH!! IT'S A LOAD OF CRAP!
MASS DECEIT FOR TOURISM!
DON'T BE DUMB, SID! THEY BROUGHT BACK OVER A MILLION DOLLARS IN GOLD ON THE FIRST BOAT! THE MAYOR OF DAWSON IN TOW WITH A SUITCASE FULL HIMSELF! I WAS THERE, SID!!
HMPH!!
IT TOOK MORE THAN ONE MAN TO CARRY EACH SACK OF GOLD.
PEOPLE ARE ALWAYS LOOKING FOR AN EASY DOLLAR. DOESN'T ANYONE WORK FOR THEIR LIVING ANYMORE?
YOU CERTAINLY ARE NAIVE, SID! IT TAKES A MAN MONTHS OF HARD WORK JUST TO GET UP TO THE KLONDIKE, THEN HE'S GOT TO DIG UP AND WASH TONNES OF DIRT WITH NO GUARANTEE OF A PAY OFF!
THAT DOESN'T SOUND EASY, DOES IT? NOT TO MENTION THE THREAT OF INDIANS, BANDITS, THIEVES, MURDERERS, FREEZING, STARVATION --
IF YOU'RE TRYING TO CONVINCE ME, YOU'RE GOING ABOUT IT ENTIRELY THE WRONG WAY.
YOU'RE ALL SET.
I'LL BE BACK TOMORROW FOR A SHAVE. THE WIFE HAS ME GOING TO HER PARENTS FOR A DINNER PARTY. MUST LOOK MY BEST.
I'LL BE HERE JUST AS SURELY AS THE SUN RISES.

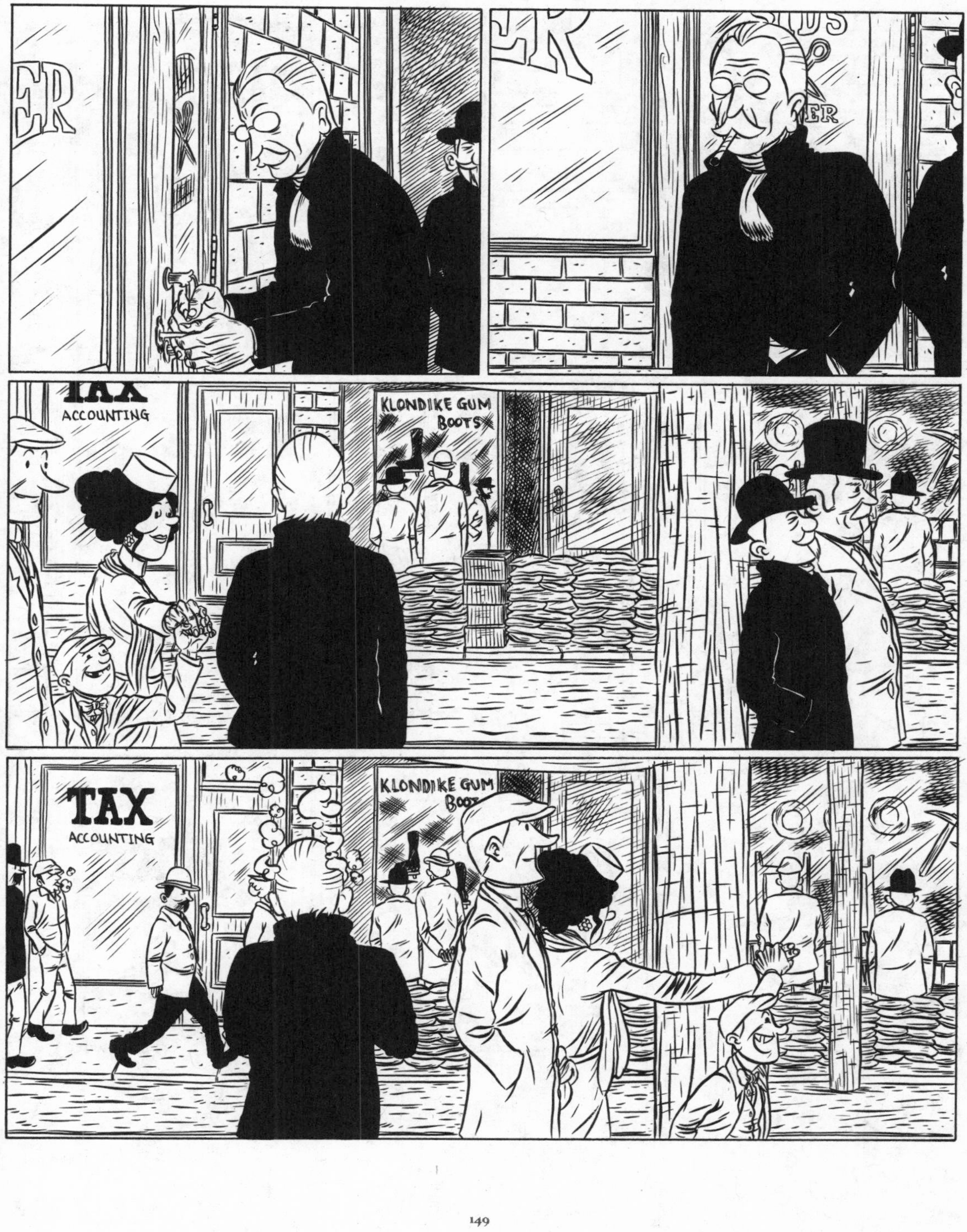
ER
ER
ER
TAX
ACCOUNTING
KLONDIKE GUM
BOOTS
TAX
ACCOUNTING
KLONDIKE GUM

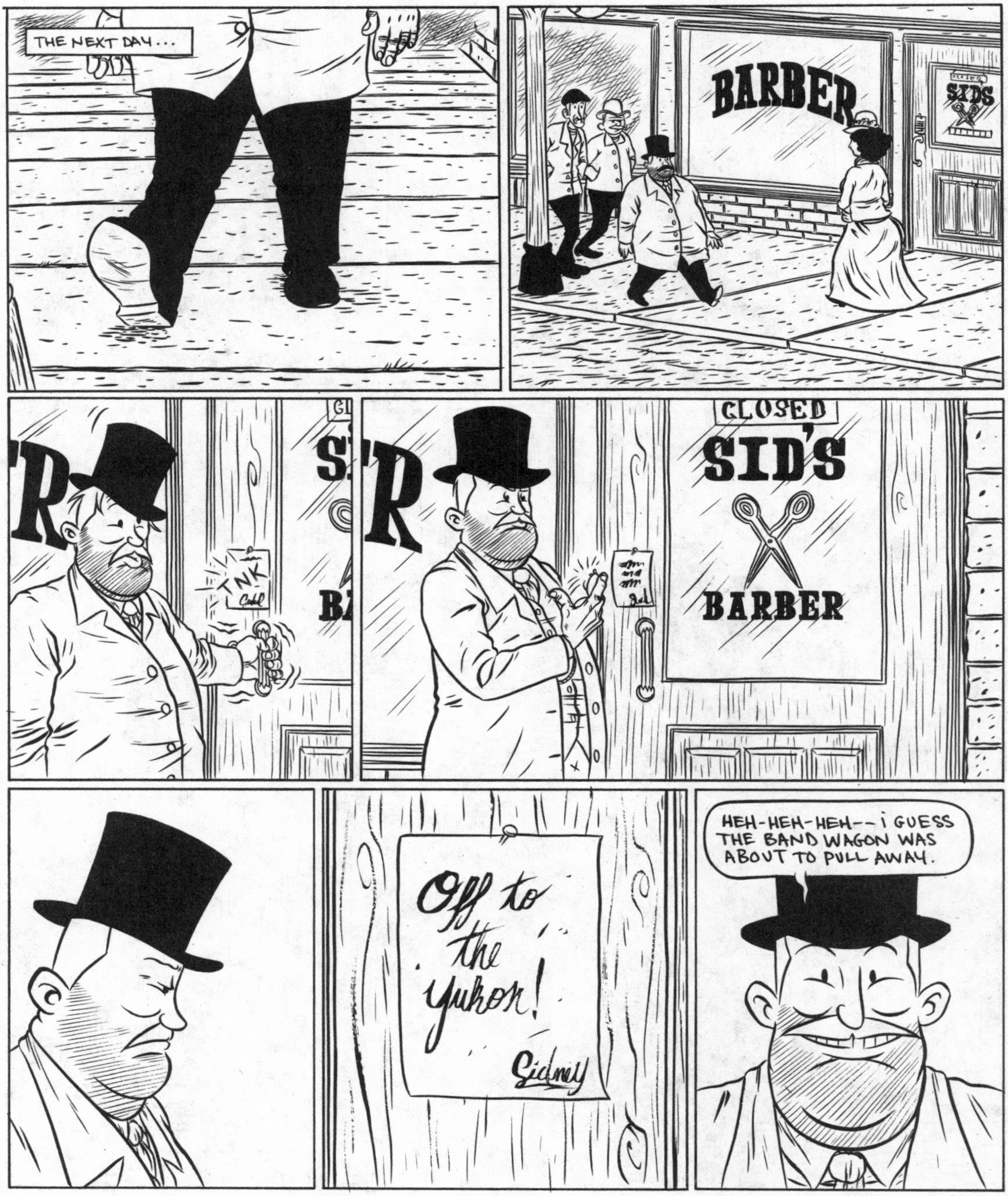
THE NEXT DAY...
BARBER
SIDS
CLOSED
SID'S
BARBER
TNK
Off to the yukon!
Sidney
HEH-HEH-HEH-- I GUESS THE BAND WAGON WAS ABOUT TO PULL AWAY.

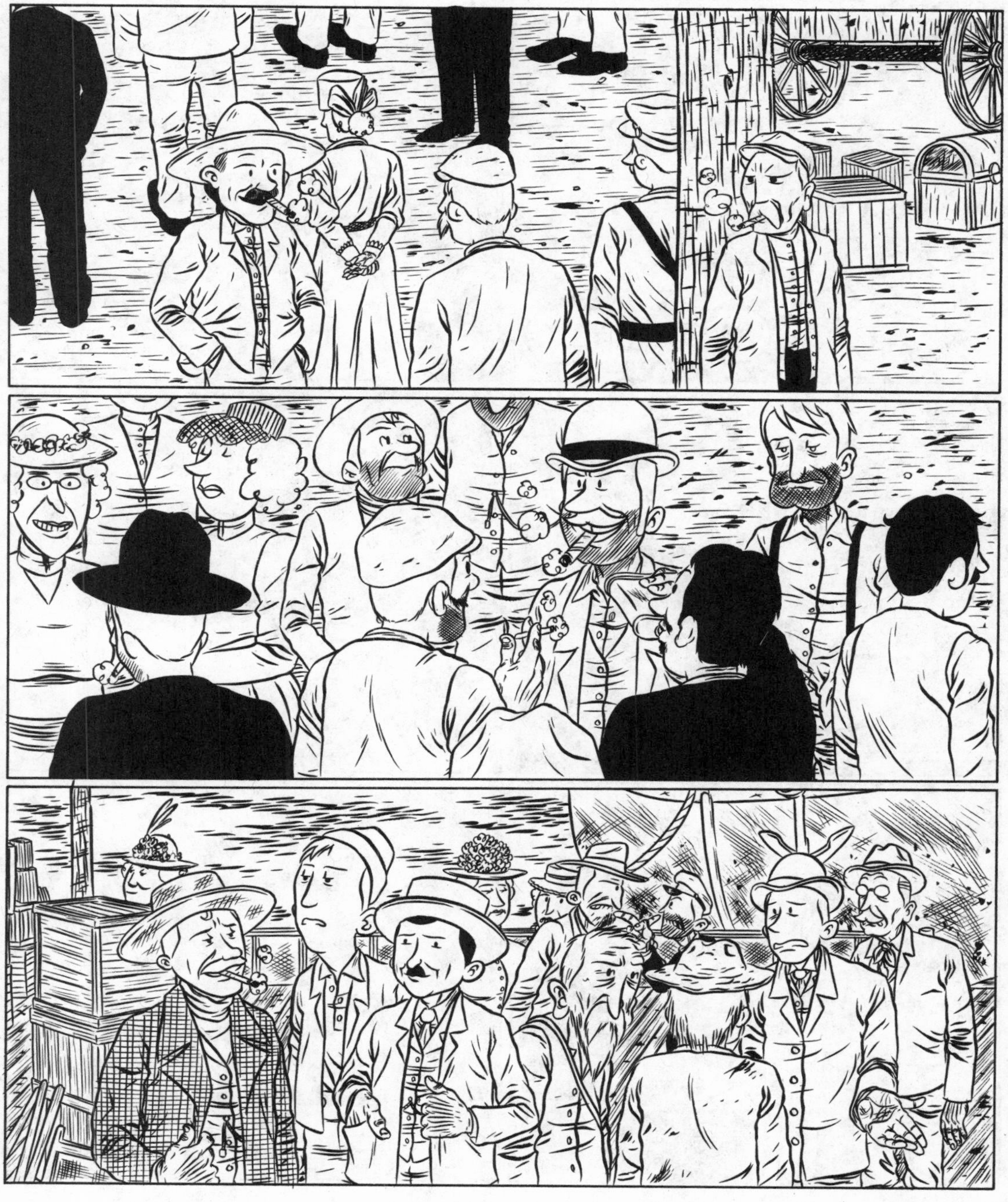

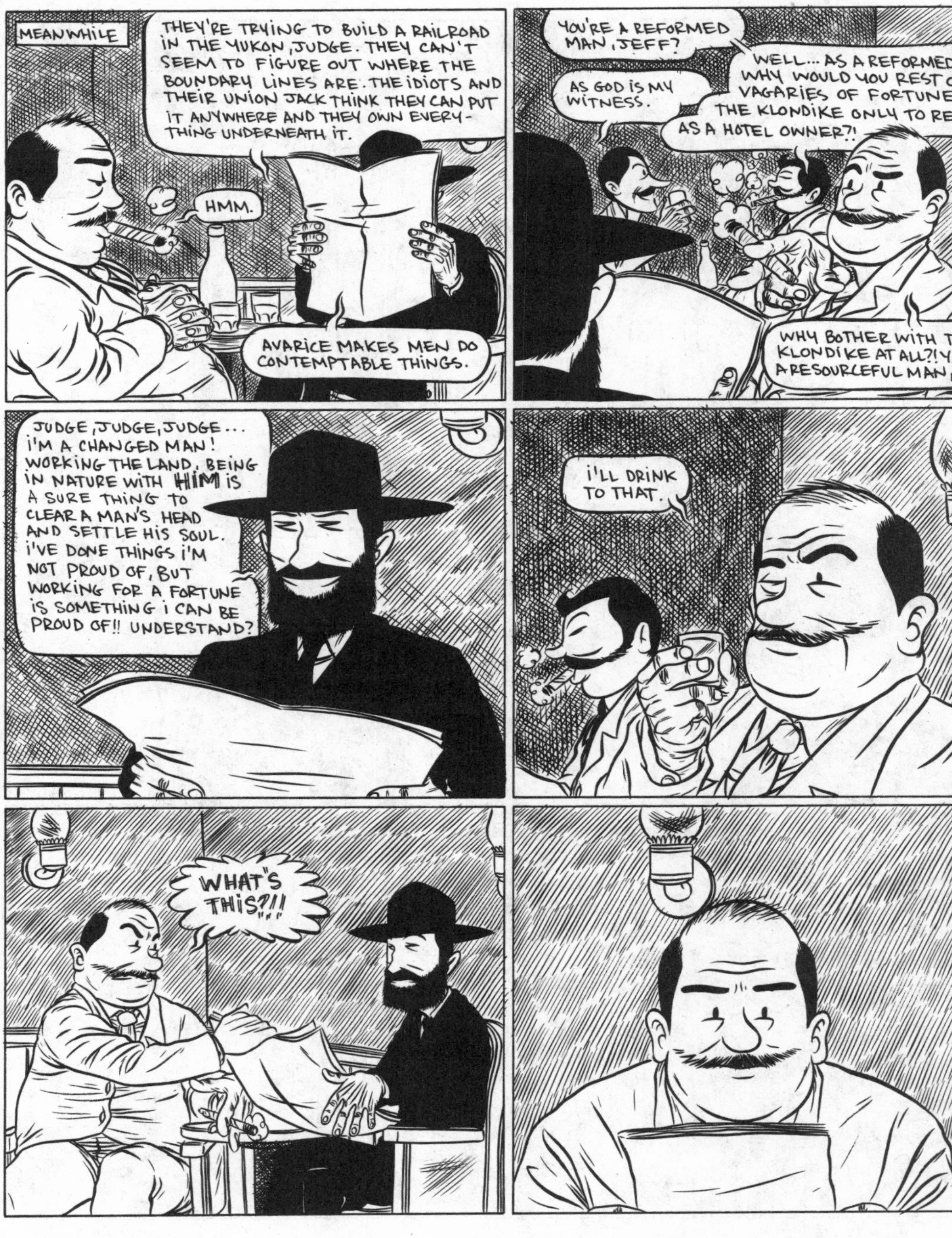
MEANWHILE
THEY'RE TRYING TO BUILD A RAILROAD IN THE YUKON, JUDGE. THEY CAN'T SEEM TO FIGURE OUT WHERE THE BOUNDARY LINES ARE. THE IDIOTS AND THEIR UNION JACK THINK THEY CAN PUT IT ANYWHERE AND THEY OWN EVERY-THING UNDERNEATH IT.
HMM.
AVARICE MAKES MEN DO CONTEMPTABLE THINGS.
YOU'RE A REFORMED MAN, JEFF?
AS GOD IS MY WITNESS.
WELL... AS A REFORMED MAN, WHY WOULD YOU REST ON THE VAGARIES OF FORTUNE IN THE KLONDIKE ONLY TO RETURN AS A HOTEL OWNER?!
WHY BOTHER WITH THE KLONDIKE AT ALL?! YOU'RE A RESOURCEFUL MAN, JEFF!
JUDGE, JUDGE, JUDGE... I'M A CHANGED MAN! WORKING THE LAND, BEING IN NATURE WITH HIM IS A SURE THING TO CLEAR A MAN'S HEAD AND SETTLE HIS SOUL. I'VE DONE THINGS I'M NOT PROUD OF, BUT WORKING FOR A FORTUNE IS SOMETHING I CAN BE PROUD OF!! UNDERSTAND?
I'LL DRINK TO THAT.
WHAT'S THIS?!!

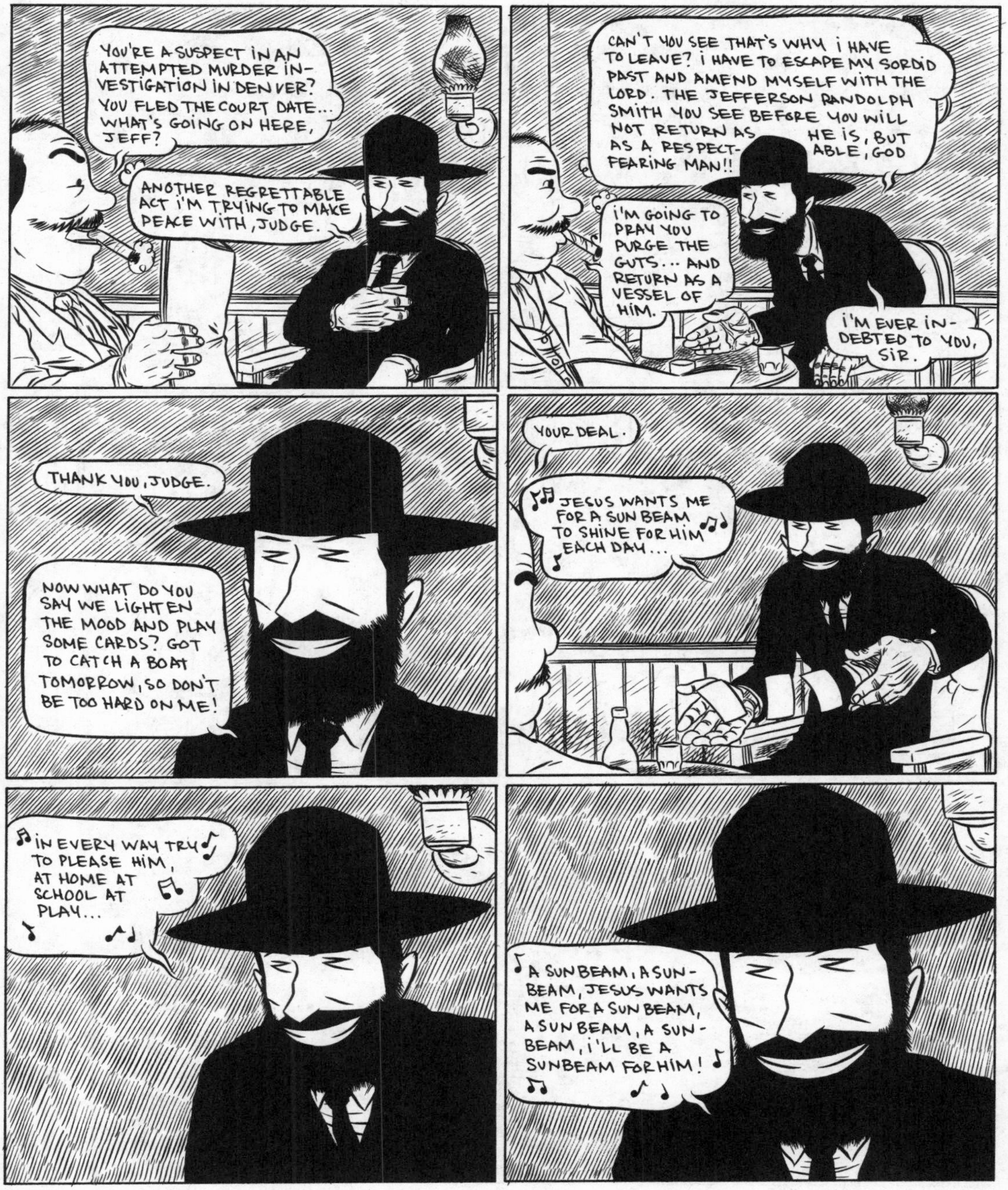
YOU'RE A SUSPECT IN AN ATTEMPTED MURDER INVESTIGATION IN DENVER? YOU FLED THE COURT DATE... WHAT'S GOING ON HERE, JEFF?
ANOTHER REGRETTABLE ACT I'M TRYING TO MAKE PEACE WITH, JUDGE.
CAN'T YOU SEE THAT'S WHY I HAVE TO LEAVE? I HAVE TO ESCAPE MY SORDID PAST AND AMEND MYSELF WITH THE LORD. THE JEFFERSON RANDOLPH SMITH YOU SEE BEFORE YOU WILL NOT RETURN AS HE IS, BUT AS A RESPECTABLE, GOD FEARING MAN!!
I'M GOING TO PRAY YOU PURGE THE GUTS... AND RETURN AS A VESSEL OF HIM.
I'M EVER INDEBTED TO YOU, SIR.
THANK YOU, JUDGE.
NOW WHAT DO YOU SAY WE LIGHTEN THE MOOD AND PLAY SOME CARDS? GOT TO CATCH A BOAT TOMORROW, SO DON'T BE TOO HARD ON ME!
YOUR DEAL.
JESUS WANTS ME FOR A SUN BEAM TO SHINE FOR HIM EACH DAY...
IN EVERY WAY TRY TO PLEASE HIM, AT HOME AT SCHOOL AT PLAY...
A SUNBEAM, A SUNBEAM, JESUS WANTS ME FOR A SUNBEAM, A SUNBEAM, A SUNBEAM, I'LL BE A SUNBEAM FOR HIM!

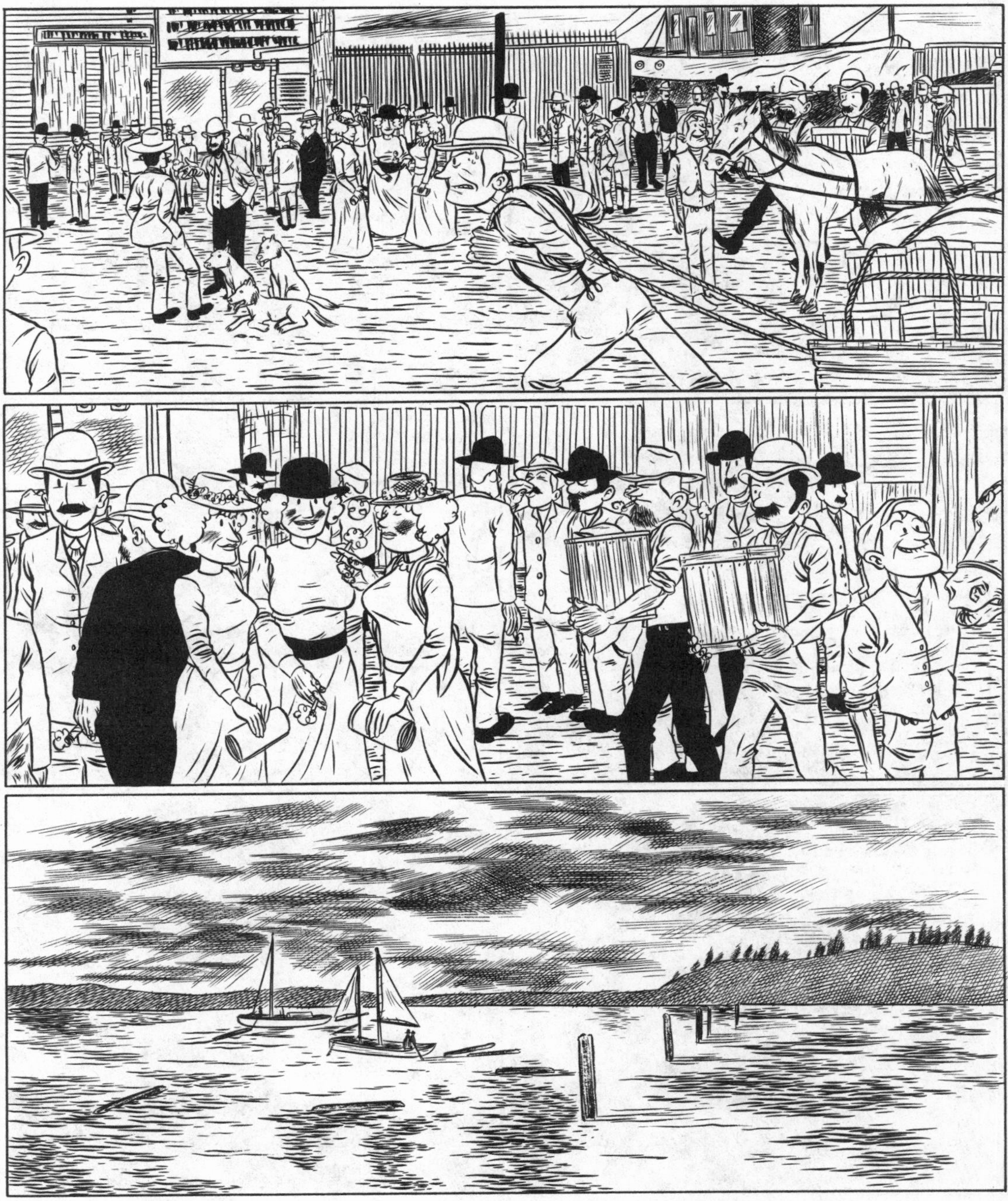

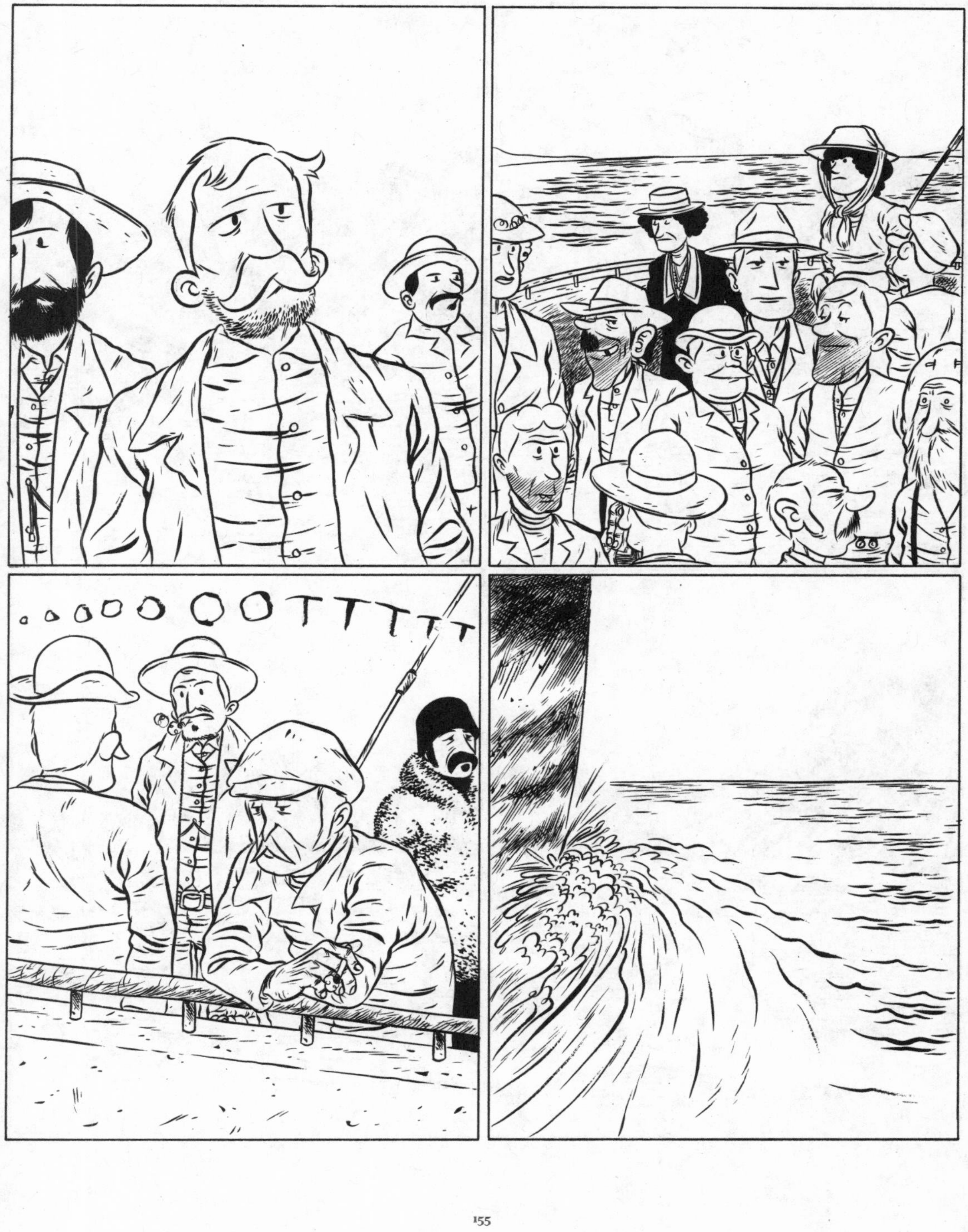
ooooooOOTTTTTT

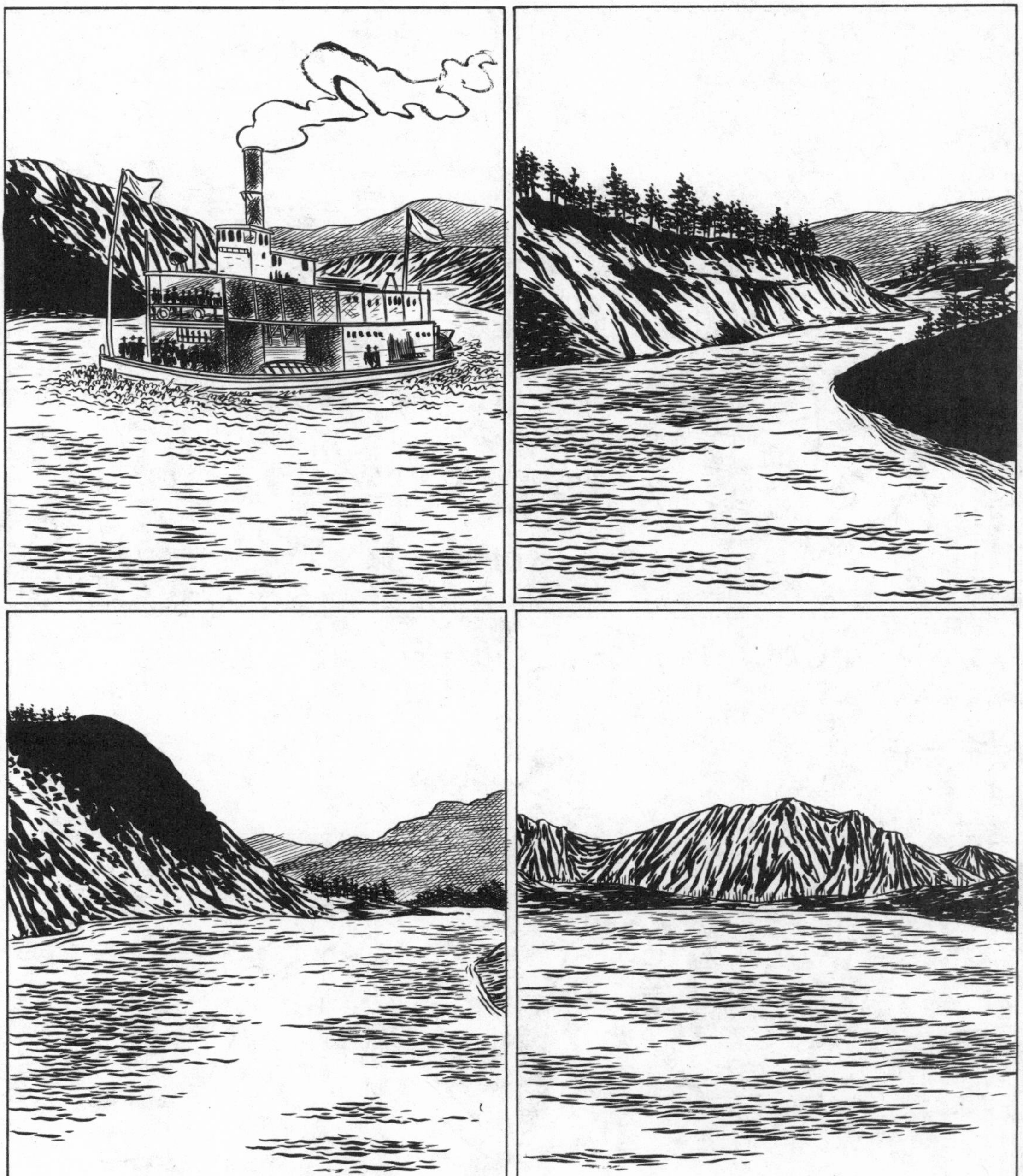

THERE WERE MANY JAPANESE MEN WORKING AS STEVEDORES DURING THE GOLD RUSH. SADLY, BUT NOT SURPRISINGLY, THEY WERE CONSIDERED TO BE SUBHUMAN BY MANY, AND THE PEOPLE THAT EMPLOYED THEM WERE NO EXCEPTION. WHEN NOT WORKING, THEY WERE KEPT CONFINED TO THEIR QUARTERS AND EVEN DURING MEALTIME THEY WERE KEPT SEPARATE FROM THE WHITES. THE JAPANESE WERE NOT TREATED ANY BETTER IN THE MINING CAMPS. COMPLAINTS OF CRIMES COMMITTED AGAINST THEM FELL ON DEAF EARS AND EVEN THOUGH THE LAWS WERE TIGHTER IN CANADA, ABUSE AND MISTREATMENT STILL RAN RAMPANT.

FRANK REID WAS DEALING WITH PROBLEMS OF HIS OWN IN SKAGWAY. REID WAS ONE OF THE FIRST TO ARRIVE IN SKAGWAY AND IMMEDIATELY TOOK ON THE POSITION OF TOWN SURVEYOR. HIS BACKGROUND AS A CONSTRUCTION ENGINEER MADE HIM PERFECT FOR THE JOB AND HE TOOK IT VERY SERIOUSLY. THE NEW INTEREST IN SKAGWAY BY GOVERNMENT OFFICIALS, HOWEVER, DID NOT SIT WELL WITH MANY LOCALS, INCLUDING CAPTAIN WILLIAM MOORE, WHO HAD BUILT A CABIN AND HAD BEEN LIVING IN SKAGWAY FOR NEARLY TEN YEARS -- LONG BEFORE REID OR THE GOVERNMENT OFFICIALS ARRIVED. THE THREAT OF LAW COMING TO CAMP CAUSED MEMBERS OF THE COMMUNITY TO ACT VIOLENTLY AGAINST REID.

SIMILAR TO REID, JOHN J. HEALY WAS A TOUGH, OLD-TIME FRONTIERSMAN WHOM IT WAS BEST NOT TO CROSS. HE FOUGHT AGAINST MINERS' MEETINGS AND WAS IN SUPPORT OF THE GOVERNMENT'S INVOLVEMENT IN KEEPING A BY-THE-BOOK STANCE ON LAW AND ORDER. HEALY WAS GENERAL MANAGER OF THE NORTH AMERICAN TRADING AND TRANSPORTATION COMPANY (N.A.T.) AND HATED TO BE SECOND GUESSED. EVEN THE PRESIDENT OF THE COMPANY, ELY WEARE, FELT THE STING OF HEALY'S WRATH WHEN HE WENT AGAINST HIS DEMANDS.

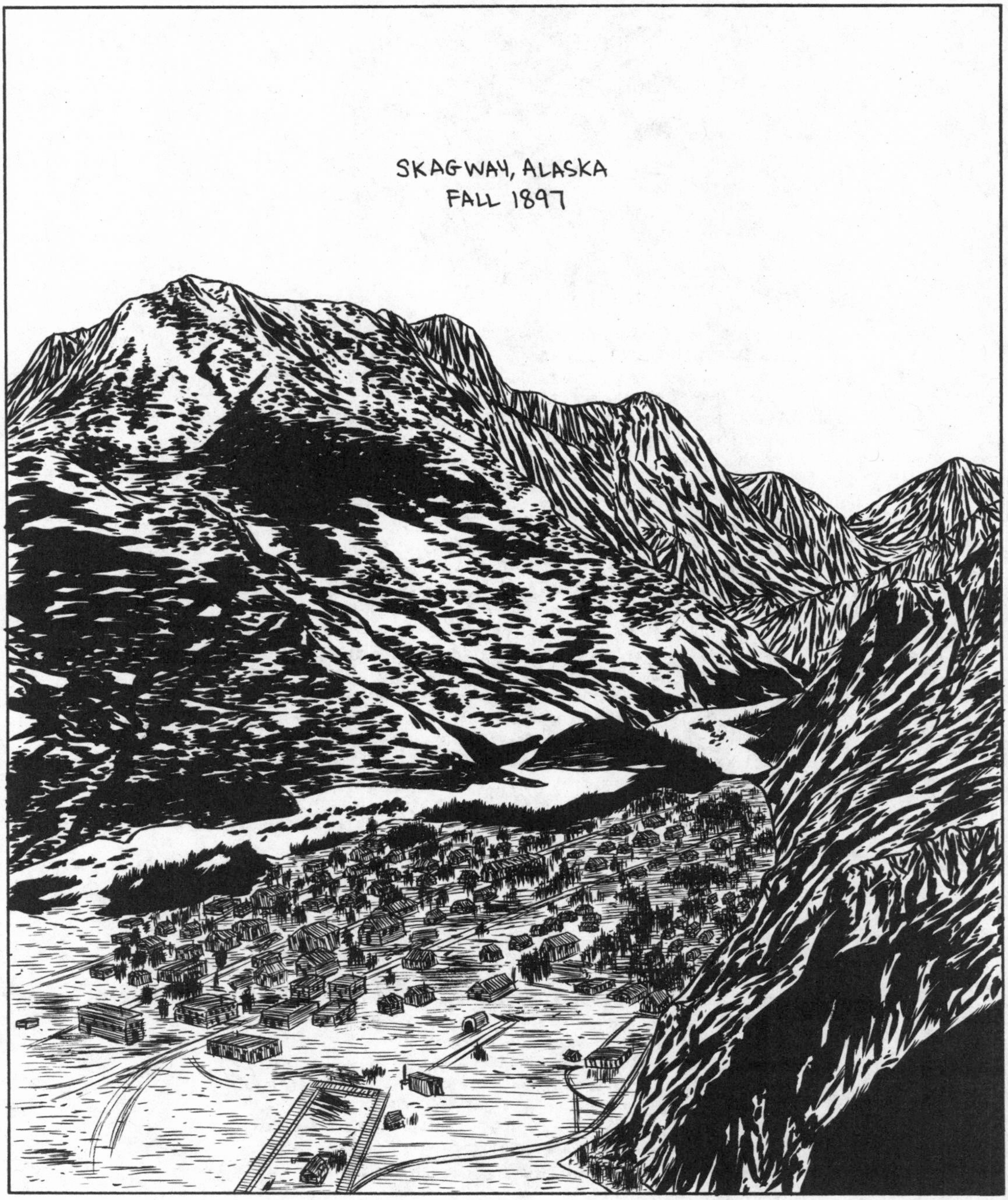
SKAGWAY, ALASKA
FALL 1897

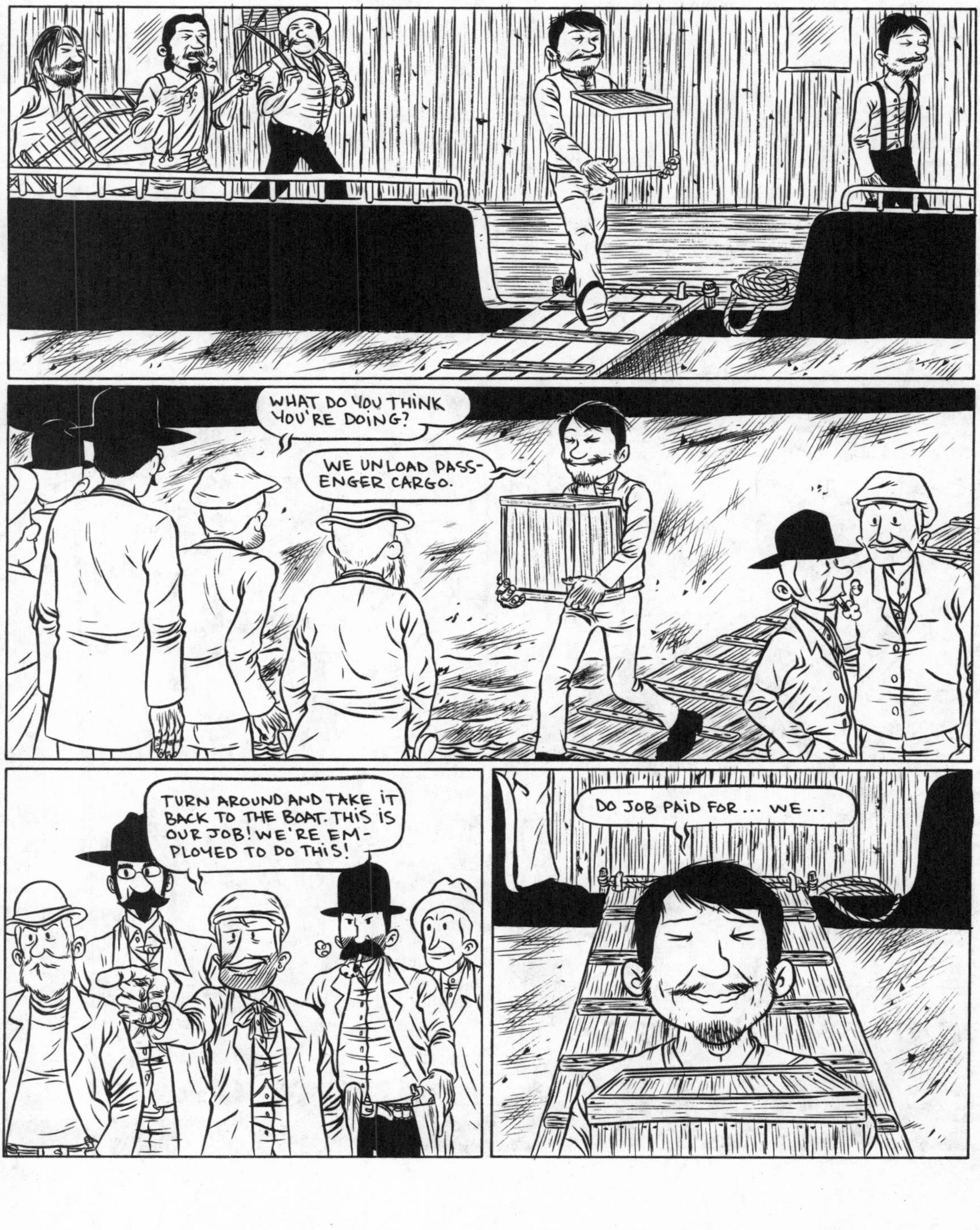
WHAT DO YOU THINK YOU'RE DOING?
WE UNLOAD PASSENGER CARGO.
TURN AROUND AND TAKE IT BACK TO THE BOAT. THIS IS OUR JOB! WE'RE EMPLOYED TO DO THIS!
DO JOB PAID FOR... WE...

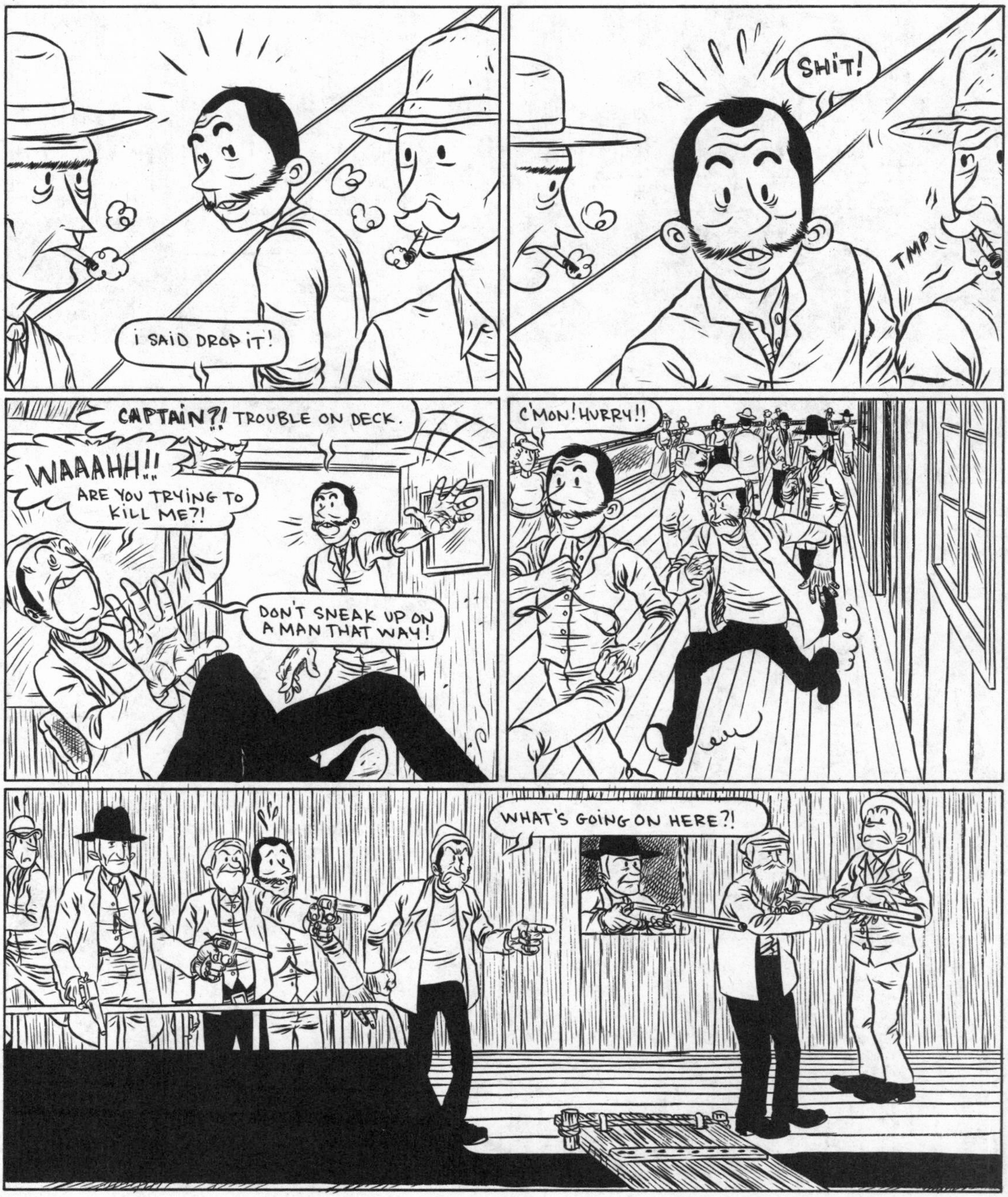
I SAID DROP IT!
SHIT!
TMP
CAPTAIN?! TROUBLE ON DECK.
WAAAHH!!
ARE YOU TRYING TO KILL ME?!
DON'T SNEAK UP ON A MAN THAT WAY!
C'MON! HURRY!!
WHAT'S GOING ON HERE?!

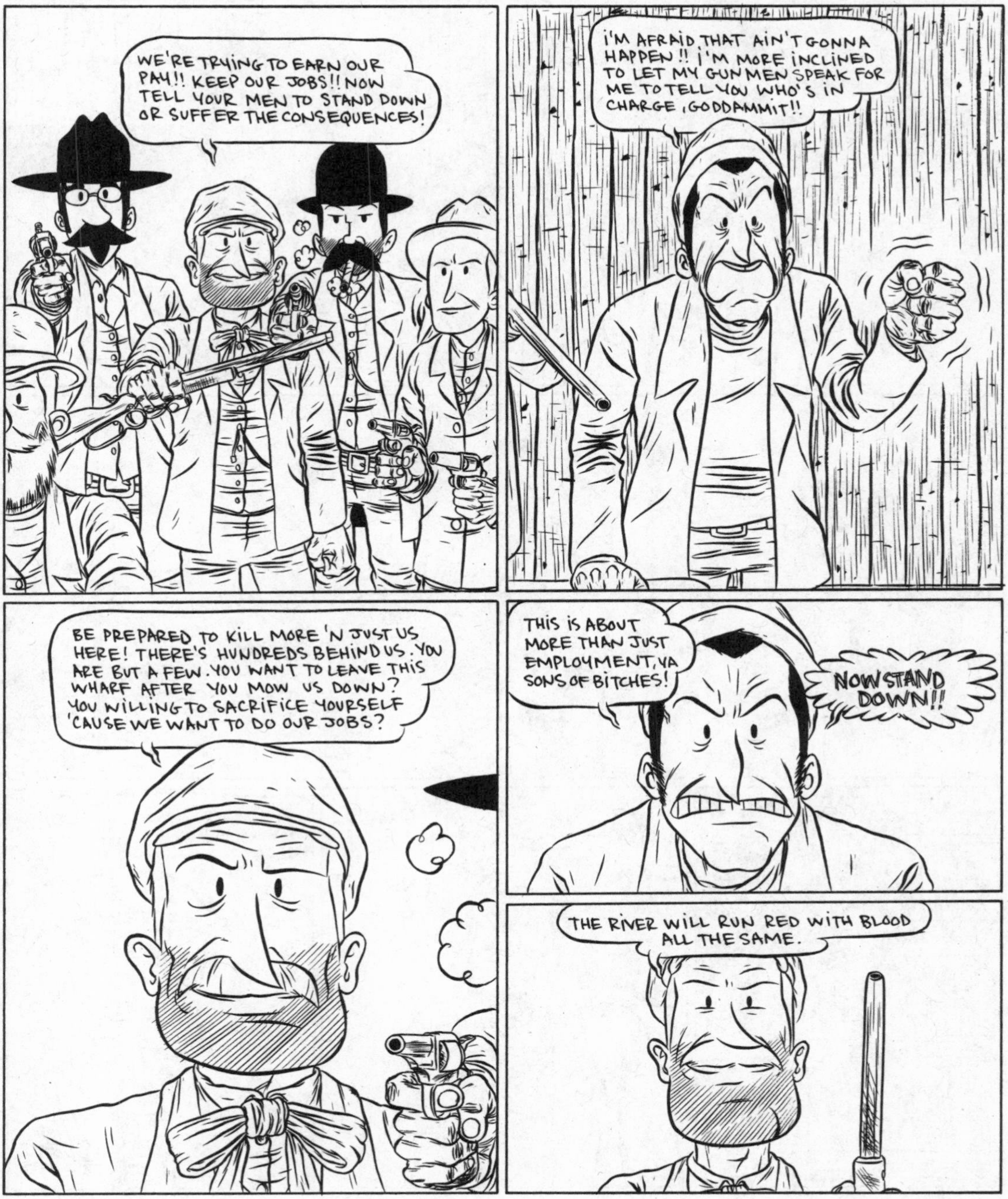
WE'RE TRYING TO EARN OUR PAY!! KEEP OUR JOBS!! NOW TELL YOUR MEN TO STAND DOWN OR SUFFER THE CONSEQUENCES!
I'M AFRAID THAT AIN'T GONNA HAPPEN!! I'M MORE INCLINED TO LET MY GUNMEN SPEAK FOR ME TO TELL YOU WHO'S IN CHARGE, GODDAMMIT!!
BE PREPARED TO KILL MORE 'N JUST US HERE! THERE'S HUNDREDS BEHIND US. YOU ARE BUT A FEW. YOU WANT TO LEAVE THIS WHARF AFTER YOU MOW US DOWN? YOU WILLING TO SACRIFICE YOURSELF 'CAUSE WE WANT TO DO OUR JOBS?
THIS IS ABOUT MORE THAN JUST EMPLOYMENT, YA SONS OF BITCHES!
NOW STAND DOWN!!
THE RIVER WILL RUN RED WITH BLOOD ALL THE SAME.

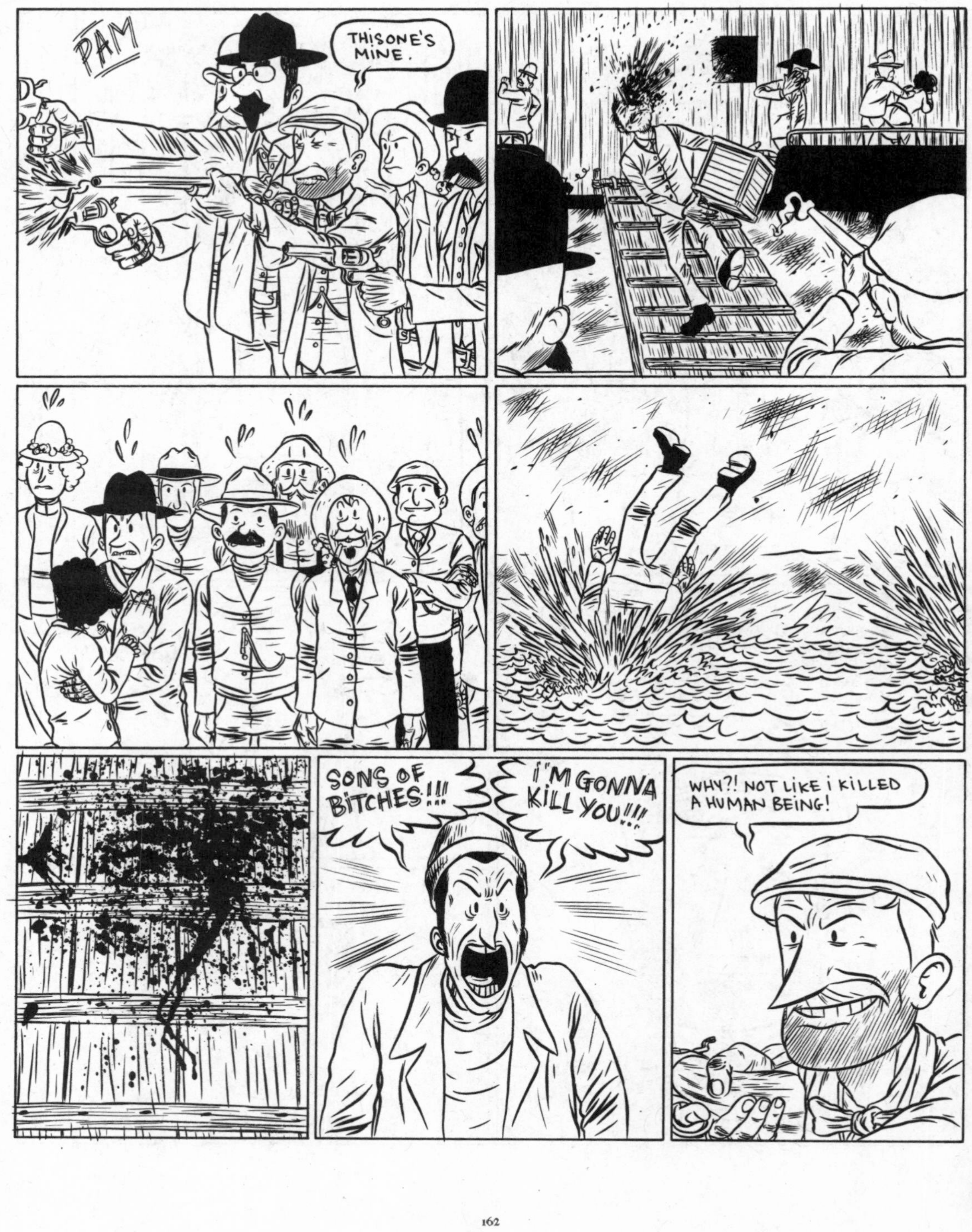
PAM
THIS ONE'S MINE.
SONS OF BITCHES!!!
I'M GONNA KILL YOU!!!
WHY?! NOT LIKE I KILLED A HUMAN BEING!

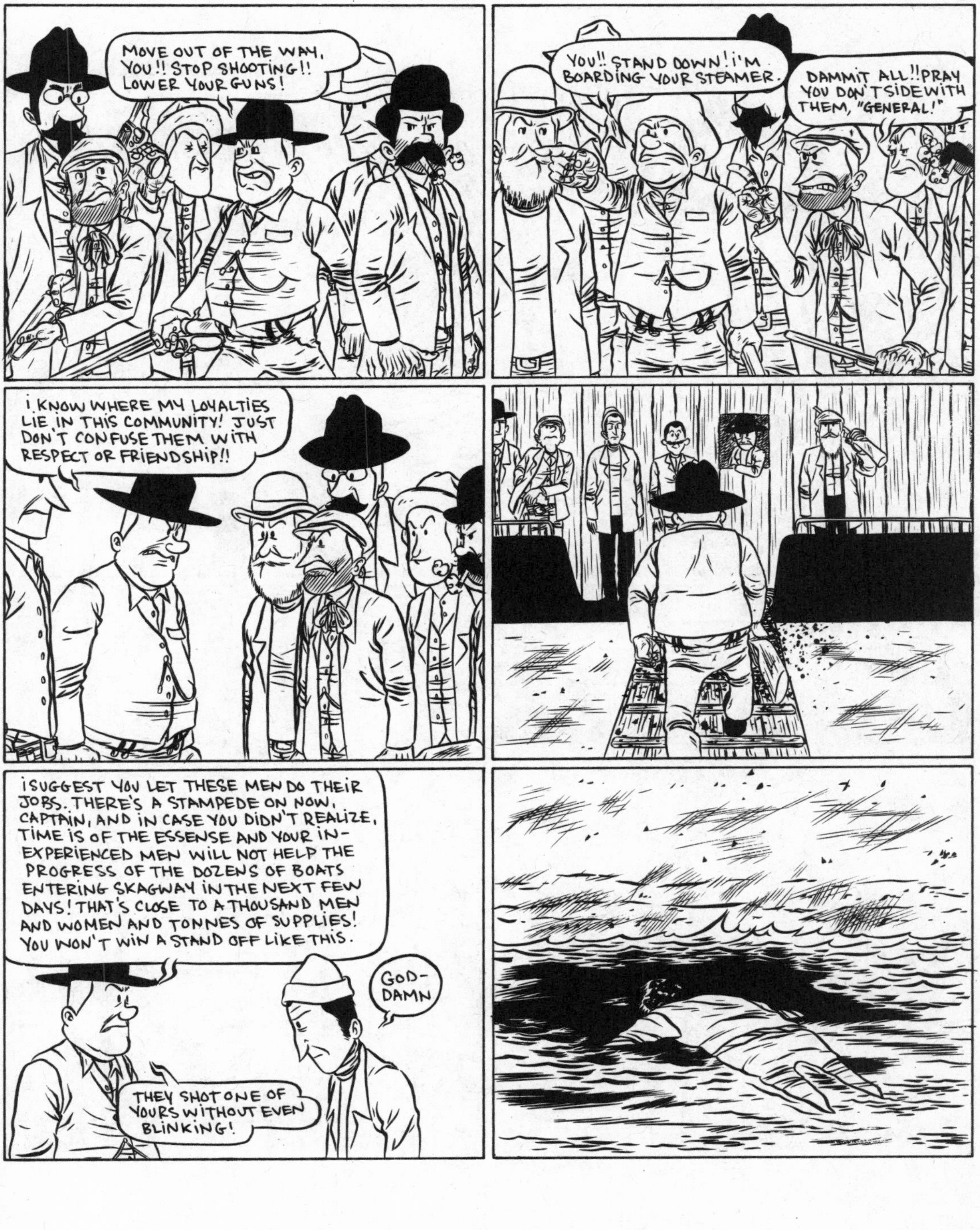
MOVE OUT OF THE WAY, YOU!! STOP SHOOTING!! LOWER YOUR GUNS!
YOU!! STAND DOWN! I'M BOARDING YOUR STEAMER.
DAMMIT ALL!! PRAY YOU DON'T SIDE WITH THEM, "GENERAL!"
I KNOW WHERE MY LOYALTIES LIE IN THIS COMMUNITY! JUST DON'T CONFUSE THEM WITH RESPECT OR FRIENDSHIP!!
I SUGGEST YOU LET THESE MEN DO THEIR JOBS. THERE'S A STAMPEDE ON NOW, CAPTAIN, AND IN CASE YOU DIDN'T REALIZE, TIME IS OF THE ESSENSE AND YOUR INEXPERIENCED MEN WILL NOT HELP THE PROGRESS OF THE DOZENS OF BOATS ENTERING SKAGWAY IN THE NEXT FEW DAYS! THAT'S CLOSE TO A THOUSAND MEN AND WOMEN AND TONNES OF SUPPLIES! YOU WON'T WIN A STAND OFF LIKE THIS.
GOD-DAMN
THEY SHOT ONE OF YOURS WITHOUT EVEN BLINKING!

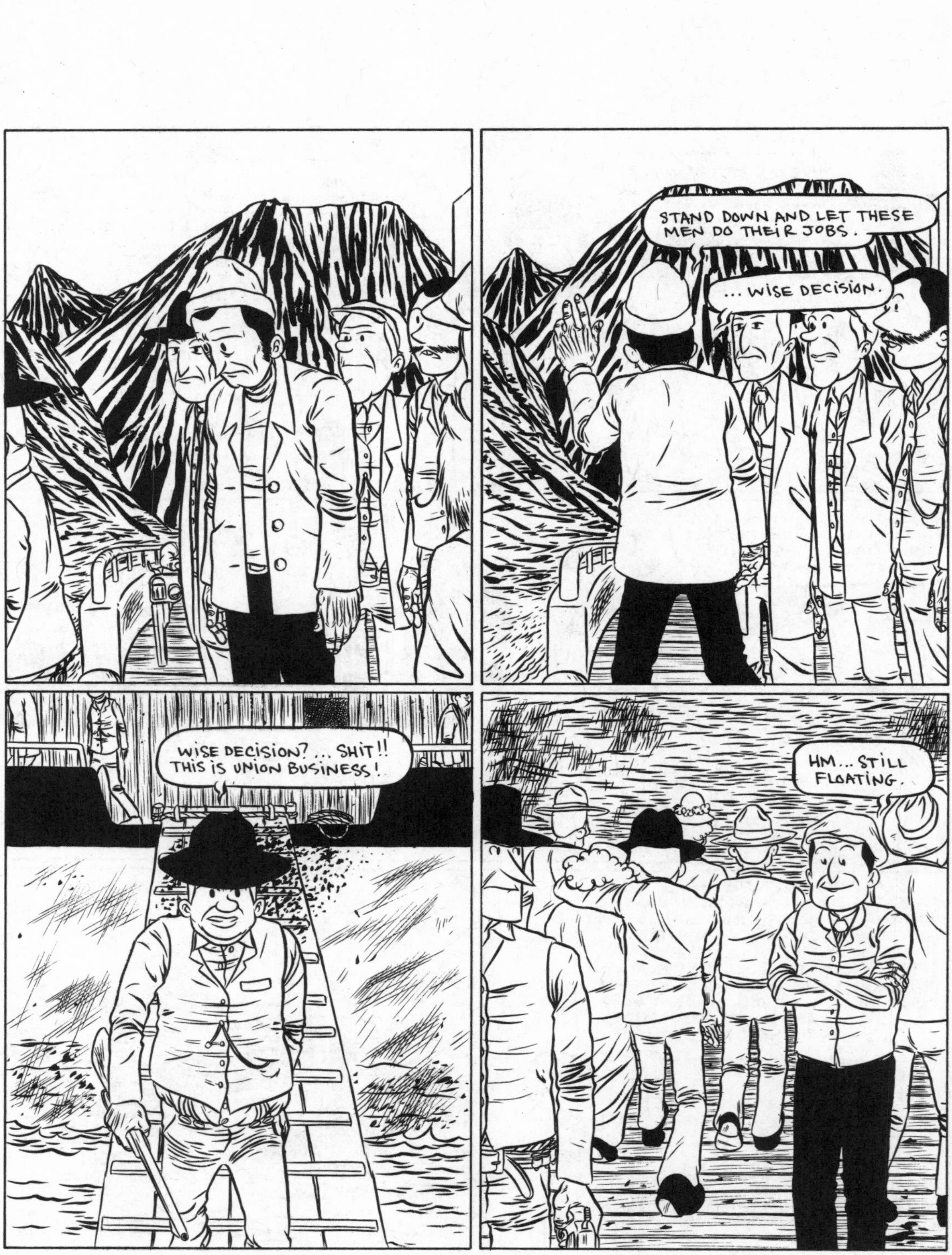
STAND DOWN AND LET THESE MEN DO THEIR JOBS.
... WISE DECISION.
WISE DECISION? ... SHIT!! THIS IS UNION BUSINESS!
HM... STILL FLOATING.

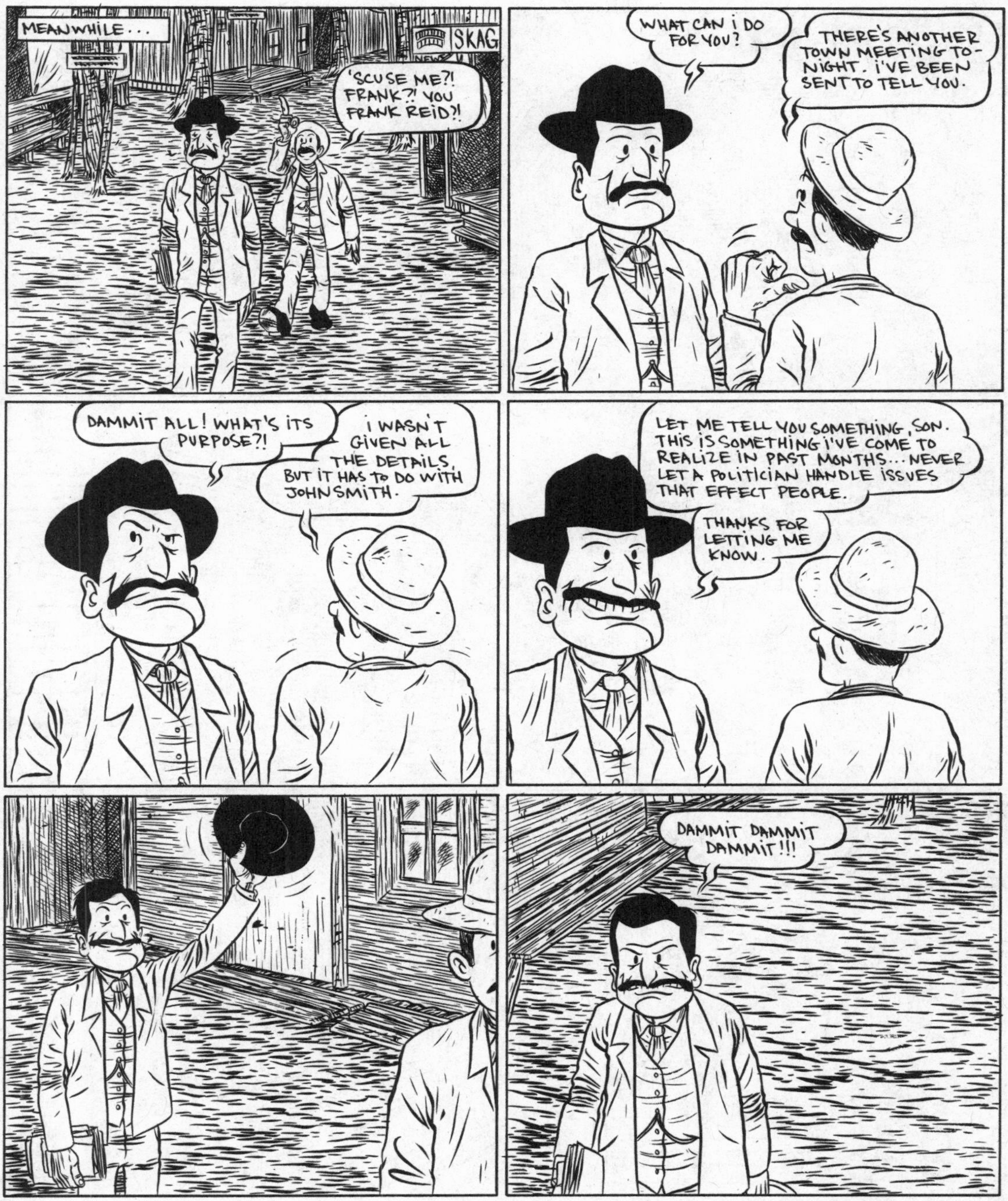
MEANWHILE...
SKAG
'SCUSE ME?! FRANK?! YOU FRANK REID?!
WHAT CAN I DO FOR YOU?
THERE'S ANOTHER TOWN MEETING TO-NIGHT. I'VE BEEN SENT TO TELL YOU.
DAMMIT ALL! WHAT'S ITS PURPOSE?!
I WASN'T GIVEN ALL THE DETAILS, BUT IT HAS TO DO WITH JOHN SMITH.
LET ME TELL YOU SOMETHING, SON. THIS IS SOMETHING I'VE COME TO REALIZE IN PAST MONTHS... NEVER LET A POLITICIAN HANDLE ISSUES THAT EFFECT PEOPLE.
THANKS FOR LETTING ME KNOW.
DAMMIT DAMMIT DAMMIT!!!

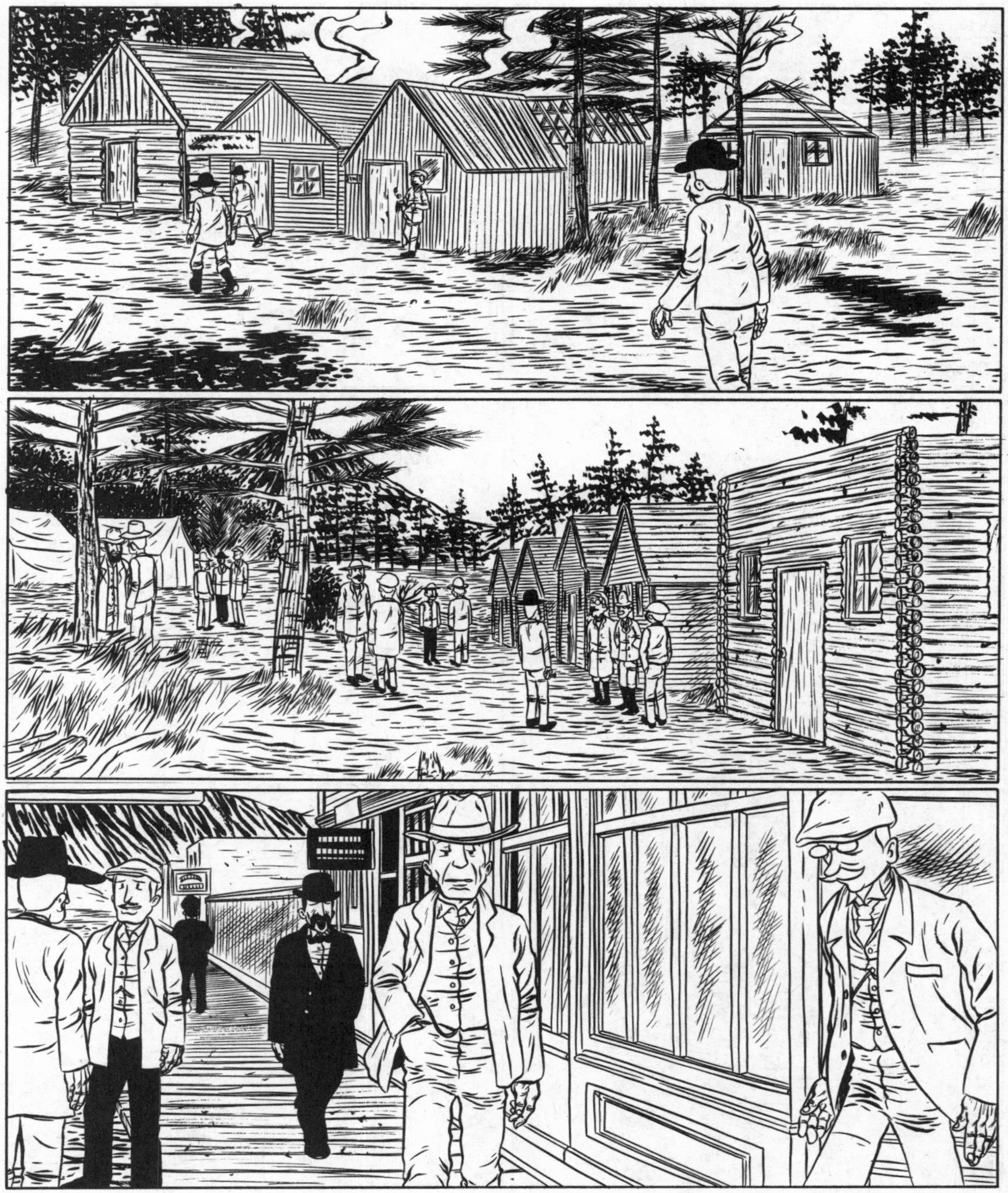

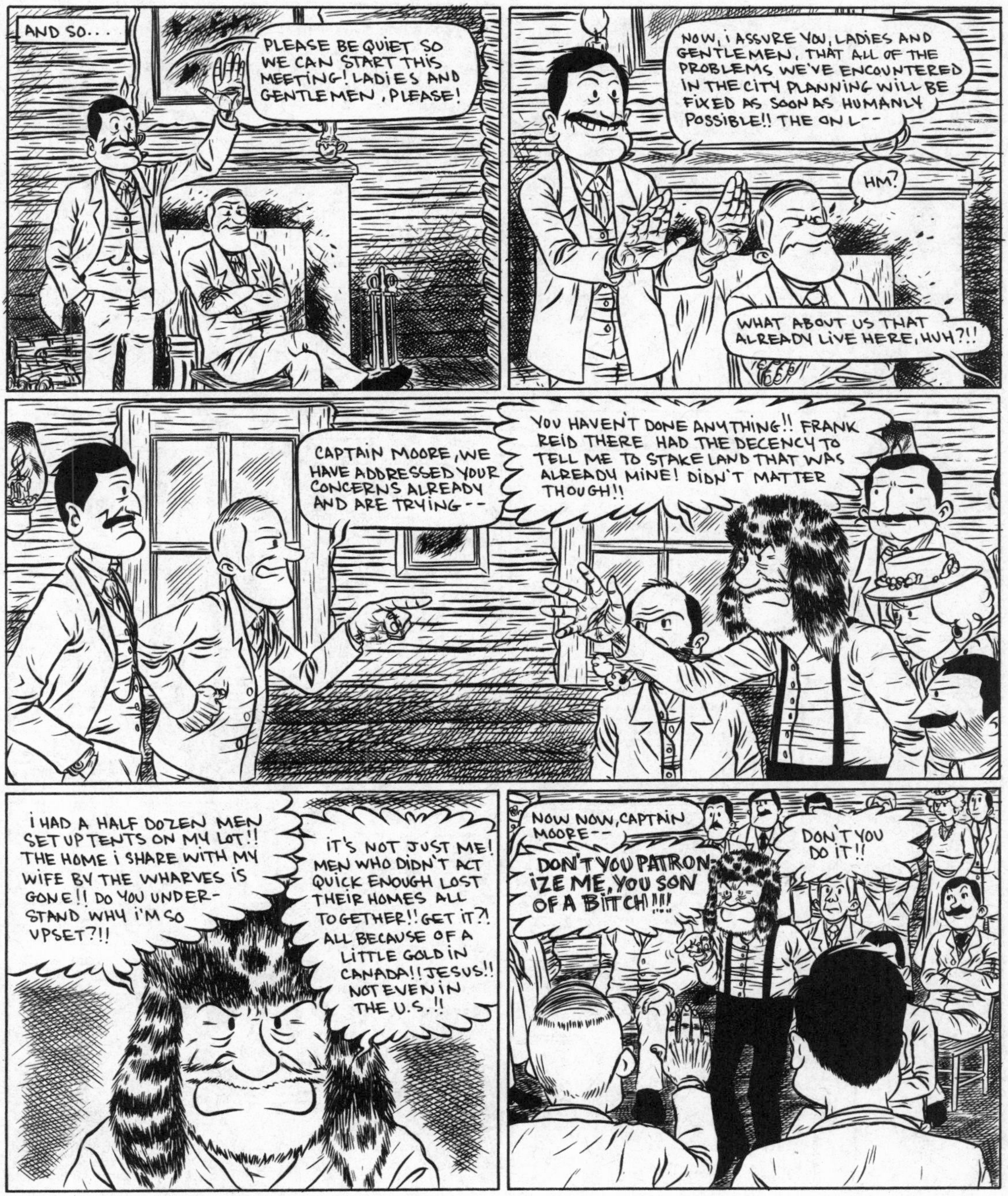
AND SO...
PLEASE BE QUIET SO WE CAN START THIS MEETING! LADIES AND GENTLEMEN, PLEASE!
NOW, I ASSURE YOU, LADIES AND GENTLEMEN, THAT ALL OF THE PROBLEMS WE'VE ENCOUNTERED IN THE CITY PLANNING WILL BE FIXED AS SOON AS HUMANLY POSSIBLE!! THE ON L--
HM?
WHAT ABOUT US THAT ALREADY LIVE HERE, HUH?!!
CAPTAIN MOORE, WE HAVE ADDRESSED YOUR CONCERNS ALREADY AND ARE TRYING--
YOU HAVEN'T DONE ANYTHING!! FRANK REID THERE HAD THE DECENCY TO TELL ME TO STAKE LAND THAT WAS ALREADY MINE! DIDN'T MATTER THOUGH!!
I HAD A HALF DOZEN MEN SET UP TENTS ON MY LOT!! THE HOME I SHARE WITH MY WIFE BY THE WHARVES IS GONE!! DO YOU UNDERSTAND WHY I'M SO UPSET?!!
IT'S NOT JUST ME! MEN WHO DIDN'T ACT QUICK ENOUGH LOST THEIR HOMES ALL TOGETHER!! GET IT?! ALL BECAUSE OF A LITTLE GOLD IN CANADA!! JESUS!! NOT EVEN IN THE U.S.!!
NOW NOW, CAPTAIN MOORE--
DON'T YOU PATRONIZE ME, YOU SON OF A BITCH!!!
DON'T YOU DO IT!!

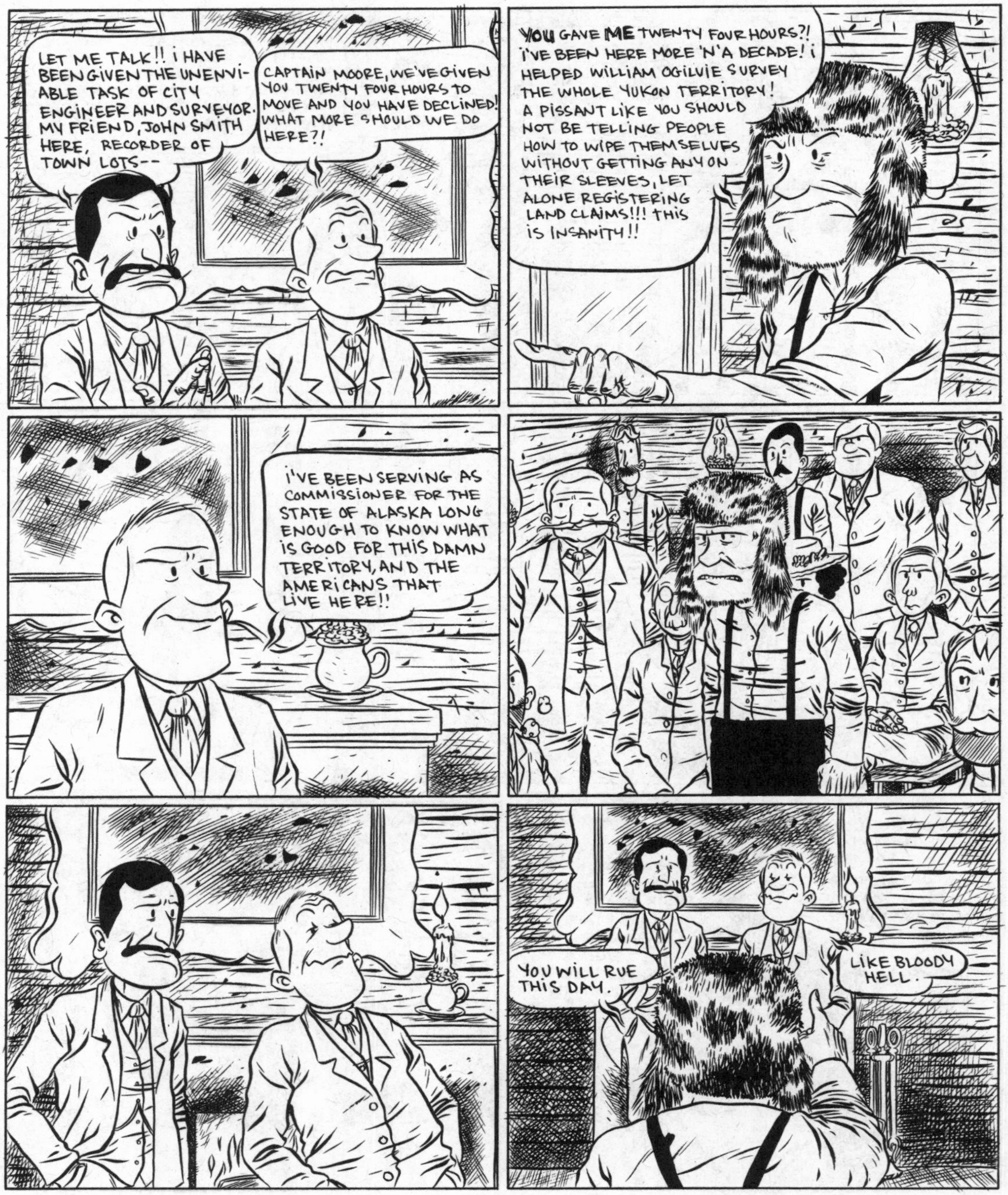
LET ME TALK!! I HAVE BEEN GIVEN THE UNENVIABLE TASK OF CITY ENGINEER AND SURVEYOR. MY FRIEND, JOHN SMITH HERE, RECORDER OF TOWN LOTS--
CAPTAIN MOORE, WE'VE GIVEN YOU TWENTY FOUR HOURS TO MOVE AND YOU HAVE DECLINED! WHAT MORE SHOULD WE DO HERE?!
YOU GAVE ME TWENTY FOUR HOURS?! I'VE BEEN HERE MORE 'N' A DECADE! I HELPED WILLIAM OGILVIE SURVEY THE WHOLE YUKON TERRITORY! A PISSANT LIKE YOU SHOULD NOT BE TELLING PEOPLE HOW TO WIPE THEMSELVES WITHOUT GETTING ANY ON THEIR SLEEVES, LET ALONE REGISTERING LAND CLAIMS!!! THIS IS INSANITY!!
I'VE BEEN SERVING AS COMMISSIONER FOR THE STATE OF ALASKA LONG ENOUGH TO KNOW WHAT IS GOOD FOR THIS DAMN TERRITORY, AND THE AMERICANS THAT LIVE HERE!!
YOU WILL RUE THIS DAY.
LIKE BLOODY HELL.

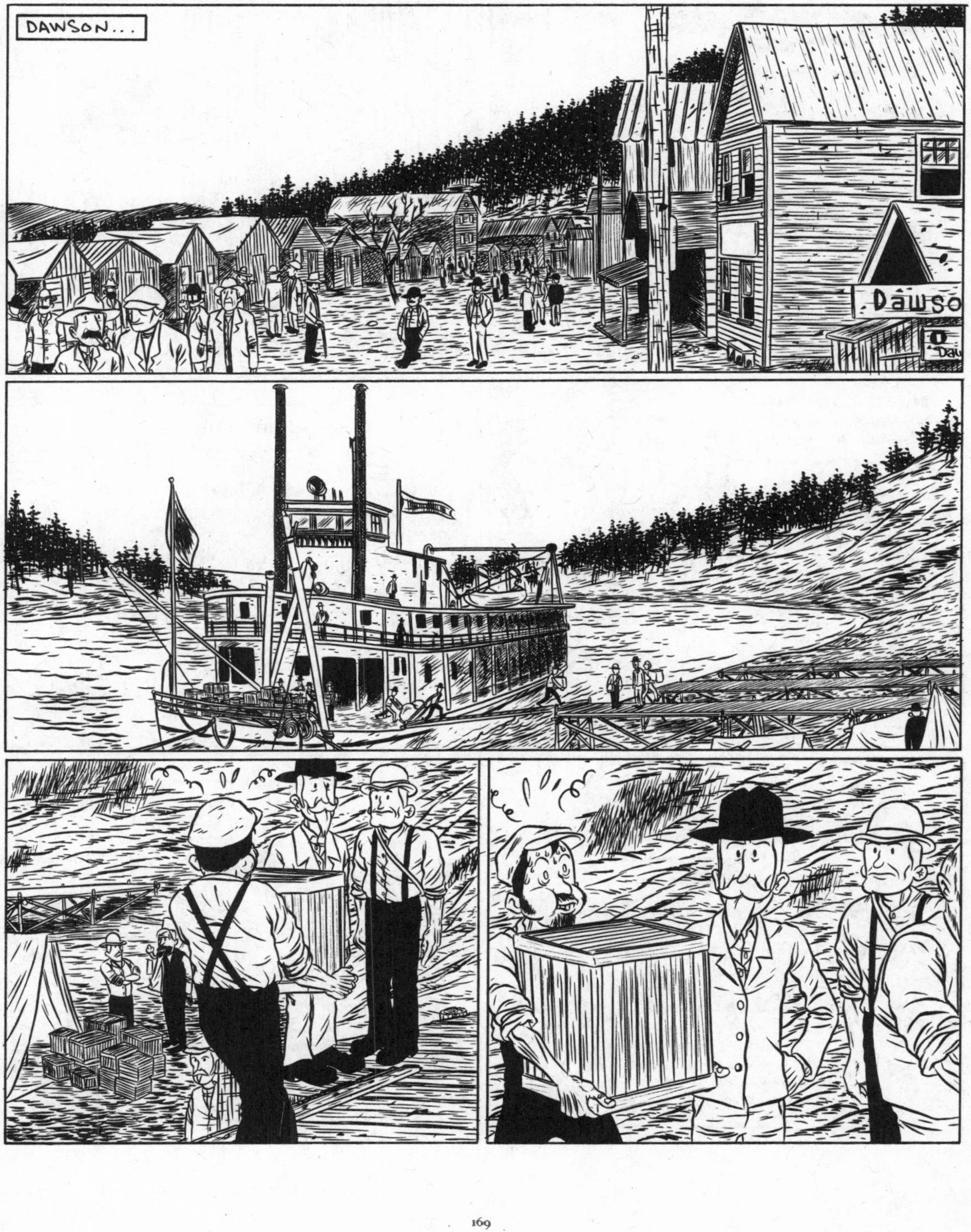
DAWSON...
Dawso
Daw

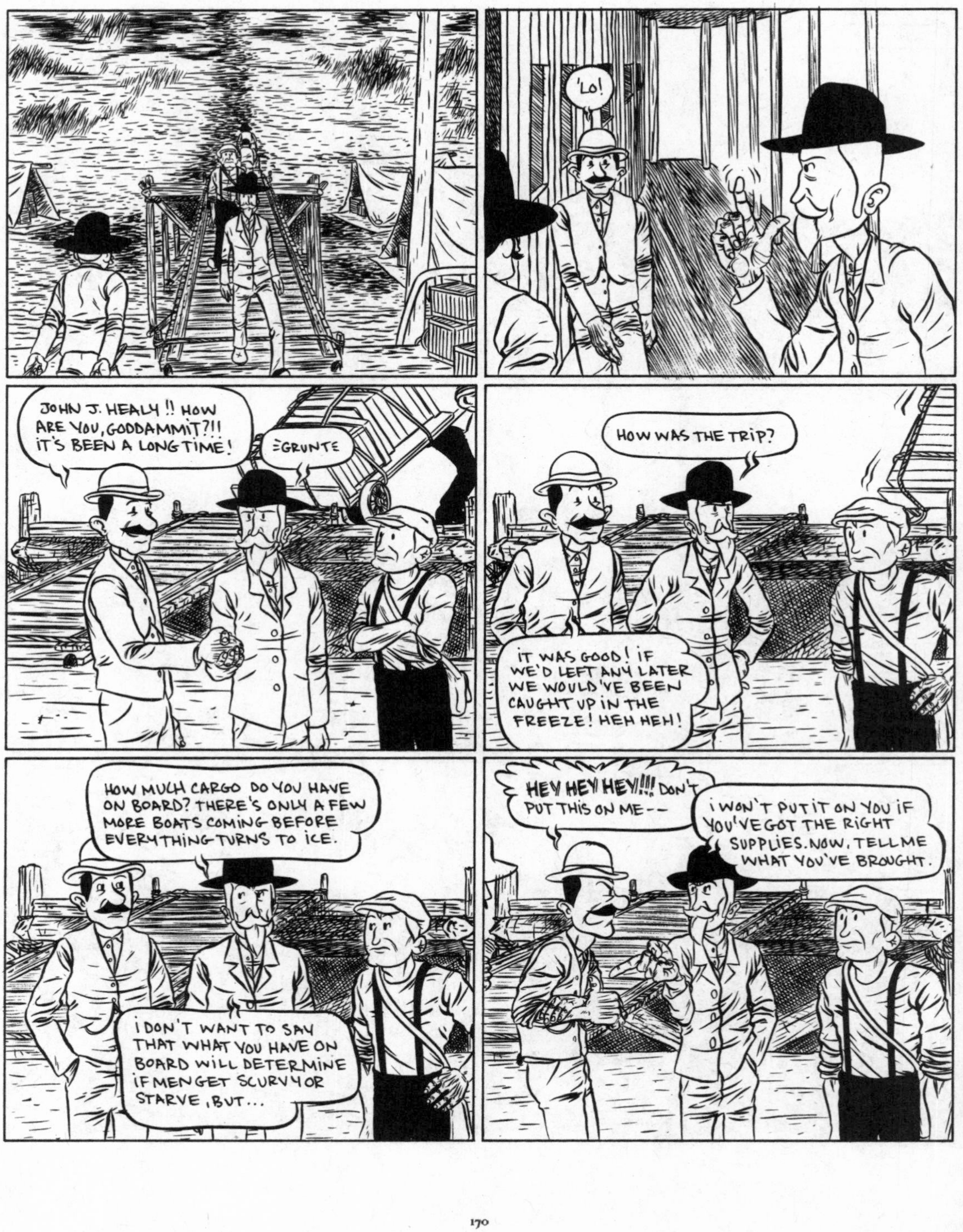

'LO!
JOHN J. HEALY!! HOW ARE YOU, GODDAMMIT?!! IT'S BEEN A LONG TIME!
GRUNT
HOW WAS THE TRIP?
IT WAS GOOD! IF WE'D LEFT ANY LATER WE WOULD'VE BEEN CAUGHT UP IN THE FREEZE! HEH HEH!
HOW MUCH CARGO DO YOU HAVE ON BOARD? THERE'S ONLY A FEW MORE BOATS COMING BEFORE EVERYTHING TURNS TO ICE.
I DON'T WANT TO SAY THAT WHAT YOU HAVE ON BOARD WILL DETERMINE IF MEN GET SCURVY OR STARVE, BUT...
HEY HEY HEY!!! DON'T PUT THIS ON ME--
I WON'T PUT IT ON YOU IF YOU'VE GOT THE RIGHT SUPPLIES. NOW, TELL ME WHAT YOU'VE BROUGHT.

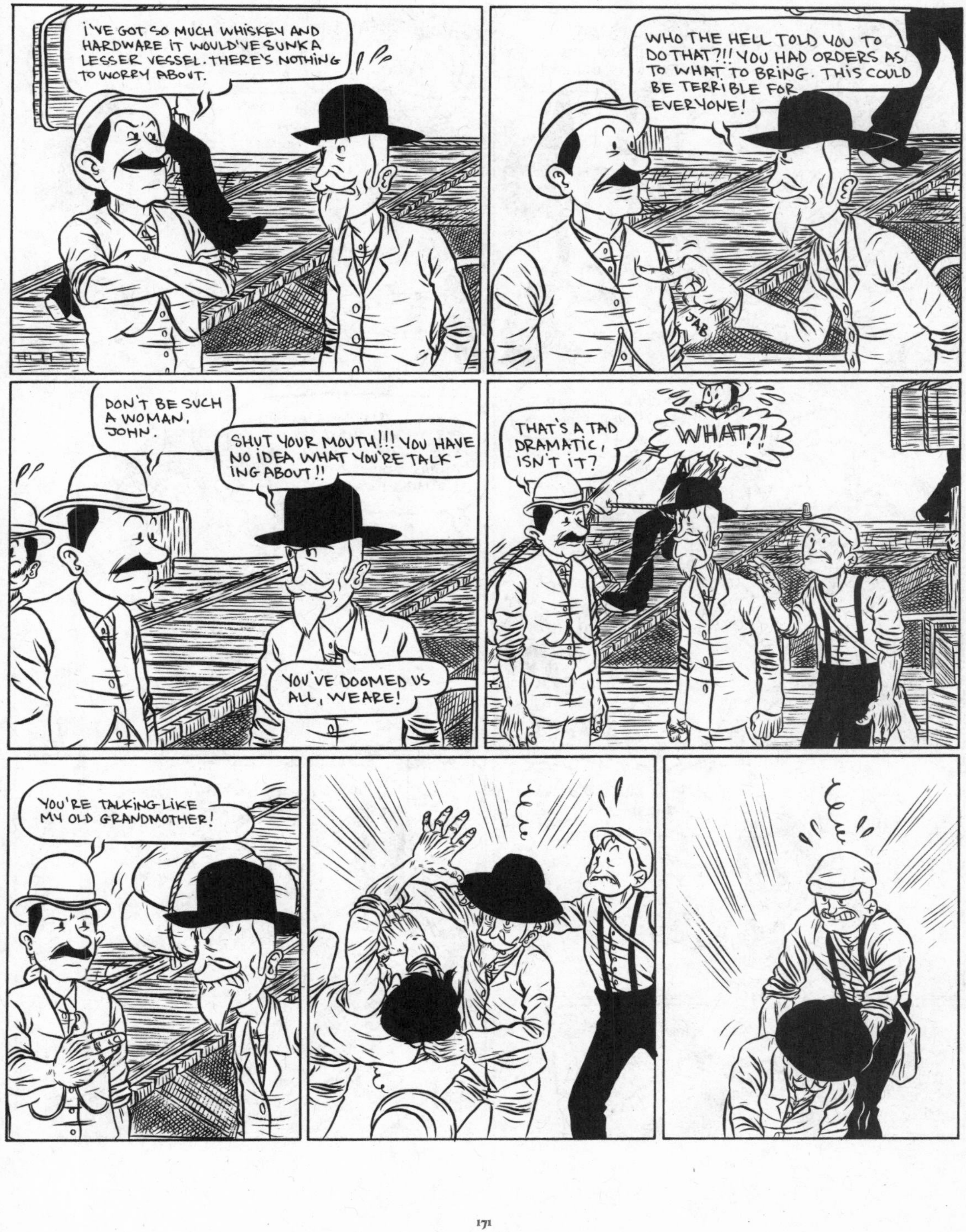
I'VE GOT SO MUCH WHISKEY AND HARDWARE IT WOULD'VE SUNK A LESSER VESSEL. THERE'S NOTHING TO WORRY ABOUT.
WHO THE HELL TOLD YOU TO DO THAT?!! YOU HAD ORDERS AS TO WHAT TO BRING. THIS COULD BE TERRIBLE FOR EVERYONE!
JAB
DON'T BE SUCH A WOMAN, JOHN.
SHUT YOUR MOUTH!!! YOU HAVE NO IDEA WHAT YOU'RE TALKING ABOUT!!
YOU'VE DOOMED US ALL, WE ARE!
THAT'S A TAD DRAMATIC, ISN'T IT?
WHAT?!
YOU'RE TALKING LIKE MY OLD GRANDMOTHER!

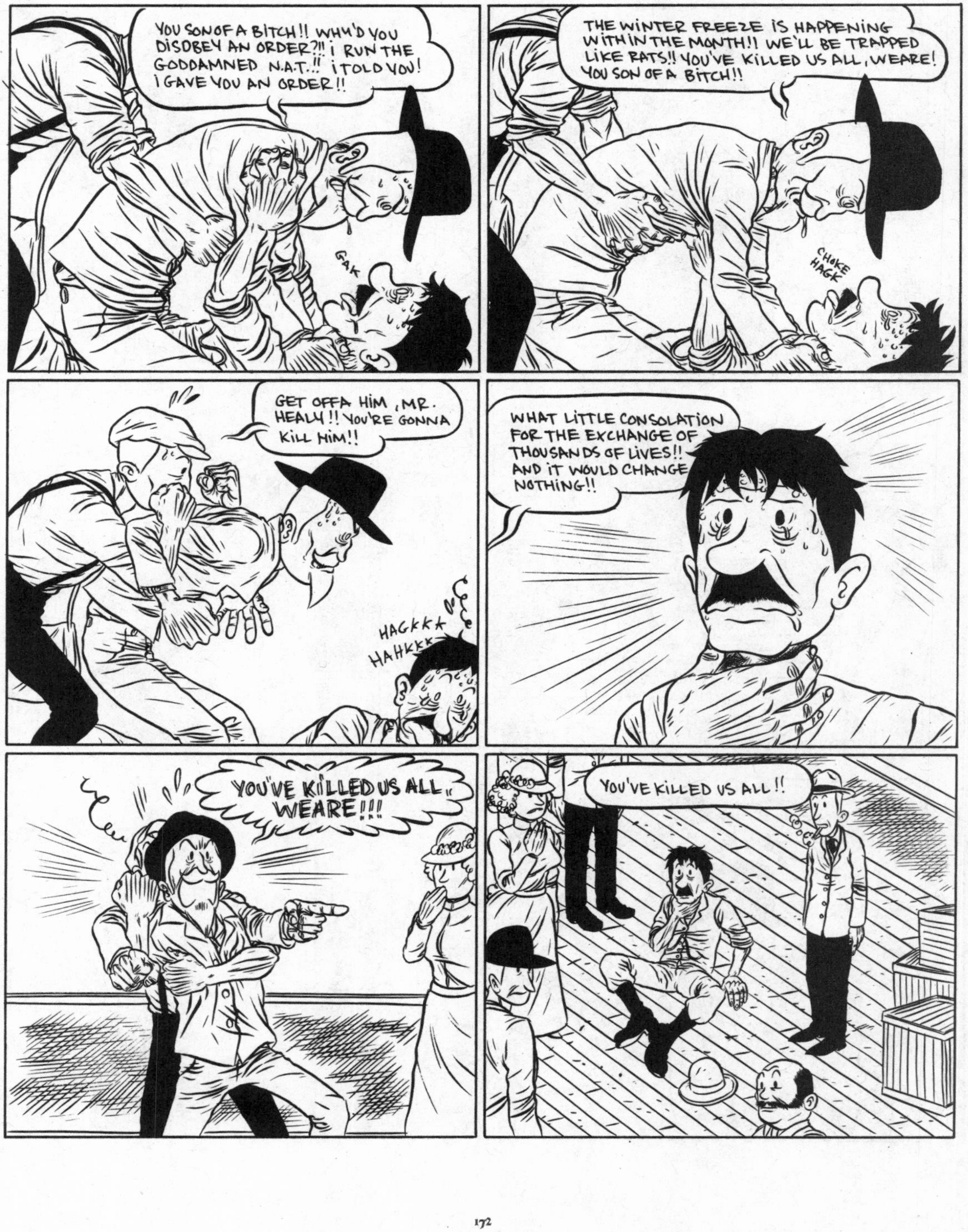
YOU SON OF A BITCH!! WHY'D YOU DISOBEY AN ORDER?!! I RUN THE GODDAMNED N.A.T.!! I TOLD YOU! I GAVE YOU AN ORDER!!
GAK
THE WINTER FREEZE IS HAPPENING WITHIN THE MONTH!! WE'LL BE TRAPPED LIKE RATS!! YOU'VE KILLED US ALL, WE ARE! YOU SON OF A BITCH!!
CHOKE HAGK
GET OFFA HIM, MR. HEALY!! YOU'RE GONNA KILL HIM!!
HAGKKK HAHKKK
WHAT LITTLE CONSOLATION FOR THE EXCHANGE OF THOUSANDS OF LIVES!! AND IT WOULD CHANGE NOTHING!!
YOU'VE KILLED US ALL, WE ARE!!!
YOU'VE KILLED US ALL!!

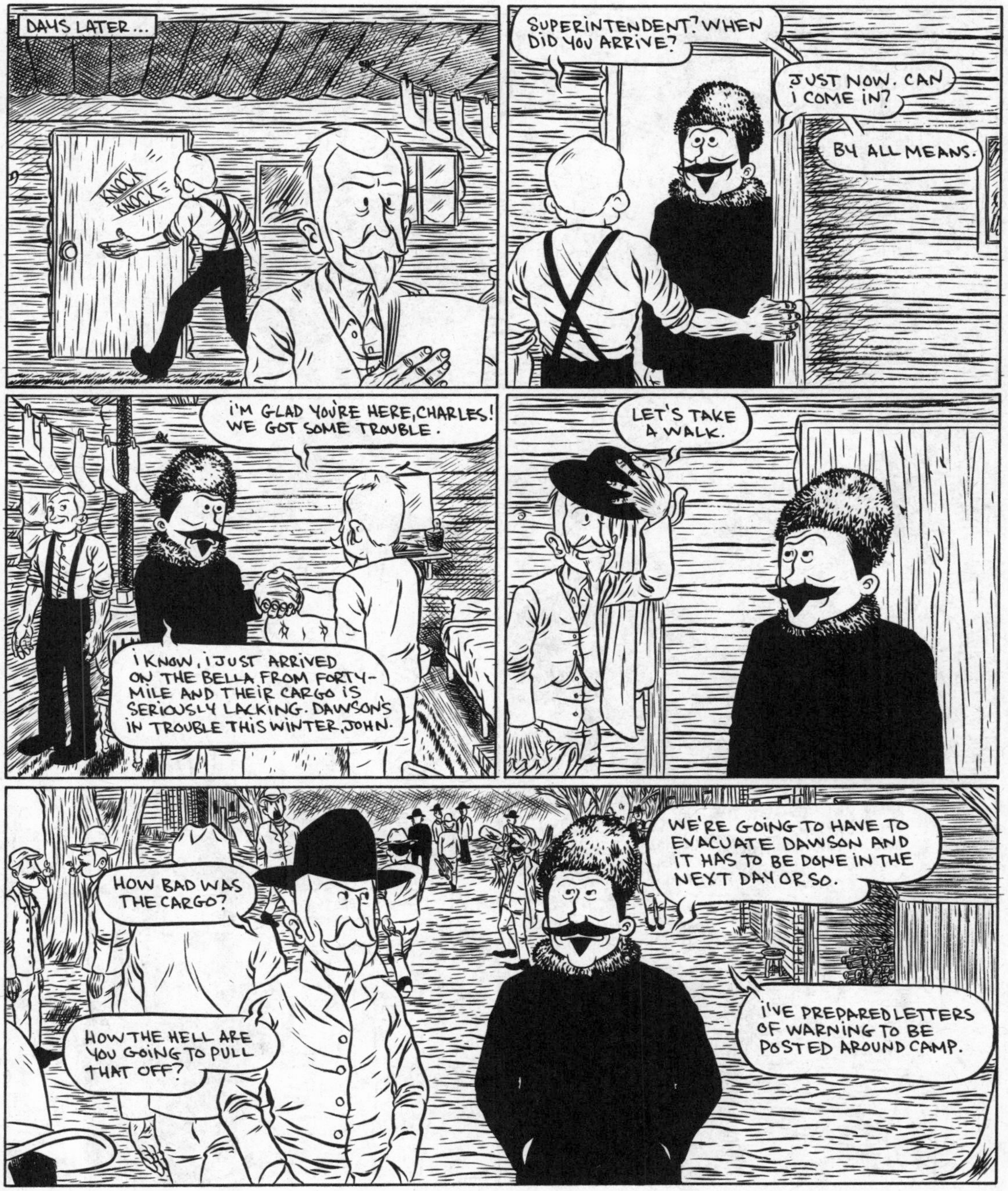
DAYS LATER...
KNOCK
KNOCK
SUPERINTENDENT? WHEN DID YOU ARRIVE?
JUST NOW. CAN I COME IN?
BY ALL MEANS.
I'M GLAD YOU'RE HERE, CHARLES! WE GOT SOME TROUBLE.
I KNOW, I JUST ARRIVED ON THE BELLA FROM FORTY-MILE AND THEIR CARGO IS SERIOUSLY LACKING. DAWSON'S IN TROUBLE THIS WINTER, JOHN.
LET'S TAKE A WALK.
HOW BAD WAS THE CARGO?
WE'RE GOING TO HAVE TO EVACUATE DAWSON AND IT HAS TO BE DONE IN THE NEXT DAY OR SO.
HOW THE HELL ARE YOU GOING TO PULL THAT OFF?
I'VE PREPARED LETTERS OF WARNING TO BE POSTED AROUND CAMP.

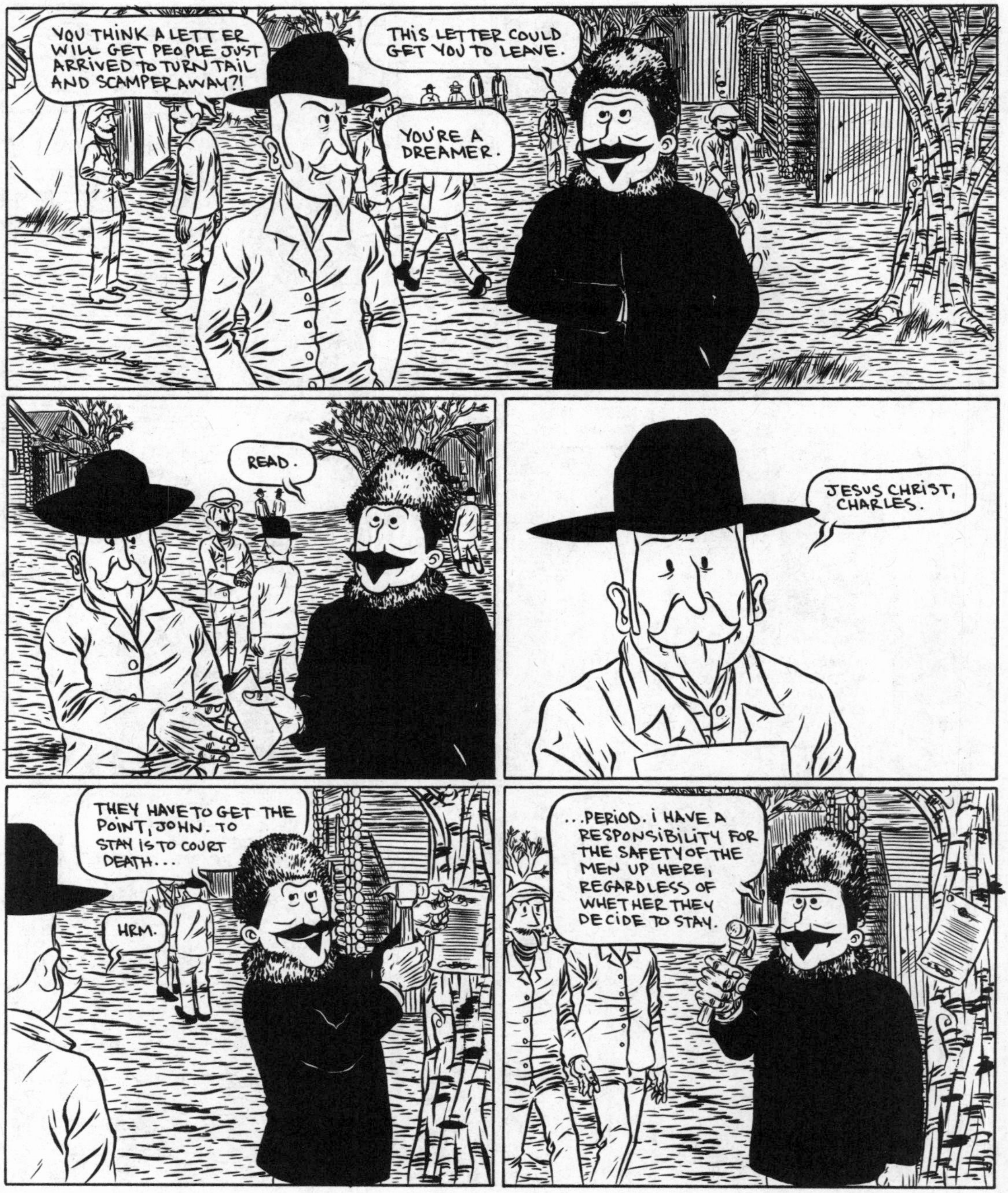

YOU THINK A LETTER WILL GET PEOPLE JUST ARRIVED TO TURN TAIL AND SCAMPER AWAY?!
THIS LETTER COULD GET YOU TO LEAVE.
YOU'RE A DREAMER.
READ.
JESUS CHRIST, CHARLES.
THEY HAVE TO GET THE POINT, JOHN. TO STAY IS TO COURT DEATH...
HRM.
...PERIOD. I HAVE A RESPONSIBILITY FOR THE SAFETY OF THE MEN UP HERE, REGARDLESS OF WHETHER THEY DECIDE TO STAY.

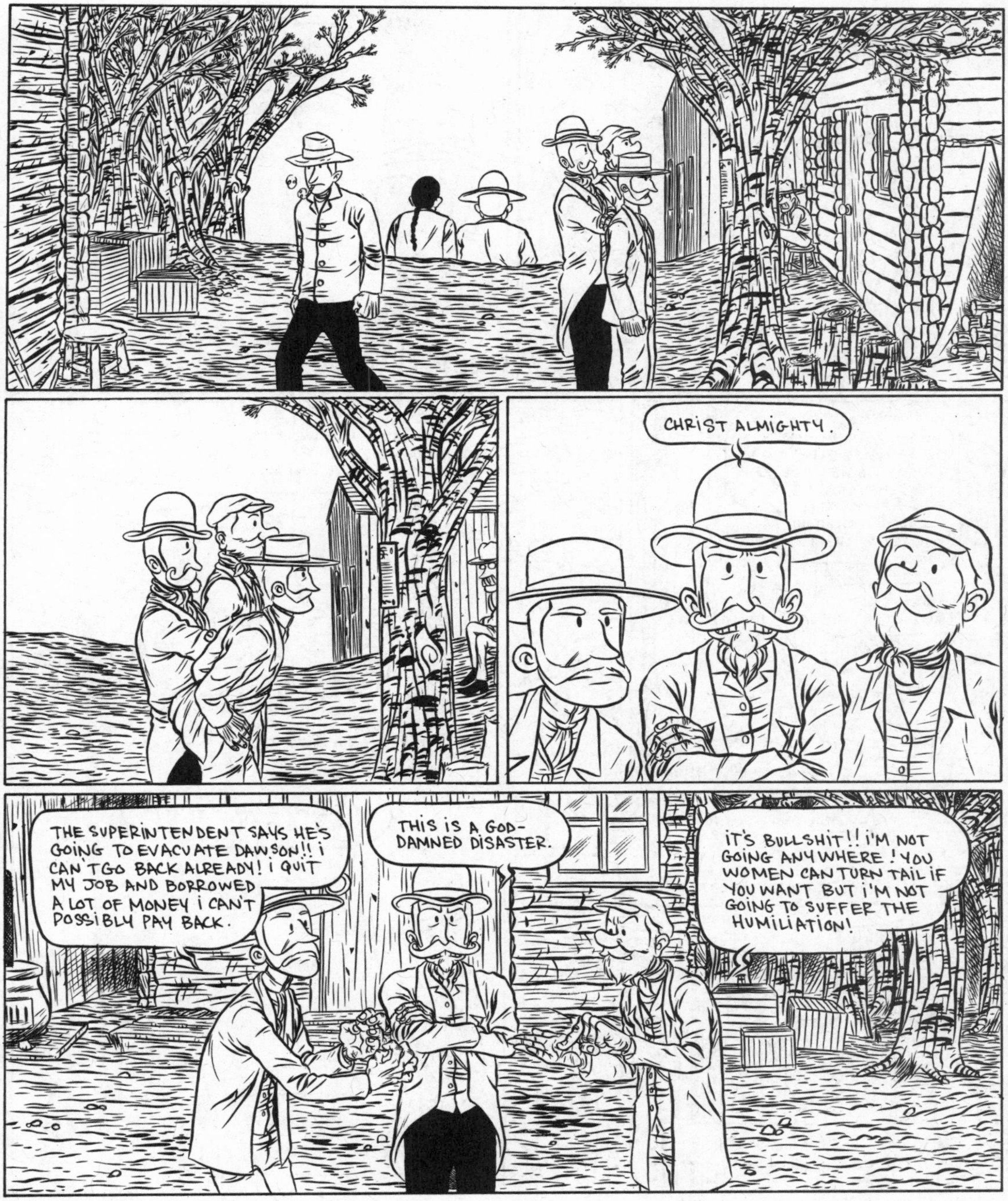
CHRIST ALMIGHTY.
THE SUPERINTENDENT SAYS HE'S GOING TO EVACUATE DAWSON!! I CAN'T GO BACK ALREADY! I QUIT MY JOB AND BORROWED A LOT OF MONEY I CAN'T POSSIBLY PAY BACK.
THIS IS A GOD-DAMNED DISASTER.
IT'S BULLSHIT!! I'M NOT GOING ANYWHERE! YOU WOMEN CAN TURN TAIL IF YOU WANT BUT I'M NOT GOING TO SUFFER THE HUMILIATION!

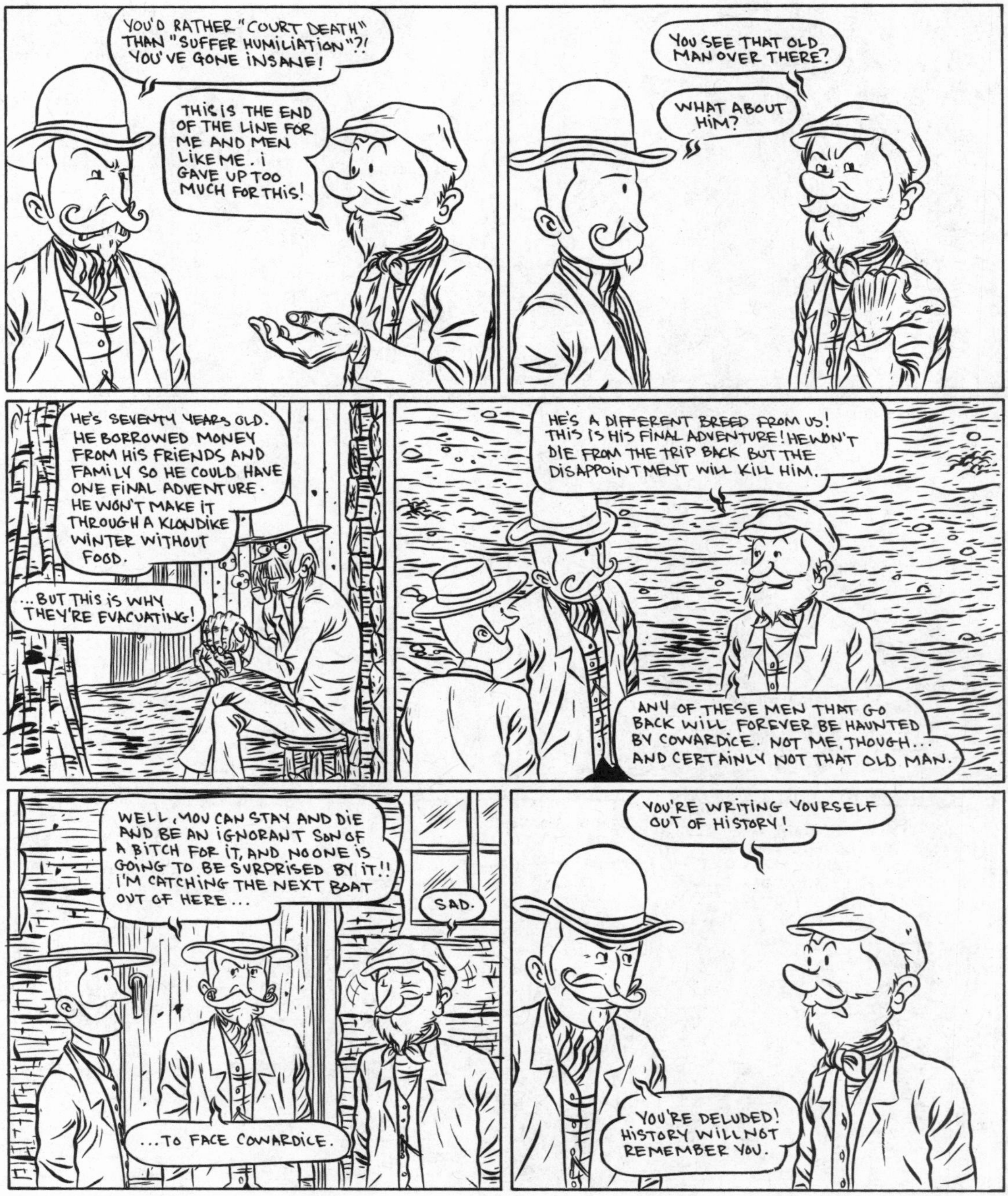
YOU'D RATHER "COURT DEATH" THAN "SUFFER HUMILIATION"?! YOU'VE GONE INSANE!
THIS IS THE END OF THE LINE FOR ME AND MEN LIKE ME. I GAVE UP TOO MUCH FOR THIS!
YOU SEE THAT OLD MAN OVER THERE?
WHAT ABOUT HIM?
HE'S SEVENTY YEARS OLD. HE BORROWED MONEY FROM HIS FRIENDS AND FAMILY SO HE COULD HAVE ONE FINAL ADVENTURE. HE WON'T MAKE IT THROUGH A KLONDIKE WINTER WITHOUT FOOD.
...BUT THIS IS WHY THEY'RE EVACUATING!
HE'S A DIFFERENT BREED FROM US! THIS IS HIS FINAL ADVENTURE! HE WON'T DIE FROM THE TRIP BACK BUT THE DISAPPOINTMENT WILL KILL HIM.
ANY OF THESE MEN THAT GO BACK WILL FOREVER BE HAUNTED BY COWARDICE. NOT ME, THOUGH... AND CERTAINLY NOT THAT OLD MAN.
WELL, YOU CAN STAY AND DIE AND BE AN IGNORANT SON OF A BITCH FOR IT, AND NO ONE IS GOING TO BE SURPRISED BY IT!! I'M CATCHING THE NEXT BOAT OUT OF HERE...
SAD.
...TO FACE COWARDICE.
YOU'RE WRITING YOURSELF OUT OF HISTORY!
YOU'RE DELUDED! HISTORY WILL NOT REMEMBER YOU.

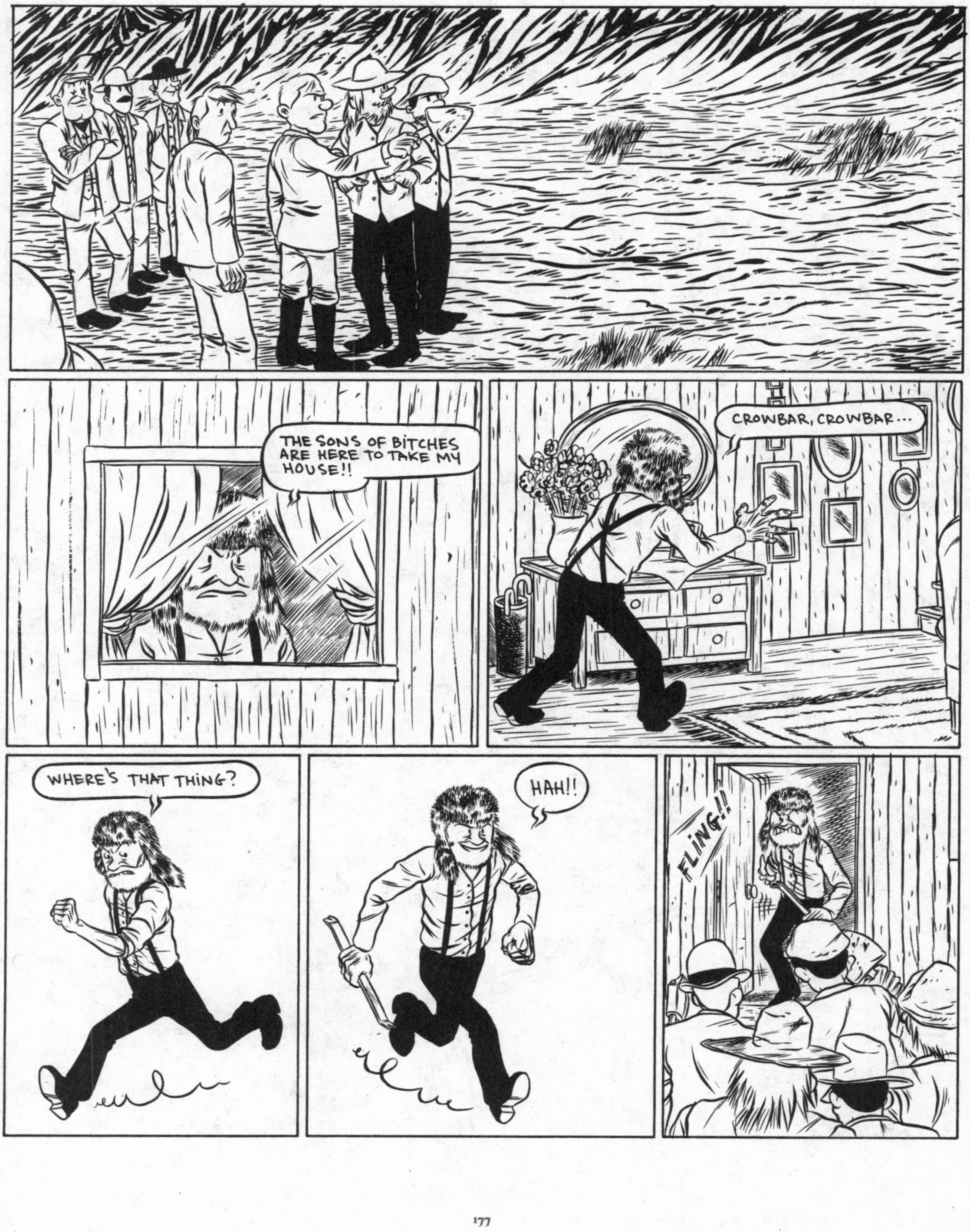
THE SONS OF BITCHES ARE HERE TO TAKE MY HOUSE!!
CROWBAR, CROWBAR...
WHERE'S THAT THING?
HAH!!
FLING!!

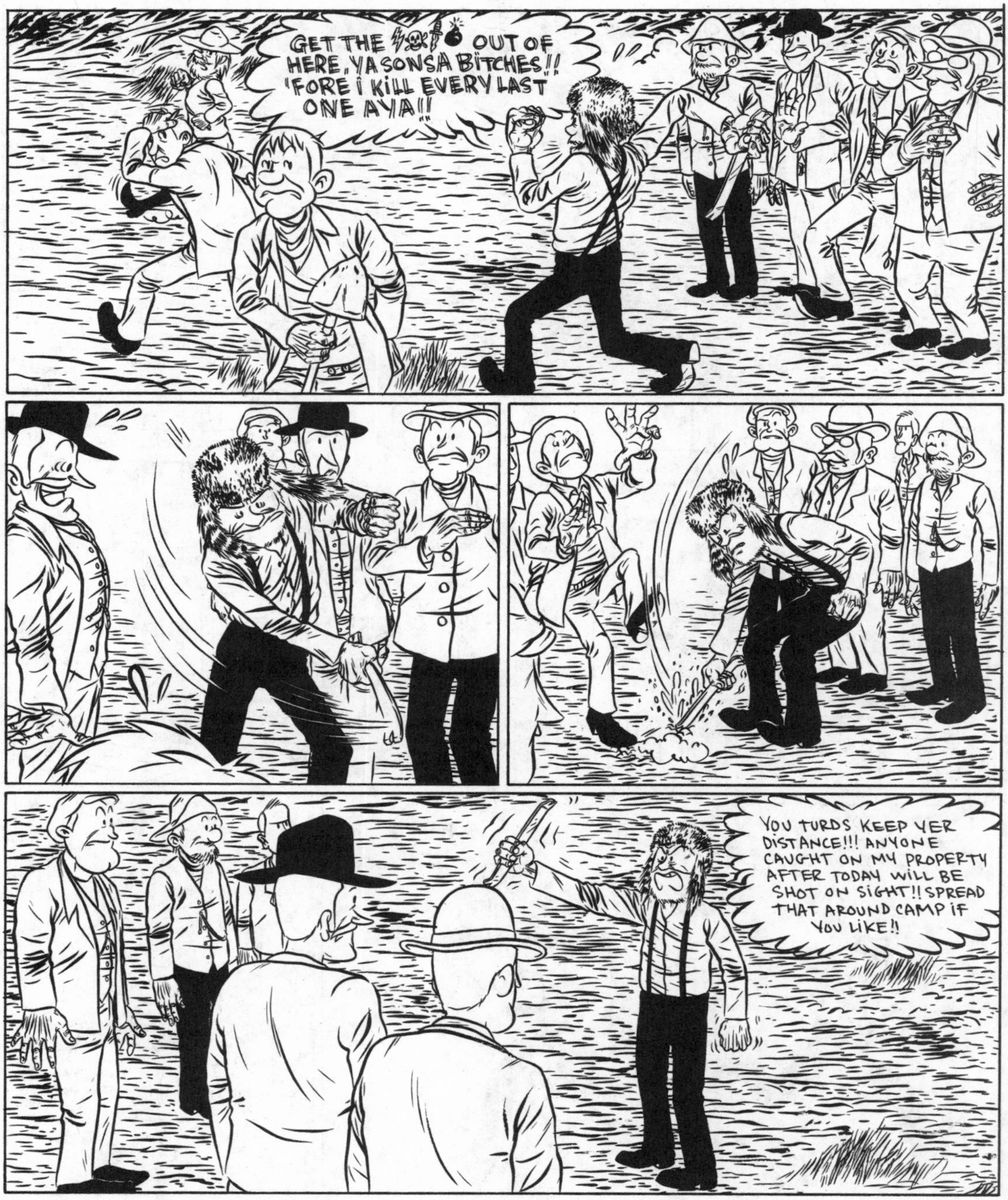
GET THE [grawlix] OUT OF HERE, YA SONSA BITCHES!! 'FORE I KILL EVERY LAST ONE AYA!!
YOU TURDS KEEP YER DISTANCE!!! ANYONE CAUGHT ON MY PROPERTY AFTER TODAY WILL BE SHOT ON SIGHT!! SPREAD THAT AROUND CAMP IF YOU LIKE!!

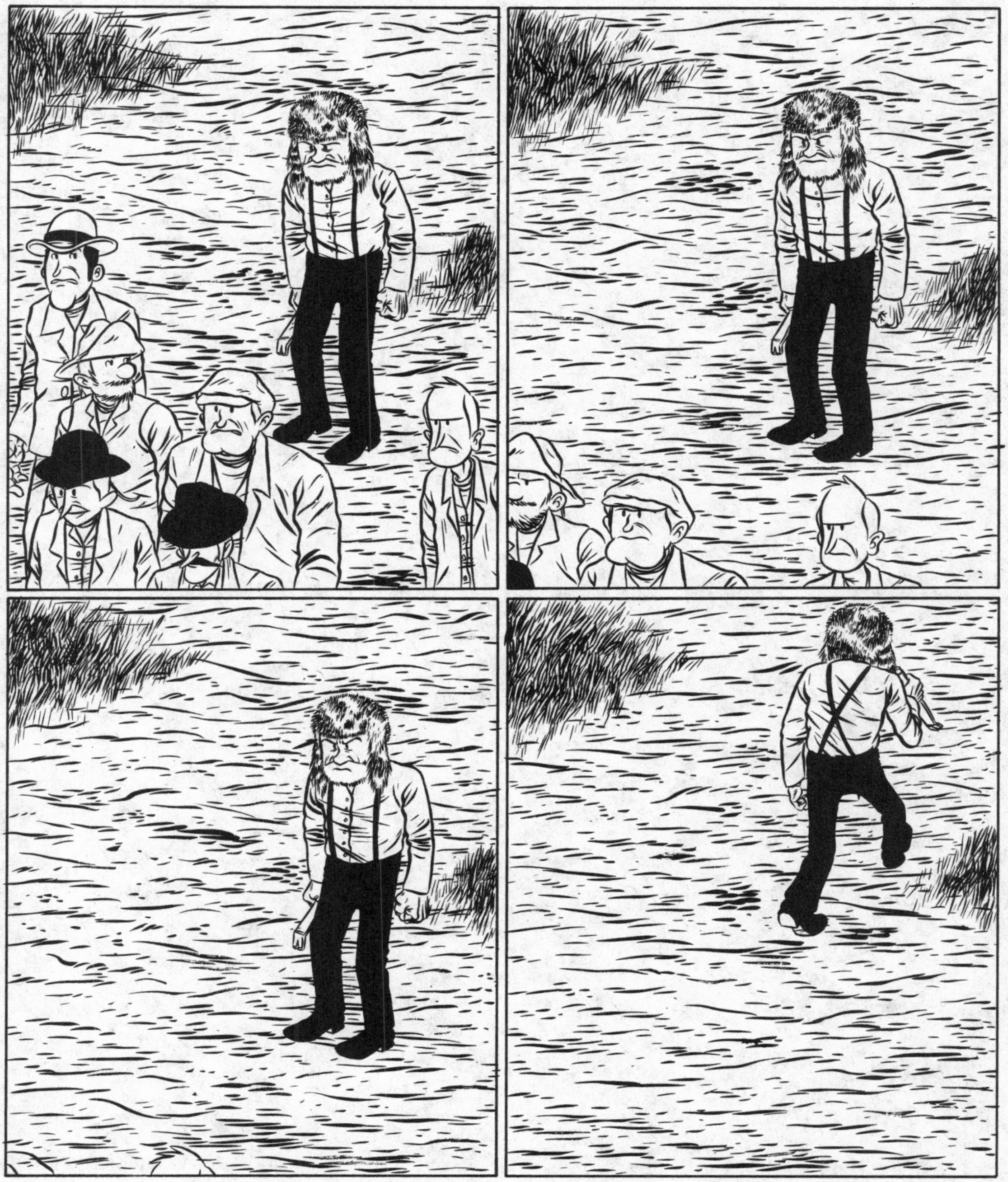

DIGGING MINES WAS AN ARDUOUS TASK IN THE
BEST OF CLIMATES, BUT IN THE SPRING AND FALL
IN THE YUKON, THE TEMPERATURE WAS, TO SAY
THE LEAST, ERRATIC. THE RISK OF THE GROUND
FREEZING AT NIGHT MADE A PROSPECTOR'S WORK
HARD. THEY WOULD WORK NIGHT AND DAY TO
SINK THEIR MINE SHAFTS BEFORE WINTER HIT.
ONCE IT DID, THE MOST ANY OF THEM COULD DO
WAS TO DIG OUT THEIR MINES AND MAKE
ENORMOUS PILES OF DIRT TO WASH IN THE
SPRING. ONE OF THE OTHER TASKS WAS TO STAND
GUARD OF ONES DIRT PILE—EVEN THOUGH THERE
WAS A MINERS' CODE, THERE WAS NONE AMONGST
THIEVES.

THE MEN ON THE TRAILS WERE STRUGGLING
A LOT WORSE THAN THE MINERS ON THE GOLD
FIELDS. THOUSANDS OF HORSES' LIVES ENDED ON
THE DEAD HORSE TRAIL BETWEEN THE BEGINNING
AND THE END OF THE GOLD RUSH. IT WAS CALLED
THE DEAD HORSE TRAIL BECAUSE OF THE
TREACHEROUS TERRAIN—CLIFFS, ROCKY RIDGES,
FALLEN TREES AND MUDDY RIVER BANKS. DOGS AND
PACK MULES FAIRED NO BETTER. THERE WERE
STORIES OF DOGS BEING SEVERELY BEATEN BY
THEIR OWNERS, WHO HAD BEEN DRIVEN MAD BY
THE DURATION AND CONDITIONS OF THE TRIP. AN OX
WAS EVEN SET ON FIRE AND BURNED ALIVE BECAUSE
IT REFUSED TO KEEP MOVING DUE TO EXHAUSTION. THE
TRAIL TURNED MEN EVIL. MURDER, SUICIDE AND SCURVY
WERE THE MOST COMMON WAYS FOR MEN TO DIE ON
THE DEAD HORSE TRAIL, BUT DESPITE ALL OF THE VIOLENCE
AND DEATH, LIFE ALSO BEGAN ON THE TRAIL.

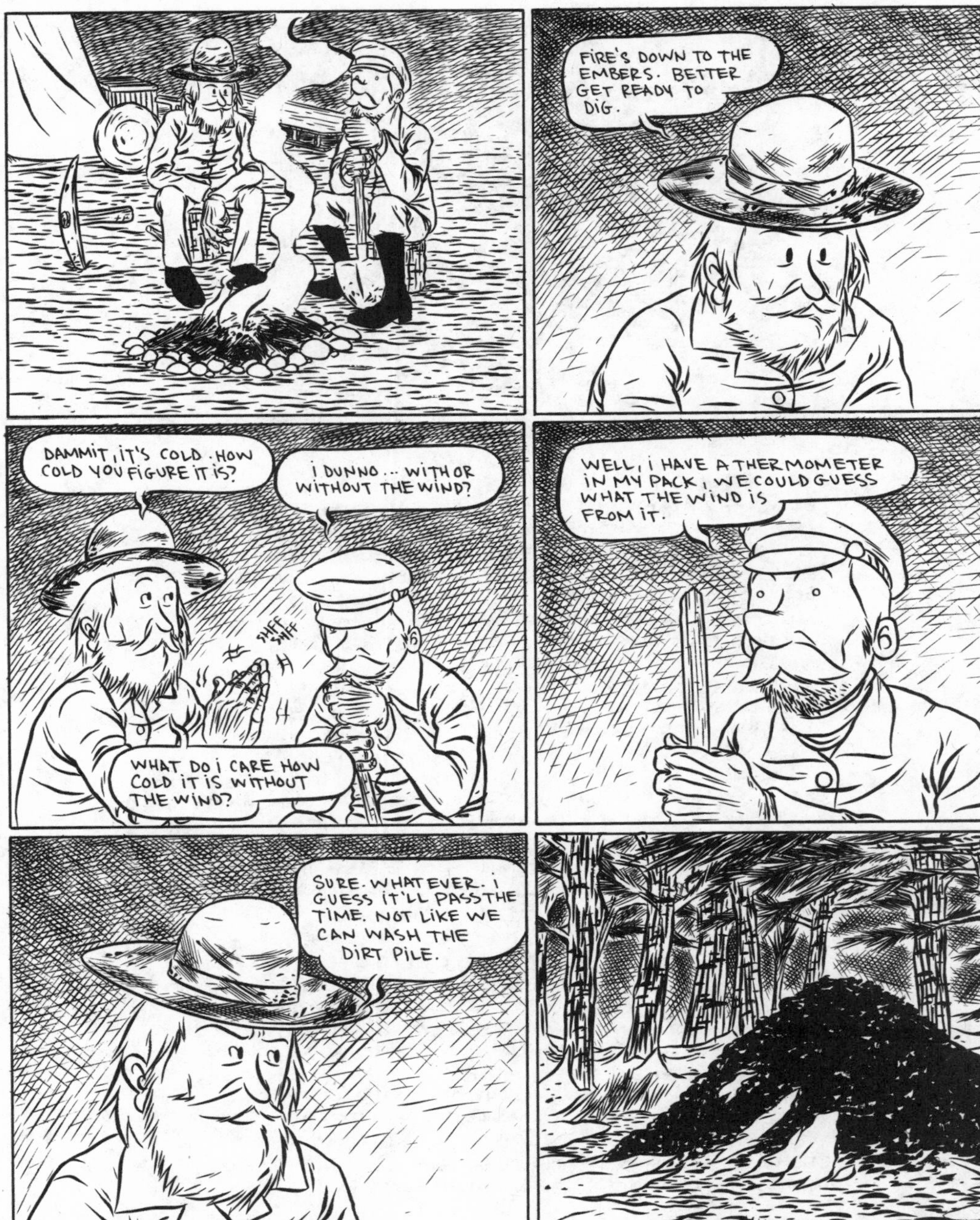
FIRE'S DOWN TO THE EMBERS. BETTER GET READY TO DIG.
DAMMIT, IT'S COLD. HOW COLD YOU FIGURE IT IS?
I DUNNO... WITH OR WITHOUT THE WIND?
SNFF SNFF
WHAT DO I CARE HOW COLD IT IS WITHOUT THE WIND?
WELL, I HAVE A THERMOMETER IN MY PACK, WE COULD GUESS WHAT THE WIND IS FROM IT.
SURE. WHATEVER. I GUESS IT'LL PASS THE TIME. NOT LIKE WE CAN WASH THE DIRT PILE.

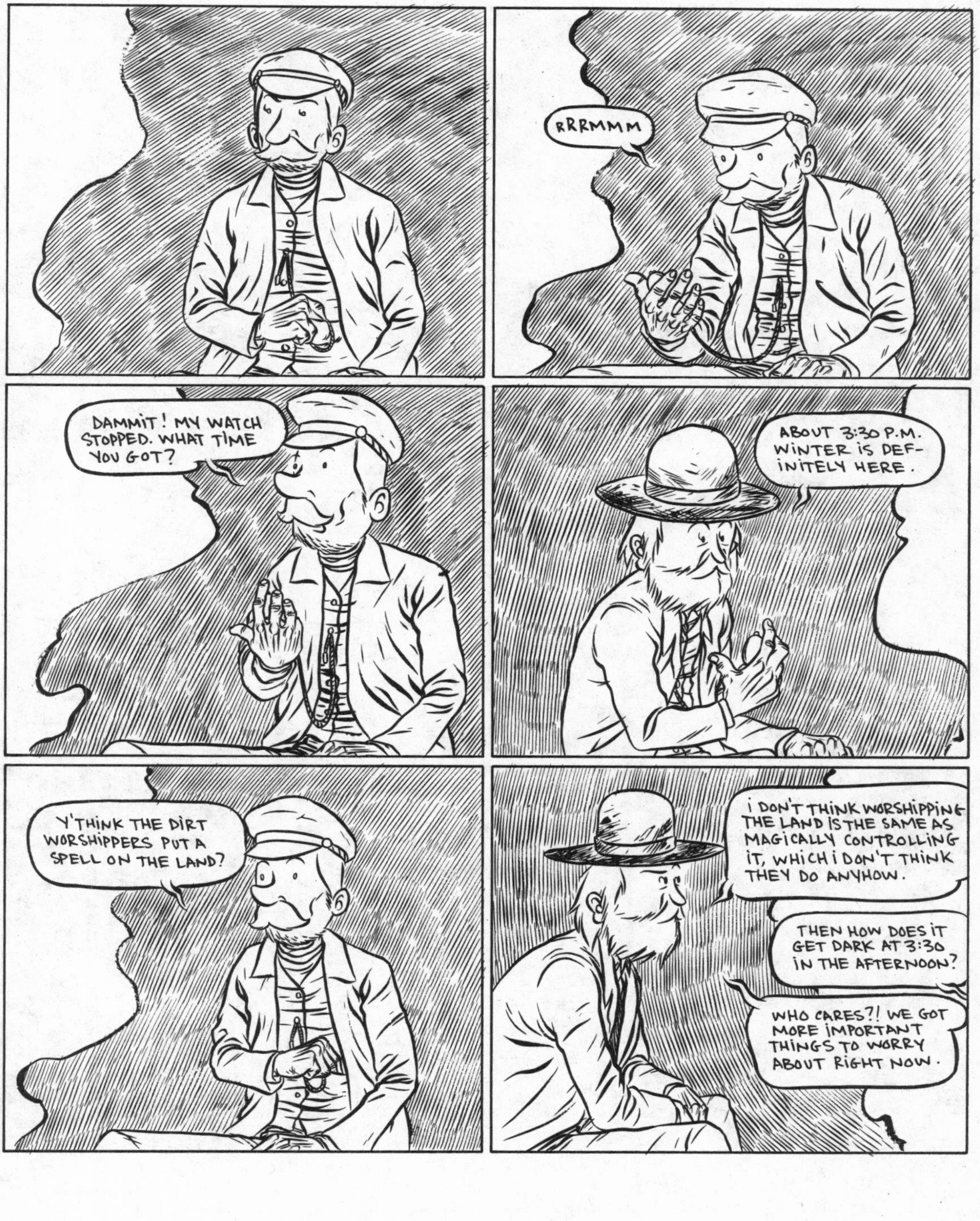
RRRMMM
DAMMIT! MY WATCH STOPPED. WHAT TIME YOU GOT?
ABOUT 3:30 P.M. WINTER IS DEF-INITELY HERE.
Y'THINK THE DIRT WORSHIPPERS PUT A SPELL ON THE LAND?
I DON'T THINK WORSHIPPING THE LAND IS THE SAME AS MAGICALLY CONTROLLING IT, WHICH I DON'T THINK THEY DO ANYHOW.
THEN HOW DOES IT GET DARK AT 3:30 IN THE AFTERNOON?
WHO CARES?! WE GOT MORE IMPORTANT THINGS TO WORRY ABOUT RIGHT NOW.

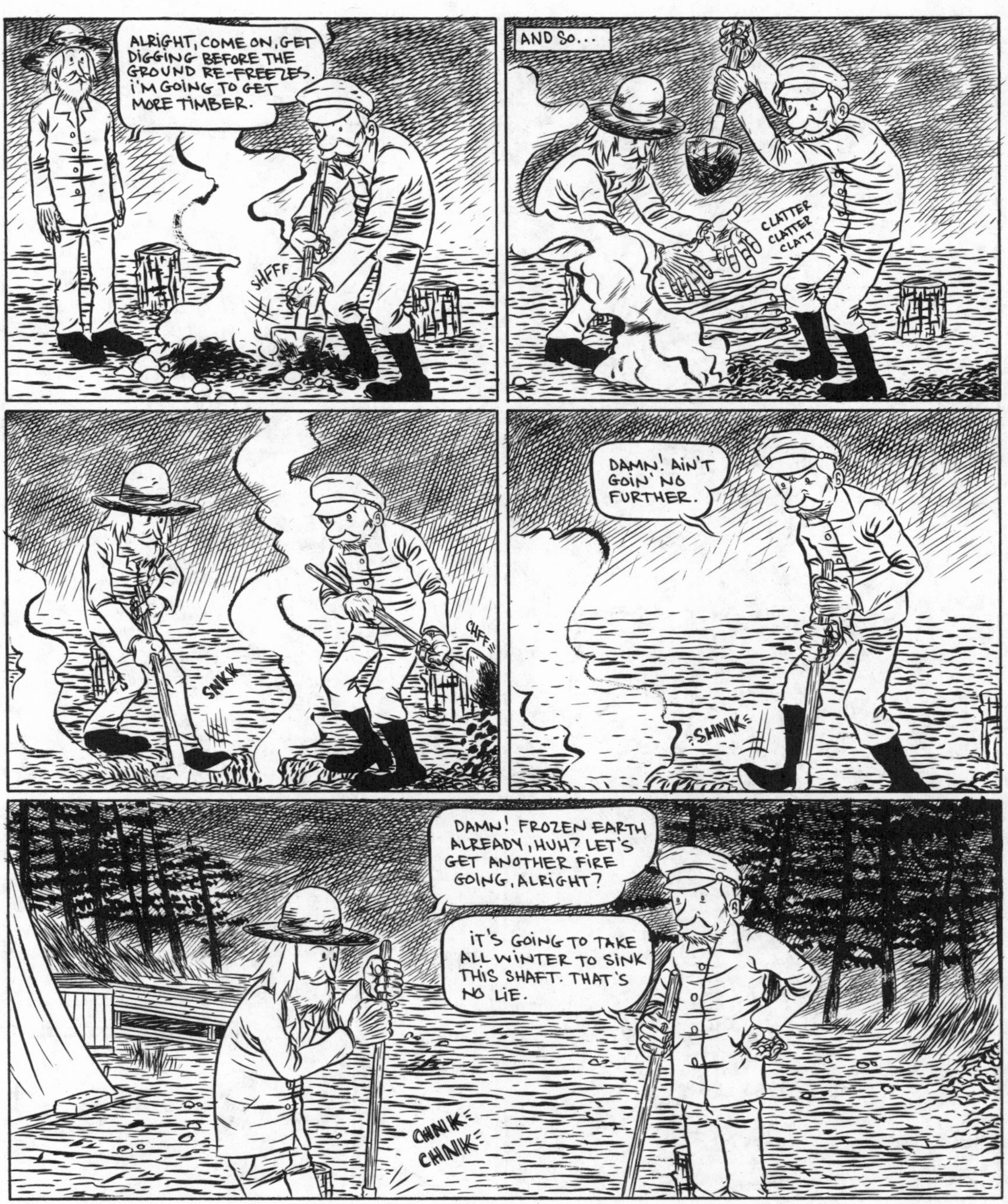
ALRIGHT, COME ON, GET DIGGING BEFORE THE GROUND RE-FREEZES. I'M GOING TO GET MORE TIMBER.
SHFFF
AND SO...
CLATTER CLATTER CLATT
SNIKK
CHFF
DAMN! AIN'T GOIN' NO FURTHER.
SHINK
DAMN! FROZEN EARTH ALREADY, HUH? LET'S GET ANOTHER FIRE GOING, ALRIGHT?
IT'S GOING TO TAKE ALL WINTER TO SINK THIS SHAFT. THAT'S NO LIE.
CHINK
CHINK

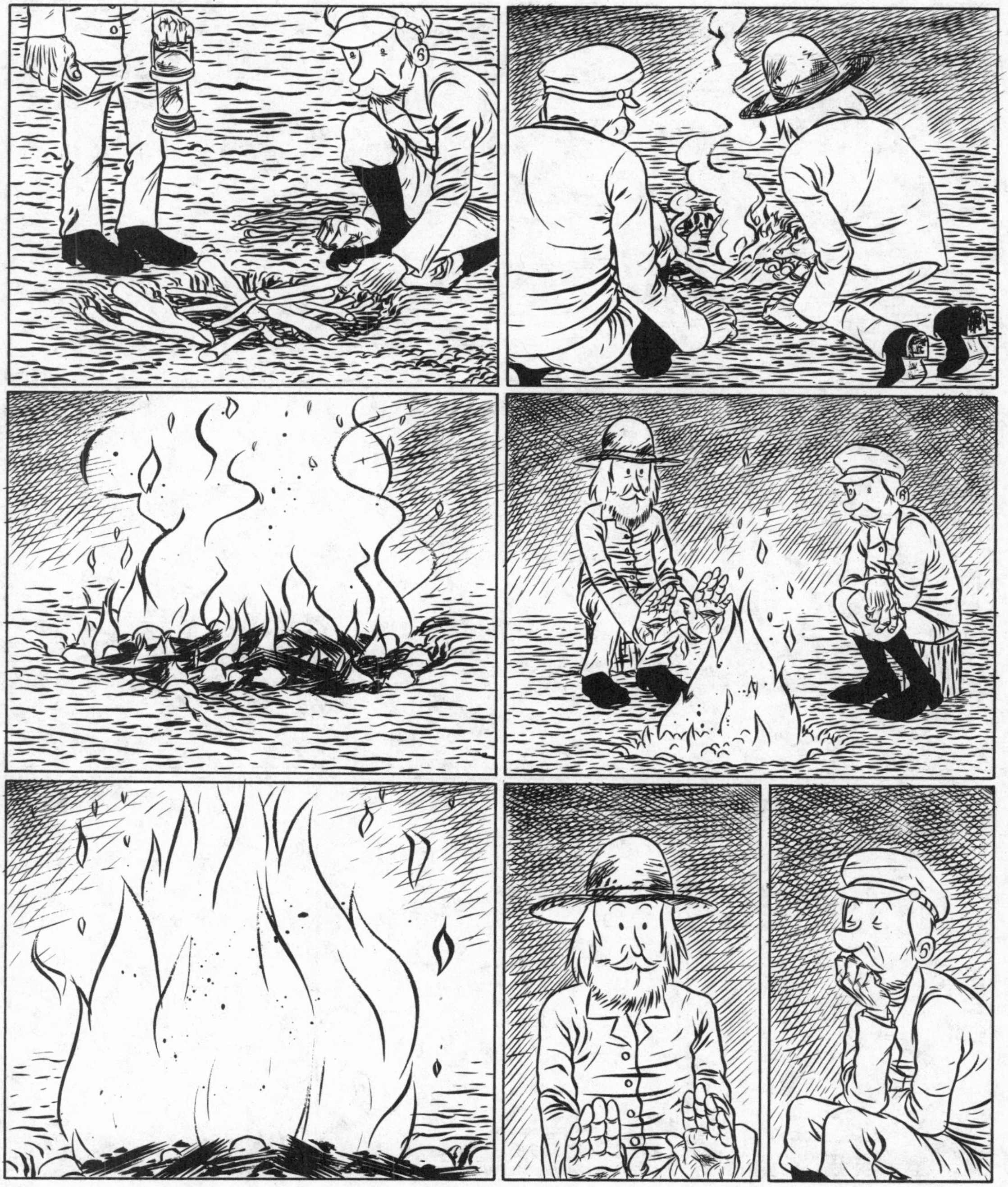

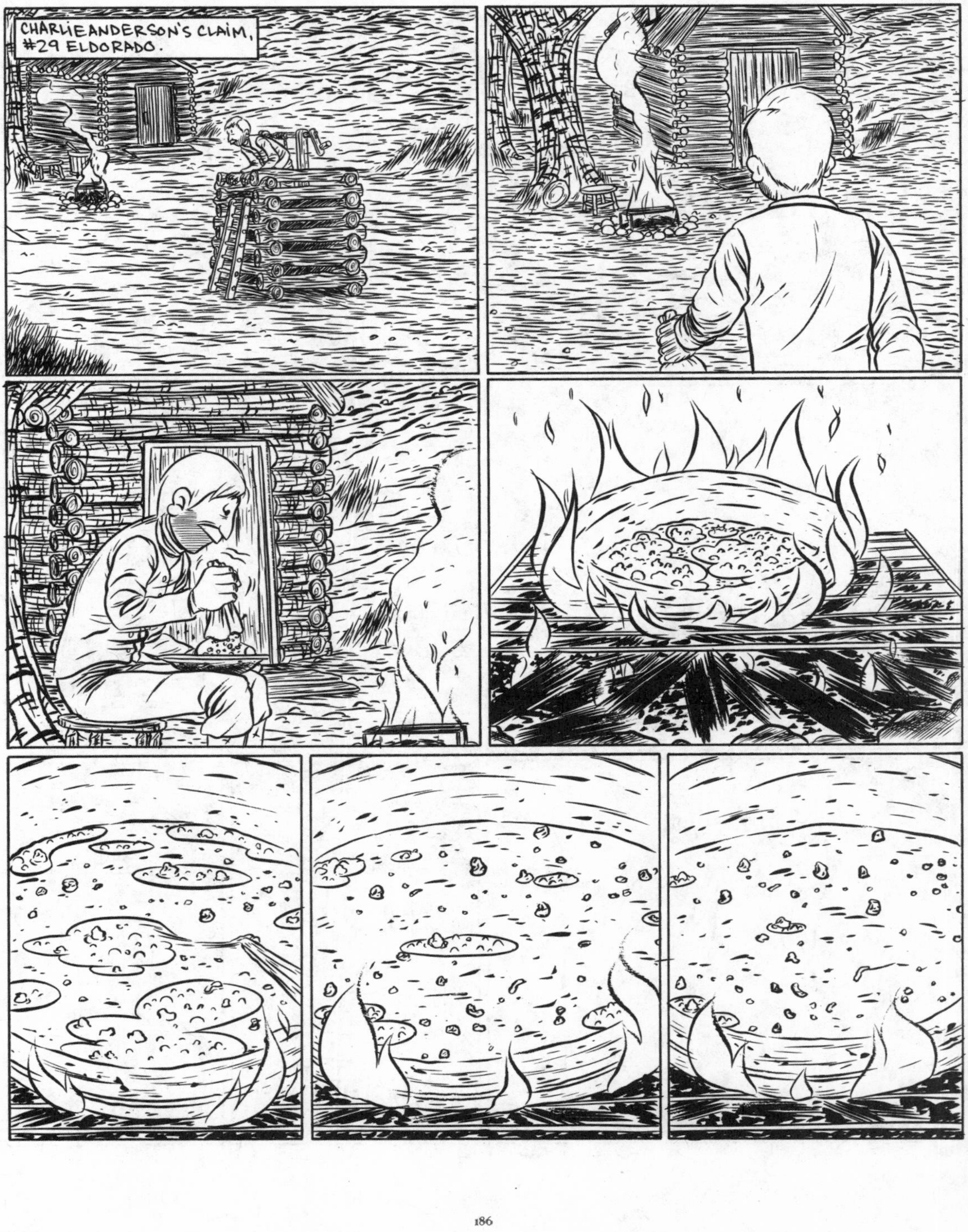
CHARLIE ANDERSON'S CLAIM, #29 ELDORADO.

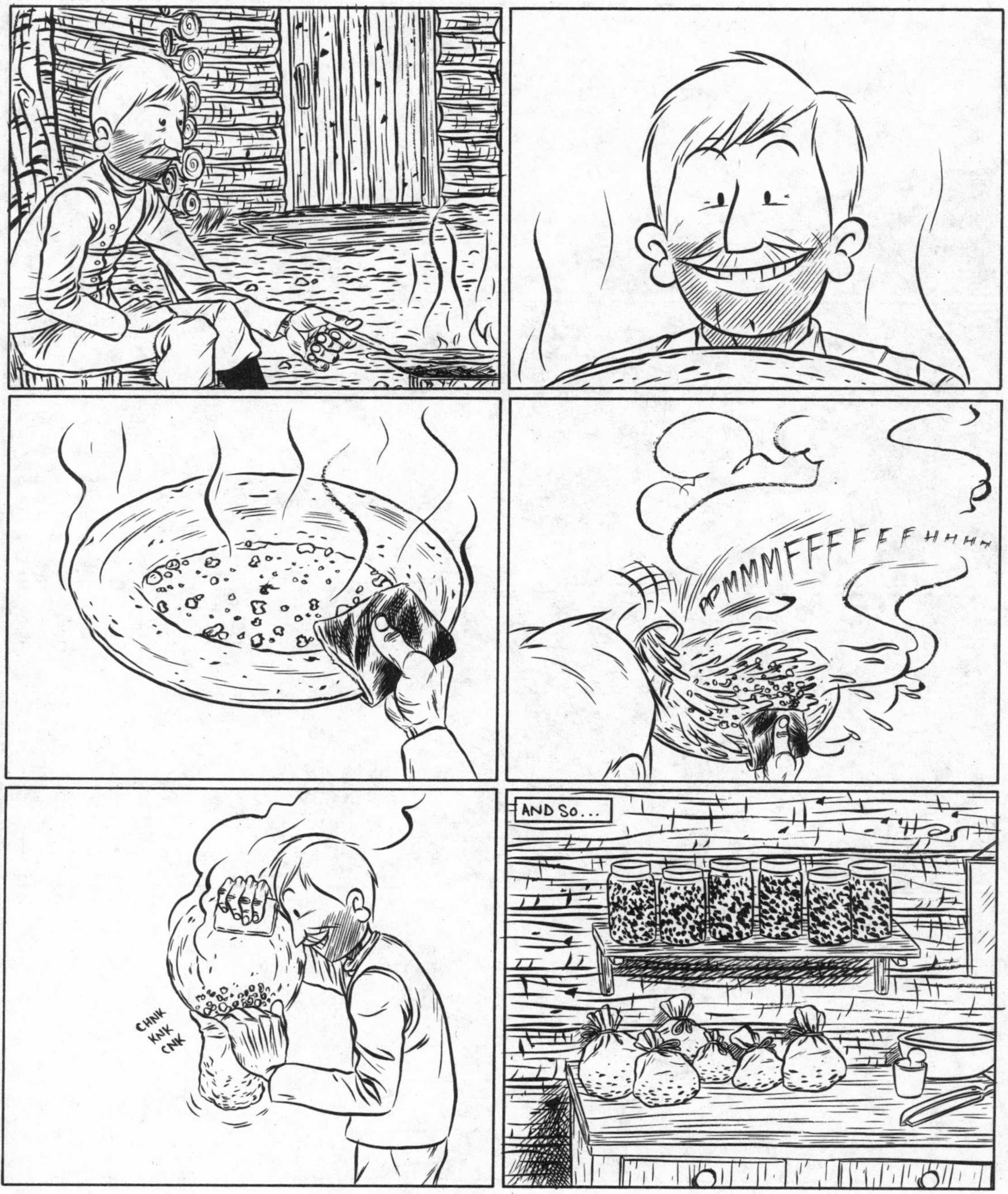
PPMMMFFFFFFFHHHH
CHNK
KNK
CNK
AND SO...

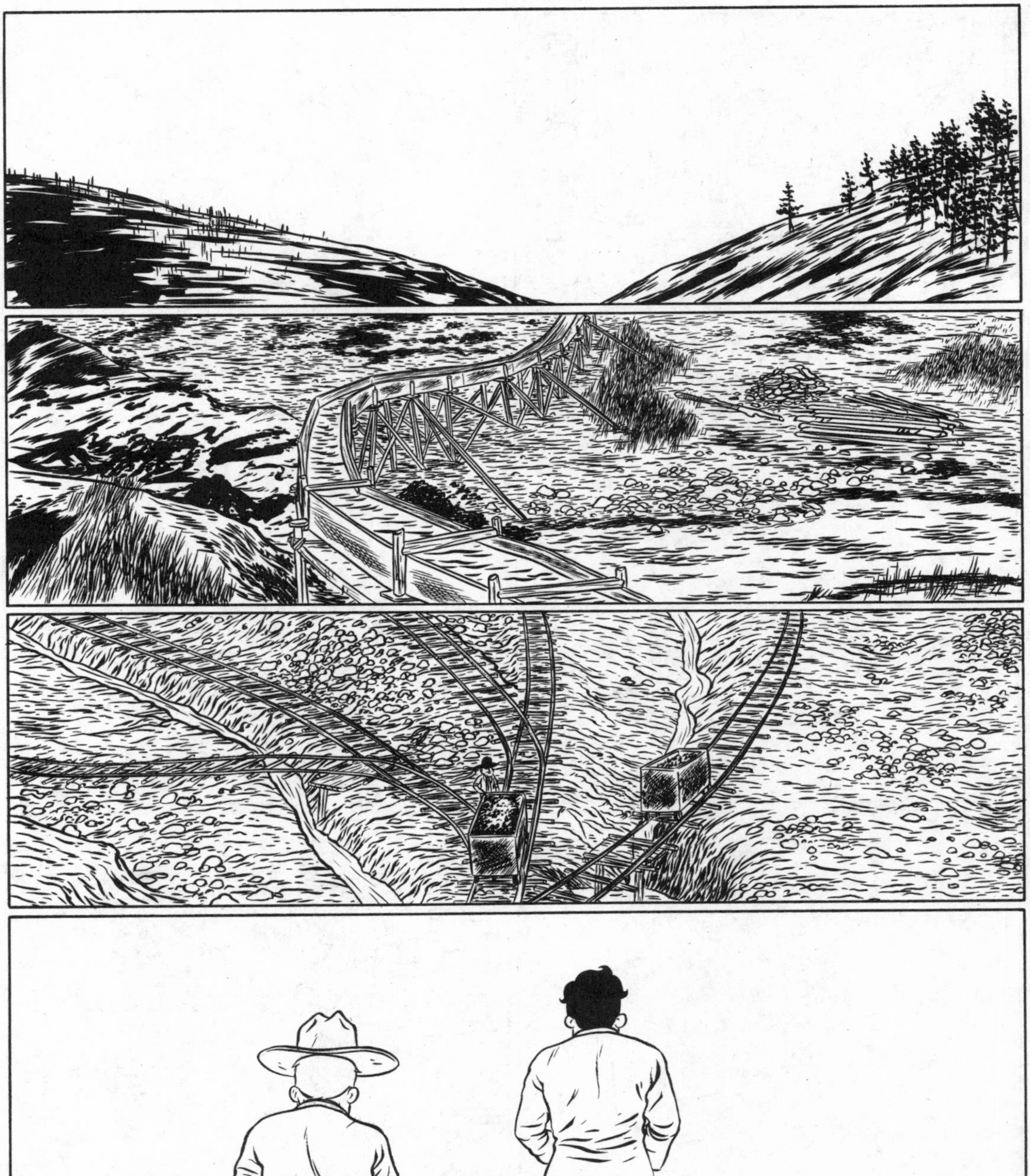

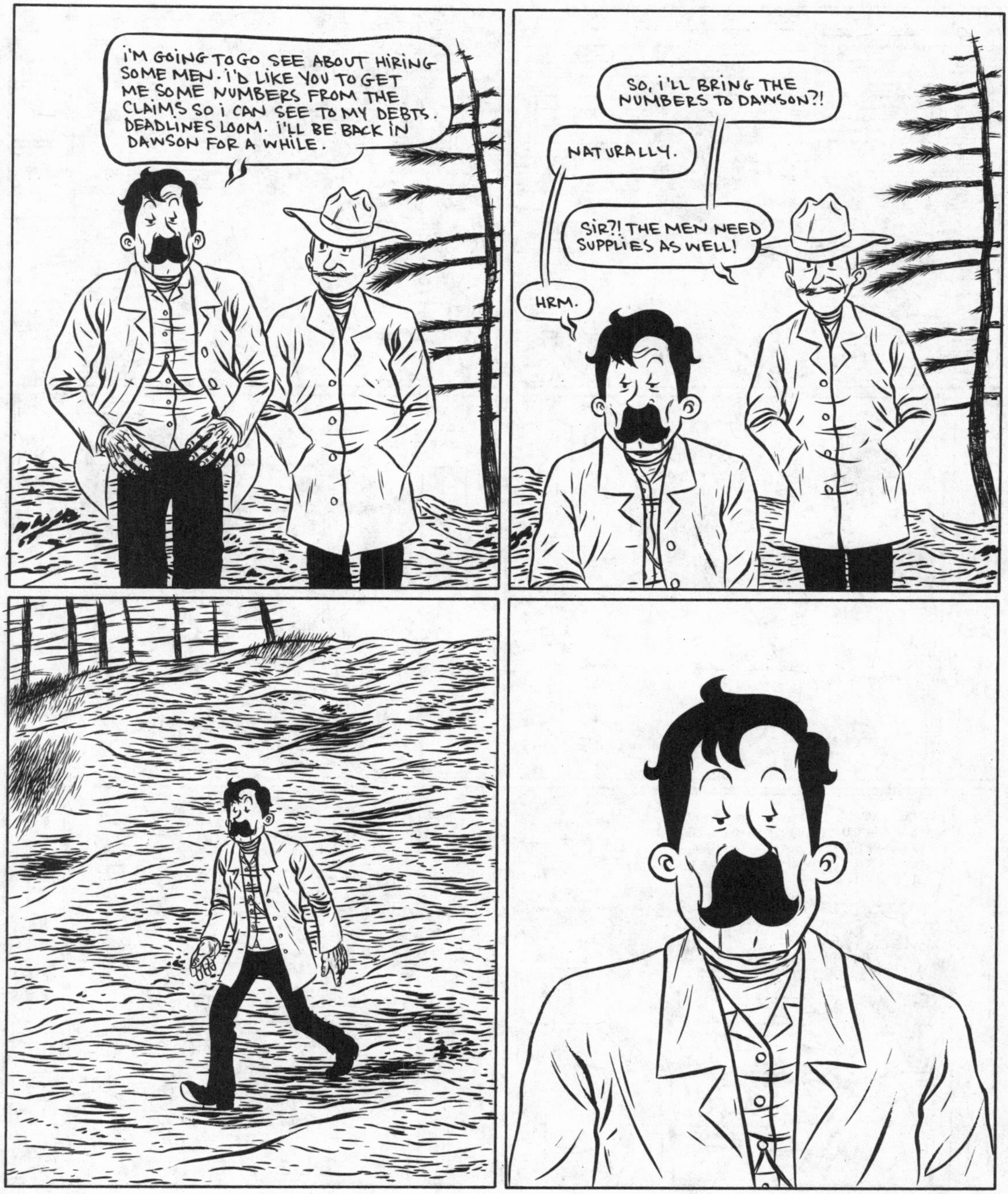
I'M GOING TO GO SEE ABOUT HIRING SOME MEN. I'D LIKE YOU TO GET ME SOME NUMBERS FROM THE CLAIMS SO I CAN SEE TO MY DEBTS. DEADLINES LOOM. I'LL BE BACK IN DAWSON FOR A WHILE.
SO, I'LL BRING THE NUMBERS TO DAWSON?!
NATURALLY.
SIR?! THE MEN NEED SUPPLIES AS WELL!
HRM.

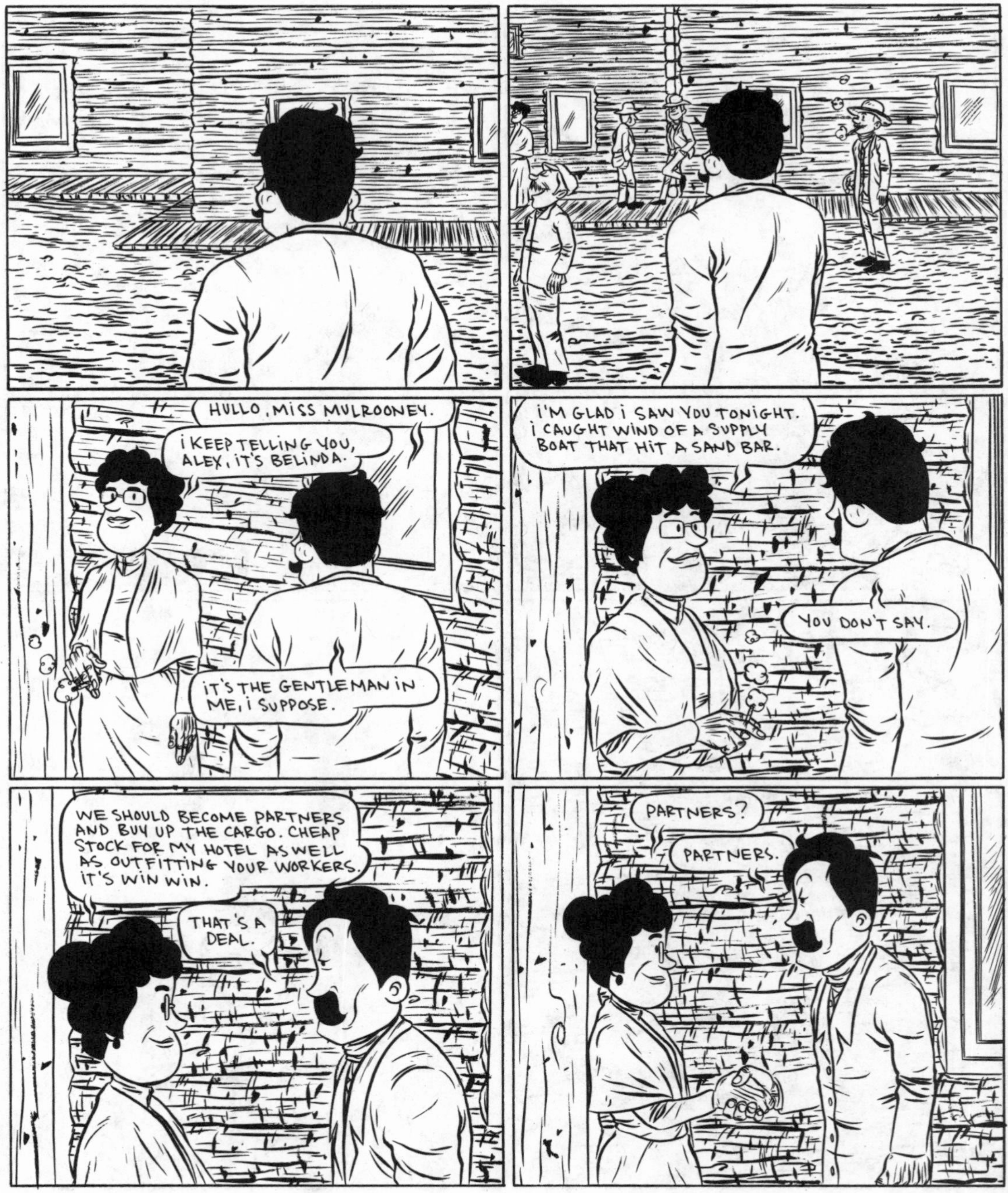
HULLO, MISS MULROONEY.
i KEEP TELLiNG YOU, ALEX, iT'S BELiNDA.
iT'S THE GENTLEMAN iN ME, i SUPPOSE.
i'M GLAD i SAW YOU TONiGHT. i CAUGHT WiND OF A SUPPLY BOAT THAT HiT A SAND BAR.
YOU DON'T SAY.
WE SHOULD BECOME PARTNERS AND BUY UP THE CARGO. CHEAP STOCK FOR MY HOTEL AS WELL AS OUTFiTTiNG YOUR WORKERS. iT'S WiN WiN.
THAT'S A DEAL.
PARTNERS?
PARTNERS.

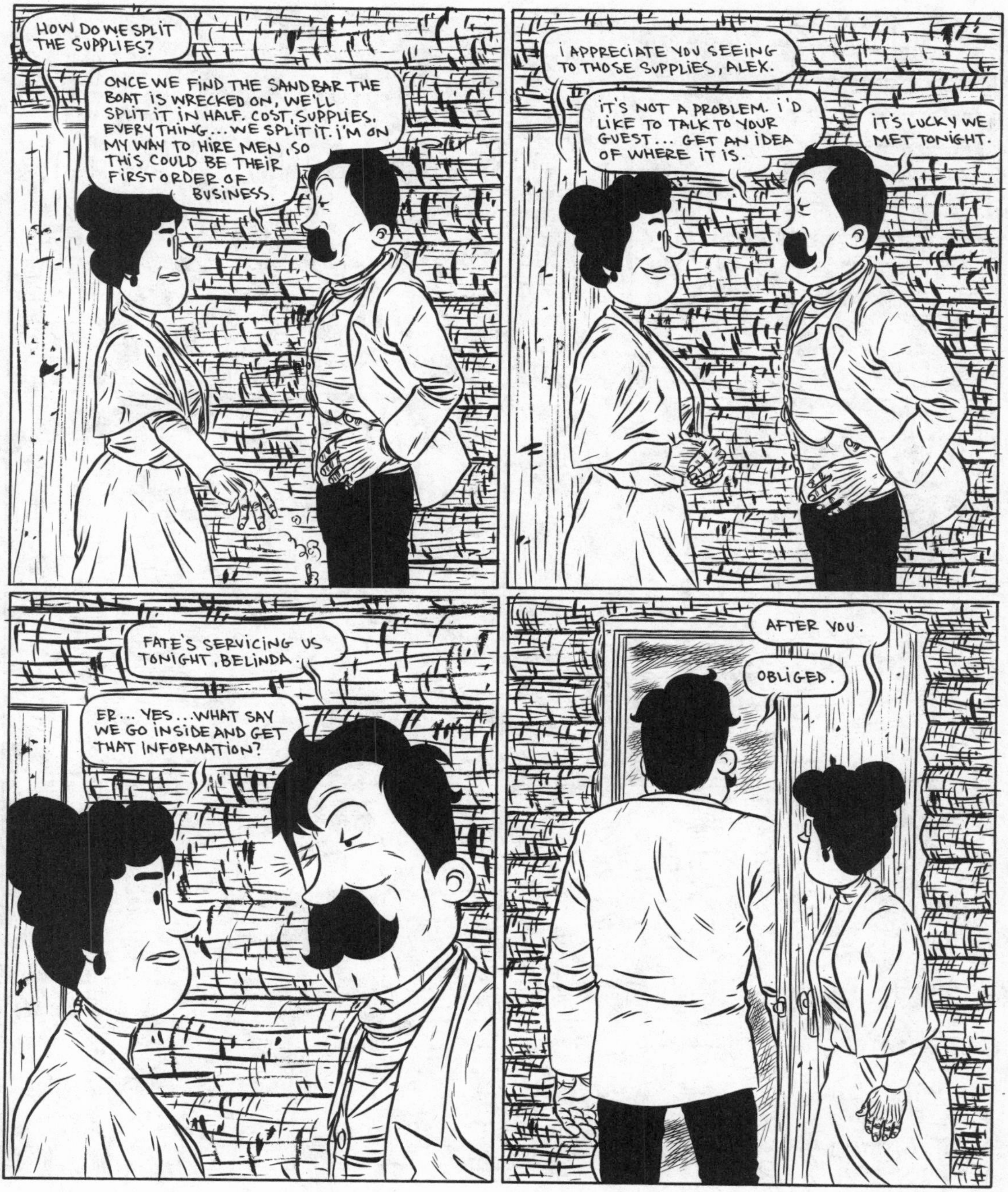
HOW DO WE SPLIT THE SUPPLIES?
ONCE WE FIND THE SANDBAR THE BOAT IS WRECKED ON, WE'LL SPLIT IT IN HALF. COST, SUPPLIES. EVERYTHING... WE SPLIT IT. I'M ON MY WAY TO HIRE MEN, SO THIS COULD BE THEIR FIRST ORDER OF BUSINESS.
I APPRECIATE YOU SEEING TO THOSE SUPPLIES, ALEX.
IT'S NOT A PROBLEM. I'D LIKE TO TALK TO YOUR GUEST... GET AN IDEA OF WHERE IT IS.
IT'S LUCKY WE MET TONIGHT.
FATE'S SERVICING US TONIGHT, BELINDA.
ER... YES... WHAT SAY WE GO INSIDE AND GET THAT INFORMATION?
AFTER YOU.
OBLIGED.

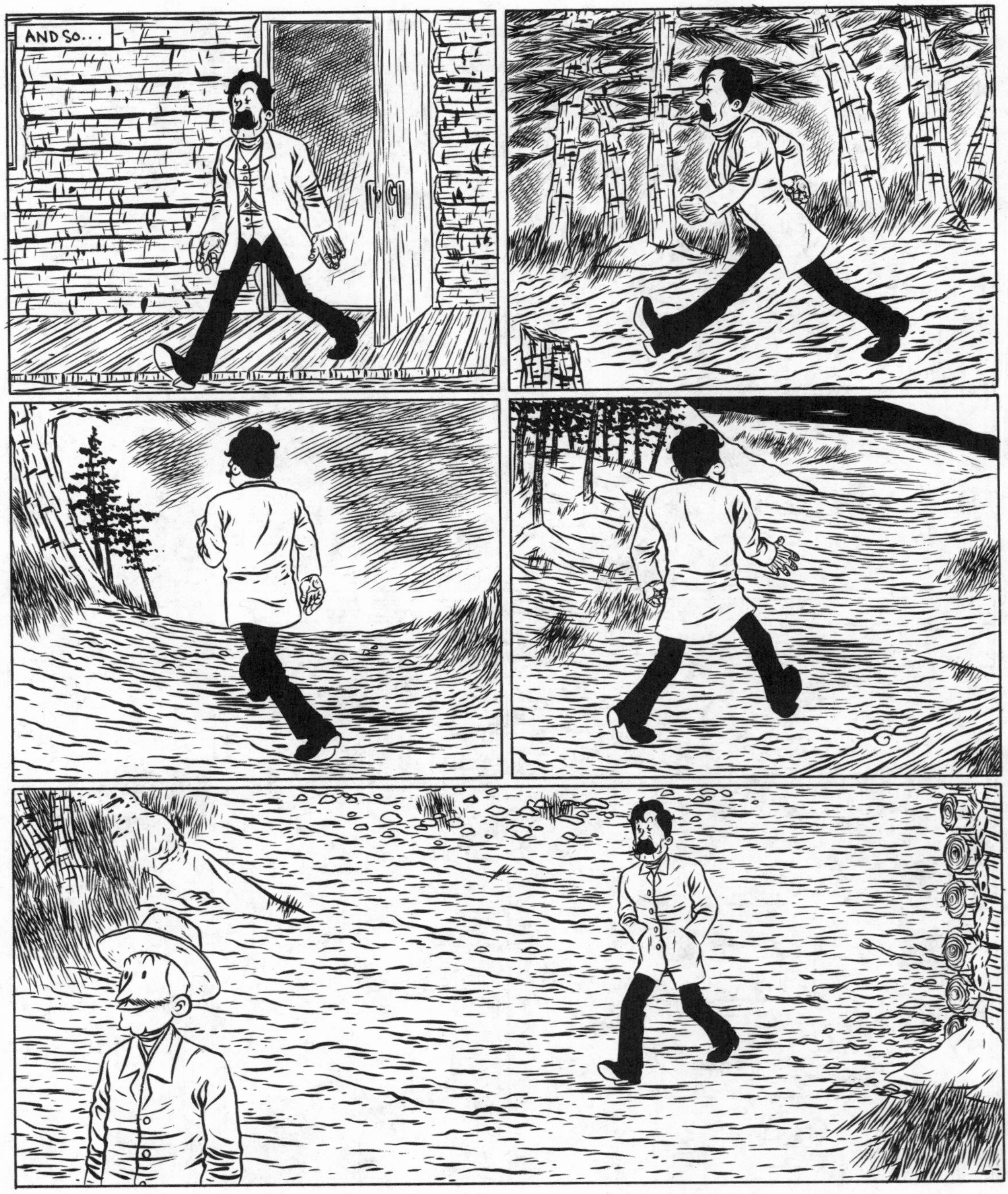
AND SO...

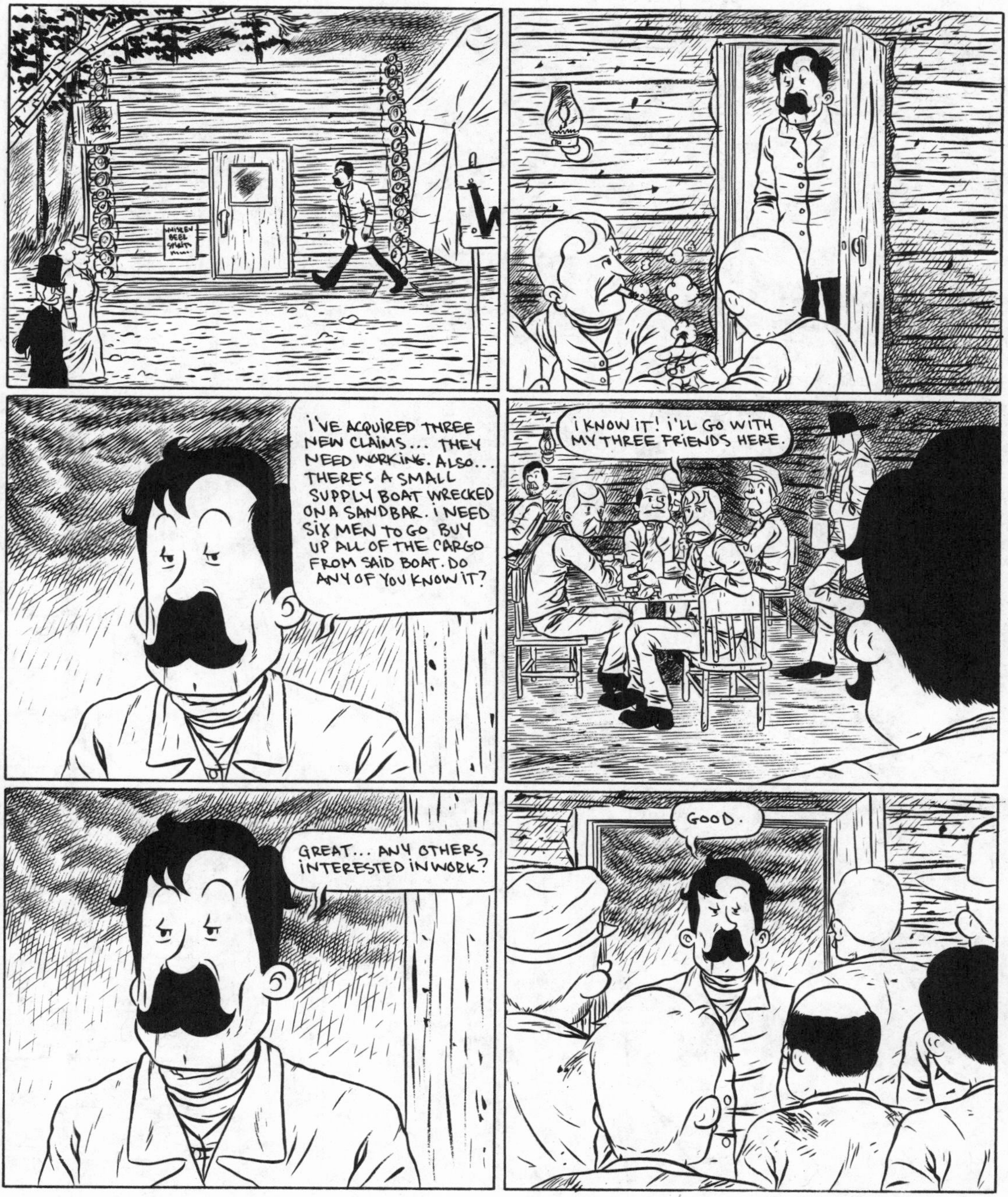
I'VE ACQUIRED THREE NEW CLAIMS... THEY NEED WORKING. ALSO... THERE'S A SMALL SUPPLY BOAT WRECKED ON A SANDBAR. I NEED SIX MEN TO GO BUY UP ALL OF THE CARGO FROM SAID BOAT. DO ANY OF YOU KNOW IT?
I KNOW IT! I'LL GO WITH MY THREE FRIENDS HERE.
GREAT... ANY OTHERS INTERESTED IN WORK?
GOOD.

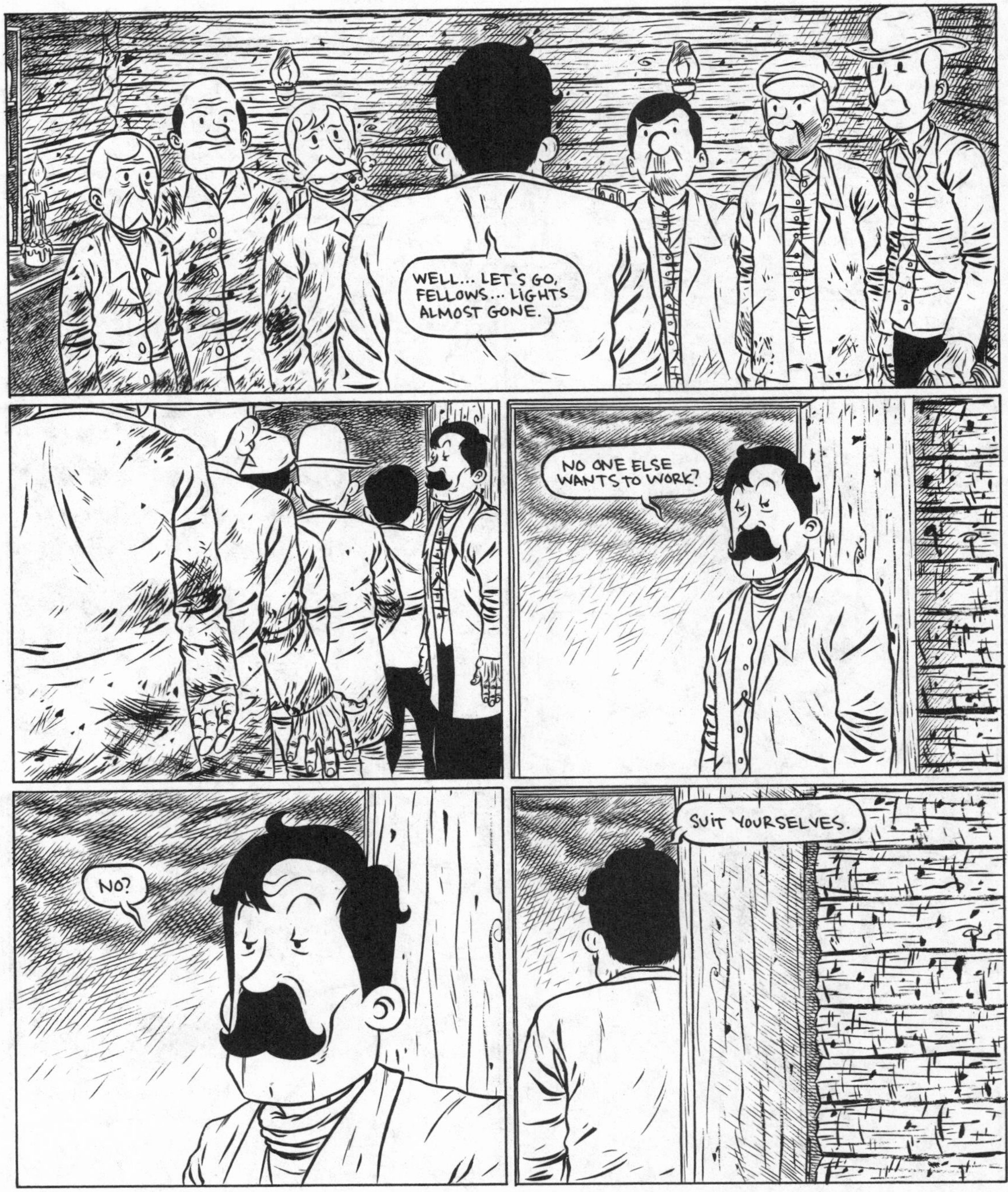
WELL... LET'S GO, FELLOWS... LIGHTS ALMOST GONE.
NO ONE ELSE WANTS TO WORK?
NO?
SUIT YOURSELVES.

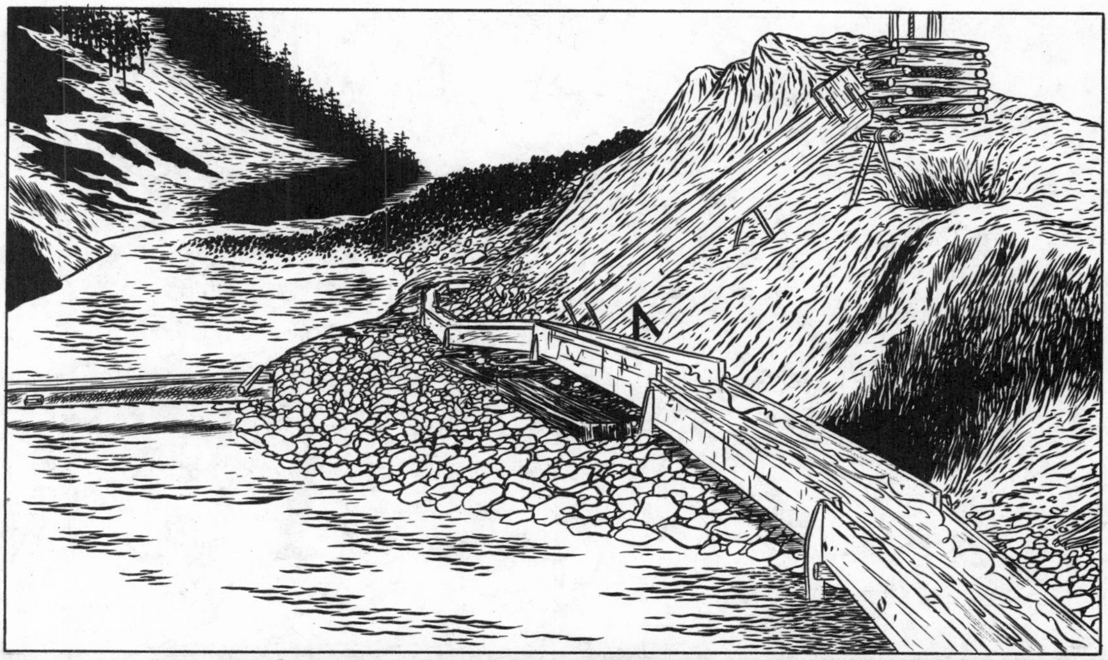

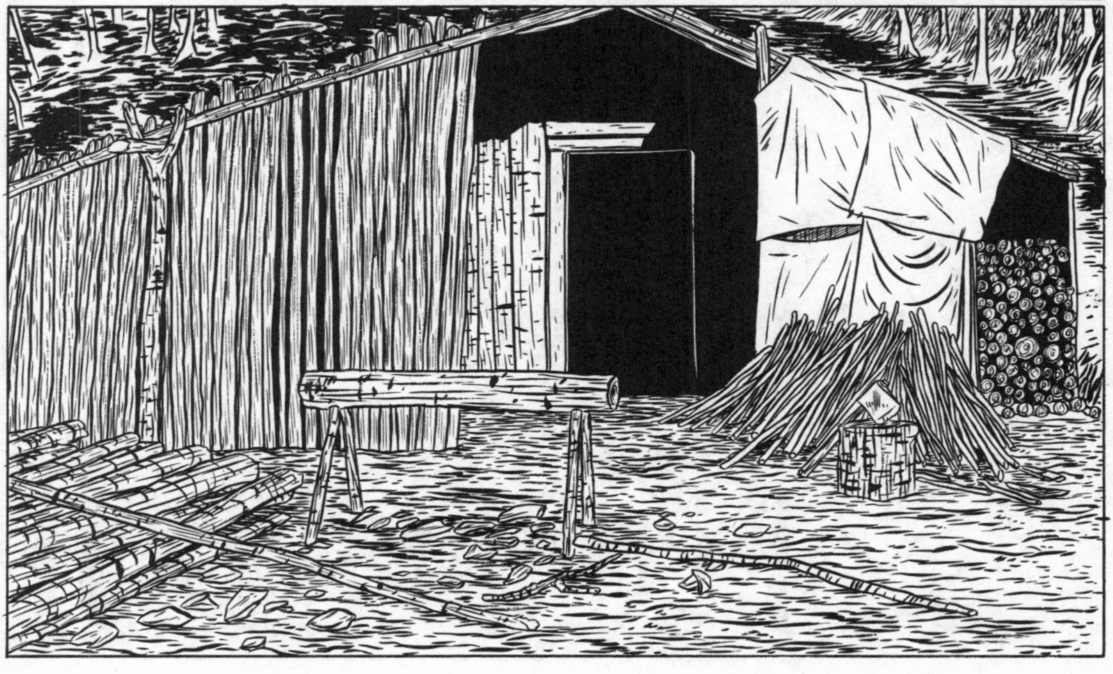

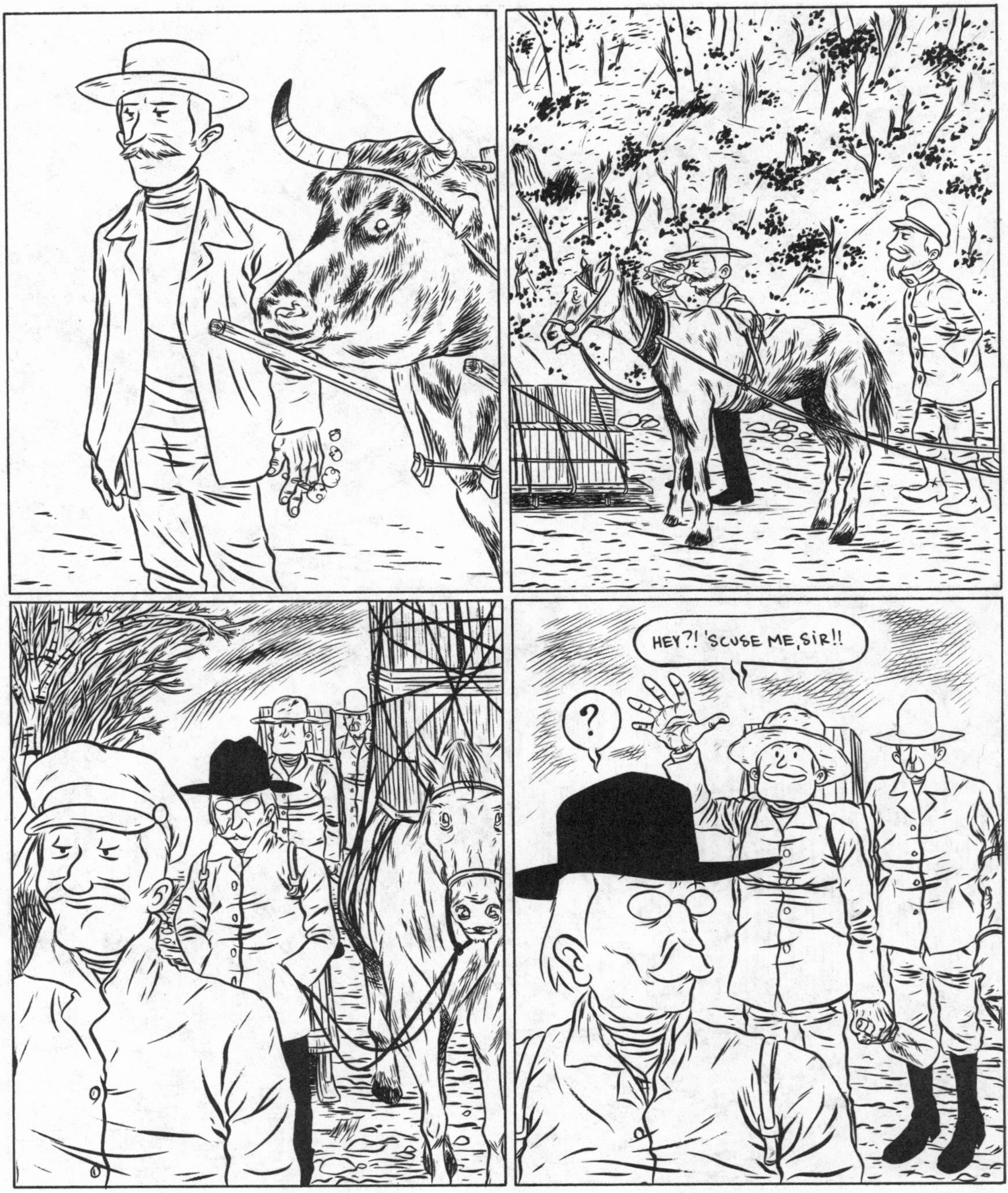
HEY?! 'SCUSE ME, SIR!!
?

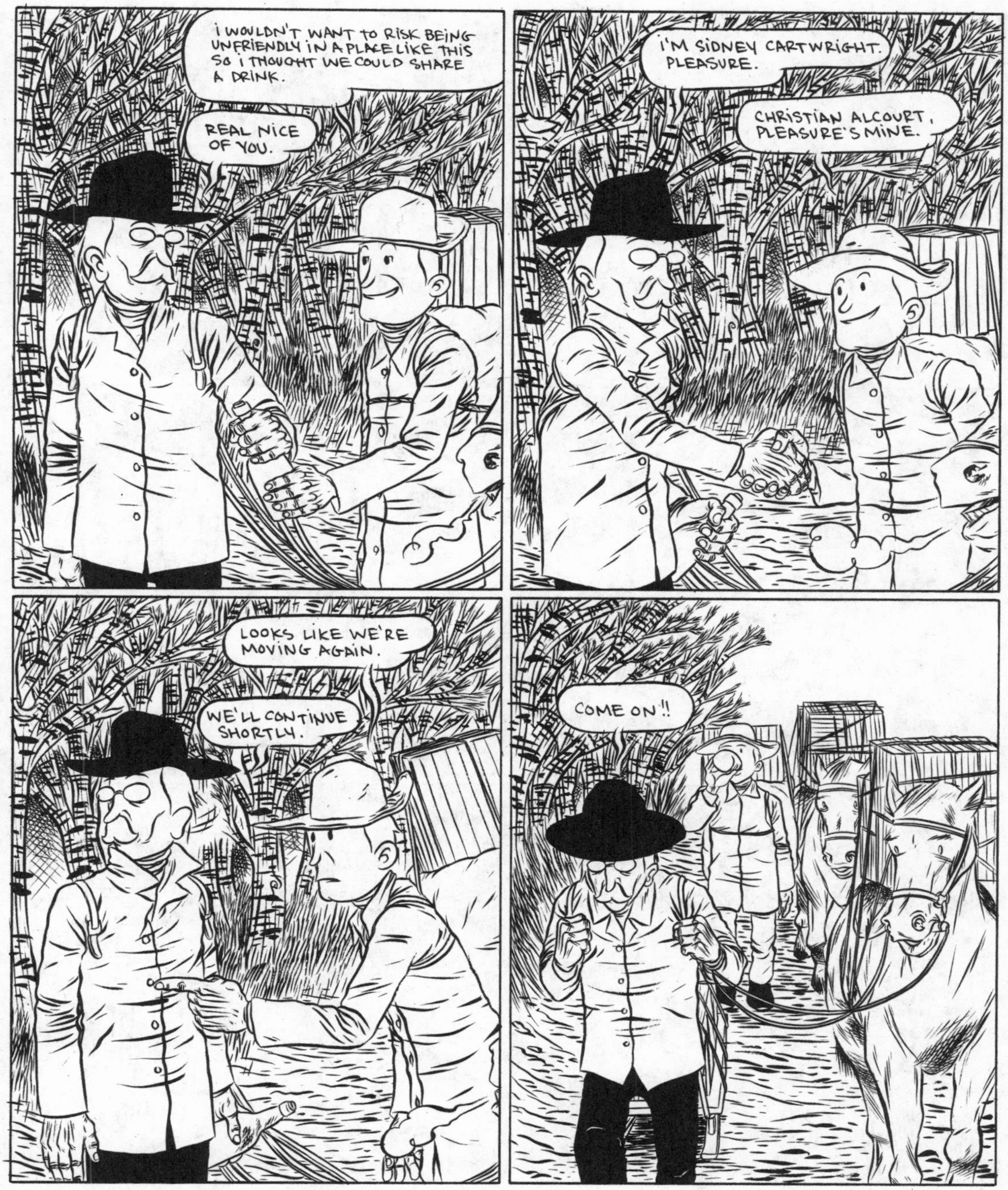
I WOULDN'T WANT TO RISK BEING UNFRIENDLY IN A PLACE LIKE THIS SO I THOUGHT WE COULD SHARE A DRINK.
REAL NICE OF YOU.
I'M SIDNEY CARTWRIGHT. PLEASURE.
CHRISTIAN ALCOURT, PLEASURE'S MINE.
LOOKS LIKE WE'RE MOVING AGAIN.
WE'LL CONTINUE SHORTLY.
COME ON!!

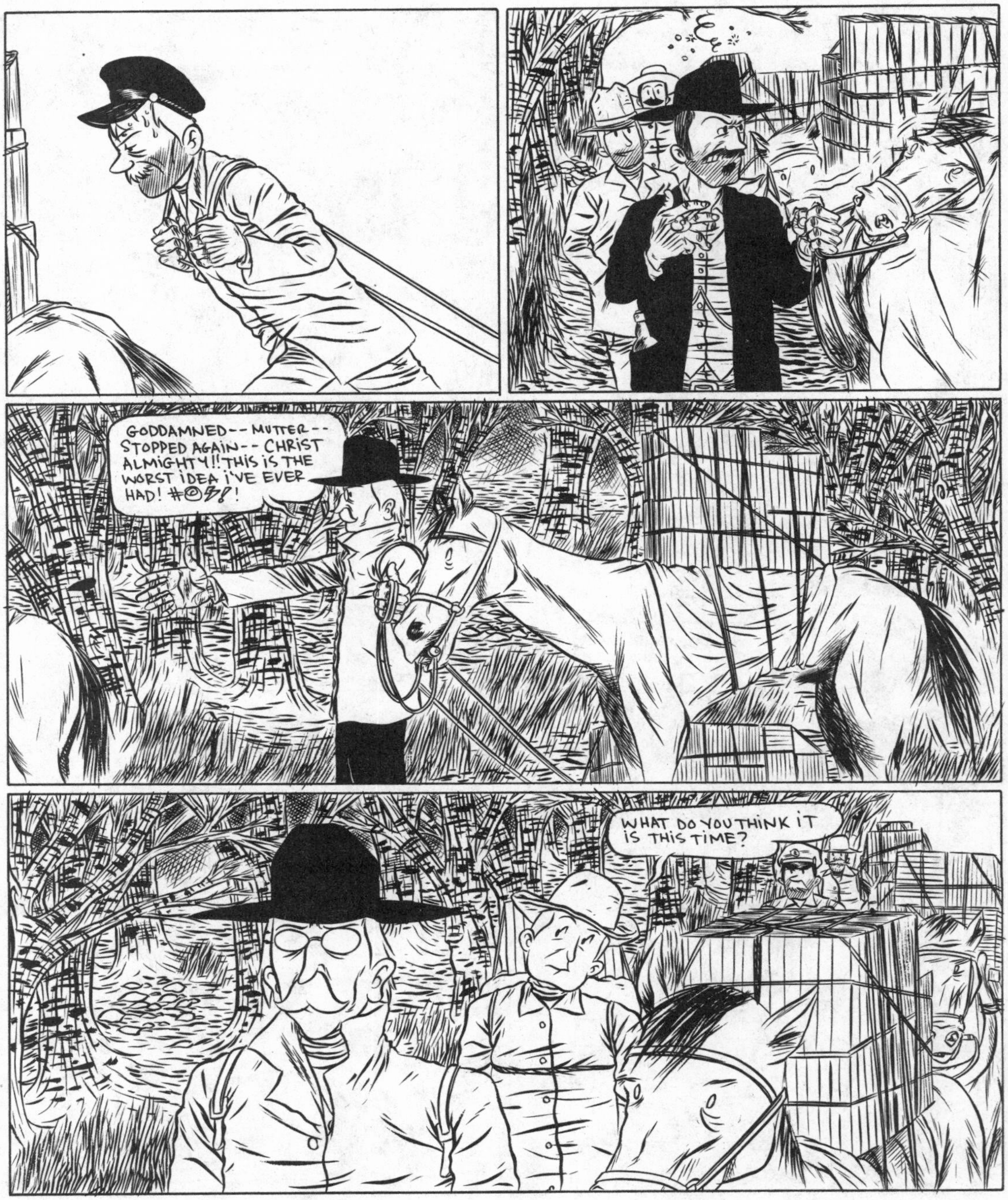
GODDAMNED-- MUTTER-- STOPPED AGAIN-- CHRIST ALMIGHTY!! THIS IS THE WORST IDEA I'VE EVER HAD! #@ϟ!!
WHAT DO YOU THINK IT IS THIS TIME?

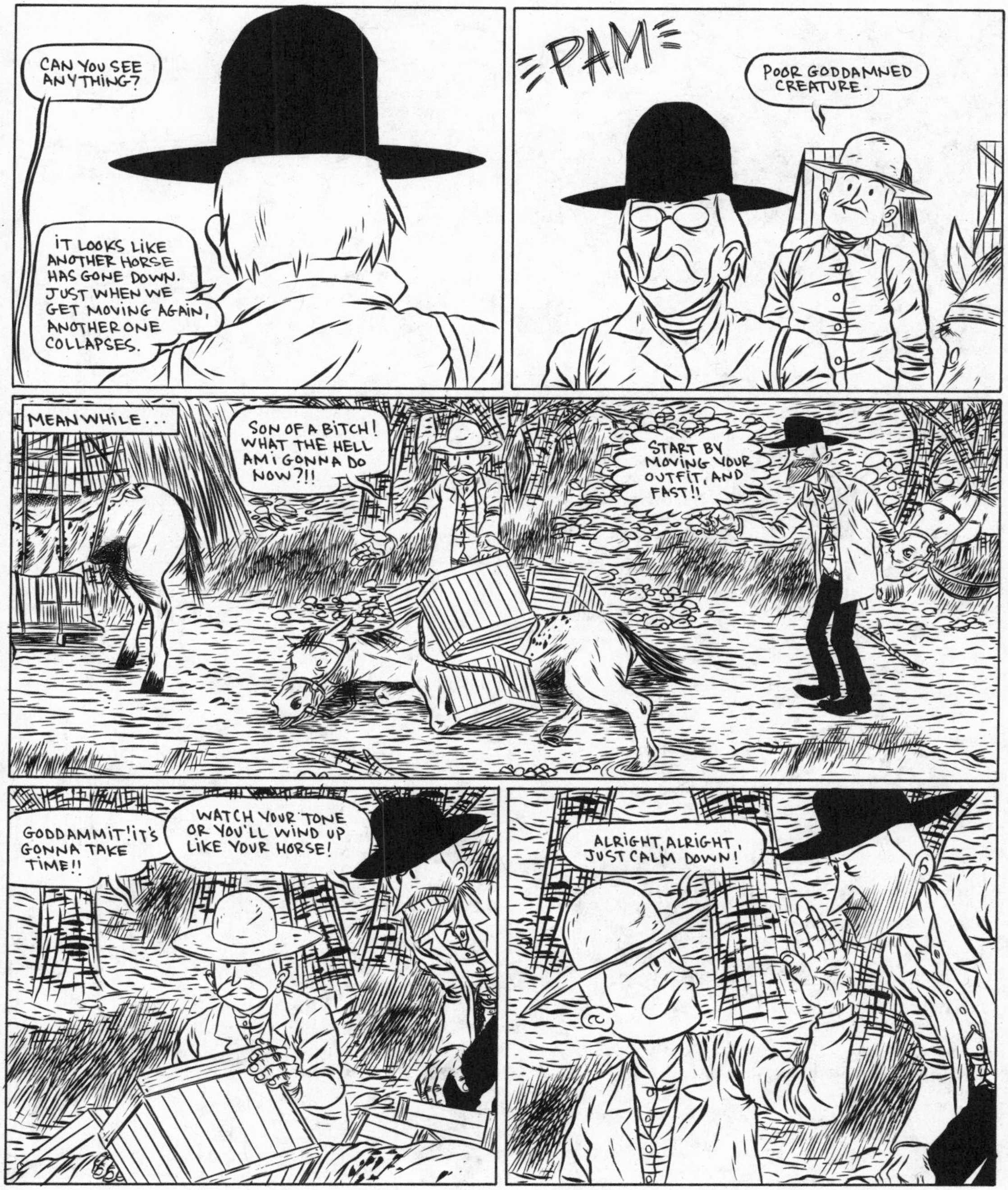
CAN YOU SEE ANYTHING?
IT LOOKS LIKE ANOTHER HORSE HAS GONE DOWN. JUST WHEN WE GET MOVING AGAIN, ANOTHER ONE COLLAPSES.
PAM
POOR GODDAMNED CREATURE.
MEANWHILE...
SON OF A BITCH! WHAT THE HELL AM I GONNA DO NOW?!!
START BY MOVING YOUR OUTFIT, AND FAST!!
GODDAMMIT! IT'S GONNA TAKE TIME!!
WATCH YOUR TONE OR YOU'LL WIND UP LIKE YOUR HORSE!
ALRIGHT, ALRIGHT, JUST CALM DOWN!

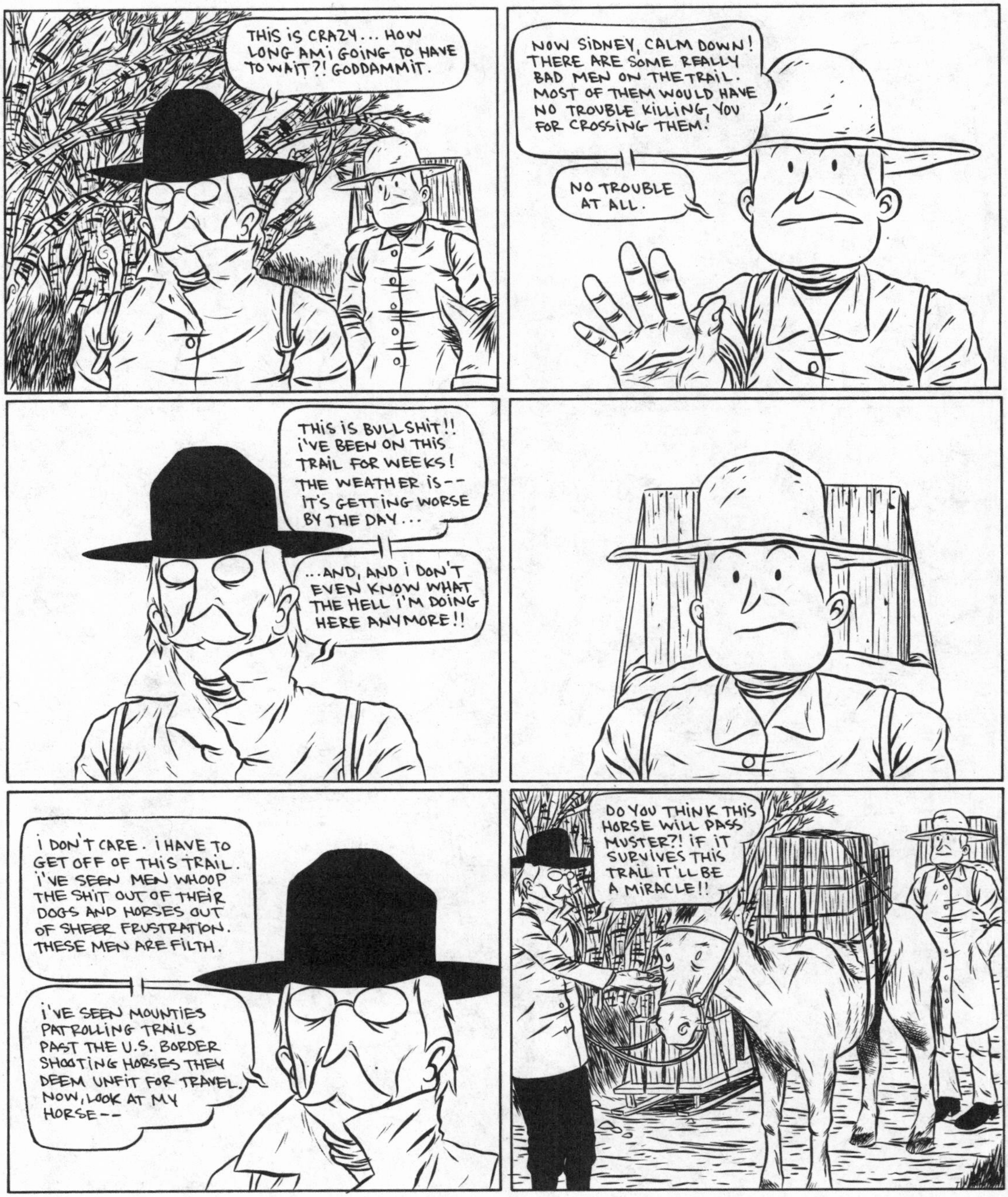
THIS IS CRAZY... HOW LONG AM I GOING TO HAVE TO WAIT?! GODDAMMIT.
NOW SIDNEY, CALM DOWN! THERE ARE SOME REALLY BAD MEN ON THE TRAIL. MOST OF THEM WOULD HAVE NO TROUBLE KILLING YOU FOR CROSSING THEM!
NO TROUBLE AT ALL.
THIS IS BULLSHIT!! I'VE BEEN ON THIS TRAIL FOR WEEKS! THE WEATHER IS-- IT'S GETTING WORSE BY THE DAY...
...AND, AND I DON'T EVEN KNOW WHAT THE HELL I'M DOING HERE ANYMORE!!
I DON'T CARE. I HAVE TO GET OFF OF THIS TRAIL. I'VE SEEN MEN WHOOP THE SHIT OUT OF THEIR DOGS AND HORSES OUT OF SHEER FRUSTRATION. THESE MEN ARE FILTH.
I'VE SEEN MOUNTIES PATROLLING TRAILS PAST THE U.S. BORDER SHOOTING HORSES THEY DEEM UNFIT FOR TRAVEL. NOW, LOOK AT MY HORSE--
DO YOU THINK THIS HORSE WILL PASS MUSTER?! IF IT SURVIVES THIS TRAIL IT'LL BE A MIRACLE!!

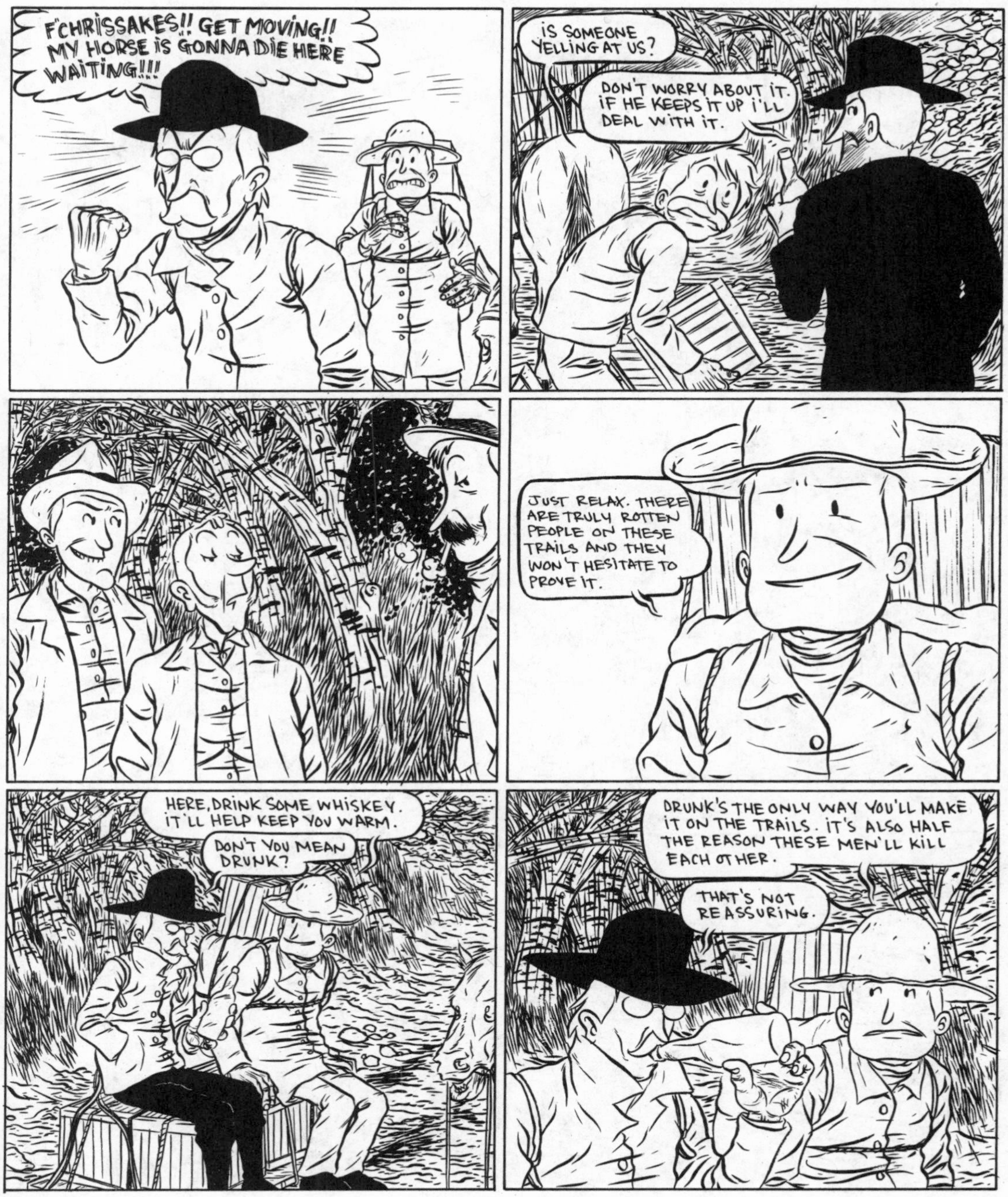
F'CHRISSAKES!! GET MOVING!! MY HORSE IS GONNA DIE HERE WAITING!!!
IS SOMEONE YELLING AT US?
DON'T WORRY ABOUT IT. IF HE KEEPS IT UP I'LL DEAL WITH IT.
JUST RELAX. THERE ARE TRULY ROTTEN PEOPLE ON THESE TRAILS AND THEY WON'T HESITATE TO PROVE IT.
HERE, DRINK SOME WHISKEY. IT'LL HELP KEEP YOU WARM.
DON'T YOU MEAN DRUNK?
DRUNK'S THE ONLY WAY YOU'LL MAKE IT ON THE TRAILS. IT'S ALSO HALF THE REASON THESE MEN'LL KILL EACH OTHER.
THAT'S NOT REASSURING.

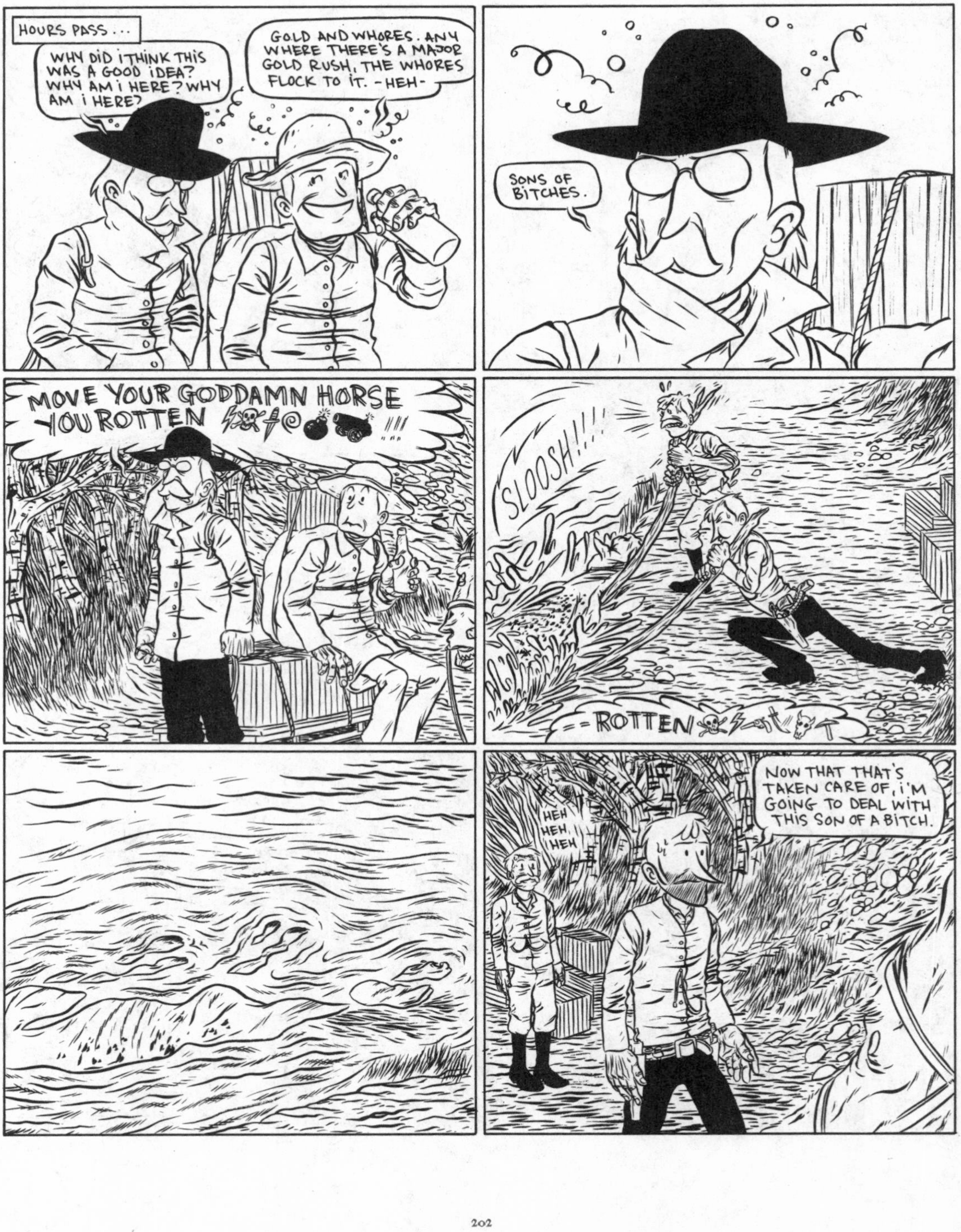
HOURS PASS...
WHY DID I THINK THIS WAS A GOOD IDEA? WHY AM I HERE? WHY AM I HERE?
GOLD AND WHORES. ANY WHERE THERE'S A MAJOR GOLD RUSH, THE WHORES FLOCK TO IT. -HEH-
SONS OF BITCHES.
MOVE YOUR GODDAMN HORSE YOU ROTTEN !!!
SLOOSH!!!!
--ROTTEN
HEH HEH HEH
NOW THAT THAT'S TAKEN CARE OF, I'M GOING TO DEAL WITH THIS SON OF A BITCH.

WHAT'S THE HOLD UP?!
LISTEN UP. I CAN TELL THAT YOU'RE DRUNK, AND JUDGING BY YER GET UP, YER NEW TO THIS! I'M GONNA GIVE YOU THE BENEFIT O' THE DOUBT. SOME MAY NOT.
JUST GET MOVING, GODDAMMIT!!
YOU WATCH YER TONE WITH ME.
GODDAMN YOU!!!
DUMB SON OF A BITCH!
THAP!!
A MAN OF YOUR YEARS SHOULD HAVE FIGURED OUT BY NOW --
-- THAT SOME FIGHTS ARE COM-PLETELY FUTILE!!

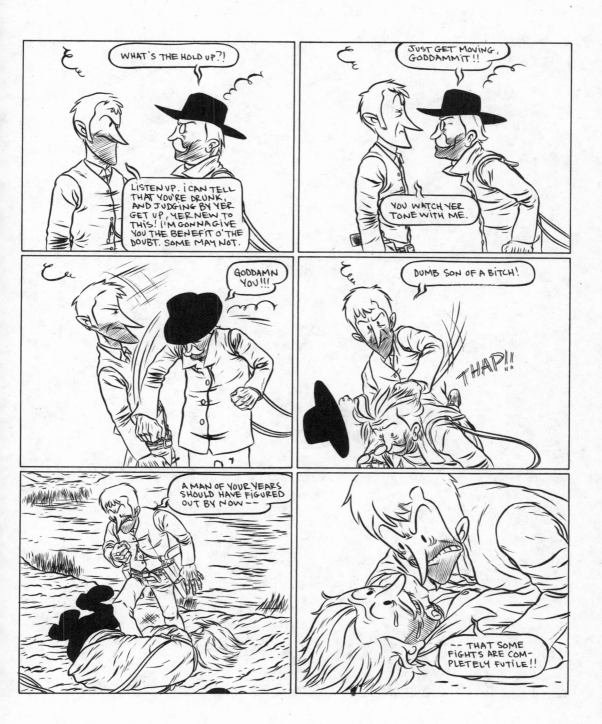

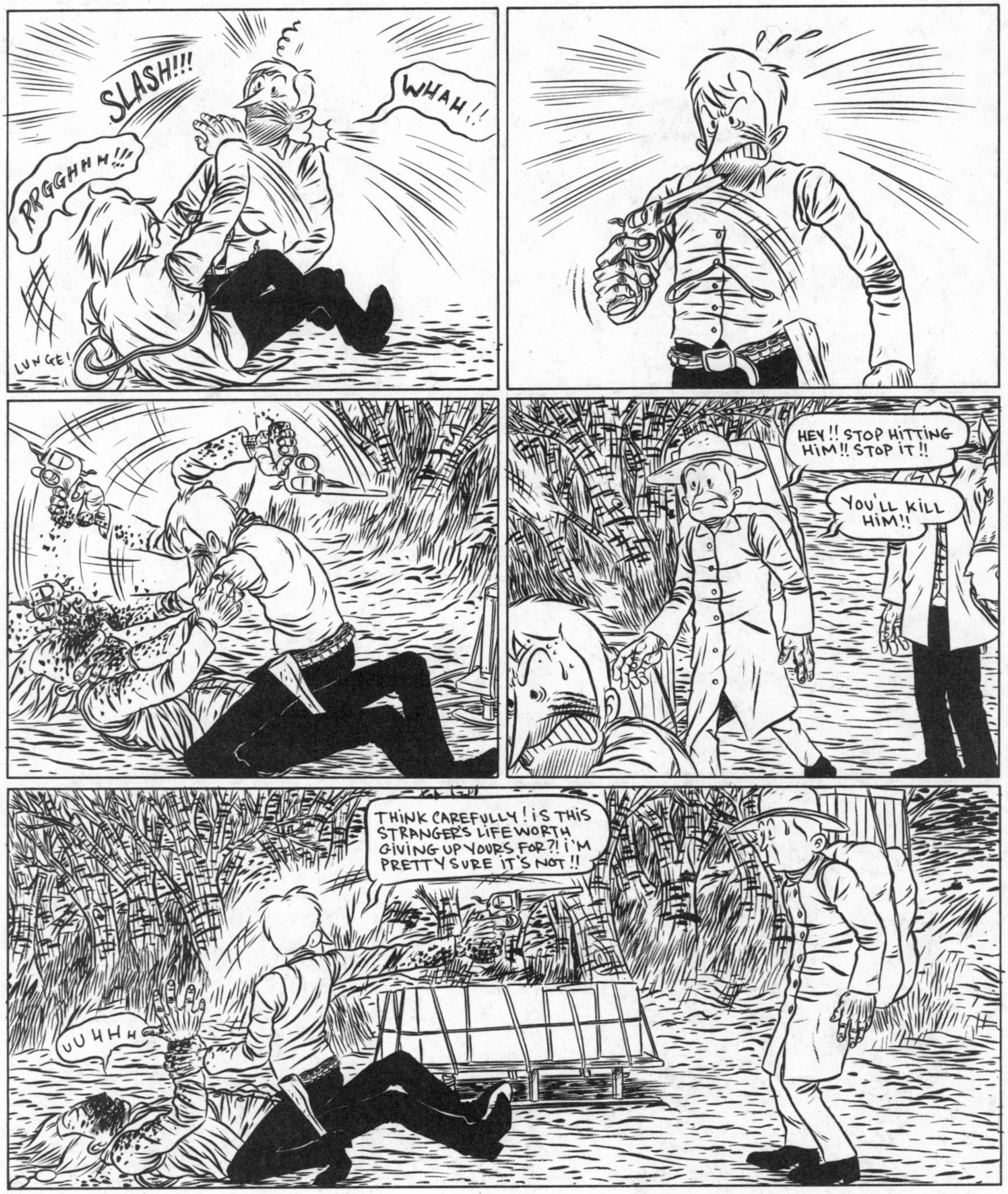
SLASH!!!
WHAH!!
RRGGHHHH!!!
LUNGE!
HEY!! STOP HITTING HIM!! STOP IT!!
YOU'LL KILL HIM!!
THINK CAREFULLY! IS THIS STRANGER'S LIFE WORTH GIVING UP YOURS FOR?! I'M PRETTY SURE IT'S NOT!!
UUHHH

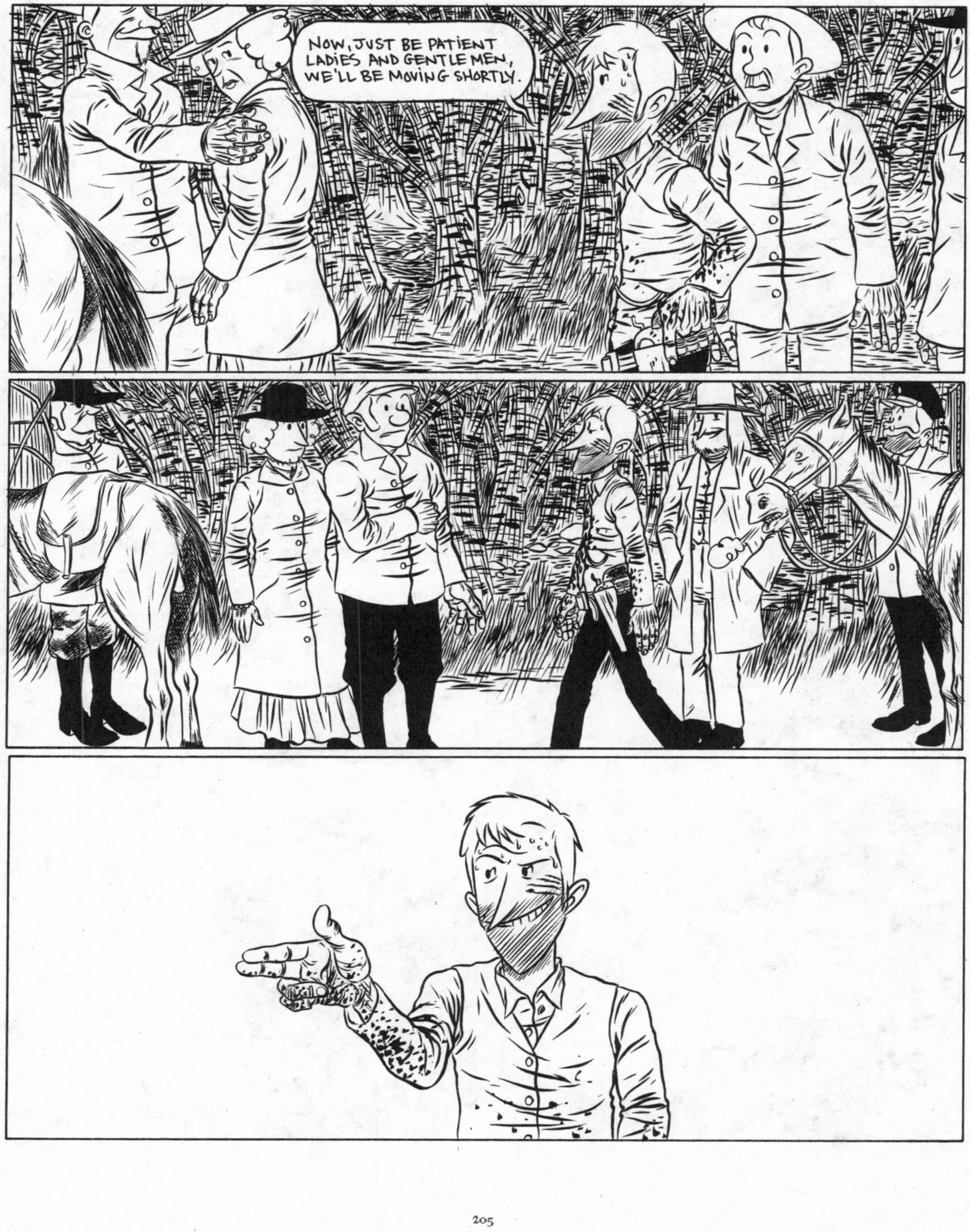
NOW, JUST BE PATIENT LADIES AND GENTLEMEN, WE'LL BE MOVING SHORTLY.

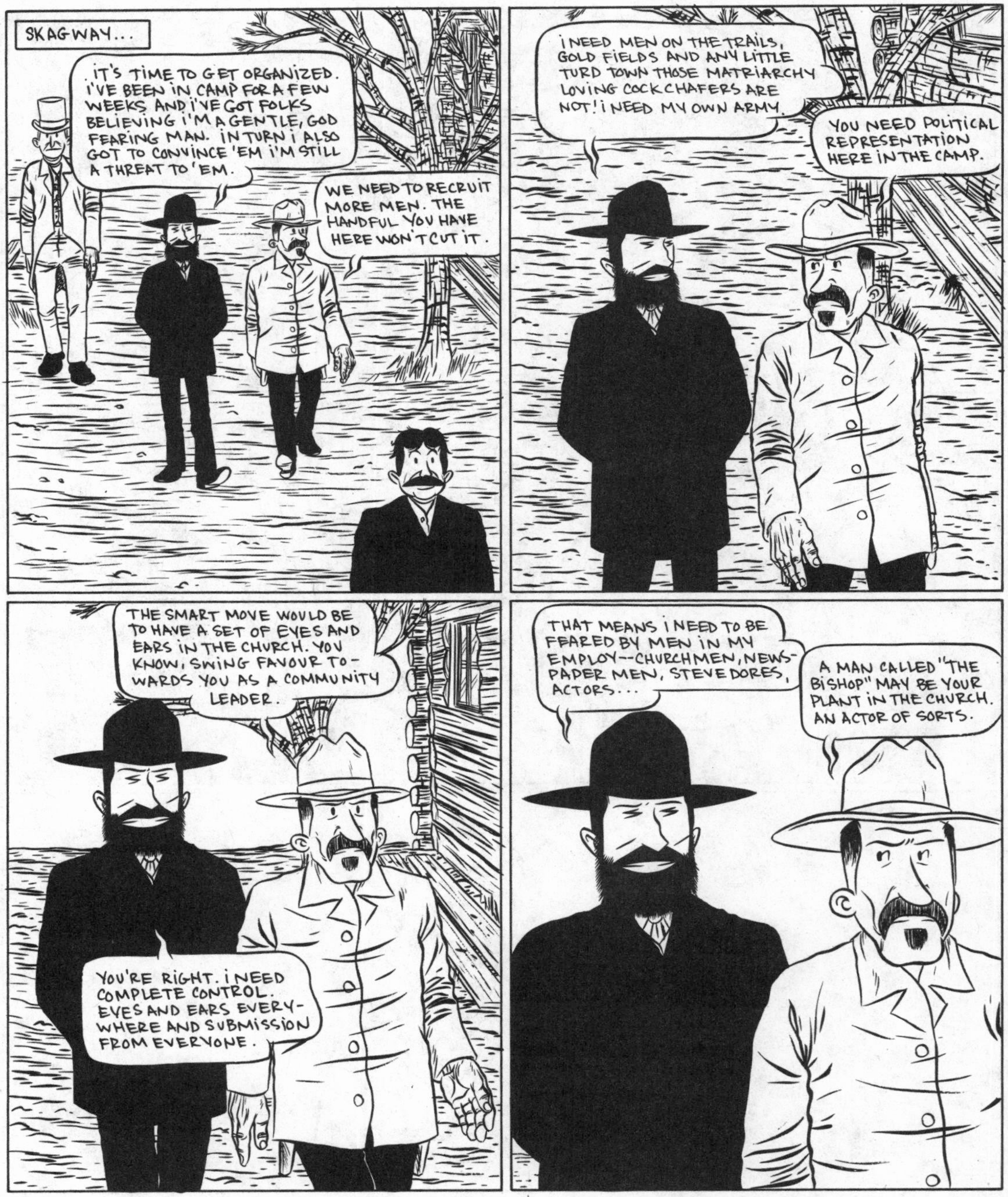
SKAGWAY...
IT'S TIME TO GET ORGANIZED. I'VE BEEN IN CAMP FOR A FEW WEEKS AND I'VE GOT FOLKS BELIEVING I'M A GENTLE, GOD FEARING MAN. IN TURN I ALSO GOT TO CONVINCE 'EM I'M STILL A THREAT TO 'EM.
WE NEED TO RECRUIT MORE MEN. THE HANDFUL YOU HAVE HERE WON'T CUT IT.
I NEED MEN ON THE TRAILS, GOLD FIELDS AND ANY LITTLE TURD TOWN THOSE MATRIARCHY LOVING COCKCHAFERS ARE NOT! I NEED MY OWN ARMY.
YOU NEED POLITICAL REPRESENTATION HERE IN THE CAMP.
THE SMART MOVE WOULD BE TO HAVE A SET OF EYES AND EARS IN THE CHURCH. YOU KNOW, SWING FAVOUR TO-WARDS YOU AS A COMMUNITY LEADER.
YOU'RE RIGHT. I NEED COMPLETE CONTROL. EYES AND EARS EVERY-WHERE AND SUBMISSION FROM EVERYONE.
THAT MEANS I NEED TO BE FEARED BY MEN IN MY EMPLOY--CHURCHMEN, NEWS-PAPER MEN, STEVEDORES, ACTORS...
A MAN CALLED "THE BISHOP" MAY BE YOUR PLANT IN THE CHURCH. AN ACTOR OF SORTS.

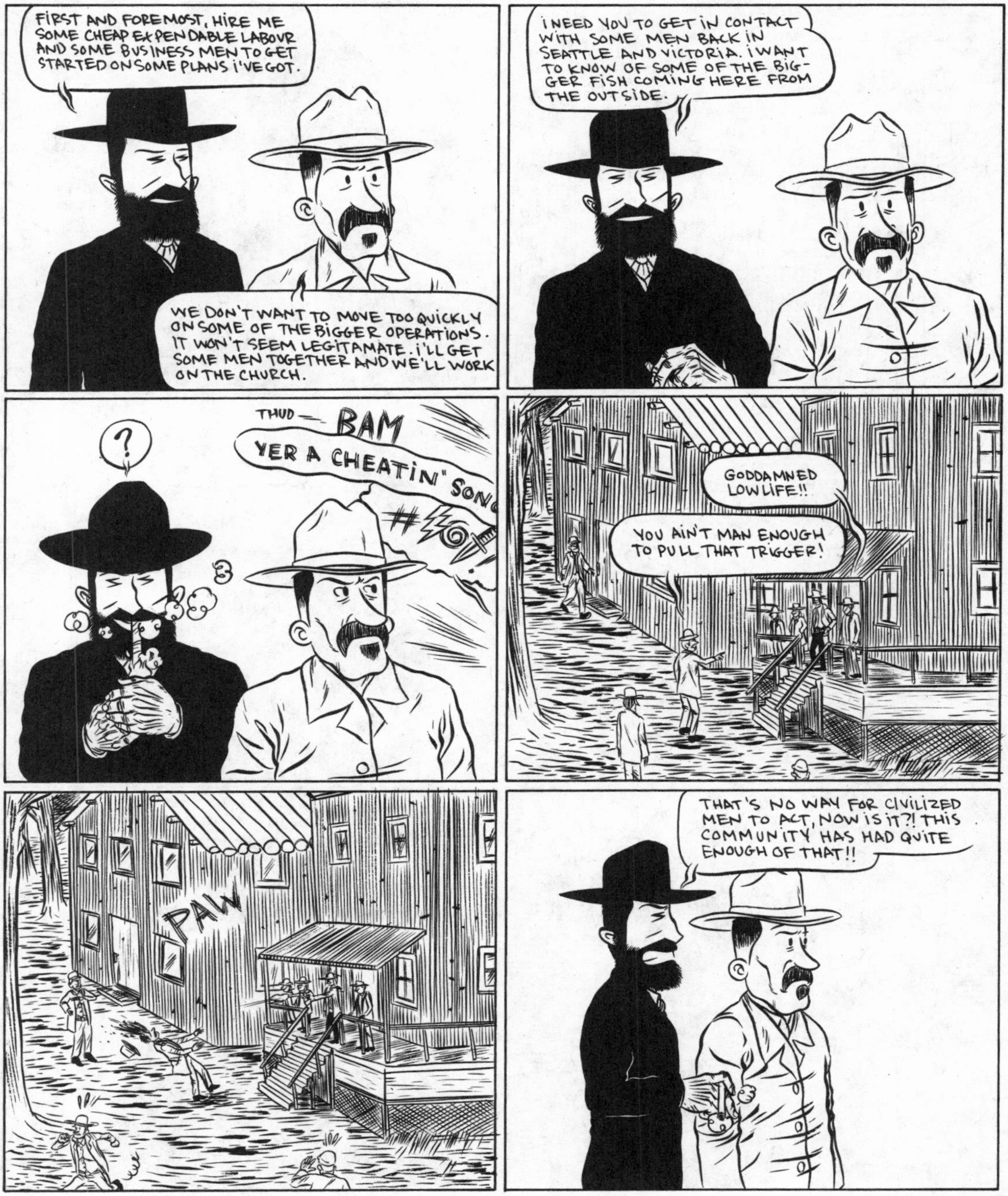
FIRST AND FOREMOST, HIRE ME SOME CHEAP EXPENDABLE LABOUR AND SOME BUSINESS MEN TO GET STARTED ON SOME PLANS I'VE GOT.
WE DON'T WANT TO MOVE TOO QUICKLY ON SOME OF THE BIGGER OPERATIONS. IT WON'T SEEM LEGITAMATE. I'LL GET SOME MEN TOGETHER AND WE'LL WORK ON THE CHURCH.
I NEED YOU TO GET IN CONTACT WITH SOME MEN BACK IN SEATTLE AND VICTORIA. I WANT TO KNOW OF SOME OF THE BIGGER FISH COMING HERE FROM THE OUTSIDE.
?
THUD— BAM
YER A CHEATIN' SON
GODDAMNED LOWLIFE!!
YOU AIN'T MAN ENOUGH TO PULL THAT TRIGGER!
PAW
THAT'S NO WAY FOR CIVILIZED MEN TO ACT, NOW IS IT?! THIS COMMUNITY HAS HAD QUITE ENOUGH OF THAT!!

WHO THE HELL ARE YOU? LAST I HEARD, LAW DIDN'T EXIST IN THESE PARTS, SO MIND YOUR DAMNED BUSINESS!!
EVERYTHING THAT GOES ON IN THIS CAMP IS MY BUSINESS.
I'M ONLY GOING TO ASK YOU ONE MORE TIME... WHO THE CHRIST ARE YOU AND WHO THE SHIT DO YOU THINK YOU ARE TO GIVE ME ORDERS?!
WHUP
I'M SOAPY SMITH.
CARE TO TAKE STEPS AGAINST ME? I'VE GOT A DOZEN MEN ON THIS THOROUGHFARE WATCHING YOU RIGHT NOW. YOU WON'T WALK AWAY FROM THIS.
BACK DOWN NOW AND SEE TO THE BURYING OF THAT MAN.

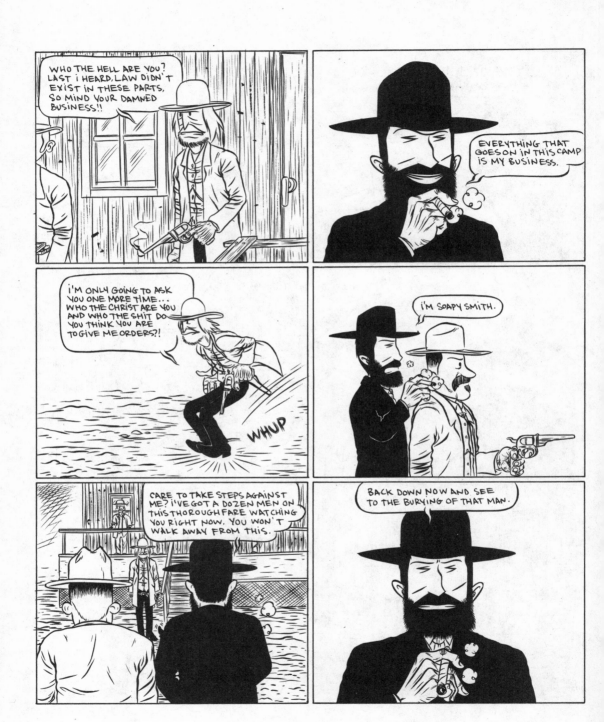

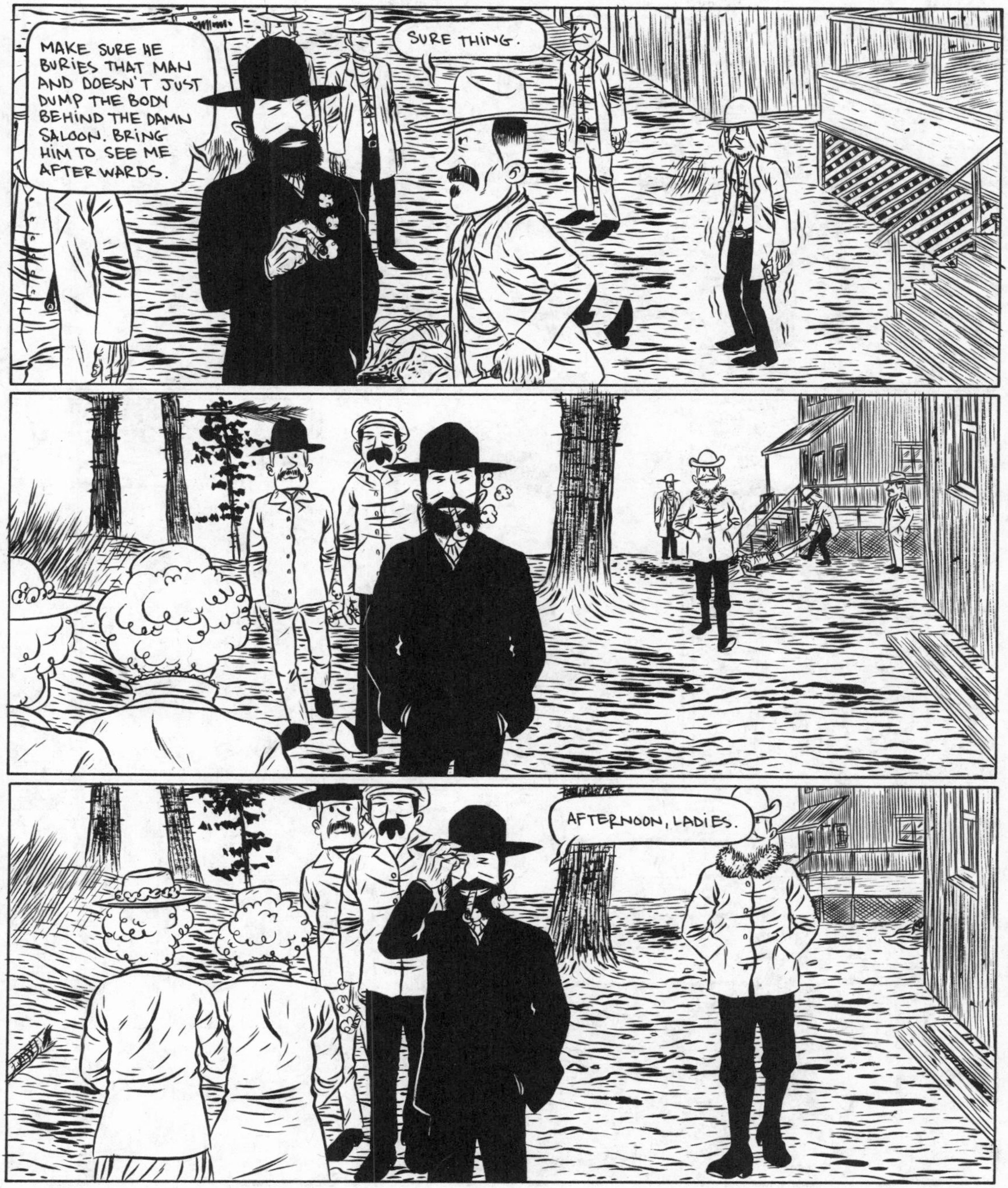
MAKE SURE HE BURIES THAT MAN AND DOESN'T JUST DUMP THE BODY BEHIND THE DAMN SALOON. BRING HIM TO SEE ME AFTERWARDS.
SURE THING.
AFTERNOON, LADIES.

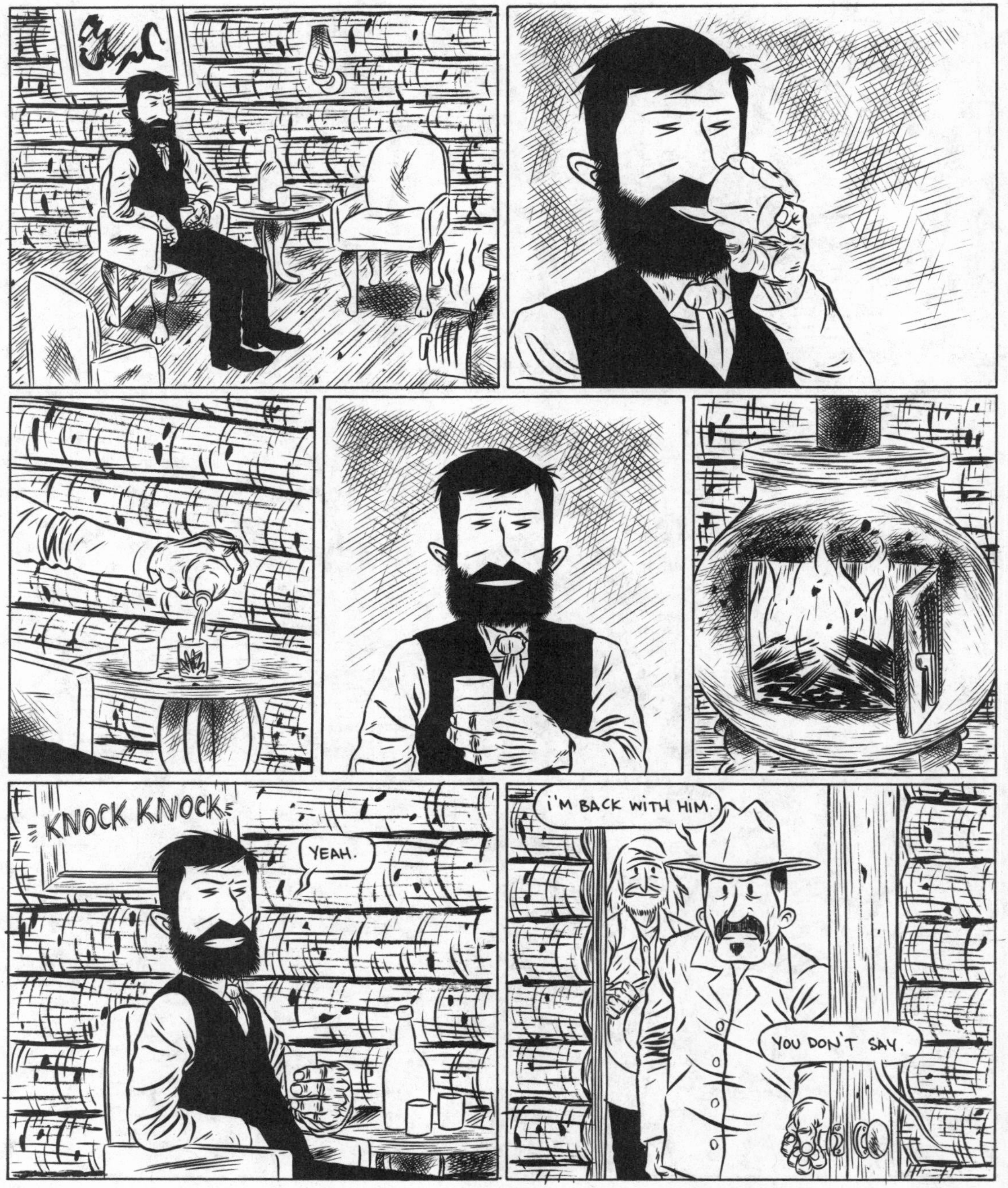
KNOCK KNOCK
YEAH.
I'M BACK WITH HIM.
YOU DON'T SAY.

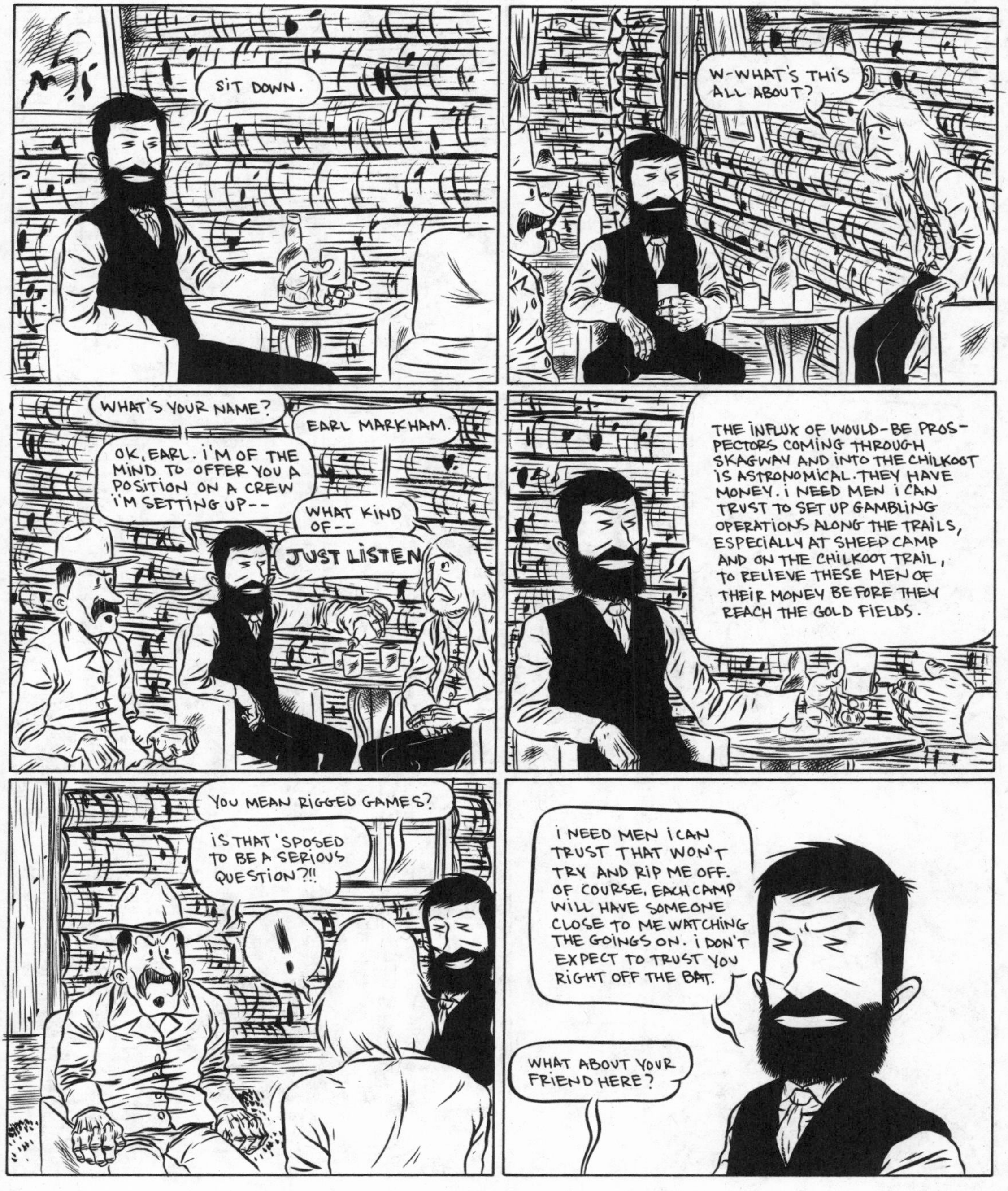
SIT DOWN.
W-WHAT'S THIS ALL ABOUT?
WHAT'S YOUR NAME?
EARL MARKHAM.
OK, EARL. I'M OF THE MIND TO OFFER YOU A POSITION ON A CREW I'M SETTING UP--
WHAT KIND OF--
JUST LISTEN
THE INFLUX OF WOULD-BE PROSPECTORS COMING THROUGH SKAGWAY AND INTO THE CHILKOOT IS ASTRONOMICAL. THEY HAVE MONEY. I NEED MEN I CAN TRUST TO SET UP GAMBLING OPERATIONS ALONG THE TRAILS, ESPECIALLY AT SHEEP CAMP AND ON THE CHILKOOT TRAIL, TO RELIEVE THESE MEN OF THEIR MONEY BEFORE THEY REACH THE GOLD FIELDS.
YOU MEAN RIGGED GAMES?
IS THAT 'SPOSED TO BE A SERIOUS QUESTION?!!
!
I NEED MEN I CAN TRUST THAT WON'T TRY AND RIP ME OFF. OF COURSE, EACH CAMP WILL HAVE SOMEONE CLOSE TO ME WATCHING THE GOINGS ON. I DON'T EXPECT TO TRUST YOU RIGHT OFF THE BAT.
WHAT ABOUT YOUR FRIEND HERE?

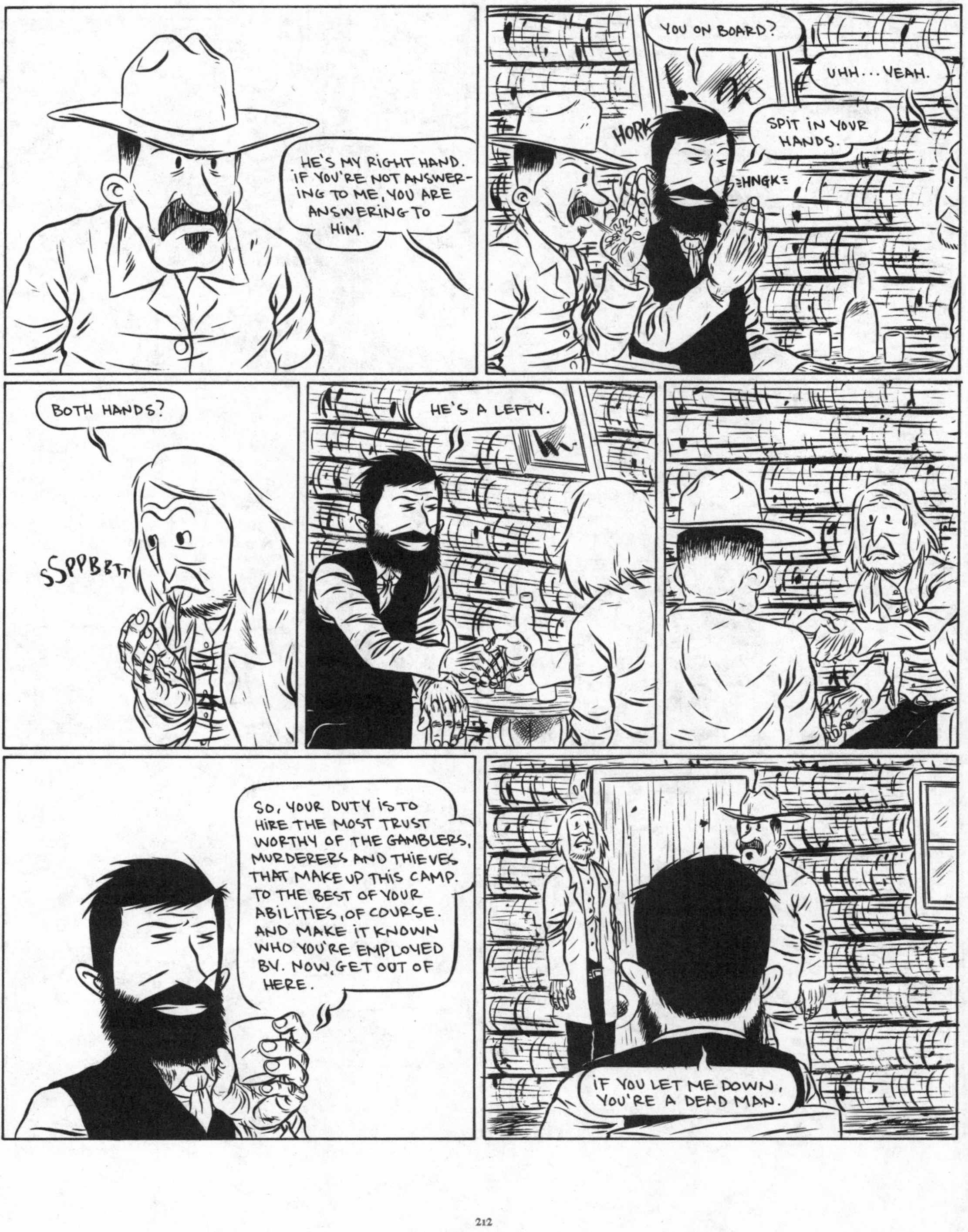
HE'S MY RIGHT HAND. IF YOU'RE NOT ANSWERING TO ME, YOU ARE ANSWERING TO HIM.
YOU ON BOARD?
UHH... YEAH.
SPIT IN YOUR HANDS.
HORK
HNGK
BOTH HANDS?
SSPPBBTT
HE'S A LEFTY.
SO, YOUR DUTY IS TO HIRE THE MOST TRUST WORTHY OF THE GAMBLERS, MURDERERS AND THIEVES THAT MAKE UP THIS CAMP. TO THE BEST OF YOUR ABILITIES, OF COURSE. AND MAKE IT KNOWN WHO YOU'RE EMPLOYED BY. NOW, GET OUT OF HERE.
IF YOU LET ME DOWN, YOU'RE A DEAD MAN.

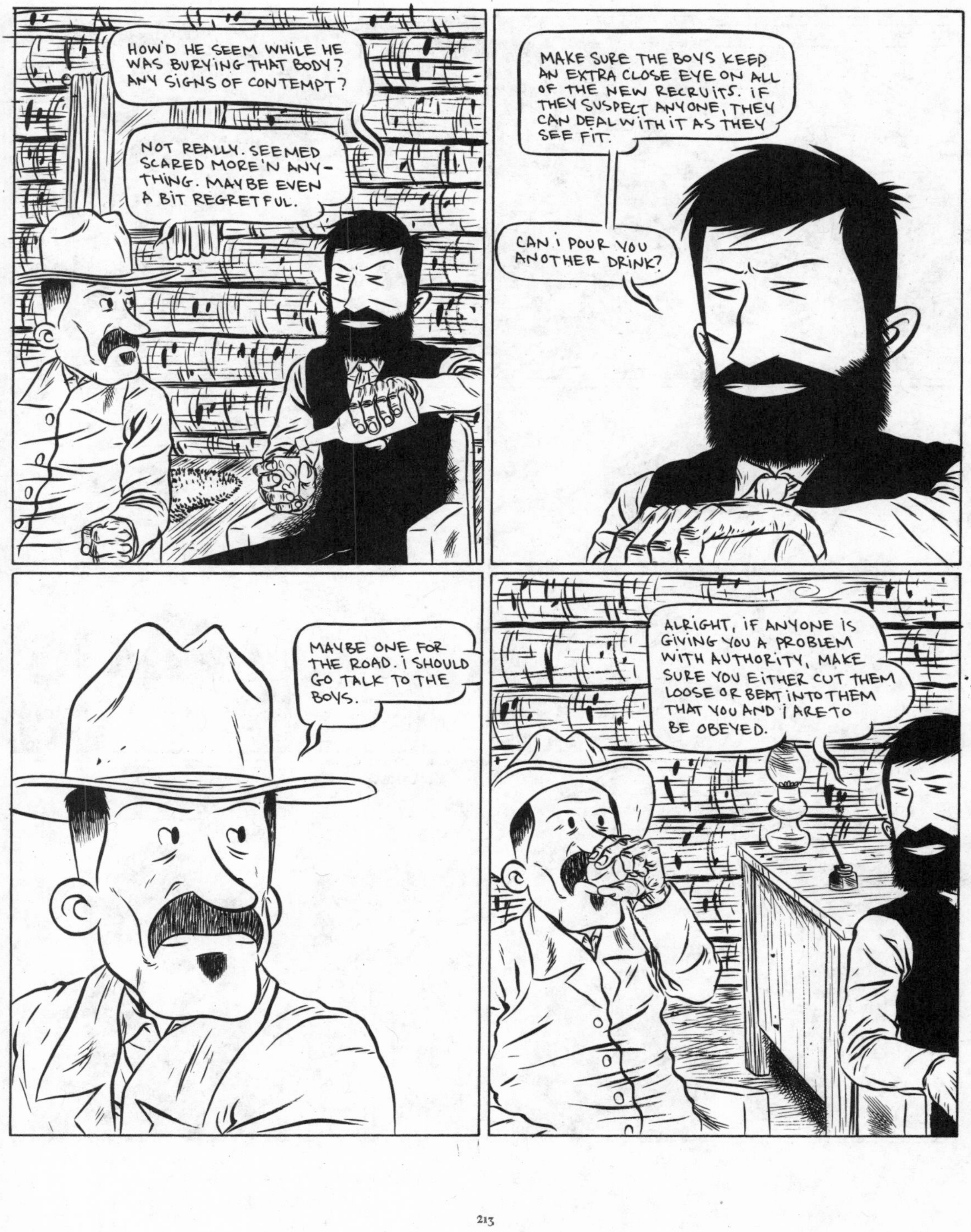
HOW'D HE SEEM WHILE HE WAS BURYING THAT BODY? ANY SIGNS OF CONTEMPT?
NOT REALLY. SEEMED SCARED MORE'N ANY-THING. MAYBE EVEN A BIT REGRETFUL.
MAKE SURE THE BOYS KEEP AN EXTRA CLOSE EYE ON ALL OF THE NEW RECRUITS. IF THEY SUSPECT ANYONE, THEY CAN DEAL WITH IT AS THEY SEE FIT.
CAN I POUR YOU ANOTHER DRINK?
MAYBE ONE FOR THE ROAD. I SHOULD GO TALK TO THE BOYS.
ALRIGHT, IF ANYONE IS GIVING YOU A PROBLEM WITH AUTHORITY, MAKE SURE YOU EITHER CUT THEM LOOSE OR BEAT INTO THEM THAT YOU AND I ARE TO BE OBEYED.

CARMACK'S DISCOVERY CLAIM...
<I HEARD KATE LEAVE THIS MORNING. WHERE WAS SHE GOING? SHE LEFT GRAPHIE BEHIND?>
<SHE WENT TO DAWSON. I THINK SHE WENT TO GO DRINK. SHE'S BEEN DRINKING A LOT MORE LATELY.>
<THIS IS NOT GOOD.>
<IT'S BAD FOR OUR DAUGHTER. SHE SHOULDN'T HAVE TO DEAL WITH HER MOTHER BEING DRUNK ALL THE TIME.>
<OH WELL... ANY RECENT NEWS?>
<BIG NEWS IN DAWSON!>

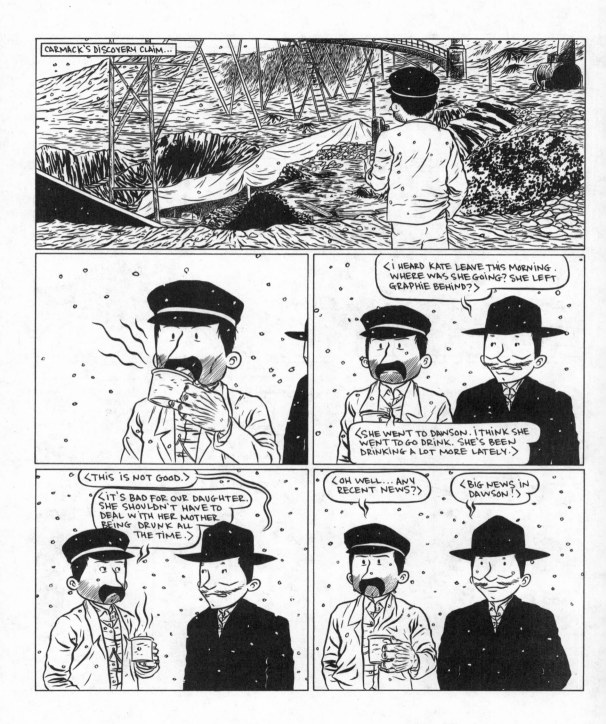

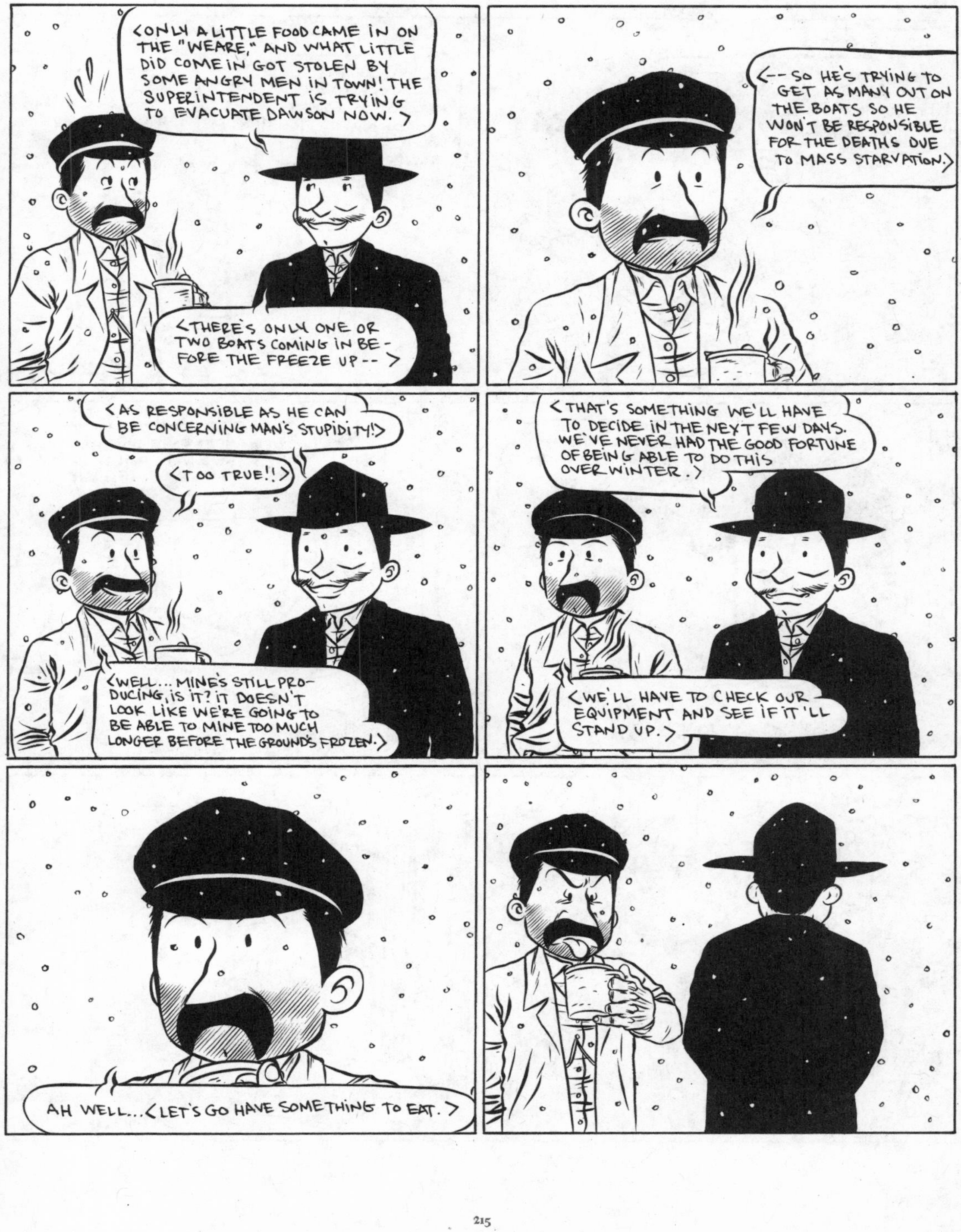

<ONLY A LITTLE FOOD CAME IN ON THE "WEARE," AND WHAT LITTLE DID COME IN GOT STOLEN BY SOME ANGRY MEN IN TOWN! THE SUPERINTENDENT IS TRYING TO EVACUATE DAWSON NOW.>
<THERE'S ONLY ONE OR TWO BOATS COMING IN BEFORE THE FREEZE UP-->
<--SO HE'S TRYING TO GET AS MANY OUT ON THE BOATS SO HE WON'T BE RESPONSIBLE FOR THE DEATHS DUE TO MASS STARVATION.>
<AS RESPONSIBLE AS HE CAN BE CONCERNING MAN'S STUPIDITY!>
<TOO TRUE!!>
<WELL... MINE'S STILL PRODUCING, IS IT? IT DOESN'T LOOK LIKE WE'RE GOING TO BE ABLE TO MINE TOO MUCH LONGER BEFORE THE GROUND'S FROZEN.>
<THAT'S SOMETHING WE'LL HAVE TO DECIDE IN THE NEXT FEW DAYS. WE'VE NEVER HAD THE GOOD FORTUNE OF BEING ABLE TO DO THIS OVER WINTER.>
<WE'LL HAVE TO CHECK OUR EQUIPMENT AND SEE IF IT'LL STAND UP.>
AH WELL... <LET'S GO HAVE SOMETHING TO EAT.>

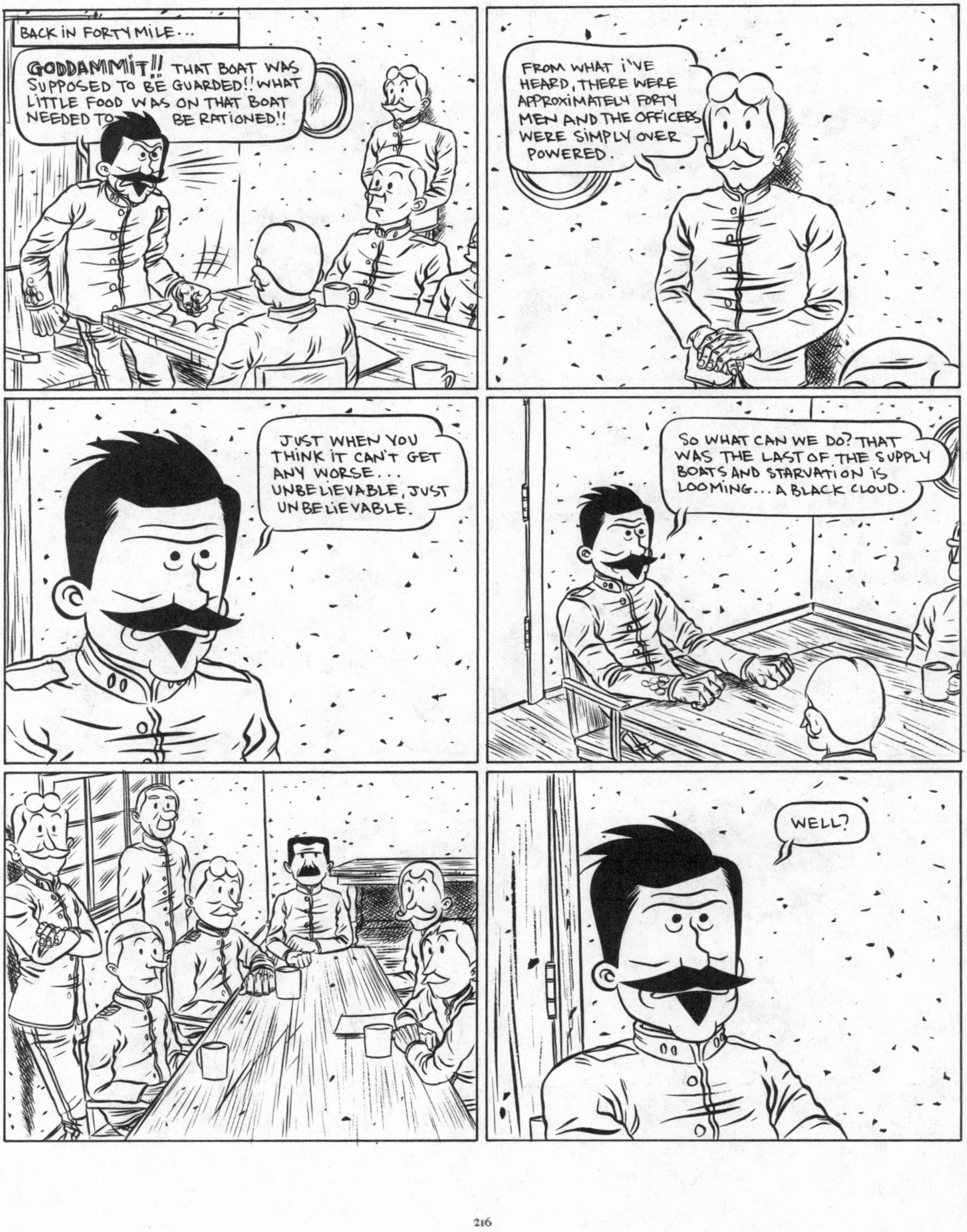
BACK IN FORTY MILE...
GODDAMMIT!! THAT BOAT WAS SUPPOSED TO BE GUARDED!! WHAT LITTLE FOOD WAS ON THAT BOAT NEEDED TO BE RATIONED!!
FROM WHAT I'VE HEARD, THERE WERE APPROXIMATELY FORTY MEN AND THE OFFICERS WERE SIMPLY OVER POWERED.
JUST WHEN YOU THINK IT CAN'T GET ANY WORSE... UNBELIEVABLE, JUST UNBELIEVABLE.
SO WHAT CAN WE DO? THAT WAS THE LAST OF THE SUPPLY BOATS AND STARVATION IS LOOMING... A BLACK CLOUD.
WELL?

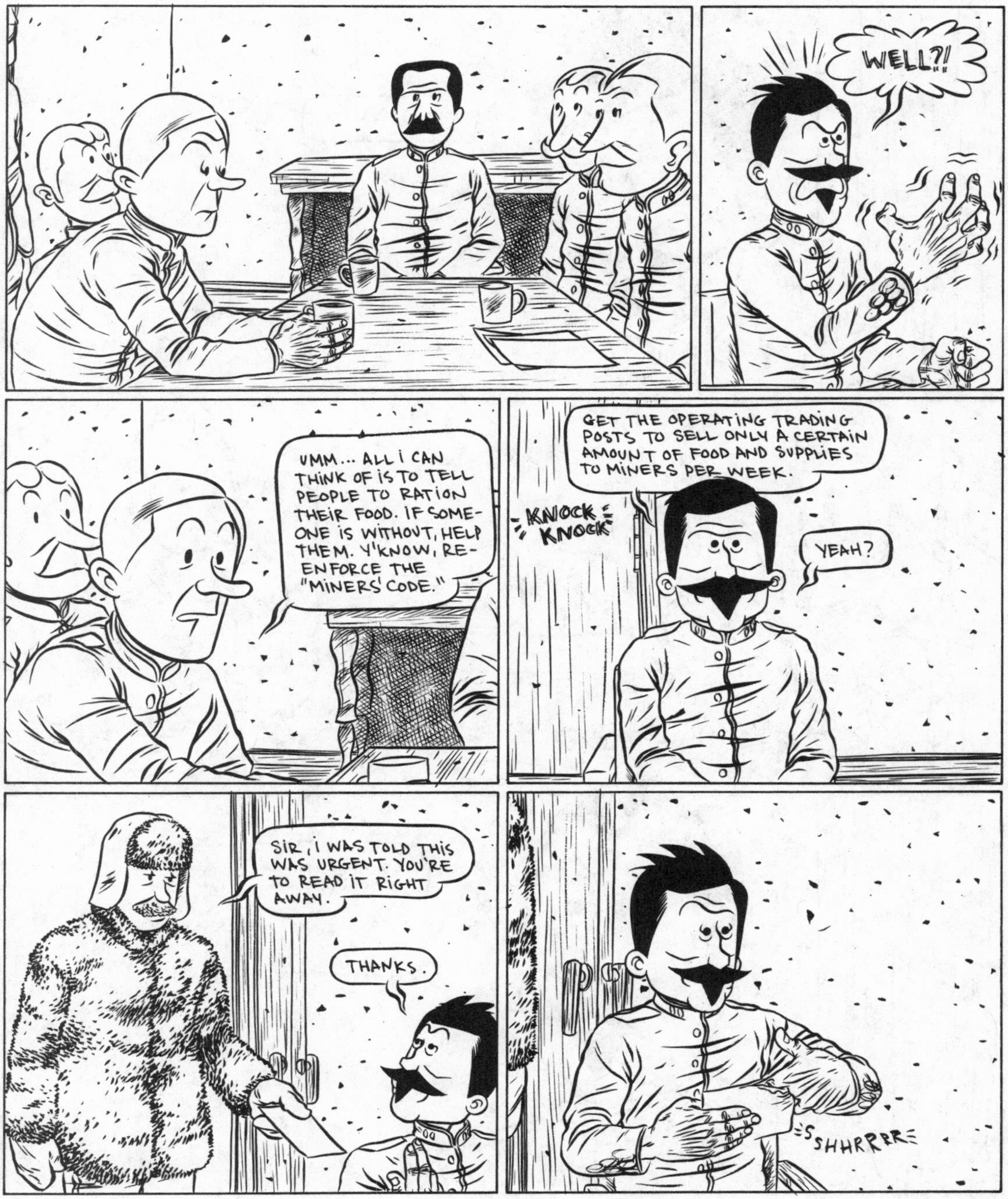
WELL?!
UMM... ALL I CAN THINK OF IS TO TELL PEOPLE TO RATION THEIR FOOD. IF SOMEONE IS WITHOUT, HELP THEM. Y'KNOW, RE-ENFORCE THE "MINERS' CODE."
GET THE OPERATING TRADING POSTS TO SELL ONLY A CERTAIN AMOUNT OF FOOD AND SUPPLIES TO MINERS PER WEEK.
KNOCK KNOCK
YEAH?
SIR, I WAS TOLD THIS WAS URGENT. YOU'RE TO READ IT RIGHT AWAY.
THANKS.
SSHHRRRR

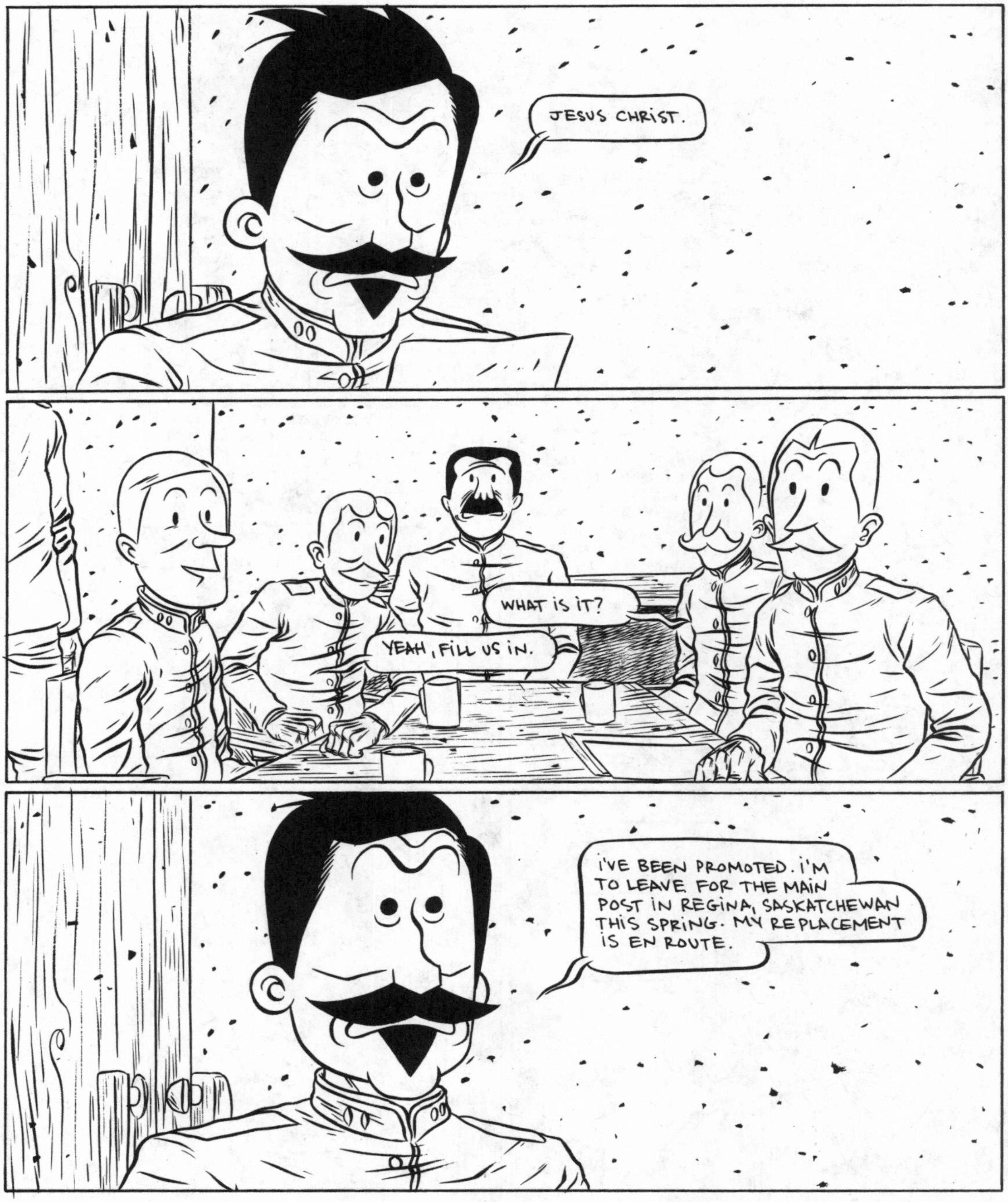
JESUS CHRIST.
WHAT IS IT?
YEAH, FILL US IN.
I'VE BEEN PROMOTED. I'M TO LEAVE FOR THE MAIN POST IN REGINA, SASKATCHEWAN THIS SPRING. MY REPLACEMENT IS EN ROUTE.

INSPECTOR SAMUEL BENFIELD STEELE WAS GIVEN THE IMMENSE TASK OF TAKING OVER CHARLES CONSTANTINE'S POST IN THE YUKON AFTER HIS PRO-MOTION TO SUPERINTENDENT. WITHIN A DAY, STEELE RELINQUISHED HIS CURRENT POST, WAS PUT ON A TRAIN AND SENT TO VANCOUVER TO CATCH A BOAT HEADED NORTH. PRIOR TO THIS APPOINTMENT, STEELE HAD BEEN IN GENERAL COMMAND OF THE MACLEOD DISTRICT. HE WAS SUCH A STICKLER FOR RULES AND ORDER THAT WITHIN A MONTH 24 MOUNTIES DESERTED. ALL OF HIS HARD WORK AND TOWING THE COMPANY LINE WENT UNNOTICED AND HE WAS PASSED OVER FOR THE POSITION OF ASSISTANT COMMISSIONER. THE MAN WHO GOT THE PROMOTION WAS J.H. MCILLREE. HE WAS KNOWN THROUGH THE N.W.M.P. BARRACKS AS "EASY GOING OLD JOHN HENRY." STEELE WAS UPSET BY THIS DECISION AS HE FELT HE WAS PERFECT FOR THE POSITION. EVEN THOUGH HE WAS A COMPANY MAN, HIS MORALS OFTEN WENT AGAINST THE POLICIES OF OTTAWA. HE WAS ACCUSED OF INTERFERING WITH THE AFFAIRS OF THE INDIAN DEPARTMENT, WANTING TO HOLD THE INDIANS OF THE TERRITORY TO THE SAME LETTER OF THE LAW AS THE WHITE MEN.

AT THE SAME TIME STEELE WAS HEADING NORTH, SOAPY SMITH WAS SETTING UP CROOKED GAMES OF CHANCE ALONG THE TRAILS AND BEGAN FLEECING MEN OUT OF THEIR MONEY AND PROSPECTING GEAR. THE WOULD-BE PROSPECTORS WERE ALLOWED TO WIN A FEW HANDS AT CARDS, THEN THEY WERE, FOR ALL INTENTS AND PURPOSES, MASSACRED. THE FALSE SENSE OF SECURITY THAT WAS OFFERED WENT A LONG WAY.

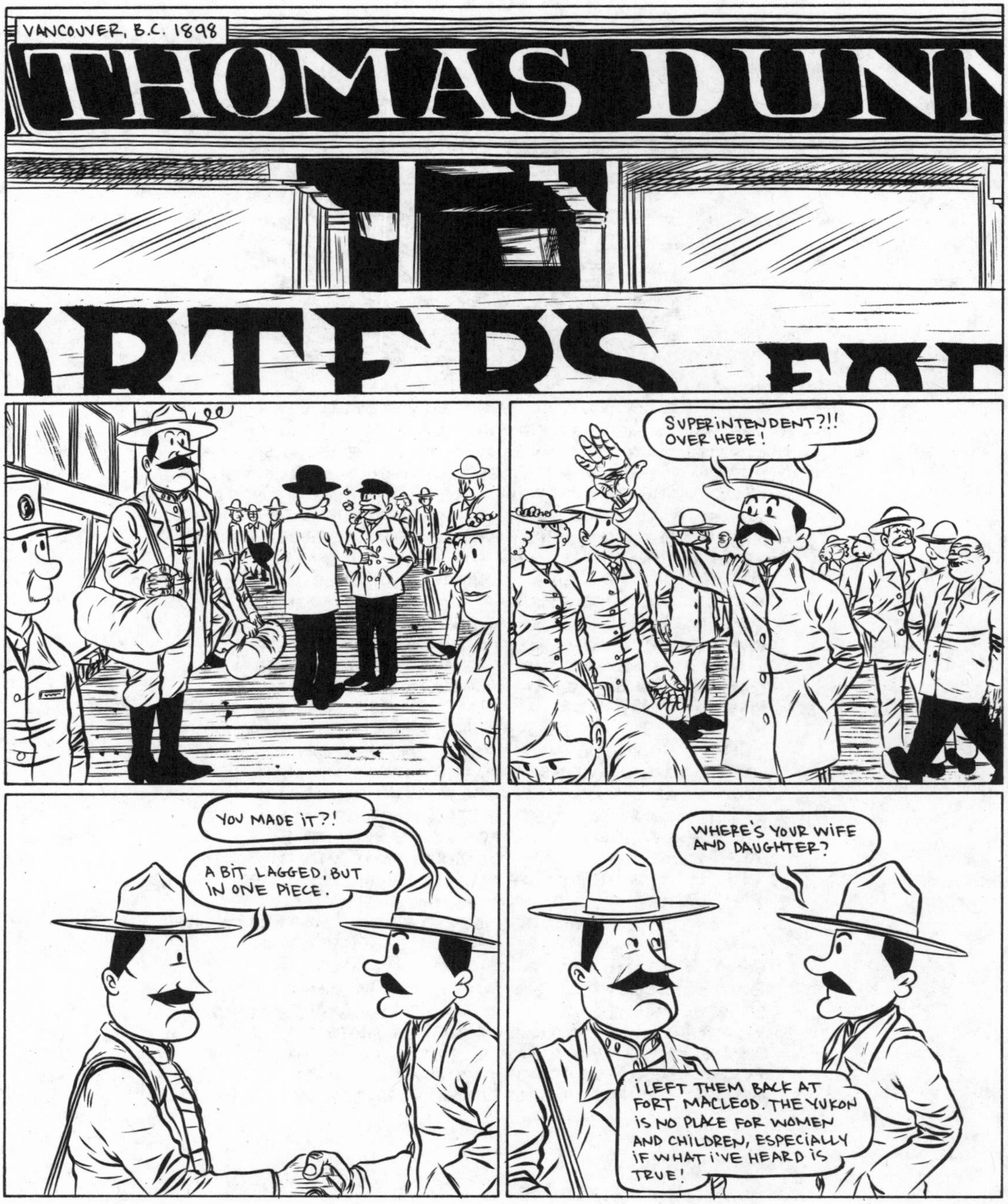
VANCOUVER, B.C. 1898
THOMAS DUNN
RTERS FOR
SUPERINTENDENT?!! OVER HERE!
YOU MADE IT?!
A BIT LAGGED, BUT IN ONE PIECE.
WHERE'S YOUR WIFE AND DAUGHTER?
I LEFT THEM BACK AT FORT MACLEOD. THE YUKON IS NO PLACE FOR WOMEN AND CHILDREN, ESPECIALLY IF WHAT I'VE HEARD IS TRUE!

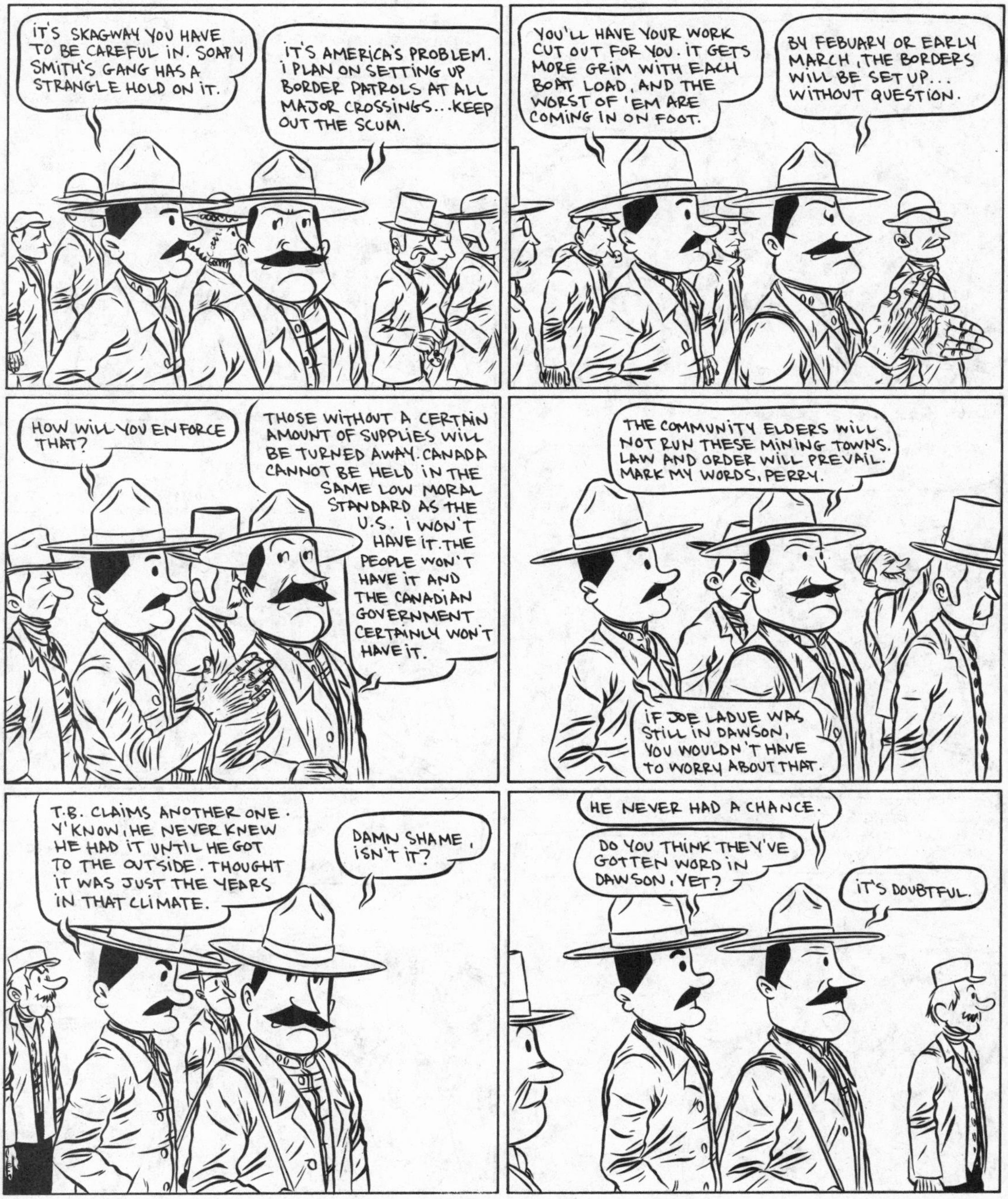
IT'S SKAGWAY YOU HAVE TO BE CAREFUL IN. SOAPY SMITH'S GANG HAS A STRANGLE HOLD ON IT.
IT'S AMERICA'S PROBLEM. I PLAN ON SETTING UP BORDER PATROLS AT ALL MAJOR CROSSINGS... KEEP OUT THE SCUM.
YOU'LL HAVE YOUR WORK CUT OUT FOR YOU. IT GETS MORE GRIM WITH EACH BOAT LOAD, AND THE WORST OF 'EM ARE COMING IN ON FOOT.
BY FEBUARY OR EARLY MARCH, THE BORDERS WILL BE SET UP... WITHOUT QUESTION.
HOW WILL YOU ENFORCE THAT?
THOSE WITHOUT A CERTAIN AMOUNT OF SUPPLIES WILL BE TURNED AWAY. CANADA CANNOT BE HELD IN THE SAME LOW MORAL STANDARD AS THE U.S. I WON'T HAVE IT. THE PEOPLE WON'T HAVE IT AND THE CANADIAN GOVERNMENT CERTAINLY WON'T HAVE IT.
THE COMMUNITY ELDERS WILL NOT RUN THESE MINING TOWNS. LAW AND ORDER WILL PREVAIL. MARK MY WORDS, PERRY.
IF JOE LADUE WAS STILL IN DAWSON, YOU WOULDN'T HAVE TO WORRY ABOUT THAT.
T.B. CLAIMS ANOTHER ONE. Y'KNOW, HE NEVER KNEW HE HAD IT UNTIL HE GOT TO THE OUTSIDE. THOUGHT IT WAS JUST THE YEARS IN THAT CLIMATE.
DAMN SHAME, ISN'T IT?
HE NEVER HAD A CHANCE.
DO YOU THINK THEY'VE GOTTEN WORD IN DAWSON, YET?
IT'S DOUBTFUL.

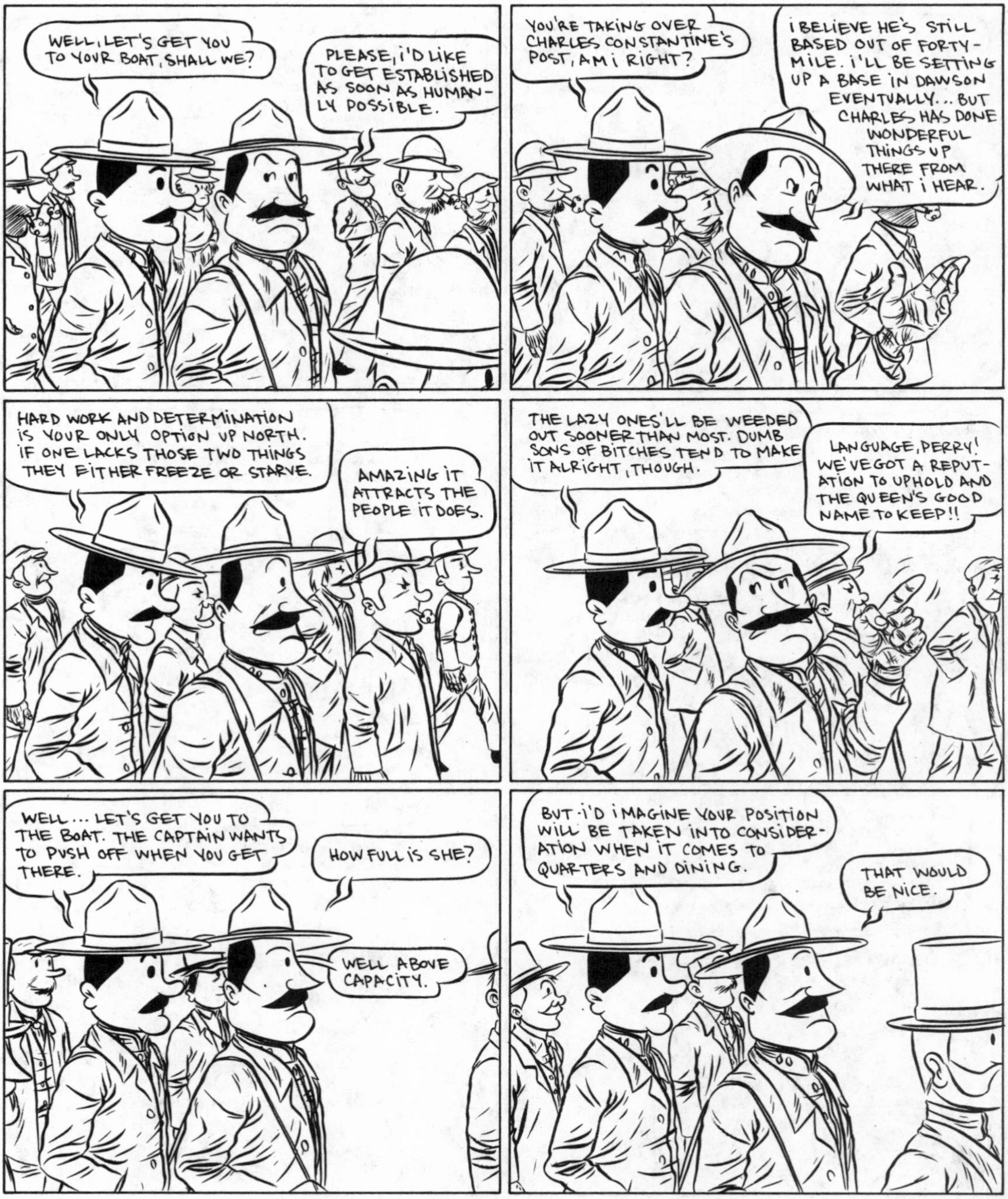
WELL, LET'S GET YOU TO YOUR BOAT, SHALL WE?
PLEASE, I'D LIKE TO GET ESTABLISHED AS SOON AS HUMANLY POSSIBLE.
YOU'RE TAKING OVER CHARLES CONSTANTINE'S POST, AM I RIGHT?
I BELIEVE HE'S STILL BASED OUT OF FORTY-MILE. I'LL BE SETTING UP A BASE IN DAWSON EVENTUALLY... BUT CHARLES HAS DONE WONDERFUL THINGS UP THERE FROM WHAT I HEAR.
HARD WORK AND DETERMINATION IS YOUR ONLY OPTION UP NORTH. IF ONE LACKS THOSE TWO THINGS THEY EITHER FREEZE OR STARVE.
AMAZING IT ATTRACTS THE PEOPLE IT DOES.
THE LAZY ONES'LL BE WEEDED OUT SOONER THAN MOST. DUMB SONS OF BITCHES TEND TO MAKE IT ALRIGHT, THOUGH.
LANGUAGE, PERRY! WE'VE GOT A REPUTATION TO UPHOLD AND THE QUEEN'S GOOD NAME TO KEEP!!
WELL... LET'S GET YOU TO THE BOAT. THE CAPTAIN WANTS TO PUSH OFF WHEN YOU GET THERE.
HOW FULL IS SHE?
WELL ABOVE CAPACITY.
BUT I'D IMAGINE YOUR POSITION WILL BE TAKEN INTO CONSIDERATION WHEN IT COMES TO QUARTERS AND DINING.
THAT WOULD BE NICE.

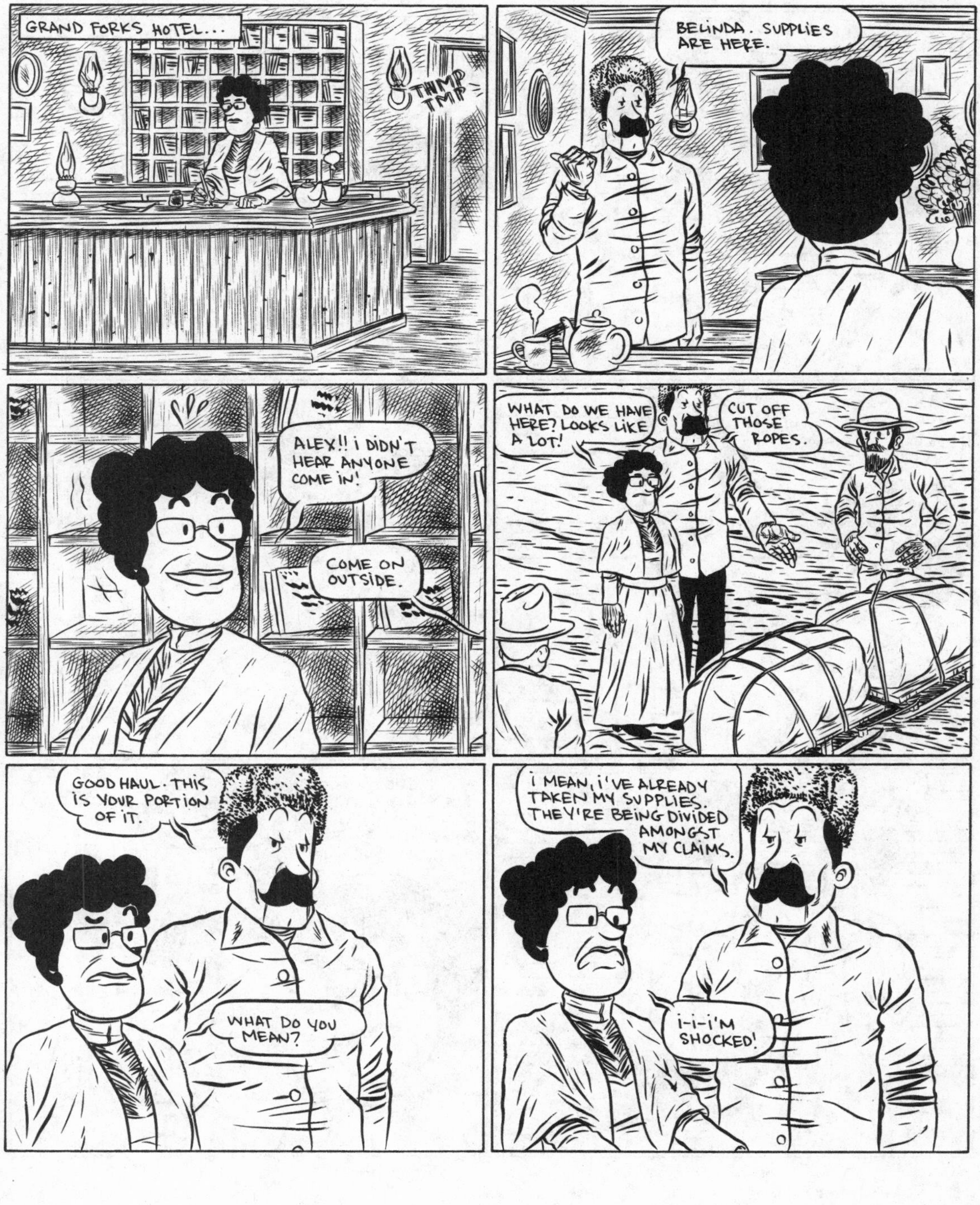
GRAND FORKS HOTEL...
THMP TMP
BELINDA. SUPPLIES ARE HERE.
ALEX!! i DIDN'T HEAR ANYONE COME iN!
COME ON OUTSIDE.
WHAT DO WE HAVE HERE? LOOKS LIKE A LOT!
CUT OFF THOSE ROPES.
GOOD HAUL. THIS iS YOUR PORTION OF iT.
WHAT DO YOU MEAN?
i MEAN, i'VE ALREADY TAKEN MY SUPPLIES. THEY'RE BEING DIVIDED AMONGST MY CLAIMS.
i-i-i'M SHOCKED!

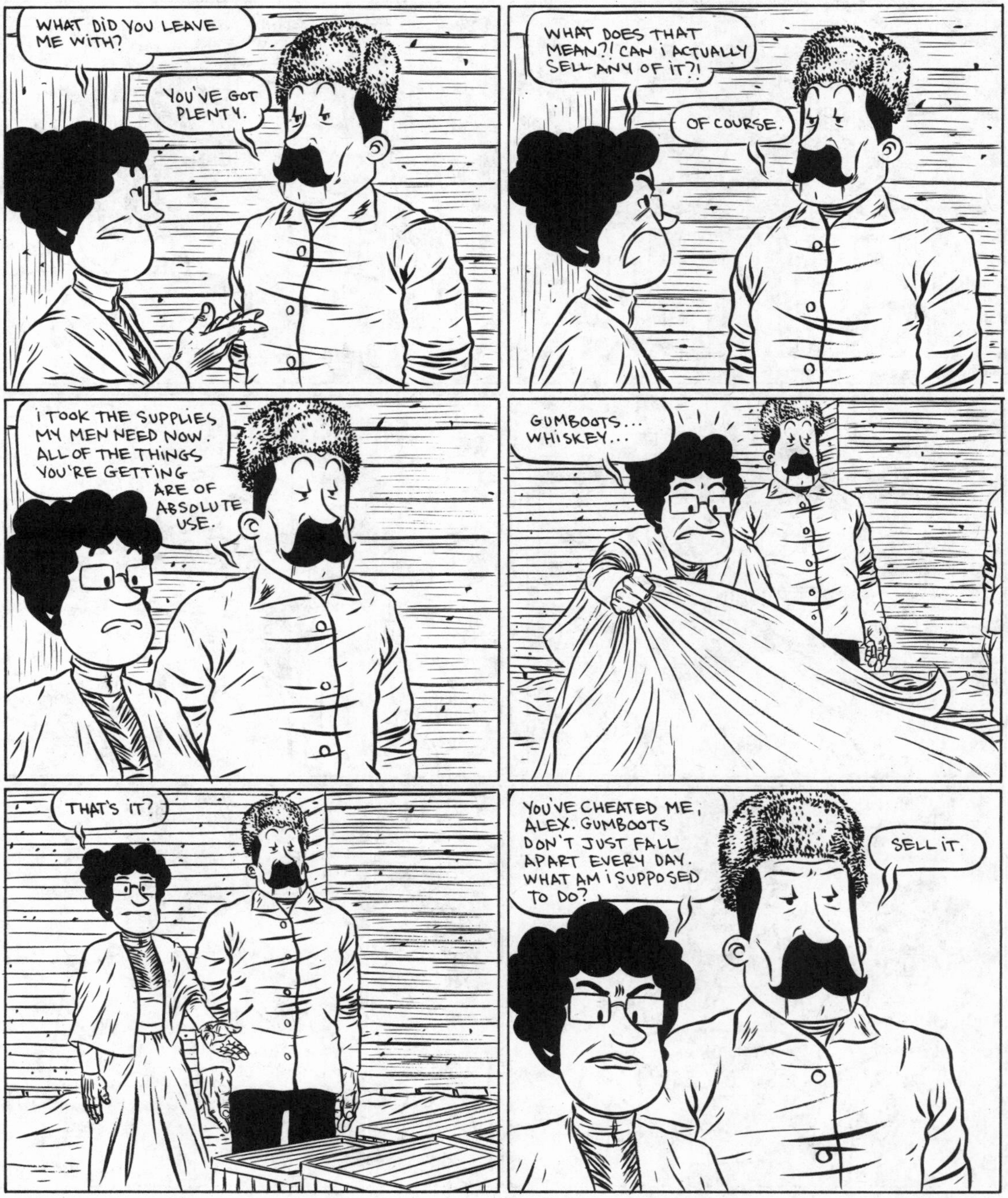
WHAT DID YOU LEAVE ME WITH?
YOU'VE GOT PLENTY.
WHAT DOES THAT MEAN?! CAN I ACTUALLY SELL ANY OF IT?!
OF COURSE.
I TOOK THE SUPPLIES MY MEN NEED NOW. ALL OF THE THINGS YOU'RE GETTING ARE OF ABSOLUTE USE.
GUMBOOTS... WHISKEY...
THAT'S IT?
YOU'VE CHEATED ME, ALEX. GUMBOOTS DON'T JUST FALL APART EVERY DAY. WHAT AM I SUPPOSED TO DO?
SELL IT.

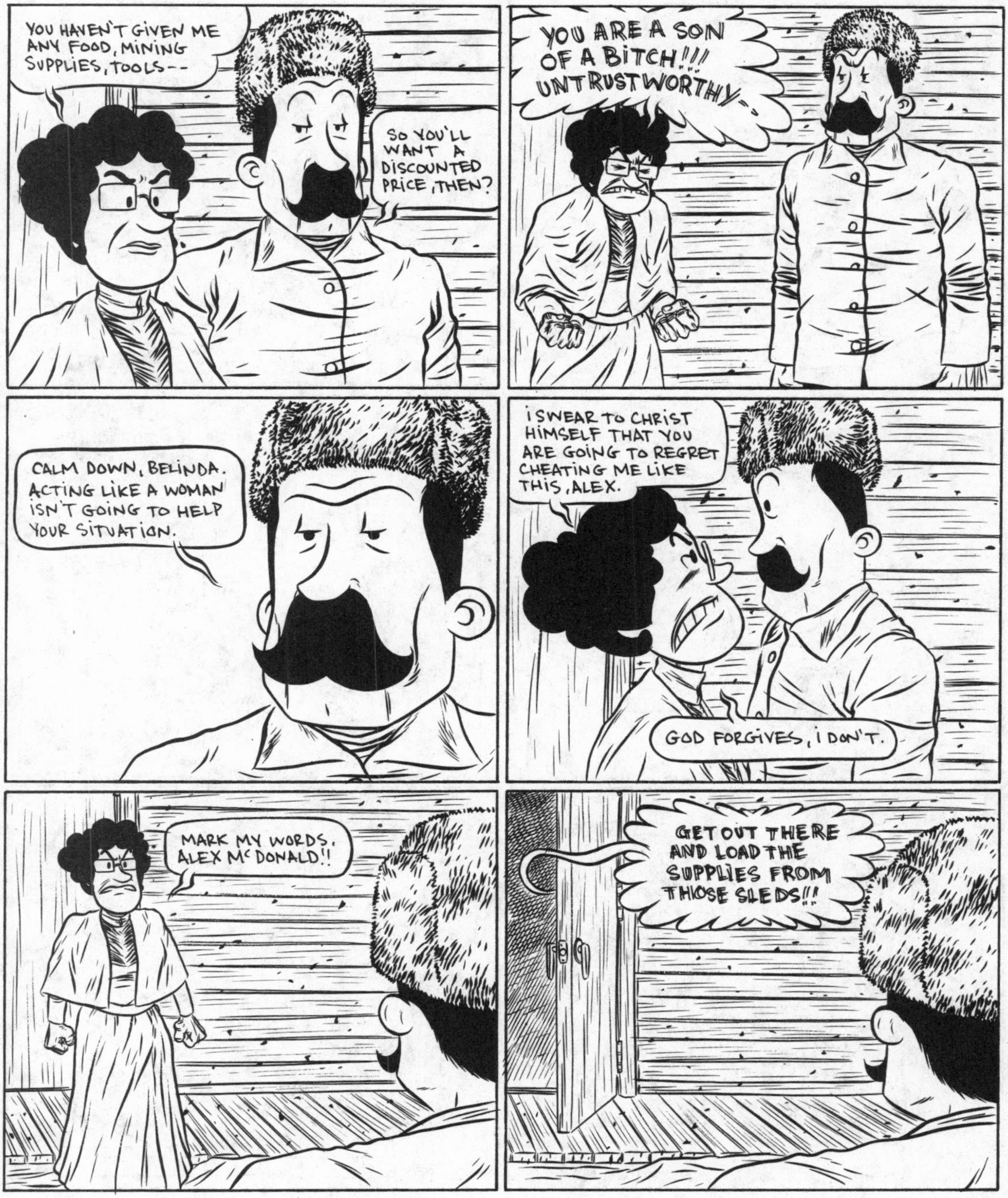
YOU HAVEN'T GIVEN ME ANY FOOD, MINING SUPPLIES, TOOLS--
SO YOU'LL WANT A DISCOUNTED PRICE, THEN?
YOU ARE A SON OF A BITCH!!! UNTRUSTWORTHY--
CALM DOWN, BELINDA. ACTING LIKE A WOMAN ISN'T GOING TO HELP YOUR SITUATION.
I SWEAR TO CHRIST HIMSELF THAT YOU ARE GOING TO REGRET CHEATING ME LIKE THIS, ALEX.
GOD FORGIVES, I DON'T.
MARK MY WORDS, ALEX McDONALD!!
GET OUT THERE AND LOAD THE SUPPLIES FROM THOSE SLEDS!!

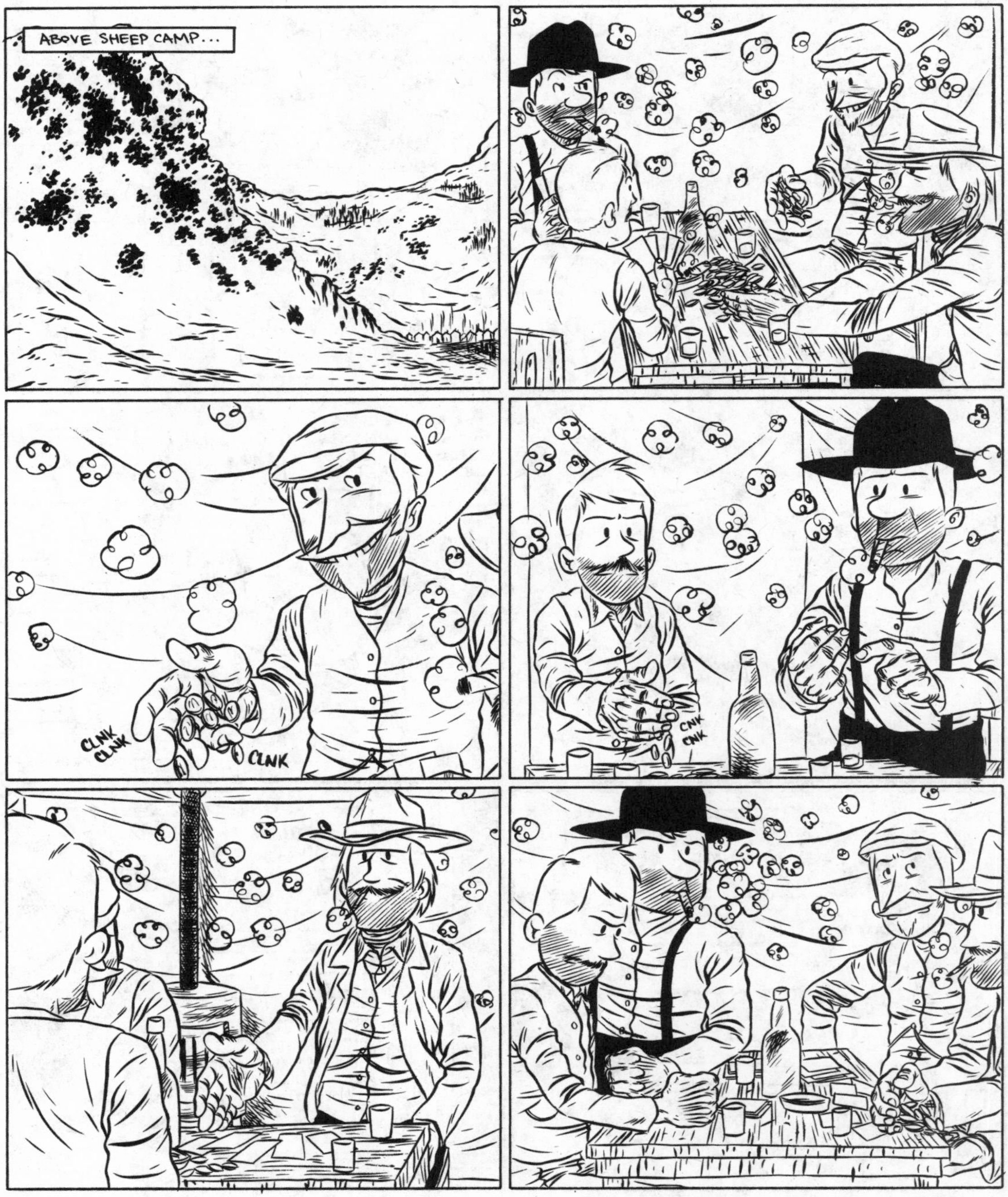
ABOVE SHEEP CAMP...
CLNK CLNK
CLNK
CNK CNK

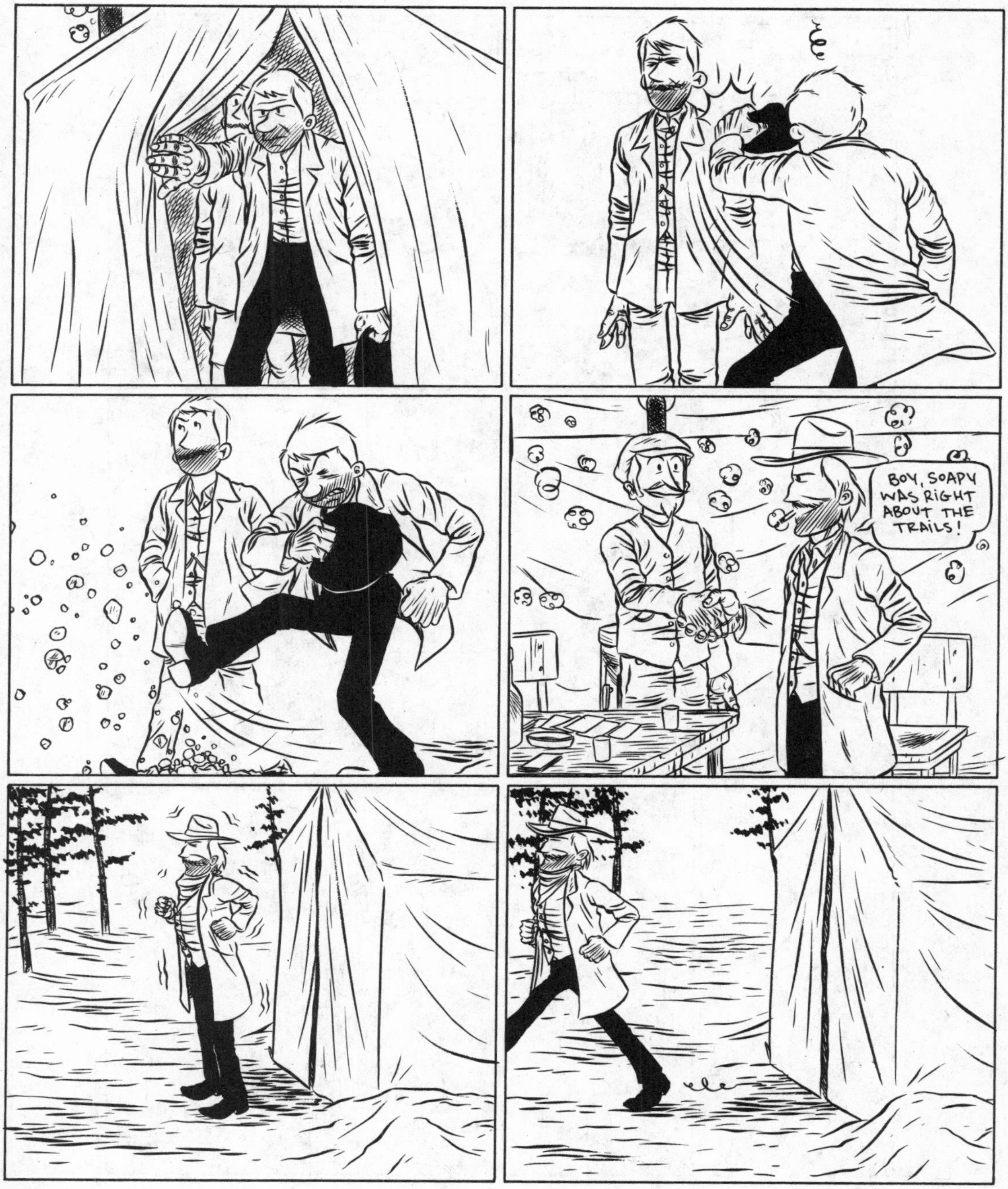
BOY, SOAPY WAS RIGHT ABOUT THE TRAILS!

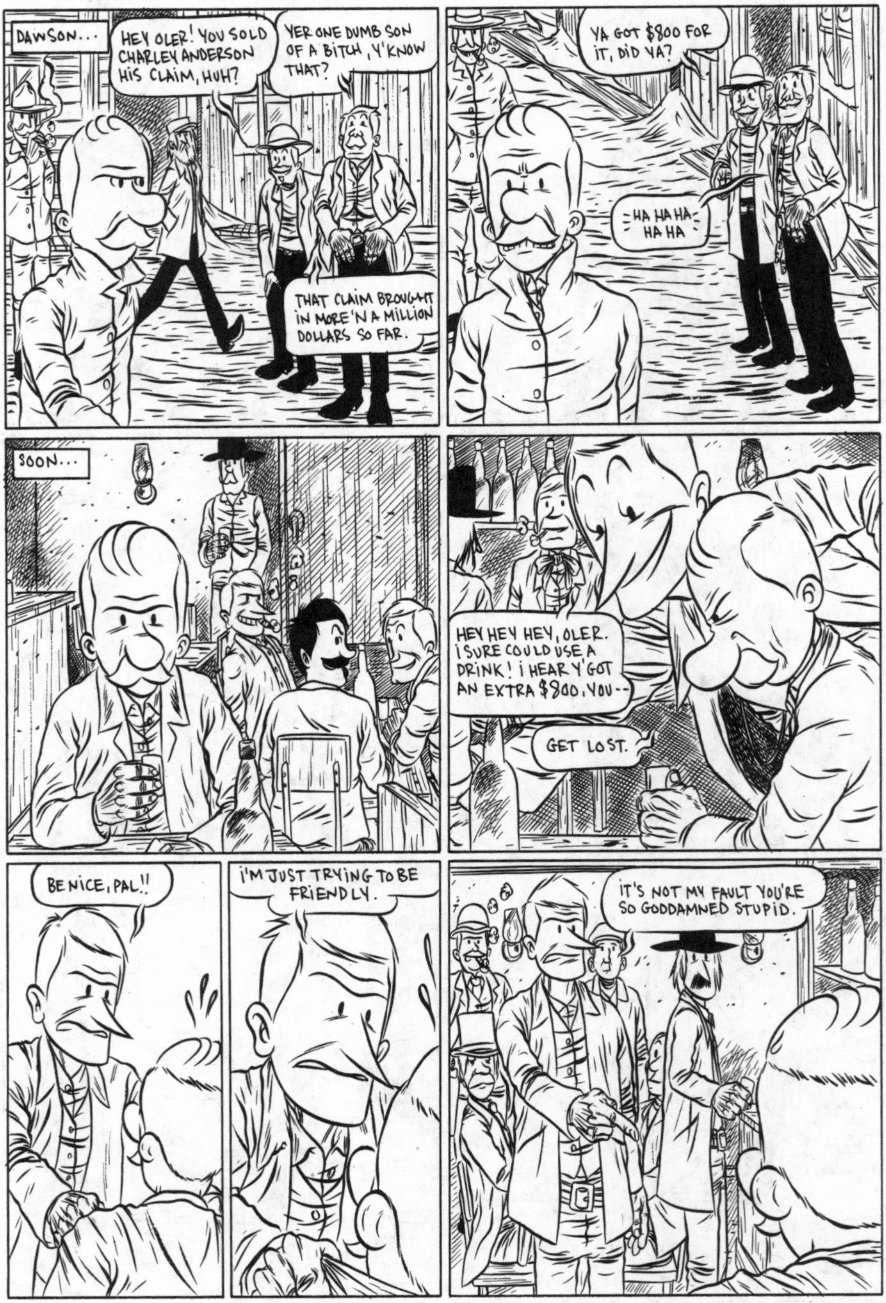
DAWSON...
HEY OLER! YOU SOLD CHARLEY ANDERSON HIS CLAIM, HUH?
YER ONE DUMB SON OF A BITCH, Y'KNOW THAT?
THAT CLAIM BROUGHT IN MORE'N A MILLION DOLLARS SO FAR.
YA GOT $800 FOR IT, DID YA?
HA HA HA HA HA
SOON...
HEY HEY HEY, OLER. I SURE COULD USE A DRINK! I HEAR Y'GOT AN EXTRA $800, YOU--
GET LOST.
BE NICE, PAL!!
I'M JUST TRYING TO BE FRIENDLY.
IT'S NOT MY FAULT YOU'RE SO GODDAMNED STUPID.

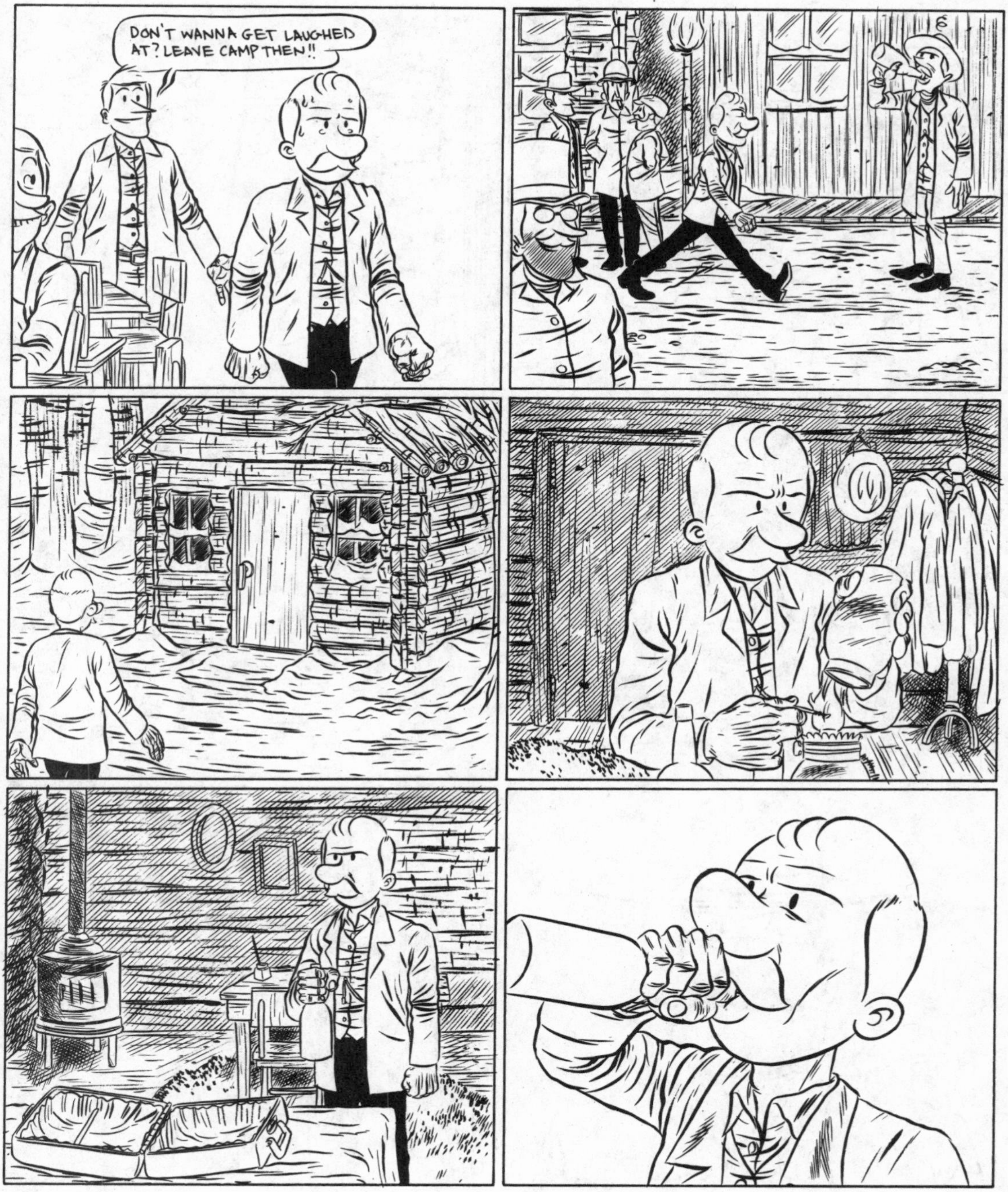
DON'T WANNA GET LAUGHED AT? LEAVE CAMP THEN!!

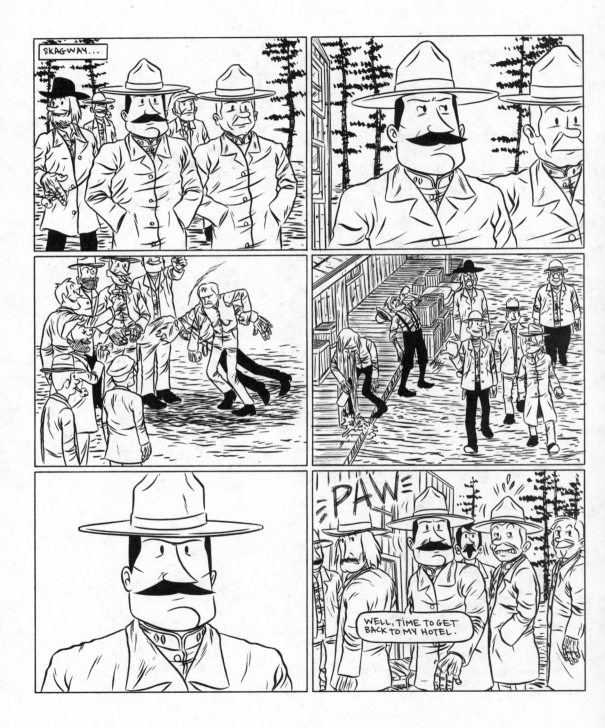

SKAGWAY...

PAW

WELL, TIME TO GET BACK TO MY HOTEL.

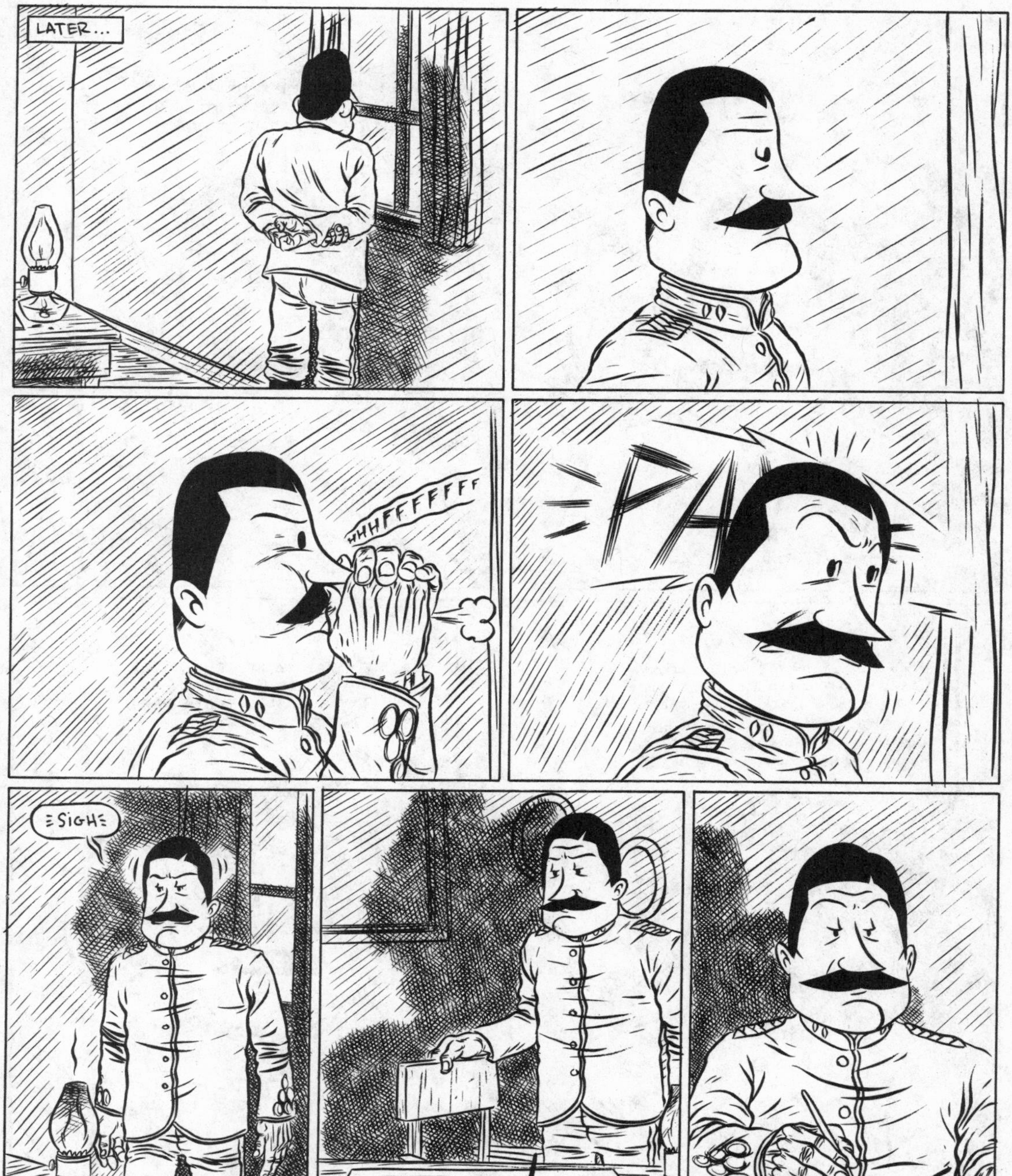
LATER...
HHHFFFFFFFF
PA
SIGH

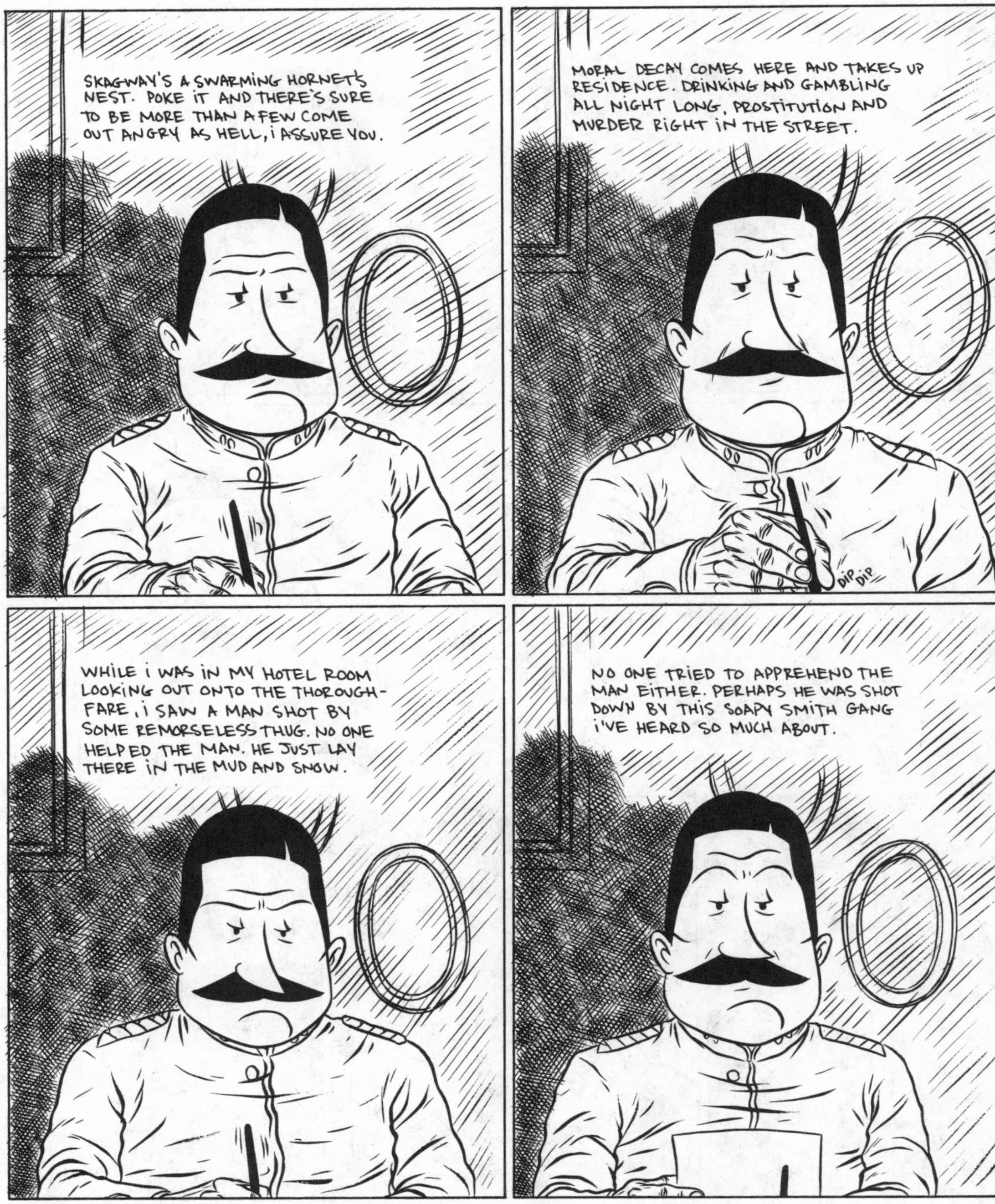
SKAGWAY'S A SWARMING HORNET'S NEST. POKE IT AND THERE'S SURE TO BE MORE THAN A FEW COME OUT ANGRY AS HELL, I ASSURE YOU.
MORAL DECAY COMES HERE AND TAKES UP RESIDENCE. DRINKING AND GAMBLING ALL NIGHT LONG, PROSTITUTION AND MURDER RIGHT IN THE STREET.
DIP DIP
WHILE I WAS IN MY HOTEL ROOM LOOKING OUT ONTO THE THOROUGH-FARE, I SAW A MAN SHOT BY SOME REMORSELESS THUG. NO ONE HELPED THE MAN. HE JUST LAY THERE IN THE MUD AND SNOW.
NO ONE TRIED TO APPREHEND THE MAN EITHER. PERHAPS HE WAS SHOT DOWN BY THIS SOAPY SMITH GANG I'VE HEARD SO MUCH ABOUT.

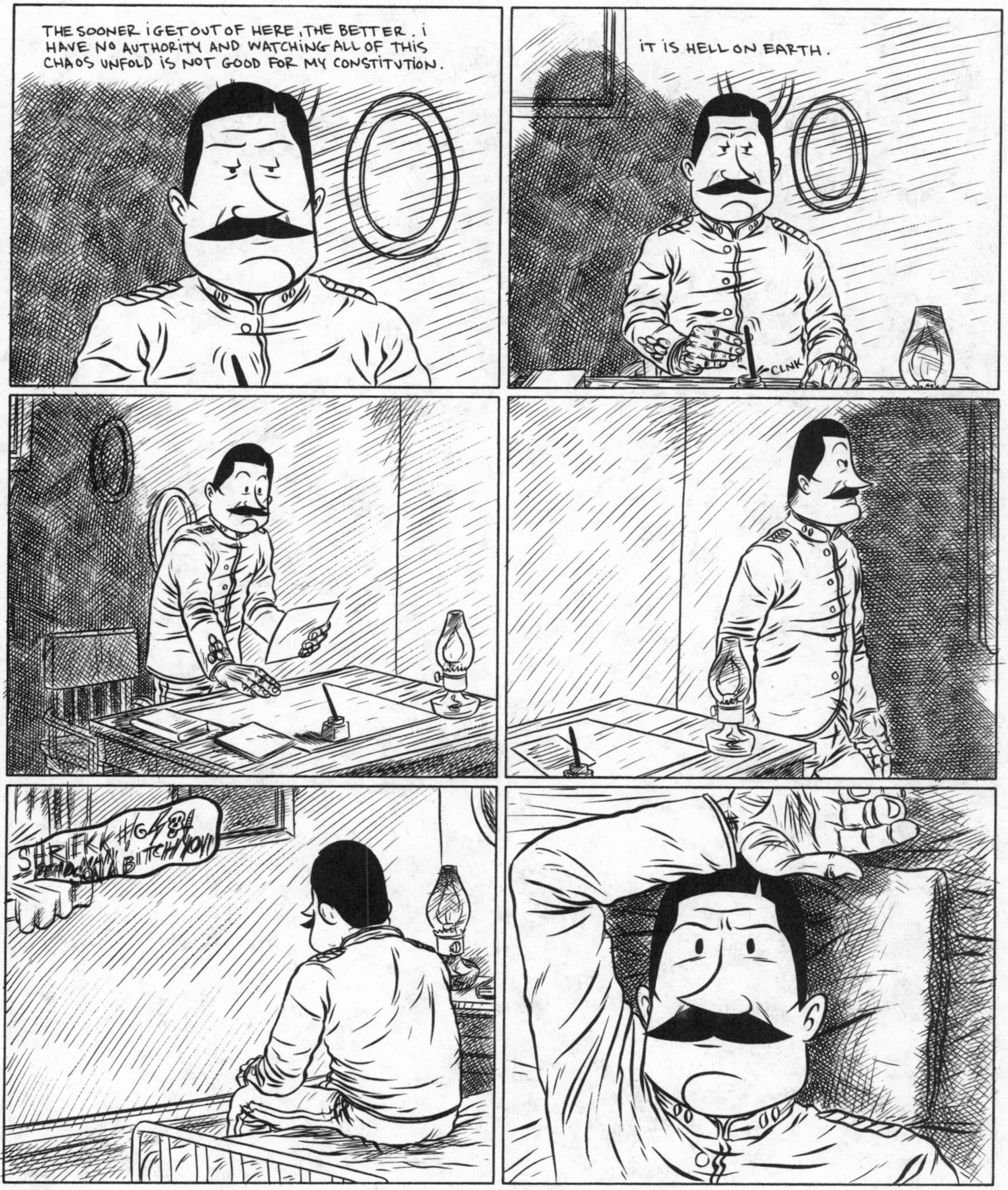
THE SOONER I GET OUT OF HERE, THE BETTER. I HAVE NO AUTHORITY AND WATCHING ALL OF THIS CHAOS UNFOLD IS NOT GOOD FOR MY CONSTITUTION.
IT IS HELL ON EARTH.
CLNK
SHRIEKK
BITCH YOU

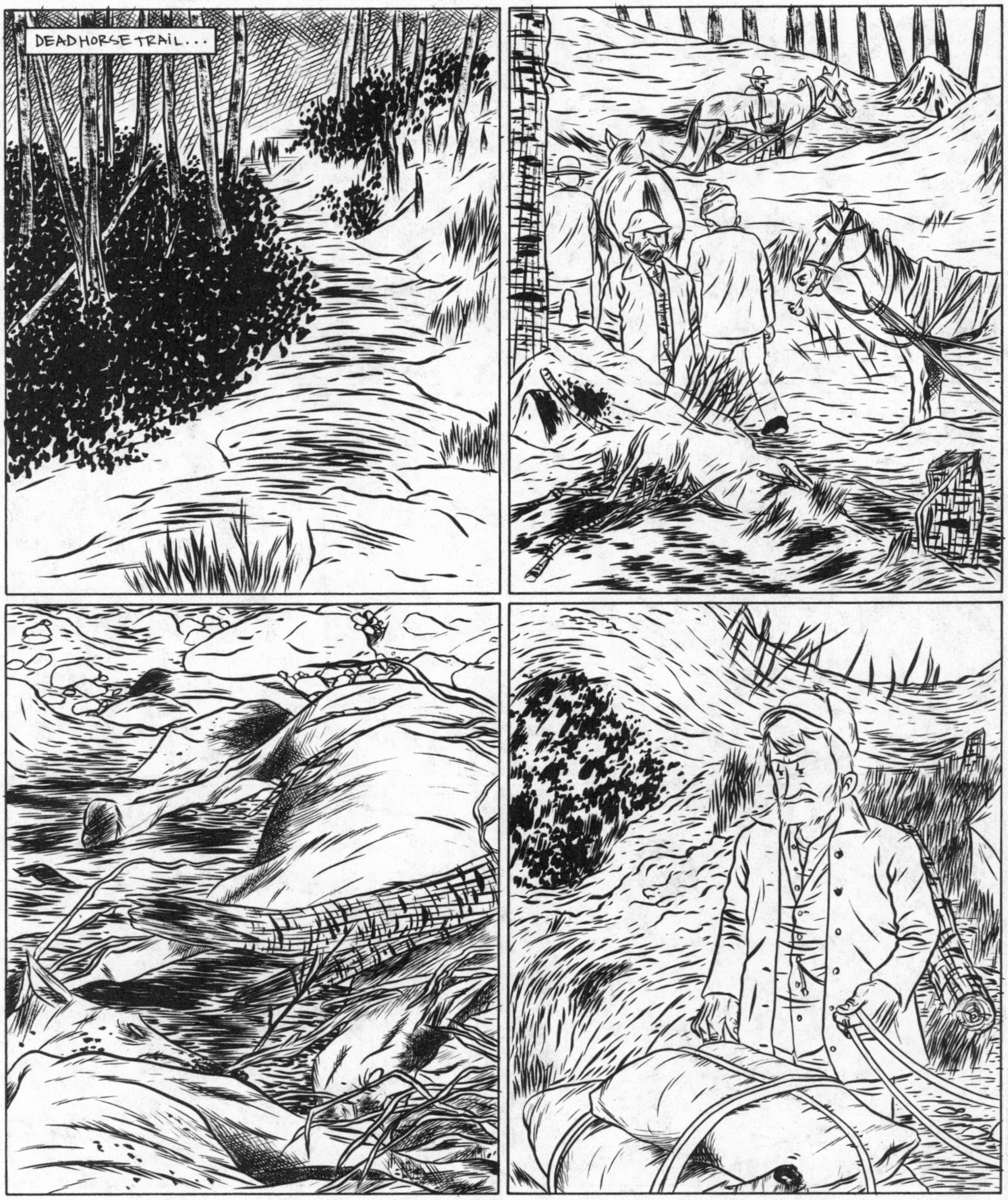
DEADHORSE TRAIL...

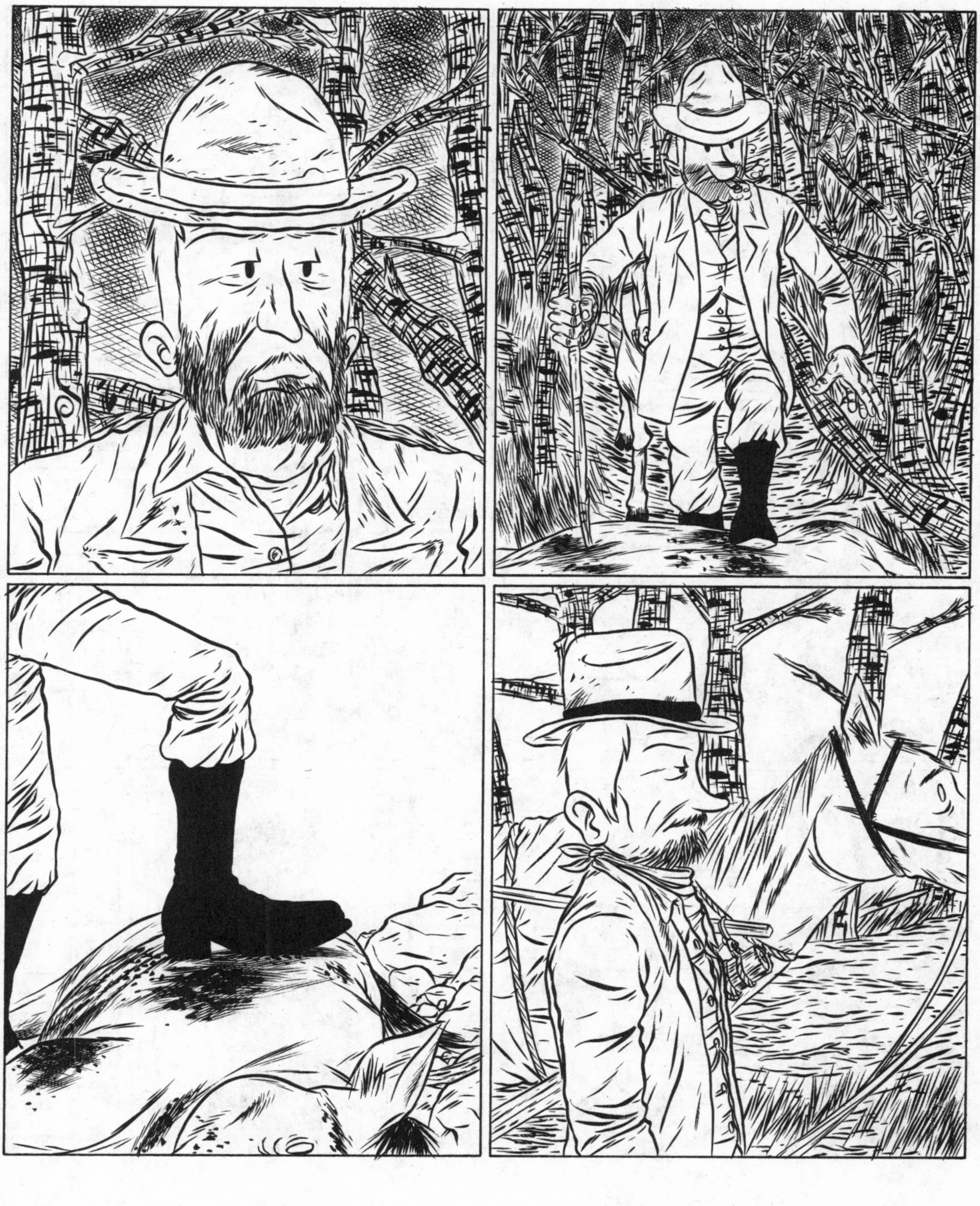

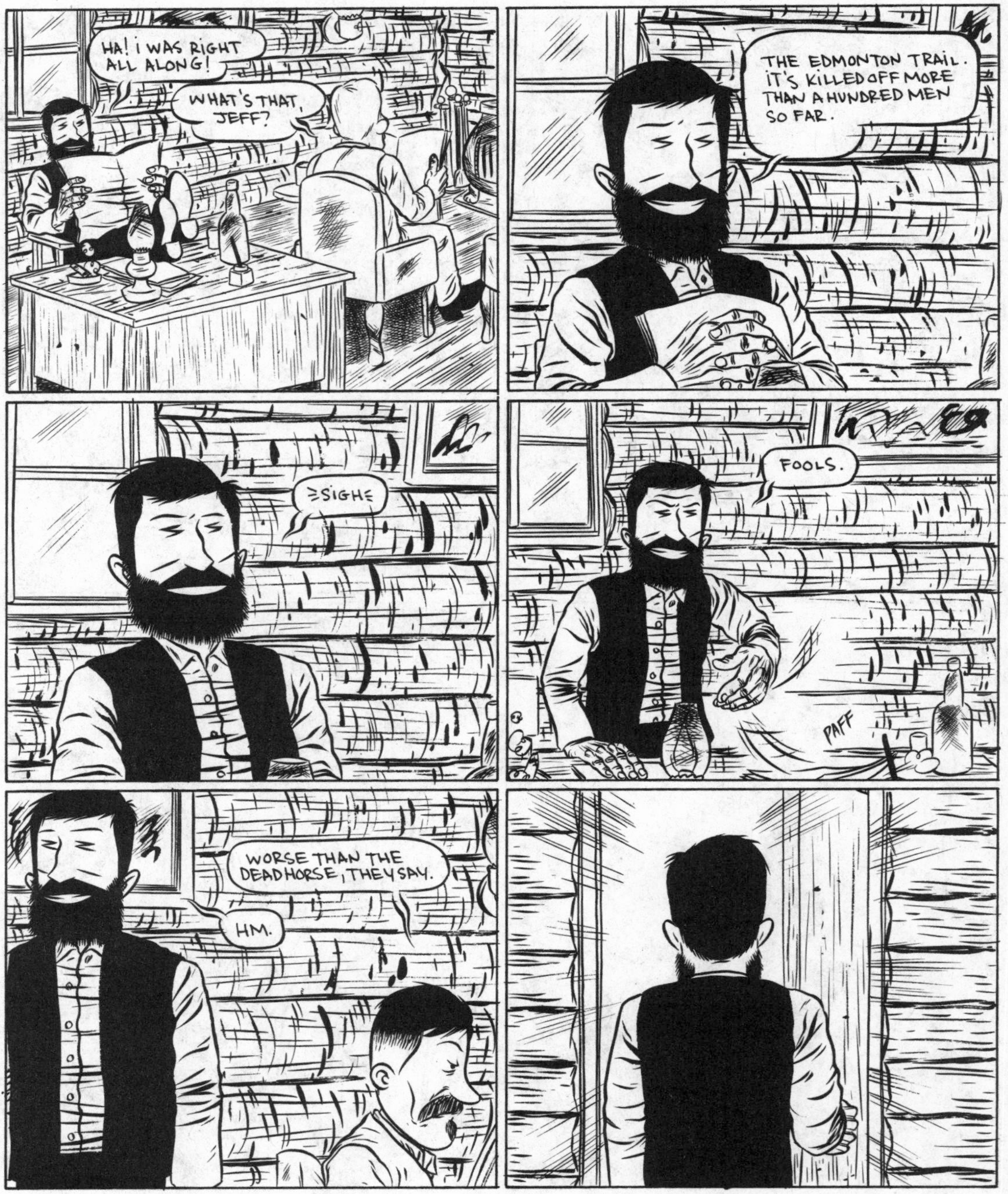

HA! I WAS RIGHT ALL ALONG!
WHAT'S THAT, JEFF?
THE EDMONTON TRAIL. IT'S KILLED OFF MORE THAN A HUNDRED MEN SO FAR.
SIGH
FOOLS.
PAFF
WORSE THAN THE DEADHORSE, THEY SAY.
HM.

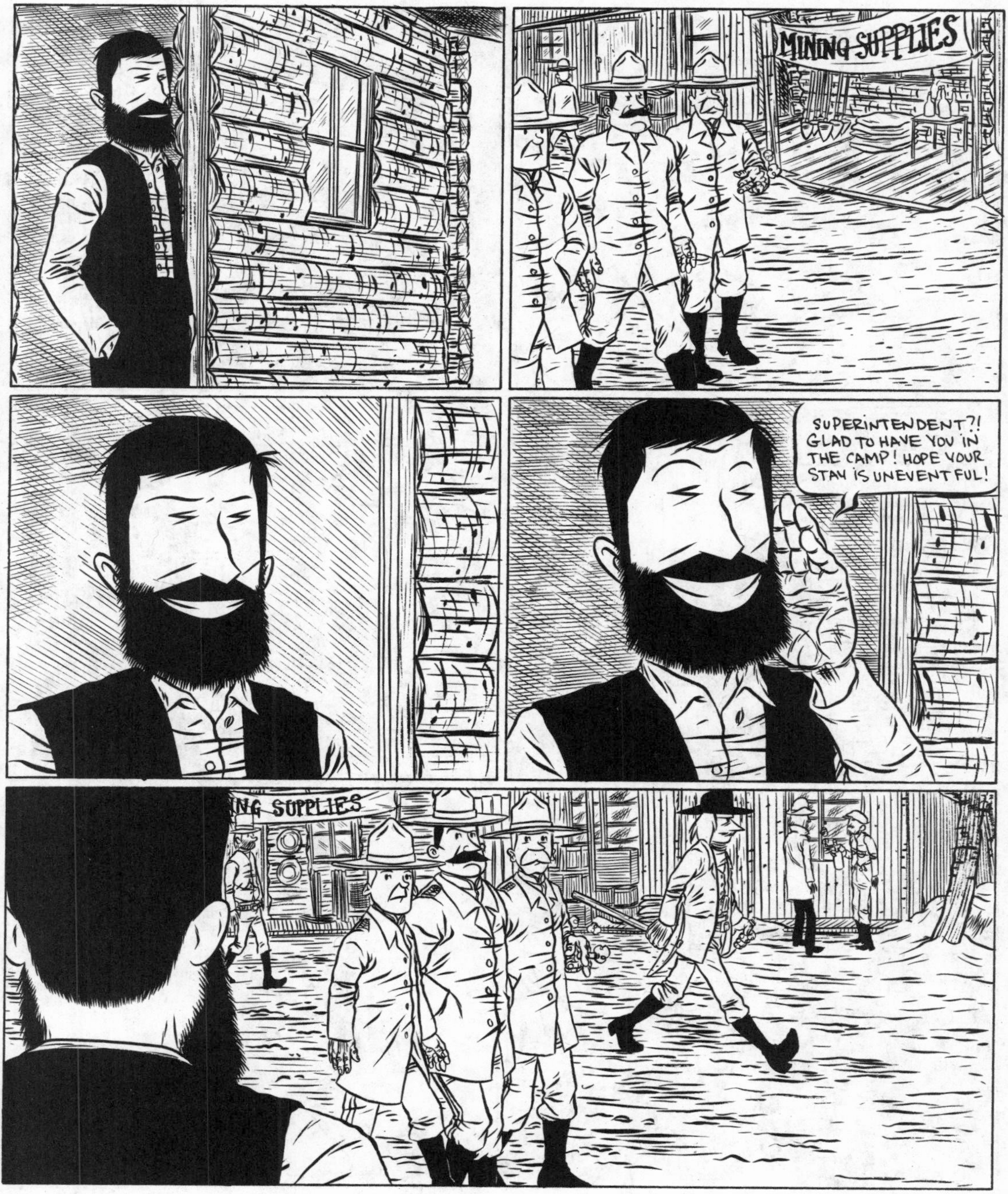
MINING SUPPLIES
SUPERINTENDENT?! GLAD TO HAVE YOU IN THE CAMP! HOPE YOUR STAY IS UNEVENTFUL!
MINING SUPPLIES

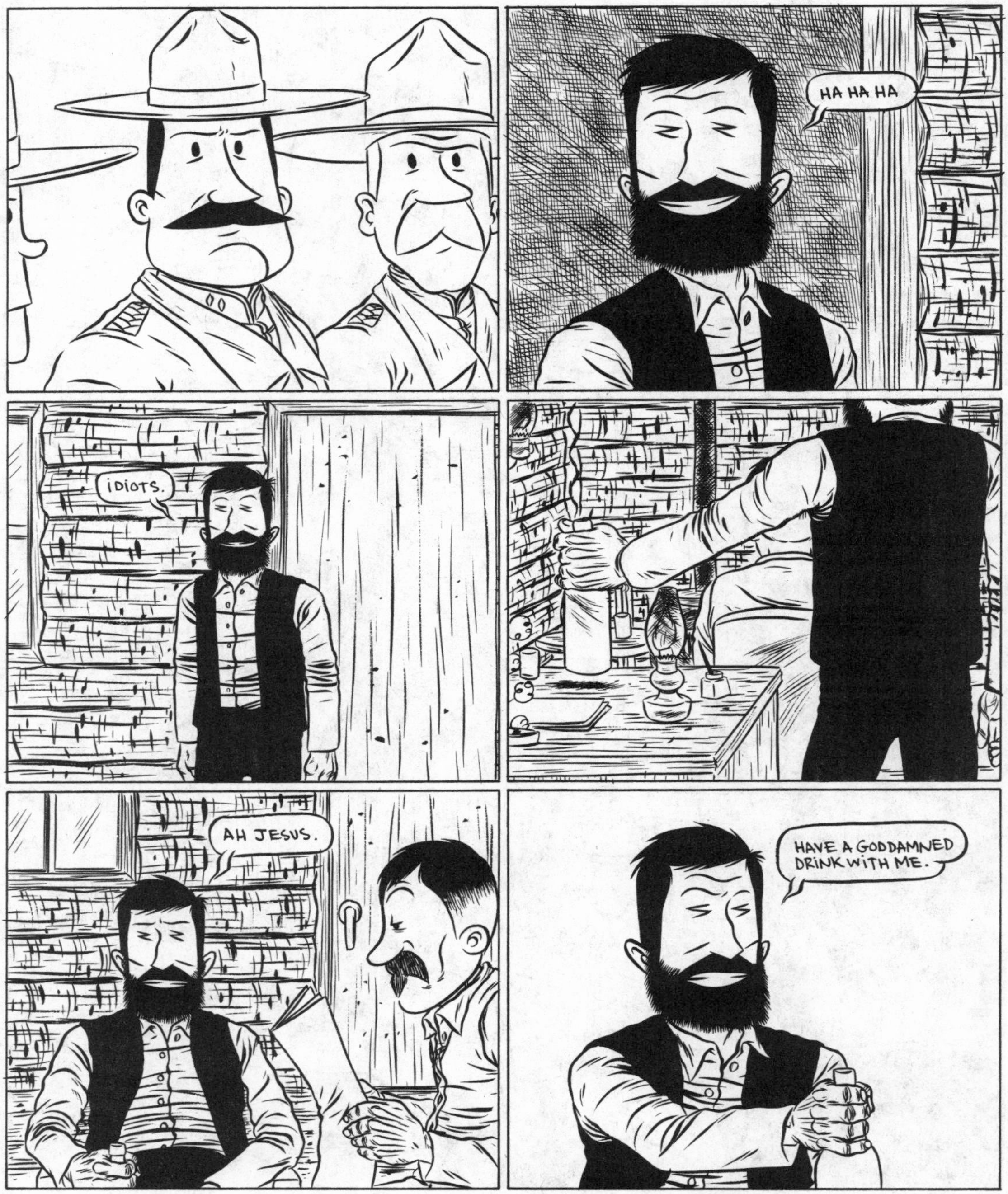
HA HA HA
IDIOTS.
AH JESUS.
HAVE A GODDAMNED DRINK WITH ME.

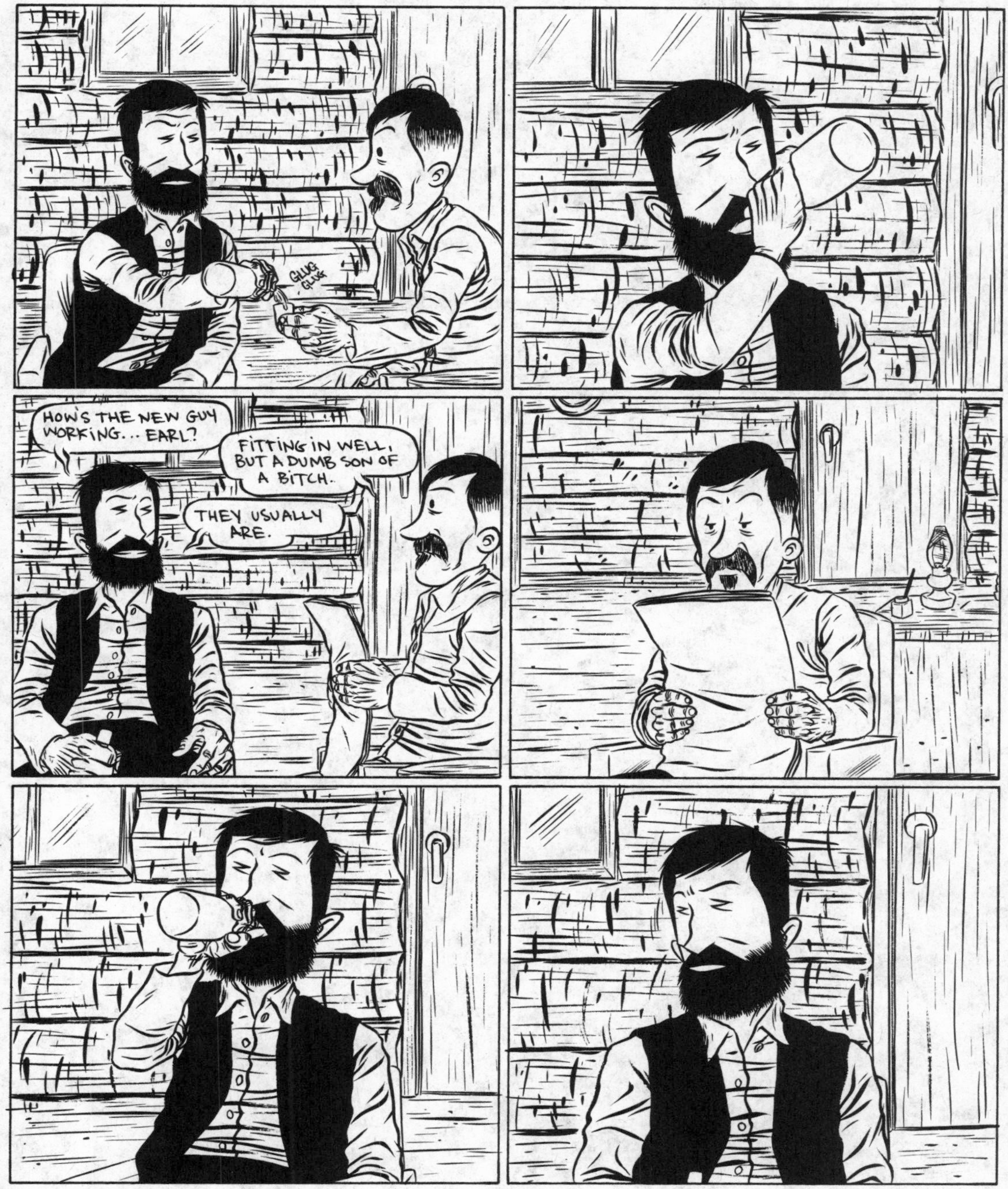
GLUG GLUG
HOW'S THE NEW GUY WORKING... EARL?
FITTING IN WELL, BUT A DUMB SON OF A BITCH.
THEY USUALLY ARE.

BRUTAL JUSTICE WAS DOLED OUT AT MINERS'
MEETINGS, BUT MEN WERE OFTEN JUST AS BRUTAL
TO THEMSELVES. WHISKEY, DRIED MEAT AND FISH,
BACON AND BREAD WAS THE DIET FOR THE WORKING
PROSPECTORS AND THE TRAVELLERS ATTEMPTING TO
REACH THE INTERIOR OF THE YUKON. COUPLING THE
INTENSE PHYSICAL STRAIN WITH THAT AWFUL DIET
WOULD DESTROY ANYONE'S HEALTH. THINGS WEREN'T GREAT
FOR THE MOUNTIES EITHER. THEY SPENT MONTHS
IN SUB ZERO TEMPERATURES PATROLLING AND
GUARDING THE PASSES, MAKING SURE PROSPECTORS
HAD THE PROPER AMOUNT OF SUPPLIES FOR THE
WINTER. THOSE WITH INSUFFICIENT OUTFITS
WEREN'T ALLOWED INTO THE YUKON. APART FROM
REGULAR PATROL WORK, SAM STEELE AND THE
MOUNTIES WERE BUSY SETTING UP A CANADIAN
BORDER LINE WHILE SUFFERING THROUGH ILLNESSES
LIKE BRONCHITIS. THE TEMPERATURE WAS FRIGID
AND STEELE AND THE OTHER MOUNTIES OFTEN
COMPLAINED THAT THEY WOULD NEVER FEEL WHAT
IT WAS LIKE TO BE WARM AGAIN. THEIR CABINS
OFFERED LITTLE RELIEF, AS COLD WINDS BLEW THROUGH
THE DOORS, WALLS AND WINDOWS. CONDITIONS WEREN'T
MUCH DIFFERENT IN DAWSON, BUT THE PERKS OF
CIVILIZATION, INCLUDING ELECTRICITY, WERE
SLOWLY INTRODUCED TO THE TOWN.
        WHILE DAWSON WAS BECOMING INCREASINGLY
CIVILIZED, SKAGWAY WAS AT A STAND STILL. THE
WAR IN SKAGWAY WAS GETTING MORE INTENSE
AS THE DAYS PASSED. FRANK REID AND THE
COMMITTEE OF 101 WERE HAVING AN EFFECT ON
SOAPY SMITH'S STRANGLE HOLD ON THE COMMUNITY.
PEOPLE BEGAN SPEAKING PUBLICLY OF THEIR DISDAIN
FOR SMITH AND HIS GANG. SMITH, HOWEVER, DID
NOT INTIMIDATE EASILY, AND THE TOWN MEMBERS'
OUTRAGE DID LITTLE MORE THAN GOAD HIM ON.

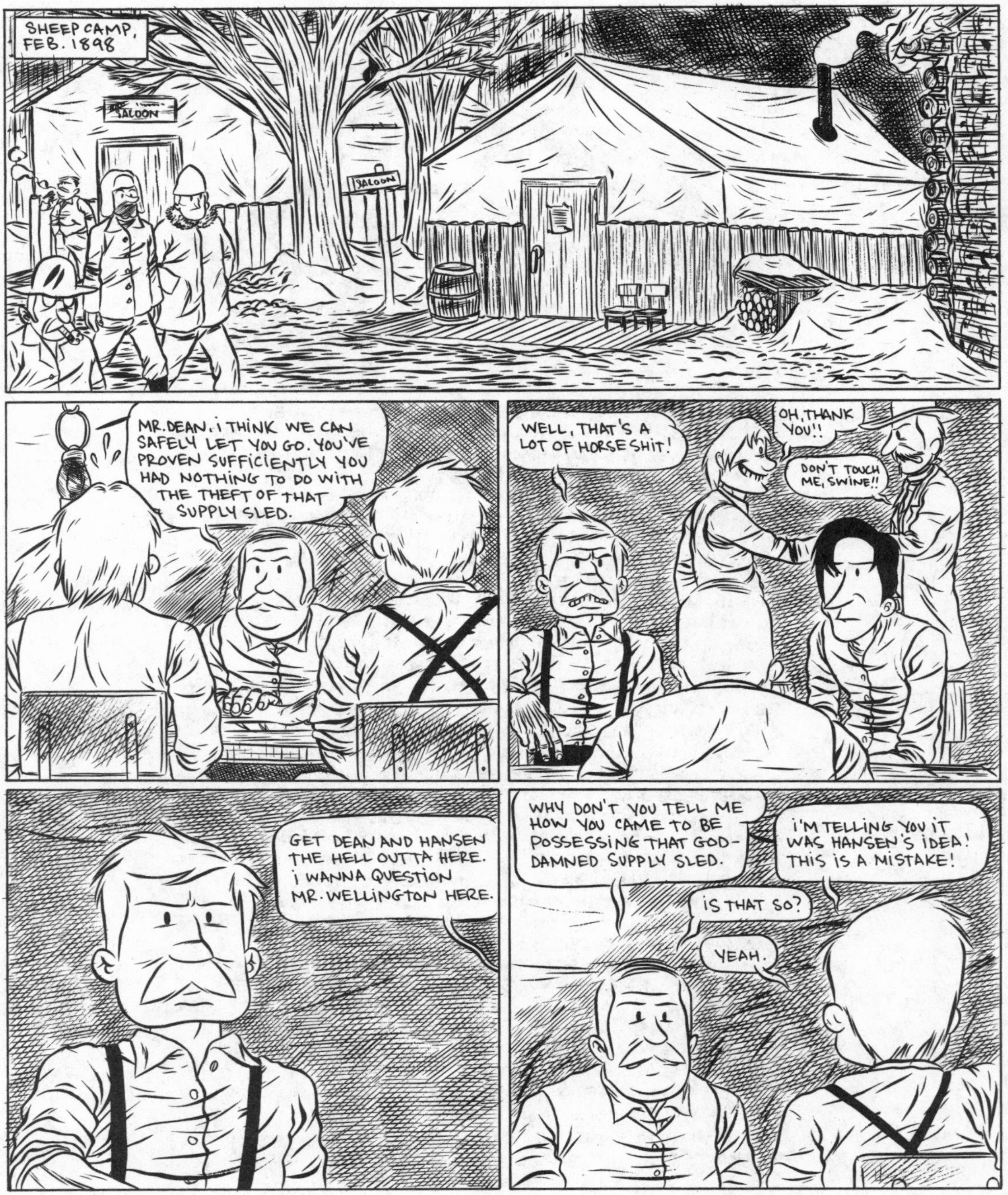

SHEEP CAMP, FEB. 1898
SALOON
SALOON
MR. DEAN, I THINK WE CAN SAFELY LET YOU GO. YOU'VE PROVEN SUFFICIENTLY YOU HAD NOTHING TO DO WITH THE THEFT OF THAT SUPPLY SLED.
WELL, THAT'S A LOT OF HORSE SHIT!
OH, THANK YOU!!
DON'T TOUCH ME, SWINE!!
GET DEAN AND HANSEN THE HELL OUTTA HERE. I WANNA QUESTION MR. WELLINGTON HERE.
WHY DON'T YOU TELL ME HOW YOU CAME TO BE POSSESSING THAT GOD-DAMNED SUPPLY SLED.
I'M TELLING YOU IT WAS HANSEN'S IDEA! THIS IS A MISTAKE!
IS THAT SO?
YEAH.

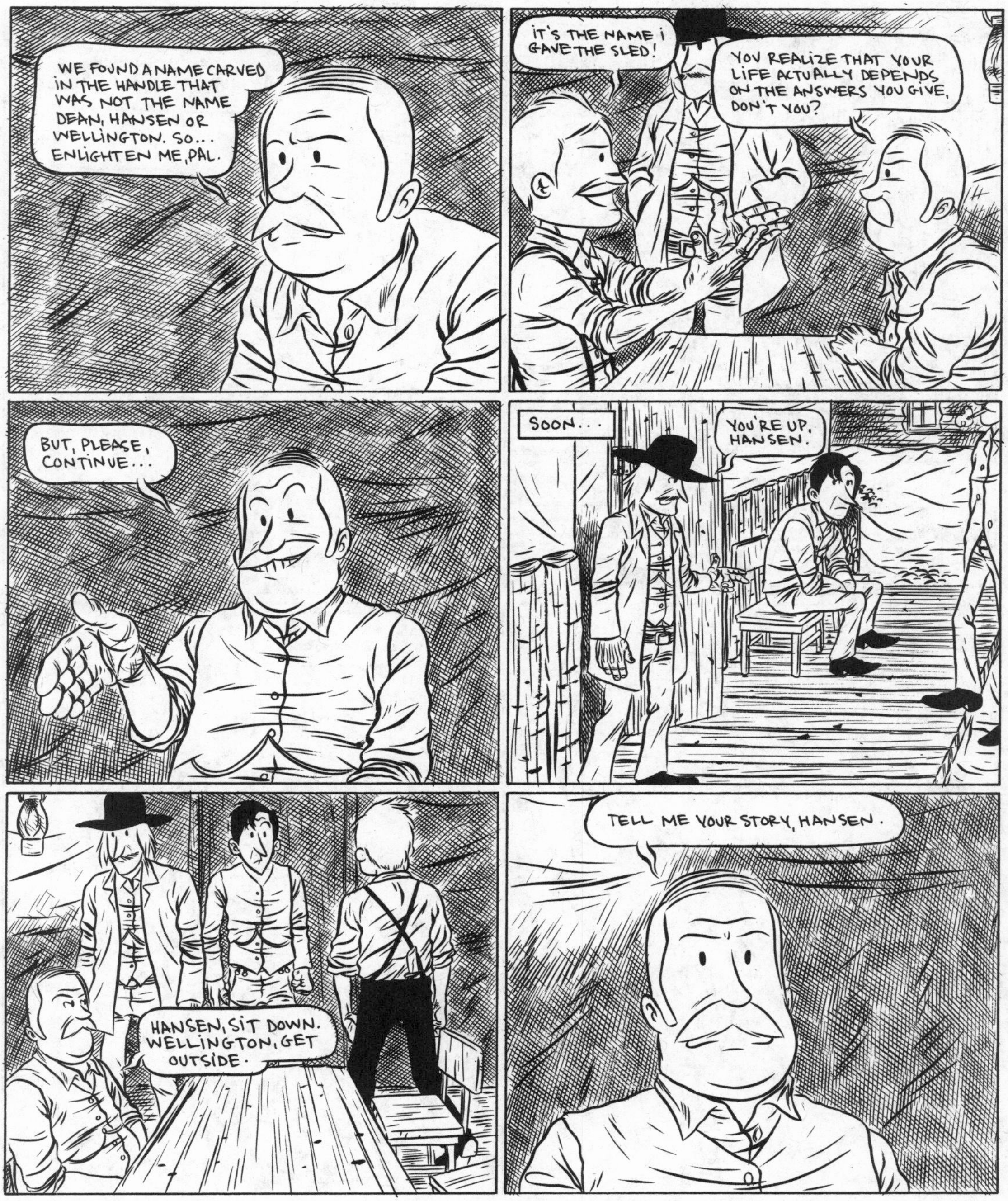
WE FOUND A NAME CARVED IN THE HANDLE THAT WAS NOT THE NAME DEAN, HANSEN OR WELLINGTON. SO... ENLIGHTEN ME, PAL.
IT'S THE NAME I GAVE THE SLED!
YOU REALIZE THAT YOUR LIFE ACTUALLY DEPENDS ON THE ANSWERS YOU GIVE, DON'T YOU?
BUT, PLEASE, CONTINUE...
SOON...
YOU'RE UP, HANSEN.
HANSEN, SIT DOWN. WELLINGTON, GET OUTSIDE.
TELL ME YOUR STORY, HANSEN.

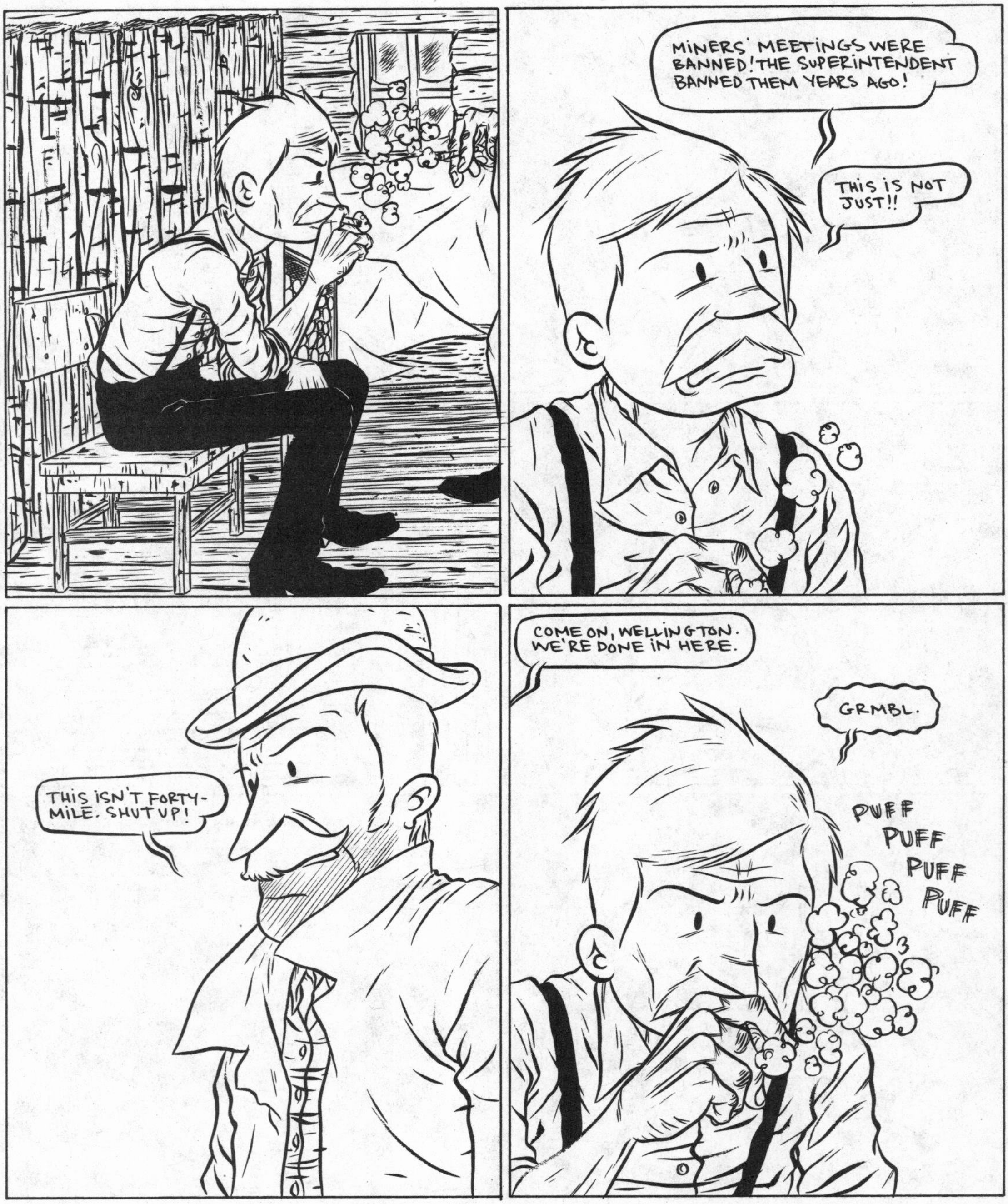
MINERS' MEETINGS WERE BANNED! THE SUPERINTENDENT BANNED THEM YEARS AGO!
THIS IS NOT JUST!!
THIS ISN'T FORTY-MILE. SHUT UP!
COME ON, WELLINGTON. WE'RE DONE IN HERE.
GRMBL.
PUFF
PUFF
PUFF
PUFF

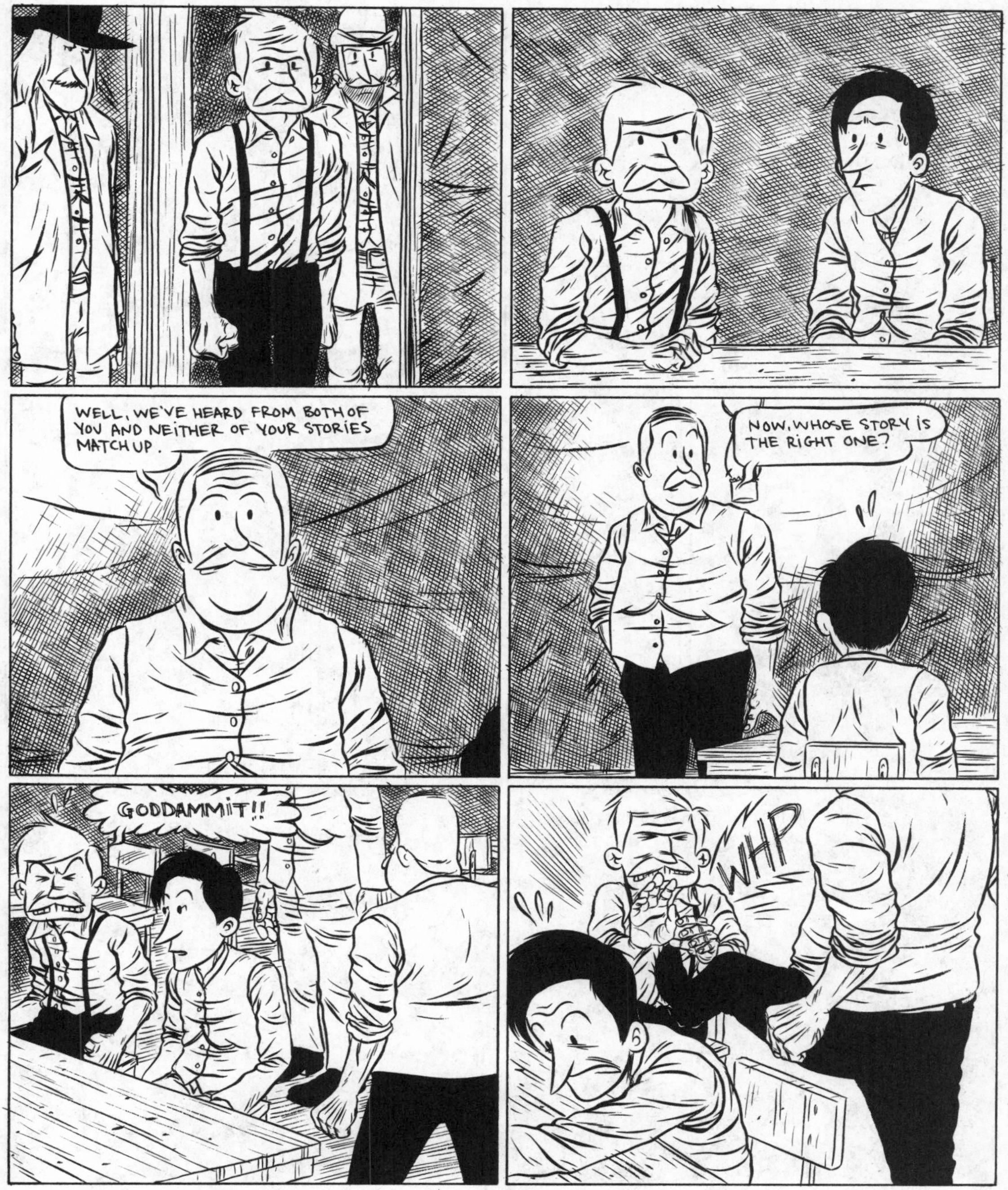
WELL, WE'VE HEARD FROM BOTH OF YOU AND NEITHER OF YOUR STORIES MATCH UP.
NOW, WHOSE STORY IS THE RIGHT ONE?
GODDAMMIT!!
WHP

FIFTY LASHES EACH!!!
GET THESE MEN OUTSIDE!!
SLICE
GIMME YOUR GUN!!!
AND DON'T NONE OF YOU SONS OF BITCHES FOLLOW ME, OKAY?!!

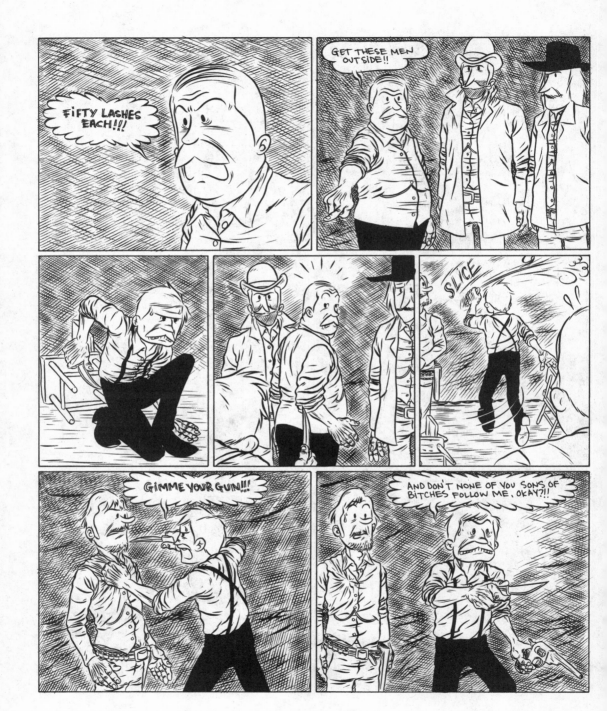

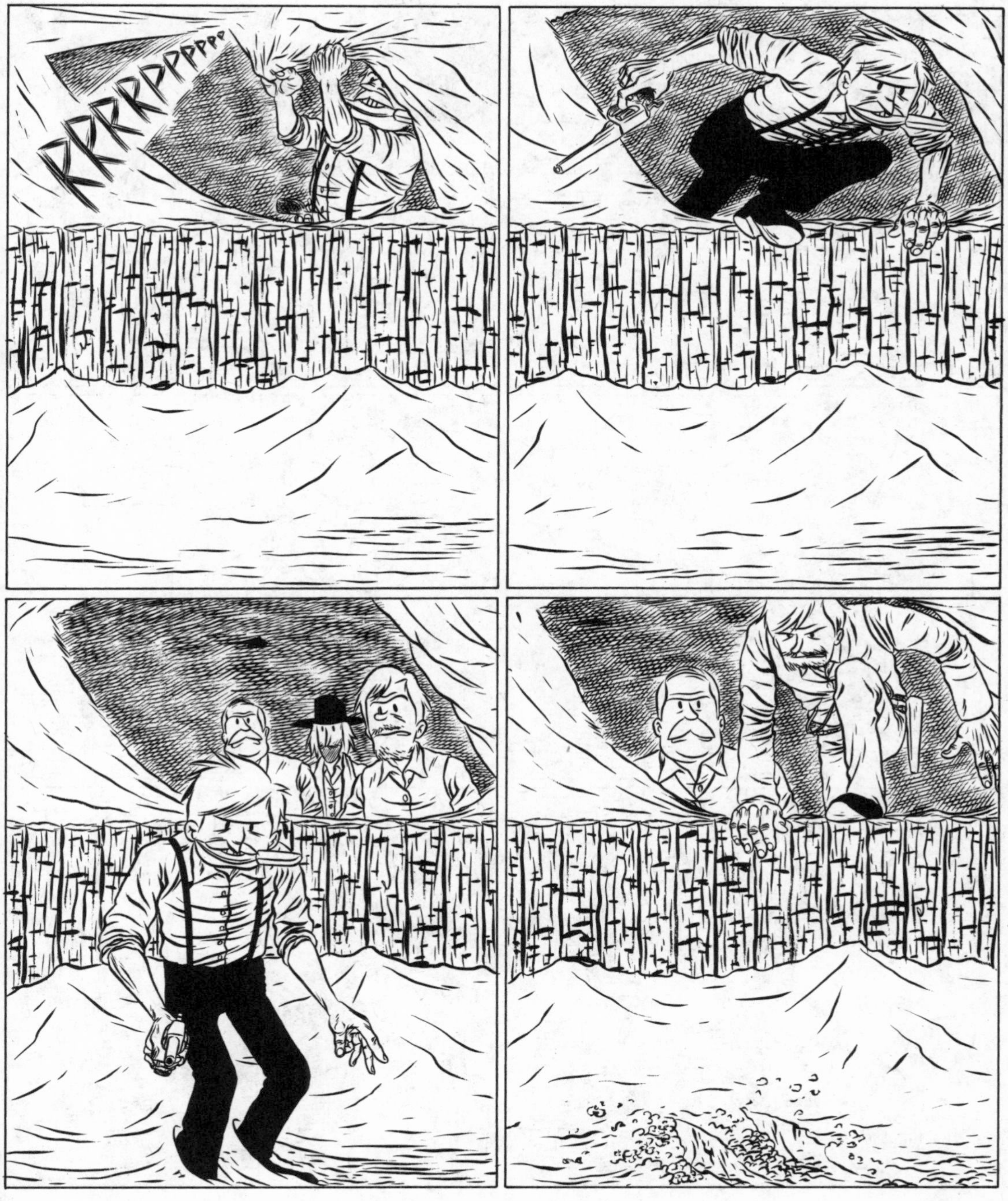
RRRRPPPPPPP

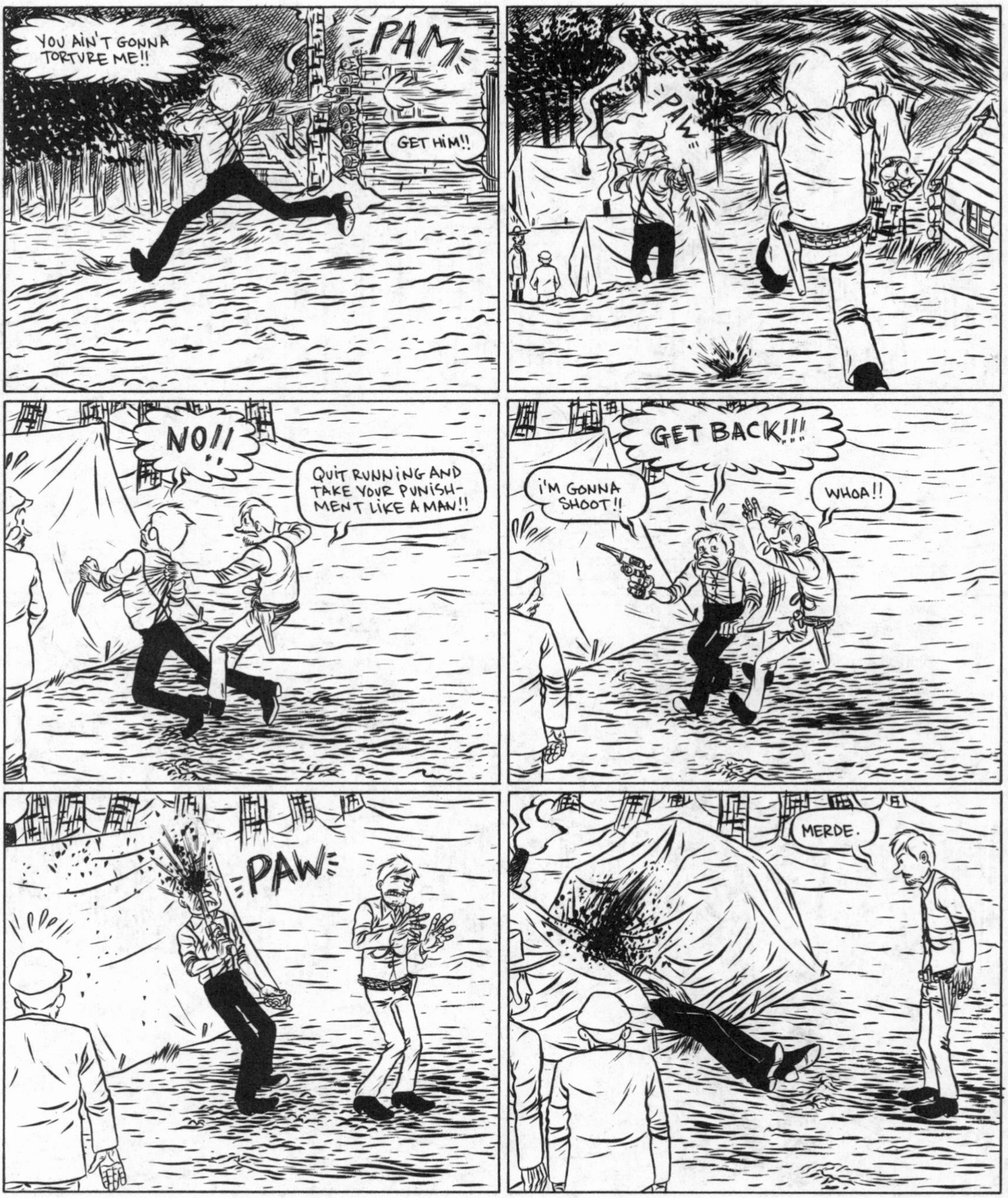
YOU AIN'T GONNA TORTURE ME!!
PAM
GET HIM!!
PAW
NO!!
QUIT RUNNING AND TAKE YOUR PUNISHMENT LIKE A MAN!!
GET BACK!!!
I'M GONNA SHOOT!!
WHOA!!
PAW
MERDE.

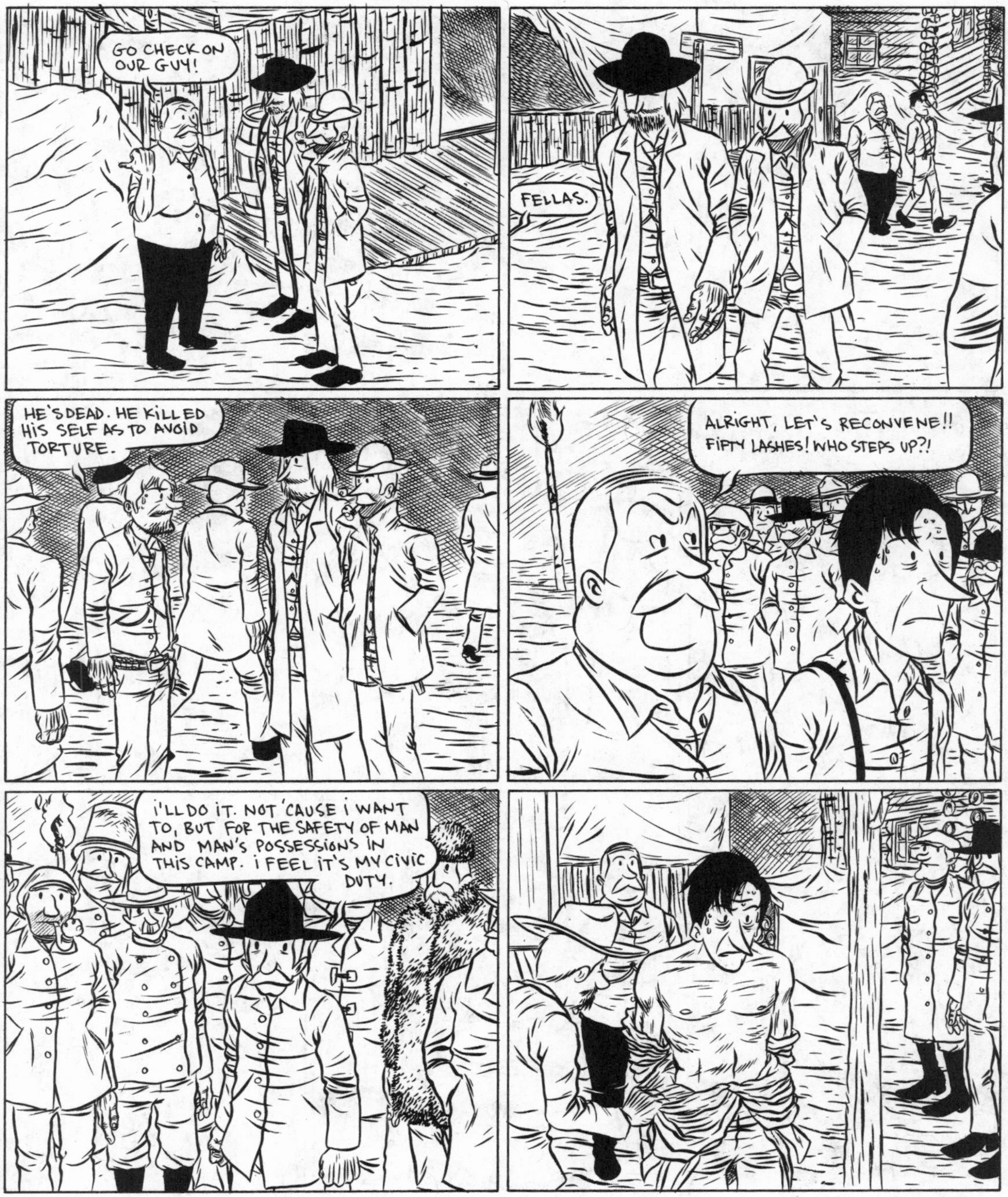
GO CHECK ON OUR GUY!
FELLAS.
HE'S DEAD. HE KILLED HIS SELF AS TO AVOID TORTURE.
ALRIGHT, LET'S RECONVENE!! FIFTY LASHES! WHO STEPS UP?!
I'LL DO IT. NOT 'CAUSE I WANT TO, BUT FOR THE SAFETY OF MAN AND MAN'S POSSESSIONS IN THIS CAMP. I FEEL IT'S MY CIVIC DUTY.

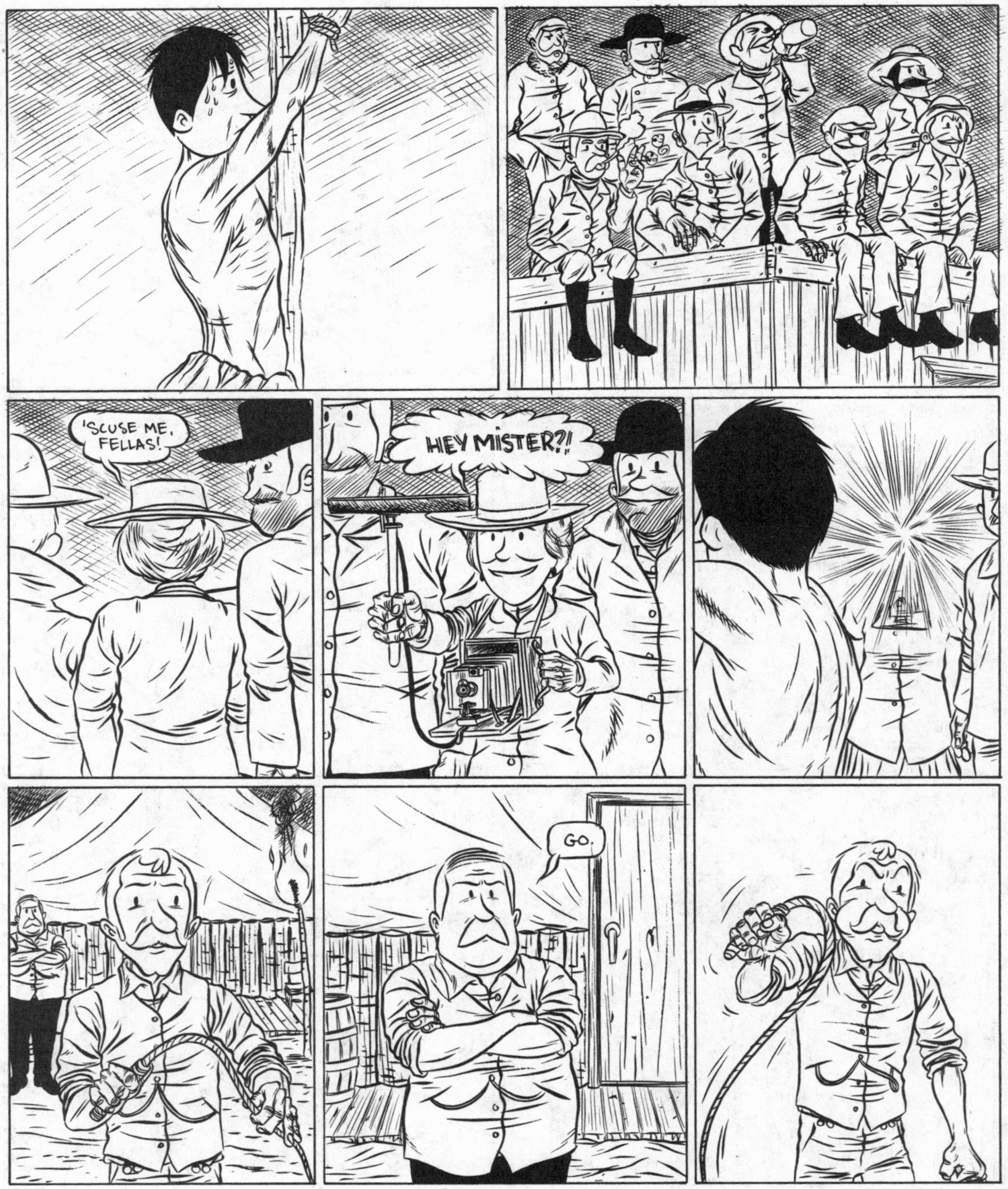

'SCUSE ME, FELLAS!
HEY MISTER?!
GO.

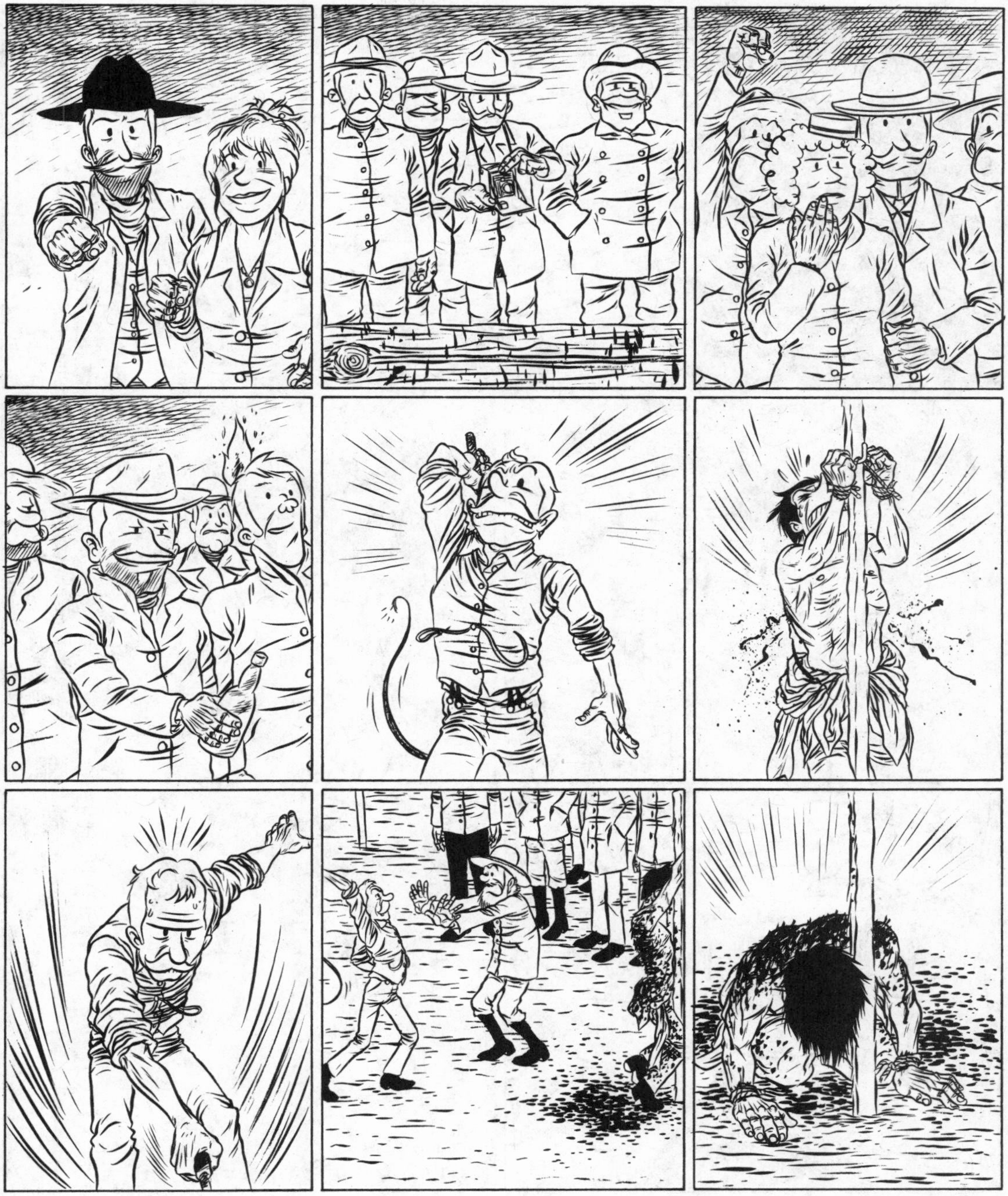

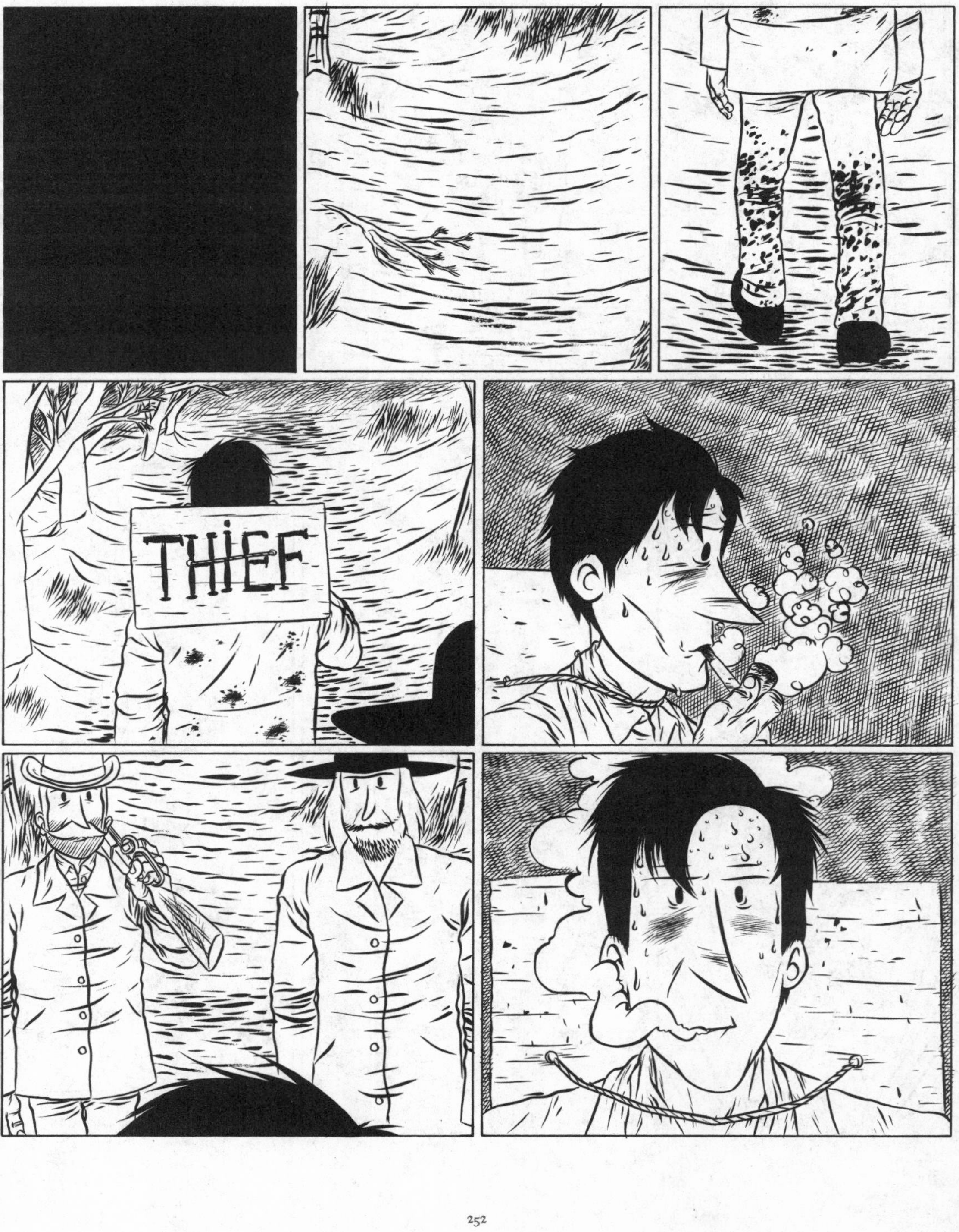
THIEF

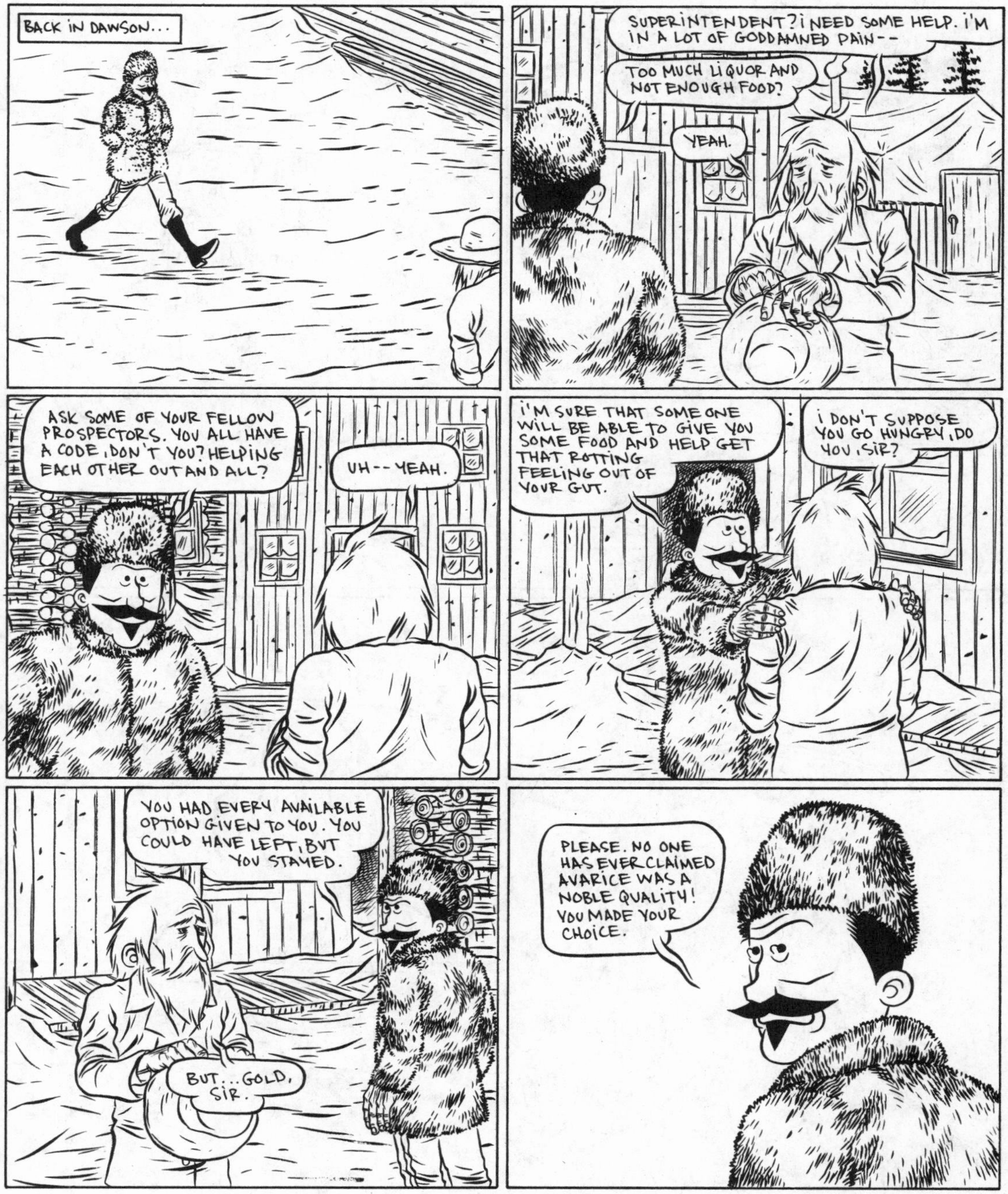
BACK IN DAWSON...
SUPERINTENDENT? I NEED SOME HELP. I'M IN A LOT OF GODDAMNED PAIN--
TOO MUCH LIQUOR AND NOT ENOUGH FOOD?
YEAH.
ASK SOME OF YOUR FELLOW PROSPECTORS. YOU ALL HAVE A CODE, DON'T YOU? HELPING EACH OTHER OUT AND ALL?
UH--YEAH.
I'M SURE THAT SOME ONE WILL BE ABLE TO GIVE YOU SOME FOOD AND HELP GET THAT ROTTING FEELING OUT OF YOUR GUT.
I DON'T SUPPOSE YOU GO HUNGRY, DO YOU, SIR?
YOU HAD EVERY AVAILABLE OPTION GIVEN TO YOU. YOU COULD HAVE LEFT, BUT YOU STAYED.
BUT...GOLD, SIR.
PLEASE. NO ONE HAS EVER CLAIMED AVARICE WAS A NOBLE QUALITY! YOU MADE YOUR CHOICE.

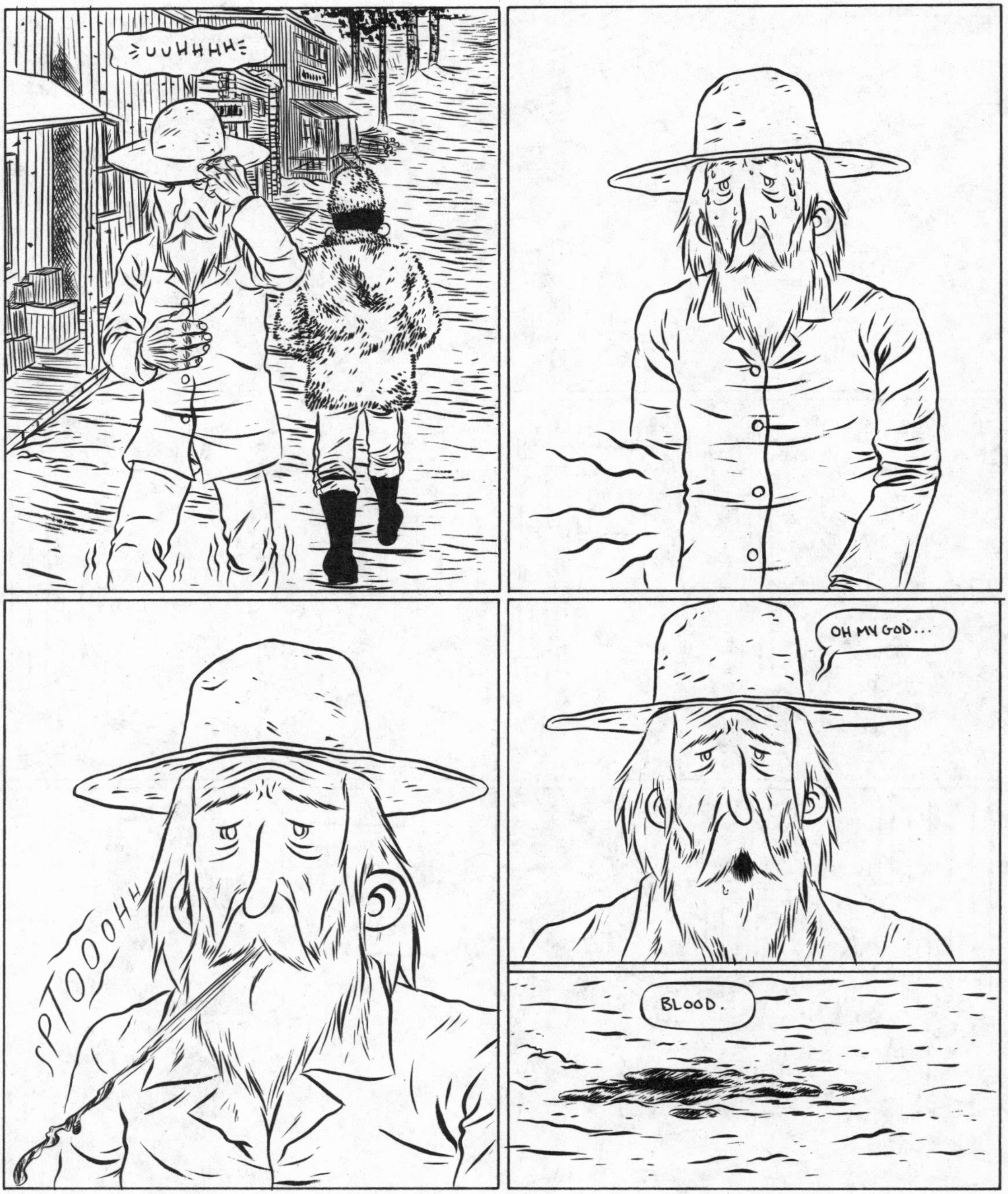
UUHHHH
SPTOOOOHH
OH MY GOD...
BLOOD.

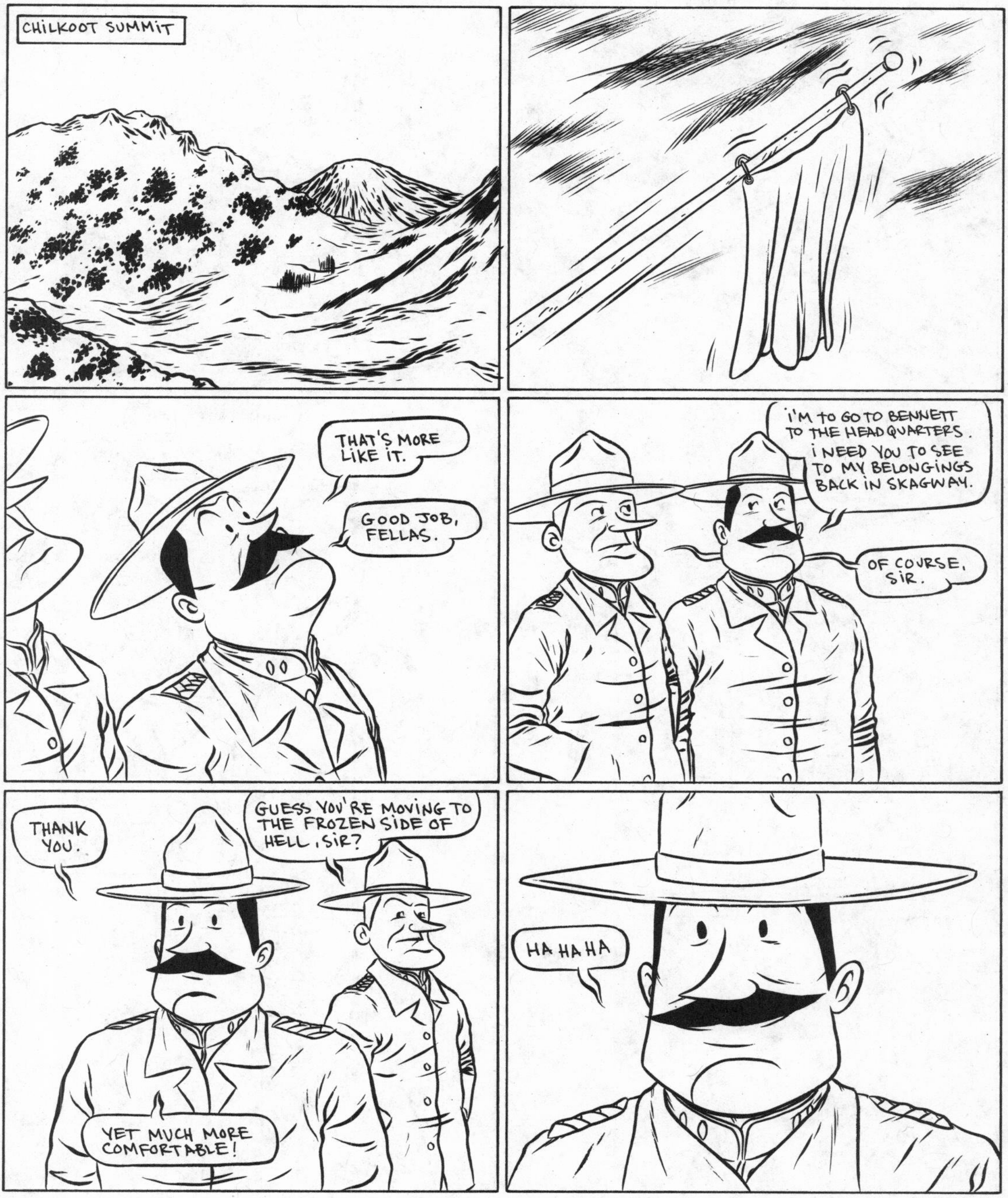
CHILKOOT SUMMIT
THAT'S MORE LIKE IT.
GOOD JOB, FELLAS.
I'M TO GO TO BENNETT TO THE HEADQUARTERS. I NEED YOU TO SEE TO MY BELONGINGS BACK IN SKAGWAY.
OF COURSE, SIR.
THANK YOU.
GUESS YOU'RE MOVING TO THE FROZEN SIDE OF HELL, SIR?
YET MUCH MORE COMFORTABLE!
HA HA HA

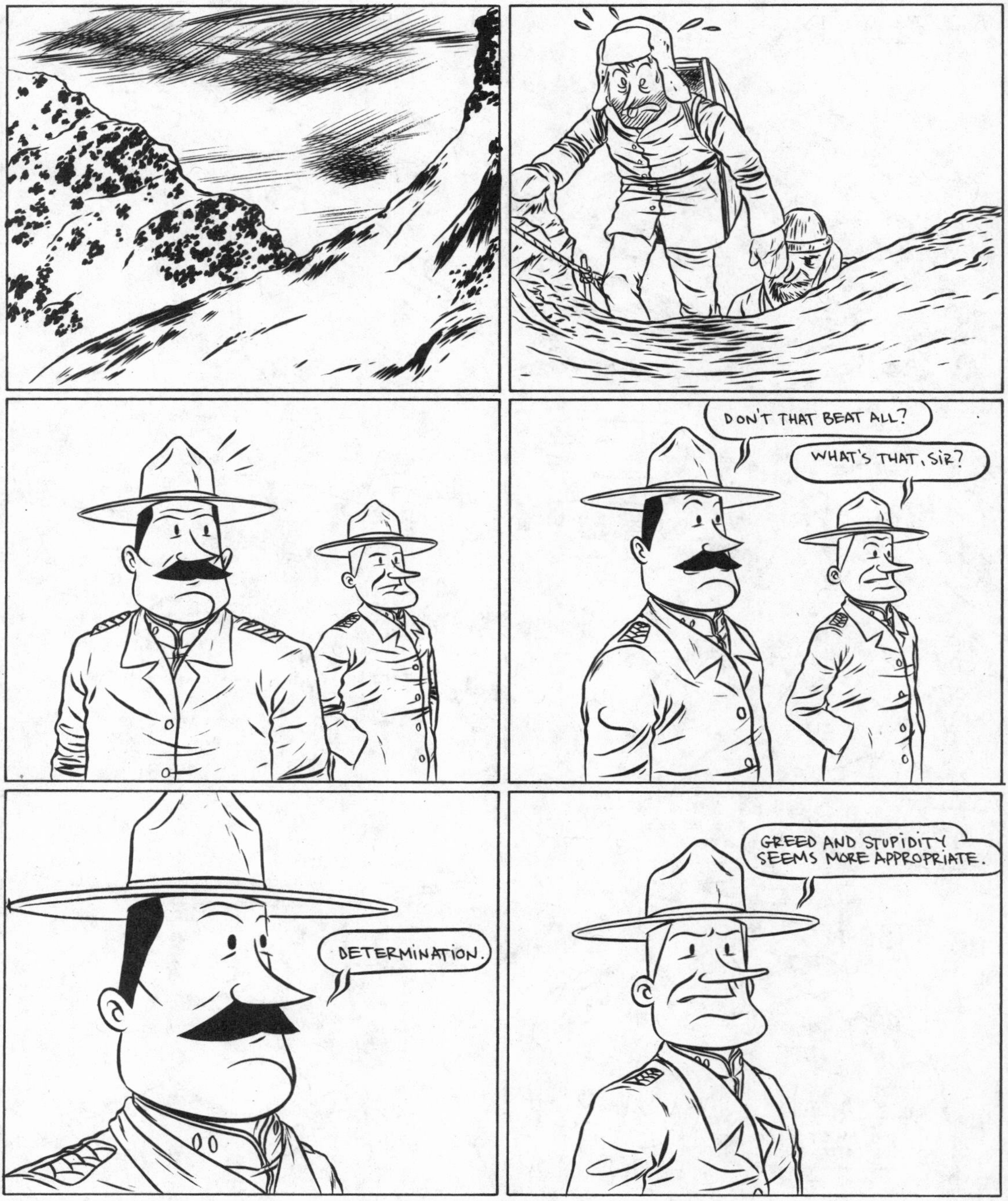
DON'T THAT BEAT ALL?
WHAT'S THAT, SIR?
DETERMINATION.
GREED AND STUPIDITY SEEMS MORE APPROPRIATE.

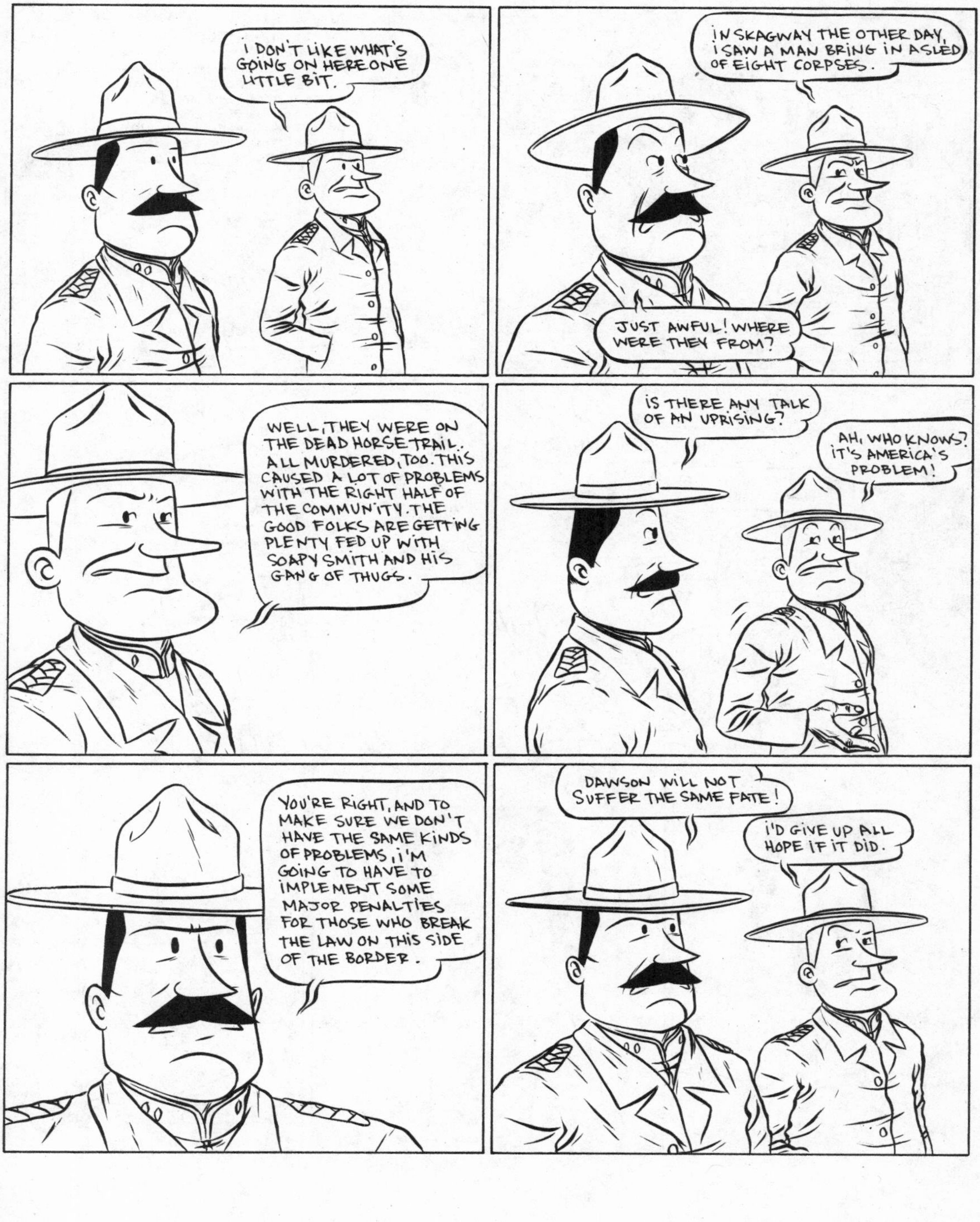
I DON'T LIKE WHAT'S GOING ON HERE ONE LITTLE BIT.
IN SKAGWAY THE OTHER DAY, I SAW A MAN BRING IN A SLED OF EIGHT CORPSES.
JUST AWFUL! WHERE WERE THEY FROM?
WELL, THEY WERE ON THE DEAD HORSE TRAIL. ALL MURDERED, TOO. THIS CAUSED A LOT OF PROBLEMS WITH THE RIGHT HALF OF THE COMMUNITY. THE GOOD FOLKS ARE GETTING PLENTY FED UP WITH SOAPY SMITH AND HIS GANG OF THUGS.
IS THERE ANY TALK OF AN UPRISING?
AH, WHO KNOWS? IT'S AMERICA'S PROBLEM!
YOU'RE RIGHT, AND TO MAKE SURE WE DON'T HAVE THE SAME KINDS OF PROBLEMS, I'M GOING TO HAVE TO IMPLEMENT SOME MAJOR PENALTIES FOR THOSE WHO BREAK THE LAW ON THIS SIDE OF THE BORDER.
DAWSON WILL NOT SUFFER THE SAME FATE!
I'D GIVE UP ALL HOPE IF IT DID.

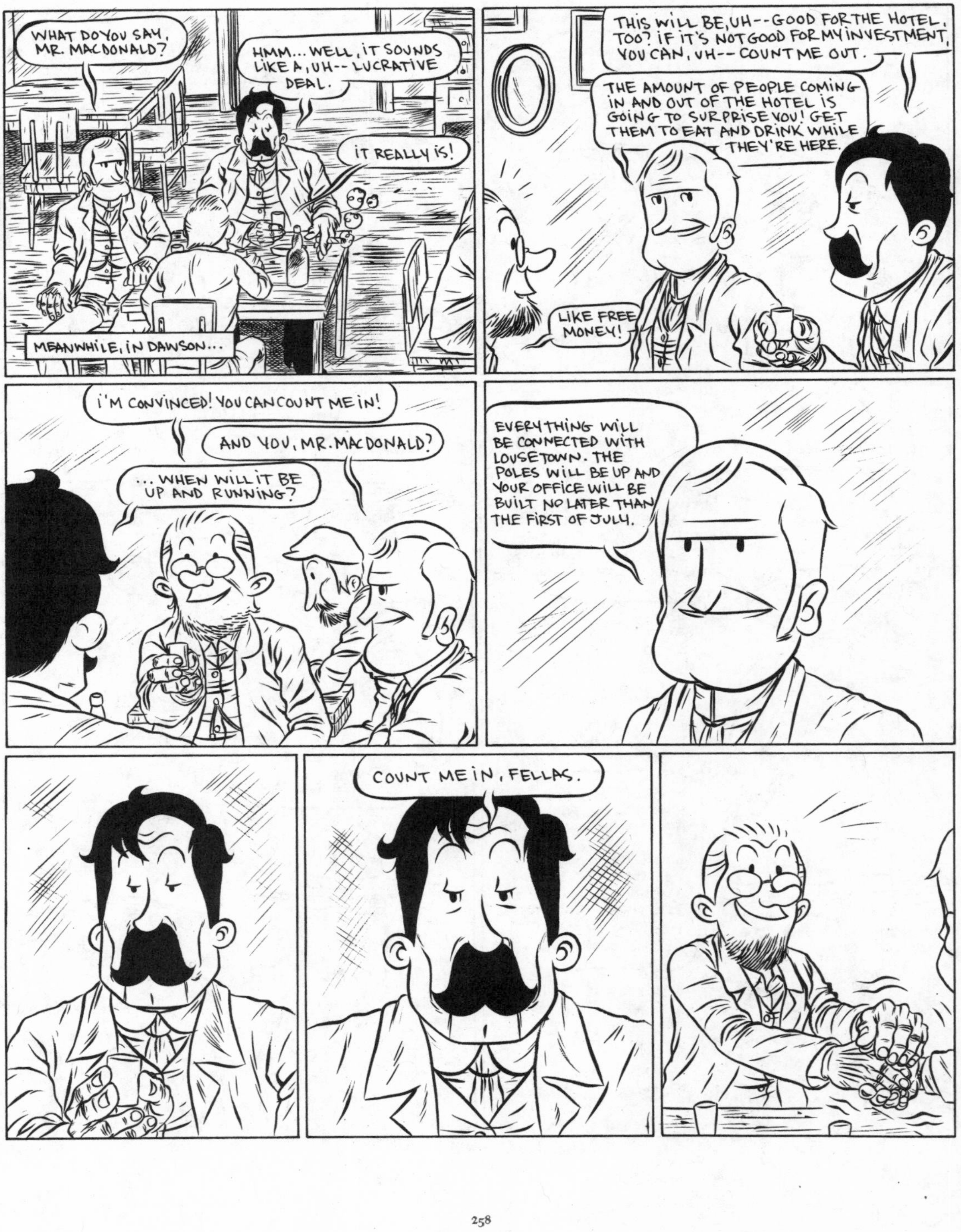

MEANWHILE, IN DAWSON...
WHAT DO YOU SAY, MR. MACDONALD?
HMM... WELL, IT SOUNDS LIKE A, UH-- LUCRATIVE DEAL.
IT REALLY IS!
THIS WILL BE, UH-- GOOD FOR THE HOTEL, TOO? IF IT'S NOT GOOD FOR MY INVESTMENT, YOU CAN, UH-- COUNT ME OUT.
THE AMOUNT OF PEOPLE COMING IN AND OUT OF THE HOTEL IS GOING TO SURPRISE YOU! GET THEM TO EAT AND DRINK WHILE THEY'RE HERE.
LIKE FREE MONEY!
I'M CONVINCED! YOU CAN COUNT ME IN!
AND YOU, MR. MACDONALD?
... WHEN WILL IT BE UP AND RUNNING?
EVERYTHING WILL BE CONNECTED WITH LOUSETOWN. THE POLES WILL BE UP AND YOUR OFFICE WILL BE BUILT NO LATER THAN THE FIRST OF JULY.
COUNT ME IN, FELLAS.

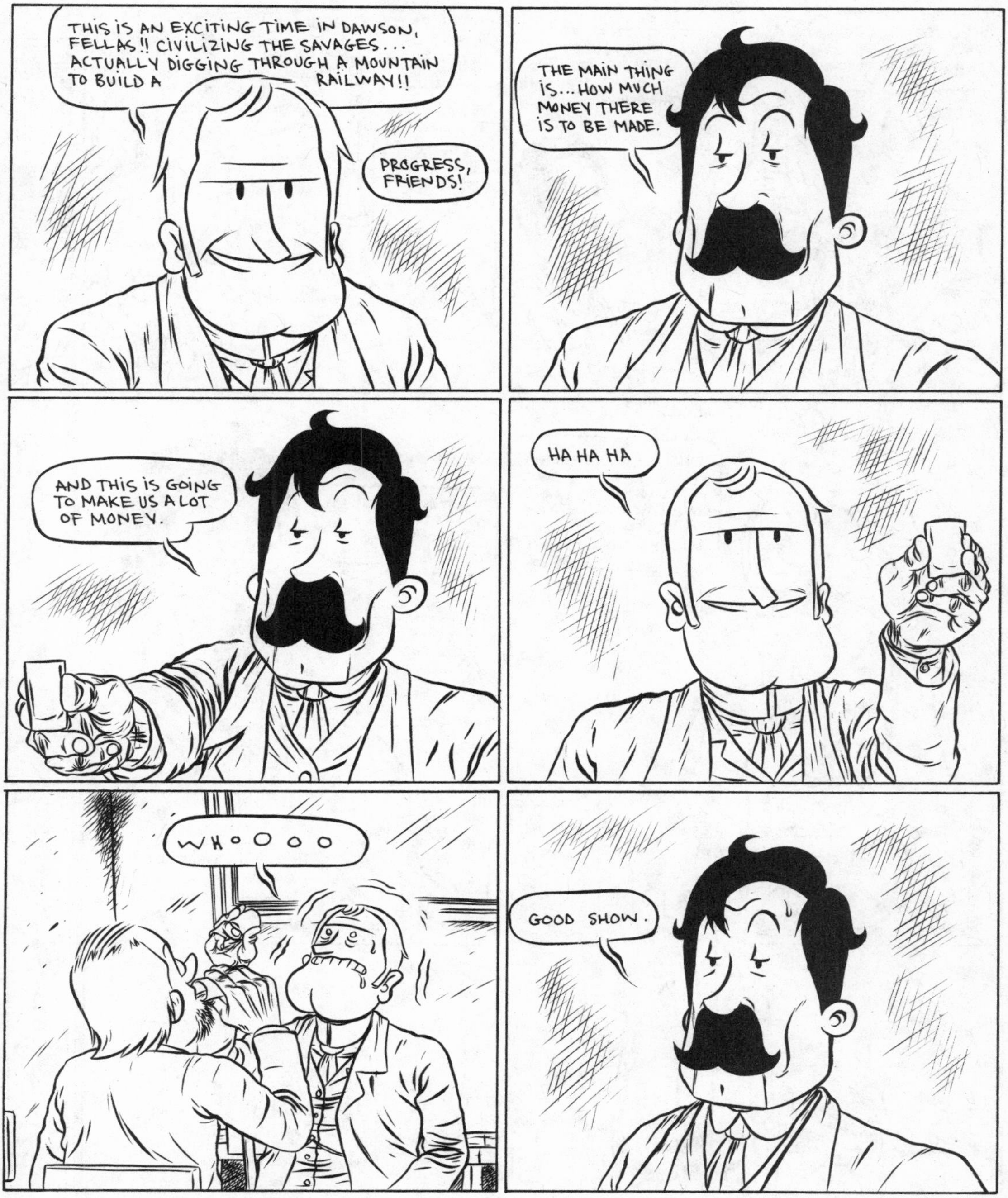
THIS IS AN EXCITING TIME IN DAWSON, FELLAS!! CIVILIZING THE SAVAGES... ACTUALLY DIGGING THROUGH A MOUNTAIN TO BUILD A RAILWAY!!
PROGRESS, FRIENDS!
THE MAIN THING IS... HOW MUCH MONEY THERE IS TO BE MADE.
AND THIS IS GOING TO MAKE US A LOT OF MONEY.
HA HA HA
WHOOOO
GOOD SHOW.

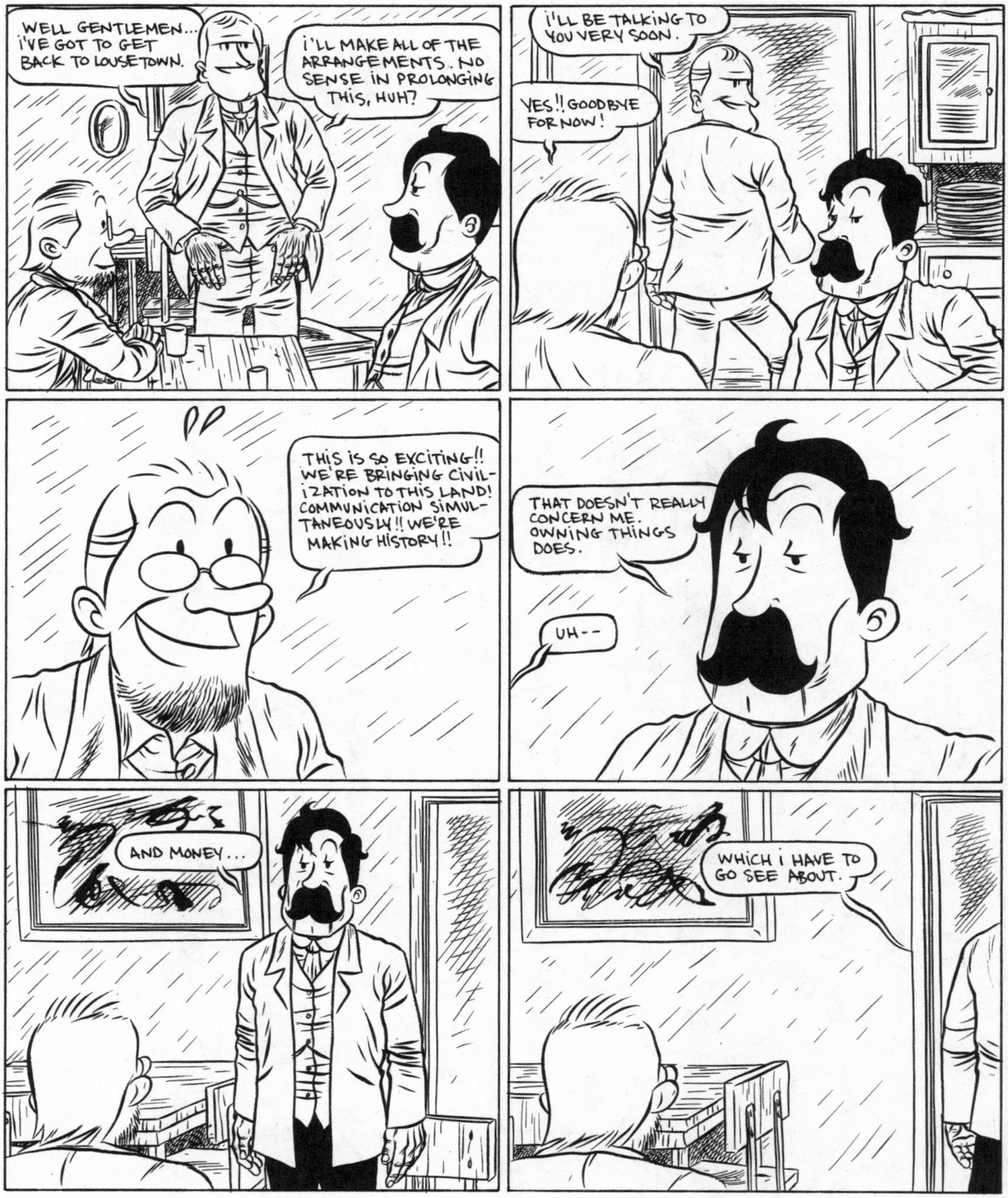
WELL GENTLEMEN... I'VE GOT TO GET BACK TO LOUSETOWN.
I'LL MAKE ALL OF THE ARRANGEMENTS. NO SENSE IN PROLONGING THIS, HUH?
I'LL BE TALKING TO YOU VERY SOON.
YES!! GOODBYE FOR NOW!
THIS IS SO EXCITING!! WE'RE BRINGING CIVILIZATION TO THIS LAND! COMMUNICATION SIMULTANEOUSLY!! WE'RE MAKING HISTORY!!
THAT DOESN'T REALLY CONCERN ME. OWNING THINGS DOES.
UH--
AND MONEY...
WHICH I HAVE TO GO SEE ABOUT.

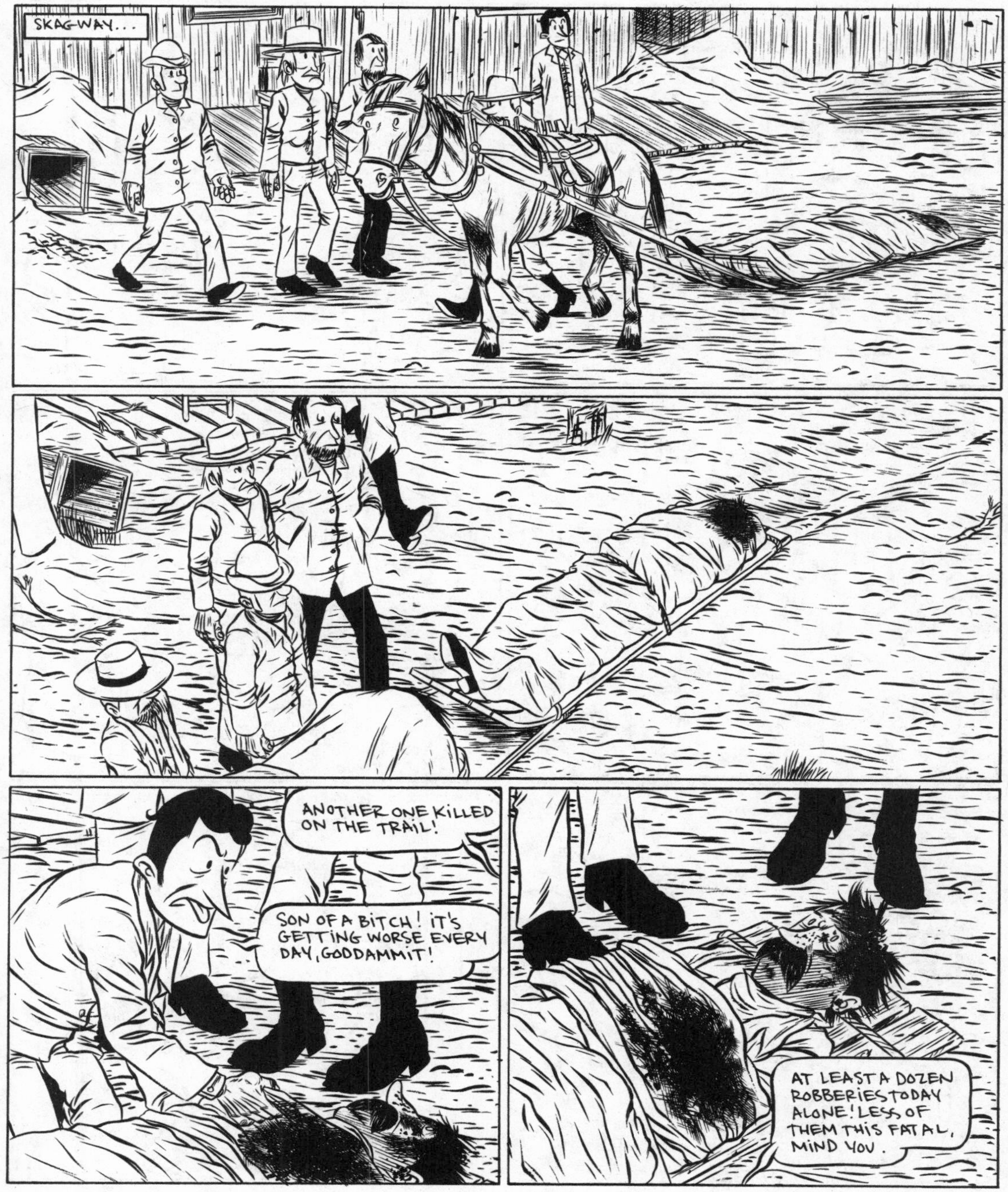
SKAG-WAY...
ANOTHER ONE KILLED ON THE TRAIL!
SON OF A BITCH! IT'S GETTING WORSE EVERY DAY, GODDAMMIT!
AT LEAST A DOZEN ROBBERIES TODAY ALONE! LESS OF THEM THIS FATAL, MIND YOU.

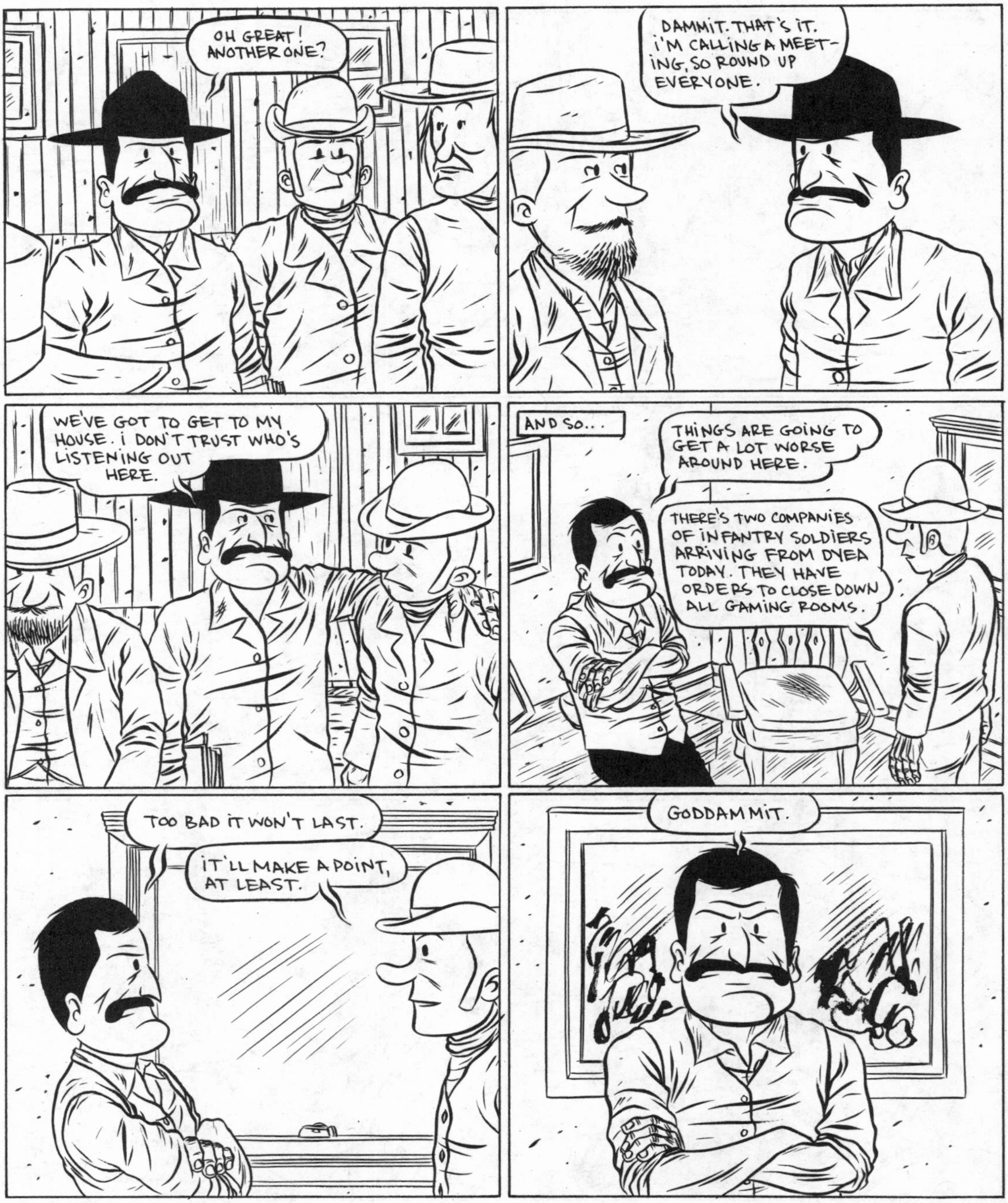
OH GREAT! ANOTHER ONE?
DAMMIT. THAT'S IT. I'M CALLING A MEETING, SO ROUND UP EVERYONE.
WE'VE GOT TO GET TO MY HOUSE. I DON'T TRUST WHO'S LISTENING OUT HERE.
AND SO...
THINGS ARE GOING TO GET A LOT WORSE AROUND HERE.
THERE'S TWO COMPANIES OF INFANTRY SOLDIERS ARRIVING FROM DYEA TODAY. THEY HAVE ORDERS TO CLOSE DOWN ALL GAMING ROOMS.
TOO BAD IT WON'T LAST.
IT'LL MAKE A POINT, AT LEAST.
GODDAMMIT.

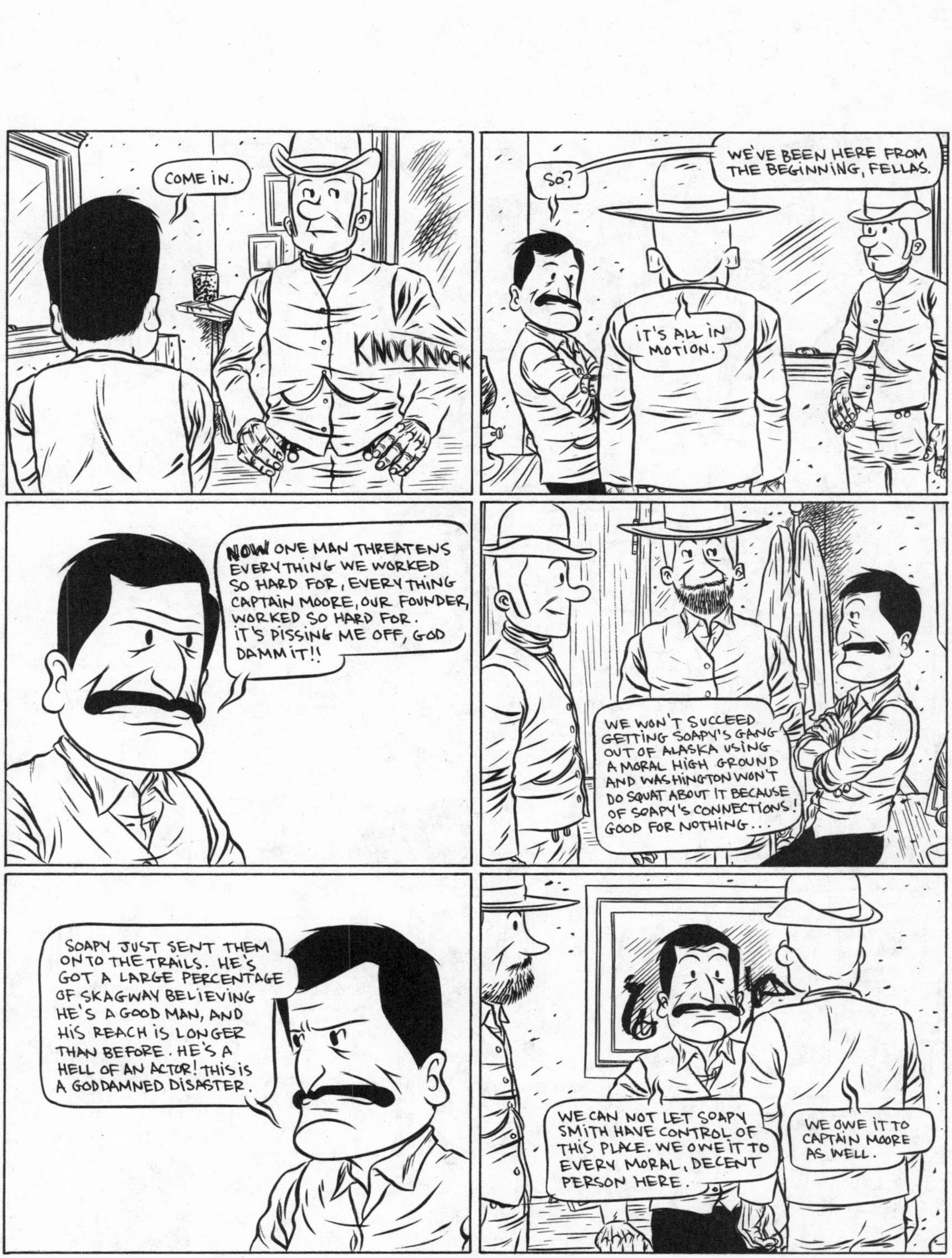
COME IN.
KNOCKNOCK
SO?
WE'VE BEEN HERE FROM THE BEGINNING, FELLAS.
IT'S ALL IN MOTION.
NOW ONE MAN THREATENS EVERYTHING WE WORKED SO HARD FOR, EVERYTHING CAPTAIN MOORE, OUR FOUNDER, WORKED SO HARD FOR. IT'S PISSING ME OFF, GOD DAMMIT!!
WE WON'T SUCCEED GETTING SOAPY'S GANG OUT OF ALASKA USING A MORAL HIGH GROUND AND WASHINGTON WON'T DO SQUAT ABOUT IT BECAUSE OF SOAPY'S CONNECTIONS! GOOD FOR NOTHING...
SOAPY JUST SENT THEM ONTO THE TRAILS. HE'S GOT A LARGE PERCENTAGE OF SKAGWAY BELIEVING HE'S A GOOD MAN, AND HIS REACH IS LONGER THAN BEFORE. HE'S A HELL OF AN ACTOR! THIS IS A GODDAMNED DISASTER.
WE CAN NOT LET SOAPY SMITH HAVE CONTROL OF THIS PLACE. WE OWE IT TO EVERY MORAL, DECENT PERSON HERE.
WE OWE IT TO CAPTAIN MOORE AS WELL.

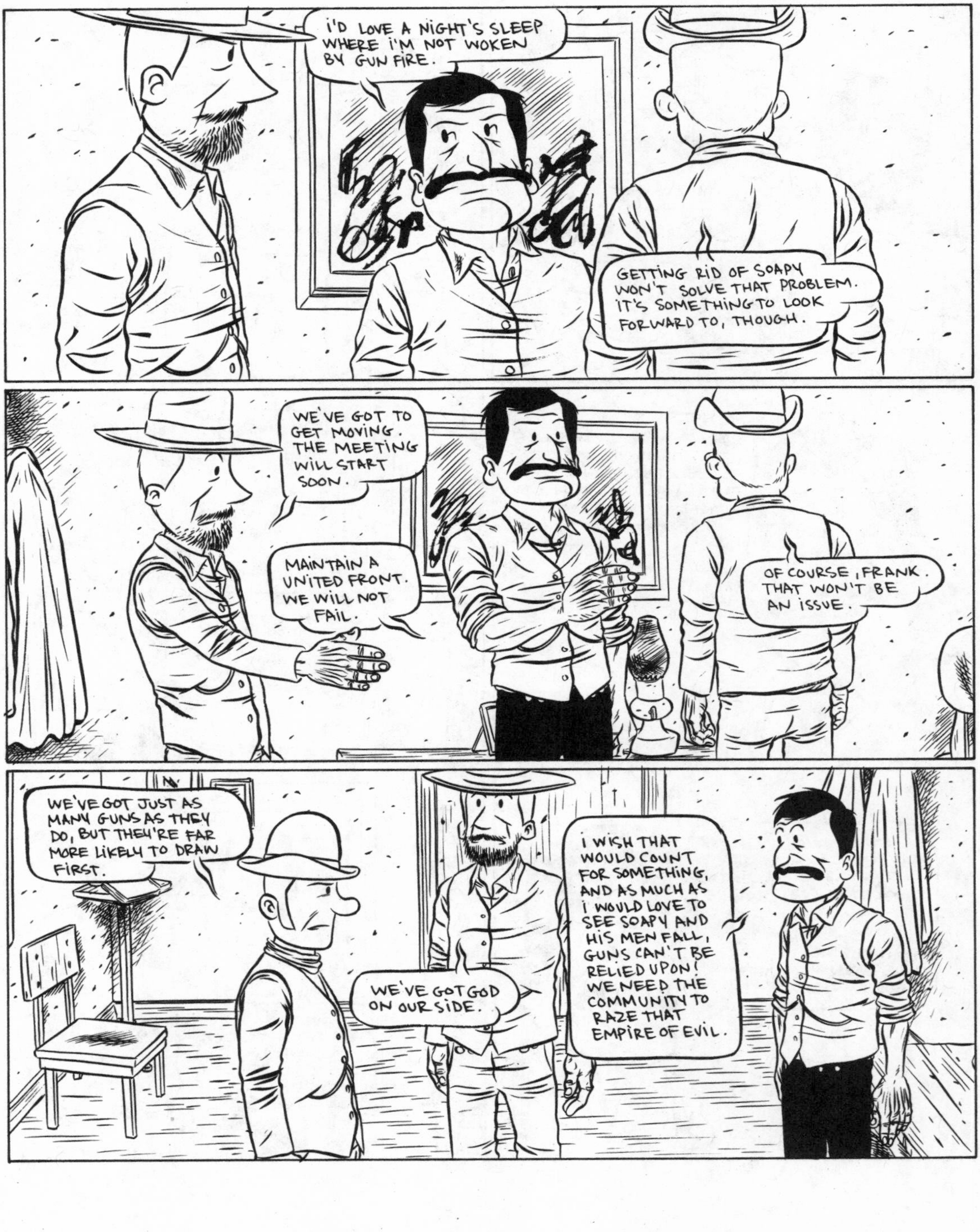
I'D LOVE A NIGHT'S SLEEP WHERE I'M NOT WOKEN BY GUN FIRE.
GETTING RID OF SOAPY WON'T SOLVE THAT PROBLEM. IT'S SOMETHING TO LOOK FORWARD TO, THOUGH.
WE'VE GOT TO GET MOVING. THE MEETING WILL START SOON.
MAINTAIN A UNITED FRONT. WE WILL NOT FAIL.
OF COURSE, FRANK. THAT WON'T BE AN ISSUE.
WE'VE GOT JUST AS MANY GUNS AS THEY DO, BUT THEY'RE FAR MORE LIKELY TO DRAW FIRST.
WE'VE GOT GOD ON OUR SIDE.
I WISH THAT WOULD COUNT FOR SOMETHING, AND AS MUCH AS I WOULD LOVE TO SEE SOAPY AND HIS MEN FALL, GUNS CAN'T BE RELIED UPON! WE NEED THE COMMUNITY TO RAZE THAT EMPIRE OF EVIL.

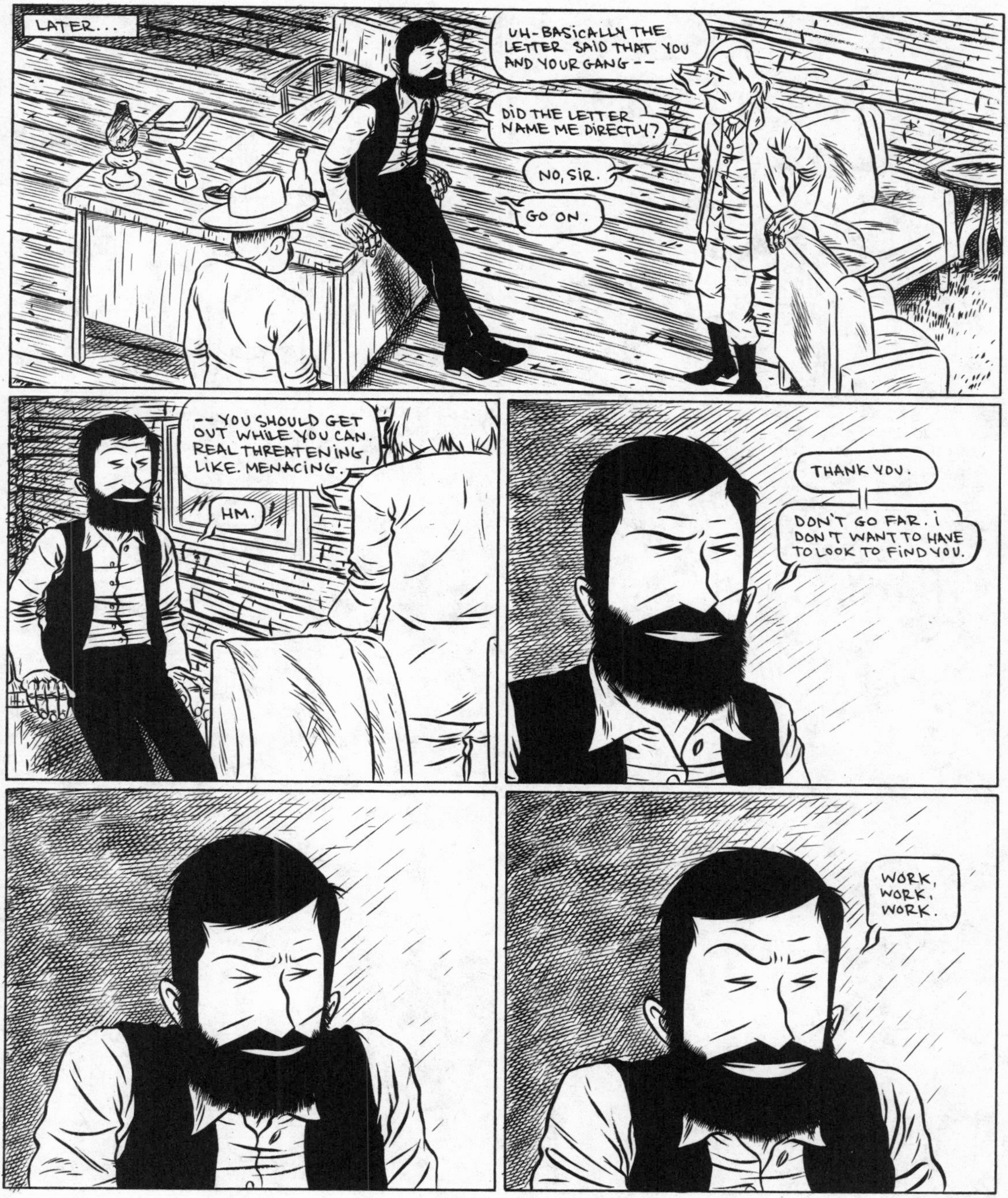
LATER...
UH-BASICALLY THE LETTER SAID THAT YOU AND YOUR GANG --
DID THE LETTER NAME ME DIRECTLY?
NO, SIR.
GO ON.
-- YOU SHOULD GET OUT WHILE YOU CAN. REAL THREATENING, LIKE. MENACING.
HM.
THANK YOU.
DON'T GO FAR. I DON'T WANT TO HAVE TO LOOK TO FIND YOU.
WORK, WORK, WORK.

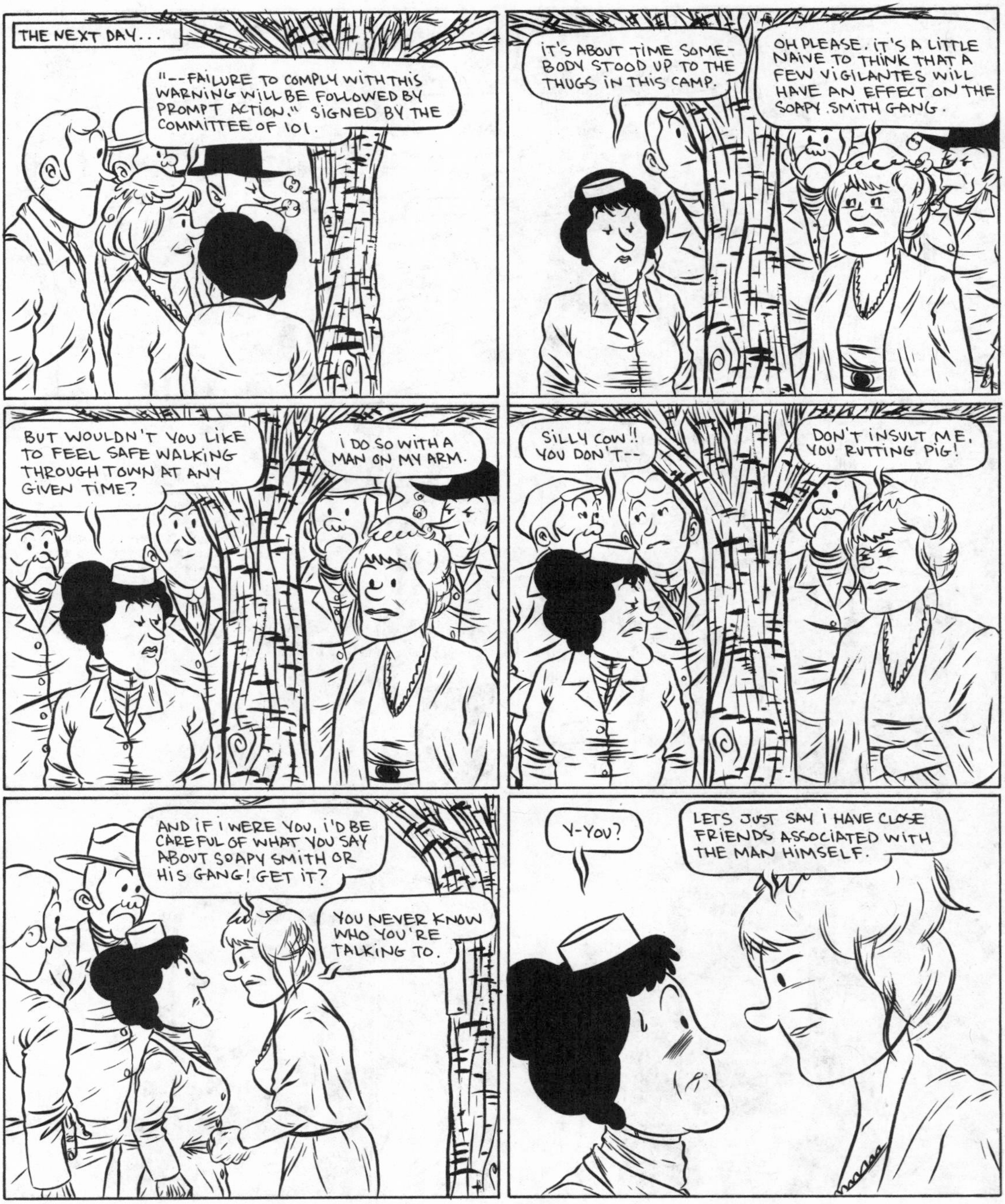
THE NEXT DAY...
"--FAILURE TO COMPLY WITH THIS WARNING WILL BE FOLLOWED BY PROMPT ACTION." SIGNED BY THE COMMITTEE OF 101.
IT'S ABOUT TIME SOMEBODY STOOD UP TO THE THUGS IN THIS CAMP.
OH PLEASE. IT'S A LITTLE NAIVE TO THINK THAT A FEW VIGILANTES WILL HAVE AN EFFECT ON THE SOAPY SMITH GANG.
BUT WOULDN'T YOU LIKE TO FEEL SAFE WALKING THROUGH TOWN AT ANY GIVEN TIME?
I DO SO WITH A MAN ON MY ARM.
SILLY COW!! YOU DON'T--
DON'T INSULT ME, YOU RUTTING PIG!
AND IF I WERE YOU, I'D BE CAREFUL OF WHAT YOU SAY ABOUT SOAPY SMITH OR HIS GANG! GET IT?
YOU NEVER KNOW WHO YOU'RE TALKING TO.
Y-YOU?
LETS JUST SAY I HAVE CLOSE FRIENDS ASSOCIATED WITH THE MAN HIMSELF.

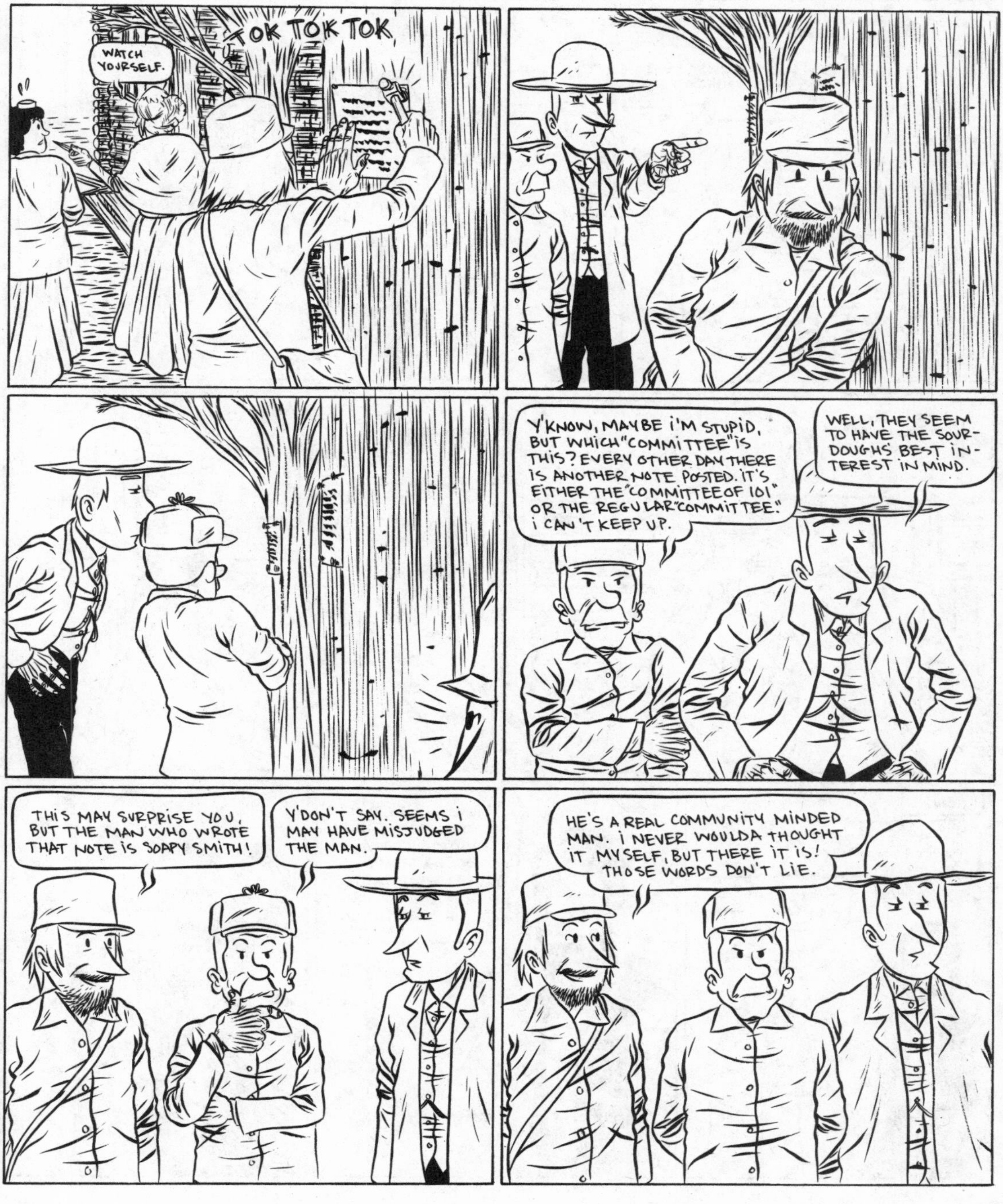
TOK TOK TOK
WATCH YOURSELF.
Y'KNOW, MAYBE I'M STUPID, BUT WHICH "COMMITTEE" IS THIS? EVERY OTHER DAY THERE IS ANOTHER NOTE POSTED. IT'S EITHER THE "COMMITTEE OF 101" OR THE REGULAR "COMMITTEE." I CAN'T KEEP UP.
WELL, THEY SEEM TO HAVE THE SOURDOUGHS BEST INTEREST IN MIND.
THIS MAY SURPRISE YOU, BUT THE MAN WHO WROTE THAT NOTE IS SOAPY SMITH!
Y'DON'T SAY. SEEMS I MAY HAVE MISJUDGED THE MAN.
HE'S A REAL COMMUNITY MINDED MAN. I NEVER WOULDA THOUGHT IT MYSELF, BUT THERE IT IS! THOSE WORDS DON'T LIE.

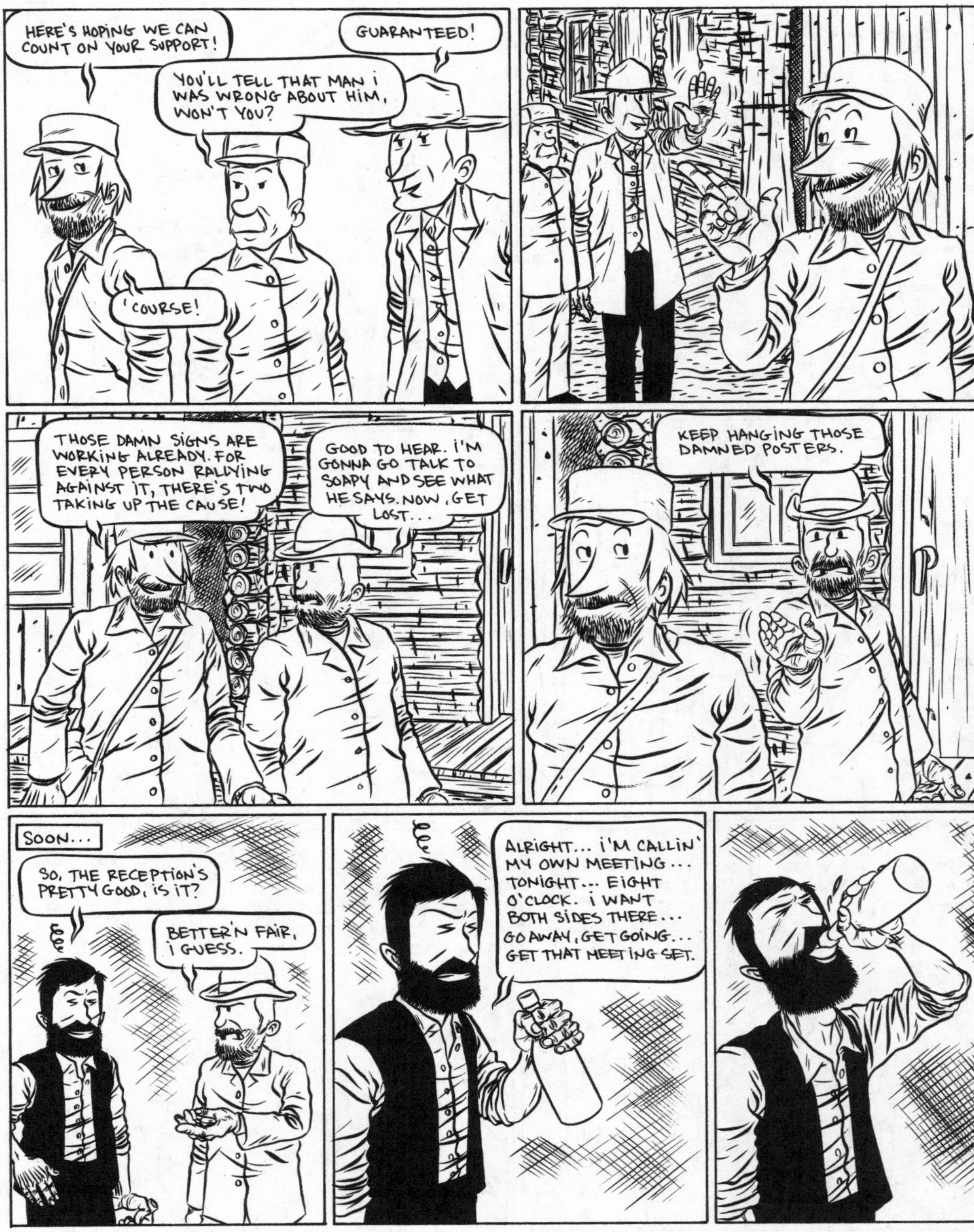
HERE'S HOPING WE CAN COUNT ON YOUR SUPPORT!
GUARANTEED!
YOU'LL TELL THAT MAN I WAS WRONG ABOUT HIM, WON'T YOU?
'COURSE!
THOSE DAMN SIGNS ARE WORKING ALREADY. FOR EVERY PERSON RALLYING AGAINST IT, THERE'S TWO TAKING UP THE CAUSE!
GOOD TO HEAR. I'M GONNA GO TALK TO SOAPY AND SEE WHAT HE SAYS. NOW, GET LOST...
KEEP HANGING THOSE DAMNED POSTERS.
SOON...
SO, THE RECEPTION'S PRETTY GOOD, IS IT?
BETTER'N FAIR, I GUESS.
ALRIGHT... I'M CALLIN' MY OWN MEETING... TONIGHT... EIGHT O'CLOCK. I WANT BOTH SIDES THERE... GO AWAY, GET GOING... GET THAT MEETING SET.

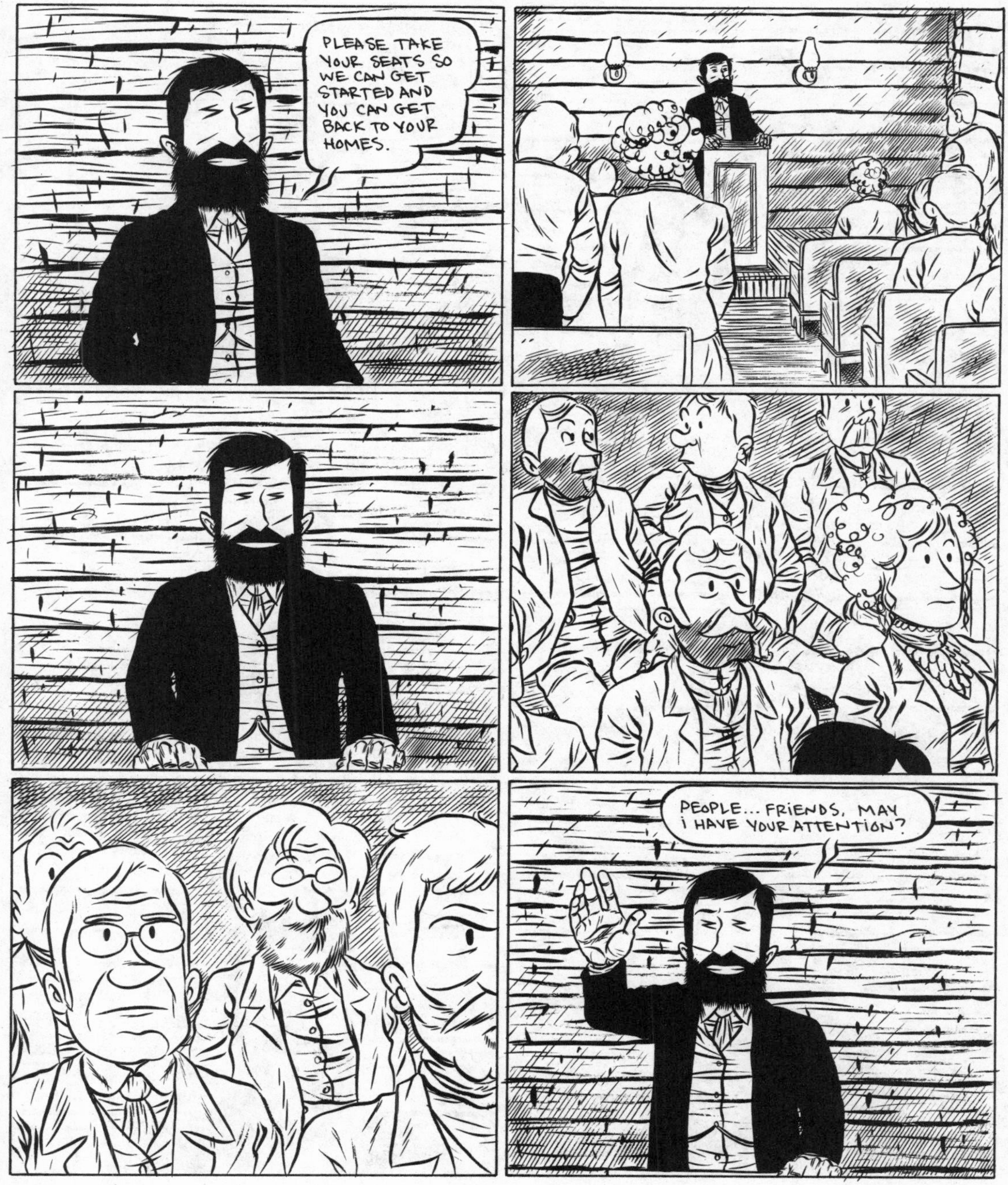
PLEASE TAKE YOUR SEATS SO WE CAN GET STARTED AND YOU CAN GET BACK TO YOUR HOMES.
PEOPLE... FRIENDS, MAY I HAVE YOUR ATTENTION?

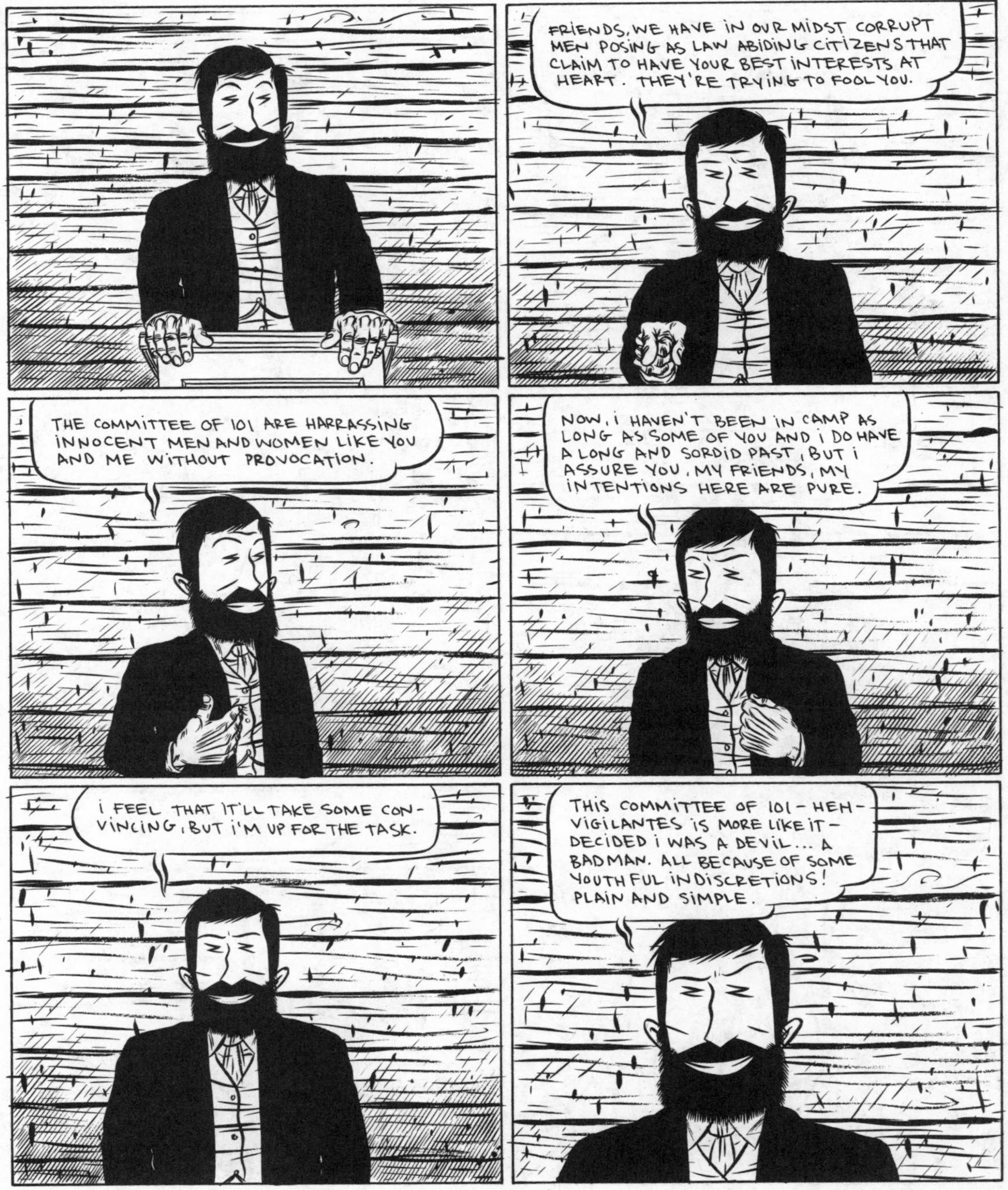

FRIENDS, WE HAVE IN OUR MIDST CORRUPT MEN POSING AS LAW ABIDING CITIZENS THAT CLAIM TO HAVE YOUR BEST INTERESTS AT HEART. THEY'RE TRYING TO FOOL YOU.
THE COMMITTEE OF 101 ARE HARRASSING INNOCENT MEN AND WOMEN LIKE YOU AND ME WITHOUT PROVOCATION.
NOW, I HAVEN'T BEEN IN CAMP AS LONG AS SOME OF YOU AND I DO HAVE A LONG AND SORDID PAST, BUT I ASSURE YOU, MY FRIENDS, MY INTENTIONS HERE ARE PURE.
I FEEL THAT IT'LL TAKE SOME CONVINCING, BUT I'M UP FOR THE TASK.
THIS COMMITTEE OF 101 - HEH - VIGILANTES IS MORE LIKE IT - DECIDED I WAS A DEVIL... A BADMAN. ALL BECAUSE OF SOME YOUTHFUL INDISCRETIONS! PLAIN AND SIMPLE.

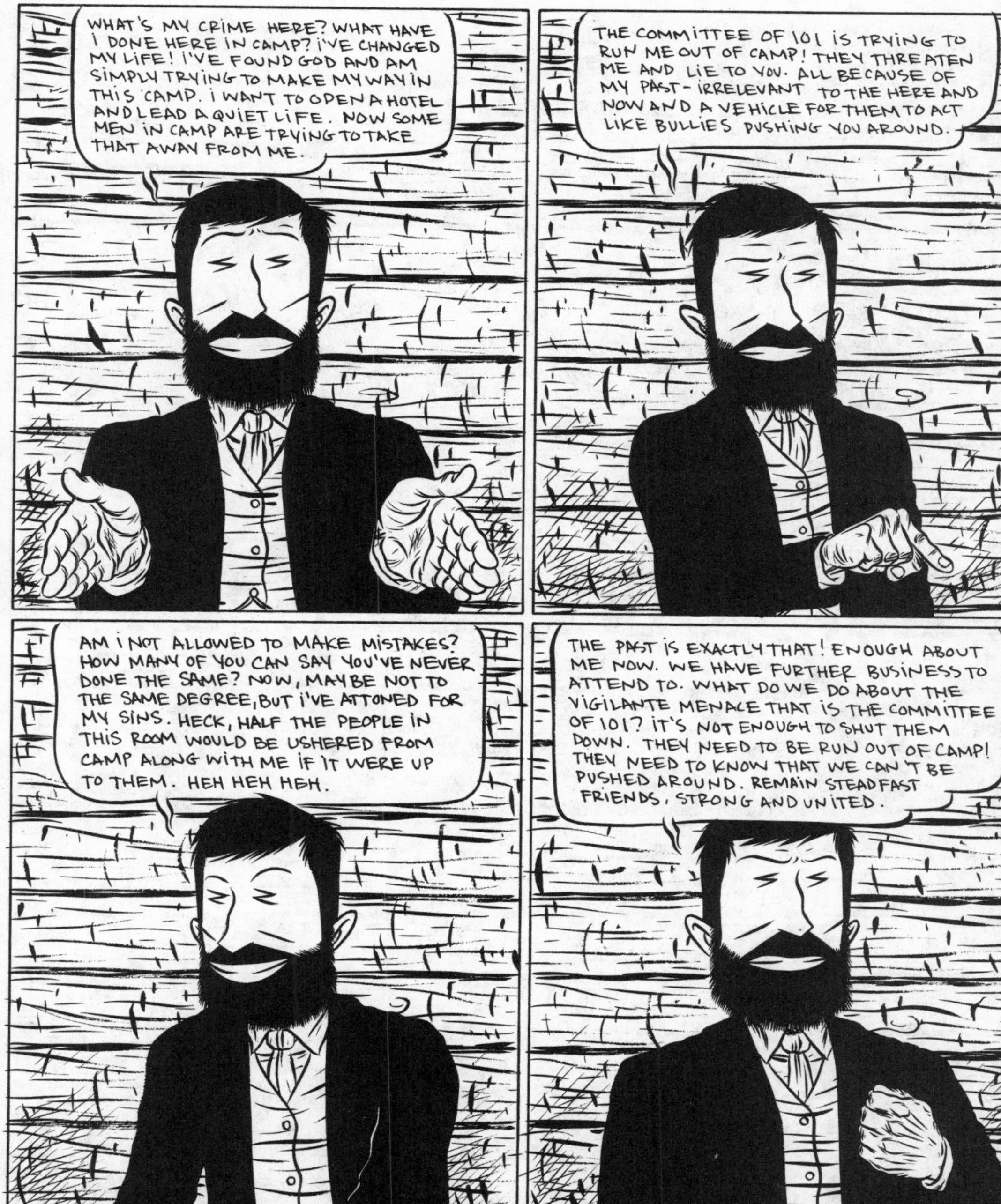
WHAT'S MY CRIME HERE? WHAT HAVE I DONE HERE IN CAMP? I'VE CHANGED MY LIFE! I'VE FOUND GOD AND AM SIMPLY TRYING TO MAKE MY WAY IN THIS CAMP. I WANT TO OPEN A HOTEL AND LEAD A QUIET LIFE. NOW SOME MEN IN CAMP ARE TRYING TO TAKE THAT AWAY FROM ME.
THE COMMITTEE OF 101 IS TRYING TO RUN ME OUT OF CAMP! THEY THREATEN ME AND LIE TO YOU. ALL BECAUSE OF MY PAST- IRRELEVANT TO THE HERE AND NOW AND A VEHICLE FOR THEM TO ACT LIKE BULLIES PUSHING YOU AROUND.
AM I NOT ALLOWED TO MAKE MISTAKES? HOW MANY OF YOU CAN SAY YOU'VE NEVER DONE THE SAME? NOW, MAYBE NOT TO THE SAME DEGREE, BUT I'VE ATTONED FOR MY SINS. HECK, HALF THE PEOPLE IN THIS ROOM WOULD BE USHERED FROM CAMP ALONG WITH ME IF IT WERE UP TO THEM. HEH HEH HEH.
THE PAST IS EXACTLY THAT! ENOUGH ABOUT ME NOW. WE HAVE FURTHER BUSINESS TO ATTEND TO. WHAT DO WE DO ABOUT THE VIGILANTE MENACE THAT IS THE COMMITTEE OF 101? IT'S NOT ENOUGH TO SHUT THEM DOWN. THEY NEED TO BE RUN OUT OF CAMP! THEY NEED TO KNOW THAT WE CAN'T BE PUSHED AROUND. REMAIN STEADFAST FRIENDS, STRONG AND UNITED.

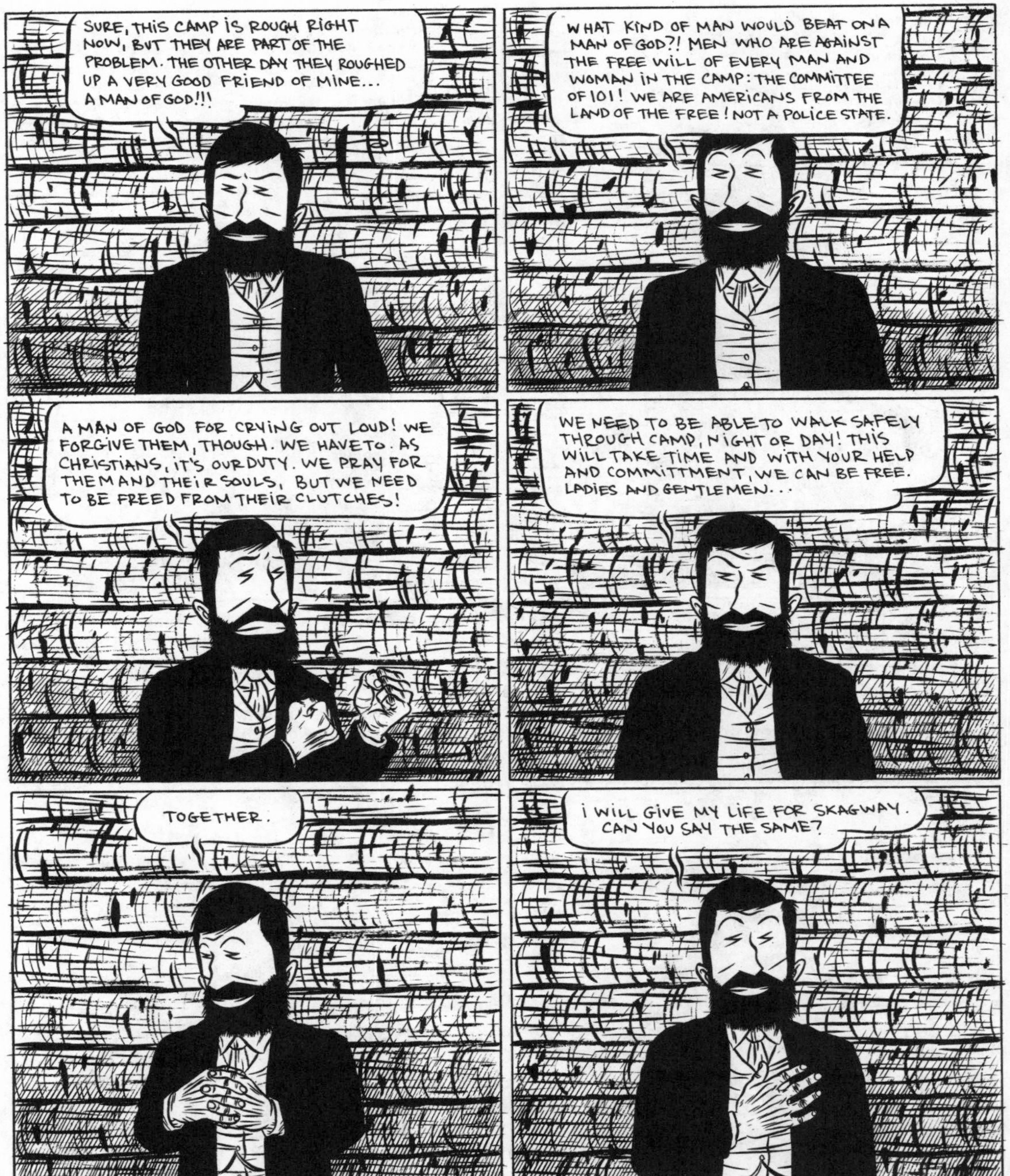
SURE, THIS CAMP IS ROUGH RIGHT NOW, BUT THEY ARE PART OF THE PROBLEM. THE OTHER DAY THEY ROUGHED UP A VERY GOOD FRIEND OF MINE... A MAN OF GOD!!!
WHAT KIND OF MAN WOULD BEAT ON A MAN OF GOD?! MEN WHO ARE AGAINST THE FREE WILL OF EVERY MAN AND WOMAN IN THE CAMP: THE COMMITTEE OF 101! WE ARE AMERICANS FROM THE LAND OF THE FREE! NOT A POLICE STATE.
A MAN OF GOD FOR CRYING OUT LOUD! WE FORGIVE THEM, THOUGH. WE HAVE TO. AS CHRISTIANS, IT'S OUR DUTY. WE PRAY FOR THEM AND THEIR SOULS, BUT WE NEED TO BE FREED FROM THEIR CLUTCHES!
WE NEED TO BE ABLE TO WALK SAFELY THROUGH CAMP, NIGHT OR DAY! THIS WILL TAKE TIME AND WITH YOUR HELP AND COMMITTMENT, WE CAN BE FREE. LADIES AND GENTLEMEN...
TOGETHER.
I WILL GIVE MY LIFE FOR SKAGWAY. CAN YOU SAY THE SAME?

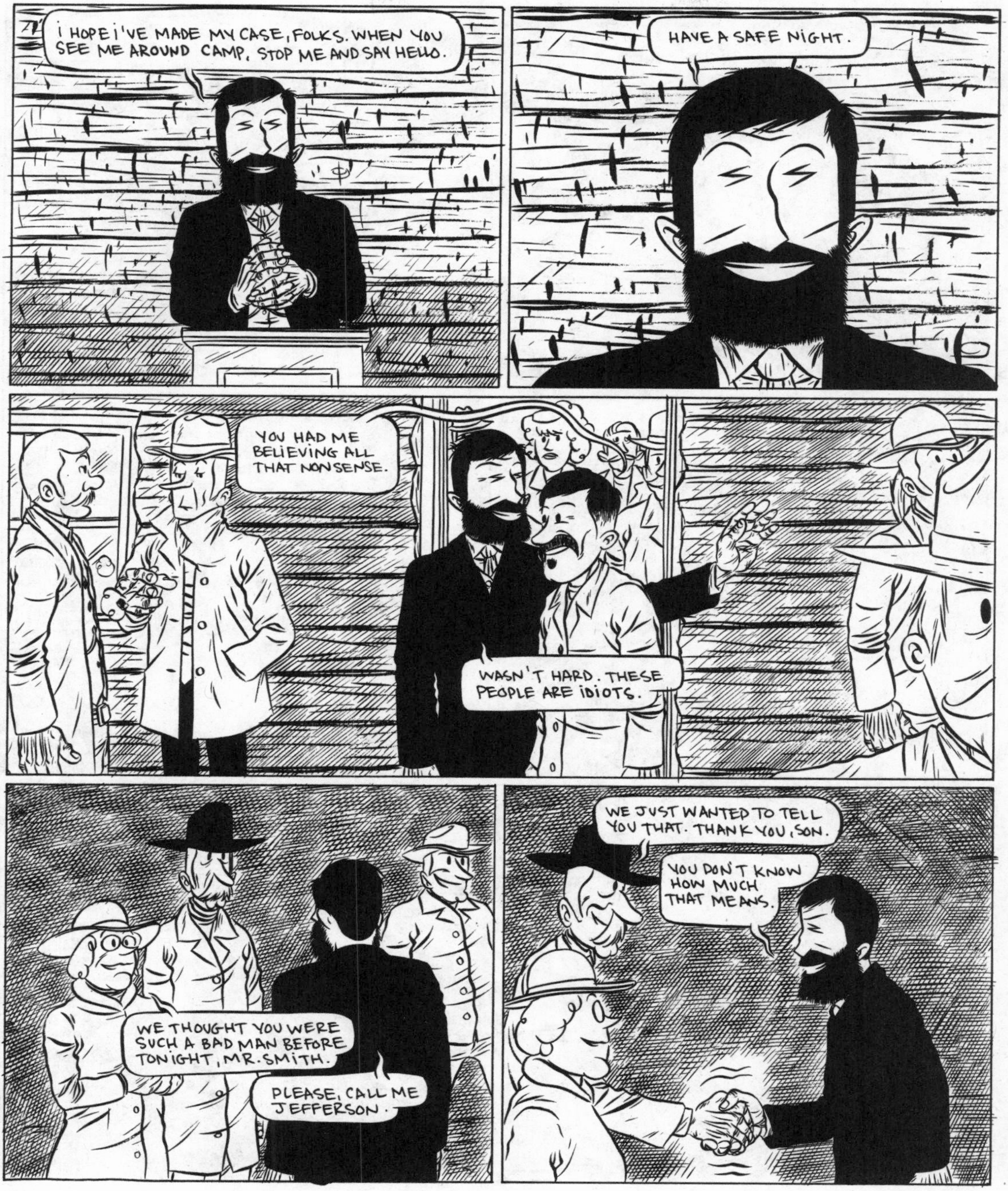
I HOPE I'VE MADE MY CASE, FOLKS. WHEN YOU SEE ME AROUND CAMP, STOP ME AND SAY HELLO.
HAVE A SAFE NIGHT.
YOU HAD ME BELIEVING ALL THAT NONSENSE.
WASN'T HARD. THESE PEOPLE ARE IDIOTS.
WE THOUGHT YOU WERE SUCH A BAD MAN BEFORE TONIGHT, MR. SMITH.
PLEASE, CALL ME JEFFERSON.
WE JUST WANTED TO TELL YOU THAT. THANK YOU, SON.
YOU DON'T KNOW HOW MUCH THAT MEANS.

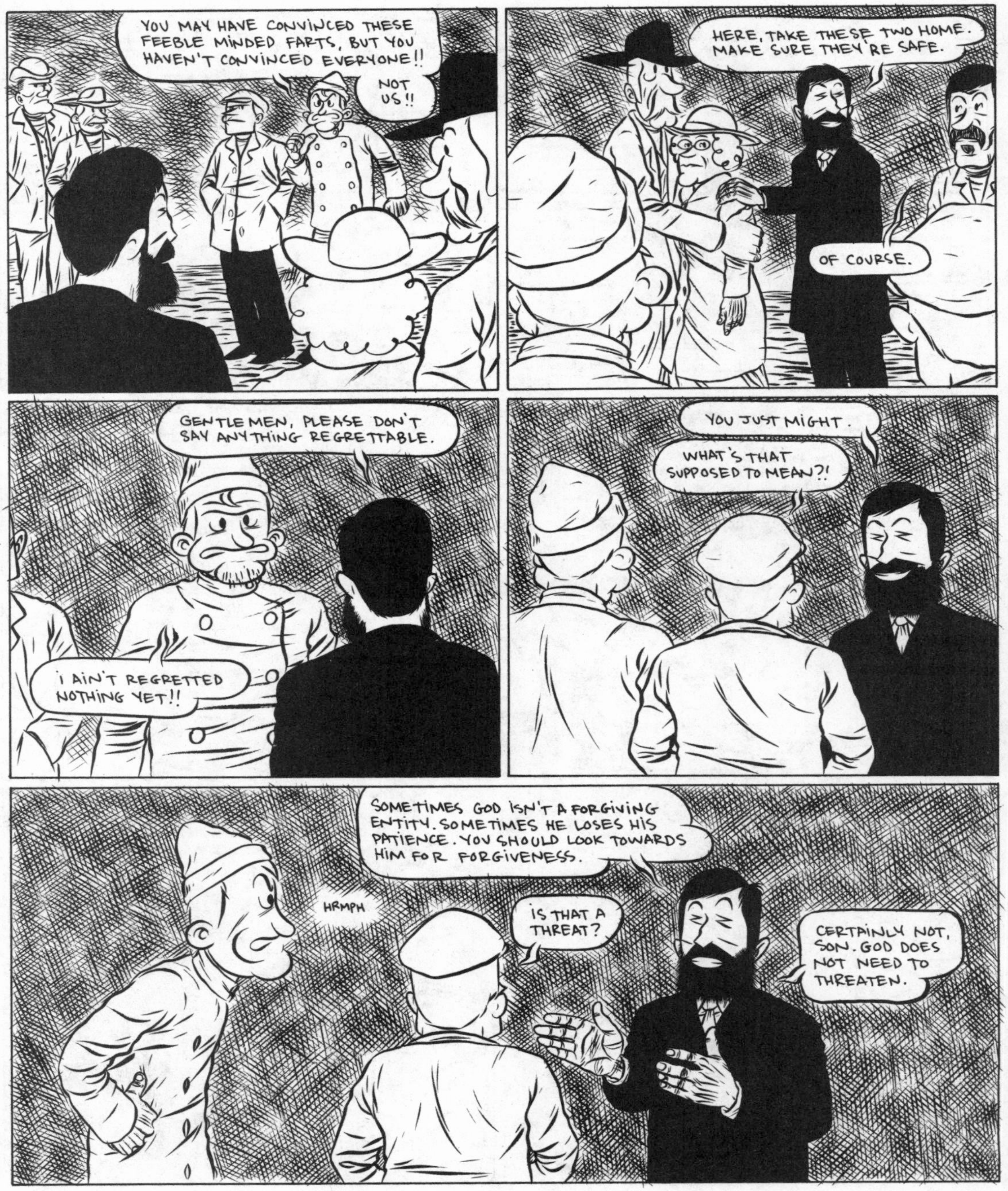
YOU MAY HAVE CONVINCED THESE FEEBLE MINDED FARTS, BUT YOU HAVEN'T CONVINCED EVERYONE!!
NOT US!!
HERE, TAKE THESE TWO HOME. MAKE SURE THEY'RE SAFE.
OF COURSE.
GENTLEMEN, PLEASE DON'T SAY ANYTHING REGRETTABLE.
I AIN'T REGRETTED NOTHING YET!!
YOU JUST MIGHT.
WHAT'S THAT SUPPOSED TO MEAN?!
SOMETIMES GOD ISN'T A FORGIVING ENTITY. SOMETIMES HE LOSES HIS PATIENCE. YOU SHOULD LOOK TOWARDS HIM FOR FORGIVENESS.
HRMPH
IS THAT A THREAT?
CERTAINLY NOT, SON. GOD DOES NOT NEED TO THREATEN.

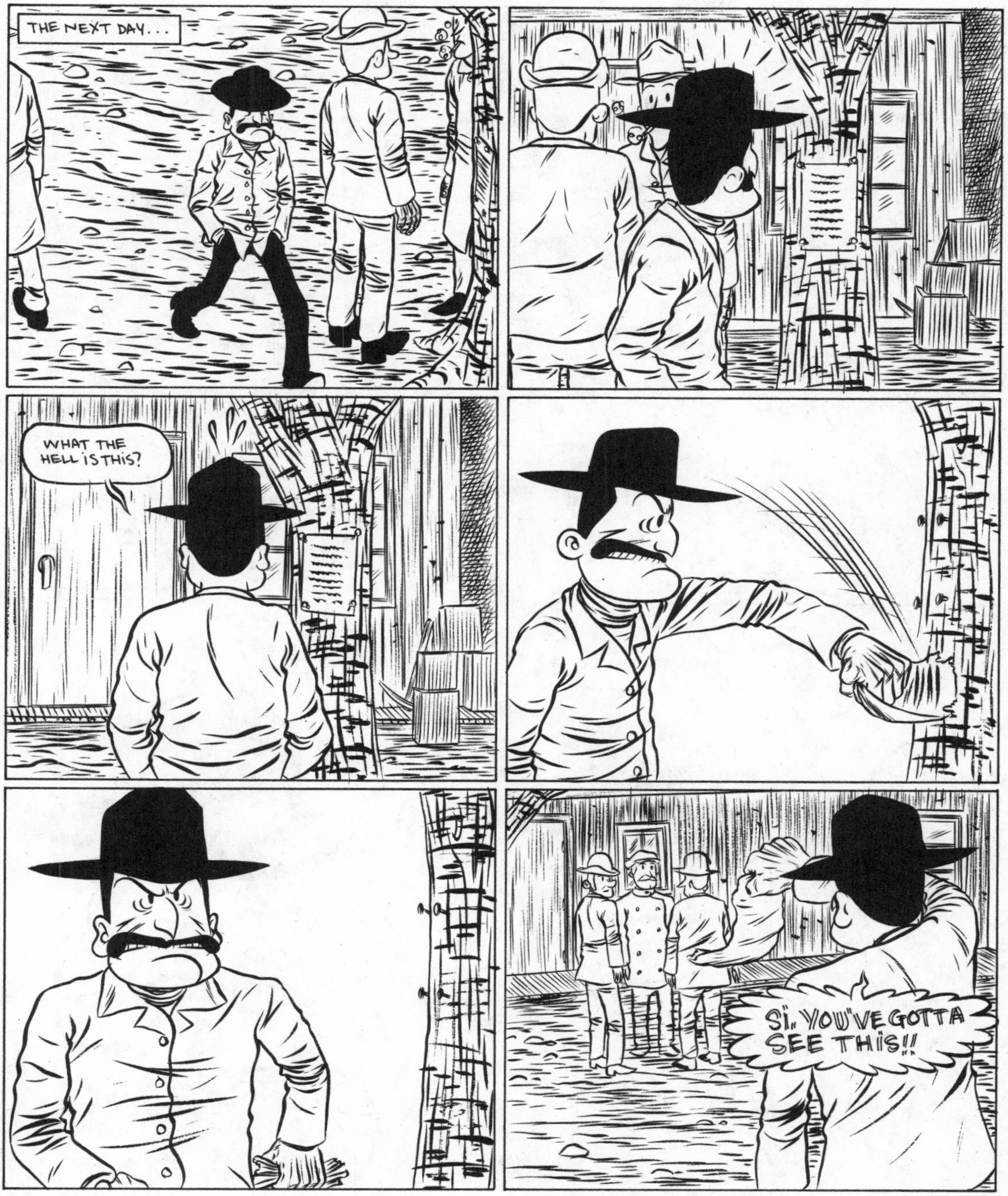
THE NEXT DAY...
WHAT THE HELL IS THIS?
SI, YOU'VE GOTTA SEE THIS!!

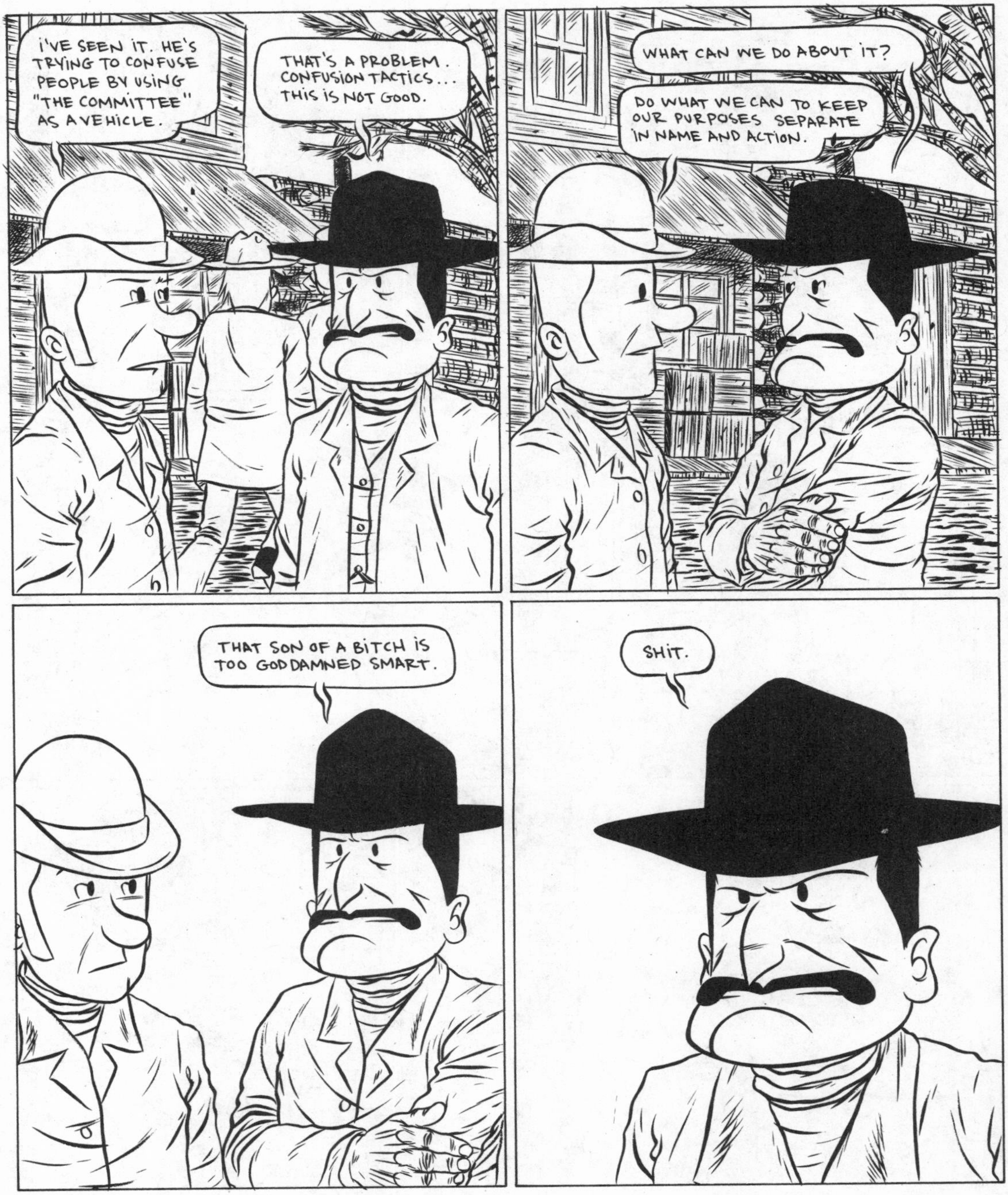
I'VE SEEN IT. HE'S TRYING TO CONFUSE PEOPLE BY USING "THE COMMITTEE" AS A VEHICLE.
THAT'S A PROBLEM. CONFUSION TACTICS... THIS IS NOT GOOD.
WHAT CAN WE DO ABOUT IT?
DO WHAT WE CAN TO KEEP OUR PURPOSES SEPARATE IN NAME AND ACTION.
THAT SON OF A BITCH IS TOO GODDAMNED SMART.
SHIT.

IT SNOWED FOR TWO MONTHS WITH NO RELIEF. HUNDREDS OF PROSPECTORS HAD BEEN ANXIOUSLY WAITING TO START CLIMBING THE PASS, SO WHEN IT STOPPED ON APRIL 3RD, THEY BEGAN DIGGING THEIR WAY OUT, PREPARING TO START THE ASCENT. THE MAJOR PROBLEM THEY FACED NOW WAS THE DRAMATIC RISE IN TEMPERATURE. MANY WERE SMART ENOUGH TO BEGIN THEIR CLIMB UP THE PASS STARTING IN THE EVENING WHEN THE TEMPERATURE DROPPED. THE EXPERIENCED INDIAN PACKERS REFUSED TO CLIMB ALL TOGETHER, KNOWING THE RISKS INVOLVED. AS THE MORNING OF APRIL 3RD TURNED INTO AFTERNOON, THE SUN HEATED THE SUMMIT, COMPROMISING ITS SO-CALLED INTEGRITY. WITH ONLY A RUMBLE AS WARNING, THE MEN AND WOMEN ON THE TRAIL HAD ALMOST NO TIME TO REACT AS A MASSIVE AVALANCHE STRUCK (A MUCH SMALLER ONE HAPPENED EARLIER THE SAME MORNING, BUT DIDN'T DETER ANYONE). HUNDREDS WERE BURIED AND THOUGHT TO BE DEAD. AS SURVIVORS WERE RESCUED, THE NUMBER OF DEAD ROSE TO MORE THAN SIXTY AND MANY WEREN'T DISCOVERED UNTIL MUCH LATER. THOUSANDS FROM THE CAMP BELOW RUSHED TO HELP WITH THE RESCUE EFFORT. THE SAME DAY, THE NEWS REACHED SKAGWAY AND SOAPY SMITH DISPATCHED HIS MEN TO GET TO THE SITE TO TAKE ADVANTAGE OF THE SIT-UATION, WHICH THEY DID WITH NO REMORSE.

THE MONTHS THAT FOLLOWED OFFERED A DIS-TURBING SIGHT TO THOSE WHO CONTINUED THEIR CLIMB UP THE CHILKOOT. THE DOZENS OF TRAVELLERS THAT WERE NEVER FOUND APPEARED THEN AS THAWED, BLOATED AND DECOMPOSING CORPSES LAYING IN SLUDGY WATER -- A SIGHT THAT NO ONE EVER FORGOT.

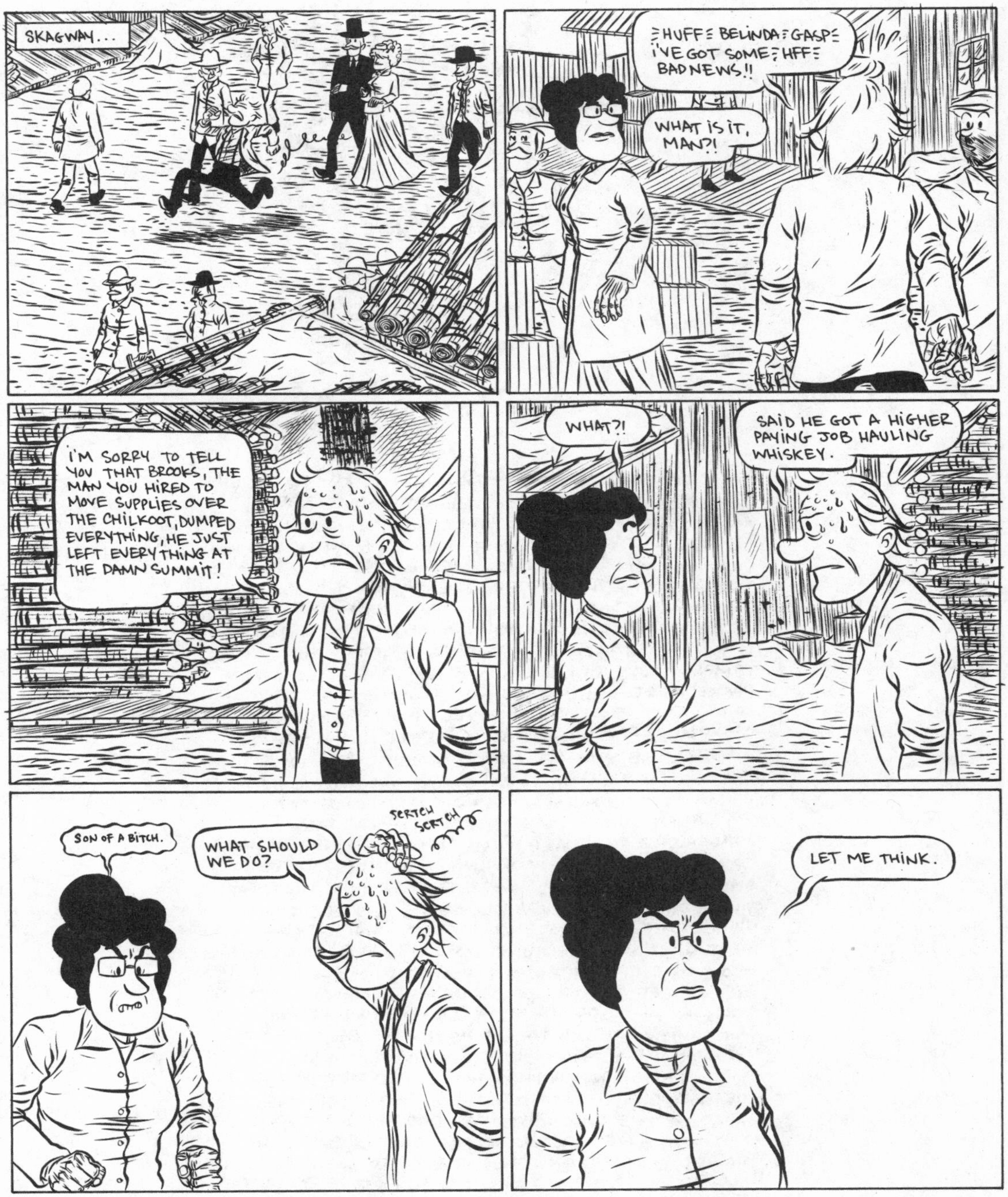
SKAGWAY...
≡HUFF≡ BELINDA ≡GASP≡ I'VE GOT SOME≡ HFF≡ BAD NEWS!!
WHAT IS IT, MAN?!
I'M SORRY TO TELL YOU THAT BROOKS, THE MAN YOU HIRED TO MOVE SUPPLIES OVER THE CHILKOOT, DUMPED EVERYTHING, HE JUST LEFT EVERYTHING AT THE DAMN SUMMIT!
WHAT?!
SAID HE GOT A HIGHER PAYING JOB HAULING WHISKEY.
SON OF A BITCH.
WHAT SHOULD WE DO?
SCRTCH SCRTCH
LET ME THINK.

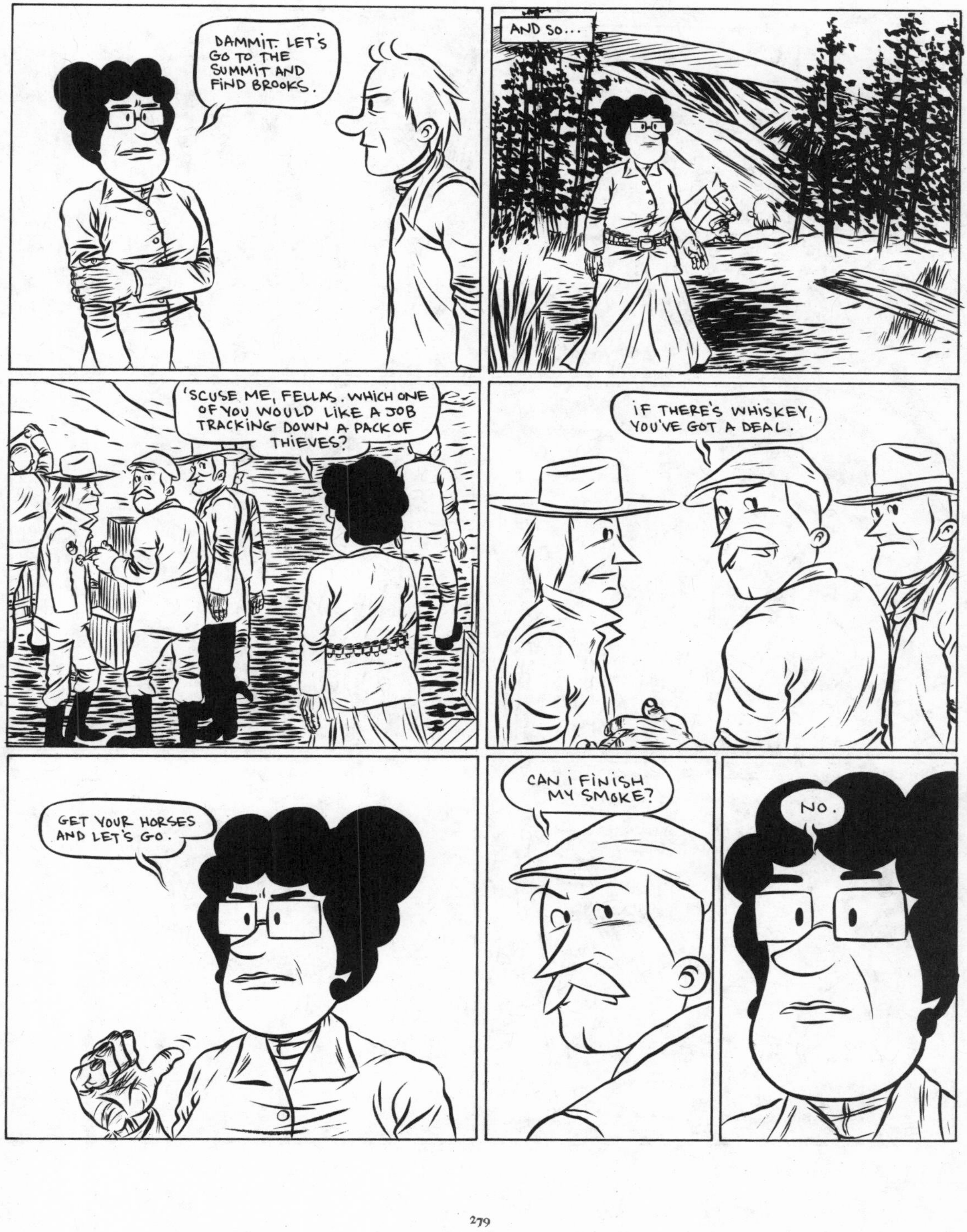
DAMMIT. LET'S GO TO THE SUMMIT AND FIND BROOKS.
AND SO...
'SCUSE ME, FELLAS. WHICH ONE OF YOU WOULD LIKE A JOB TRACKING DOWN A PACK OF THIEVES?
IF THERE'S WHISKEY, YOU'VE GOT A DEAL.
GET YOUR HORSES AND LET'S GO.
CAN I FINISH MY SMOKE?
NO.

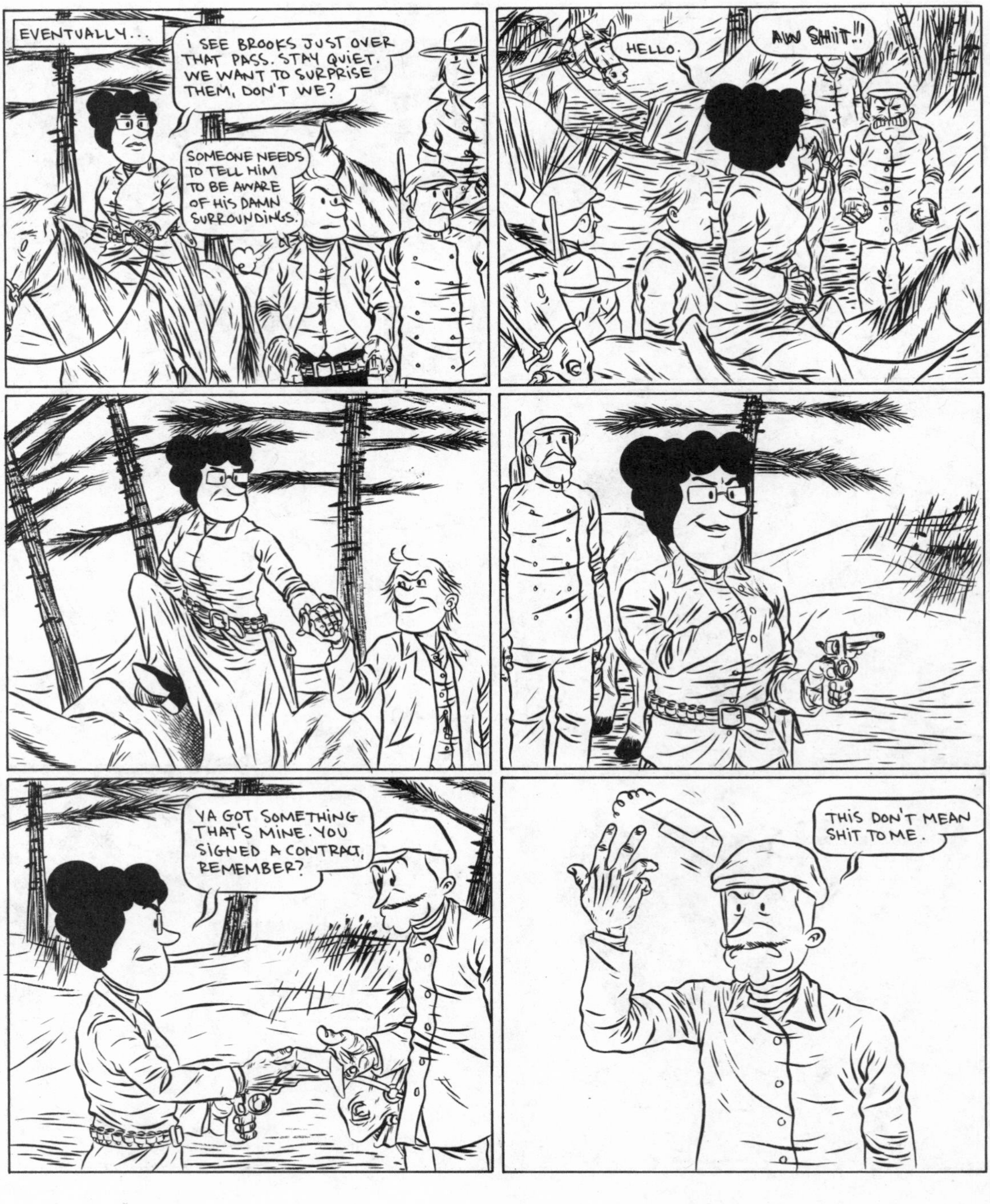
EVENTUALLY...
I SEE BROOKS JUST OVER THAT PASS. STAY QUIET. WE WANT TO SURPRISE THEM, DON'T WE?
SOMEONE NEEDS TO TELL HIM TO BE AWARE OF HIS DAMN SURROUNDINGS.
HELLO.
AW SHIT!!
YA GOT SOMETHING THAT'S MINE. YOU SIGNED A CONTRACT, REMEMBER?
THIS DON'T MEAN SHIT TO ME.

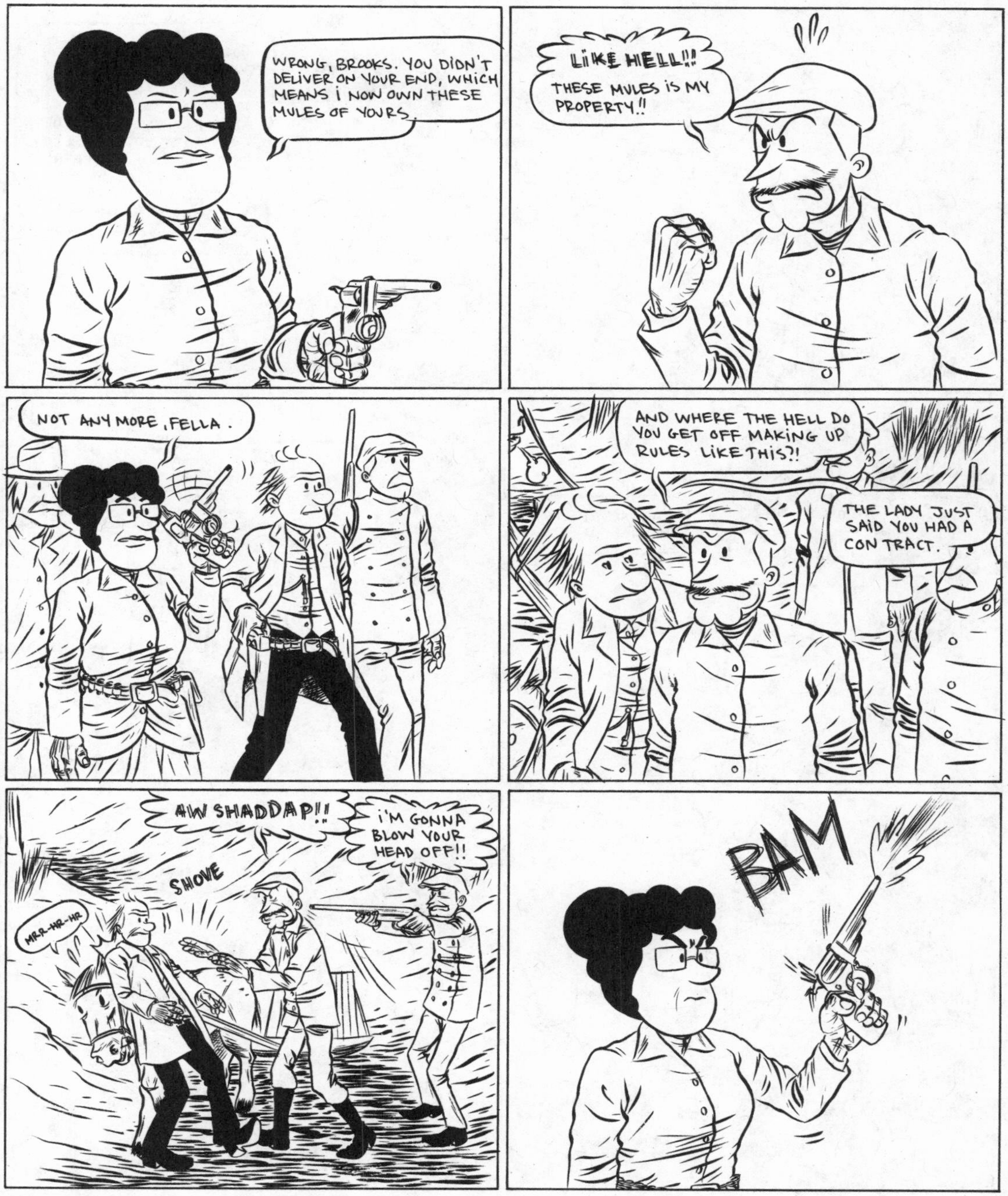
WRONG, BROOKS. YOU DIDN'T DELIVER ON YOUR END, WHICH MEANS I NOW OWN THESE MULES OF YOURS.
LIKE HELL!!
THESE MULES IS MY PROPERTY!!
NOT ANY MORE, FELLA.
AND WHERE THE HELL DO YOU GET OFF MAKING UP RULES LIKE THIS?!
THE LADY JUST SAID YOU HAD A CONTRACT.
AW SHADDAP!!
I'M GONNA BLOW YOUR HEAD OFF!!
SHOVE
MRR-HR-HR
BAM

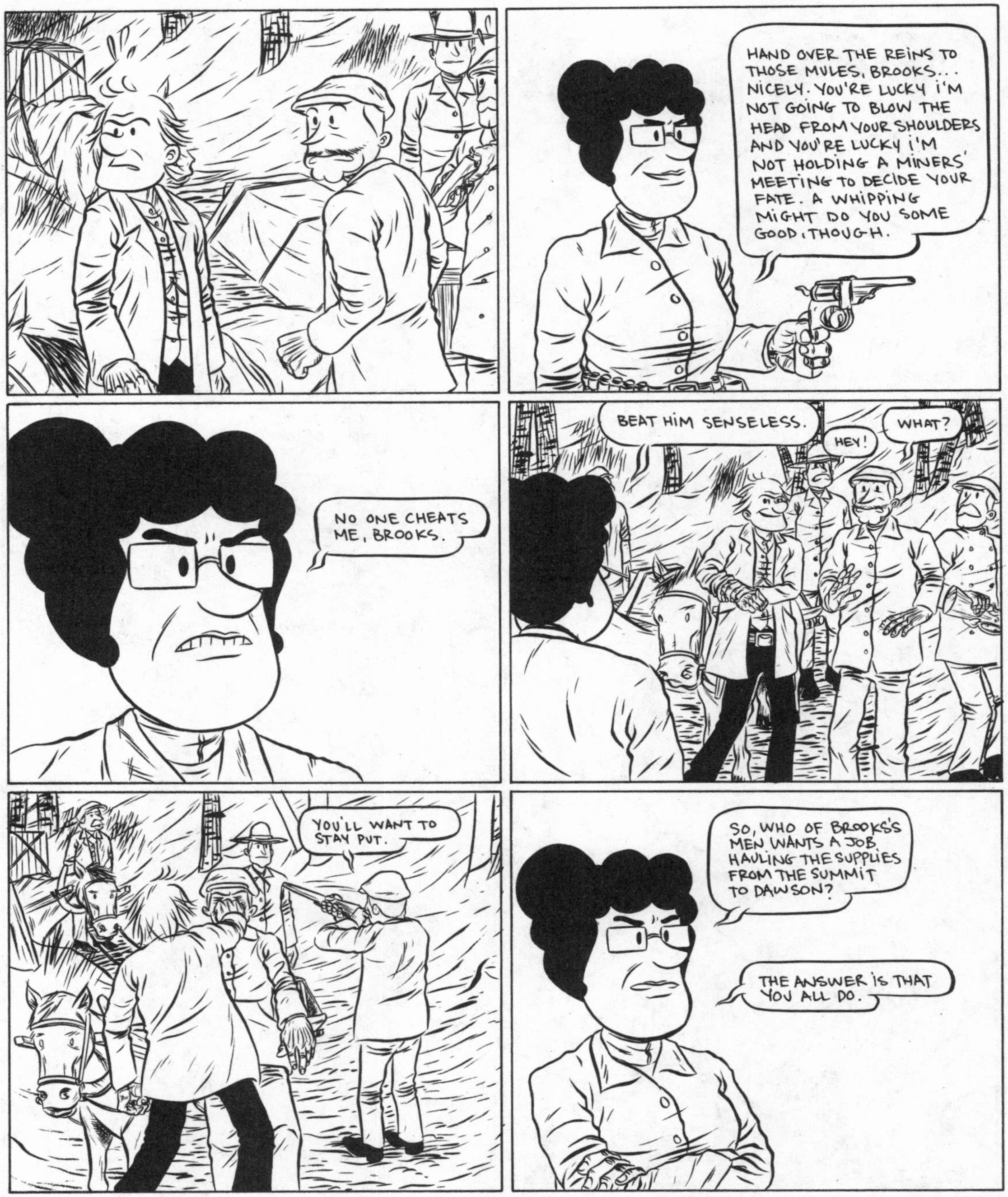
HAND OVER THE REINS TO THOSE MULES, BROOKS... NICELY. YOU'RE LUCKY I'M NOT GOING TO BLOW THE HEAD FROM YOUR SHOULDERS AND YOU'RE LUCKY I'M NOT HOLDING A MINERS' MEETING TO DECIDE YOUR FATE. A WHIPPING MIGHT DO YOU SOME GOOD, THOUGH.
NO ONE CHEATS ME, BROOKS.
BEAT HIM SENSELESS.
HEY!
WHAT?
YOU'LL WANT TO STAY PUT.
SO, WHO OF BROOKS'S MEN WANTS A JOB HAULING THE SUPPLIES FROM THE SUMMIT TO DAWSON?
THE ANSWER IS THAT YOU ALL DO.

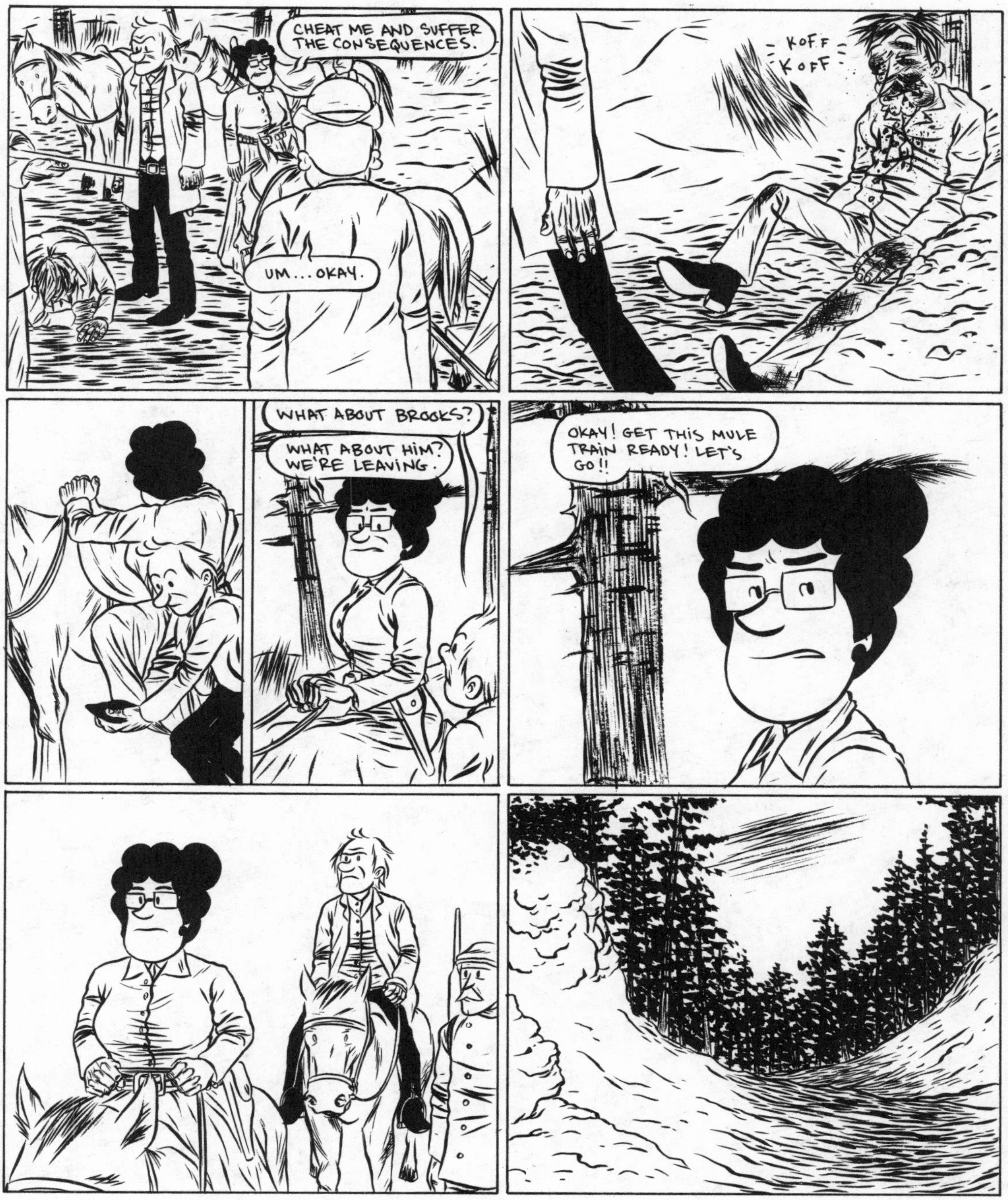
CHEAT ME AND SUFFER THE CONSEQUENCES.
UM... OKAY.
KOFF KOFF
WHAT ABOUT BROOKS?
WHAT ABOUT HIM? WE'RE LEAVING.
OKAY! GET THIS MULE TRAIN READY! LET'S GO!!

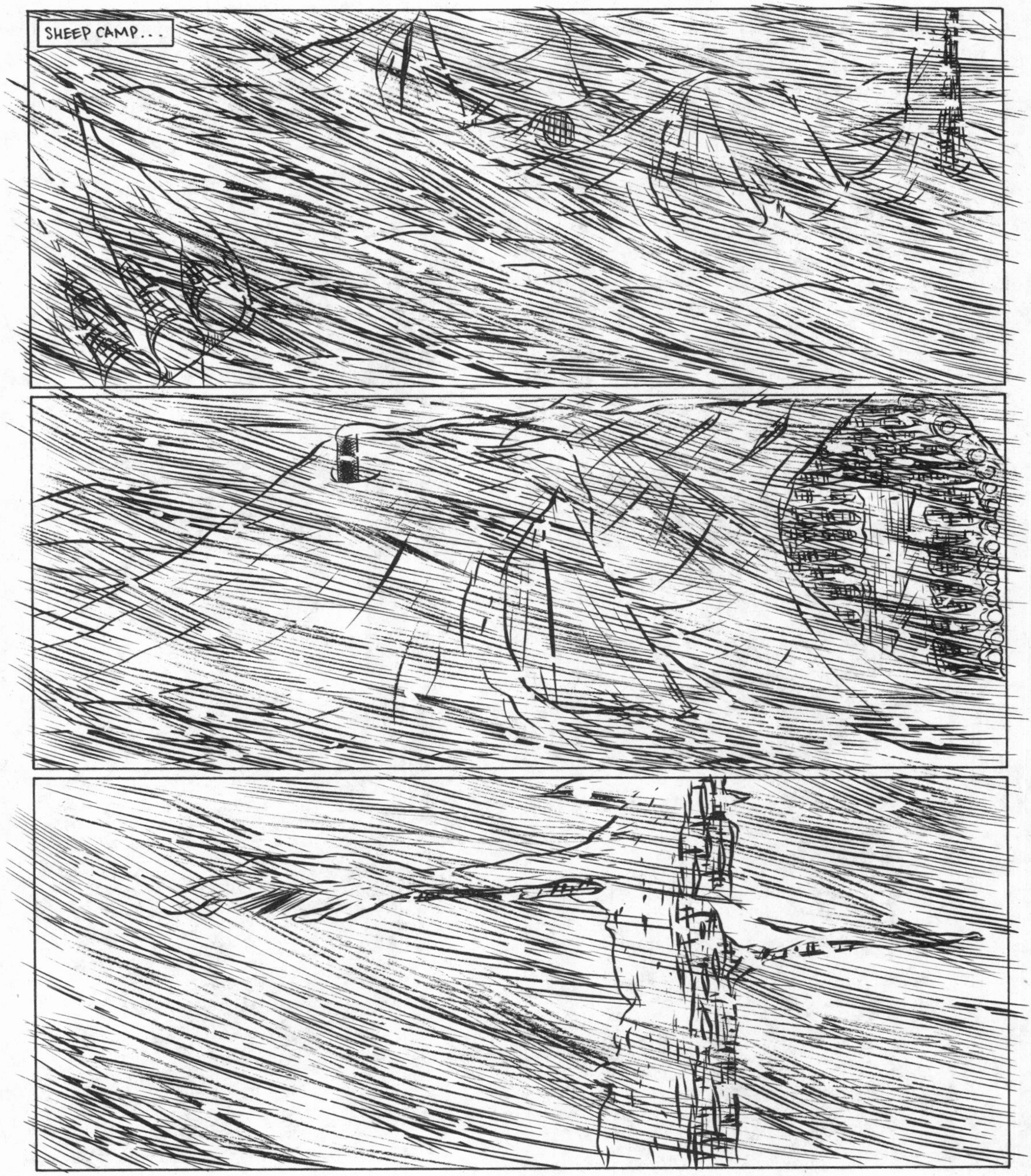
SHEEP CAMP...

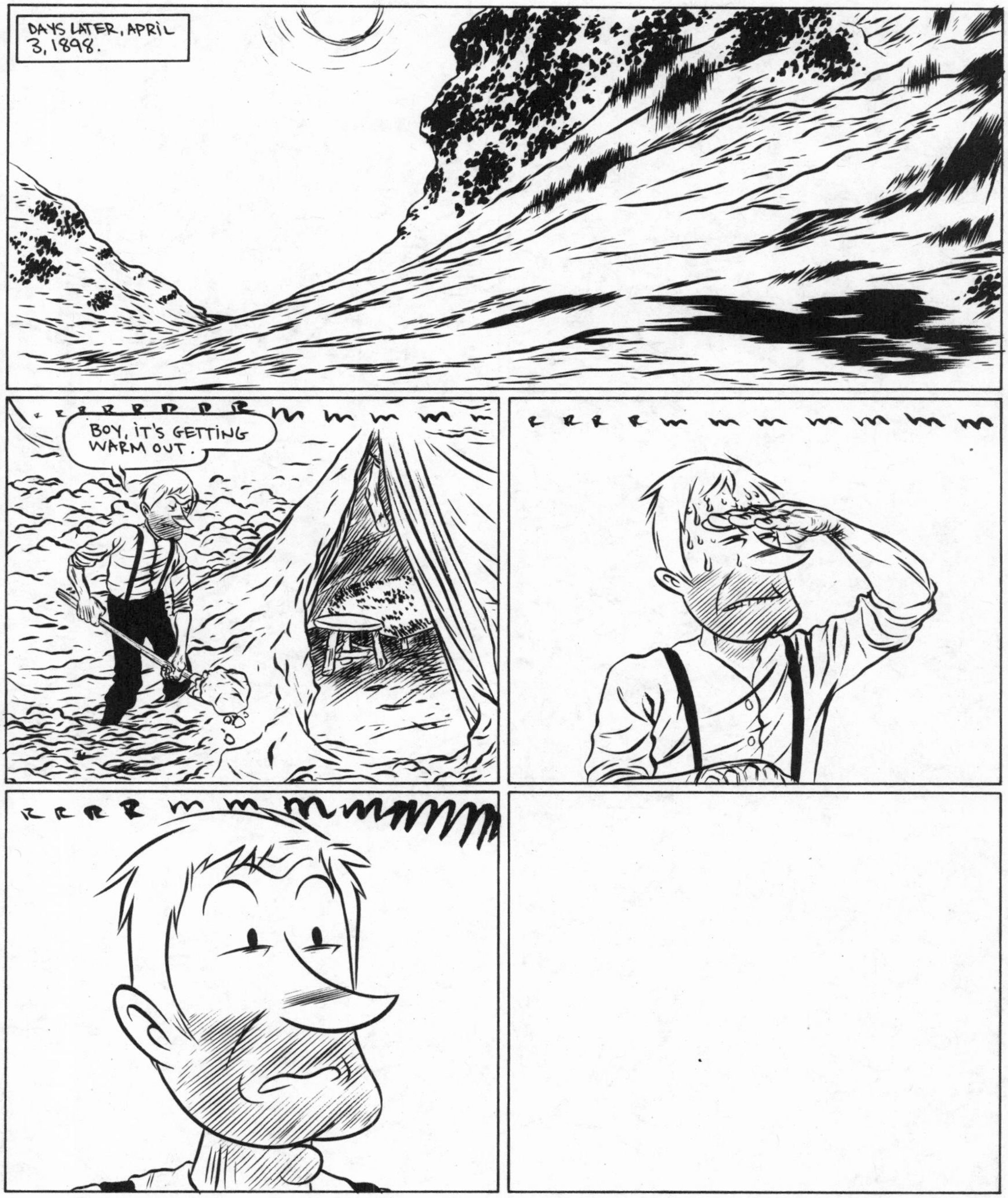
DAYS LATER, APRIL 3, 1898.
RRRRRRRR mmmmmm
BOY, IT'S GETTING WARM OUT.
RRRR mmmmmmmmm
RRRR mmmmmmm

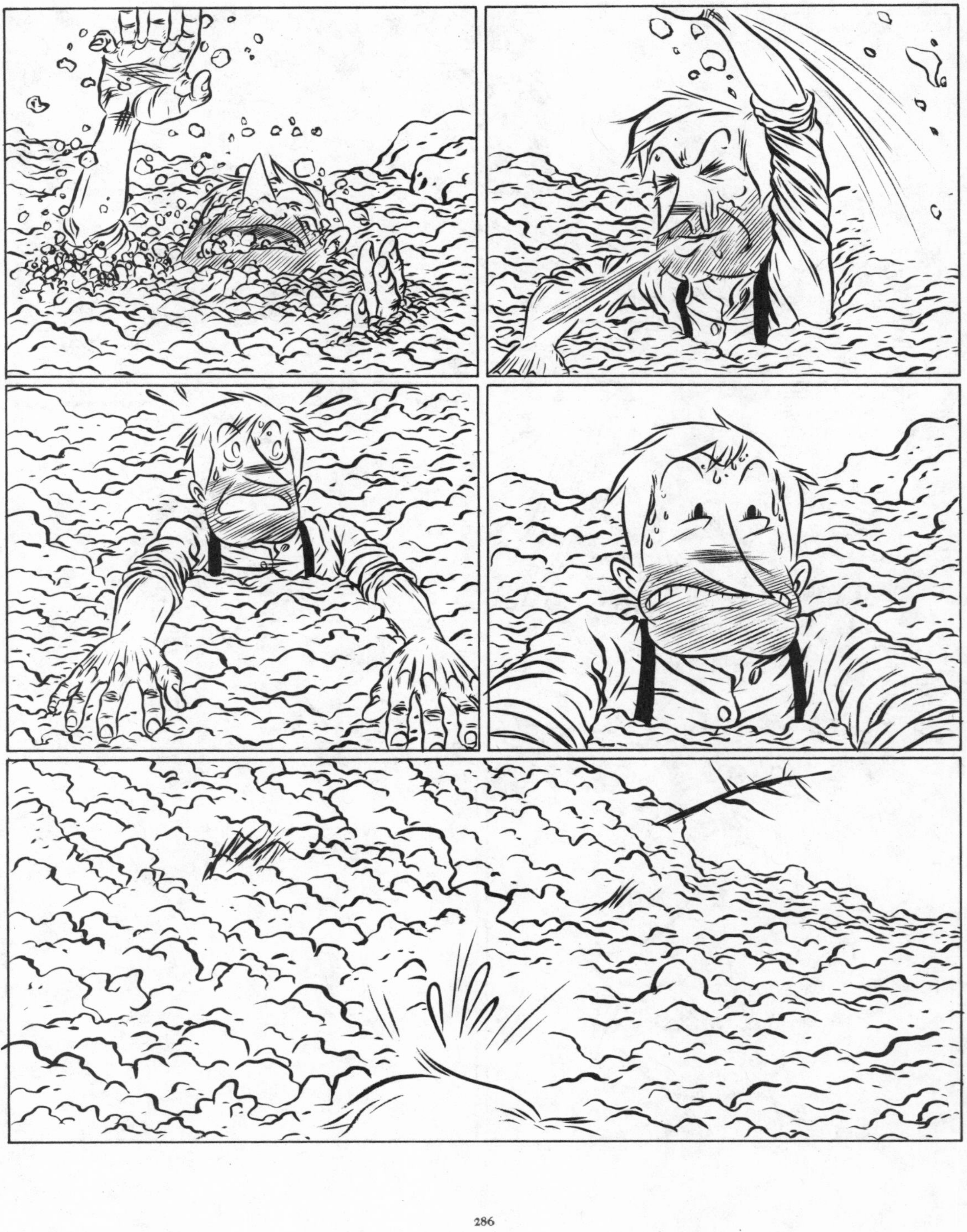

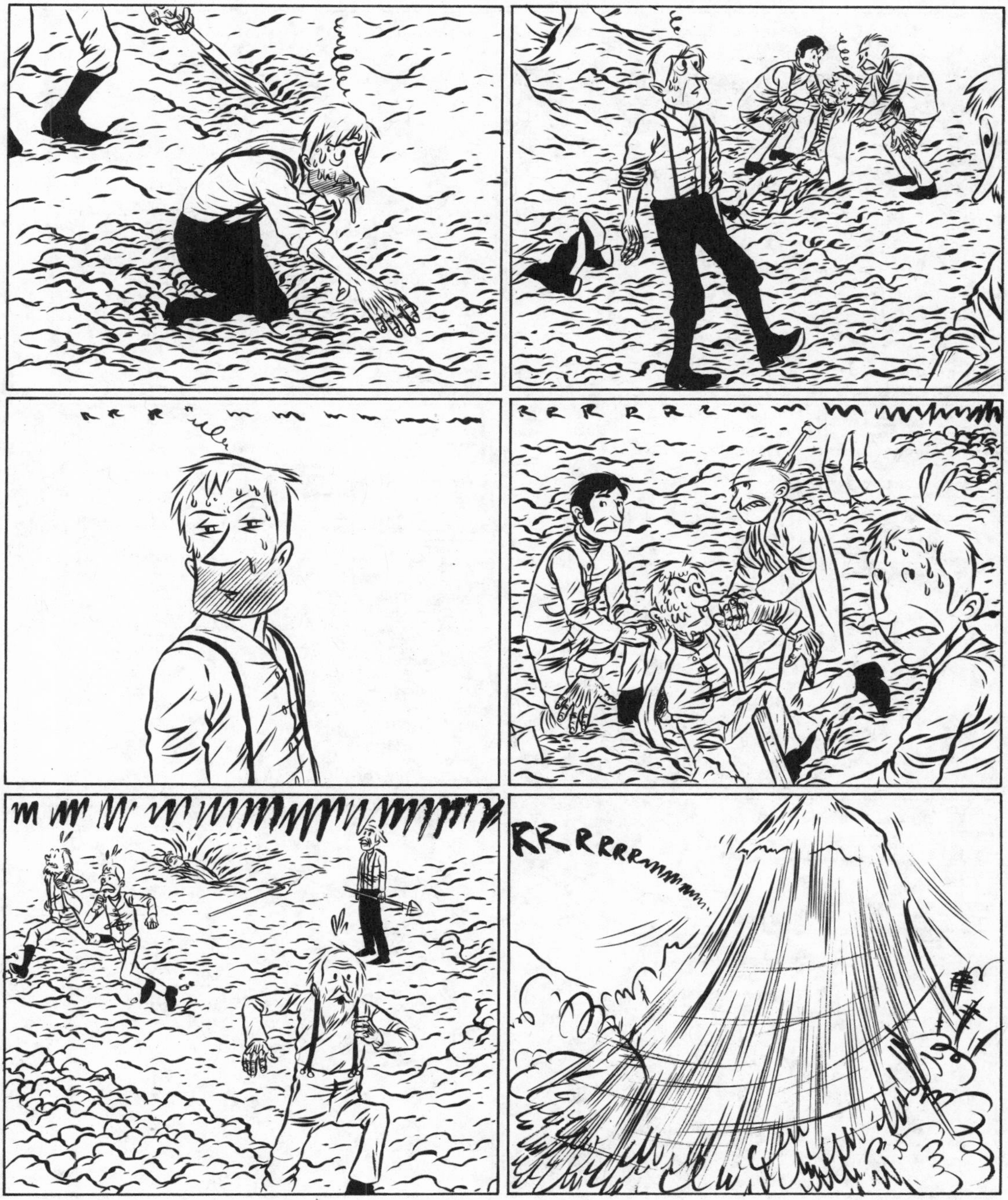

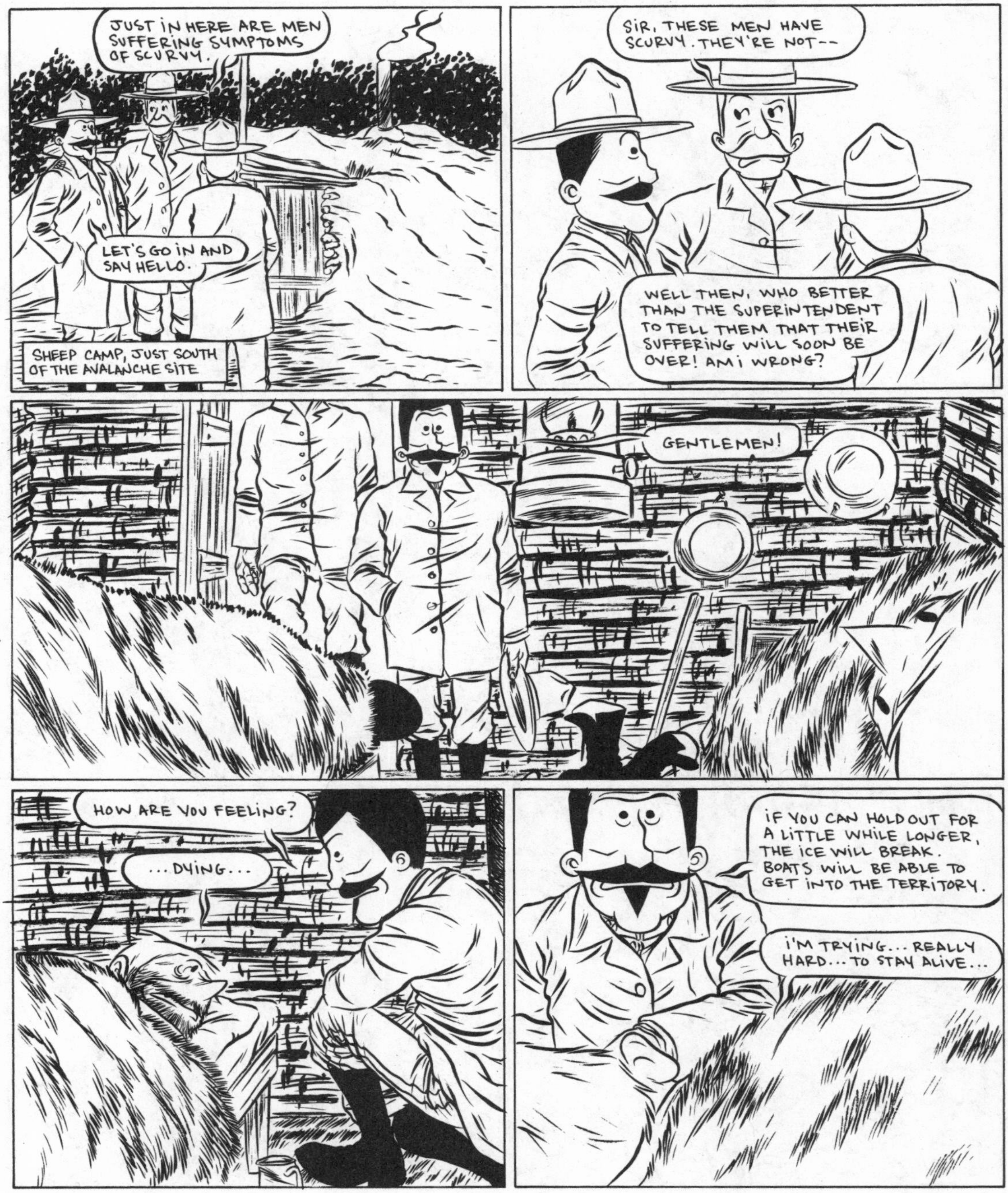
JUST IN HERE ARE MEN SUFFERING SYMPTOMS OF SCURVY.
LET'S GO IN AND SAY HELLO.
SHEEP CAMP, JUST SOUTH OF THE AVALANCHE SITE
SIR, THESE MEN HAVE SCURVY. THEY'RE NOT--
WELL THEN, WHO BETTER THAN THE SUPERINTENDENT TO TELL THEM THAT THEIR SUFFERING WILL SOON BE OVER! AM I WRONG?
GENTLEMEN!
HOW ARE YOU FEELING?
...DYING...
IF YOU CAN HOLD OUT FOR A LITTLE WHILE LONGER, THE ICE WILL BREAK. BOATS WILL BE ABLE TO GET INTO THE TERRITORY.
I'M TRYING... REALLY HARD... TO STAY ALIVE...

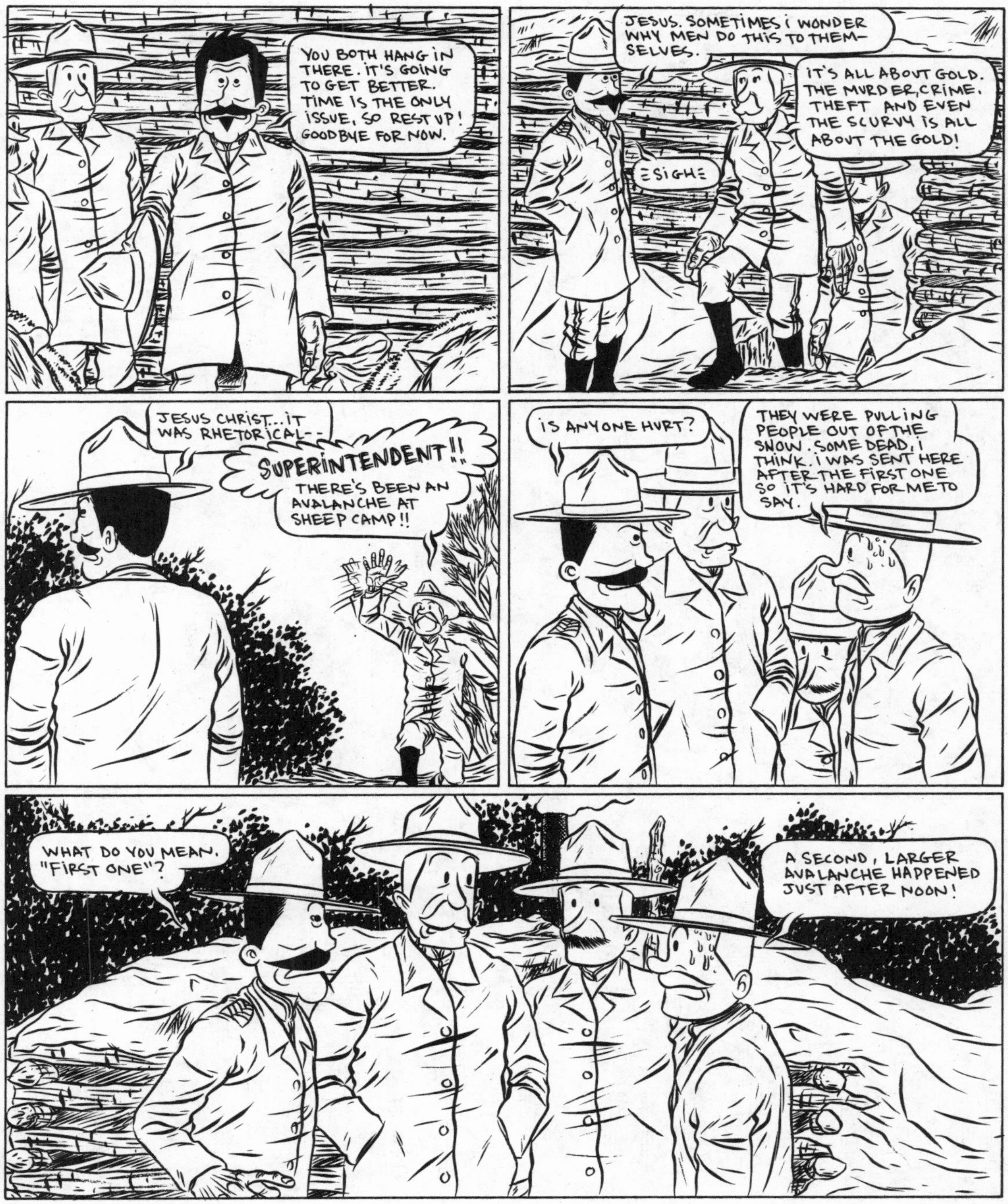
YOU BOTH HANG IN THERE. IT'S GOING TO GET BETTER. TIME IS THE ONLY ISSUE, SO REST UP! GOODBYE FOR NOW.
JESUS. SOMETIMES I WONDER WHY MEN DO THIS TO THEMSELVES.
IT'S ALL ABOUT GOLD. THE MURDER, CRIME, THEFT AND EVEN THE SCURVY IS ALL ABOUT THE GOLD!
=SIGH=
JESUS CHRIST... IT WAS RHETORICAL--
SUPERINTENDENT!! THERE'S BEEN AN AVALANCHE AT SHEEP CAMP!!
IS ANYONE HURT?
THEY WERE PULLING PEOPLE OUT OF THE SNOW. SOME DEAD, I THINK. I WAS SENT HERE AFTER THE FIRST ONE SO IT'S HARD FOR ME TO SAY.
WHAT DO YOU MEAN, "FIRST ONE"?
A SECOND, LARGER AVALANCHE HAPPENED JUST AFTER NOON!

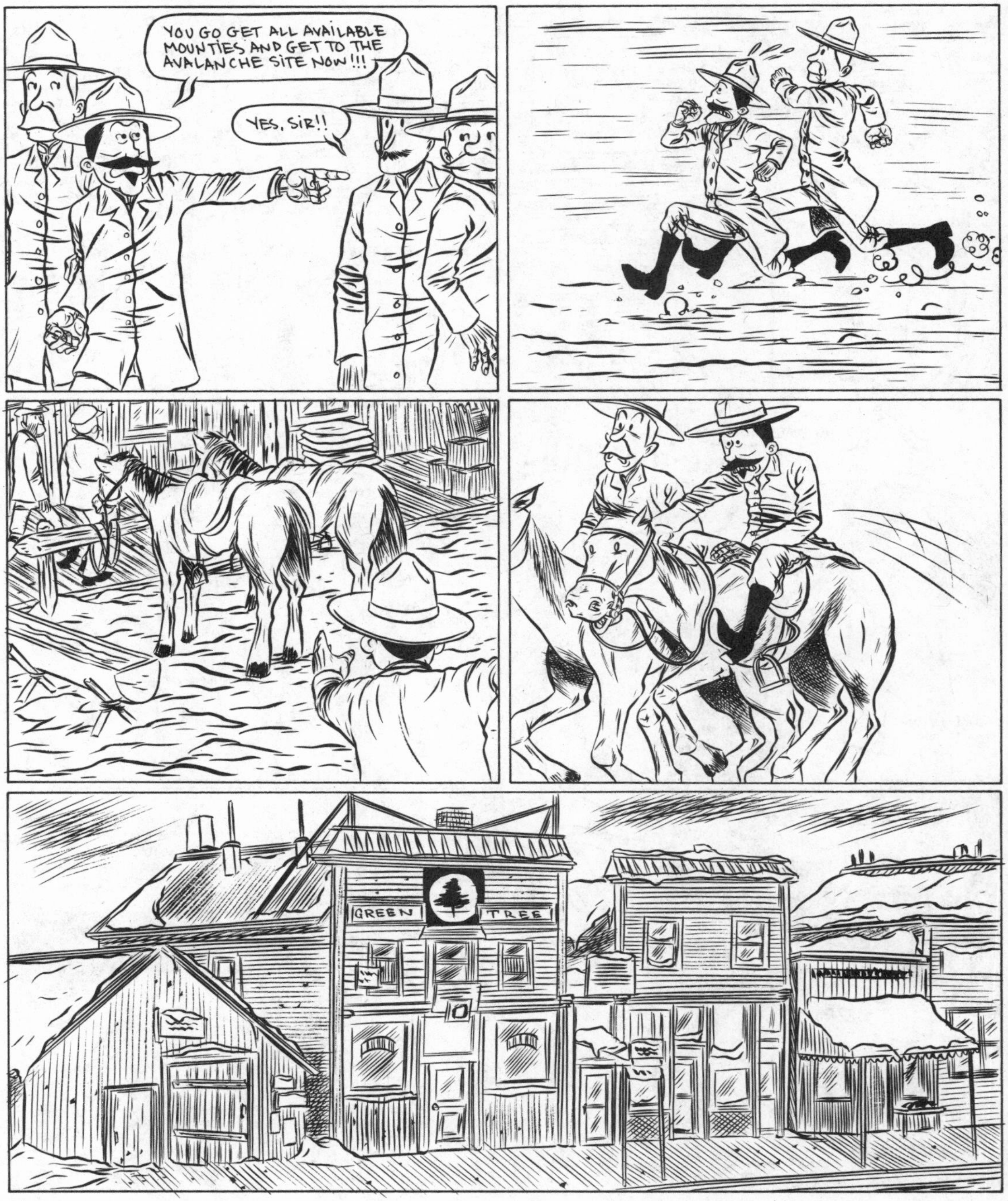
YOU GO GET ALL AVAILABLE MOUNTIES AND GET TO THE AVALANCHE SITE NOW!!!
YES, SIR!!
GREEN TREE

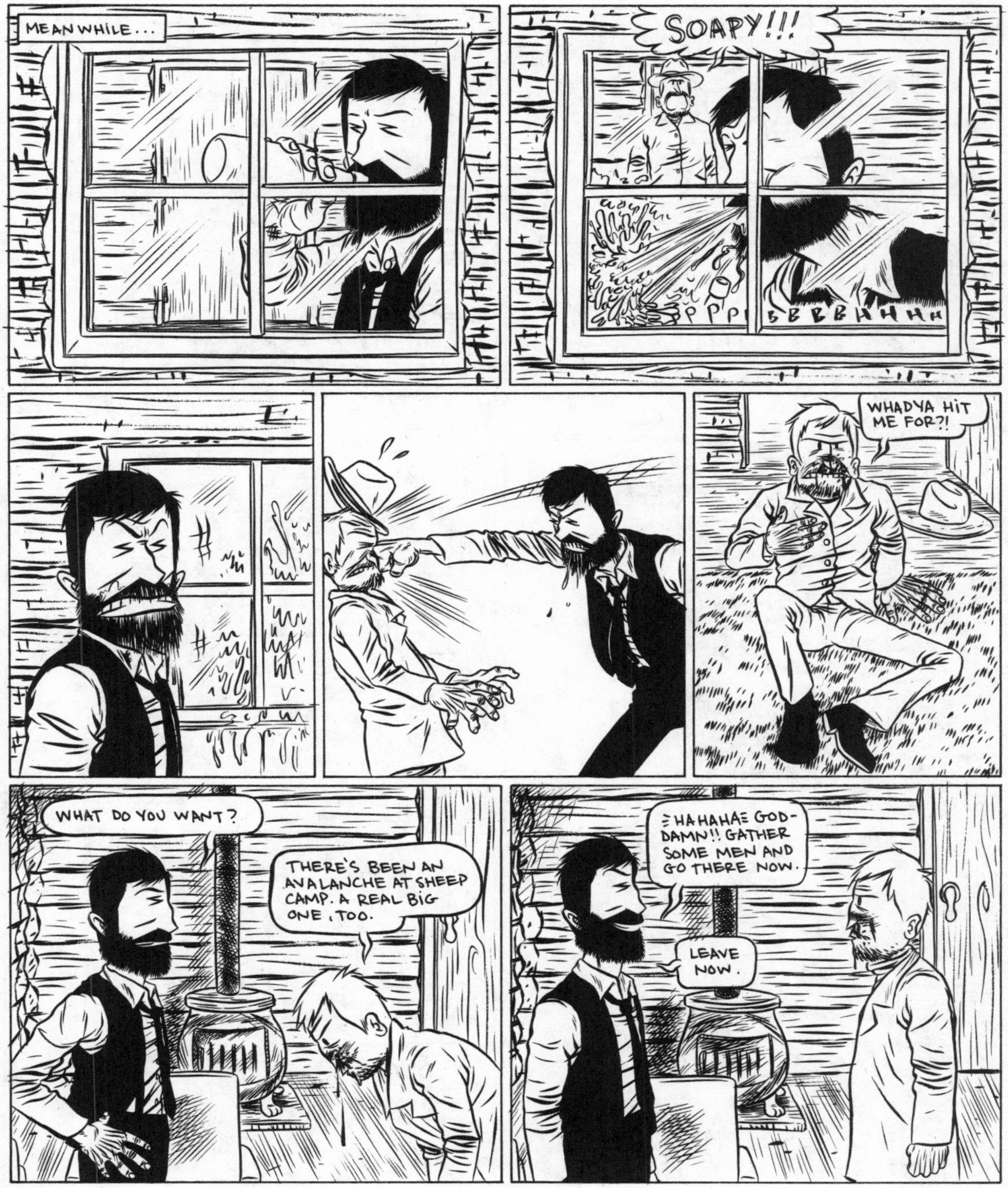
MEANWHILE...
SOAPY!!!
PPP BBBHHHH
WHADYA HIT ME FOR?!
WHAT DO YOU WANT?
THERE'S BEEN AN AVALANCHE AT SHEEP CAMP. A REAL BIG ONE, TOO.
HAHAHA GOD-DAMN!! GATHER SOME MEN AND GO THERE NOW.
LEAVE NOW.

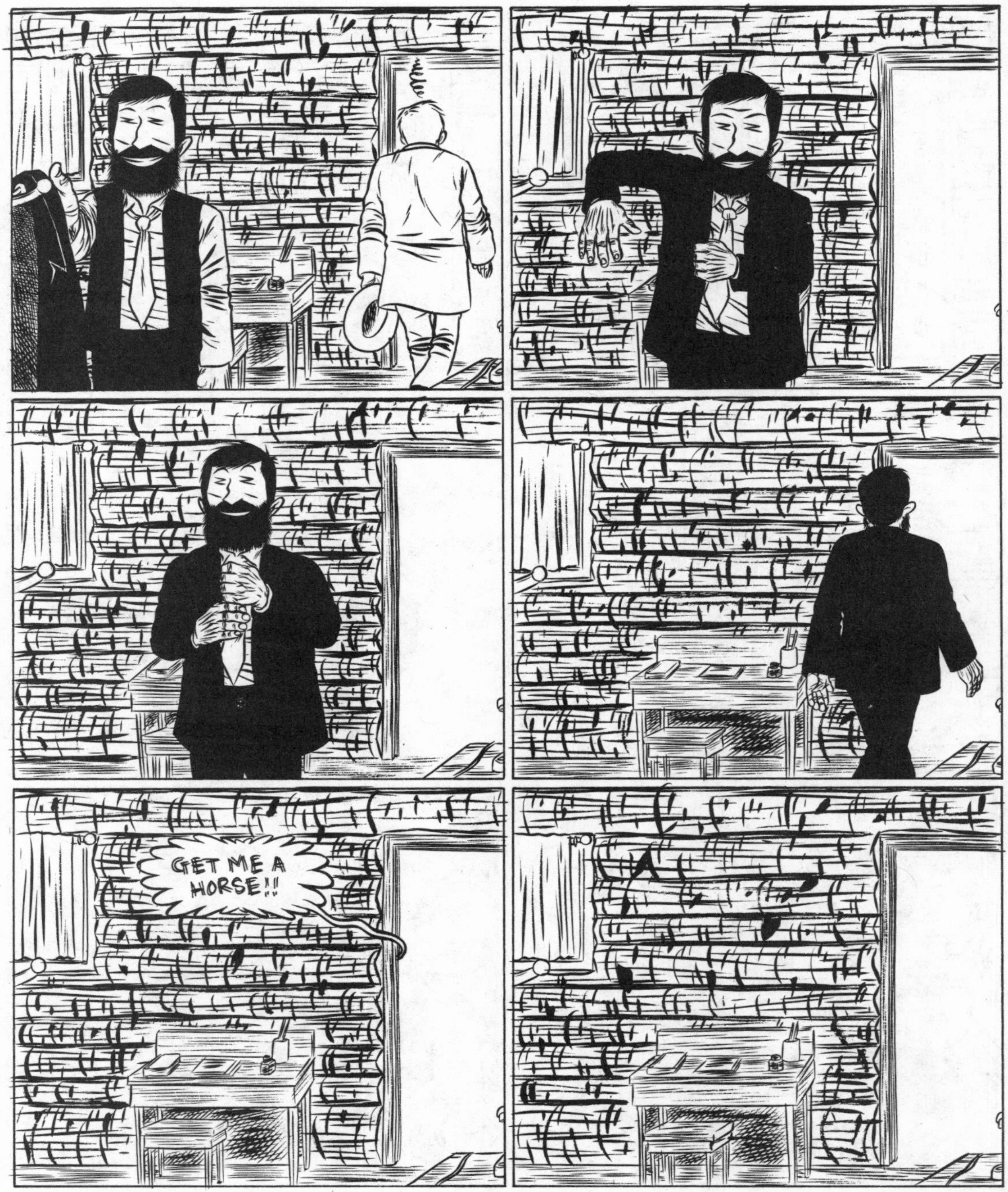
GET ME A HORSE!!

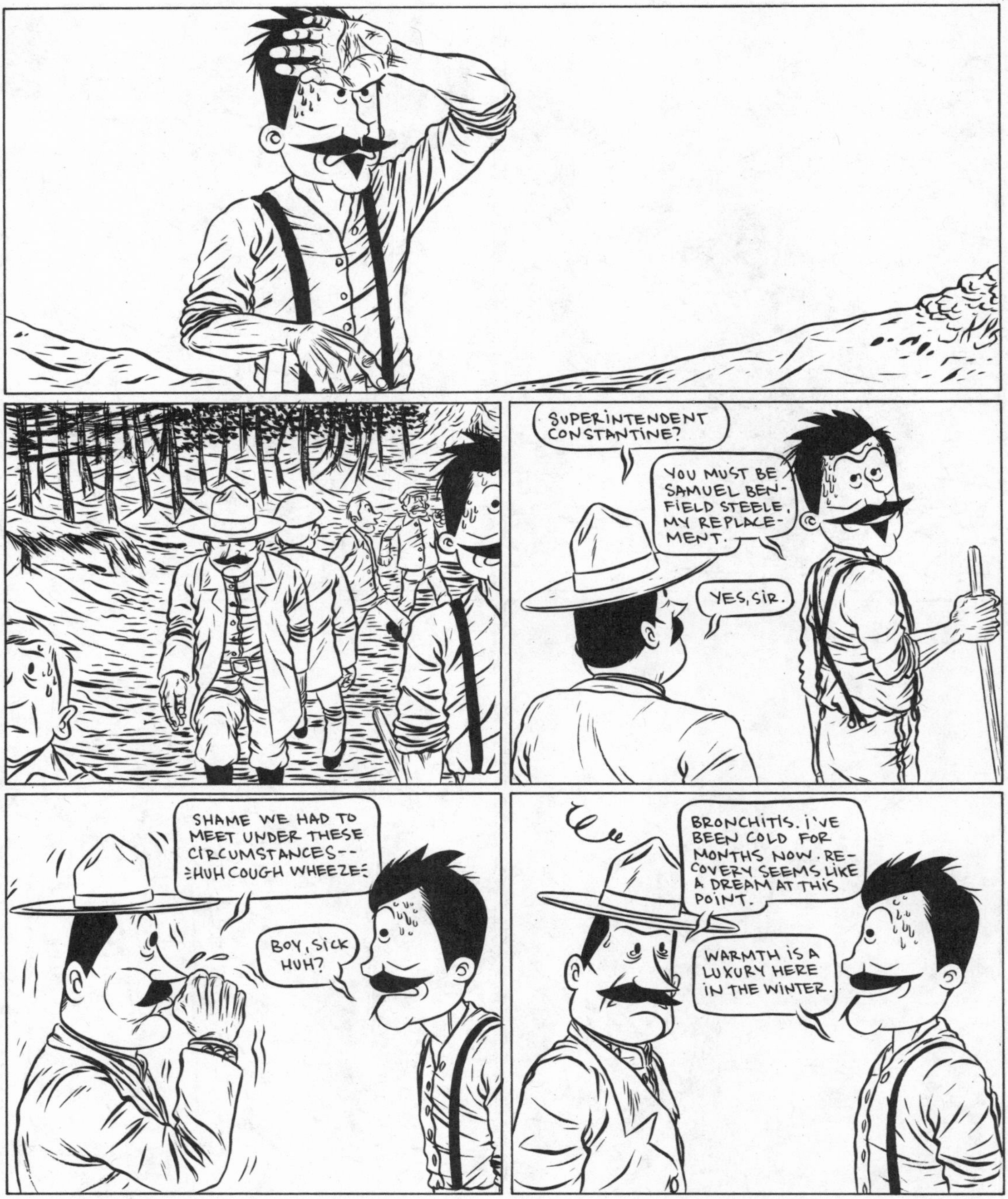
SUPERINTENDENT CONSTANTINE?
YOU MUST BE SAMUEL BENFIELD STEELE, MY REPLACEMENT.
YES, SIR.
SHAME WE HAD TO MEET UNDER THESE CIRCUMSTANCES-- HUH COUGH WHEEZE
BOY, SICK HUH?
BRONCHITIS. I'VE BEEN COLD FOR MONTHS NOW. RECOVERY SEEMS LIKE A DREAM AT THIS POINT.
WARMTH IS A LUXURY HERE IN THE WINTER.

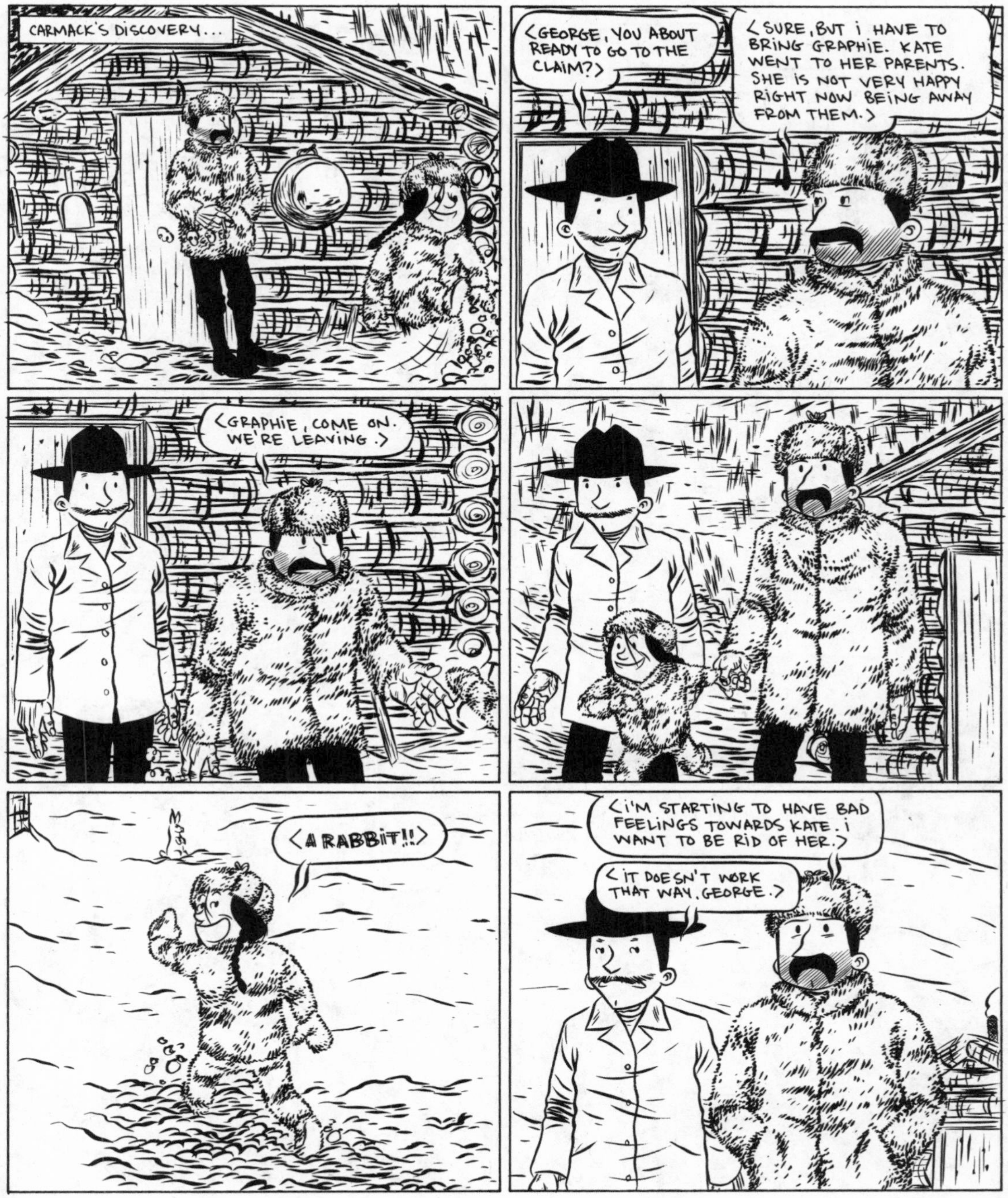
CARMACK'S DISCOVERY...
<GEORGE, YOU ABOUT READY TO GO TO THE CLAIM?>
<SURE, BUT I HAVE TO BRING GRAPHIE. KATE WENT TO HER PARENTS. SHE IS NOT VERY HAPPY RIGHT NOW BEING AWAY FROM THEM.>
<GRAPHIE, COME ON. WE'RE LEAVING.>
<A RABBIT!!>
<I'M STARTING TO HAVE BAD FEELINGS TOWARDS KATE. I WANT TO BE RID OF HER.>
<IT DOESN'T WORK THAT WAY, GEORGE.>

<HOW DOES IT WORK THEN?>
<YOU CAN'T JUST DIVORCE HER BECAUSE OF SOME HARD TIMES, GEORGE.>
<THE LAWS OF THE TAGISH DON'T APPLY TO ME, JIM.>
<YOU'VE LIVED AS AN INDIAN! YOU'VE MARRIED AS AN INDIAN! THE LAWS OF OUR TRIBE STILL APPLY TO YOU, GEORGE!>
<I'M WHITE, JIM. THEREIN LIES THE DIFFERENCE.>
<YOUR LAWS DON'T MEAN SHIT TO ME ANYMORE. I'M THROUGH WITH THIS! THE ONLY LAW I'LL BEND TO HERE IS THE MINERS'.>

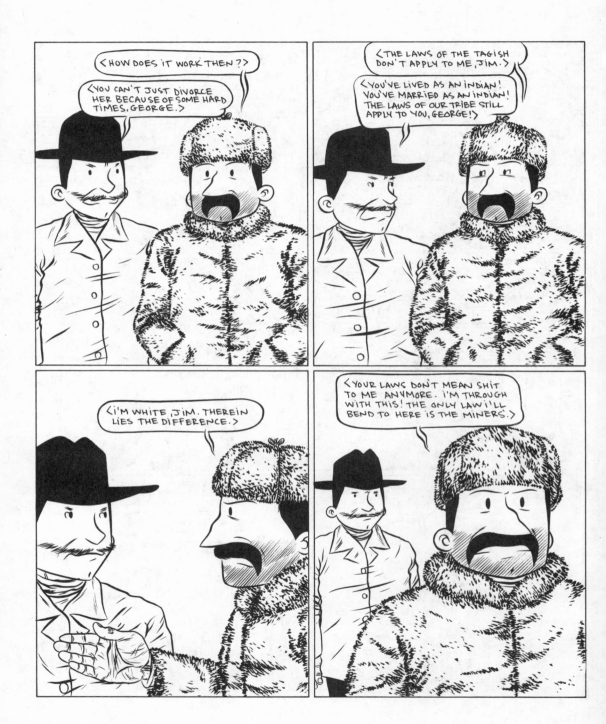

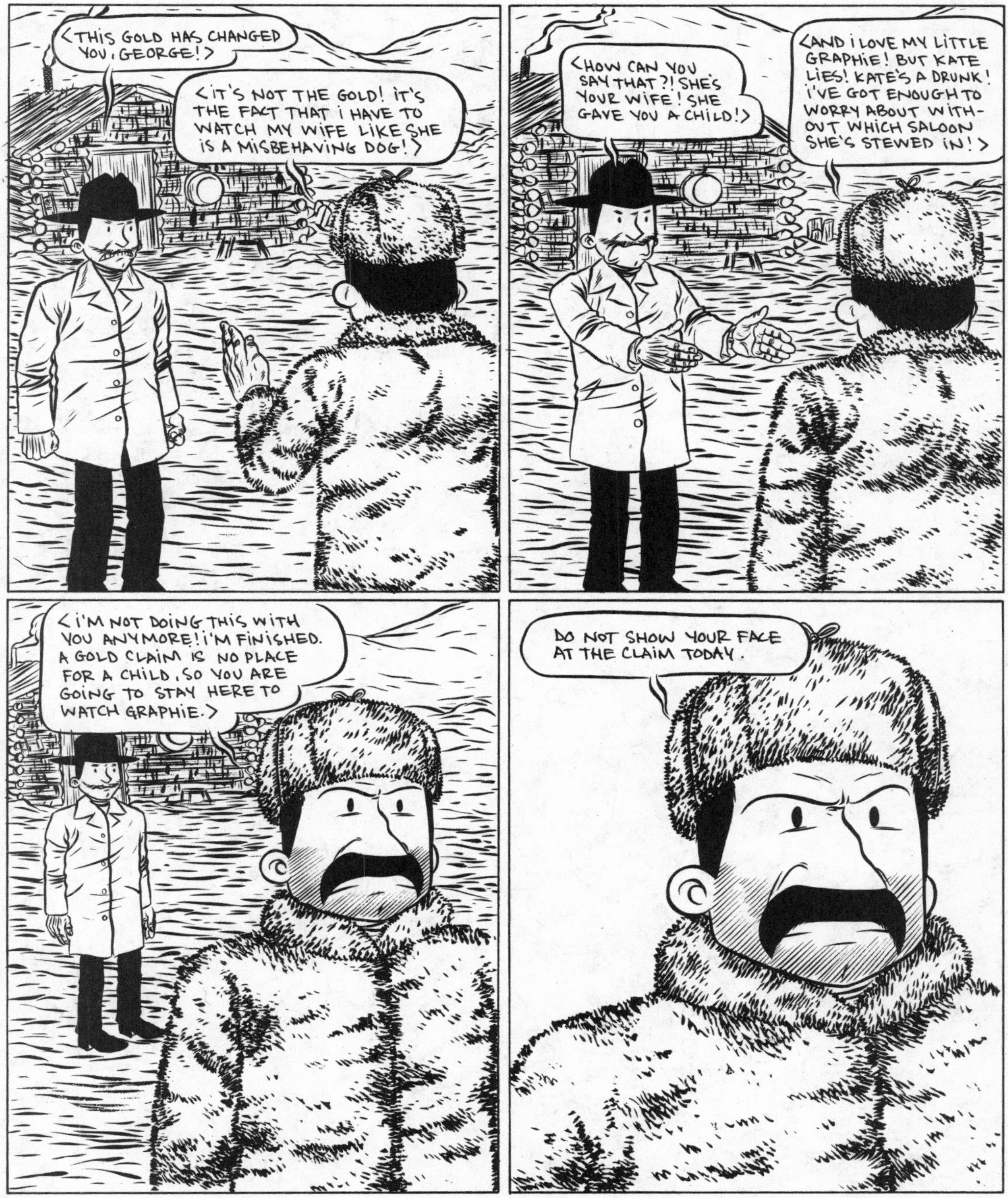
<THIS GOLD HAS CHANGED YOU, GEORGE!>
<IT'S NOT THE GOLD! IT'S THE FACT THAT I HAVE TO WATCH MY WIFE LIKE SHE IS A MISBEHAVING DOG!>
<HOW CAN YOU SAY THAT?! SHE'S YOUR WIFE! SHE GAVE YOU A CHILD!>
<AND I LOVE MY LITTLE GRAPHIE! BUT KATE LIES! KATE'S A DRUNK! I'VE GOT ENOUGH TO WORRY ABOUT WITH-OUT WHICH SALOON SHE'S STEWED IN!>
<I'M NOT DOING THIS WITH YOU ANYMORE! I'M FINISHED. A GOLD CLAIM IS NO PLACE FOR A CHILD, SO YOU ARE GOING TO STAY HERE TO WATCH GRAPHIE.>
DO NOT SHOW YOUR FACE AT THE CLAIM TODAY.

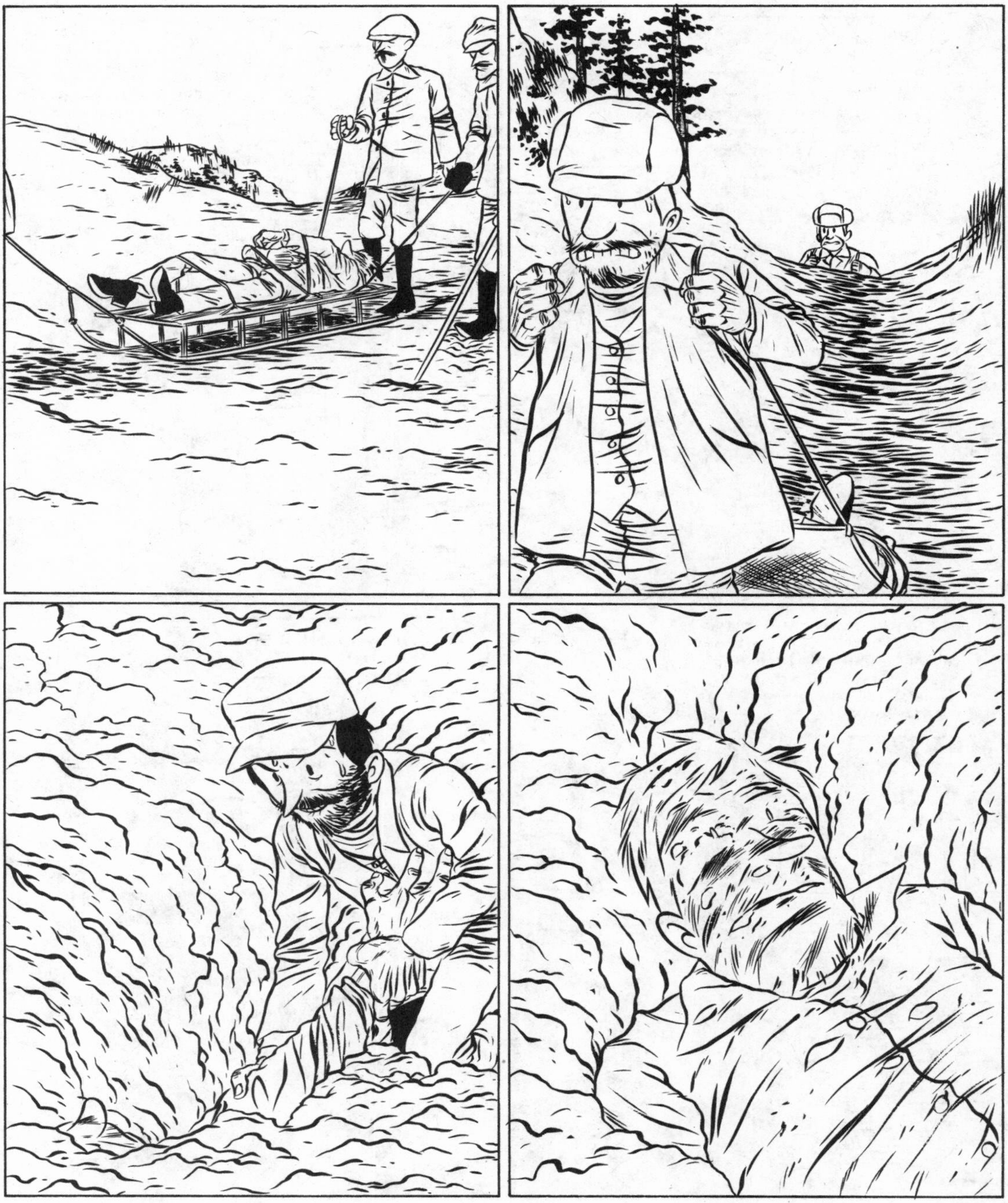

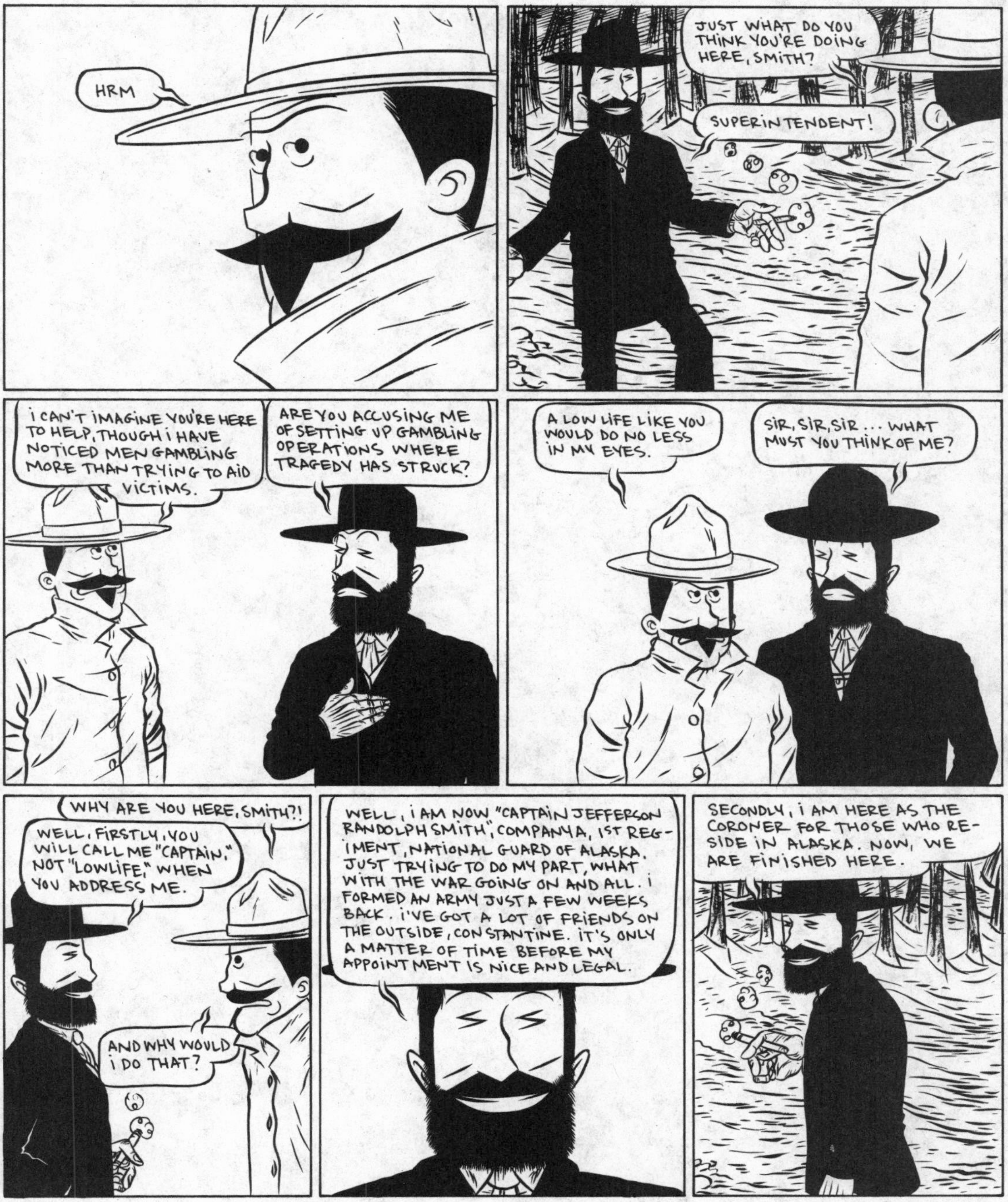

HRM
JUST WHAT DO YOU THINK YOU'RE DOING HERE, SMITH?
SUPERINTENDENT!
I CAN'T IMAGINE YOU'RE HERE TO HELP, THOUGH I HAVE NOTICED MEN GAMBLING MORE THAN TRYING TO AID VICTIMS.
ARE YOU ACCUSING ME OF SETTING UP GAMBLING OPERATIONS WHERE TRAGEDY HAS STRUCK?
A LOW LIFE LIKE YOU WOULD DO NO LESS IN MY EYES.
SIR, SIR, SIR ... WHAT MUST YOU THINK OF ME?
WHY ARE YOU HERE, SMITH?!
WELL, FIRSTLY, YOU WILL CALL ME "CAPTAIN," NOT "LOWLIFE," WHEN YOU ADDRESS ME.
AND WHY WOULD I DO THAT?
WELL, I AM NOW "CAPTAIN JEFFERSON RANDOLPH SMITH", COMPANY A, 1ST REGIMENT, NATIONAL GUARD OF ALASKA. JUST TRYING TO DO MY PART, WHAT WITH THE WAR GOING ON AND ALL. I FORMED AN ARMY JUST A FEW WEEKS BACK. I'VE GOT A LOT OF FRIENDS ON THE OUTSIDE, CONSTANTINE. IT'S ONLY A MATTER OF TIME BEFORE MY APPOINTMENT IS NICE AND LEGAL.
SECONDLY, I AM HERE AS THE CORONER FOR THOSE WHO RESIDE IN ALASKA. NOW, WE ARE FINISHED HERE.

J.D. STEWART WAS EN ROUTE TO NANAIMO, B.C. FROM DAWSON WITH A TWENTY-EIGHT-HUNDRED-DOLLAR SACK OF GOLD DUST WHEN HE STOPPED IN SKAGWAY. HE, OF COURSE, WAS NONE THE WISER THAT HE WOULD BE INADVERTANTLY INSTRUMENTAL IN SOAPY SMITH'S FATE. PRIOR TO STEWART'S ARRIVAL IN THE CAMP, SMITH STARTED RECRUITING MEN FOR HIS VERY OWN MILITARY UNIT. THIS WAS A RESULT OF THE SPANISH-AMERICAN WAR THAT BROKE OUT ON APRIL 24TH. HE DECLARED HIMSELF CAPTAIN OF "COMPANY A, 1ST REGIMENT, NATIONAL GUARD OF ALASKA" AND OPENED A RECRUITING OFFICE. THIS WAS MORE OF AN EXCUSE TO ARM AND ORGAN- IZE HIS GANG. ON MAY 1ST, HE MARCHED AT THE HEAD OF A PROCESSION TWO BLOCKS LONG WHILE OVER 2000 PEOPLE CHEERED ON. AFTER THE PARADE, SMITH WAS CALLED OUT BY SEVERAL PROSTITUTES TO START A WOMEN'S AUXILIARY UNIT, SMITH MADE A SPEECH, THEN PRODUCED AND BURNED AN EFFIGY OF GENERAL WEYLER, THE SPANISH GENERAL IN CUBA. SMITH CONTINUED TO USE PATRIOTISM FOR PROFIT, EVEN AFTER THE SECRETARY OF WAR TURNED DOWN HIS OFFER TO SERVE IN THE WAR EFFORT.

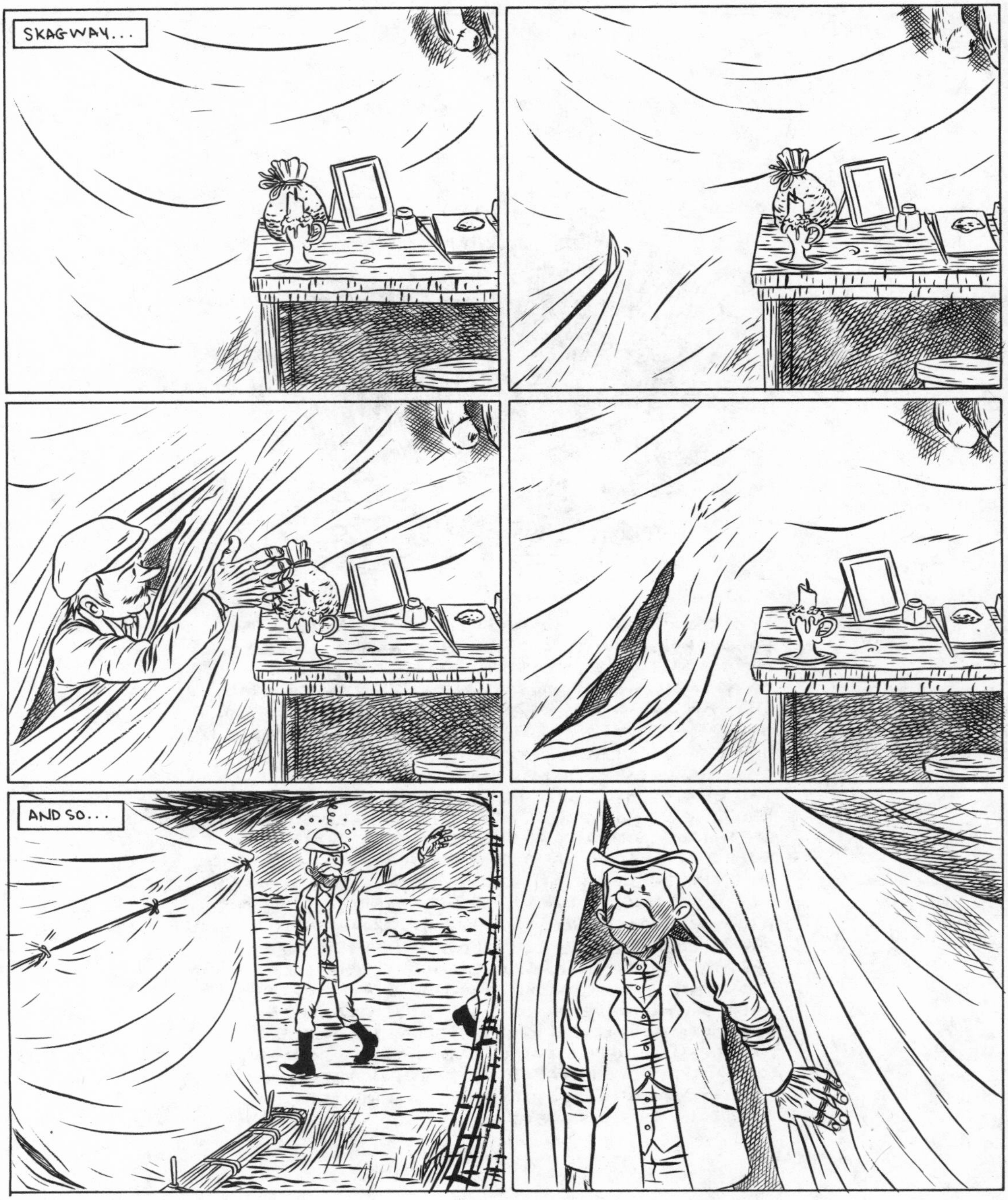
SKAGWAY...
AND SO...

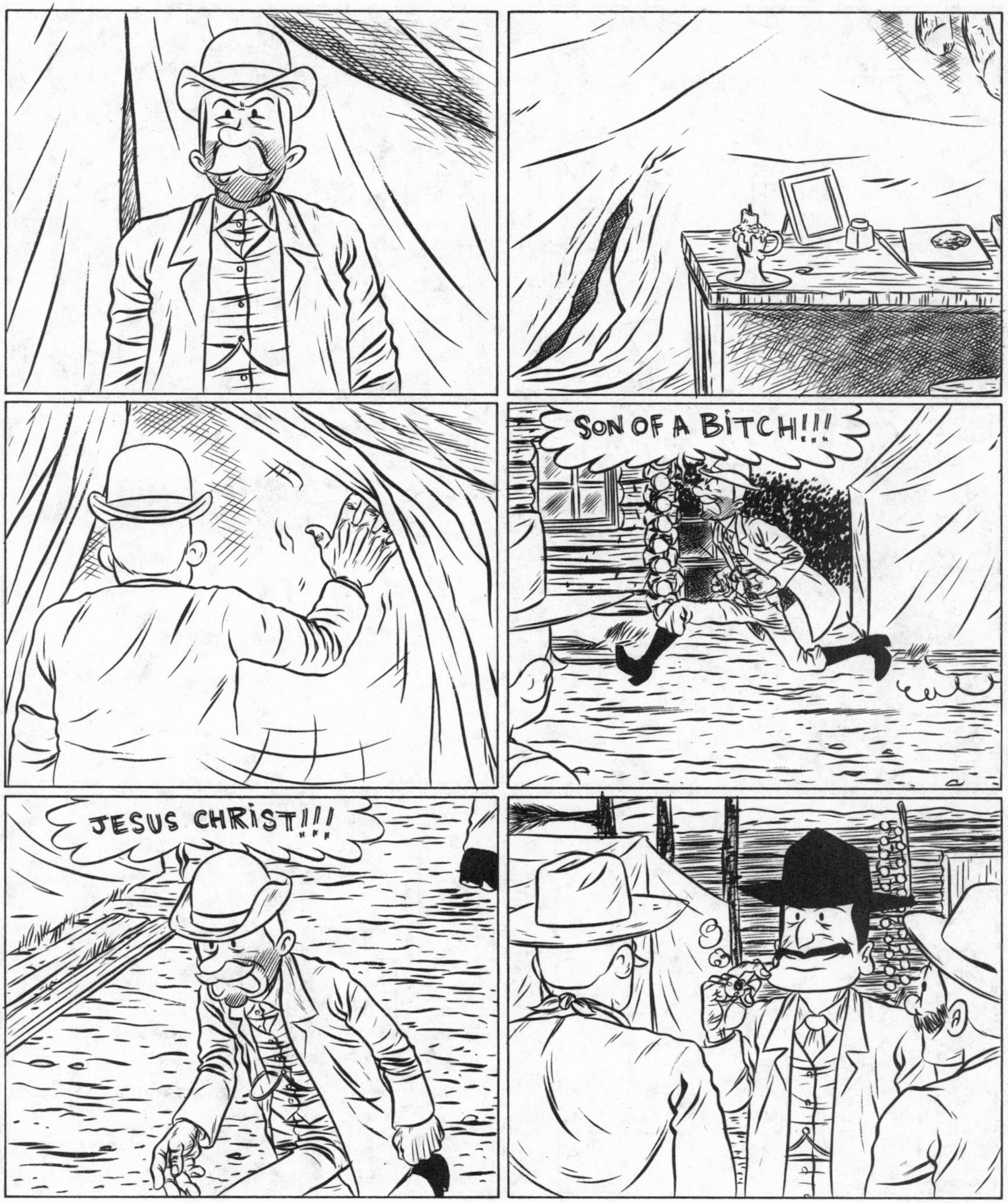
SON OF A BITCH!!!
JESUS CHRIST!!!

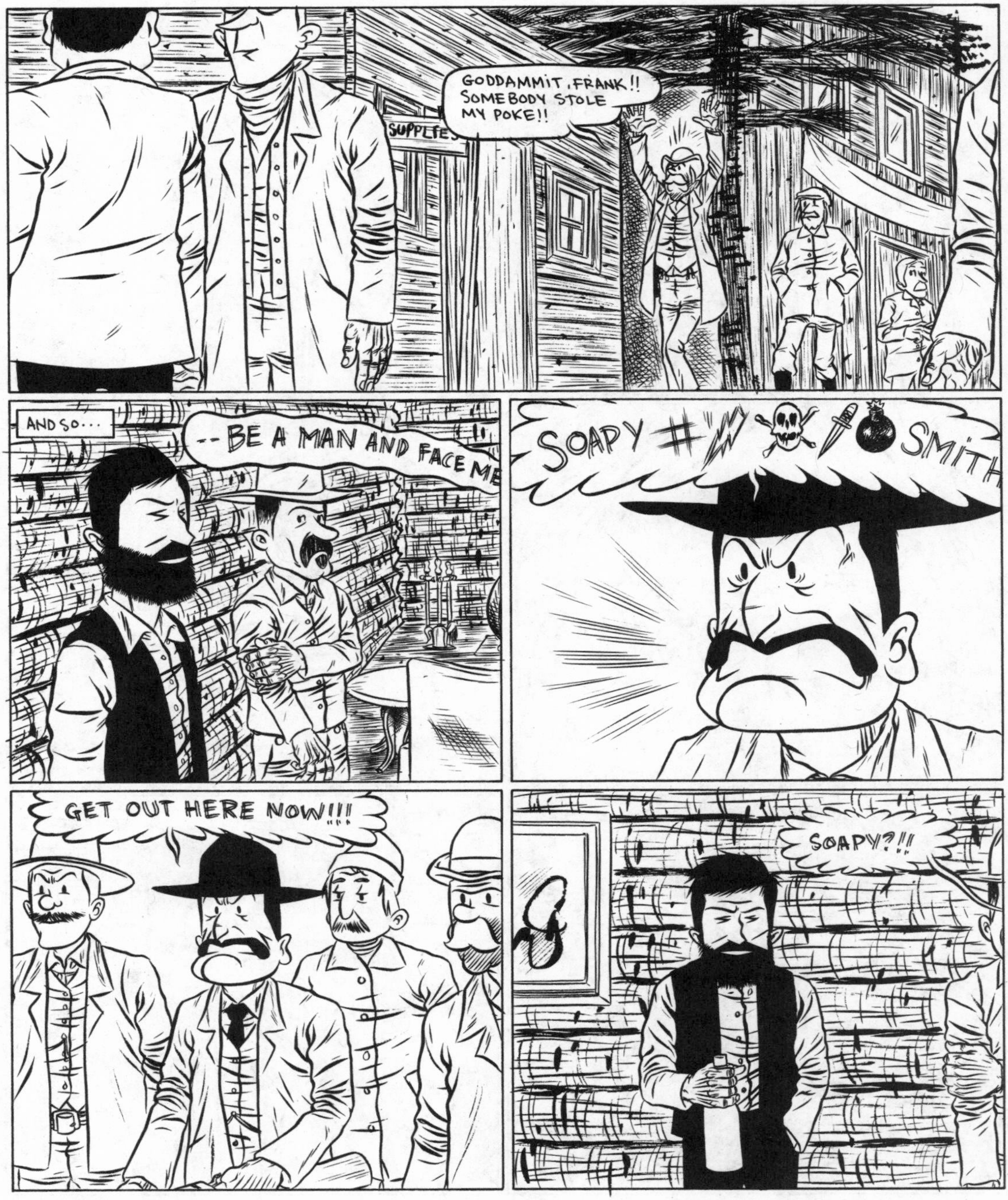
GODDAMMIT, FRANK!! SOMEBODY STOLE MY POKE!!
SUPPLIES
AND SO...
--BE A MAN AND FACE ME
SOAPY #!@*! SMITH
GET OUT HERE NOW!!!
SOAPY?!!

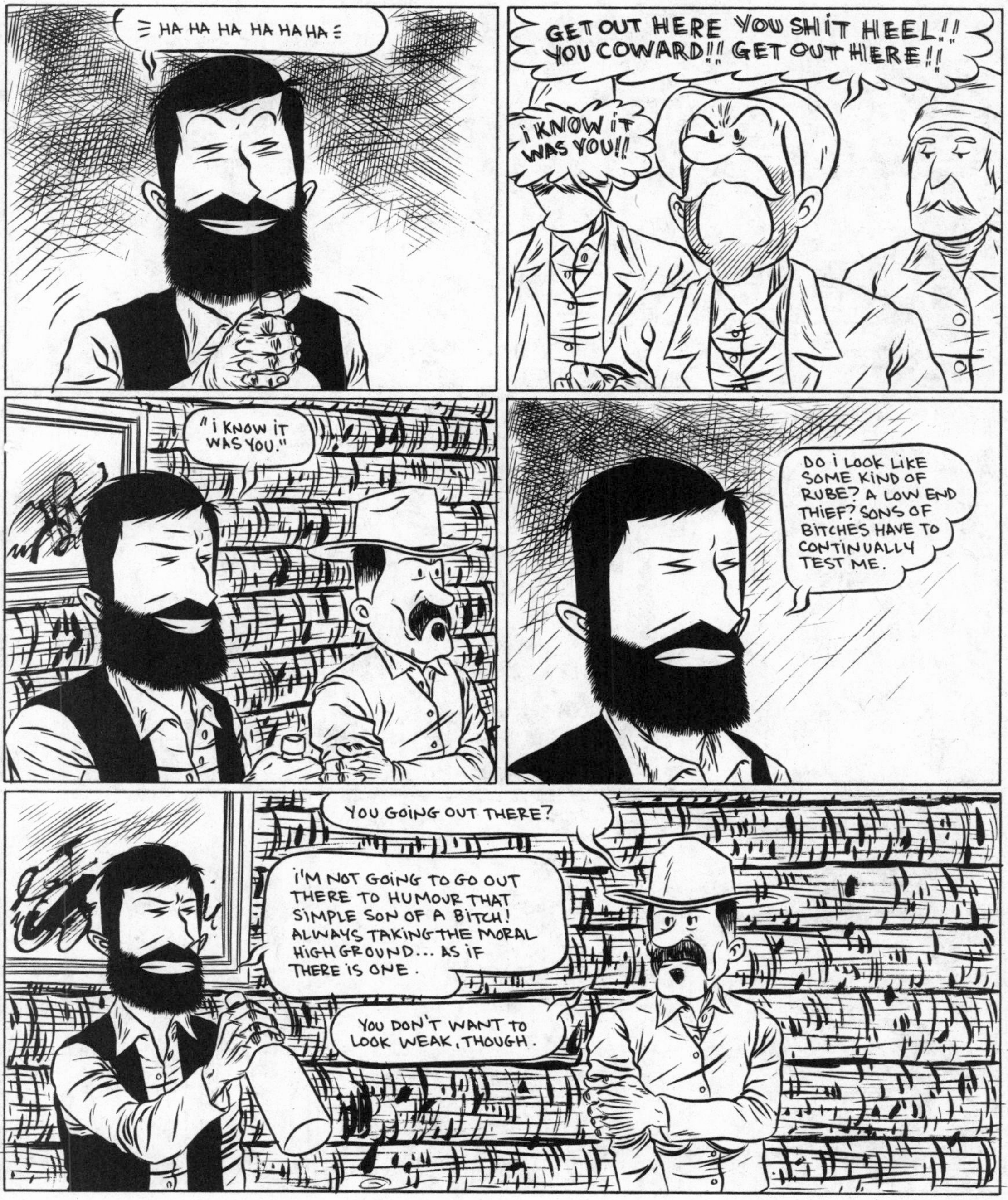
HA HA HA HA HA HA
GET OUT HERE YOU SHIT HEEL!! YOU COWARD!! GET OUT HERE!!
I KNOW IT WAS YOU!!
"I KNOW IT WAS YOU."
DO I LOOK LIKE SOME KIND OF RUBE? A LOW END THIEF? SONS OF BITCHES HAVE TO CONTINUALLY TEST ME.
YOU GOING OUT THERE?
I'M NOT GOING TO GO OUT THERE TO HUMOUR THAT SIMPLE SON OF A BITCH! ALWAYS TAKING THE MORAL HIGH GROUND... AS IF THERE IS ONE.
YOU DON'T WANT TO LOOK WEAK, THOUGH.

WEAKNESS IS SHOWING YOUR ASS LIKE HE IS.
THE MAN IS COWERING!! HE WON'T FACE ME!!
HE HAD HIS MEN STEAL FROM ME!! NOW I HAVE NOTHING!
YOU'RE CALLING OUT SOAPY RIGHT HERE IN THE STREET?
NOT AFRAID OF WHO'S AROUND?
I AM NOT AFRAID OF WEASELS.
-HEH- NO HARM. JUST WANNA GET PAST YOU. NEED A DRINK.

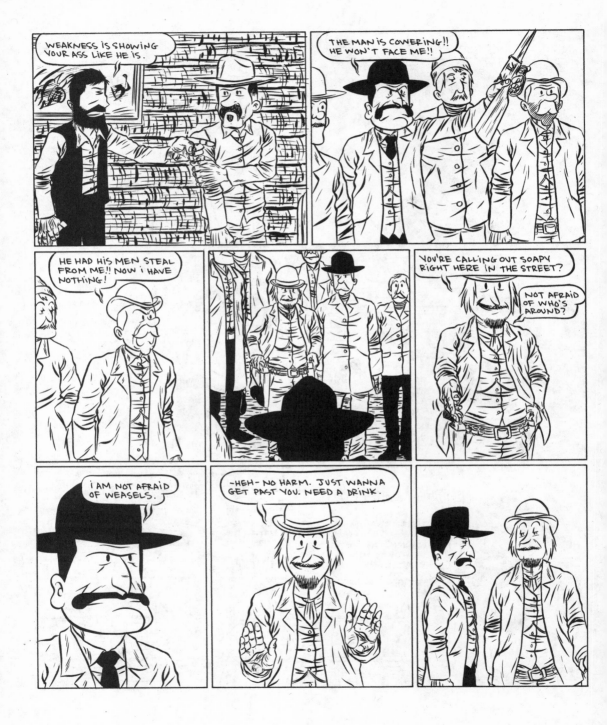

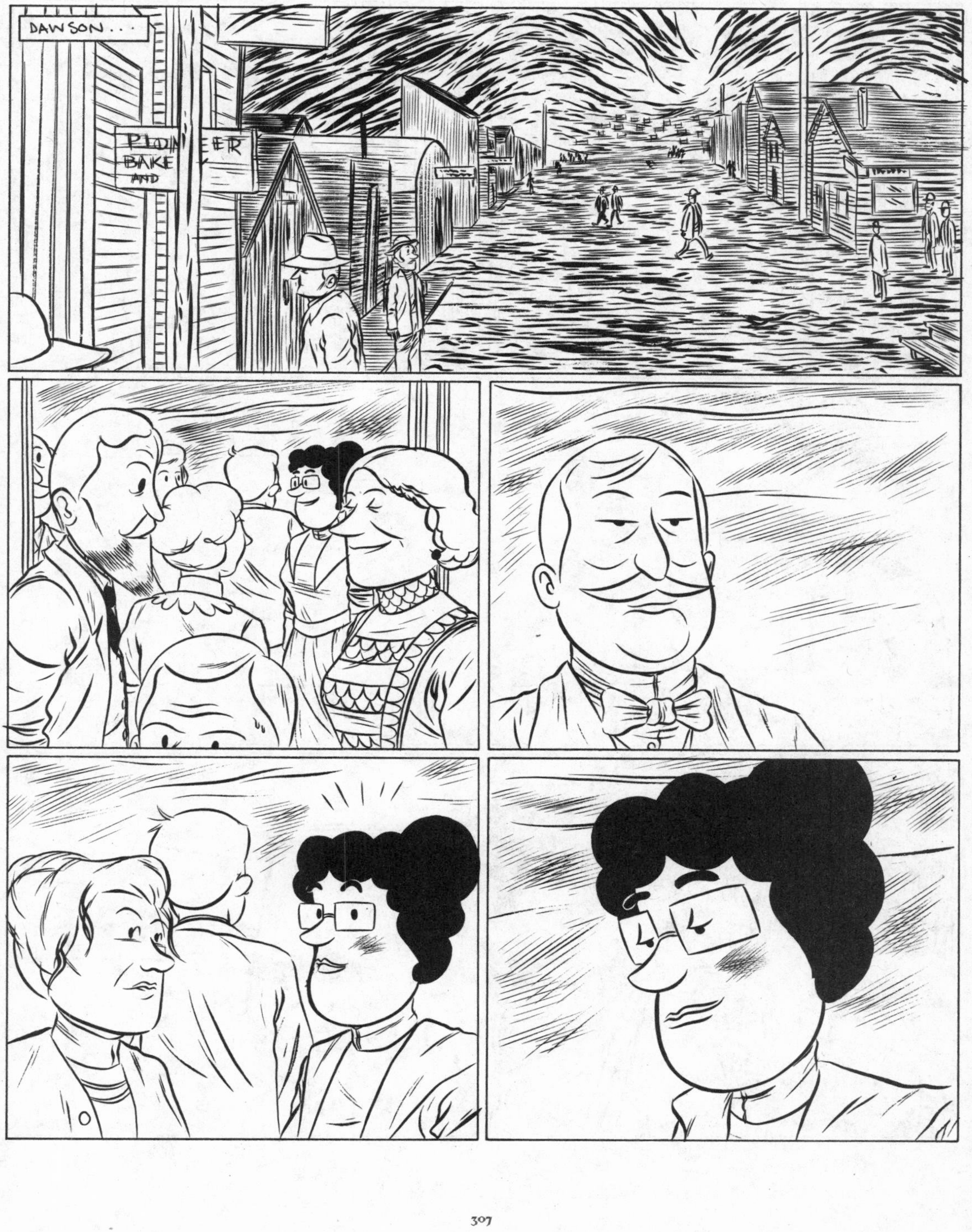
DAWSON...
PIONEER
BAKE
AND

SALOON
GOOD LUCK, SUPERINTENDENT!
THANK YOU!
SUPERINTENDENT CONSTANTINE?
SALOON
SUPERINTENDENT NOW, I HEAR. CONGRATULATIONS!
IT'S BEEN A PLEASURE, CHARLES. BE SAFE.
I HAVEN'T HAD TO DRAW MY GUN IN YEARS. I FEEL CONFIDENT THINGS WON'T CHANGE TOO MUCH.
WELL, THINGS IN THE PRAIRIES HAVE BEEN GETTING PRETTY TUMULTUOUS LATELY— NOT LIKE HERE.
WELL, AT LEAST IT'S NOT SKAGWAY. GOOD LUCK, SAM.
I'LL DO MY BEST TO KEEP THE PEACE.

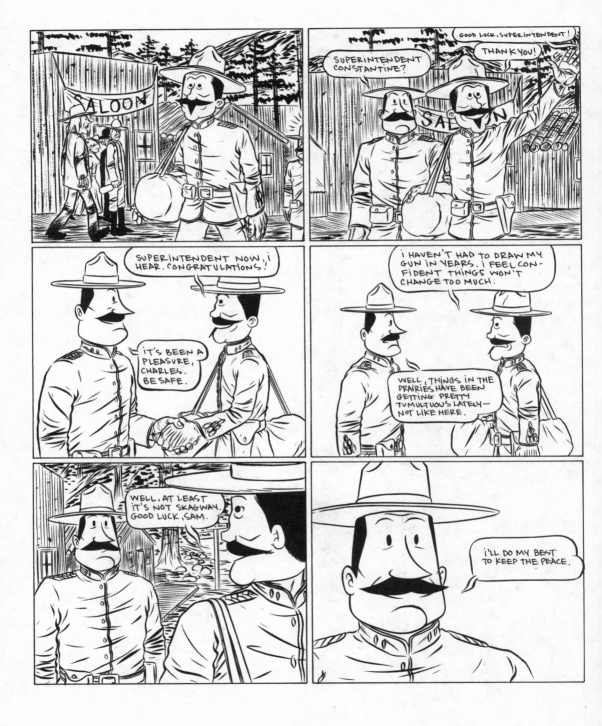

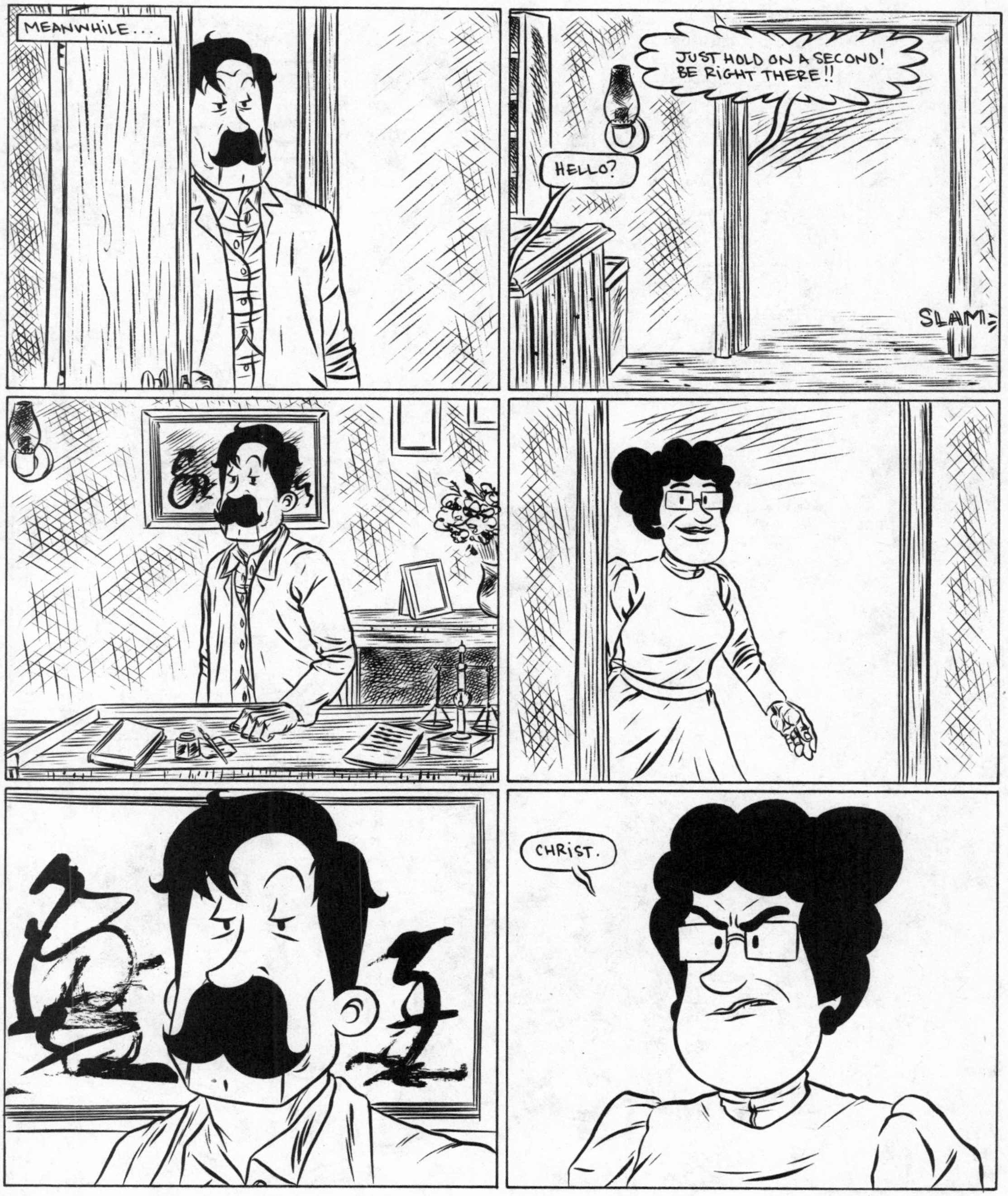
MEANWHILE...
HELLO?
JUST HOLD ON A SECOND! BE RIGHT THERE!!
SLAM
CHRIST.

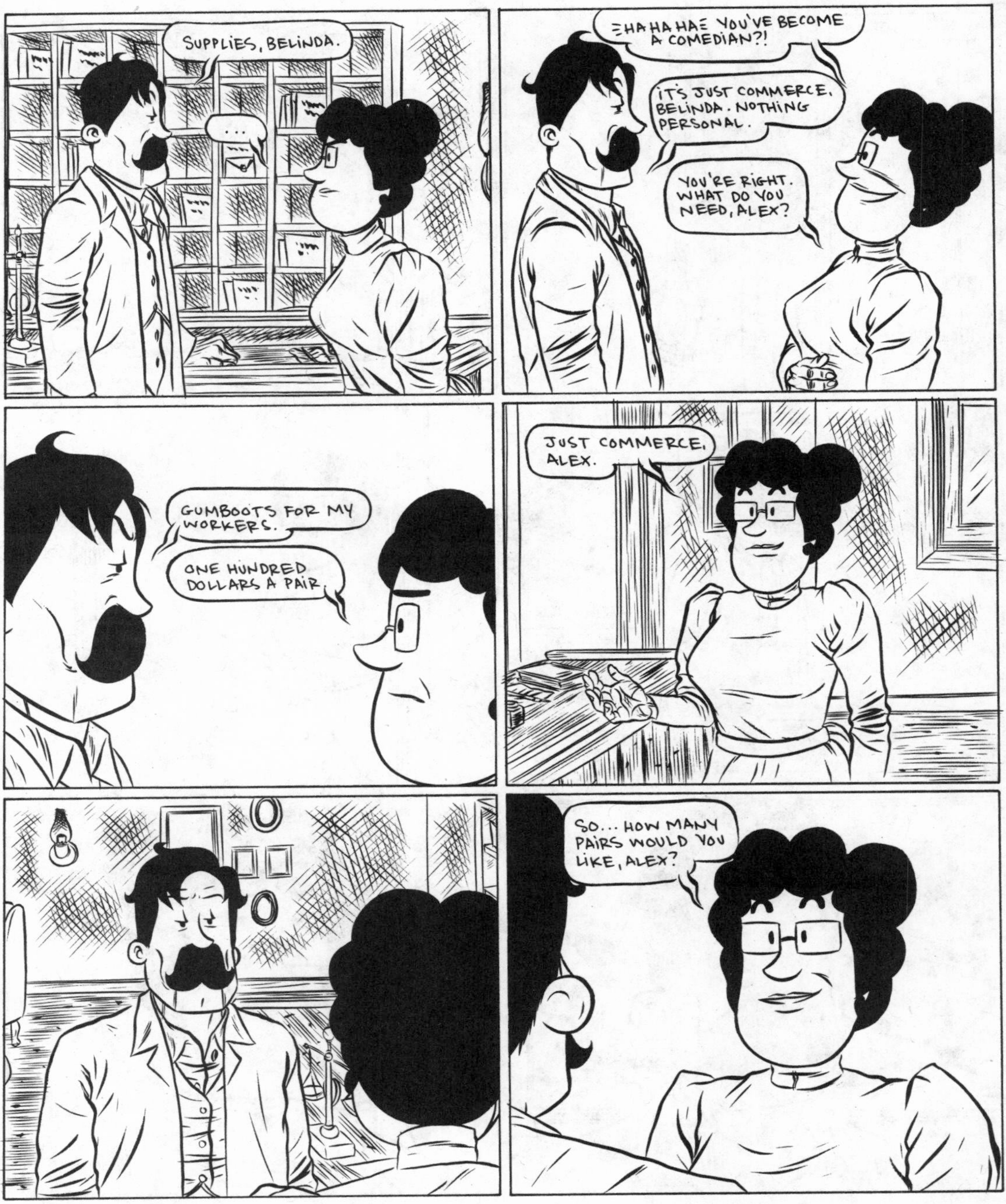
SUPPLIES, BELINDA.
...
≡HA HA HA≡ YOU'VE BECOME A COMEDIAN?!
IT'S JUST COMMERCE, BELINDA. NOTHING PERSONAL.
YOU'RE RIGHT. WHAT DO YOU NEED, ALEX?
GUMBOOTS FOR MY WORKERS.
ONE HUNDRED DOLLARS A PAIR.
JUST COMMERCE, ALEX.
SO... HOW MANY PAIRS WOULD YOU LIKE, ALEX?

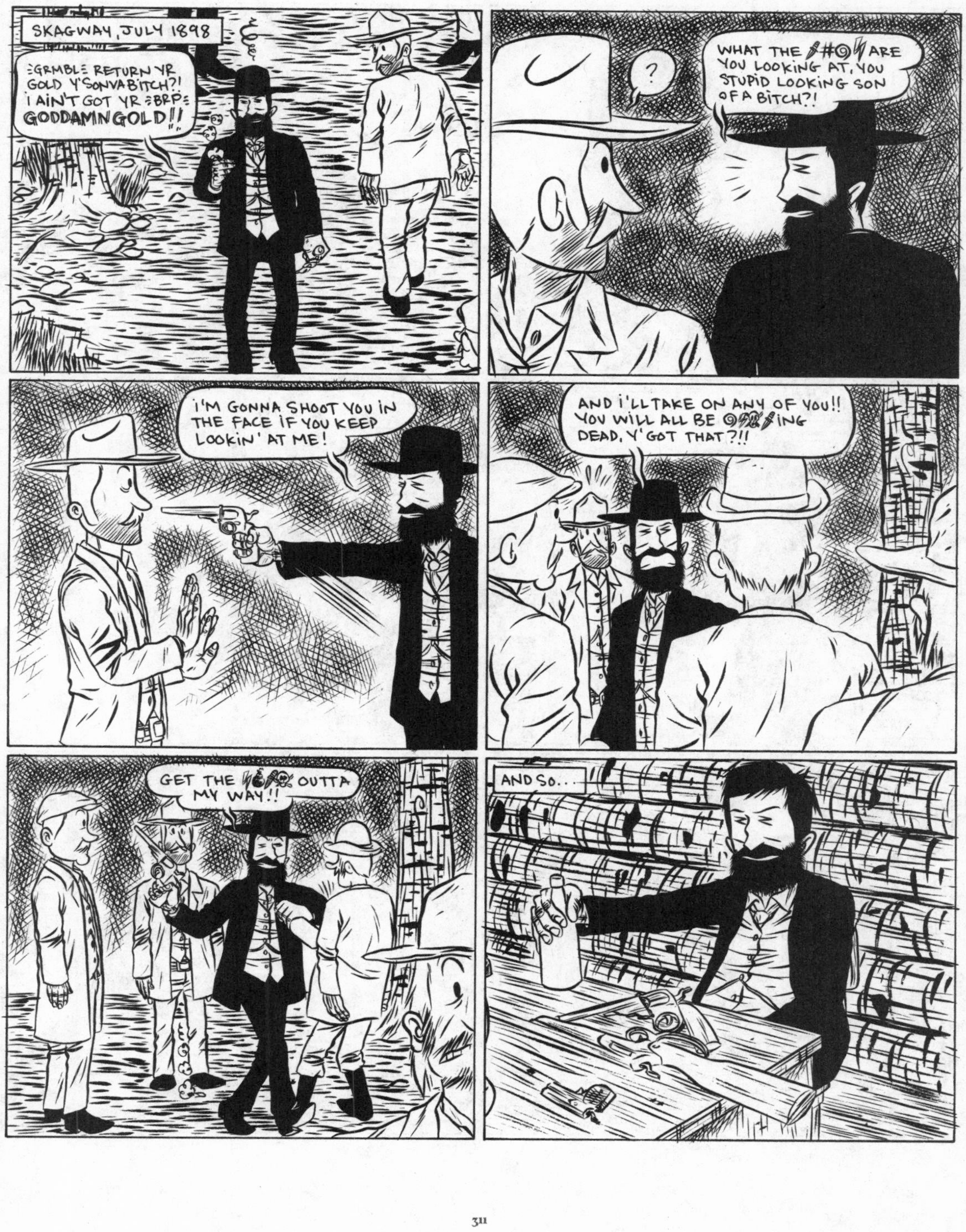
SKAGWAY, JULY 1898
GRMBLE RETURN YR GOLD Y'SONVABITCH?! I AIN'T GOT YR BRP GODDAMN GOLD!!
?
WHAT THE ARE YOU LOOKING AT, YOU STUPID LOOKING SON OF A BITCH?!
I'M GONNA SHOOT YOU IN THE FACE IF YOU KEEP LOOKIN' AT ME!
AND I'LL TAKE ON ANY OF YOU!! YOU WILL ALL BE ING DEAD, Y'GOT THAT?!!
GET THE OUTTA MY WAY!!
AND SO...

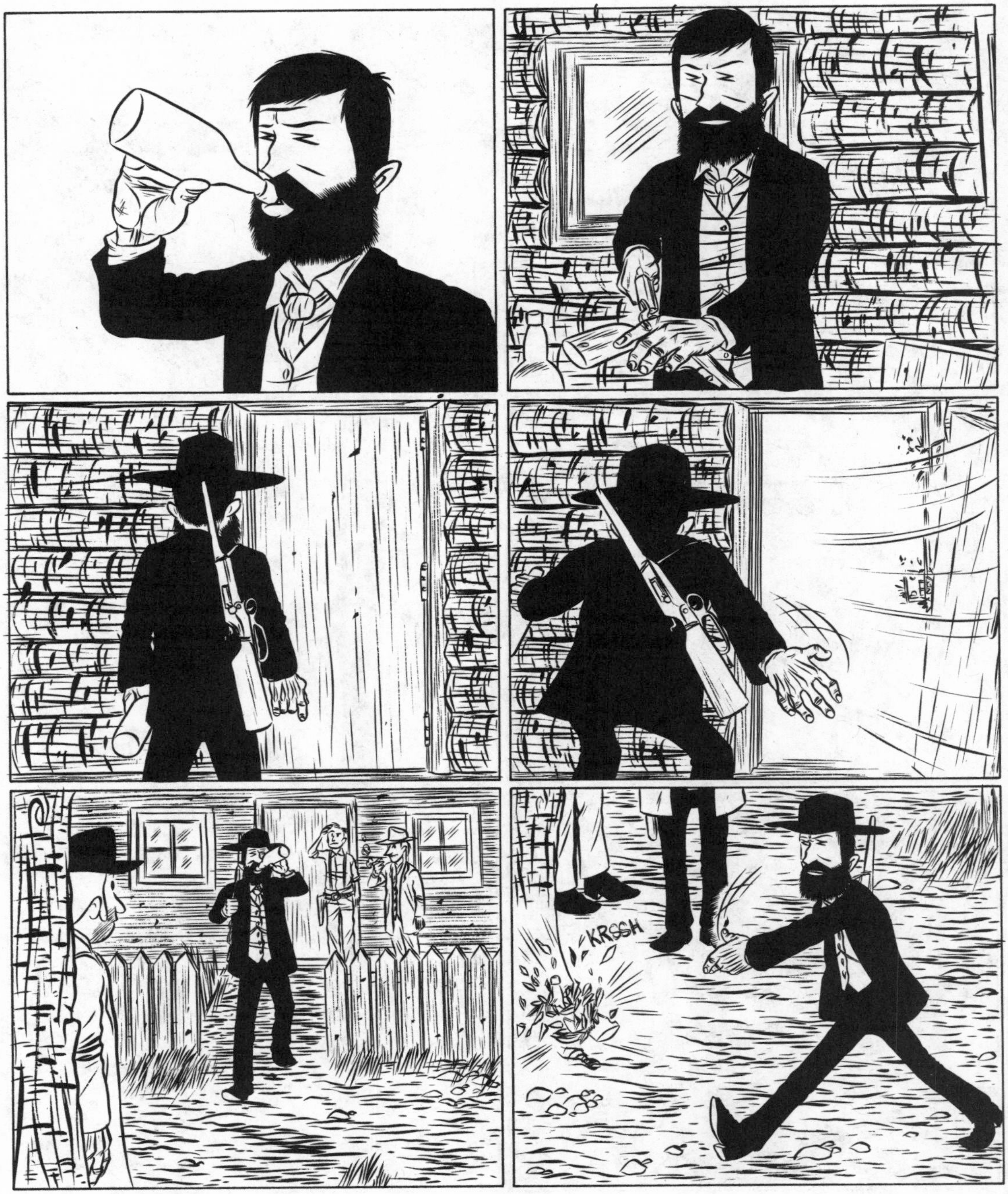
KRSSH

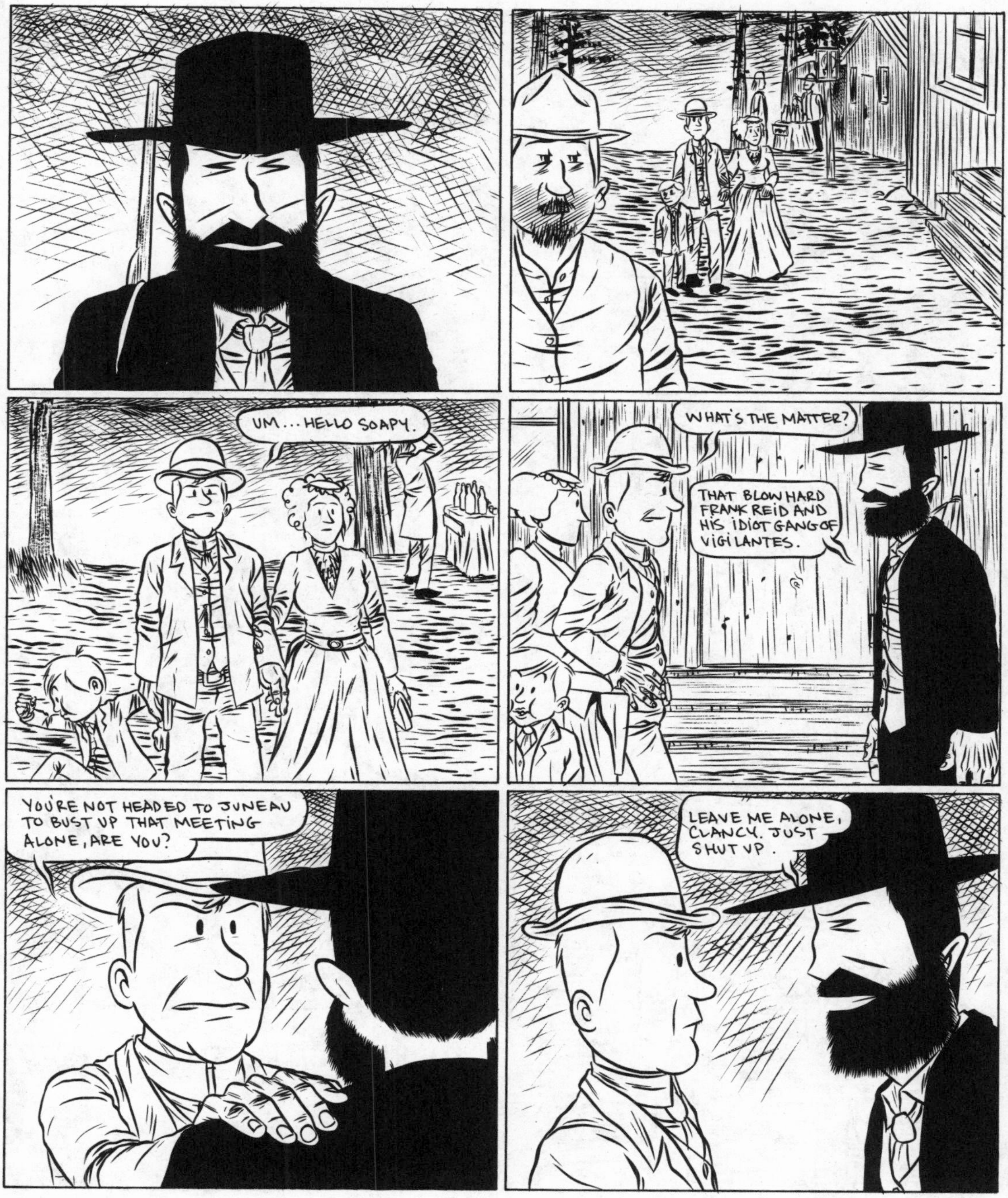
UM... HELLO SOAPY.
WHAT'S THE MATTER?
THAT BLOWHARD FRANK REID AND HIS IDIOT GANG OF VIGILANTES.
YOU'RE NOT HEADED TO JUNEAU TO BUST UP THAT MEETING ALONE, ARE YOU?
LEAVE ME ALONE, CLANCY. JUST SHUT UP.

≡PFFT≡ FINE! IF YOU WANT TO GET YOURSELF KILLED, DON'T LET ME STAND IN YOUR WAY!!
BMP
YOU CAN'T GO DOWN THERE, SMITH!!
A COMMITTEE OF 101 MEETING IS ABOUT TO COMMENCE!

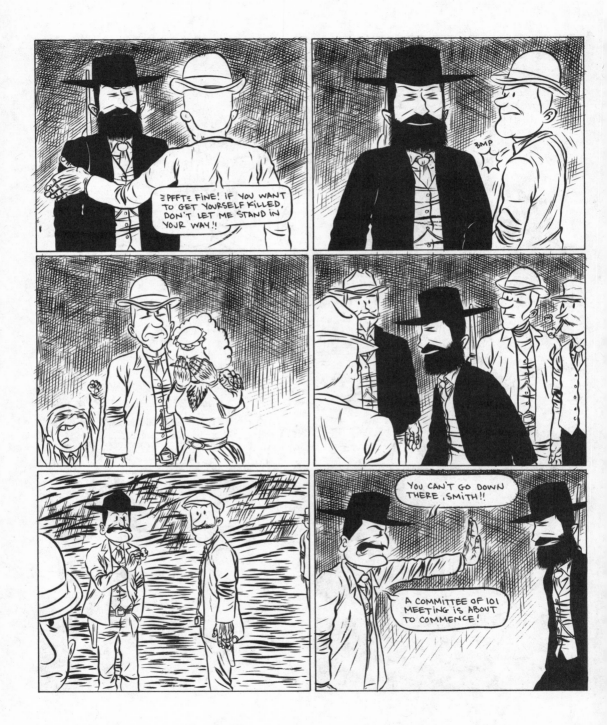

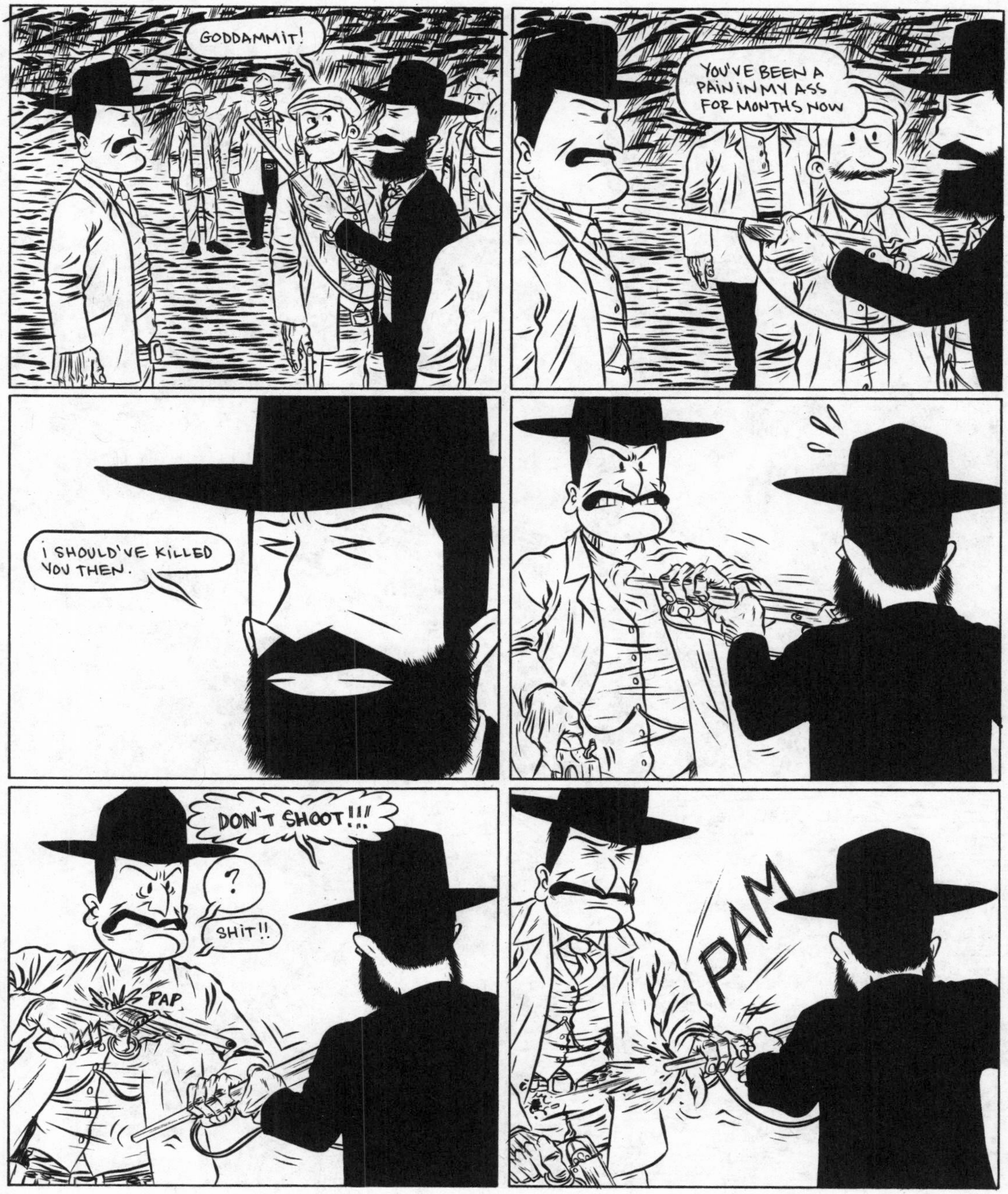
GODDAMMIT!
YOU'VE BEEN A PAIN IN MY ASS FOR MONTHS NOW
I SHOULD'VE KILLED YOU THEN.
DON'T SHOOT!!!
?
SHIT!!
PAP
PAM

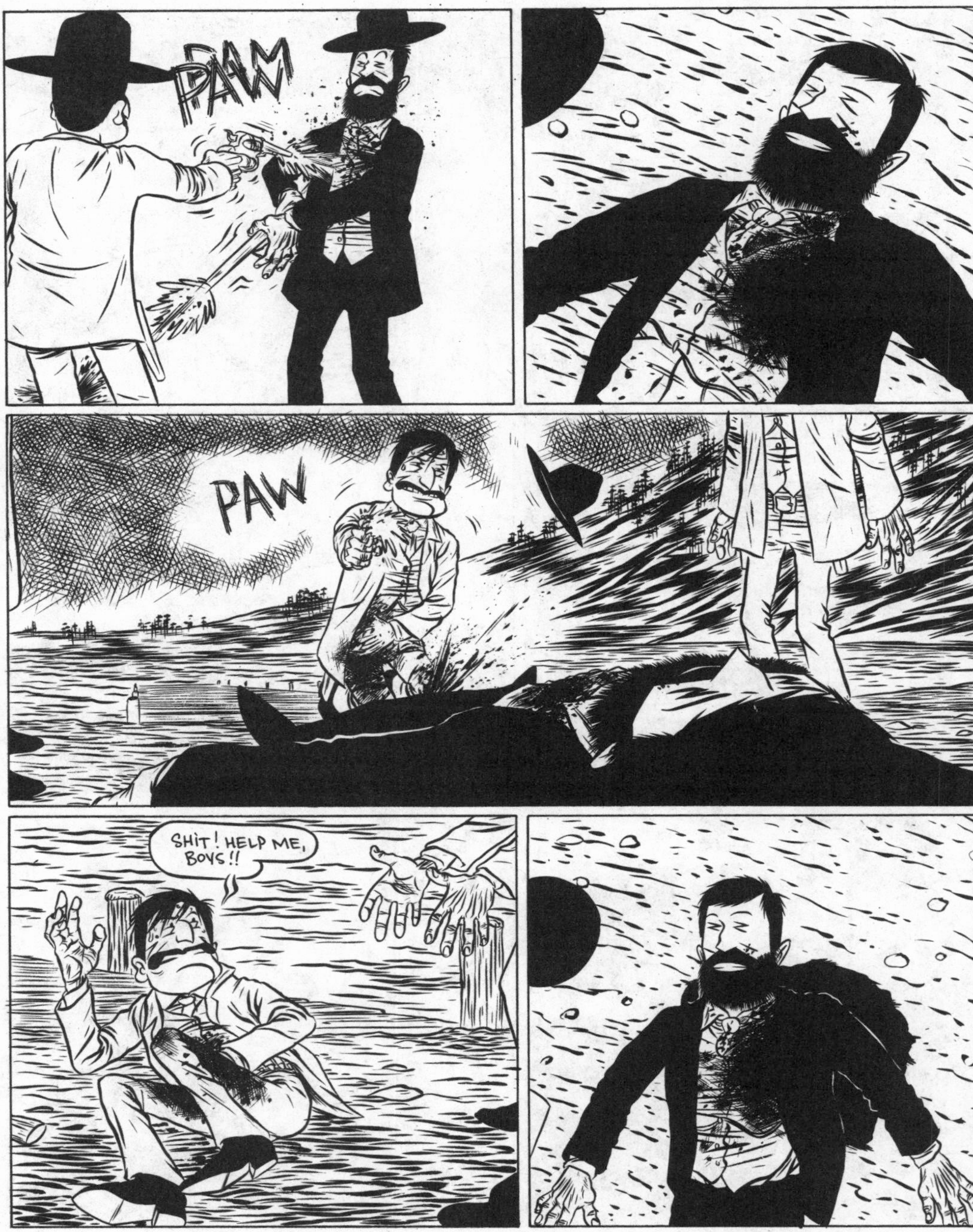
PAW
PAW
SHIT! HELP ME, BOYS!!

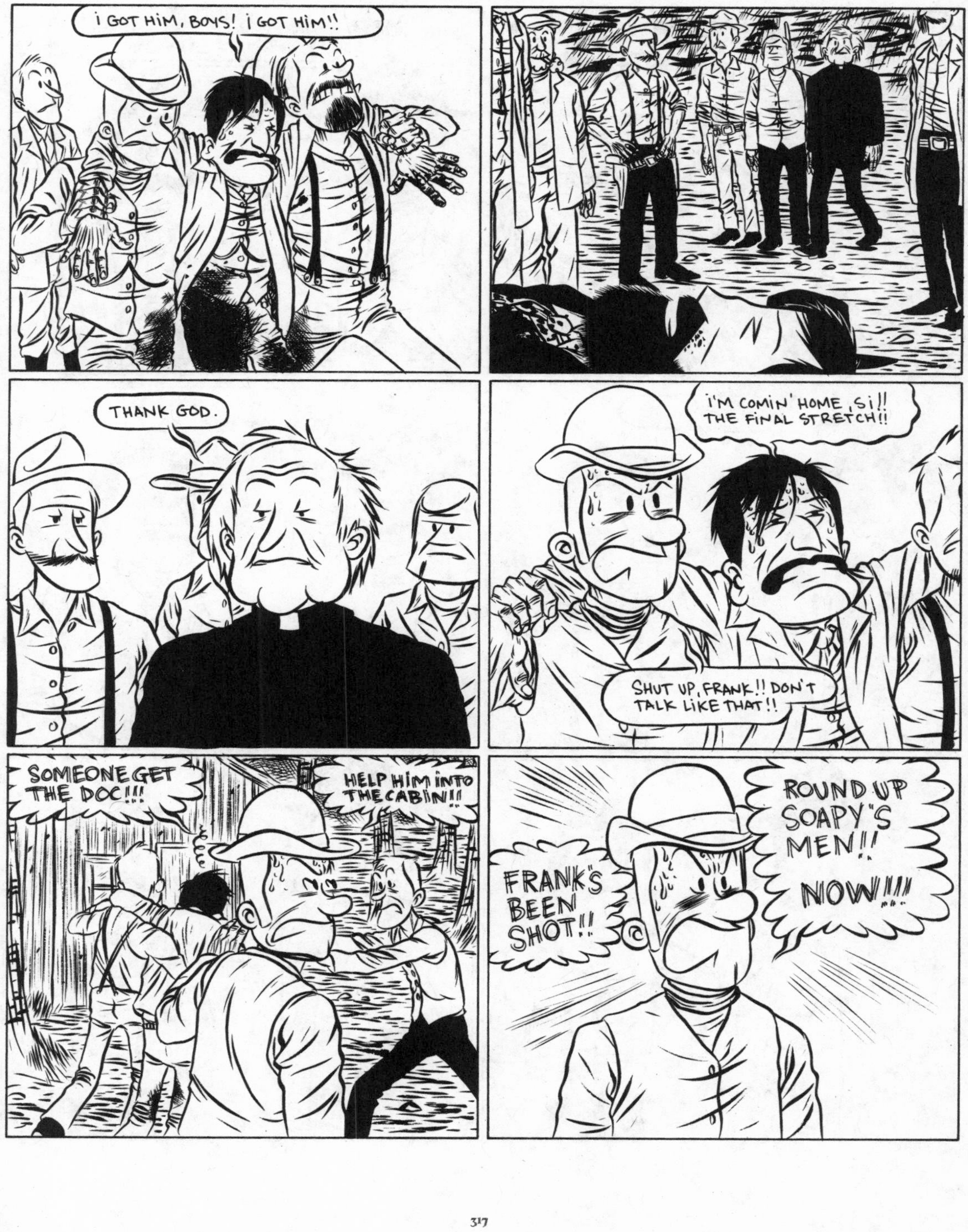
I GOT HIM, BOYS! I GOT HIM!!
THANK GOD.
I'M COMIN' HOME, SI!! THE FINAL STRETCH!!
SHUT UP, FRANK!! DON'T TALK LIKE THAT!!
SOMEONE GET THE DOC!!!
HELP HIM INTO THE CABIN!!
FRANK'S BEEN SHOT!!
ROUND UP SOAPY'S MEN!!
NOW!!!

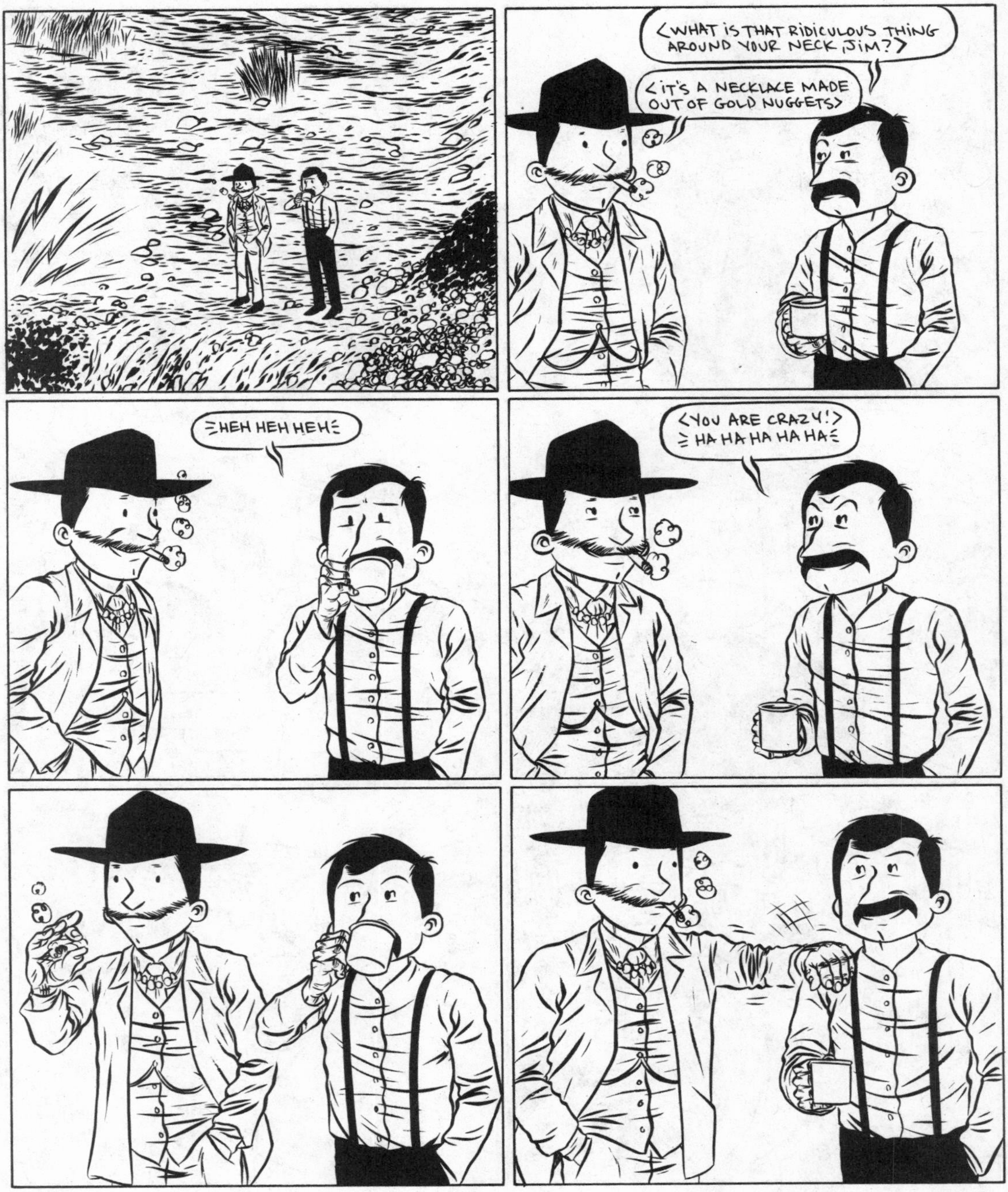
<WHAT IS THAT RIDICULOUS THING AROUND YOUR NECK, JIM?>
<IT'S A NECKLACE MADE OUT OF GOLD NUGGETS>
HEH HEH HEH
<YOU ARE CRAZY!> HA HA HA HA HA

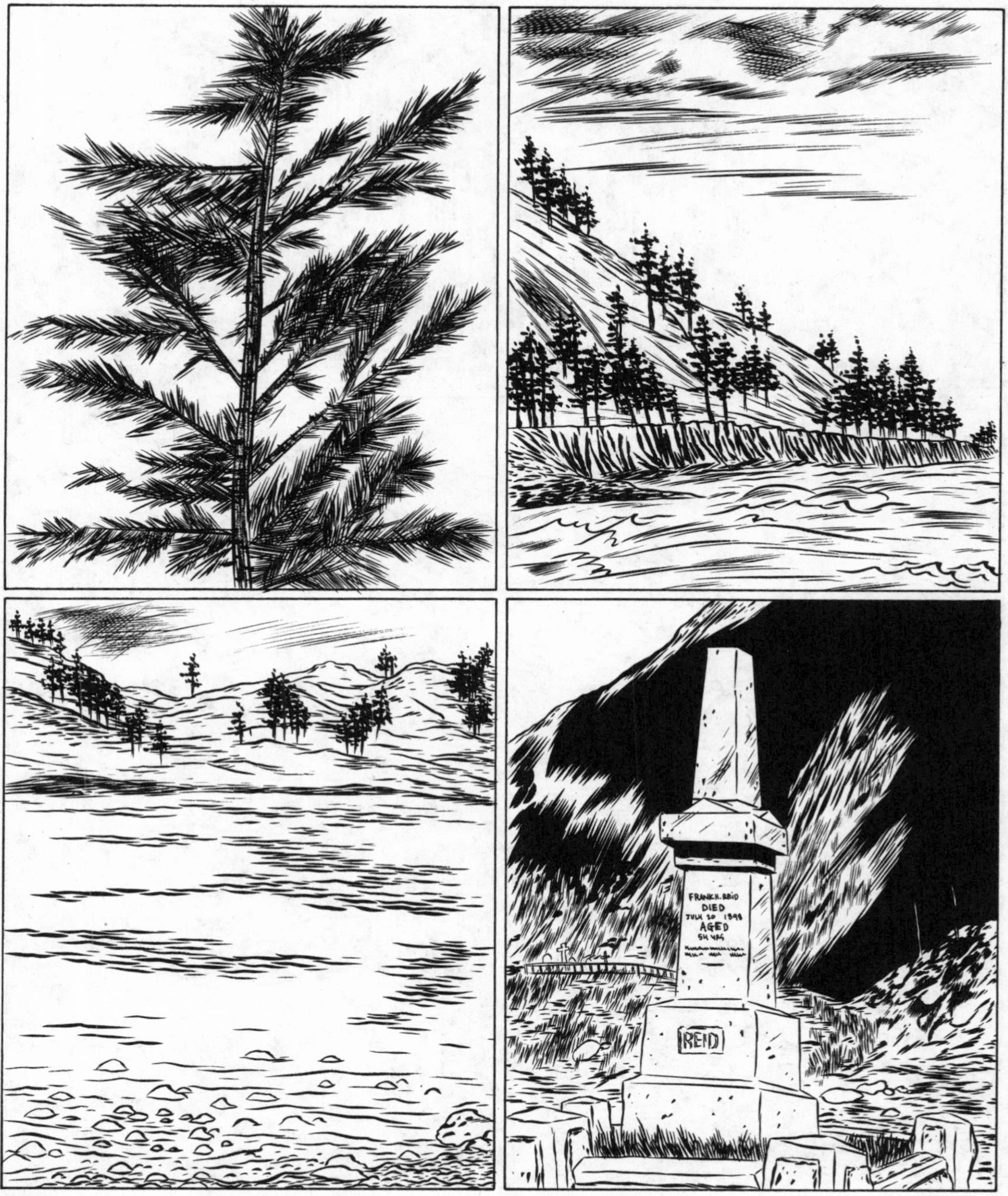
FRANK H. REID
DIED
JULY 20 1898
AGED
54 YRS
REID

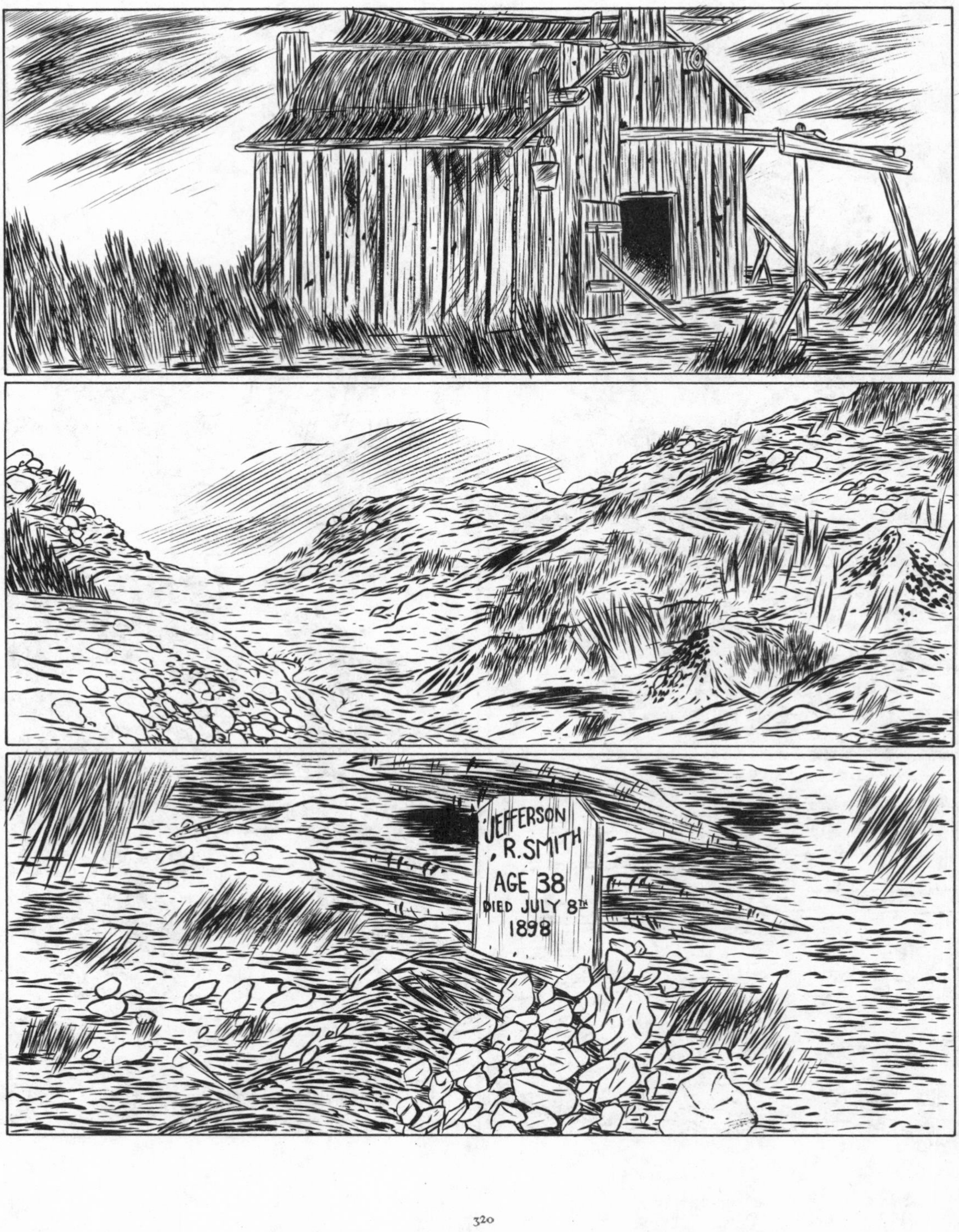
JEFFERSON R. SMITH
AGE 38
DIED JULY 8TH
1898

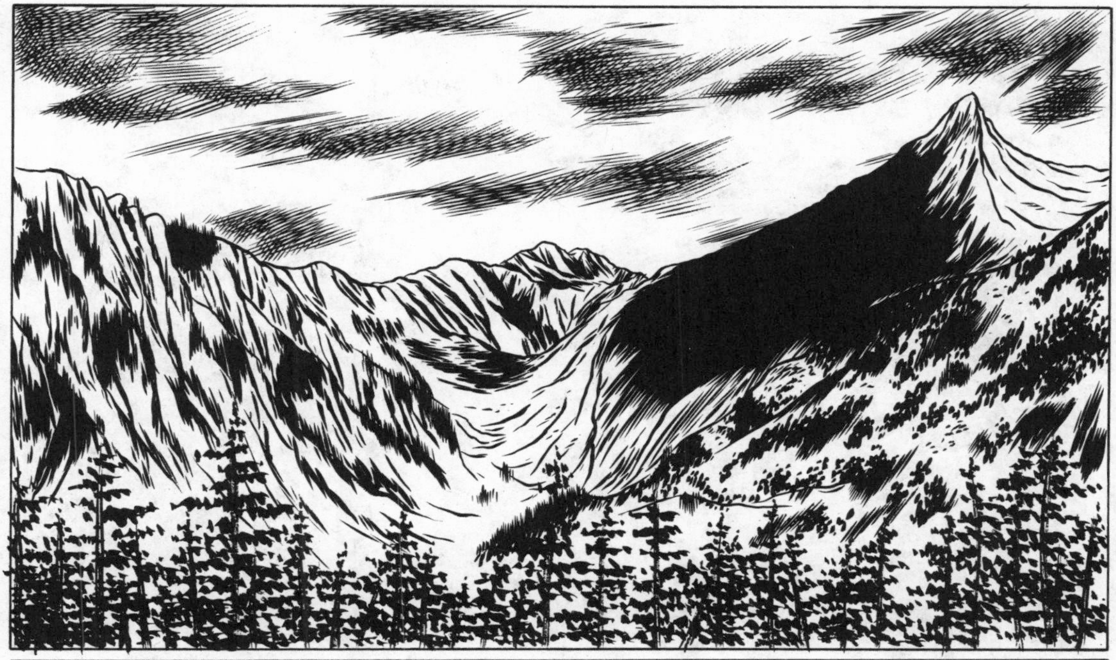

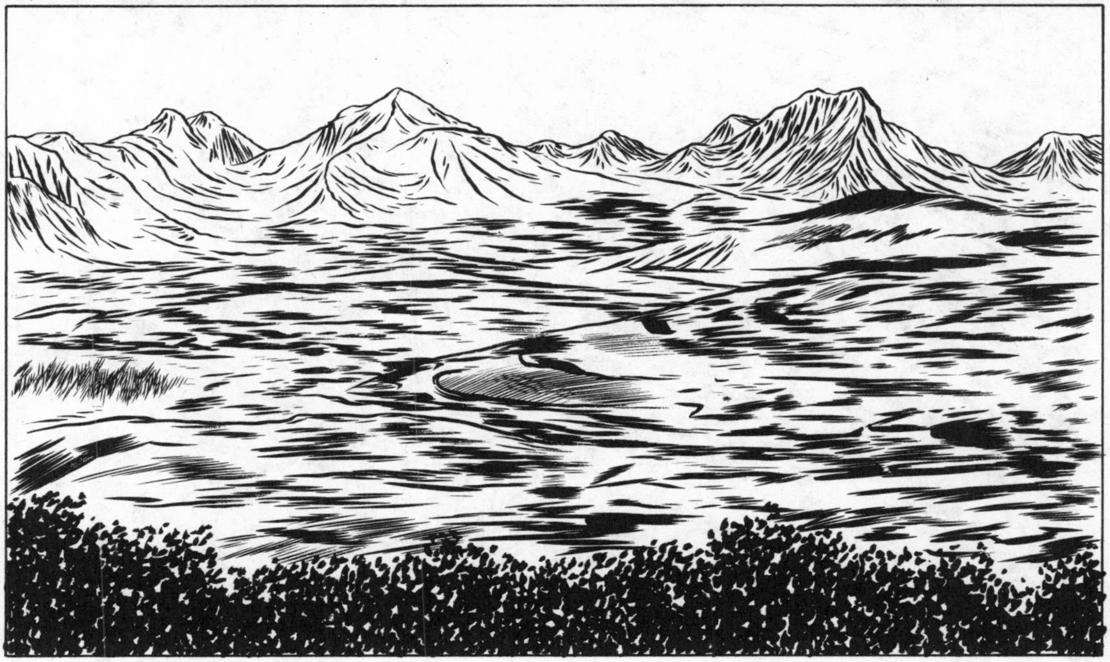

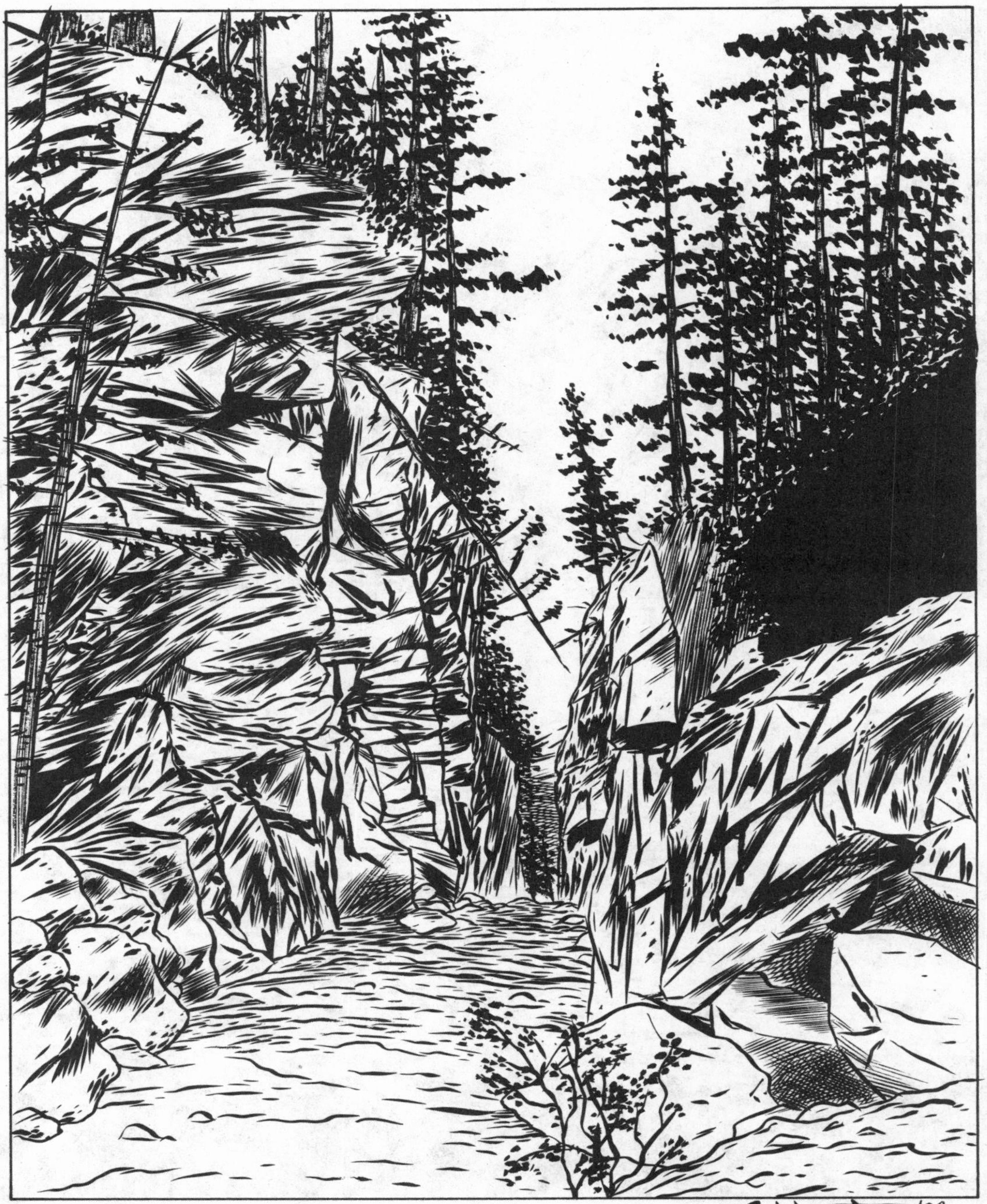

THANKS...
C. OLIVEROS, T. DEVLIN, P. BURNS, T. HURREN,
R. ROSEN, J. CAMPBELL, C. BENNET, ALL OF THE
INTERNS, B. GRIEVE, K. WORTON, B. WORTON,
J. AZZOPARDI, P. BIRKEMOE, K. TABAJARA,
C. BUTCHER, C. BROWN, SETH + T. GALLANT,
S. GREEN, J. KIRKPATRICK, B. ROSENFELD,
N. HRAB, E. KIM, D. HALLIDAY, G. FIRANSKI,
B. AIKMAN, J. MOSER-AIKMAN, C. MOSER-PRPICH,
C. PRPICH, J. MOSER, R. MOSER, S. MANALE
K. ROMAIN, R. SCOBLE, P. KILTHEI, A. HOFFMAN,
M. RENNER, D. KUZENKO, L. ELLIOT, R. ALGERA,
M. LACOMBE, A. WOODROW-BUTCHER,
J. ZUBKAVICH, A. ULLEDAL, D. TILLVSZ,
D. COOKE, R. ELINSKY, P. TASSONE, A. MUIR,
K. MALO, B+G SAVAGE, G. BELL, K. HUIZENGA,
J. LEMIRE + L.A. GREENE, J. MARTZ, A. COSTAIN,
R. GOWMAN, C. ROSS-OPAZO, B. SUGAR, A. ETHIER,
D. SLATOR + M. AIDE, D.S. GRAY, H. LIN.
M. FORSYTHE, J+S ASPERT, N. FLANAGAN,
D. TAMBLYN, P. KYLE, C. KUZMA, G. LAPALME,
(WOWEE ZONK), M. COLEK, P. SHEWCHUK,
J. RESENDES, E. MATTHESON, AND OF COURSE,
P. BERTON...
            SPECIAL THANKS TO K. SAVAGE

        IN MEMORY OF:
    D. STEPHENSON 1971-2006
            AND
        M. AIDE 1951-2007

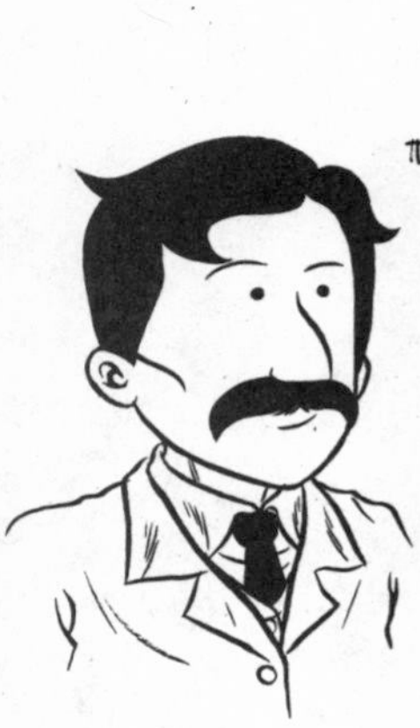

TAPPAN ADNEY

THOUGH APPEARING IN THE BOOK BRIEFLY, ADNEY WAS AN IMPORTANT PART OF KLONDIKE GOLD RUSH HISTORY. HE WAS A CORRESPONDENT FOR "HARPER'S ILLUSTRATED WEEKLY" AND PUBLISHED ONE OF THE BEST, THOUGH INCOMPLETE, ACCOUNTS OF THE KLONDIKE GOLD RUSH: "THE KLONDIKE STAMPEDE OF 1897–1898."

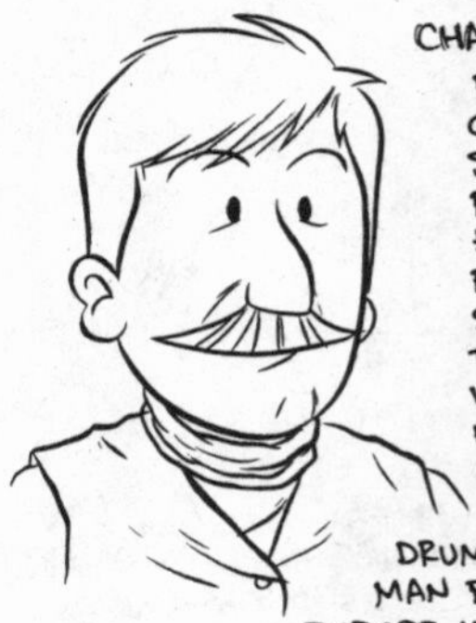

CHARLEY ANDERSON

BEFORE HIS FAMOUS STRIKE ON #29 ELDORADO, ANDERSON SPENT $800 ON A SMALL BARREL OF BENT AND BLACKENED NAILS RECOVERED FROM A FIRE TO BUILD A SLUICE BOX – THIS PROVED TO BE A SMART INVESTMENT. WITHIN A COUPLE OF YEARS, HE HAD MONEY TO SPARE. HE TEMPTED A DANCE HALL GIRL NAMED GRACIE DRUMMOND AWAY FROM ANOTHER MAN FOR $50,000. AFTER A TRIP TO EUROPE, HE SPENT AN ADDITIONAL $20,000 TO BUILD HER A TURRETED CASTLE ON THE OUTSKIRTS OF SAN FRANCISCO.

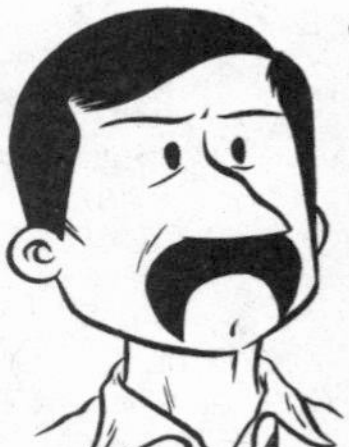

GEORGE CARMACK

AFTER HE LEFT THE KLONDIKE, THE MAN ONCE CALLED "LYING GEORGE," LEFT HIS WIFE KATE AFTER MARRYING MARGUERITE LAIMEE. SINCE THERE WERE NO LEGAL PAPERS INVOLVED WITH HIS MARRIAGE TO KATE, HE WAS FREE TO MARRY MARGUERITE (WHO RAN A BAWDY HOUSE IN DAWSON, INCIDENTALLY). WHILE ON THE OUTSIDE, HE INVESTED HEAVILY IN SEATTLE REAL ESTATE, OPERATED A MINE IN CALIFORNIA AND WAS A WELL RESPECTED MEMBER OF THE MASONIC ORDER. CARMACK LIVED WELL ON THE OUTSIDE. HE DROVE HIS EXPENSIVE CAR AROUND SEATTLE WITH A BANNER THAT SAID: "GEORGE CARMACK, DISCOVERER OF GOLD IN THE KLONDIKE." HE DIED IN VANCOUVER IN 1922, STILL MARRIED TO MARGUERITE LAIMEE.

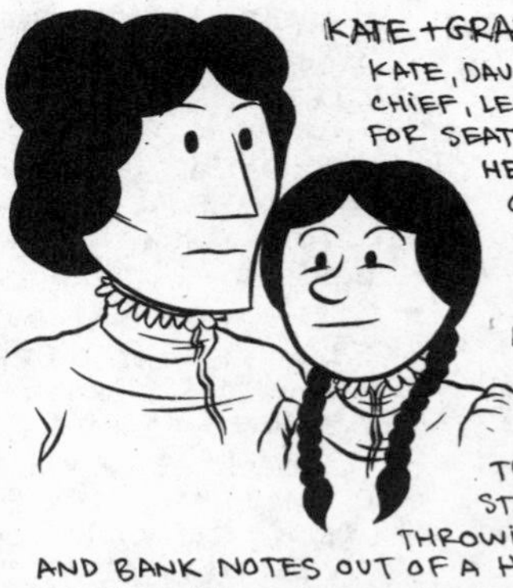

KATE + GRAPHIE CARMACK

KATE, DAUGHTER OF A TAGISH CHIEF, LEFT THE KLONDIKE FOR SEATTLE WITH GEORGE, HER DAUGHTER, GRAPHIE, JIM AND CHARLEY. TIMES WEREN'T GREAT FOR ANY OF THEM AS KATE, JIM AND CHARLEY OFTEN GOT ARRESTED FOR DRUNKENNESS. THEY ONCE NEARLY STARTED A RIOT BY THROWING GOLD NUGGETS AND BANK NOTES OUT OF A HOTEL WINDOW. BY 1900, KATE AND GRAPHIE WERE LIVING WITH GEORGE'S SISTER ROSE, BUT WERE SOON SENT AWAY AT THE REQUEST OF GEORGE. IN HER LATER YEARS, KATE LIVED ON A GOVERNMENT PENSION, BUT STILL WORE THE GOLD NUGGET NECKLACE SHE HAD BEEN WEARING SINCE GEORGE AND JIM'S GOLD DISCOVERY. KATE DIED ON MARCH 29, 1920 IN CARIBOU CROSSING.

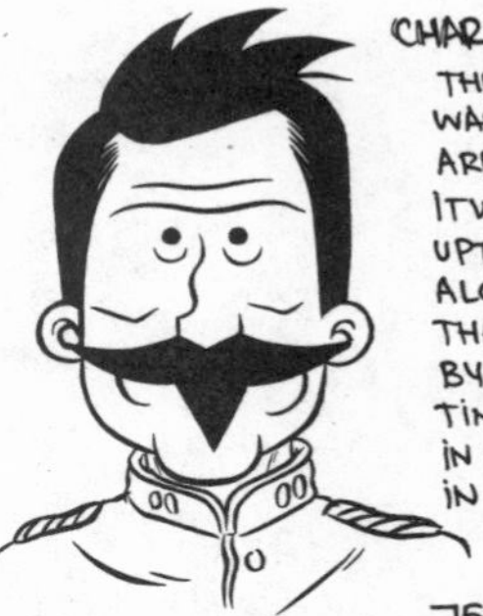

CHARLES CONSTANTINE

THE INCORRUPTIBLE INSPECTOR WAS THE FIRST MOUNTIE TO ARRIVE IN THE YUKON IN 1894. IT WAS THE WHITE MEN CORRUPTING THE INDIANS WITH ALCOHOL AND GAMBLING THAT BROUGHT HIM THERE. BY 1898, INSPECTOR CONSTANTINE RELINQUISHED HIS POST IN FORTYMILE AND WAS PUT IN CHARGE OF THE ATHABASCA DISTRICT. IN 1905, HE OVERSAW THE BUILDING OF A 750 MILE TRAIL FROM PEACE RIVER TO TESLIN LAKE, BUT AFTER THREE YEARS THE GOVERNMENT ABANDONED THE PROJECT. IT DESTROYED THE HEALTH OF MANY MEN, INCLUDING INSPECTOR CONSTANTINE. HE DIED IN SAN FRANCISCO IN 1912 AFTER YEARS OF DECLINING HEALTH.

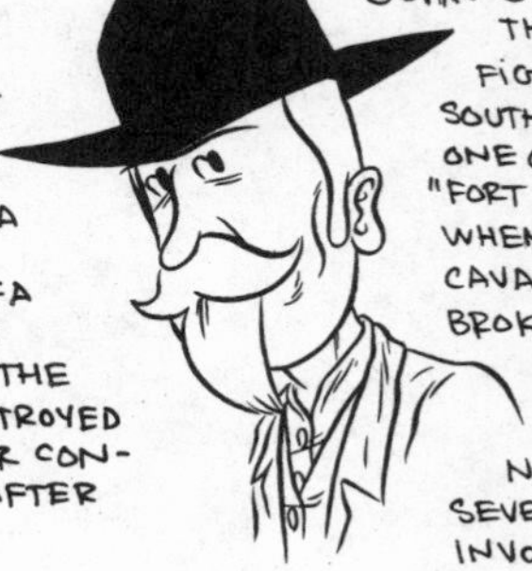

JOHN J. HEALY

THIS TOUGH-AS-LEATHER INDIAN FIGHTER MOVED FROM MONTANA UP TO SOUTHERN ALBERTA IN 1860. HE BUILT ONE OF THE FAMOUS WHISKEY FORTS, "FORT WHOOP-UP," IN CANADIAN TERRITORY. WHEN AN ARMY CALLED THE "SPITZEE CAVALRY" ATTACKED THE FORT, HEALY BROKE IT UP BY HOLDING A LIT CIGAR OVER AN OPEN BARREL OF GUNPOWDER. HE WAS ALSO THE FIRST PERSON TO REQUEST THE PRESENCE OF THE N.W.M.P. INTO THE YUKON AFTER SEVERAL CONFRONTATIONS WITH MEN INVOLVED WITH MINERS' MEETINGS.

ROBERT HENDERSON

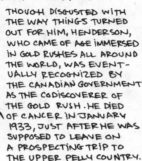

Though disgusted with the way things turned out for him, Henderson, who came of age immersed in gold rushes all around the world, was eventually recognized by the Canadian government as the codiscoverer of the gold rush. He died of cancer in January 1933, just after he was supposed to leave on a prospecting trip to the upper Pelly country.

GEORGE HOLT

The only reason anyone remembered Holt was the fact that he somehow managed to cross the heavily guarded Chilkoot Pass and survived to tell the tale. Little else is known about him.

JOHN THE RUSSIAN + HENRY THE SCOT

John and Henry represent the wide breadth of miners and prospectors that came from around the globe to take part in the rush.

JOE LADUE

The Klondike gold rush could not have happened without the presence of Joe Ladue. He had posts all over the Yukon; he was involved in the extensive exploration of the rivers and country. He guided prospectors to ideal spots and extended almost unlimited credit to the prospectors in his employ. Prior to the Klondike, Ladue got his start in the Black Hills (Dakota Territory) operating a steam engine in a mine (within eighteen months, he was foreman) and studied mining at night to further his career. Within a few months he was promoted to superintendent.

"BIG" ALEX McDONALD

The only use the "King of the Klondike" had for gold was to buy more land, and he was panning $5000 worth a day at his #30 Eldorado claim. He had twenty-eight claims all over the Yukon Valley, but twenty of them were pinched out before he even broke ground. Aside from being a shrewd businessman, McDonald was also charitable. He helped raise $35,000 to build a hospital that, at one point, housed forty-five miners suffering from scurvy. He also lent his physical strength to help build a church. While on a trip to Rome, McDonald was granted an audience with the Pope and made a "Knight of St. Gregory."

BILL McPHEE

Generous in nature, this old-time Fortymile saloon keeper housed miners and prospectors in his "Pioneer Saloon" during the starvation winter. The homeless men slept wherever they could, including on benches, tables and chairs. In his declining years, McPhee lived on a pension paid out by Clarence Berry, a Klondiker McPhee grubstaked (someone who gives money to a prospector to buy a claim and supplies).

"SKOOKUM" JIM MASON

JIM ALWAYS WANTED TO BE TREATED LIKE A WHITE MAN; AFTER HE AND HIS PARTNER, GEORGE CARMACK, MADE THE DISCOVERY THAT STARTED THE GOLD RUSH, HE FINALLY WAS. BY 1901, JIM'S MINING CONCERN WAS PAYING, AND PAYING BIG. $90,000 A YEAR IN ROYALTIES WAS BIG MONEY AT THE TIME, BUT HE STILL LIVED THE TOUGH LIFE OF THE PROSPECTOR. HE TRAVELLED ALMOST NON-STOP FOR YEARS, OFTEN GOING WITHOUT FOOD FOR DAYS. BY 1911, JIM, THE MAN WHO'D ONCE HELPED CAPTAIN MOORE SURVEY SKAGWAY AND THE WHITE PASS TRAIL, COULDN'T CONTINUE ON. HIS ONCE MASSIVE FRAME GAVE OUT. HE DIED ON JULY 11.

BELINDA MULROONEY

BEFORE THE "QUEEN OF THE KLONDIKE" MADE THE TRIP NORTH, THIS COAL MINER'S DAUGHTER FROM SCRANTON, PA WAS A STEWARDESS ON THE "CITY OF TOPEKA" AND WAS PUT IN CHARGE OF ORDERING ALL OF THE SHIP'S SUPPLIES FOR A TEN PERCENT COMMISSION AND ANSWERED ONLY TO THE CAPTAIN (WHO WAS LIKELY SCARED OF THIS HARD-AS-NAILS BUSINESS WOMAN). IN 1900, BELINDA MARRIED A CHAMPAGNE SALESMAN, COUNT CHARLES EUGENE CARBONNEAU, AND BECAME A COUNTESS HERSELF. BY 1910, THE COUPLE RETIRED TO YAKIMA, WA. CHARLES WAS KILLED DURING A GERMAN SHELLING IN WWI AND BELINDA REMAINED IN YAKIMA UNTIL HER DEATH ON SEPTEMBER 3, 1967. SHE WAS 97 YEARS OLD.

CAPT. WILLIAM MOORE

IN ADDITION TO BEING THE FOUNDER OF SKAGWAY, ALASKA, CANADIAN BORN MOORE ALSO BROUGHT THE MAIL TO TOWN FROM THE OUTSIDE BY DOGSLED. WHEN THE YOUNGER (AND ONLY OTHER) MAILMAN COULDN'T HANDLE THE LONG, INTENSE JOURNEY, MOORE TOOK OVER FOR HIM. HE WAS 73 AT THE TIME.

WINFIELD OLER + AL THAYER

WINFIELD OLER, THE ORIGINAL OWNER OF #29 ELDORADO ACTUALLY FLED THE COUNTRY TO ESCAPE THE DAILY HUMILIATION THE OTHER PROSPECTORS DOLED OUT TO HIM BECAUSE OF HIS HASTY AND FOOLISH SALE. NOT MUCH ELSE IS KNOWN ABOUT AL THAYER. HIS INVOLVEMENT WAS MORE ANECDOTAL THAN ANYTHING.

FRANK REID

ASIDE FROM STARTING THE "COMMITTEE OF 101," REID WAS ALSO IN CHARGE OF SURVEYING SKAGWAY AT ITS INCEPTION. PART OF HIS JOB WAS TAKING FIVE DOLLARS FOR REGISTERING PLOTS OF LAND. THOSE WHO LIVED IN SKAGWAY BEFORE THE SURVEYING BEGAN HAD TO PAY THE FEE AS WELL, AND IN SOME CASES, HAD THEIR HOMES TORN DOWN IN ORDER TO COMPLY WITH THE NEW STREET PATTERN. YEARS LATER, AFTER THE SHOOT OUT WITH SOAPY SMITH, REID DIED FROM HIS WOUNDS. HIS FUNERAL WAS THE LARGEST IN SKAGWAY HISTORY.

ED SCHIEFFELIN

BEFORE FOUNDING TOMB-STONE, ARIZONA (SCENE OF THE FAMOUS SHOOT OUT AT THE O.K. CORRAL), SCHIEFFELIN WAS AN INDIAN SCOUT FOR CAMP HUACHUCA. AFTER HIS FLIGHT FROM THE FRIGID TEMPERATURES OF THE NORTH, HE SOLD HIS STEAMBOAT, "NEW RACKET," TO JOE LADUE, PRESUMABLY TAKING A COMPANY BOAT FROM ST. MICHAEL TO A MORE CIVILIZED LOCATION, LIKELY SEATTLE OR SAN FRANCISCO.

JEFFERSON RANDOLPH "SOAPY" SMITH

BY 1892, DENVER WAS ENTRENCHED IN ANTI-GAMBLING AND SALOON REFORMS, SO CRIME BOSS SOAPY SMITH SOLD HIS "TIVOLI" CLUB AND MOVED TO THE SILVER MINING BOOM-TOWN OF CREEDE, COLORADO. HIS GANG MOVED IN AS WELL, BUT SIMILAR REFORMS SOON CAME TO CREEDE AND SOAPY RETURNED TO DENVER. HE QUICKLY ROSE BACK TO POWER, BUYING CITY OFFICIALS AND EVEN ADMITTING TO THE PRESS THAT HE WAS A CON MAN, WHICH HE BELIEVED TO BE MORE HONOURABLE THAN THE AVERAGE POLITICIAN. IN 1896, HIS POSITION AS CRIME BOSS WAS LOST TO THE BLONGER BROS. AFTER SOAPY AND HIS BROTHER, BASCOMB, WERE CHARGED WITH THE AT-TEMPTED MURDER OF A SALOON MANAGER. WHILE BASCOMB WAS JAILED, SOAPY ESCAPED AND HEADED WEST.

SID THE BARBER

SID REPRESENTS THE GREENHORNES – THE OVER ZEALOUS AND OFTEN GREEDY MEN WHO MADE THE TREK TO THE YUKON WITH LITTLE OR NO EX-PERIENCE. THERE WERE, HOWEVER, MANY MEN AND WOMEN WHO WENT PURELY FOR THE ADVEN-TURE. SADLY, MANY DID NOT MAKE IT PAST THE WHITE PASS TRAIL. CITY DWELLERS COULDN'T BEGIN TO IMAGINE THE HARDSHIPS THEY WOULD FACE ON THE TRAILS.

SOAPY'S CAPTAIN

SOAPY'S CAPTAIN WAS CREATED TO CUT BACK ON CONFUSION – HE'S A COMPOSITE OF SEVERAL OF SOAPY'S MEN: JOHN BOWERS, "SLIM JIM" FOSTER AND "OLD MAN" TRIPLETT. ALL THIEVES AND THUGS ACTING AS BENEVOLENT MEN.

SAMUEL BENFIELD STEELE

AFTER STEELE BECAME SUPERINTENDENT IN 1898, THE LAWS IN THE YUKON BECAME RIGID. DAWSON BE-CAME SO SAFE THAT ONE COULD LEAVE A SACK OF GOLD UNATTENDED IN AN OPEN CABIN OR TENT WITH-OUT FEAR OF THEFT. SIDE ARMS WERE FORBIDDEN WITHOUT A LICENSE AND ONE COULD BE FINED FOR USING FOUL LANGUAGE. GAMBLING AND PROSTITUTION WERE ALLOWED IF IT WAS CONTAINED TO "PARADISE ALLEY," BUT CHEATING AT CARDS GOT YOU THREE MONTHS CHOPPING WOOD. PROSPECTING AND MINING, ALONG WITH GAMBLING AND PROSTITUTION, WERE BANNED ON SUNDAYS. BREAKING THAT RULE GOT YOU KICKED OUT OF THE YUKON OR TIME ON THE WOOD PILE.

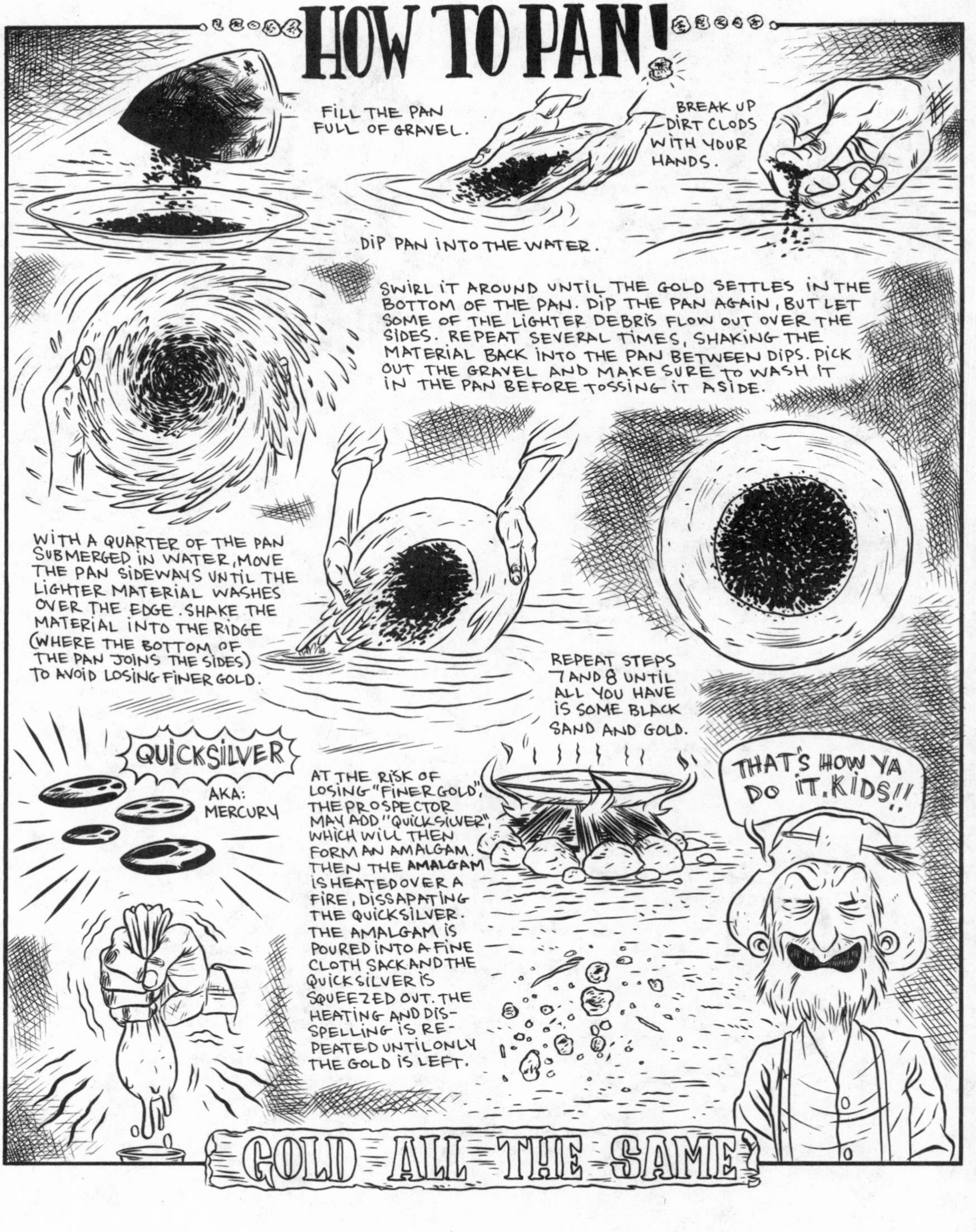
HOW TO PAN!
FILL THE PAN FULL OF GRAVEL.
BREAK UP DIRT CLODS WITH YOUR HANDS.
DIP PAN INTO THE WATER.
SWIRL IT AROUND UNTIL THE GOLD SETTLES IN THE BOTTOM OF THE PAN. DIP THE PAN AGAIN, BUT LET SOME OF THE LIGHTER DEBRIS FLOW OUT OVER THE SIDES. REPEAT SEVERAL TIMES, SHAKING THE MATERIAL BACK INTO THE PAN BETWEEN DIPS. PICK OUT THE GRAVEL AND MAKE SURE TO WASH IT IN THE PAN BEFORE TOSSING IT ASIDE.
WITH A QUARTER OF THE PAN SUBMERGED IN WATER, MOVE THE PAN SIDEWAYS UNTIL THE LIGHTER MATERIAL WASHES OVER THE EDGE. SHAKE THE MATERIAL INTO THE RIDGE (WHERE THE BOTTOM OF THE PAN JOINS THE SIDES) TO AVOID LOSING FINER GOLD.
REPEAT STEPS 7 AND 8 UNTIL ALL YOU HAVE IS SOME BLACK SAND AND GOLD.
QUICKSILVER
AKA: MERCURY
AT THE RISK OF LOSING "FINER GOLD", THE PROSPECTOR MAY ADD "QUICKSILVER", WHICH WILL THEN FORM AN AMALGAM. THEN THE AMALGAM IS HEATED OVER A FIRE, DISSAPATING THE QUICKSILVER. THE AMALGAM IS POURED INTO A FINE CLOTH SACK AND THE QUICKSILVER IS SQUEEZED OUT. THE HEATING AND DIS-SPELLING IS RE-PEATED UNTIL ONLY THE GOLD IS LEFT.
THAT'S HOW YA DO IT, KIDS!!
GOLD ALL THE SAME

QUARTZ OR BEDROCK MINING: DONE BY CRUSHING THE VEIN ROCK WHERE THE GOLD IS PLACED. A MINE IS DUG INTO THE GROUND TO THE BEDROCK. IF THERE'S GOLD, IT'S EXTRACTED AND LIFTED OUT IN A WINDLASS. IT'S THEN PUT INTO THE DUMP FOR SPRING CLEAN UP.

PLACER MINING: ALSO KNOWN AS "POOR MAN'S MINING". WATER PASSES THROUGH OR OVER BEDROCK, CARRYING THE GOLD WORN OFF THE VEIN INTO THE STREAM BEDS AND CREEKS. AS GOLD IS NOT EXCLUSIVELY FORMED IN BEDROCK, IT CAN ALSO BE FORMED IN THE DENSE CLAY OF CREEK BEDS. THE CREEK BEDS ARE DUG UP REGARDLESS OF WHETHER THE GOLD FORMED THERE OR NOT. IT'S THEN PANNED AND SEPARATED. PROSPECTORS KNEW THAT GOLD WAS APPX. 19.3 TIMES HEAVIER THAN WATER, SO THEY FOLLOWED THE RIVERS, STREAMS AND CREEKS TO PAN THEM.

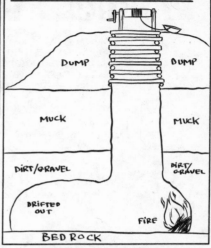
TYPICAL MINE SHAFT SEEN ON CLAIMS

DUMP — DUMP
MUCK — MUCK
DIRT/GRAVEL — DIRT/GRAVEL
DRIFTED OUT
FIRE
BED ROCK

PANNING

REFER TO "HOW TO PAN" STRIP.

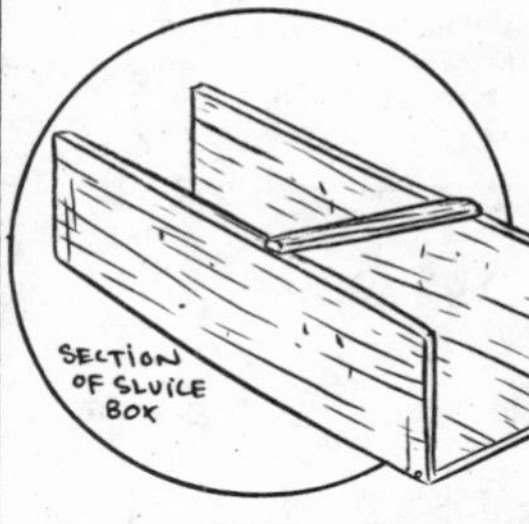

SLUICING

BUILT IN SECTIONS, ONE END NARROWER THAN THE OTHER SO MORE SECTIONS CAN BE ADDED. THE FLOOR OF THE BOX IS CALLED A "RIFFLE", WHICH IS MADE TO BE LIFTED OUT WHEN WATER CAN NO LONGER PASS THROUGH. THE WATER FLOW IS DIVERTED FROM THE SLUICE BOX AND THE RIFFLE REMOVED. WATER IS SLOWLY POURED BY HAND INTO THE RIFFLE THE GOLD IS SEPARATED.

SECTION OF SLUICE BOX

SEE BOTTOM OF THE PAGE FOR AN EXAMPLE OF A RIFFLE.

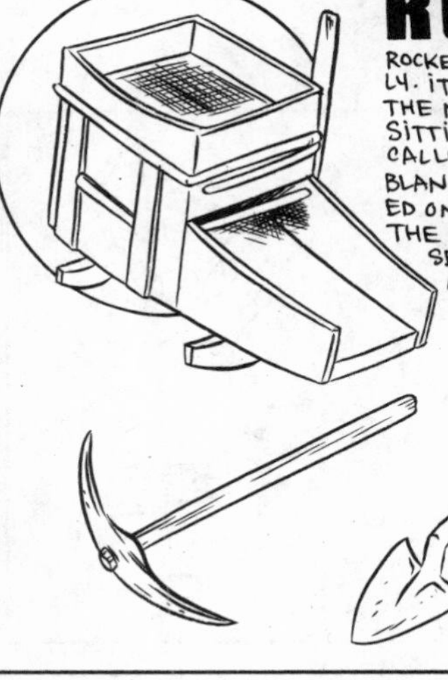

ROCKING

ROCKERS WERE BUILT FOR WASHING GRAVEL QUICKLY. IT HAS A ROUNDED BASE SO ONE COULD ROCK THE MATERIAL AROUND AND BREAK UP THE DIRT SITTING ON THE PERFORATED METAL GRATE, CALLED A "HOPPER". INSIDE IS A SLOPING BLANKET CALLED AN "APRON". THE DIRT SHOVELED ON, WATER'S POURED OVER IT AND ROCKED. THE APRON IS REMOVED AND THE GOLD SEPARATED. THE CONTENTS OF THE APRON IS PUT IN A BUCKET WITH QUICKSILVER, THEN COOKED OFF.

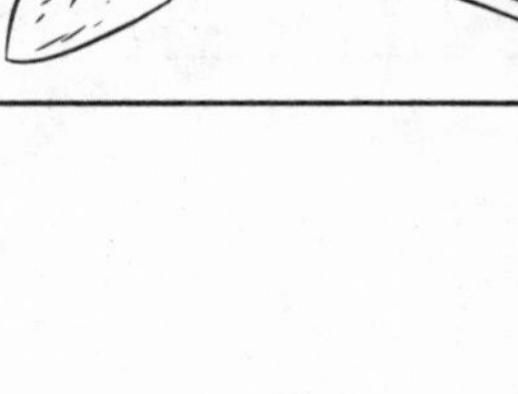

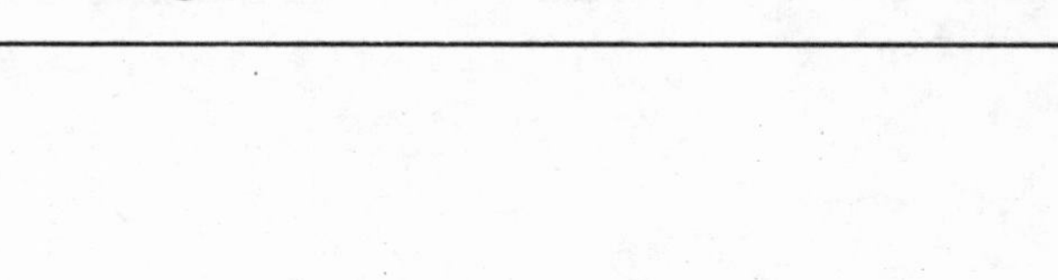

THAWING ON BEDROCK MINING

MINERS BUILT FIRES AND LEFT THEM ON THE POTENTIAL MINE SHAFT OVER NIGHT TO HEAT THE EARTH. BY MORNING THE MINER COULD DIG BETWEEN 4-9 INCHES. THE PROCESS WOULD BE REPEATED UNTIL THE MINERS REACHED BED ROCK. THE DIRT FROM THE MINESHAFT IS PUT INTO A PILE CALLED A "DUMP" TO BE CLEANED UP IN THE SPRING. ON OCCASION, THE MINER WOULD HIT AN UNDERGROUND STREAM WHILE DIGGING THE SHAFT. THE WATER WOULD FILL UP THE SHAFT AND FREEZE WITHIN TWENTY MINUTES, MAKING MONTHS OF WORK FOR NOTHING. THE PROCESS WOULD BEGIN AGAIN ON A DIFFERENT LOCATION OF THE CLAIM. ANOTHER ISSUE WAS THE GROUND GETTING TOO HOT, MELTING SNOW DRIFTS AND FILLING THE SHAFT WITH WATER.

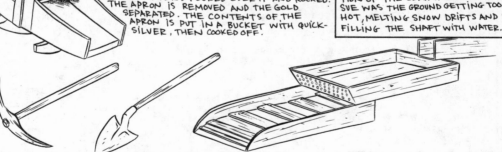

VARIOUS FORMS

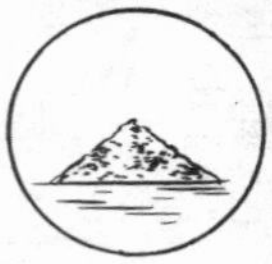

FLOUR GOLD

CAN BE SO FINE THAT IT IS BARELY SEEN BY THE NAKED EYE. QUICK SILVER IS ESSENTIAL SO AS NOT TO LOSE ANY OF THIS TYPE OF GOLD.

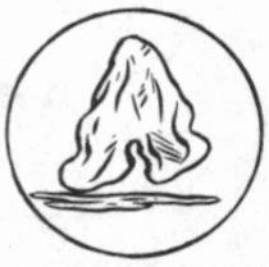

LEAF GOLD

THIN, FLATTENED PIECES OF GOLD UP TO HALF AN INCH OR MORE SQUARED.

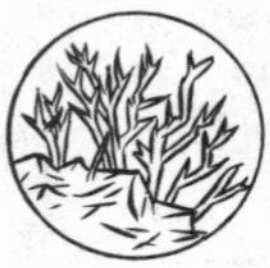

WIRE GOLD

SHORT, WIRE LIKE PIECES OF GOLD.

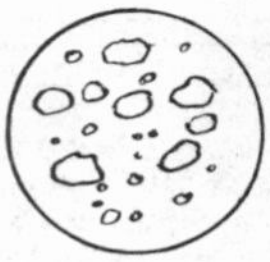

COARSE GOLD

A GENERAL TERM USED TO DESCRIBE ANYTHING FROM FLOUR TO PIECES THE SIZE OF CORNMEAL, GRAINS OF WHEAT OR LARGER.

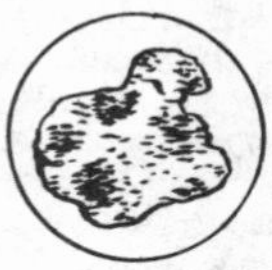

NUGGET GOLD

ALSO A FLEXIBLE TERM. INCLUDES SIZES FROM THE WEIGHT OF A PENNY TO A NUGGET SO LARGE A MAN CAN BARELY CARRY IT.

WHEN GOLD IS SMACKED WITH A HAMMER IT SMUSHES. FOOLS GOLD BREAKS.

TRIVIA!

HERE ARE A FEW TOOLS WE USED ON A CLAIM.

AXE: SELF EXPLANATORY

BUTCHER KNIFE: USED FOR CUTTING MEAT

BROAD HATCHET: GENERALLY FOR CUTTING TIMBER

DRAWKNIFE: A BLADE WITH HANDLES ON EITHER END

GALVANIZED BUCKET: USED FOR GOLD AND QUICKSILVER AS WELL AS WATER

GOLD SCALES: SELF EXPLANATORY

HAMMER: FOR BUILDING OR TESTING WHETHER GOLD IS REAL OR NOT

HANDSAW: ESSENTIAL FOR BUILDING SLUICE BOXES

CANVAS BAG: TRANSPORTING BLACK SAND AND GOLD

QUICKSILVER (MERCURY): FOR MAKING AN AMALGAM WITH GOLD

PICK: BREAKING UP EARTH AND BED ROCK

WHIPSAW: A LARGE SAW MANNED BY TWO MEN

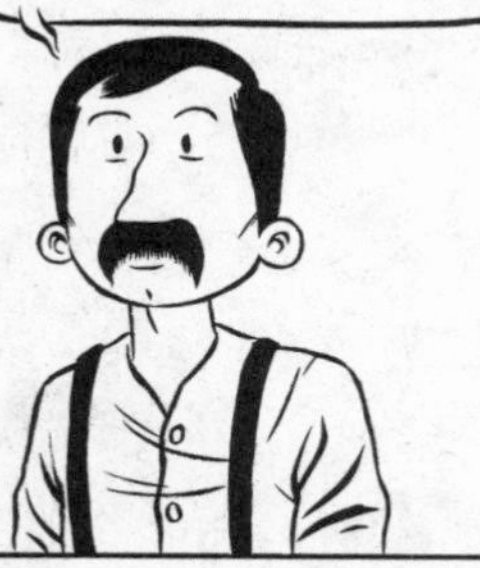

OTHER ROCKS GOLD IS FOUND IN

MICA SCHIST:

SCHIST IS A FORM OF METAMORPHIC ROCK. A PLATY ROCK WHERE THE GOLD COULD BE FOUND SANDWICHED BETWEEN THE SLABS. "SCHIST" IS DERIVED FROM THE GREEK WORD MEANING, TO SPLIT.

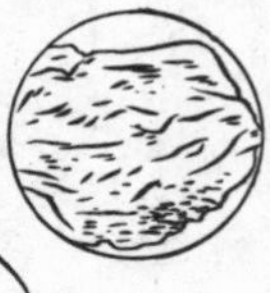

FELDSPAR:

MAKES UP SOME 60% OF THE EARTH'S CRUST, AND IS A COMMON, RAW MATERIAL IN THE PRODUCTION OF CERAMICS.

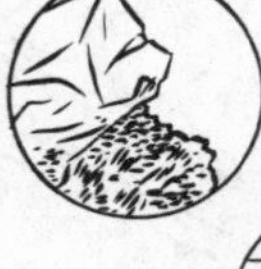

GNEISS:

RESEMBLES SCHIST. THE MINERALS ARE FORMED IN BANDS RATHER THAN PLATES. SOMETIMES IT'S DIFFICULT TO TELL THE DIFFERENCE BETWEEN THE TWO. OTHER TYPES OF METAMORPHIC ROCK, LIKE SCHIST AND GNEISS, ARE SLATE AND MARBLE.

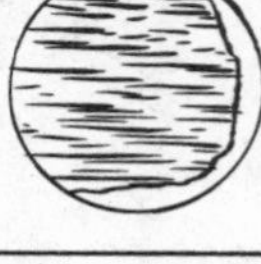

AUTHOR'S NOTE

OVER THE FIVE YEARS I SPENT WORKING ON THIS COMIC, I DISCOVERED A LOT OF THINGS ABOUT WHAT MAKES A STORY WORK WHEN USING HISTORY AS THE BACKBONE. THE MAIN THING IS THAT THE TRUTH, THOUGH BEING INFORMATIVE, IS NOT ALWAYS ENTERTAINING AND THE THINGS THAT ARE ENTERTAINING ARE NOT NECESSARILY IMPORTANT. THIS IS HISTORICAL FICTION. I WASN'T THERE TO OVERHEAR CONVERSATIONS OR OBSERVE THE GOOD AND BAD TIMES OF THOSE MINING CAMPS, GOLD FIELDS AND TRAILS. I HAD TO SPECULATE ON EVENTS BOTH TO MOVE THE STORY FORWARD AND TO HELP INCORPORATE FACTS. I'VE ADDED FICTIONAL CHARACTERS TO THE STORY AS A VEHICLE TO DELIVER INFORMATION THAT DIDN'T HAPPEN TO ANY OF THE KEY PLAYERS IN THE STORY. FOR EXAMPLE, NONE OF THE TERRIBLE THINGS THAT HAPPENED ON THE DEAD HORSE TRAIL INVOLVED BIG ALEX McDONALD OR GEORGE CARMACK, SO IT WAS OBVIOUS TO ME THAT IN ORDER TO GET THAT INFORMATION ACROSS, I HAD TO BRING IN FICTIONAL CHARACTERS. IF YOU WERE TO ASK ME WHAT PERCENTAGE IS REAL AND WHAT IS MADE UP, I WOULD SAY ABOUT EIGHTY TO TWENTY — AND THAT'S A CONSERVATIVE ESTIMATION.

ANOTHER DIFFICULTY WAS DETERMINING WHO OF THE NON-FICTIONAL CHARACTERS INVOLVED HAD INTERESTING STORIES THAT FOLLOWED THE TONE OF THE STORY I WANTED TO TELL. THAT TOOK A WHILE. I DID A LOT OF READING AND NOTE TAKING TO TRY AND FIGURE THIS OUT, AND IN THE END, THE REASON I EXCLUDED THE PEOPLE I DID WAS BECAUSE I THOUGHT THEIR STORIES WERE ON THE DRY SIDE, OR THAT THEY WERE ONLY USEFUL FOR COMIC RELIEF, WHICH WAS NOT THE POINT OF THIS BOOK (SIDE NOTE: FOR THOSE WHO ARE UNFAMILIAR WITH THE SELF-PUBLISHED COMICS I'D MADE PRIOR TO AND DURING THE WRITING OF THE KLONDIKE, I WAS REALLY ONLY INTERESTED IN BLACK COMEDY. SO LEAVING OUT SOME OF THE MORE HILARIOUS PEOPLE AND MOMENTS WAS NOT A DECISION I TOOK LIGHTLY. I LOVE WRITING AND DRAWING THOSE KINDS OF STORIES, BUT I KNEW FROM THE START THAT THIS WAS NOT THE VENUE). THE LAST CONCERN I HAD WAS HOW MANY PEOPLE COULD I, OR YOU,

THE READER, KEEP TRACK OF: THERE WERE
MORE PEOPLE WHO PLAYED A ROLE IN THE
KLONDIKE THAN I COULD POSSIBLY INCLUDE IN
ONE BOOK.

I WAS VERY DELIBERATE WITH MY APPROACH
AND IMMEDIATELY SAW THE STORY I WANTED
TO TELL WHEN I BEGAN READING PIERRE BERTON'S
"KLONDIKE: THE LAST GREAT GOLD RUSH 1896-1899."
I DIDN'T WANT IT TO BE AN ADVENTURE BOOK, SO
WHILE I WAS RESEARCHING AND WRITING I HAD
TO LOOK AT THE SMALLER PICTURES WITHIN THE
BIGGER STORY. I HAD TO BREAK EVERYTHING
DOWN INTO WHAT WAS IMPORTANT TO THE STORY
AND WHAT WAS FRIVOLOUS. DON'T GET ME WRONG,
I LOVE A GOOD ADVENTURE STORY AND THERE WERE
PLENTY OF MOMENTS THAT WOULD HAVE LENT
THEMSELVES TO THAT GENRE, BUT I SAW THE
KLONDIKE GOLD RUSH AS A LOT MORE THAN JUST
ADVENTURE. IT WAS NEVER ABOUT CANADA VS.
THE U.S., GOOD VS. EVIL OR EVEN MAN VS. NATURE.
WHAT FASCINATED ME WAS HOW FAR THESE PEOPLE
WENT, AND HOW FAR THEY PUSHED THEMSELVES
FOR THE SLIM CHANCE OF STRIKING IT RICH. WHAT
DROVE THESE MEN AND WOMEN TO RISK DEATH IN
SEARCH OF GOLD? WAS IT ADVENTURE? AVARICE? I
CAN'T SAY, AND IN ALL GOOD CONSCIENCE, WON'T.
PERHAPS YOU CAN FIGURE IT OUT.

BIBLIOGRAPHY...

• AKRIGG, G. P.V. + HELEN B. - BRITISH COLUMBIA CHRONICLE - GOLD + COLONISTS, DISCOVERY PRESS - 1977
• ADNEY, TAPPAN - THE KLONDIKE STAMPEDE OF 1897-98, UBC PRESS - 1994
• BARLEE, N.L. - GOLD CREEKS + GHOST TOWNS, CANADA WEST MAGAZINE - 1970
• BELL, KEN + STACEY, C.P. - 100 YEARS: THE ROYAL CANADIAN REGIMENT 1883-1983, COLLIER MACMILLAN CANADA INC. - 1983
• BERTON, PIERRE - KLONDIKE: THE LAST GREAT GOLD RUSH 1896-99, McCLELLAND + STEWART LTD. - 1958
• BERTON, PIERRE - THE KLONDIKE QUEST: A PHOTOGRAPHIC ESSAY / 1897-99, THE BOSTON MILLS PRESS - 1997
• BERTON, PIERRE - THE GOLDEN TRAIL, FIFTH HOUSE LTD. - 2004
• BERTON, PIERRE - THE WILD FRONTIER, McCLELLAND + STEWART LTD. - 1978
• BLOWER, JAMES - GOLD RUSH: A PICTORAL HISTORY, McGRAW-HILL COMPANY OF CANADA - 1971
• CHARTERS, DEAN - MOUNTIE: 1873-1973, COLLIER MACMILLAN CANADA LTD. - 1973
• COATES, KENNETH - BEST LEFT AS INDIANS: NATIVE-WHITE RELATIONS IN THE YUKON TERRITORIES 1840-1973, McGILL-QUEEN'S UNIVERSITY PRESS - 1991
• COATES, KEN + MORRISON, WILLIAM R. - LAND OF THE MIDNIGHT SUN, McGILL-QUEEN'S UNIVERSITY PRESS - 2005
• DUNCAN, JENNIFER - FRONTIER SPIRIT, DOUBLE DAY CANADA - 2003
• FAULK, ODIE B. - TOMBSTONE: MYTH + REALITY, OXFORD UNIVERSITY PRESS - 1972
• FETHERLING, DOUGLAS - THE GOLD CRUSADES, MACMILLAN OF CANADA - 1988
• GIBBONS, TONY (GENERAL EDITOR) - ENCYCLOPEDIA OF SHIPS, THUNDER BAY PRESS - 2001
• GOUGH, BARRY M. - GOLD RUSH, GROLIER LTD. - 1983
• GRAHAM, HARRY - ACROSS CANADA TO THE KLONDYKE, METHUEN PUBLICATIONS - 1984
• HALL, E. (COMPILED BY) - EARLY CANADA, QUEEN'S PRINTER - 1967
• JOHNSON, JAMES ALBERT - GEORGE CARMACK; THE MAN OF MYSTERY WHO SET OFF THE KLONDIKE GOLD RUSH, WHITE CAP BOOKS - 2001
• LOUDON, W.J. - A CANADIAN GEOLOGIST, MACMILLAN CO. OF CANADA - 1930
• MACDONALD, IAN + O'KEEFE, BETTY - THE KLONDIKE'S DEAR LITTLE NUGGET, HORSDAL + SCHUBART PUBLISHERS - 1996
• MACGREGOR, J.G. - THE KLONDIKE GOLD RUSH THROUGH EDMONTON 1897-98, McCLELLAND + STEWART LTD. - 1970
• MORGAN, LAEL - GOOD TIME GIRLS, EPICENTRE PRESS - 1999

• MORRISON, WILLIAM R. — TRUE NORTH, OXFORD UNIVERSITY PRESS — 1998

• MORSE, KATHRYN — NATURE OF GOLD, AN ENVIRONMENTAL HISTORY OF THE KLONDIKE GOLD RUSH, UNIVERSITY OF WASHINGTON PRESS — 2003

• OLIVE, W.H.T. — THE RIGHT WAY ON, TIMBER HOLME BOOKS — 1999

• OPPEL, FRANK (COMPILED BY) — TALES OF ALASKA + THE YUKON, CASTLE — 1986

• OPPEL, FRANK (COMPILED BY) — TALES OF THE CANADIAN NORTH, CASTLE — 1986

• PORSILD, CHARLENE — GAMBLERS + DREAMERS, UBC PRESS — 1998

• SAWYER, ROBERT — SAM STEELE: LION OF THE FRONTIER, CENTAX BOOKS — 1999

• STEELE, SIR SAMUEL BENFIELD — FORTY YEARS IN CANADA, PROSPERO BOOKS — 2000

• SYMINGTON, FRASER — THE CANADIAN INDIAN: THE ILLUSTRATED HISTORY OF THE GREAT TRIBES OF CANADA, MCCLELLAND + STEWART LTD. — 1969

• TATLEY, RICHARD — NORTHERN STEAM BOATS, THE BOSTON MILLS PRESS — 1996

• WILSON, GRAHAM — PADDLE WHEELERS OF ALASKA AND THE YUKON, WOLF CREEK BOOKS LTD. — 1999

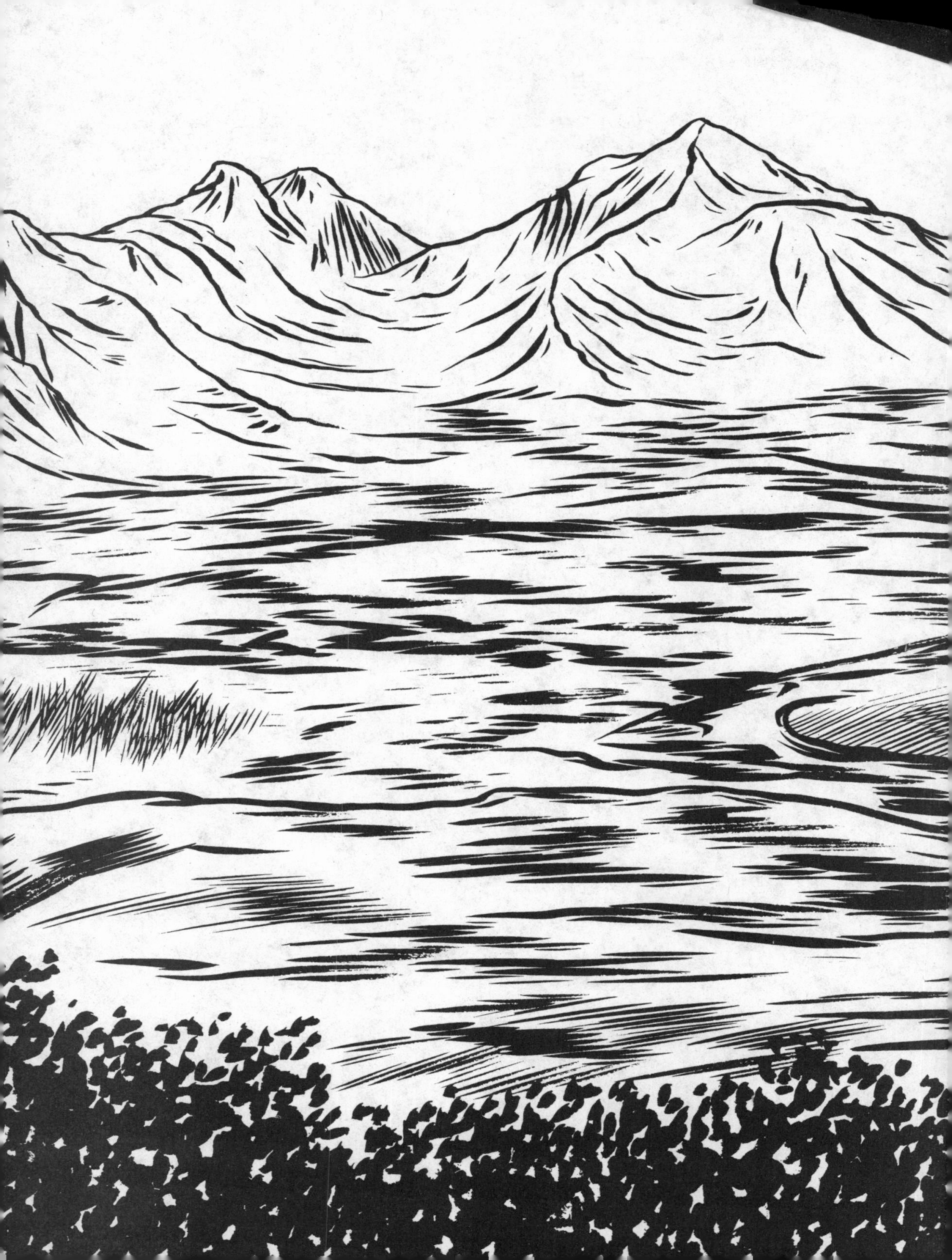